11-13

20, 22, 23

Vwiranani Mtika
May 30, 2005

Mike Mtika
April 1, 2005.

Tables 2.3 and 2.4 not in.

African Economic
Development

African Economic Development

Edited by

Emmanuel Nnadozie

Department of Economics
Truman State University
Kirksville, Missouri 63501

 **ACADEMIC PRESS**

An imprint of Elsevier Science

Amsterdam   Boston   London   New York   Oxford   Paris
San Diego   San Francisco   Singapore   Sydney   Tokyo

This book is printed on acid-free paper. ♾

Copyright © 2003, Elsevier Science (USA).

All Rights Reserved.
No part of this publication may be reproduced or transmitted in any
form or by any means, electronic or mechanical, including photocopy,
recording, or any information storage and retrieval system, without
permission in writing from the publisher.

Permissions may be sought directly from Elsevier's Science &
Technology Rights Department in Oxford, UK: phone: (+44) 1865
843830, fax: (+44) 1865 853333, e-mail:
permissions@elsevier.com.uk. You may also complete your request
on-line via the Elsevier Science homepage (http://elsevier.com), by
selecting "Customer Support" and then "Obtaining Permissions."

Academic Press
An imprint of Elsevier Science
525 B Street, Suite 1900, San Diego, California 92101-4495, USA
http://www.academicpress.com

Academic Press
84 Theobald's Road, London WC1X 8RR, UK
http://www.academicpress.com

Library of Congress Catalog Card Number: 2002116536

International Standard Book Number: 0-12-519992-9

PRINTED IN THE UNITED STATES OF AMERICA
03 04 05 06 07 08   8 7 6 5 4 3 2 1

For Martin O. Ijere and Marcel Mazoyer—
my eternal mentors—for their invaluable guidance, and
to the people of Africa for their unusual resilience in the face of
seemingly insurmountable challenges.

African Economic Development

Edited by

Emmanuel Nnadozie

Department of Economics
Truman State University
Kirksville, Missouri 63501

ACADEMIC PRESS

An imprint of Elsevier Science

Amsterdam   Boston   London   New York   Oxford   Paris
San Diego   San Francisco   Singapore   Sydney   Tokyo

This book is printed on acid-free paper. ⊚

Academic Press
An imprint of Elsevier Science
525 B Street, Suite 1900, San Diego, California 92101-4495, USA
http://www.academicpress.com

Academic Press
84 Theobald's Road, London WC1X 8RR, UK
http://www.academicpress.com

Library of Congress Catalog Card Number: 2002116536

International Standard Book Number: 0-12-519992-9

PRINTED IN THE UNITED STATES OF AMERICA
03 04 05 06 07 08   8 7 6 5 4 3 2 1

For Martin O. Ijere and Marcel Mazoyer—
my eternal mentors—for their invaluable guidance, and
to the people of Africa for their unusual resilience in the face of
seemingly insurmountable challenges.

CONTENTS

PART **I**

Introduction to Africa and African Economic Development

1 Why Study African Economic Development?
Emmanuel Nnadozie

2 Overview of African Development

Emmanuel Nnadozie

3 Definition and Measurement of Growth and Development

Emmanuel Nnadozie

PART II

Africa's Characteristics and Development Challenges

4 Geo-Economy and History

Mario J. Azevedo

5 Engines of Growth and Africa's Economic Performance

Marcel Fafchamps

6 Population

Jacob Adetunji

7 Poverty and Development

Nick Vink and Norma Tregurtha

PART III
Critical Issues

8 Implications of Ethnic Diversity

Paul Collier

9 Health and Economic Development

Mario J. Azevedo

10 Education

Mario J. Azevedo and Emmanuel Nnadozie

11 Democracy and Development

John J. Quinn

12 Political Instability

Kwabena Gyimah-Brempong

13 Inequality and Conflict

E. Wayne Nafziger

14 Corruption and Economic Development

John Mukum Mbaku

PART **IV**

Sector Analyses

15 Land Tenure, Agriculture, and Economic Development

Nii O. Tackie, Arthur Siaway, and Ntam Baharanyi

16 Financial Markets and Economic Development

Léonce Ndikumana

17 Saving, Investment, and Growth in Sub-Saharan Africa

Seymour Patterson

PART **V**

Africa and the International Environment

18 Trade and Economic Development

Victor Iwuagwu Oguledo

19 Regionalism and Economic Development

Femi Babarinde

20　Globalization and Development

Richard E. Mshomba

21　Information and Communication Technologies

Francis A.S.T. Matambalya

PART **VI**

Development Challenges, Policies, and Strategies

22 Economic Policies, Stabilization, and Reforms

Sarah Bryant Bower

23 Restarting and Sustaining Growth and Development

James S. Duesenberry, Arthur A. Goldsmith, and Malcolm F. McPherson

CONTRIBUTORS

Numbers in parentheses indicate the pages on which the authors' contributions begin.

JACOB ADETUNJI (99) United States Agency for International Development, Bureau for Global Health, Washington, D.C. 20523

MARIO J. AZEVEDO (47, 181, 207) Department of African American and African Studies, University of North Carolina, Charlotte, North Carolina 28223

FEMI BABARINDE (473) American Graduate School of International Business, Thunderbird University, Glendale, Arizona 85306

NTAM BAHARANYI (353) Department of Agriculture Sciences, Tuskegee University, Tuskegee, Alabama 36088

SARAH BRYANT BOWER (549) College of Business Administration, Clarion University, Clarion, Pennsylvania 16214

PAUL COLLIER (149) The World Bank, Washington, D.C. 20433

JAMES S. DUESENBERRY (565) Department of Economics, Harvard University, Cambridge, Massachusetts 02138

MARCEL FAFCHAMPS (65) Center for the Study of African Economics, University of Oxford, Oxford, OX 12JD, England

ARTHUR A. GOLDSMITH (565) Department of Management, University of Massachusetts 02125

KWABENA GYIMAH-BREMPONG (259) Department of Economics, University of South Florida, Tampa, Florida 33620

PETER KILBY (xxxi) Department of Economics, Wesleyan University, Middletown, Connecticut 06459

FRANCIS A. S. T. MATAMBALYA (519) Department of Marketing, University of Dar es Salaam, Dar es Salaam, Tanzania

JOHN MUKUM MBAKU (313) Department of Economics, Weber State University, Ogden, Utah 84408

MALCOLM F. McPHERSON (565) Belfer Center for Science and International Affairs, John F. Kennedy School of Government, Harvard University, Cambridge, Massachusetts 02138

RICHARD E. MSHOMBA (499) Department of Economics, LaSalle University, Philadelphia, Pennsylvania 19141

E. WAYNE NAFZIGER (295) Department of Economics, Kansas State University, Manhattan, Kansas 66506

LÉONCE NDIKUMANA (373) Department of Economics, University of Massachusetts, Amherst, Massachusetts 01003

EMMANUEL NNADOZIE (3, 15, 29, 207) Department of Economics, Truman State University, Kirksville, Missouri 63501

VICTOR IWUAGWU OGULEDO (441) Department of Economics, College of Arts and Sciences, Florida Agricultural and Mechnaical University, Tallahassee, Florida 32307

SEYMOUR PATTERSON (405) Department of Economics, Truman State University, Kirksville, Missouri 63501

JOHN J. QUINN (231) Department of Political Science, Truman State University, Kirksville, Missouri 63501

ARTHUR SIAWAY (353) Department of Agriculture Sciences, Tuskegee University, Tuskegee, Alabama 36088

NII O. TACKIE (353) Department of Agriculture Sciences, Tuskegee University, Tuskegee, Alabama 36088

NORMA TREGURTHA (121) Department of Agricultural Economics, University of Stellenbosch, Matieland 7602, Stellenbosch, South Africa

NICK VINK (121) Department of Agricultural Economics, University of Stellenbosch, Matieland 7602, Stellenbosch, South Africa

ACRONYMS AND ABBREVIATIONS

ACP African, Caribbean, and Pacific (group of States)
ADB African Development Bank
ADI African Development Indicators
AEC African Economic Community
AERC African Economic Research Consortium
AFESD Arab Fund for Economic and Social Development
AGOA African Growth and Opportunities Act
AID Agency for International Development US
AIDS Acquired Immune Deficiency Syndrome
AMU Arab Maghreb Union
APPER African Priority Programme for Economic Recovery
AU African Union
BADEA Arab Bank for Economic Development in Africa
BDEAC Banque de Développement des Etats de l'Afrique Centrale (Central African States Development Bank)
BEAC Bank of Central African States
BOAD Banque Ouest-Africaine de Développement (West African Development Bank)

CBI Cross Border Initiative
CEAO Communauté Economique de l'Afrique de l'Ouest (West African Economic Community)
CEEAC Communauté Economique des Etats de l'Afrique Centrale (Economic Community of Central African States)
CEMAC Economic and Monetary Community of Central Africa
CFA Communauté Financière Africane (franc zone)
CI Competitiveness Indicator
CIDA Canadian International Development Agency
CILSS Permanent Interstate Committee on Drought Control in the Sahel
CMEA Council for Mutual Economic Assistance
COMESA Common Market for Eastern and Southern Africa
CPI Consumer Price Index
DAC Development Assistance Committee of the OECD
DDG Development Data Group, World Bank
DFI Direct Foreign Investment
EAC East African Cooperation

EADB   East African Development Bank
EC   European Community
ECA   Economic Commission for Africa (UN)
ECCAS   Economic Community of Central African States
ECOWAS   Economic Community of West African States
EDA   European Development Bank
ELF   Ethno-linguistic fractionalization
EMU   Economic and Monetary Union
EU   European Union
f.o.b.   Free on board
FAGACE   Fonds Africain de Garantee et de Coopération Economique
FAO   Food and Agricultural Organization of the United Nations
FAOSTAT   Food and Agriculture Organization of the United Nations Statistical Database
FDI   Foreign Direct Investment
G8   Canada, France, Germany, Italy, Japan, Russia, the United Kingdom, and the United States
GATS   General Agreement on Trade in Services
GDI   Gross Domestic Investment
GDP   Gross Domestic Product
GDS   Gross Domestic Saving
GFS   Government Finance Statistics (IMF)
GNFS   Goods and Nonfactor Services
GNP   Gross National Product
GNS   Gross National Saving
GSP   Generalized System of Preferences
GTAP   Global Trade Analysis Project
HDI   Human Development Index

HIPC   Heavily Indebted Poor Countries
HIV   Human Immunodeficiency Virus
HPI   Human Poverty Index
IBRD   International Bank for Reconstruction and Development
ICFTU-AFRO   International Confederation of Free Trade Unions (Africa)
ICP   International Comparison Project
IDA   International Development Association
IDDA   Industrial Development Decade for Africa
IDS   Institute of Development Studies
IEA   International Energy Agency
IFAD   International Fund for Agricultural Development
IFS   International Financial Statistics (IMF)
IGAD   Intergovernmental Authority on Development
IL   International Labor Organization
ILO   International Labour Organization
IMF   International Monetary Fund
IOC   Indian Ocean Commission
IS   Import Substitution
ISIC   UN International Standard Industrial Classification
ITU   International Telecommunications Union
IUCN   International Union for Conservation of Nature and Natural Resources
LDC   Less Developed Country
LDCs   Least Developed Countries
LIBOR   London Interbank Offered Rate

LIC   Low Income Countries
LIMI   Low-Income and Middle-Income Countries
LPA   Lagos Plan of Action
MAP   Millennium Partnership for the African Recovery Programme
MENA   Middle East and North Africa (region)
METMIN   Metals and Minerals Database (World Bank)
MIC   Middle Income Countries
MIGA   Multilateral Investment Guarantee Agency
NAI   New African Initiative
NEPAD   New Partnership for African Development
NIC   Newly Industrialized Countries
NIEs   Newly Industrializing Economies
OAU   Organization of African Unity
ODA   Official Development Assistance
ODCCP   Office for Drug Control and Crime Prevention
OECD   Organization for Economic Cooperation and Development
OIC   Organization of the Islamic Conference
OPEC   Organization of Petroleum Exporting Countries
OPIC   Overseas Private Investment Corporation (U.S.)
ORS   Oral Rehydration Solution
PE   Public Enterprise
PHC   Primary Health Care
PI   Political Instability
PPP   Purchasing Power Parity
PQLI   Physical Quality of Life Index
RSA   Republic of South Africa
SACU   Southern African Customs Union

SADC   Southern African Development Community
SAF   Structural Adjustment Facility
SAP   Structural Adjustment Program
SDA   Social Dimensions of Adjustments
SDR   Special Drawing Right
SIMA   Statistical Information Management and Analysis Database World Bank
SITC   UN Standard International Trade Classification
SOE   State Owned Enterprises
SSA   Sub-Saharan Africa
TFR   Total Fertility Rate
TNCs   Transnational Corporations
TOT   Terms of Trade
TRIMs   Trade-Related Investment Measures
TRIPs   Trade-Related Intellectual Property Rights
UDEAC   Union Douanière et Economique de l'Afrique Centrale (Central African Customs and Economic Union)
UMC   Upper Middle Income
UNCHS   United Nations Centre for Human Settlement
UNCTAD   United Nations Conference on Trade and Development
UNDP   United Nations Development Programme
UNECE   United Nations Economic Commission for Europe
UNEP   United Nations Environmental Programme
UNESCO   United Nations Education Scientific and Cultural Organizations
UNFPA   United Nations Population Fund

UNHCR   United Nations High Commission for Refugees

UNICEF   United Nations Children's Fund

UNIDO   United Nations Industrial Development Organization

UN-NADAF   United Nations New Agenda for the Development of Africa in the 1990s

UNPAAERD   United Nations Program of Action for African Economic Recovery and Development

UNSO   United Nations Statistical Office

UNTA   United Nations Technical Assistance

UNTACDA   United Nations Transport and Communications Decade for Africa

USDA   United States Department of Agriculture

USDC   United States Department of Commerce

WADB   West African Development Bank

WAEMU   West African Economic and Monetary Union

WB   World Bank

WFP   World Food Programme

WHO   World Health Organization

WRI   World Resources Institute

WTO   World Trade Organization

AFRICAN AND OTHER
ORGANIZATIONS

REGIONAL AND SUPRA-REGIONAL ORGANIZATIONS

African Economic Community (AEC)
African Union (AU)
African, Caribbean, and Pacific Group of States (ACP Group)
Arab Maghreb Union (AMU)
Central African Customs and Economic Union (UDEAC)
Common Market for Eastern and Southern Africa (COMESA)
Communauté Economique de l'Afrique de l'Ouest (CEAO) [*West African Economic Community*]
Communauté Economique des Etats de l'Afrique Centrale (CEEAC) [*Economic Community of Central African States*]
Communauté Financière Africaine (CFA) [*Franc Zone*]
Cross Border Initiatives (CBI)
East African Cooperation (EAC)
Economic and Monetary Community of Central Africa (CEMAC)
Economic Community of Central African States (ECCAS)
Economic Community of West African States (ECOWAS)
Indian Ocean Commission (IOC)
Inter-Governmental Authority for Government (IGAD)
Mano River Union
Nile River Basin
Organization of African Unity (OAU)
Organization of Petroleum Exporting Countries (OPEC)

Permanent Interstate Committee on Drought Control in the Sahel (CLISS)
Southern African Customs Union (SACU)
Southern African Development Community (SADC)
Union Douanière et Economique de l'Afrique Centrale (UDEAC) [*Central African Customs and Economic Union*]
West African Economic and Monetary Union (WAEMU)
West African Economic Community (CEAO)

MULTINATIONAL BANKS

Arab Fund for Economic and Social Development (AFESD)
Arab Bank for Economic Development in Africa (BADEA)
African Development Bank (ADB)
Bank of Central African States (BEAC)
Banque de Développement des Etats de l'Afrique Centrale (BDEAC) [*Central African States Development Bank*]
Banque Ouest-Africaine de Développement (BOAD) [*West African Development Bank*]
East African Development Bank (EADB)
West African Development Bank (WADB)

MULTILATERAL ORGANIZATIONS

General Agreement on Tariffs and Trade (GATT)
International Bank for Reconstruction and Development (IBRD)(World Bank)
International Development Association (IDA)
International Labor Organization (ILO)
International Monetary Fund (IMF)
United Nations (UN)
United Nations Commission for Trade and Development (UNCTAD)
United Nations Development Program (UNDP)
United Nations Economic Commission for Africa (UNECA) or (ECA)
United Nations Economic Commission for Europe (UNECE)
United Nations Educational Scientific and Cultural Organization (UNESCO)
United Nations Environment Program (UNEP)
United Nations Food and Agricultural Organization (FAO)
United Nations High Commission on Refugees (UNHCR)
United Nations Industrial Development Organization (UNIDO)
United Nations International Children's Emergency Fund (UNICEF)

United Nations Program of Action for African Economic Recovery and
  Development (UNPAAERD)
United Nations Technical Assistance (UNTA)
World Bank (WB)
World Food Program (WFP)
World Health Organization (WHO)
World Trade Organization (WTO)

OTHER ORGANIZATIONS

Agency for International Development (AID) US
European Community (EC)
European Development Bank (EDA)
European Union (EU)
Organization for Economic Cooperation and Development (OECD)
Overseas Private Investment Corporation (OPIC) US
United States Department of Agriculture (USDA)
United States Department of Commerce (USDC)
G8 [Canada, France, Germany, Italy, Japan, Russia, the United Kingdom, and the
  United States]

FOREWORD

Africa is suffering. In the 40 years since the ending of colonialism, the continent has been smitten by three catastrophic droughts, civil war in countries that encompass more than half of all its inhabitants, the Tutsi genocide, six wars between African states, an AIDS epidemic of vast proportion, and adverse movements in its terms of trade. If we may describe these events as "external shocks" over which those in charge of the management of Sub-Saharan economies had little control, there were a variety of "internal factors" that have also contributed. Thus advances in national output have been repressed by economic policies that often include expenditure on grandiose projects and quick-fix economic controls. The former has drained precious tax proceeds and the latter has worked to destroy incentives to produce. And African economies have further been weakened by a blanket of theft cast by their national leaders and public servants. Such theft takes the form of fiduciary looting by those at the top and by pervasive corrupt exactions by those below charged with administering the nation's social and economic programs.

Yet the picture is not one of unmitigated gloom. Despite the common perception, Africa is not "a continent under intolerable strain, poised between crisis and catastrophe."[1] A true social and economic crisis would produce a fall in life expectancy—yet, AIDS notwithstanding, life expectancy is up by almost a quarter since 1960. Child mortality has been cut in half. Female literacy, with all it entails for health and childcare, at 48% is greater than in south Asia or North Africa. Higher up the ladder, female enrolment in secondary schools has risen from about 3 to 23%. Access to potable water is now over 30% as compared to

---

[1]From the *Financial Times*, July 24th, 1996 as cited by John Sender (1999) "Africa's Economic Performance: Limitations of the Current Consensus," *Journal of Economic Perspectives*, Summer, 13(3), 96. Most of the statistics cited in this paragraph are drawn from this excellent Marxist dissent from the conventional wisdom as to Africa's situation.

10% in 1970. As one of Adam Smith's primary determinants of the market's size, and hence advances in the division of labor, the network of paved roads between 1970 and 1990 had risen from 3.8 to 8.9 kilometers per thousand square kilometers. Agricultural yields per acre for most of the basic staple crops are up substantially since the early 1960s—29% for cassava, 43% for wheat, 57% for corn and 65% for rice. And Africa has had its own information explosion in terms of newspaper circulation, radio and TV ownership with expansions of five- to fifteenfold in the past 25 years. With more information disseminated across society, the foundations for improved decision making are laid, not only in matters of economics but also for politics. A better informed electorate makes it that much harder for authoritarian regimes to retain power. Such regimes have recently been replaced by multiparty electoral systems in Nigeria and Ghana— joining six smaller countries—so that over a quarter of all Africans now live in functioning democracies, as fragile and imperfect as they may be.

For the students of this volume, these disparate elements of gloom and hope, of progress and stagnation will become part of an intelligible whole. Borrowing Sir Frederick Lugard's term, its authors have set themselves a "dual mandate." The first part of that mandate is to provide a comprehensive survey of Africa's economic development. Early chapters by Emmanuel Nnadozie and Mario Azevedo set out the essential facts, diversity, and unique features of its climate, topography and history that have shaped the post-colonial experience. In the chapters that follow virtually every sector of the economy—agriculture, health, education, communications, labor, financial markets, and trade—are described and their performance over the past 40 years evaluated. No other book on African economies can boast such breadth. Indeed one would have to go back to Lord Hailey's magisterial 1800-page *An African Survey* of 1945 for comparable scope. Interestingly, Lord Hailey's opening paragraph setting out his objectives applies equally well to the present undertaking:

> This work is not limited to a discussion of the state of our knowledge regarding the problems which are involved in the development of Africa; it attempts also to describe the physical and social background out of which these problems have arisen, and to analyze the factors which, so far as can now be seen, must determine their solution.

The second part of the mandate set by our authors relates to Lord Hailey's final point, analyzing the factors which must determine the solution to Africa's current ills. Leading scholars in their field—Paul Collier, John Quinn, John Mbaku, E. Wayne Nafziger, Kwabena Gyimah-Brempong, Marcel Fafchamps, James Duesenberry—probe deeply into the adequacy of contemporary economic and political theory as they apply to Africa's problems. The focus is on economic policy and the empirical testing of policy prescriptions. How the formulation, adoption, and implementation of those policies are impacted by ethnic diversity, political instability, corruption, and globalization are closely scrutinized.

Few stones are left unturned. Other topics explored include the continent's experience with structural adjustment programs, the potential of regional cooperation and of utilization of the Internet, and the economics of conflict and humanitarian emergencies.

"Seek ye first the political kingdom." In the final chapter of this volume, Arthur Goldsmith and his co-authors offer the proposition that the leaders of Africa have, in effect, run Thomas Hobbes' *Leviathan* in reverse. In a state of nature it is "all against all," where no rules prevail, uncertainty reigns supreme. Here human life is "nasty, poor, brutish and short" and, it hardly need be added, the returns to effort and enterprise, to savings and investment are highly problematic. To escape this predicament a *social contract* is struck where the people submit themselves to an independent political authority that provides in exchange social peace and "commodious living." No mean attainment, Adam Smith judged this state of things to be in itself the necessary *and* sufficient condition for economic development: "Little else is requisite to carry a state to the highest degree of opulence from the lowest barbarism but peace, easy taxes, and tolerable administration of justice; all the rest being brought about by the natural course of things." During the late 1960s and the 1970s Africa's leaders breached the social contract, sewing disorder and compelling their subjects to fall back on traditional and informal mechanisms. Once the contract is securely reinstated, once the extraordinarily difficult task of returning good government to Africa has been accomplished, then and only then will a sustained development process be possible. This book makes important scholarly and policy contributions by providing a multitude of insights into Africa's development conditions. African decision makers must be open to learn from and act upon the type of analysis and policy prescriptions set forth in this volume which point to the roads to be avoided and the roads to be taken.

Peter Kilby
Middletown, Connecticut
January, 2003

PREFACE

The African Economic Development textbook is prepared for use at the university level for such courses such as African Economic Development, Economic Development, and International and African Studies. The book is comprehensive and eclectic; therefore, accessible to a wide audience. It pays great attention to maintaining balance among the economic development theoretical constructs. The text also identifies critical African development issues in a comparative, cross-sectional, and sound pedagogical procedure using appropriate theoretical tools.

The book is structured and written both for students who have had some basic training in economics and for those with little or no formal economics background. The textbook may also be useful to undergraduate and graduate students and others who are interested in African development. It highlights and explains, at appropriate points, essential principles and concepts of economics that are particularly relevant for the understanding of African development problems and issues. These concepts are also defined in a detailed and extensive glossary. Thus, the book should be of special value in undergraduate and international courses that attract students from a variety of disciplines. In addition, the coverage is broad in scope and rigorous enough to satisfy any undergraduate and certain graduate economics requirements in the field of economic development.

WHAT THIS BOOK CONTAINS

APPROACH

This book contains chapters from prominent scholars, which focus on African economic development. These articles examine both the political and institutional framework in which economic development takes place. Furthermore, they consider the economic situations in African countries, including their relationship with rich nations.

The book provides answers to four fundamental questions: (1) What is African development and how is it unique? (2) What appears to have caused development to occur in more advanced regions and do current economic theories explain Africa's performance? (3) How can we bring about development in Africa and what is the role of the state? (4) In the current era of globalization, what should be the relationship between richer nations and African countries, especially with regard to aid, debt, and trade?

Hence, the articles included in this book are publications that deal with such issues as the causes of Africa's underdevelopment, poverty, income distribution and income inequality, development and human welfare, the theories of development, and strategies for Africa's economic development. The articles contained in the text recognize the historical realities of African countries and adopt a pragmatic approach that balances the different schools of thought within the spectrum of African development thinking, to make the book comprehensive and more holistic. Hence, the book contains articles that do the following:

- Provide a comparative approach to elucidate real-world development issues using appropriate theoretical tools.
- Emphasize a problem-solving scenario by characterizing the problems and identifying the best solutions.
- Use cross-sectional and time series data from various parts of Africa.
- Are multidimensional and interdisciplinary works that present the different dimensions of the issues.
- Deal, from an economic point of view, with the critical issues relating to women and development, the environment, wars, famine, and AIDS.
- Recognize development problems and solutions from institutional and structural perspectives.
- Understand the growing global interdependence and the role of the information age in Africa's economic development.

ORGANIZATION AND CONTENT

The book is organized into six parts. Part I introduces Africa and African economic development. This segment is designed to provide the reader with the basic development concepts, the characteristics of the African continent, and African development.

Part II deals with Africa's theoretical, demographical, and poverty-related challenges. In Chapter 4, "Geo-Economy and History," Mario Azevedo provides the reader with a brief history and geography of Africa. Azevedo's chapter presents a minimal but useful set of basic information for the reader. Marcel Fafchamps presents a well-developed expose on the usefulness of economic theory in explaining the African development experience. Fafchamps argues that geographical proximity is key and Africa is penalized by its geographical isolation. Jacob Adetunji's chapter focuses on demography and the labor market. The importance of this chapter lies in the fact that population—which should engender development and for whom development is meant—is at the center of the development discussion. Adetunji argues that higher population growth rates, which lead to higher labor force growth rates, constitutes one of the major challenges to African development. Nick Vink's and Norma Tregurtha's contribution focuses on the challenges of poverty. Essentially, Vink and Tregurtha illustrate how basic choices or capabilities can be accounted for in the measurement of poverty to ensure a policy more suited to understanding the plight of poor people. This was accomplished through a case study of farm workers on commercial farms in South Africa.

Part III of the book discusses critical issues in Africa economic development in the areas of ethnic diversity, health, education, democracy, political instability, conflict and corruption. Paul Collier's "Implications of Ethnic Diversity" sets the tone by providing a refreshing view on the consequences of ethno-linguistic fractionalization in Africa. Collier highlights the role of primary commodity, the degree of fractionalization, and the diaspora in explaining conflict and provides useful policy suggestions. Azevedo addressess the subject of health, while Azevedo and Nnadozie address education. Azevedo argues that Africa is in a health crisis which is depleting both the human and economic resources needed for development and disease eradication. According to Azevedo, factors responsible for the crisis include: natural climatic conditions, the colonial legacy, unwise policies introduced by the African leadership, and Africa's international debt burden.

On education, Azevedo and Nnadozie conclude that education contributes both directly and indirectly to economic development by improving human capital, productivity of labor, economic growth, and human and social welfare. They argue that despite recent accomplishments in literacy rates, like the colonial educational system, the post-colonial African educational systems have been inadequate and have had difficulty adapting to the development needs of the African people.

In Chapter 11, John Quinn explores the relationship between democracy and development and examines how the two are linked. In his view, although democracy has been a much studied issue, the direction of causation is still much in debate: Does development lead to democracy, or does democracy promote development? Or both? Quinn concludes that the literature supports both sides.

Kwabena Gyimah-Brempong investigates the relationship between political instability and economic development in African countries and confirms what most studies have found, that political instability has a negative and statistically significant impact on economic growth in Africa. In his estimation, political instability affects growth both directly and indirectly through a reduction in capital formation. He also found that slow economic growth causes political instability, which in turn leads to further economic stagnation.

Given the proliferation of conflict in Africa, Nafziger's chapter, "Inequality and Conflict," is very germane to the development question. This chapter focuses on how economic factors affect complex humanitarian emergencies, comprising a human-made crisis in which large numbers of people die and suffer from war, physical violence (often by the state), and refugee displacement. In Nafziger's view, the crisis is complex because it is multidimensional, politicized, and persistent.

In Chapter 14, John Mukum Mbaku discusses the problem of corruption in Africa and its negative effects on economic development. Mbaku argues that while corruption is a serious development problem for most of the countries on the continent, several countries, notably Botswana, Mauritius, Namibia, Tunisia, and South Africa, are making significant progress in fighting this scourge.

Part IV, "Sectoral Analysis," begins with a chapter entitled "Land Tenure, Agriculture, and Economic Development" by Nii O. Tackie, Arthur Siaway, and Ntam Baharanyi. The authors present the different land tenure systems in Africa and their impact on economic development by way of agricultural production. According to the authors, existing land tenure systems have been blamed for the lack of increase in agricultural productivity, and hence, lack of economic development in Africa. They recommend selective or guarded land tenure reform as a solution to the land tenure problem. In Chapter 16, Léonce Ndikumana examines the role of financial markets in economic development and argues that, although evidence on Africa is still limited, the results from existing empirical work supports the view that financial development has a positive effect on economic growth in African countries.

Following the chapter on financial markets, Seymour Patterson presents Africa's capital investment- and saving-related problems. According to him, African countries have a saving gap, which means that investment requirements of an African country are greater than the country's capacity to finance them from domestic savings alone. He also presents evidence of the positive correlation between growth and investment, and argues that, for African countries, the solution to low growth is physical capital formation.

Part V deals with "Africa and the International Environment" by looking at trade, regionalism, globalization, and communications and information technology. Victor Oguledo shows the mutually reinforcing influence that trade and development have on each other. He also provides a detailed analysis of the static and dynamic benefits of trade and argues that, on balance, African countries stand to benefit from trade, especially if they pursue credible liberal trade policie and increase public investment in economic and social infrastructure. In Chapter 19, Femi Babarinde continues the discussion by employing regionalism as a tool for explaining why economic development in all of its manifestations has eluded the African people. In that same vein, Babarinde shows how regionalism can be utilized to advance the continent's economic development. Following Babarinde's chapter, Richard Mshomba considers the trend toward greater globalization and discusses the benefits and challenges of globalization to African countries. He suggests ways in which African countries can work to increase the benefits and meet the challenges of globalization. Mshomba also suggests how the benefits associated with globalization can be used to foster real economic development.

Finally, Francis Matambalya assesses how investments in information and communications technology ICTs can potentially affect Africa's economic development prospects and concludes that ICTs prop up productivity-propelled growth. Matambalya argues that ICTs enable economic units to increase productivity, thus building a base for sustainable growth.

In Part VI, the final segment of the book, Sarah Bryant Bower points out that almost every country on the continent has been involved in structural adjustment programs with the World Bank and IMF. Economic theory, she argues, has developed to guide policy prescriptions for the reforms needed to improve growth conditions.

This book attempts to provide a multidimensional perspective on ways of bringing development to Africa. There are abundant recommendations on how to bring about economic development in Africa—from World Bank publications, to texts and scholarly articles used in intellectual circles. Indeed, in 1991, the World Bank devoted its *World Development Report* to the "Challenge of Development" to explain how development occurred in the developed world and how it would occur in developing countries. In another publication, the World Bank (2000) asks: *Can Africa Claim the 21st Century?* Each year, the World Bank publishes the *World Development Report* and the United Nations Development Program publishes the *Human Development Report*. It is, therefore, a difficult task to synthesize these myriad prescriptions in a single, brief chapter. The prescriptions can be categorized into three groups: those that are part and parcel of the development theories presented in the preceding section and in Marcel Fafchamps' chapter; those that have been perennially prescribed by the multilateral organizations—the World Bank, United Nations, and IMF—and their experts; and those found in literature written by scholars and development practitioners. By and large, the generally recommended approach has been to target growth as a means of bringing about economic development. More recently, poverty reduction has emerged as the main target.

Based on the foregoing discussions, the principal goal of this book is to demonstrate how Africa's development dilemma is multifaceted and not solely dependent on economic variables. In reality, however, the prescriptions for Africa's development problems have not matched the diagnosis. With few exceptions, the underlying prescriptions and its modus operandi have remained a one-size-fits-all neo-liberal structural adjustment program prescribed mostly by outsiders. Since the 1960s, Africa has suffered from faulty and inappropriate advice by well-meaning but often uninformed, biased, and sometimes politically motivated "expert" advisers from the developed world, assisted by the World Bank, the IMF, and the United Nations. The bottom line of this book is that Africa's performance is influenced by its history and its geography. More eclectic approaches and models of growth must be developed in order to better understand the significance of other non-economic variables, including historical, political, socio-cultural, geographical and environmental, and international.

From this book we can identify five other key issues:

1. There are no absolute solutions to Africa's problems, especially since many of the largely economic development prescriptions for African countries are of little relevance to the continent. We also learn that ethnic diversity, colonial legacy, political instability, democracy, culture and geography are being raised as possible causes of Africa's underdevelopment within the mainstream of economic thinking.

2. There is a need for increased pragmatism and lessened ideological or political focus. Each African country must adopt a pragmatic choice of policies based on its historical, social, political, economic, and environmental realities. Policies could carefully mix interventionist and laissez-faire.

3. In many respects, the economic environment is improving in Africa as we see in Chapter 2. The macroeconomic policy environment is changing through economic reform and financial institutions are also reforming. Labor market reforms are underway but need to intensify. There is a need to invest heavily in infrastructure.

4. Regionalism and such regional organizations as AEC, ECOWAS, and SADC are, in spite of their numerous problems, slowly beginning to address the problems of market size, multiplicity of inconvertible currencies, and inadequate infrastructure.

The passage of time has shown that dire predictions about other regions have been wrong. The performance of other regions, coupled with the achievements of a number of African countries, suggests that a significant reduction in poverty is possible in Africa. Nonetheless, what is needed for Africa to develop (according to the World Bank) are leadership, better governance, human and physical capital investment, and international support.

Emmanuel Nnadozie
Kirksville, Missouri
January, 2003

ACKNOWLEDGMENTS

The production of such an important work as *African Economic Development* requires a momentous level of contribution by many people. Indeed, this book would not have been possible without the invaluable assistance, noteworthy support, and limitless kindness of several individuals. Prominent among these are the contributors to this volume to whom I am greatly indebted: Jacob Adetunji, Mario Azevedo, Femi Babarinde, Ntam Baharanyi, Sarah Bryant Bower, Paul Collier, James Duesenberry, Marcel Fafchamps, Arthur A. Goldsmith, Kwabena Gyimah-Brempong, Francis Matambalya, John Mukum Mbaku, Malcolm F. McPherson, Richard Mshomba, E. Wayne Nafziger, Léonce Ndikumana, Victor Oguledo, Seymour Patterson, John Quinn, Arthur Siaway, Nii Tackie, Norma Tregurtha, and Nick Vink. I am exceptionally grateful to Peter Kilby for his invaluable support and for writing this book's Foreword.

The development of this book also benefited from the wisdom and professional review of many experts. I am especially grateful to the anonymous reviewers in the United States and abroad whose detailed and insightful commentaries and critique of the proposal and manuscripts proved immensely helpful in shaping the fine product that *African Economic Development* has become.

Deserving of a great deal of gratitude are J. Scott Bentley and Paul Gottehrer of Academic Press, an imprint of Elsevier Science; Harsha Vasisht of Cepha Imaging Pvt Ltd.; and Paula Presley of Truman State University Press for their immense help and guidance throughout the production of this textbook. I am equally indebted to my esteemed colleagues Chudi Uwazurike, Ebere Onwudiwe, Richard Sklar, Martin Onwu, Una Okonkwo-Osili, Chuma Obidegwu, Dwayne Smith, Bertha Thomas, John Ishiyama, Mark Abani, Bob Shermann, Yaw Nyarko, Kasirim Nwuke, and Chuma Soludo. Their support and generosity was especially vital.

Over the course of its development, the assistance of the following indefatigable student assistants was vital for the realization of *African Economic Development*: Karin Ernst, Mary McCarville Brown, Sara Durham, Maria Augusta Carasco, Fadzai Doreen Smout, Lisa Miller, Carrie Puckett, Valerie Hopkins, Martha Miricho, Lindsay Sims, Anita Stoyanova, Andrea Isbell, Thokozile Kachipande, Franita Smith, Olesya Paramonova, Hristina Toshkova, Anette Hoskins, Natasha Jones, Todor Stavrev, Pamela Agbevey, and Antoneta Tacheva. Likewise, I am greatly indebted to Sarah A. Hass, Teresa York, and Summer Battles whose unwavering professional support, kindness, and generosity were as extremely important to the success of the project as their editorial support. I am also very appreciative of my former students in the United States for helping in shaping the ideas of this textbook.

Family support was also essential in keeping me grounded and focused. My gratitude, therefore, goes to Adaeze, Ozy, Chukwuma, Meg, Cecilia, Brian, Vic, Sam, Tessy, Igna, Zeek, Kent, and especially my mother Lolo Susanna Adanma Nnadozie. I am grateful to the Social Science Division and the McNair Program at Truman State University for providing me with the institutional arrangement that made possible such a huge undertaking as this book project. I am also indebted to the Afro-American African Studies Department at University of North Carolina at Charlotte where the original idea was developed, as well as the African Finance and Economics Association (AFEA) and the Akagu Foundation—the two organizations that provided me with great inspiration and through which I learned the true meaning of African development.

PART I

Introduction to Africa and African Economic Development

Why Study African Economic Development?

EMMANUEL NNADOZIE

Department of Economics, Truman State University, Kirksville, Missouri 63501

KEY TERMS

African dummy	Growth rates
Balanced growth	Illiteracy rates
Colonial legacy	Import substitution (IS)
Culture	Indicators of development
Democracy	Indicators of growth
Ethnic diversity	Neoclassical tradition
Export promotion	Neo-Marxist paradigm
Externalities	Orthodoxy
Gender gap	Per capita income
Geography	Political instability
Gross domestic product (GDP)	Primary school enrollment

I. INTRODUCTION

The problem of economic development is not new nor did it originate in Africa, as all countries of the world were at one time or another developing countries. Yet, it is not so difficult to see why the concept of development is so essential to Africanists and the study of Africa in general. After all, African economic development involves growth and the general improvement in quality of life and overall human welfare. Yet, by many measures of human welfare, Africa has not performed well, lagging behind the rest of the world.[1] For instance, Collier and Gunning[2] estimate that, during the 1980s, Africa's per capita gross domestic product (GDP) declined by 5% below the average for all low-income developing countries and 6.2% during the 1990–1994 period.

In reality, the concept or nature of development throughout the world does not differ; what is different is Africa's development experience vis-à-vis the rest of the world and the fact that global change may have a differential impact on Africa.

3

Based on Africa's unique economic performance record and because Africa is the least developed continent, with 70% of the countries being low income, it merits special attention. In the view of some researchers, Africa's growth experience is unique because of the so-called African dummy. These researchers, using cross-country regressions that find a significant negative African dummy variable, or so-called Africa effect, have concluded that being an African country has an adverse impact on growth.[3] Bloom and Sachs do not find a significant African dummy and argue that Africa's unique geographical characteristics explain its dismal growth experience.[4]

A. Africa's Development Experience

Because growth is central to development, we need to examine the growth experience of African countries. Some *indicators of growth* in the last two decades, 1977–1999, are presented in Table 1.1, Figure 1.1 shows a great diversity of growth experience, with some countries showing sustained and rapid growth and others declining over the two decades. As Table 1.1 and 1.2 and Fig. 1.1 show, Africa's development experience is unsatisfactory. The *growth rates* also reflect a great deal of inter-country diversity, with some countries achieving modest results, while others show significant losses. Overall, growth rates across Africa in the last two decades are disappointing.

Although many countries recorded significant increases between 1977 and 1999, per capita gross national product (GNP) growth was either small or negative, which is indicative of the high population growth rates evident in Table 2.1 (Chapter 2). Growth of over 4% per year was achieved, for instance, by Egypt, Tunisia, Botswana, Lesotho, Mauritius, and Seychelles. Morocco, Benin, Burkina Faso, Cape Verde, Ethiopia, The Gambia, Guinea, Guinea Bissau, Malawi, Mali, Swaziland, Tanzania, Uganda, and Zimbabwe all showed growth rates in income per capita above 2.4%. Unfortunately, pictures of rapid decline abound on the continent. Many economists believe that "countries with more rapid growth in incomes have indeed been those with higher savings rates and more industrialization."[5]

Because development implies economic structural change, we take an intertemporal look at the structure of the economies as presented in Table 1.1. Here, the picture is equally mixed—a shift out of agriculture over time alongside no shifts at all. Neither the manufacturing nor service sector in Africa is well developed. Overall, manufacturing contributes the least value added to the GDP.

Figure 1.1 shows that, with the exception of the outliers—Equatorial Guinea, which grew significantly during the period under review, and Congo and Sierra Leone, ravaged by civil war—the majority of African countries had growth rates within a 5-percentage-point spread. Indeed, the large majority of African countries grew by an average of less than 5% between 1990 and 1997.

Undoubtedly, this low growth explains to a large extent the lack of development on the continent.

Other indicators of development show a similar picture for Sub-Saharan Africa (SSA), especially when compared with other developing regions and all developing countries in general (see Table 1.2).

Using the *indicators of development*, we can determine the development performance of African countries within the context of other developing countries. In Table 1.2, we compare some development indicators of SSA, the Arab States, South Asia, and all developing countries. Table 1.2 shows that SSA has the lowest *per capita income* and *primary school enrollment*, the widest gender gaps, and the most inadequate communications infrastructure. *Illiteracy rates* are comparable between SSA and the Arab States, but they are outperformed by South Asia. On a brighter note, SSA has the lowest CO_2 emissions which is indicative of a low level of industrialization and consequent pollution in Africa. Overall, SSA has not had a successful development experience, as shown by various indicators. Africa remains the least developed of all the regions of the world. In 2000, 36% of African countries were considered not to be free, compared to 28% for Asia, 22% for Central and Eastern Europe and the former Soviet Union, and 6% for Latin America.[6] Until recently, Africa had made remarkable achievements in areas such as education and life expectancy, but cross-country comparisons (as well as intercontinental analysis) show that in the last 30 years, Africa has not performed as well as the rest of the world. There is, therefore, an urgent need to establish the appropriate framework to bring about development in Africa.

B. THE NEED FOR THE STUDY OF AFRICAN DEVELOPMENT

Aside from permitting us to focus on Africa's seemingly intractable state of underdevelopment, there are many other reasons why a study of African economic development is important. Specifically, the study of the economics of African development will help us to:

1. Become aware of the realities and disparities that exist between African countries and the rest of the world, especially with regard to distribution of income, resource endowment, and resource management.
2. Understand and grasp the economic, financial, and cultural circumstances of African countries and the causes and effects of poverty.
3. Understand the implications of decisions made by donor countries and institutions insofar as they affect African countries and the implications for wealthier countries of the socioeconomic difficulties of African countries

TABLE 1.1 Growth Rates 1977–1999

	GNP per capita (constant 1995 US$)	GNP per capita (% average annual growth rate) 1977–1997	GDP in billions, PPP (current international $)		GDP average annual growth rate (%)		Agriculture value added (% of GDP)		Industry value added (% of GDP)		Manufacturing value added (% of GDP)		Service value added (% of GDP)	
			1977	1997	1977–1990	1990–1997	1977	1997	1977	1997	1977	1997	1977	1997
Seychelles	7021	3.1	—	—	4.5	4.1	9.2	4.1	13.8	23.3	5.5	13.1	77.0	72.6
Gabon	3985	-3.1	3.2	8.7	-0.9	3.6	5.5	7.5	58.3	55.4	4.7	4.6	36.3	37.1
Mauritius	3796	3.5	1.8	10.6	4.6	5.3	19.7	8.9	25.4	33.0	14.6	24.7	54.9	58.1
South Africa	3377	-0.4	86.7	299.5	2.0	1.1	7.8	4.5	42.5	38.5	22.3	23.9	49.6	56.9
Botswana	3307	5.7	0.88	11.7	10.7	5.2	20.9	3.4	33.3	48.0	8.0	4.7	45.8	48.6
Namibia	2196	0.8	—	8.1	0.7	3.5	—	10.7	—	33.4	—	14.0	—	55.8
Tunisia	2092	2.0	8.7	48.8	4.3	5.0	15.8	13.1	25.7	28.5	10.6	18.5	58.4	58.3
Swaziland	1555	2.1	0.51	3.2	5.9	3.7	29.9	18.7	25.0	41.6	—	34.2	45.1	39.6
Algeria	1409	-0.3	33.9	130.7	3.5	0.6	10.0	11.4	51.2	49.4	9.3	9.1	38.8	39.2
Morocco	1281	1.5	19.4	90.3	4.4	2.5	16.4	15.3	32.6	33.2	16.6	17.6	51.1	51.5
Cape Verde	1108	1.5	—	1.2	6.0	3.2	—	8.7	—	21.4	—	0.5	—	69.9
Egypt	1097	3.8	26.7	184.0	6.4	4.2	27.1	17.7	27.2	31.8	14.9	25.2	45.7	50.5
Equatorial Guinea	892	11.0	—	—	1.4	18.0	—	23.1	—	67.2	—	9.7	—	9.7
Lesotho	734	1.7	0.58	3.7	6.1	6.9	34.3	11.5	15.5	42.0	5.0	17.2	50.2	46.5
Cote d'Ivoire	727	-1.6	8.0	26.1	1.2	2.5	24.3	27.3	15.2	21.2	7.6	17.6	60.6	51.5
Zimbabwe	656	-0.1	5.8	26.9	3.8	2.7	18.1	18.6	31.1	25.2	19.3	17.7	50.8	56.2
Congo, Rep.	633	0.3	0.77	4.3	5.5	1.0	15.4	9.5	31.6	57.1	—	6.1	52.9	33.4
Cameroon	587	1.0	7.1	26.4	5.4	-0.7	33.6	40.9	18.4	21.5	9.0	10.3	48.0	37.6
Senegal	554	-0.5	3.9	15.2	2.1	2.8	27.1	18.5	14.4	22.2	—	14.8	58.5	59.3
Guinea	552	2.0	—	13.0	3.7	4.7	—	22.6	—	35.3	—	4.4	—	42.1
Mauritania	452	-0.2	1.0	4.2	1.6	3.3	29.2	25.5	29.8	29.0	—	9.7	41.0	45.5
Comoros	413	-1.1	—	0.79	3.0	0.2	—	38.7	—	12.8	—	5.3	—	48.5
Zambia	387	-2.0	3.0	9.0	0.5	1.1	16.4	16.4	37.7	31.4	17.8	12.3	46.0	52.2
Ghana	384	0.0	7.0	29.4	2.2	4.2	56.2	35.8	15.8	25.7	10.8	9.1	28.0	38.5
Benin	381	0.8	1.4	7.3	3.6	3.9	31.9	38.4	12.6	13.9	9.0	8.4	55.6	47.7
Gambia, The	342	-0.2	0.38	1.7	3.7	2.7	35.5	29.9	10.9	14.8	4.6	6.1	53.6	55.4
Central African Republic	341	-1.5	1.7	4.5	0.7	0.7	40.2	54.1	19.7	18.0	6.5	8.6	40.1	27.8
Togo	337	-0.4	1.7	6.4	2.8	2.0	35.4	41.8	19.5	20.8	6.3	8.7	45.1	37.4

Kenya	330	0.8	6.8	33.9	5.0	2.3	42.0	28.8	18.0	15.5	11.0	10.1	40.1	55.6
Uganda	326	2.4	—	23.6	3.4	7.0	74.0	43.8	7.0	17.3	5.8	8.2	19.0	38.9
São Tomé and Principe	297	0.4	1.9	—	1.0	1.0	61.4	23.3	11.0	18.7	5.8	2.9	27.7	58.0
Mali	259	0.2	11.1	7.6	2.4	3.1	39.9	49.2	12.4	17.3	6.0	7.0	47.7	33.5
Sudan	255	-0.2	2.2	43.3	0.6	6.4	34.3	35.4	24.4	26.8	18.2	20.3	41.3	37.8
Burkina Faso	250	0.8	30.7	10.5	3.1	3.4	29.6	32.7	31.4	46.9	4.6	4.8	39.0	20.4
Nigeria	239	-0.8	—	107.9	1.8	3.8	46.2	53.8	22.6	11.0	—	7.0	31.2	35.2
Guinea-Bissau	232	0.7	4.6	—	3.1	3.9	32.8	31.6	17.0	13.5	—	11.2	50.2	54.9
Madagascar	229	-1.8	1.8	13.1	1.2	0.9	—	9.3	—	29.5	—	15.6	—	61.2
Eritrea	222	3.6	1.6	3.0	—	5.0	35.2	38.8	13.6	14.8	—	12.2	51.3	46.4
Chad	218	0.1	2.6	6.1	0.7	4.6	51.1	37.5	23.3	26.0	10.8	19.0	25.6	36.5
Rwanda	207	-0.4	—	5.1	3.8	0.4	51.8	38.0	14.0	18.0	15.6	6.6	34.2	44.1
Niger	202	-1.5	1.6	8.2	2.0	1.2	—	47.3	—	17.5	5.1	13.6	—	46.1
Tanzania	183	0.9	—	18.0	4.7	3.2	41.8	36.3	18.7	62.0	—	4.2	39.6	28.7
Malawi	163	0.5	1.0	7.2	3.0	4.6	—	9.3	—	20.8	11.7	6.9	—	29.1
Angola	159	-5.2	1.3	16.7	3.3	0.4	37.2	50.1	19.9	16.7	5.5	9.7	42.9	30.0
Sierra Leone	150	-3.0	—	1.9	1.4	-4.7	63.8	53.3	14.0	24.3	9.1	9.5	22.2	44.8
Burundi	141	-0.6	25.0	4.0	4.2	-1.9	—	31.0	—	16.9	—	—	—	25.2
Mozambique	131	0.2	—	12.3	0.5	4.7	23.0	57.9	—	—	—	—	52.0	—
Congo, Democratic Republic of	114	-5.1	—	40.8	0.5	-6.1	—	55.5	25.0	—	—	—	—	—
Ethiopia	112	0.3	—	30.1	2.5	3.6	1.6	3.6	—	6.7	2.2	0.3	—	37.9
Libya	—						—	—	72.3	—	—	—	26.1	—
Djibouti	—					-2.6	31.9	—	32.7	20.5	6.4	5.7	35.5	75.8
Liberia	—						—	—	—	—	—	—	—	—
Mayotte	—													
Reunion	—													
Somalia	—						—	61.0	12.0	—	5.1	—	27.0	—

Source: World Bank (2001) *World Development Indicators 2001* (CD-ROM), Washington, D.C.: The World Bank.

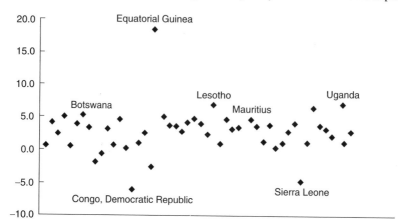

FIGURE 1.1 Average annual growth rate (%) of African countries, 1990–1997. (Based on data collected from World Bank (2001), *World Development Indicators 2001*, (CD-ROM), Washington, D.C.: The World Bank.)

TABLE 1.2 Indicators of Development in Sub-Saharan Africa and Other Regions

	Per capita GDP	Primary school enrollment	Infant mortality (per 1000 live births)	Adult illiteracy rates (age 15 and above) (%)	Carbon dioxide emissions	Gender-related development index (GDI)	Communication (main telephone lines/1000 1996–1998)
Sub-Saharan Africa	1607	56.2	138	40.6	2.0	0.459	14
Arab States	4140	86.4	126	40.3	3.8	0.612	65
South Asia	2112	78.0	130	45.7	5.8	0.532	24
All developing countries	3270	85.7	110	27.6	36.4	0.634	58

Source: United Nations Development Program (2000) *Human Development Report 2000*, London: Oxford University Press.

within the context of international relations, geopolitical concerns, national security, military power, strategic questions, etc., which are affected by the economic development or lack of it in Africa.

4. Become aware of how to apply economics in our analysis and understanding of the economies of African countries.

5. Become fully prepared and equipped for the dynamic global economy and the tremendous interrelationships or lack thereof involved in the economic functioning of the international scene.

6. Prepare and train future African development practitioners for the onerous task of generating economic development on the continent of Africa.

A study of African economic development is equally important because Africa's role and participation in the global marketplace are increasing. African countries are all members of global organizations (e.g., United Nations or World Trade Organization), albeit often in a nominal manner. As of November 2000, 41 of the 140 members of the World Trade Organization (WTO) were African countries, with the majority of them joining the organization at its inception in January 1995. They form part of and participate in the programs of (global) multilateral organizations (World Bank, International Monetary Fund (IMF), etc.). It is important, therefore, to determine how African countries are influenced by global phenomena. Notably, Africa's external debt has more than doubled in the past two decades. From a mere $93 billion in 1980, Africa's external debt grew to $240 billion in 1991 and rose to $285 billion in 1993. With a population of over 700 million people, Africa is an emerging market that cannot be ignored by the international community. Africa is dynamic, and many political, economic, and social changes are taking place around the continent. Consequently, the continent deserves serious attention.

Trade agreements such as the General Agreement on Tariffs and Trade (GATT), the subsequent creation of the World Trade Organization, and the emergence of trade-led growth by trade in Asia have brought international trade to the forefront of the development discourse. What impact does this trend have on Africa's development prospects? Of what relevance is the Asian development experience to Africa? These are the types of questions that this book addresses.

Furthermore, the explosion in communications technology has dramatically altered views on the limitations that nations face in their quest for economic progress. Could this mean that, finally, African countries could bridge the information gap and leapfrog into veritable 21st century economic miracles? It is equally important to inquire as to whether Africa can, or even must, attempt to cope with the pace of technological development. If the technological gap is inevitable, what lag size is permissible? This book on African economic development provides answers to this and other questions.

Globalization and the shift to market-based economic systems by many African countries, championed by international financial institutions, present many challenges for the state and for economic development and international relations. Not that Africa is having a bigger impact on the world, but global changes may have a differential impact on Africa. For precisely this reason, a book that deals specifically with African economic development is important.

Finally, ". . .the great diversity in the circumstances, attainments and difficulties across the world's countries" makes such simple distinctions as "North and South, developed and underdeveloped, and so on, extremely misleading."[7] Hence, one must minimize this high degree of diversity through the sort of regional focus on Africa that this book provides. A focus on Africa will enable us to shed more light on the uniqueness of the African continent and its development difficulties and their global implications and to determine whether Africa-specific remedies are necessary to bring about development on the African continent.

II. PRINCIPAL MESSAGES

This book examines a multiplicity of theories and models, from classical and Marxist to neoclassical, neo-Marxist, structural, and other combinations, while recognizing the widespread disagreement among economists as to why development occurs or fails to occur in a country or region. The book helps us to understand Africa's development experience and its underlying theories. Until recently, economists (mostly of the orthodox school) tended to provide a uniquely economic explanation for Africa's underdevelopment. In fact, the original interest in growth, be it in Africa or in the developing world as a whole, has little to do with underdevelopment.[8] Consequently, research on Africa's development has focused on economic variables; as a result, development prescriptions have remained largely economic in nature. There has been an unbridled reign of orthodoxy based on the aforementioned models, which in most cases have had little or no relevance to Africa.

For instance, Arthur Lewis, a pioneer development economist and Nobel Laureate, developed a theory to explain the mechanism by which underdeveloped economies transform their domestic economies. As a structuralist, Lewis focuses mostly on internal sources of underdevelopment and uses a two-sector surplus labor model to show that the dualistic nature of developing economies made up of urban (modern) and rural (traditional and agricultural) sectors create differential marginal products of labor. This means that investment in the urban sector is necessary to reduce the rural surplus labor and increase the rural marginal product of labor. Following Lewis's focus on structural transformation from predominantly agricultural to industrial, other economic analysts focused on such areas as source of productivity, the role of trade, import substitution, balanced growth, and export promotion. Much of these development analyses focused on the issues considered central to growth: accumulation, technical change, human capital, population, and, later, trade. Another issue that has preoccupied development economists is the role of the market versus that of government. In the neoclassical tradition, the state's role is strictly limited to the provision of essential services and to the definition of property rights within the economic system, with the goal being to reduce externalities and promote and diffuse information about existing economic opportunities. In the neo-Marxist paradigm, the state is expected to become more activist in the development process, owning resources, producing goods and services, and planning development. When economic analysts of development began focusing on developing countries, they centered on cross-country regression analysis of mostly economic variables and growth was used as a proxy for development.[9]

At the dawn of the 21st century, there seems to be a new awakening to noneconomic variables in African development analysis. We now see such factors as ethnic diversity, colonial legacy, political instability, democracy, culture, and geography being raised within the mainstream of economic thinking as possible explanators of Africa's underdevelopment. Econometric models now incorporate noneconomic variables and economists are seeking to discern noneconomic sources of Africa's underdevelopment.

The starting point of this new wave was the opposing viewpoints about the existence of the so-called Africa effect or negative African dummy.[10] While some researchers posited that the Africa effect could be used to explain Africa's dismal growth, other economists found that colonial heritage explains African growth and rendered the African dummy insignificant.[11] Hence, they concluded that colonialism and colonial legacies have adversely affected growth in the former colonies in Sub-Saharan Africa even though differences exist among anglophone, francophone, and lusophone Africa.[12]

Aside from the role of geography and history, there is also the impact of sociocultural and political variables. Many economists and social scientists have determined that ethnic and cultural diversity lead to slow growth and, in fact, hold a country in a state of low growth, especially when coupled with economic distress, significant income inequality, limited political rights, and undemocratic systems. For instance, they have concluded that ethno-religious conflict and instability are bad for growth and development, and Africa has been bedeviled by ethnic conflict throughout its history.[13] Barro finds the existence of a nonlinear effect of democracy on growth.[14] This is in line with other findings based on rigorous studies which conclude that economic growth is unlikely to occur in the absence of political stability and democratic entrenchment.[15]

Early on, Scully concluded that "nations that have chosen to suppress economic, political, and civil liberties have gravely affected the standard of living of their citizens."[16] Today, emphasis is also being placed on social capital and geography[17] in the study of growth and development in Africa and elsewhere. Collier and Gunning[18] discuss lack of social capital, lack of openness to trade, deficient public service, geography and risk, lack of financial depth, and high aid dependence. Missing from their analysis is the historical legacy of colonialism and exploitation and external dimensions as sources of Africa's underdevelopment.

Perhaps none captures the dramatic shift in African development thinking better than the following statement from The World Bank:[19]

> The debate on Africa's slow growth has offered many explanations. Some factors—such as geography (tropical location, a low ratio of coastline to interior and the resulting high transport costs), small states, high ethnic diversity, unpredictable rainfall, and terms of trade shocks—are taken to represent "destiny," or exogenous factors beyond the control of African policymakers. Others, such as poor policies (including trade and exchange rate policies, nationalization, and other restraints on economic

activity) can, in principle, be changed. A second dimension distinguishes such factors depending on whether they are primarily domestic or external.

We can only conclude that the study of the economics of African development is in flux and based on cross-country studies. Africa's underdevelopment is caused by a complex mixture of factors, some of which lie in the continent's history of exploitation and colonialism, its postcolonial misgovernance and political instability, its location, and unfavorable external relations.[20] Also, Africa is more or less in a confused state, having served as the experimental laboratory for competing and often ruinous development ideologies, paradigms, and theories, imposed mostly from the outside. No unified theory of African development takes into consideration the continent's unique historical experience and legacy, the extreme levels of economic, sociocultural, and political diversity and demographic realities, resource endowment, and relations with the outside world.

DISCUSSION QUESTIONS

1. Why do we need to study African economic development?
2. Why does Africa's development experience make it necessary for us to study African economic development?
3. Describe the growth experience of African countries in the 1990s.
4. Do you think that Africa's growth experience differs from the rest of the world? If so, how?
5. Until recently, economists (mostly of the orthodox school) tended to provide a uniquely economic explanation for Africa's underdevelopment. How has this focus changed in recent times?
6. Do you think that the current explosion in information technology and globalization would help African countries leapfrog into veritable 21st century economic miracles?
7. Use examples to explain what we mean when we say that the study of African economic development is in a flux.
8. In the 1980s and 1990s, there was a significant shift in African development thinking. What is this shift in thinking and how has it unfolded?
9. Table 1.2 presents information on basic indicators for African countries. Describe Africa's growth and development experience based on this table. Do you see any direct and inverse relationships between economic growth and any other variables?

NOTES

[1]For more information on how Africa has performed *vis-à-vis* the rest of the developing world in the last three decades and on the explanation for Africa's poor economic performance, see Collier, P. and

Gunning, J.W. (1999) "Explaining African Economic Performance," *Journal of Economic Literature,* 37: 64–111; and Easterly, W. and Levine, R. (1997) "Africa's Growth Tragedy: Policies and Ethnic Divisions," *Quarterly Journal of Economics,* 112: 1203–1250.

[2]Collier, P. and Gunning, J.W. (1999) "Explaining African Economic Performance," *Journal of Economic Literature,* 37: 64–111.

[3]Grier, K., and Tullock, G. (1989). "An Empirical Analysis of Cross-National Economic Growth, 1951–1980." *Journal of Monetary Economics,* 24: 259–276; Barro, R.J. (1991) "Economic Growth in a Cross Section of Countries," *Quarterly Journal of Economics,* 106: 407–443; See also Easterly and Levine (1997) and Collier and Gunning (1999).

[4]Bloom, D.E. and Sachs, J.D. (1998) "Geography, Demography, and Economic Growth in Africa," *Brookings Papers on Economic Activity,* 2: 207–295.

[5]Stern, N. (1989) "The Economics of Development: A Survey," *The Economic Journal,* 99 (September): 612.

[6]Freedom House (2002) "Freedom in the World 2001–2002: Select Data from Freedom House's Annual Global Survey of Political Rights and Civil Liberties," www.freedomhouse.org/research/survey2002.htm; see also

[7]Stern (1989), p. 606.

[8]Basu, K. (1997) *Analytical Development Economics: The Less Developed Economies Revisited,* Cambridge, MA: MIT Press, p. 43.

[9]Stern (1989) provides us with invaluable insight on the origin and development of cross-country analysis of growth. According to him, early contributors include Clark, C. (1940) *The Conditions of Economic Progress,* London: Macmillan, Kuznets, S. (1961) "Quantitative Aspects of the Economic Growth of Nations: IV. Long-Term Trends in Capital Formation Proportions," *Economic Development and Cultural Change,* 11(2): 1–80; Kuznets, S. (1971) *Economic Growth of Nations: Total Output and Production Structure,* Cambridge, MA: Harvard University Press. Leading figures are Chenery, H.B. and Syrquin, M. (1975) *Patterns of Development, 1950–1970,* London: Oxford University Press; Chenery, H.B. (1979) *Structural Change and Development Policy,* New York: Oxford University Press; Chenery, H.B., Robinson, S. and Syrquin, M. (1986) *Industrialization and Growth: A Comparative Study.* Washington, D.C.: The World Bank. Also, Adelman, I. and Morris, C. (1973) *Economic Growth and Social Equity in Developing Countries,* Stanford, CA: Stanford University Press; Morris C. and Adelman, I. (1988) *Comparative Patterns of Economic Development 1850–1914,* Baltimore, MD: The Johns Hopkins University Press.

[10]See, for instance, Grier and Tullock (1989), Barro (1991), Easterly and Levine (1997), and Collier and Gunning (1999).

[11]Bertocchi, G., and Canovo, F. (1991) Economics Working Papers 202, Department of Economics and Business, Universitat Pompeu Fabra; Sala-i-Martín, X. (1997). "Empirics of Economic Growth: Cross-Sectional Analysis." *Zagreb Journal of Economics,* 1(1), 103–132.

[12]Price, G.N. (2000) "Economic Growth in a Cross Section of Non-Industrial Countries: Does Colonial Heritage Matter for Africa?," paper presented at the Allied Social Science Association Meeting, New Orleans, LA, January 4–7.

[13]Easterly and Levine (1997); Rodrick, D. (1998) "Where Did All the Growth Go? External Shocks, Social Conflict, and Growth Collapses," NBER Working Paper 6350; Collier, P. (1998) "The Political Economy of Ethnicity," paper presented at the Annual Bank Conference on Development Economics. Washington, D.C., April.

[14]Barro, R.J. (1997) *Determinants of Economic Growth: A Cross Country Empirical Study,* Cambridge, MA.: The MIT Press.

[15]See, for instance, Gyimah-Brempong and Corley, M. (2001) "Civil Wars and Economic Growth in Sub-Saharan Africa," paper presented at Allied Social Science Association Annual Meeting, New Orleans, LA, January 4–7.

[16]Scully, G.W. (1988) "Institutional Framework and Economic Development," *The Journal of Political Economy*, 96(3): 652–662.

[17]Collier and Gunning (1999) emphasize social capital while researchers who emphasize geography include Bloom and Sachs (1998); Collier and Gunning (1999); and Frankel, J.A. and Romer, D. (1999). "Does Trade Cause Growth?," *American Economic Review*, 89(3): pp. 379–398.

[18]see Collier and Gunning (1999).

[19]The World Bank (2000) *World Development Report 2000: Entering the 21st Century*. New York: Oxford University Press, p. 23.

[20]Many of the variables that have been found to be important in cross-country growth analysis are relevant for Africa. Temple, J. (1999) "The New Growth Evidence," *Journal of Economic Literature*, 37: 112–156, provides us with these variables: investment in physical capital, investment in human capital, investment in research and development, population growth, international trade, financial systems, macroeconomic policy, government size, infrastructure/public capital, income/wealth inequality, and social and political factors.

Overview of African Development

EMMANUEL NNADOZIE

Department of Economics, Truman State University, Kirksville, Missouri 63501

KEY TERMS

Anglophone	Italophone
Central Africa	Low income
Colonial experience	Lusophone
Colonialism	Middle income
East Africa	Political diversity
Economic diversity	Regional classification
Fancophone	Sociocultural diversity
High Income	Southern Africa
Hispanophone	Sub-Saharan Africa
Income-based classification	West Africa

I. INTRODUCTION

A. DIVERSITY AND CLASSIFICATION OF AFRICAN COUNTRIES

The map of Africa is like a giant jigsaw puzzle, indeed a tapestry of countries. In fact, it is a giant geopolitical puzzle created during the scramble for and partitioning of Africa among Belgium, France, Germany, Great Britain, and Italy.[1] Consequently, Africa has 53 countries, most of which were artificially created. Based on their geopolitical artificiality, these countries bear no resemblance to the historical, sociocultural, economic, and political realities of African societies, and one could argue that these African countries were set up for failure from the start.

Africa is more than three times the size of the United States and contains about 22% of the world's total land area. Covering about 11,699,000 mi[2], Africa is the second largest of the world's seven continents, following Asia. In 1995, about 12% of the world's population, an estimated 718 million people, lived in Africa, making it the world's second-most populous continent, after Asia. As a whole, Africa encompasses at least 53 nations, ranging from Nigeria, a country with an estimated 127 million people, to small island republics such as Comoros, with a population just over 500,000. As a developing continent, Africa presents the characteristics, opportunities, and challenges of developing regions.

II. THE DIVERSITY OF AFRICA

Africa is a very diverse continent—indeed, the *most* diverse—in political, environmental, sociocultural, and economic terms. We can differentiate among African countries in terms of their environmental, sociocultural, political, and economic diversity, as well as the diversity of their colonial experience and legacy. The 53 African countries differ in population and geographic size, resources, types of industry, role of government, state enterprise, and the degree of international dependency on international economic affairs. Furthermore, Africa's diversity extends to its physical environment in terms of size, climate, and vegetation. In terms of land area, Sudan is the largest country with 2,505,000 km^2, while Seychelles Island is the smallest country with only 45,000 km^2. The climatic and vegetational diversity includes temperate (Mediterranean), desert, savanna, humid tropical, and highland. There are over 2000 named African societal groupings in all, and more than 1000 African languages that differ from each other as much as English differs from French.

A. ECONOMIC DIVERSITY IN AFRICA

We can look at Africa's economic diversity through well-known basic indicators: population, population growth, infant mortality, per capita gross national product (GNP), life expectancy at birth, daily caloric supply per capita, gross domestic savings as percent of gross domestic product (GDP), Official Development Assistance (ODA) net disbursements or ODA receipts as percent of GDP, primary education as percent of age group enrolled in education, and real GDP per capita measured in terms of purchasing power parity (PPP).[2] These basic indicators are shown in Table 2.1.

From Table 2.1, we note that rich and poor countries coexist, as shown by per capita incomes in 1999: Seychelles, $10,600; Botswana, $6872; and Rwanda, $448. It is equally clear from this table that African countries are characterized by high population growth rates, high levels of infant mortality, and, with a few exceptions, low life expectancies at birth. Not shown are notable gender gaps in social and economic attainment. In general, life expectancies and savings rates seem to vary directly with income across the countries to a large extent, while infant mortality seems to vary inversely with per capita income, as Figure 2.1 suggests.

Figure 2.1 shows partial associations between life expectancy, infant mortality, and GDP per capita. Panel A shows the partial association between per capita GDP and life expectancy, while Panel B shows the partial association between per capita GDP and the infant mortality rate. The figure shows that per capita GDP is, in fact, highly correlated to both life expectancy and infant mortality. That is, African countries with higher per capita income tend to have higher life expectancy and lower infant mortality. The figure also shows that the relationship is positive for life expectancy and negative for infant mortality.

Although there is considerable diversity on the continent, the fact that all African countries are either middle- or low-income developing nations gives them some common characteristics. For example, common economic characteristics include low standards of living, such as low incomes, high inequality, poor health, inadequate education, and low levels of productivity. Other factors are high rates of population growth and dependency burdens, high and rising levels of unemployment and underemployment, and significant dependence on agricultural production and primary exports.

African countries also tend to have landlocked population concentrations and poor infrastructures, which negatively affect their growth prospects. Sachs and Warner[3] argue that, in addition to poor economic policy and lack of openness to international markets, geographical factors such as lack of access to the sea and tropical climate have also contributed to Africa's slow growth. In general, African countries are characterized by dominance, dependence, and vulnerability in international relations. Notwithstanding this unsatisfactory reality, development is underway in many countries.

Figure 2.1 (Panels A and B) and Table 2.2 show that in many respects, including literacy, infant mortality, and life expectancy rates, most African countries have progressed at remarkably rapid rates from a historical perspective.

III. CLASSIFICATION OF AFRICAN COUNTRIES

African countries can be classified on the basis of the region in which they are located, their income levels, and their colonial experience.

A. REGIONAL CLASSIFICATION

There are five generally accepted political regions in Africa: East, West, Central, North, and Southern (Table 2.3).

TABLE 2.1 Basic Indicators (1999)

	Total Population	Annual Population Growth (%)	Infant Mortality Rates (per 1000 live births)	GDP per capita PPP (Current International $)	Life Expectancy at Birth (Total Years)	Gross Domestic Savings (% of GDP)	Aid (Official Development Assistance as % of GNP, 1997)	Primary School Enrollment (% of Total School Age)	GDP per capita (Constant 1995 US$)	GNP per capita (Constant 1995 US$)
Seychelles	0.08	1.5	9	10,600	72	20	2.8	—	7177	6831
Mauritius	1.10	1.3	19	9107	71	23	1.0	96.5	4120	4054
South Africa	42.10	1.7	62	8908	48	18	0.4	99.9	3904	3819
Botswana	1.50	1.7	58	6872	39	14	2.6	80.1	3711	3563
Libya	5.40	2.2	22	6697	71	—	—	99.9	—	—
Gabon	1.20	2.3	84	6024	53	35	0.9	—	4369	3877
Tunisia	9.40	1.3	24	5957	73	24	1.1	99.9	2390	2286
Namibia	1.70	2.3	63	5468	50	9	5.0	91.4	2097	2145
Algeria	29.90	1.5	34	5063	71	32	0.6	96.0	1569	1495
Equatorial Guinea	0.40	2.6	104	4677	51	58	5.0	79.3	1149	959
Cape Verde	0.40	3.0	39	4490	69	10	26.2	99.9	1461	1447
Swaziland	1.00	2.9	64	3987	46	21	2.0	94.6	1394	1518
Egypt	62.60	1.8	47	3420	67	14	2.5	95.2	1191	1204
Morocco	28.20	1.7	48	3419	67	20	1.4	76.6	1359	1322
Angola	12.30	2.9	127	3179	47	—	9.9	34.7	520	233
Zimbabwe	11.90	1.8	70	2876	40	11	3.9	93.1	703	652
Guinea	7.20	2.3	96	1934	46	15	10.3	45.6	603	591
Ghana	18.70	2.3	57	1881	58	6	7.4	43.4	410	403
Lesotho	2.10	2.3	92	1854	45	—	7.4	68.6	513	658
Cote d'Ivoire	15.40	2.6	111	1654	46	23	4.7	58.3	787	730
Mauritania	2.50	2.7	88	1609	54	7	23.9	62.9	483	467
Gambia, The	1.20	2.8	75	1580	53	2	10.3	65.9	365	358
Cameroon	14.60	2.7	77	1573	51	19	5.9	61.7	656	626
São Tomé and Principe	0.10	2.3	47	1469	65	-9	86.3	—	337	300
Comoros	0.50	2.5	61	1429	61	0	14.5	50.1	388	388
Senegal	9.20	2.7	67	1419	52	13	9.6	59.5	591	582
Togo	4.50	2.4	77	1410	49	4	8.6	82.3	327	321

Country									
Sudan	28.90	2.3	67	1370	56	—	2.1	—	—	—
Djibouti	0.60	1.9	109	1266	47	—	17.5	31.9	—	—
Uganda	21.40	2.7	88	1167	42	5	12.8	—	347	348
Central African Republic	3.50	1.7	96	1166	44	7	9.2	46.2	347	341
Kenya	29.40	2.1	76	1022	48	7	4.6	65.0	337	332
Burkina Faso	10.90	2.4	105	965	45	10	15.5	32.3	267	266
Benin	6.10	2.7	87	933	53	6	10.7	67.6	402	399
Rwanda	8.30	2.5	123	885	40	−1	32.0	78.3	235	234
Eritrea	3.90	2.8	60	881	50	−21	14.8	29.3	173	205
Mozambique	17.20	1.9	131	861	43	7	37.4	39.6	198	185
Nigeria	123.80	2.5	83	853	47	18	0.5	39.6	250	229
Chad	7.40	2.7	101	850	49	−3	14.3	47.9	218	216
Madagascar	15.00	3.1	90	799	54	5	24.3	58.7	242	238
Congo, Democratic Republic of	49.70	3.2	85	760	46	—	3.2	58.2	—	—
Zambia	9.80	2.2	114	756	38	−1	16.9	72.4	389	374
Mali	10.50	2.4	120	753	43	10	18.4	38.1	280	275
Niger	10.40	3.4	116	753	46	4	18.6	24.4	209	206
Congo Republic	2.80	2.7	89	727	48	30	14.7	78.3	840	630
Guinea-Bissau	1.10	2.0	127	678	44	−2	49.9	52.3	183	166
Ethiopia	62.70	2.4	104	628	42	3	10.1	35.2	112	111
Malawi	10.70	2.4	132	586	39	−1	14.1	98.5	156	153
Burundi	6.60	2.0	105	578	42	0	12.6	35.6	143	141
Tanzania	32.90	2.4	95	501	45	2	13.1	47.4	188	188
Sierra Leone	4.90	1.9	168	448	37	−6	16.0	44.0	138	134

Note: All figures are 1999 figures unless otherwise indicated. Liberia, Mayotte, and Somalia were not included for lack of data. GDP = gross domestic product; PPP = purchasing power parity; GNP = gross national product.

Source: World Bank (2001) *World Development Indicators 2001* (CD-ROM), Washington, D.C.: The World Bank, except for the per capita GDP figures for Seychelles, Libya, Equatorial Guinea, São Tomé and Príncipe, Guinea Bissau, and Djibouti, which were 1998 PPP US$ obtained from United Nations Development Program (2000) *Human Development Report 2000*, New York: Oxford University Press, pp. 158–159.

In addition to the regional classification shown in Table 2.3, many development experts and organizations subdivide Africa into North Africa and Sub-Saharan Africa. This classification aggregates all other African countries with the exception of Algeria, Djibouti, Egypt, Libya, Morocco, and Tunisia.[4] Because South Africa is

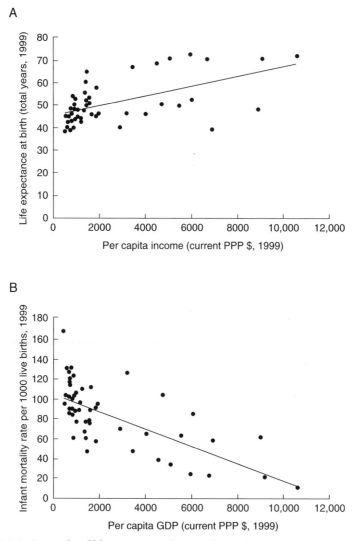

FIGURE 2.1   Scatter plot of life expectancy, infant mortality, and income in Africa, 1999. (A) Life expectancy and per capita GDP. (B) Infant mortality and per capita GDP. (From World Bank (2001) *World Development Indicators 2001* (CD-ROM), Washington, D.C.: The World Bank.)

TABLE 2.2   Changes in Illiteracy Rates, Life Expectancy, Birth Rates, and Infant Mortality in Selected African Countries

	Adult Illiteracy Rate (% of People Ages 15 and Above)		Life Expectancy		Birth Rate		Infant Mortality Rate	
	1970	1999	1960	1990	1960	1999	1960	1999
Algeria	76	33	47.28	67.37	51	25	166	34
Botswana	54	24	46.69	56.76	52	33	115	58
Cameroon	69	25	39.46	54.18	44	38	161	77
Chad	91	59	34.86	46.16	45	45	193	101
Comoros	58	41	42.69	55.97	40[a]	34	84[a]	61
Cote d'Ivoire	84	54	39.46	49.80	53	37	164	111
Egypt	69	45	46.37	62.81	45	26	178	47
Ethiopia	87	63	36.11	45.00	51	44	174	104
Gabon	—	—	40.88	51.88	31	36	169	84
Ghana	71	30	45.22	57.16	48	30	131	57
Kenya	59	19	44.95	57.11	53	35	123	76
Mauritius	33	16	59.40	69.64	43	17	68	19
Mozambique	83	57	37.49	43.44	47	40	189	131
Nigeria	80	37	39.66	49.05	51	40	189	83
Senegal	85	64	37.91	49.54	49	38	171	67
Uganda	64	34	44.06	46.75	49	46	131	88
Zambia	52	23	41.78	49.15	50	41	134	114
Zimbabwe	43	12	45.46	56.16	52	30	109	70

Source: World Bank (2001) *World Development Indicators 2001* (CD-ROM), Washington, D.C.: The World Bank.
[a]1990 figures; previous years were unavailable.

very different from other African countries south of the Sahara (accounting formore than 40% of Sub-Saharan Africa GDP), it is often excluded from Sub-Saharan Africa.

B. INCOME-BASED CLASSIFICATION OF AFRICAN COUNTRIES

The World Bank classifies economies based on per capita GNP:

- Low-income economies ($755 or less)
- Middle-income economies ($756–9265)
- Lower-middle-income economies ($756–2995)
- Upper-middle-income economies ($2996–9265)
- High-income economies ($9266 or greater)

TABLE 2.5   Cross-Classification Based on Income and Region in 2000

Income Group	Subgroup	East and Southern Africa	Central and West Africa	North Africa
		Sub-Saharan Africa		
Low income (38)		Angola	Benin	
		Burundi	Burkina Faso	
		Comoros	Cameroon	
		Congo, Democratic Republic of	Central African Repulic	
		Eritrea	Chad	
		Ethiopia	Congo Republic	
		Kenya	Cote d' Ivoire	
		Lesotho	Gambia, The Ghana	
		Madagascar	Guinea	
		Malawi	Guinea-Bissau	
		Mozambique	Liberia	
		Rwanda	Mali	
		Somalia	Mauritania	
		Sudan	Niger	
		Tanzania	Nigeria	
		Uganda	São Tomé and Principe	
		Zambia	Senegal	
		Zimbabwe	Sierra Leone	
Middle income	Lower (9)	Namibia	Togo	
		Swaziland	Cape Verde	Algeria
			Equatorial Guinea	Djibouti
				Egypt
				Morocco
				Tunisia
	Upper (7)	Botswana	Gabon	Libya
		Mauritius		
		Mayotte		
		Seychelles		
		South Africa		
Total		25	23	6

francophone countries (23) outnumber the rest. The anglophone countries, or former British colonies, follow with 20 countries. An exception has to be made for Liberia, which was established partly by freed slaves who returned from the Americas. Likewise, we need to note that the South African and Namibian experience with colonialism was different from that of the rest of Africa. Former Portuguese colonies, or lusophone countries, as they are generally called, are only five in number, while both hispanophones (former Spanish

TABLE 2.6   Classification Based on Colonial Experience

Francophone (23)	Anglophone (20)	Lusophone (5)
Algeria	Botswana	Angola
Benin	Egypt	Cape Verde
Burkina Faso	The Gambia	Mozambique
Burundi	Ghana	São Tomé and Principe
Cameroon	Kenya	Guinea Bissau
Central African Republic	Lesotho	
Chad	Liberia	**Hispanophone (2)**
Comoros	Malawi	Equatorial Guinea
Congo Republic	Mauritius	Western Sahara
Congo, Democratic	Namibia	
Republic of Zaire	Nigeria	**Italophone (2)**
Cote d'Ivoire	Seychelles	Eritrea
Djiouti	Sierra Leone	Somalia
Gabon	South Africa	
Guinea	Sudan	**Afrophone (1)**
Madagascar	Swaziland	Ethiopia
Mali	Tanzania	
Mauritania	Uganda	**Anglo/Franco (1)**
Morocco	Zambia	Libya
Niger	Zimbabwe	
Reunion		
Rwanda		
Senegal		
Togo		
Tunisia		

colonies) and italophones (former Italian colonies) have two countries each. Libya had both English and French colonial experience.

These countries tend to maintain the legacy of their colonial experience in terms of trade and relations with each other. This classification is relevant because it helps us understand differential contemporary cultures and worldview. According to Nnadozie,[6]

> The British colonial administration applied a system of "indirect rule," whereby they ruled their former colonies indirectly through local African leaders. [This] differed sharply from the more centralized assimilationist approach—in which the Africans were to be assimilated into European culture adopted by the French and Portuguese. The result was that anglophone countries obtained independence with a greater proportion of their culture intact than the francophone and lusophone African countries.

The Portuguese were also less inclined to grant independence to their African colonies, as in the case of Angola and Mozambique, which obtained their independence only in 1975.

Principe, Senegal, Seychelles, Sierra Leone, Somalia, South Africa, Sudan, Swaziland, Tanzania, Togo, Uganda, Zambia, and Zimbabwe.

[5]For more information on Africa's economic performance see Easterly, W. and Levine, R. (1997) "Africa's Growth Tragedy: Policies and Ethnic Divisions," *Quarterly Journal of Economics*, 112: 1203–1250.

[6]Nnadozie, E. (1998) *African Culture and American Business in Africa*, Kirksville, MO: Afrimax, p. 77.

CHAPTER 3

Definition and Measurement of Growth and Development

EMMANUEL NNADOZIE

Department of Economics, Truman State University, Kirksville, Missouri 63501

KEY TERMS

Basic needs	Human welfare
Clothing	Income poverty
Economic development	Inequality
Economic growth	Lorenz curve
Educational services	Physical Quality of Life Index
Food	Population below the poverty line
Gini ratio	Poverty
Gross national product (GNP)	Poverty rates
Health	Purchasing power
Housing	Purchasing power parity
Human Development Index	Quality of life
Human poverty	Real per capita GNP
Human Poverty Index	Structural transformation

I. INTRODUCTION

The problem of economic development is not new nor did it originate in Africa, as all countries of the world were at one time or another developing countries. In fact, the subject of development is so important in the history of human thought that many renowned thinkers have discussed it in their work. Adam Smith and Thucydides judged economic improvement in terms of increasing opulence, the growth of capital reserves, the expansion of commerce, and the enlarged power in war or peace which greater wealth bestowed.[1] Karl Marx saw economic progress as a movement from a primitive and slave society through feudalism, capitalism, and socialism to the ideal classless society of communism, which improves the status and conditions of labor. In the Marxist views, economic progress involves the final liberation of labor from its oppressors through dialectical materialism, which consequently makes economic progress inevitable.

Until recently, economic development had been viewed mostly in terms of increase in per capita income. This narrow definition of development was abandoned when evidence, especially in the 1950s and 1960s, showed that countries can grow significantly without an improvement in the standard of living of the masses of people. More economists adopted a people-centered development view and broadened their definition to include issues of redistribution. Hence, in 1991, the World Bank, recognizing this shift in development thinking, described development as "a sustainable increase in living standards that encompass material consumption, education, health and environmental protection."[2] This chapter defines the economics of African development and provides a way in which it can be measured.

II. THE ECONOMICS OF AFRICAN DEVELOPMENT DEFINED

African economic development, or the economics of African development, is the study of the conditions, factors, and processes that bring about or prevent economic development in Africa. African economic development focuses on the application of economic analysis to the understanding of the economies of African countries. According to this definition, the economics of development is, in particular, concerned with "how standards of living in the population are determined and how they change over time,"[3] and how policy can or should be used to influence these processes. African development economics cannot be considered independently of the political, environmental, sociocultural, and historical dimensions of the human experience. After all, "the overall goal of development is ... to increase the economic, political, and civil rights of all people across gender, ethnic groups, religions, races, regions, and countries."[4] African development economics entails a study of development objectives, development policies, and the development process.

A. DEFINITION OF DEVELOPMENT IN AFRICA

Based on this background information, we can provide a working definition of economic development in Africa. We define development in Africa as *a multi-dimensional process involving an increase in income, improvement in the quality of life of Africans, and transformation in the structure of African economies, social structures, and popular attitudes.*[5] Hence, African development involves three mutually reinforcing dynamics: *growth, improvement in quality of life,* and *structural economic* and *social transformation.*

1. Growth

Growth, which involves expansion of opulence and improvement in living conditions, is made possible by an increase in gross domestic product (GDP) or gross national product (GNP) and employment. Growth—increase in real per capita GDP or GNP—should be considered in relation to distribution. Both the GNP and the GDP can be defined as the market value of final goods and services produced by a country at a given period.[6] GDP measures the total value of the final use of output produced by an economy, by both residents and nonresidents. Thus, GNP is the GDP plus the difference between the incomes residents receive from abroad for factor services (labor and capital) less payments made to nonresidents who contribute to the domestic economy. Where there is a large nonresident population playing a major role in the domestic economy (such as foreign corporations), these differences can be significant. In 1999, the total national product of all the nations of the world was valued at more than U.S. $29 trillion, of which more than $22.9 trillion originated in high-income countries, and only $320.6 billion (roughly 1% of the world GNP) was generated in Sub-Saharan Africa.

2. Improvement in Quality of Life

Improvement in the *quality of life* includes fulfillment of *basic needs* and improvement in *human welfare*, an expansion of and improvement in access to food, clothing, housing, health, educational services, safe environment, and richer cultural life. For development to occur, there must, in addition to higher incomes and structural economic transformation, be an improvement in the quality of life, which, according to the World Bank involves better education, higher standards of health and nutrition, less poverty, a cleaner environment, more equality of opportunity, and greater individual freedom.[7] In other words, there must be a clear choice between life and death, well-being and illness, happiness and misery, freedom and vulnerability.[8]

- Higher incomes are measured in terms of increases in real per capita GDP or GNP.
- Better education involves increases in primary, secondary, and tertiary school enrollments and completion; increases in adult literacy rates; and a higher education index. Better education has both quality and quantity dimensions.
- Higher standards of health involve an increase in public health expenditures, improvement (lowering) of the population-per-physician ratio (or population-per-nurse ratio), higher immunization rates, increase in population with access to safe water, and improved outcomes such as an increase in life expectancy at birth or a reduction in child and

maternal mortality. Higher standards of nutrition involve an increase in caloric intake, an increase in per capita food production, and a reduction in child malnutrition.

- Less poverty entails a tangible and significant reduction of both income and relative and absolute poverty through a reduction in the population below the poverty line or a reduction of the population below $1 a day in purchasing power parity (PPP) dollars.[9] It also involves a reduction in the human poverty index and income inequality. Poverty has both relative (inequality) and absolute dimensions.
- A cleaner environment results from a reduction in total and per capita carbon dioxide (CO_2) emissions and a reduction in the rate of deforestation.
- More equality of opportunity involves a reduction in income, gender, racial inequality, and more equitable access to resources.
- Greater individual freedom is measured in terms of increased democratization and democratic elections, increases in political freedom, and increases in political and economic reforms.[10]

3. Economic and Social Structural Transformation

Economic and social structural transformation is the transformation of the productive structure of the economy from mostly agrarian to industrial or service based. This is also called structural change.[11] Structural transformation involves industrialization, agricultural transformation, migration, and urbanization, as well as reciprocal interactions between rising incomes and changing proportions of demand and supply. Finally, it also entails changes in the behavior of individuals, households, and institutions and the various markets in which they are involved.[12]

Institutions are central to holistic and sustainable development. *Institutions* refer to sets of formal rules, including constitutions, laws, regulations, and contracts, and social capital and informal rules, such as values and social norms that govern the actions of individuals and organizations and the interactions of participants in the development process.[13] Institutions are important because they establish the organizational and regulatory environment for the economic system, a favorable environment for development to occur, and development services. For instance, civil service and judiciary institutions are necessary for efficient government action. Governance institutions provide human development services such as education and safety nets. Institutions also provide physical services, such as electricity.[14] Because of their centrality to the development process, institutions must change and improve in appropriate ways to ensure sustainable development. For instance, sustained growth requires that institutions improve their efficiency in coordinating economic activity and making policy and in enforcing property rights and contracts, as well as in providing security, and predictability. Therefore, development occurs in an economy when it is growing and transforming and people's welfare is enhanced:

> *African economic development*
>
> $=$ *economic growth and improvement in human welfare*
>
> *accompanied by economic and social structural transformation*

Improvement in the quality of life results from economic growth and improvement in welfare:

> *Improvement in the quality of life*
>
> $=$ *economic growth and improvement in human welfare*

The values of African development are also embodied in the advancement of human rights and human development.[15] After all, development is meant for humans—to improve the dignity of humans. According to the United Nations' declaration, human rights and human development involve:

- *Freedom from discrimination* and progress toward equality regardless of gender, race, religion, ethnicity, or age
- *Freedom from want* and improvement in the standard of living
- *Freedom to develop and realize one's human potential*
- *Freedom from fear, with no threats to personal security*
- *Freedom of speech, participation, and association*
- *Freedom from exploitation and for decent work*
- *Sustenance*, the ability to meet basic needs of food, shelter, health, and protection
- *Self-esteem*, to be a person, to have authenticity, identity, dignity, respect, honor, or recognition
- *Freedom from servitude*, to be able to choose

B. GROWTH VERSUS DEVELOPMENT

Economic growth and economic development are two terms that are often confused. *Economic growth* refers to a rise in national or per capita income and the GNP. *Economic development* refers to a rise in per capita income, improvement in quality of life, reduction in poverty, and fundamental changes in the structure of the economy. For development to occur, citizens must take part in the process of structural change and must benefit from the fruits of change. Hence, growth can occur without development, but *development without growth* is not likely. However, one must recognize that it is probably possible to achieve development without growth in some parts of Africa. When an African country's income and consumption increase due to the discovery of huge mineral deposits, it is experiencing economic growth not development.

III. HOW DEVELOPMENT IS MEASURED

African development can be measured directly and indirectly in a variety of ways. We can use the components of quality of life as measures of development. Likewise, we can measure it by looking at other social indicators that help us measure human development and human outcomes. These indicators include life expectancy at birth, infant mortality, child malnutrition, private consumption, and female net primary enrollment ratio. Others are energy use per capita, population growth rate, and agriculture share in GDP. In its annual *World Development Report,* The World Bank provides World Development Indicators, while the United Nations Development Program reports Human Development Indicators in its annual *Human Development Report.* These publications provide information on people, the environment, the economy, states, and markets, as well as global links.

A. QUALITY OF LIFE AS A MEASURE OF DEVELOPMENT

According to the World Bank, the challenge of development is to improve the quality of life. Quality of life calls for higher incomes but involves some other ends. In addition to higher incomes, quality of life also involves better education, higher standards of health, and nutrition, less poverty, a cleaner environment, more equality of opportunity, and greater individual freedom. One can measure each of these components of quality of life using such established measures as per capita income, life expectancy rates, literacy rates or primary school enrollment, caloric intake, human poverty index, CO_2 emission or greenhouse gases, or a democracy index.

Conventionally, quality of life can be measured by means of the *Physical Quality of Life Index* (PQLI) using the social indicators that were identified to construct the simple composite index. PQLI values range from 1–100, where 1 represents the worst performance for any country and 100 the best performance. In general, a country with a low PQLI tends to have a low per capita GDP. The PQLI is seldom used, having been superceded by the Human Development Index.

B. HUMAN DEVELOPMENT AS A MEASURE OF ECONOMIC DEVELOPMENT

Measurement of human outcomes is another way to measure economic development. To do this, we can use the indicator of development derived from basic human needs, known as the *Human Development Index* (HDI).

In 1990, the United Nations Development Program (UNDP) developed the Human Development Index as a composite index based on three indicators. According to the UNDP (2001), the human development index is "a composite index measuring average achievement in three basic dimensions of human development—a long and healthy life, knowledge, and a decent standard of living." The three indicators of the HDI are:

- *Life expectancy*, which measures longevity, is defined as the average number of years a newborn baby would live if patterns of mortality prevailing for all people at the time of its birth were to stay the same throughout its life.
- *Educational attainment* encompasses adult literacy (two-thirds weight) and the combined gross primary, secondary, and tertiary enrolment ratio (one-third weight).
- *GNP per capita* is estimated in terms of purchasing power parity in U.S. $, which measures a decent standard of living.

Each year, the UNDP publishes the *Human Development Report*, which provides a number of human development indicators, including the HDI. The HDI ranges from 0–1, with a value of 1 being the highest. Many Organization for Economic Cooperation and Development (OECD) countries have an HDI value of about 0.9, while the HDI values for Sub-Saharan African countries are between 0.4 and 0.5. The UNDP classifies countries on the basis of human development indexes into high human development (HDI 0.800 and above), medium human development (HDI 0.500–0.799), and low human development (HDI below 0.500). As Table 3.1 shows, in 2001, no African country was classified as high human development, 19 countries were classified as medium human development, and 29 were classified as low human development.

The HDI rankings and values are for 1999. The rankings are based on 162 countries, which means that war-ravaged Sierra Leone (162nd) ranks lowest among all countries with an HDI of 0.258. Libya (59th) with an HDI of 0.770 is the highest ranked African country, followed by Mauritius (63rd) with an HDI of 0.765. In 1999, African countries constituted 80% of the 36 low HDI countries and only 24% of the 78 medium HDI countries. In fact, the 28 lowest HDI-ranked countries in the world are in Africa. These countries need to take concerted actions to improve life expectancy, educational attainment, and incomes of their citizens.

TABLE 3.1   Classification of African Countries According to Human Development Aggregates (1999)

High Human Development (HDI 0.800 and above)	Medium Human Development (HDI 0.500–0.799)			Low Human Development (HDI below 0.5000)		
	Rank	Country	HDI	Rank	Country	HDI
None	59	Libya	0.770	128	Togo	0.489
	63	Mauritius	0.765	135	Madagascar	0.462
	89	Tunisia	0.714	136	Nigeria	0.455
	91	Cape Verde	0.708	137	Djibouti	0.447
	94	South Africa	0.702	138	Sudan	0.439
	100	Algeria	0.693	139	Mauritania	0.437
	105	Egypt	0.635	140	Tanzania	0.436
	109	Gabon	0.617	141	Uganda	0.435
	110	Equatorial Guinea	0.610	142	Democratic Republic of Congo	0.426
	111	Namibia	0.601	143	Zambia	0.427
	112	Morocco	0.596	144	Cote d'Ivoire	0.429
	113	Swaziland	0.583	145	Senegal	0.423
	114	Botswana	0.577	146	Angola	0.422
	117	Zimbabwe	0.554	147	Benin	0.420
	119	Ghana	0.542	148	Eritrea	0.416
	120	Lesotho	0.541	149	Gambia	0.398
	123	Kenya	0.514	150	Guinea	0.397
	125	Cameroon	0.506	151	Malawi	0.397
	126	Congo Republic	0.502	152	Rwanda	0.395
				153	Mali	0.378
				154	Central African Republic	0.372
				155	Chad	0.359
				156	Guinea-Bissau	0.339
				157	Mozambique	0.323
				158	Ethiopia	0.321
				159	Burkina Faso	0.320
				160	Burundi	0.309
				161	Niger	0.274
				162	Sierra Leone	0.258

Source: UNDP (2001) Human Development Report 2001, New York: Oxford University Press, pp. 142–144, 257.

C. Measuring Income Inequality and Poverty

Another indirect way of measuring development is through income distribution and the rate of poverty. Remember that, among other things, development entails a reduction in income inequality and poverty. Because increases in income do not necessarily lead to a reduction in poverty, it is important to look at the rate of poverty as a measure of development: "Whereas poverty is concerned with the absolute standard of living of a part of the society—the poor—inequality refers to relative living standards across the whole society."[16]

1. Measures of Income Inequality

Measures of inequality such as the Gini index and income distribution data presented in Table 3.2 or the Lorenz curve shown Figure 3.1 can also be used to

TABLE 3.2   Income Inequality and Distribution among African Countries

Country	Year	Gini Index	Percentage Distribution of Income or Consumption				
			Lowest 20%	Second 20%	Third 20%	Fourth 20%	Highest 20%
Egypt	1995	28.9	9.8	13.2	16.6	21.4	39.0
Rwanda	1983–85	28.9	9.7	13.2	16.5	21.6	39.1
Ghana	1997	32.7	8.4	12.2	15.8	21.9	41.7
Burundi	1992	33.3	7.9	12.1	16.3	22.1	41.6
Algeria	1995	35.3	7.0	11.6	16.1	22.4	42.6
Cote d'Ivoire	1995	36.7	7.1	11.2	15.6	21.9	44.3
Tanzania	1993	38.2	6.8	11.0	15.1	21.6	45.5
Mauritania	1995	38.9	6.2	10.8	15.4	22.0	45.6
Uganda	1992–93	39.2	6.6	10.9	15.2	21.3	46.1
Morocco	1998–99	39.5	6.5	10.6	14.8	21.3	46.6
Mozambique	1996–97	39.6	6.5	10.8	15.1	21.1	46.5
Ethiopia	1995	40.0	7.1	10.9	14.5	19.8	47.7
Tunisia	1990	40.2	5.9	10.4	15.3	22.1	46.3
Guinea	1994	40.3	6.4	10.4	14.8	21.2	47.2
Senegal	1995	41.3	6.4	10.3	14.5	20.6	48.2
Kenya	1994	44.5	5.0	9.7	14.2	20.9	50.2
Madagascar	1993	46.0	5.1	9.4	13.3	20.1	52.1
Burkina Faso	1994	48.2	5.5	8.7	12.0	18.7	55.0
Zambia	1996	49.8	4.2	8.2	12.8	20.1	54.8
Mali	1994	50.5	4.6	8.0	11.9	19.3	56.2
Niger	1995	50.5	2.6	7.1	13.9	23.1	53.3
Nigeria	1996–97	50.6	4.4	8.2	12.5	19.3	55.7
Lesotho	1986–87	56.0	2.8	6.5	11.2	19.4	60.1
Zimbabwe	1990–91	56.8	4.0	6.3	10.0	17.4	62.3
South Africa	1993–94	59.3	2.9	5.5	9.2	17.7	64.8
Central African Republic	1993	61.3	2.7	4.9	9.6	18.5	65.0
Sierra Leone	1989	62.9	1.1	2.0	9.8	23.7	63.4

Source: World Bank (2001) World Development Report 2000/2001: Attacking Poverty, New York: Oxford University Press, pp. 282–283.
Note: Countries are ranked from low to high in terms of their Gini indexes. These are countries for which data are available.

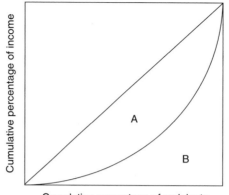

FIGURE 3.1   The Lorenz curve.

measure development. Income inequality data is difficult to obtain in Africa. Consequently, the distribution of income and consumption among African countries shown in Table 3.2 should be read with some caution. Notwithstanding the problem of data, Table 3.2 ranks selected African countries according to their Gini index from low to high. The Gini index measures the extent to which the distribution of income among individuals or households within a country deviates from a perfectly equal distribution. A value of 0 represents perfect equality; a value of 1, perfect inequality. From Table 3.2 we see that Egypt has the lowest Gini index, while Sierra Leone has the highest Gini index of the selected countries. This means that income inequality is higher in Sierra Leone than in Egypt.

We can use the income distribution data presented in Table 3.2 to construct the Lorenz curve shown in Figure 3.1. The Lorenz curve shows the percentage of total income accounted for by any cumulative percentage of recipients. The further the Lorenz curve (the convex line) bends away from the 45° line, the greater the inequality of income distribution. Dividing A by the total area (A + B) under the 45° line gives the Gini index.

We can construct Lorenz curves for Ghana, Ethiopia, and Nigeria using the data presented below on percentage share of household income going to each quintile.

	Poorest 20%	Second Quintile	Third Quintile	Fourth Quintile	Richest 20%
Ghana	8.4	12.2	15.8	21.9	41.7
Ethiopia	7.1	10.9	14.5	19.8	47.7
Nigeria	4.4	8.2	12.5	19.3	55.7

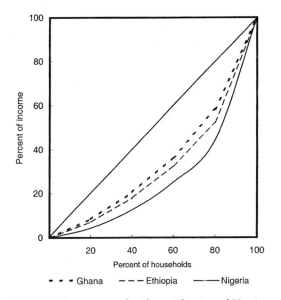

FIGURE 3.2   Lorenz curves for Ghana, Ethiopia, and Nigeria.

From the above data, we can calculate the cumulative income shares, taking the poorest households first:

Cumulative Ratio of Households	Cumulative Ratio of Income Received(%)		
	Ghana	Ethiopia	Nigeria
20% of the households receive	8.4	7.1	4.4
40% of the households receive	20.6	18	12.6
60% of the households receive	36.4	32.5	25.1
80% of the households receive	58.3	52.3	44.4
100% of the households receive	100	100	100

We then plot the points corresponding to these data observations and draw the Lorenz curves for Ghana, Ethiopia, and Nigeria (see Figure 3.2). When we compare the three Lorenz curves in Figure 3.2, we see that the Lorenz curves for Ethiopia and Ghana both lie above that for Nigeria, indicating that both Ghana and Ethiopia have a more equal size distribution of income. But, because Ethiopia's Lorenz curve lies below that of Ghana, Ethiopia has more income inequality than Ghana. This reality is confirmed by the fact that Ghana has a substantially lower Gini coefficient (32.6 compared to Nigeria's 50.6), which indicates a less unequal size distribution of income, which is just what the Lorenz curve shows.

In general less developed countries have higher Gini indexes than more developed countries, with the exception of the United States. The fundamental economic argument for income equality is that it is necessary as an economic incentive for production. Recent cross-country regression analyses indicate that greater inequality adversely affects economic growth.[17] Aghion and others examined how inequality affects growth (and vice versa) using cross-country regression analysis and concluded that inequality affects growth negatively, whereas redistribution affects growth positively. This is because "...wealth inequality determines investment in physical or human capital which in turn affects the long-run growth."[18] They also looked at how growth may increase inequality and argue that it is possible that trade liberalization may increase inequality by enhancing the skills of skilled labor further worsening earnings distribution. Likewise, due to imperfections in the capital market, efficiency may not lead to equity, which means that although more equality is good for growth, growth may not lead to more equality. Government policies, such as taxes and transfers, significantly reduce income inequality by redistributing income from higher income groups to lower income groups.

2. Measuring Poverty

One of the fundamental objectives of economic development is the reduction of poverty. Poverty—an extremely degrading condition of living—is a major economic development problem in Africa and other developing countries. According to the United Nations, in 1997 25% of the world's 6 billion people lived in severe poverty, with approximately 1.3 billion people living on incomes of less than $1 a day.[19] These numbers are similar to the World Bank data presented in Table 3.3, which shows that nearly 50% of the Sub-Saharan Africa

TABLE 3.3   Income Poverty in Sub-Saharan Africa Compared with Other Regions Selected Years, 1987–1998

Region	Share of Population Living on Less Than $1 a Day				
	1987	1990	1993	1996	1998
Sub-Saharan Africa	46.6	47.7	49.7	48.5	46.3
East Asia and Pacific	26.6	27.6	25.2	14.9	15.3
Europe and Central Asia	0.2	1.6	4.0	5.1	5.1
Latin America and the Caribbean	15.3	16.8	15.3	15.6	15.6
Middle East and North Africa	4.3	2.4	1.9	1.8	1.9
South Asia	44.9	44.0	42.4	42.3	40.0
Total	28.3	29.0	28.1	24.5	24.0

Source: World Bank (2001) World Development Report 2000/2001, New York: Oxford University Press, p. 23.

population live on less than $1 a day. The number has remained above 46% since 1987 (see Table 3.3).

However, poverty is a difficult concept to define and measure because it goes beyond a lack of money. Over the years, poverty has been defined in a variety of ways, more recently as ". . . the inability to attain a minimal standard of living."[20] It is necessary to be familiar with the terms *income poverty* and *human poverty*. Income poverty refers to the lack of a minimum level of financial resources to satisfy basic needs, while human poverty involves the absence or denial of choices and opportunities to live a tolerable life.

South Asia has the most people affected by human poverty, but Africa has the most people affected by income poverty. In Africa, human poverty is pervasive in Niger, Sierra Leone, Burkina Faso, Ethiopia, Mali, and Mozambique—more than half of the people live in human poverty. Women and children are disproportionately poor in African countries.

The World Bank measures poverty by using consumption or income data collected through household surveys. Poverty can be measured by means of the *Human Poverty Index* (HPI), which is a composite index measuring deprivations in the three basic dimensions of the Human Development Index: longevity, knowledge, and standard of living. The HPI can be used to rank a country's standing in relation to other countries. Another measure of poverty is the *population living below the income poverty line*, which is defined as the percentage of the population living below the poverty line of $1 a day, adjusted for purchasing power parity. In addition to the general poverty line, each country can set up a national poverty line based on what it considers appropriate. In this case, we can measure poverty by determining the ratio of *population living below the national poverty line* (as shown in Table 3.3).

IV. SUMMARY

African economic development can mean either the economic development of Africa, the process of increasing incomes, improving human welfare, and changing the economic structure of African societies, or the economics of African development, the application of economic analysis to the understanding of the economies of African countries. In the latter case (with which we are mostly concerned), we study the processes and factors that bring about or prevent economic development in Africa: "how standards of living in the population are determined and how they change over time" and how policy can or should be used to influence these processes.[21]

Economic growth refers to a rise in national or per capita income and the gross national product, whereas economic development refers to the rise in per capita income, improvement in quality of life, reduction in poverty, and fundamental changes in the structure of the economy and society. Development includes economic growth, which is an increase in national output or per capita income. Development can be measured by means of the Physical Quality of Life Index, Human Development Index, income inequality ratios, and poverty indexes.

Poverty, the inability to attain a minimum standard of living, is a major problem facing developing countries and Africa in particular. Africa has the most people in income poverty but human poverty is pervasive in many countries. Poverty can be measured in many ways, most commonly by the percentage of the population below the poverty line. Although both poverty and inequality are consequences of underdevelopment, they are also its causes. For development to occur, African policy makers must focus on poverty and the elimination of income inequality.

DISCUSSION QUESTIONS

1. How do you define economic development? Why?
2. Write out a clear statement of how one can judge a country's economic development performance; that is, what country characteristics and data indicators should one examine?
3. Select two African countries and write a 5-page comparative analysis of development in the two countries using available data, based on your understanding of the measurement of development.
4. Why is development more than simple economic growth?
5. How does economic development differ from economic growth?
6. Economic development can be measured in a variety of ways; discuss two approaches that can be used to measure development.
7. What are the Lorenz curve and Gini index and how can they be used to measure income inequality?
8. Using the data presented in Table 3.2, construct Lorenz curves for Egypt, Senegal, and South Africa. Compare and contrast the patterns of income inequality in these three countries based on their Lorenz curves.
9. Why is inequality bad for growth?
10. How do we measure poverty?

NOTES

[1]Adler, M. Ed. (1994) *Great Books of the Western World*, Chicago: Encyclopaedia Britannica, p. 351.
[2]World Bank (1991) *World Development Report 1991: The Challenge of Development*, New York: Oxford University Press, p. 31.
[3]Stern, N. (1989) "The Economics of Development: A Survey," *The Economic Journal*, 99, 597–685.

[4]World Bank (1991), p. 31.

[5]This definition was adapted from Todaro, M.P. (2000) *Economic Development*, 7th ed., Reading, MA: Addison-Wesley, p. 16.

[6]They are gross because deductions are not made for depreciation of capital stock. When they are adjusted for capital depreciation, they become net domestic product (NDP) and net national product (NNP). GNP consists of both domestic and foreign value added claimed by a country's residents.

[7]World Bank (1991).

[8]Sen, A. (1988) "The Concept of Development," in C. Hollis and T. N. Srinivasan, Eds., *Handbook of Development Economics*, Vol. 1, North-Holland: Elsevier.

[9]The PPP method converts GNP per capita into international dollars. The international dollar is obtained when the exchange rates are converted by purchasing power parities to account for differences in prices across countries. Consequently, an international dollar buys the same amount of goods and services in a country's domestic market as one dollar would buy in the United States. Measuring GNP at PPP is a conversion of GNP to international dollars using the purchasing power parity exchange rate or real price levels between countries. This measure helps to resolve the problem of nominal exchange rates not always reflecting international differences in prices. The World Bank uses PPP data from the International Conversion Program (ICP) of the UN and World Bank as conversion factors.

[10]These are some of the ways in which to measure these dimensions. They are by no means the only or even necessarily the definitive ones.

[11]Sen (1988).

[12]Chenery, H. (1988), "Introduction to Part 2" in C. Hollis and T.N. Srinivasan, Eds., *Handbook of Development Economics*, Vol. 1, North-Holland: Elsevier, p. 197.

[13]World Bank (2000), p. 22.

[14]World Bank (2000) *World Development Report 2000: Entering the 21st Century*, New York: Oxford University Press.

[15]UNDP (2000) *Human Development Report 2000*, New York: Oxford University Press, pp. 3–6.

[16]World Bank (1990) *World Development Report 1990*, New York: Oxford University Press, p. 26.

[17]See for instance Aghion, P., Caroli, E., and C. Garcia-Peñalosa (1999) "Inequality and Economic Growth: The Perspective of the New Growth Theories," *Journal of Economic Literature*, 37: pp. 1615–1660; Alesina, A. and Rodrik, D. (1994) "Distributive Politics and Economic Growth," *Quarterly Journal of Economics*, 109(2): 465–490; Perroti, R. (1993) "Political Equilibrium, Income Distribution and Growth," *Review of Economic Studies*, 60(4): 755–756; Persson, T. and Tabellini, G. (1994) "Is Inequality Harmful for Growth?" *American Economic Review*, 84(3): 600–621.

[18]See footnote 17.

[19]UNDP (1997) *Human Development Report 1997*, New York: Oxford University Press.

[20]World Bank (1990), p. 26.

[21]Stern (1989), p. 597, considers the economics of development as the application of economic analysis to the understanding of the economies of poor or developing countries.

PART II

Africa's Characteristics and Development Challenges

Geo-Economy and History

MARIO J. AZEVEDO

*Department of African American and African Studies, University of
North Carolina, Charlotte, North Carolina 28223*

KEY TERMS

Assimilation	Neolithic
Colonialism	Plateau
Homo erectus	Servitude
Homo habilis	Stateless society
Homo sapiens	Traditional
Indirect rule	Triangle trade

I. INTRODUCTION

This chapter is divided into two distinct sections, one describing the geographical features of the African continent and their impact on economic development and the other outlining the unfolding history of Africa over the centuries,
both serving as prerequisites to an understanding of the contemporary African
continent, particularly in reference to economic development, the focus of this
textbook. In regard to salient geographical features, the following pages underscore the difficult natural conditions under which most Africans live, exacerbated
by climate, topography, disease, distance, cultural resilience rooted in a constant
struggle for survival, and internal and external geopolitical adverse conditions.
Yet, even while pointing out the continent's difficult geographic conditions, the
author stresses the economic potential reflected in the abundance of long rivers
and lakes and the existence of the world's most important mineral reserves.

The history section starts with the evolution of mankind and examines the
complex intermingling of peoples of various racial, ethnic, and religious
backgrounds. It supports the thesis that the present underdeveloped economic
conditions in Africa have been largely brought about by the effects of the slave
trade and subsequent colonization of the continent by Europeans and Arabs.
This supposition, however, does not camouflage the failure of African leadership

47

during the post-independence period, especially in the areas of economic policy and democratic tolerance.

II. GEO-ECONOMY

Inhabited by some 750 million people, Africa is the second largest continent in the world and is comprised of 11,650,000 square miles, measuring 5000 miles from north to south and 4600 from east to west. Africa is best described as a continent of geographical and demographic diversity. Yet, life has not been easy on the continent. Even at the dawn of the third millennium, about 75% of the African population engage in and live off subsistence agriculture, producing primarily to feed the family rather than to sell their yield in the marketplace. Given that only about 6% of the land is arable, most of the farming is still agriculture intensive rather than extensive, characterized by shifting and slash and burn practices, in which the tools are still simple and resources, such as fertilizers, are often nonexistent. In the arable areas, parts of the savanna and highlands of East Africa, a pastoral lifestyle, at times combined with nomadic life, is a way of life for the population. By contrast, a tiny percentage of people in central Africa (as among the Bambuti and Twa) and in the Namib and the Kalahari deserts lives essentially from hunting activities.

As a result of the harsh reality of life in the farms of the countryside and the lure of urban lifestyle brought on by Western colonization, African cities are bursting at the seams. Waves of rural immigrants make life even more miserable in these urban enclaves, as reflected by overcrowding, poverty, slums, and increasing violent crime rates in such cities as Cairo (Africa's largest), Johannesburg, Lagos, Lusaka, Abidjan, Luanda, and Kinshasa. In Zambia, for example, urbanization has occurred so rapidly that over 50% of the country's population live in the urban areas.

The African continent has been described by geographers as a high plateau, with 90% of its land mass located 500 feet above sea level (compared to Europe's 50%), 80% of it within the tropics of Cancer and Capricorn and divided almost in half by the Equator.

Some experts have characterized the soil of Africa as a virtual "chunk of iron ore," although of lower grade but rendering agricultural activity more difficult and less productive. Major geographical features include the Great Rift Valley which extends from the Red Sea through the Ethiopian Mountains to East Africa's lakes and out to the Indian Ocean in Mozambique. Parts of its plateau are made up of isolated mountains or mountain chains: Kilimanjaro (19,340 ft), Rwenzori (16,000 ft), Kenya (17,000 ft), Cameroon (13,000 ft), the Drakensberg of South Africa (11,000 ft), the Atlas mountain chains of Northwest Africa (13,000 ft), and the Manica Plateau of Mozambique and Zimbabwe.

Africa's long rivers (Nile, 4000 miles; Congo, 2718 miles; Niger, 2600 miles; Zambezi, 1600 miles) and large freshwater lakes (Victoria, Tanganyika [450 miles long], Rudolf, and Chad) have created several internal basins, such as the Djouf Basin of the middle Upper Niger River; the Chad Basin around Lake Chad; the Sudan Basin of the Upper Nile; the Congo Basin, mainly in Congo-Kinshasa; and the Kalahari Basin of southern Africa. Although Africa's rivers range in length from over 4000 miles, as is the case with the Nile, to over 1600 miles for the Zambezi, they are not entirely navigable. But, where they are, they constitute an important means of communication, transportation, and trading activities. Both rivers and lakes provide fishing opportunities for their surrounding populations and offer great hydroelectric potential for the entire continent. Unfortunately, except for the Aswan Dam in Egypt, the Cahora Bassa Dam in Mozambique, and the Upper Volta Dam in northern Ghana, Africa has been unable to effectively harness the tremendous resources its waters offer. Some years ago, Hance wrote:[1]

> The water power resources of Africa are tremendous and are estimated at about 40 percent of the world's total (275 of 688 million horsepower). It is somewhat ironic that this continent, plagued with aridity over such great areas, should at the same time have such a magnificent hydroelectric potential. The high rainfall in the rainforest and savanna areas, and their high average elevation, combine to explain this wealth. About 18 percent of the world total and 45 percent of the total African potential are in the Congo Basin. The 217-mile stretch of the Lower Congo River from Leopoldville to Matadi has an estimated potential of 85 million horsepower.

The problem is, of course, related to the topography, which forces rivers to meander through flat regions. Dams are also very costly and are rarely efficient options. The unpredictability of heavy rain and the absence or short duration of rain in many parts of the continent makes life difficult. Grove expressed this complexity this way:[2]

> In January inflows of unstable moist air from the South Atlantic bring rain to the Congo/Zaire basin while the Indian Ocean is the source of rain for the countries stretching from Natal to Tanzania. As the sun moves north, so the inter-tropical converging zone (ITCZ) follows. By March the rainy season is over in Botswana and Zimbabwe and is beginning in a zone stretching across the continent from Kenya to Sierra Leone. By July/August the ITCZ has reached furthest north and Atlantic air occupies much of the continent between a few degrees north of the equator and the tropic of Cancer; rain falls over most of west Africa and Ethiopia with occasional showers even on the Tibesti mountains in the Sahara. In September and October the rain belt moves rapidly south again, bringing a second rainy season to the equatorial zone. Then the cycle starts again.

The laymen can best understand the geographical complexity of Africa by examining its four or five almost distinct climatic and vegetation zones. First comes the tropical rainforest (with the highest population density in Africa, up to 500 people per km^2 or 1500 per mi^2 which straddles the equator from the

Atlantic Ocean up to the start of the East African highlands, where temperatures never fall below 68°F throughout the year. This region is characterized by heavy and constant rainfall, receiving over 50 inches (127 mm) of rain per year; therefore, it has no dry season. Because the constant heavy clouds reflect the sunlight, average temperatures remain between 84° and 90°F in this zone.

The vegetation is made up of thick, heavy trees, at times becoming a jungle (covering 15% of Africa), brushes, ferns (as tall as 10 ft), palm trees, wood climbers or lianas that may reach a height of 60 ft, and a canopy of broadleaved evergreens up to 150 ft tall. Soils of the tropical rainforest are not the best because they lack humus and are low in organic nutrients and essential minerals, but they can sustain enough agricultural activity to feed millions of people. Rainforest crops include cassava; yams; sweet potatoes; grains, such as rice and corn; fruits, including plantains and bananas; coffee; cotton; palm oil; sesame; squash; melon; peanuts; peas; beans; onions; tomatoes; tobacco; mushrooms; edible leaves; snails; and termites. Mahogany and ebony trees are abundant in this region and constitute important export items in the form of wood. Rubber trees also produce sap, and quinine is extracted from certain known trees in the forest, while livestock and poultry include goats, sheep, pigs, and chicken. Mineral resources include iron, uranium, copper, gold, petroleum, diamonds, gold, zinc, bauxite, and titanium, among others.

Next comes the savanna, which covers most of Africa's land mass and lies just above and below the (equatorial) tropical rainforest, on the so-called "poleward sides" of Africa. Here, the rainy season, called the *high sun*, is long, and is followed by a short dry season, called the *low sun*, the coolest period of the year but with temperatures never dropping below 65°F. The soils are capable of high agricultural yields, and crops include sorghum, wheat, cotton, bananas, and cashew nuts. Livestock production includes cattle and sheep, which are sources of milk, butter, and blood, and are high in protein content. Minerals range from phosphates and chromite to diamonds, tin, gold, coal, zinc, copper, manganese, iron, and petroleum (some of which is exported). Vegetation in the savanna is varied but the essential features are shrubs, grasses, scattered thorn trees, and acacias in the dry areas.

Life in the savanna is pleasant, and most of the large game (elephants, lions, rhinoceroses, and hippopotami) are found here, some of which live in national parks, as is the case in Kenya, Tanzania, Uganda, and South Africa. Unfortunately, many areas of the savanna are infested with mosquitoes, flies, and other insects that cause such diseases as malaria (the greatest killer of African children), yellow fever, river blindness, sleeping sickness, and others (see Chapters 9 and 10 for more details on the health conditions in Africa).

The desert or low-lying zone contains the Sahara Desert (about 3 million mi^2) in the north. The Namib and the Kalahari deserts are located in Southern Africa and form part of the countries of Namibia, Botswana, Zimbabwe, and

South Africa. The desert, especially the Sahara, is hot during the day, reaching over 120°F, but can be as cool as 50°F at night. In the Sahara, resources such as oil, gas, uranium, and phosphate have been found, while the Kalahari and the Namib deserts are rich in diamonds, copper, coal, nickel, asbestos, kijamite, manganese, gold, barite, limestone, and chrome. Vegetation is almost non-existent here; if present, it is very sparse. The few meager crops include sorghum, millet, beans, cowpea peanuts, and sunflowers in the Namib and Kalahari deserts and dates and livestock, such as sheep and goats, in the Sahara Desert.

The fringes of the Sahara Desert are less barren, and receive between 8 and 80 inches of rain yearly, but droughts are recurring phenomena negatively affecting such countries as Senegal, Mali, Niger, Mauritania, Chad, Burkina Faso, Kenya, Somalia, and Sudan. The Sahel constitutes a transition zone between the desert and the savanna, located between 0° and 150° north latitude and extending from the east to the west coasts of Africa. Sahelian soils lack humus and are much less productive than elsewhere, except when irrigated. Crops include peanuts, millet, corn, sesame, tobacco, barley, wheat, and cotton. The Sahel hosts many nomadic groups, such as the Tuareg and the Tubu, who raise camels, cattle, sheep, and goats along the sparse oases. Phosphate, iron, and salt, as well as oil, have been found in several areas of the zone.

The Mediterranean climate zone is found on both extremities of Africa—Morocco, Algeria, Libya, Tunisia, and part of northern Egypt—and South Africa, at the southern tip. The major climatic feature of the Mediterranean zone is the existence of two distinct seasons—a dry long summer and a cold rainy winter—with rainfalls at times exceeding 20 inches a year. Citrus fruits, grapes, apples, peaches, wheat, olives, cotton, rice, dates, and onions are grown in both northern and southern Africa's Mediterranean zones. Cattle and sheep flourish here, although desert winds from the southern interior called *sirocco*, *khamigin*, or *ghibili* have been very devastating economically. Oil, natural gas, manganese, cobalt, lead, and mercury are found in the northern zone, whereas in South Africa gold and diamonds are abundant.

Finally, the East African highlands found in Ethiopia, Uganda, Kenya, Tanzania, Rwanda, and Burundi constitute the best climatic zone for human habitat in Afrrica with moderate to very cool temperatures. The land here is generally fertile, one of the reasons why Europeans preferred to live in this zone, and is capable of producing a variety of crops, such as millet, sorghum, corn (or maize), cassava, bananas, potatoes, yams, beans, sugar, tobacco, coffee, tea, sisal, coconuts, sesame, and cashew nuts. The soil is said to contain diamonds, copper, gold, tin, beryl, soda, ash, tungsten, copper, phosphate, iron, coal, and uranium. Cattle, sheep, goats, and poultry also supplement the diet of the people, who are fortunate to live in these areas where, compared to the rest of the continent, the most important soil feature is its high organic content.

One can argue whether the geographical conditions of the continent are a hindrance or a facilitator to economic development. Griffiths hastens to note that:[3]

> Africa is a continent of wide horizons on broad, flat plateau surfaces. . . .The plateau consists of a number of vast, shallow basins separated often by barely discernible watersheds, occasionally by mountainous tracts of considerable height in the Tibesti [Chad], Air and Hoggan mountains of the Sahara. In Southern Africa the Kalahari basin presents an outward-facing scarped rim, the Great Escarpment, which in places rises to 10,000 feet (300 m) proving a formidable obstacle to transport development.

Over the centuries, people have tried to tame the geography of Africa, but the struggle has always been an uphill one. Soil erosion, deforestation, intermittent fires, desertification, and the apparent rise in temperatures over the continent constitute perhaps the most serious problems Africans face regarding their continent. In this context, the many rivers and lakes notwithstanding, long distances from these waters present a major problem for at least 15 landlocked African countries that share a common legacy of colonial disinterest and neglect and continue to be very poor and underdeveloped, showing per capita incomes of less than $400, except for Zimbabwe, Botswana, Lesotho, and Swaziland.[4] Evidently, the geography of a continent determines to a large degree not only the type of economic activity and wealth of its people but also the course of their history, as the following section illustrates.

III. THE HISTORY OF AFRICA

Summarizing adequately 8000 years of Africa's history in a few pages is not an easy task. This can only be done by focusing on a few but important landmarks in the history of the continent. The author hopes that students will learn the historical details from other classes and their own reading. The following discussion will remain faithful to the objective of the textbook, namely, examining how history or human past experiences have shaped the continent's economic conditions and vice versa.

A balanced historical account of world history puts the African continent at center stage. It is widely believed in scientific circles that East Africa is the birthplace of humans, whether one adheres to creationism or to the evolutionary theory, the tenet that creatures evolved from the simplest to more complex forms in a process that began millions of years ago. The oldest fossils of hominids and their ancestors, most likely the apes, have been discovered in parts of eastern and southeastern Africa, an area that was well suited to human habitation, given its temperate climate, the relative absence of vector diseases compared to the tropical rainforest, the abundance of water from lakes and rivers, and the potential for a nomadic life based on pastoral activities. In summary, economically speaking, East Africa was suited to sustain human life even thousands of years ago.

If, indeed, Africa is the cradle of mankind, it is also the cradle of culture and the place where the first tools, made out of wood, bone, and stone, emerged. Perfecting their tools, hominids evolved from *Homo habilis* (able to make tools) 3–5 million years ago to *Homo erectus* (already migrating) 800,000 years ago, and to *Homo sapiens* perhaps 200,000 years ago. This was the way the continent of Africa was populated, and the new creatures with well-developed brains began to migrate to other continents during the Neolithic age, 10–12,000 years ago. Some of these new Stone Age humans developed what is believed by many historians to be the first human civilization around 5000 B.C. By 3000 B.C., the Egyptians had created the first writing system (hieroglyphics), begun building the pyramids, invented the solar calendar, mummified the bodies of their pharaohs, and perfected geometry. In the process, they had devised the first organized institutions—a government, schools, hospitals, churches, an army, and an economic system—all presumably made possible by the development of farming, which allowed people to settle permanently in one area, giving second priority to hunting and a nomadic life.

The introduction of metal tools and weapons for war and agriculture made existence on the planet more complex and perhaps made the people more adept in dealing with new social and physical challenges. The Egyptian civilization lasted almost 3000 years, finally destroyed by continuous invasions by Nubians, Assyrians, Persians, Greeks, and Romans. Besides Egypt, the kingdom of Kush or Nubia in northern Sudan also flourished but was conquered by Egypt perhaps after 1500 B.C. Yet, Kush freed itself and occupied Egypt proper around 800 B.C. Kush's proximity to another early kingdom, Axum (in today's Ethiopia), represented a danger to its national existence, and indeed a major battle between the two occurred around 350 A.D., annihilating Kush's capital, Meroe. Says Fairservis of Meroe's debacle: "Meroe, completely cut off from Egypt and increasingly so from Africa (probably by the Nobatae and almost certainly by the Axumites), completely collapsed and its royal remnants retreated westward into Kordofan and Darfur where tantalizing traditions among the living people tell of their final refuge."[5]

Kush, like Egypt, had survived for many centuries; had created its own writing system, the Meroetic cursive (unfortunately, not yet deciphered); built small pyramids; and perfected the art of iron smelting, which may have diffused from Kush to Axum and other parts of Africa. As a result, Meroe became, for a time, a major trading center, where people from many parts of Africa came to exchange items and to learn how to extract iron, smelt it, and use it for agricultural tools and as a potent weapon.

Migrations were constant on the continent, leading to the establishment of new communities of hunters, farmers, pastoralists, state and stateless societies, and empires. The major and better known movement of people was the Bantu migration, which may have started where modern Nigeria is located, occurring between the first and tenth centuries of our era. From here, the migration spread to East and Southern Africa, where similar languages emerged with time, now classified as the Bantu linguistic group. Axum, founded around 1000 B.C. (later to expand into what became Ethiopia), converted early to Christianity and has remained independent ever since, except for a brief interlude from 1936–1941, when Benito Mussolini of Italy occupied it. Ethiopia developed its own writing system, perfected terracing on the slopes of its mountains, domesticated animals such as elephants (as Kush or Nubia had done), and carved churches inside rocks.

In West Africa, one would have encountered the then-famous kingdoms of Ghana, Mali, and Songhay, which emerged during the 8th century and was destroyed during the 16th century as a result of Islamic invasions led by the Almoravids. The Almoravids so weakened Ghana that Mali, a small vassal state, was able to conquer it and subdue it during the 13th century. Mali, in turn, was overpowered by Songhay during the next century. An invasion by Morocco and the nefarious slave trade initiated by the Europeans led to the demise of Songhay. Songhay was the greatest west African empire at the time, ruled by such famous African emperors as Mansa Mussa and Askia Muhammed. Mali developed sophisticated learning centers considered by some to have been the first institutions of higher learning in Africa: the universities of Senkore and Djene, centered at Timbuktu, capital of ancient Mali, and Djene, respectively.

These three kingdoms developed an extensive trans-Saharan trade system based on gold, silver, horses, camels, fish, salt, weapons, and agricultural products, which eventually created two distinct classes—the urbanites and the rural population. Following the conversion of the rulers of Mali and Songhay to Islam, the people remained by and large religious traditionalists, although they may have followed and practiced the external trappings of the Qur'an and the Sharia (the laws of Islam). Yet, just as its rival, Christianity, did centuries later, Islam had a tremendous impact on West Africa (and East Africa), from the standpoint of both culture and economics. Says Curtin *et al.*:[6]

> As the importance of trade increased in Western Sudan, from the eleventh century onward, the Muslim long-distance traders carried their network of commerce southward from the desert ports of the Sahel. They spread as a trade disapora, sending out emigrants to settle at all the principal points of trade so as to be assured of trustworthy business contacts.

Other states worth mentioning emerged in West Africa. Included are the kingdom of Benin (800 A.D) which enacted a democratic form of government; the Yoruba states of Ile-Ife and Oyo, well known for their artistic creations; 18th-century Dahomey, a despotic state; the several 15th-century Hausa states

(Zamfara, Goba, Kano, and Katsina), which flourished from trade and links with the Muslim world; the 19th-century Sokoto empire, which resulted from the unification of the Hausa states by Islamic crusader Usman Dan Fodio; and the Ashanti Confederation of the Akan people of present-day Ghana created by visionary Osei Tutu during the 17th century.

In southwest and central Africa emerged the Congo and Angola kingdoms, which established strong trading, religious, and diplomatic ties with the Portuguese as early as the 15th-century, as well as the 17th-century Lunda empire in present Zaire, with its well developed and structured administration of justice and tax collection. Kanem-Bornu (800–1890), Bagirmi (1500–1897), and Wadai (1500–1912), in present-day Chad, were the most powerful Islamic states. They perfected the art of war in order to expand their territory and acquire various commodities such as slaves, horses, wax, fish, gold, guns, kola nuts, cloth, and salt as exchange items for their trans-Saharan economic intercourse with North Africa.

Moving to East and Southern Africa, one would have encountered the various city-states and cosmopolitan entrepots along the Indian Ocean—Sofala, Malindi, Kilwa, Mombasa, Mogadiscio, Zanzibar, Pemba, Brava, Mafia, and Mozambique Island, at times known as the Swahili coastal towns—which resulted from centuries of trading and intermarriage among Africans, Arabs, Persians, Europeans, and Indians. All coastal towns and cities, spurred by commerce and trade enhanced by Islam (introduced here since the 7th century), remained economically vibrant from the 8th century to the 17th century, trading in ivory, cloves, gold, silver, animal skins, cloth, carpets from the middle East, guns and gun powder, incense, and myrrh. The kingdoms of Bunyioro and Buganda in east-central Africa, which emerged during the 17th and 18th centuries, have been well remembered for their elaborate investiture pageantry, for patronizing the arts, and for controlling the area's ivory trade.

The Mwenemutapa and Zimbabwe empires in modern Mozambique and Zimbabwe, which reached their zenith during the 17th century, have been noted for their masonry skills. Great Zimbabwe contains massive stone structures and was the capital of a major state from about 1250–1450 A.D. The Zulu kingdom, established by Shaka during the 19th century, withstood British and Boer incursions for decades before succumbing and is remembered for its techniques and mastery of warfare. Zulu economic livelihood depended primarily on cattle livestock and pillage of an enemy's women and agricultural fields. There were, of course, many other societies and states, including the stateless societies found among the peoples such as the Ibo of Nigeria, the Sara of Chad, and the Bambuti of the Ituri forest in the Congo, where decisions were made by chiefs, elders, selected individuals, or by consensus. Several of the states and stateless societies were actually democratic and well organized.

Overall, the preceding discussion proves that, long before the arrival of Europeans, Africans maintained vibrant political and economic systems; developed writing systems; domesticated animals; used iron; traded in many major commodities, such as gold, silver, cloth, guns, horses, camels, fish, salt, cloves, wax, and agricultural produce; and even developed institutions of higher learning. Pottery, glassmaking, basketry, and sculpture were widespread on the continent to the extent that, when the Europeans landed off their caravels and other wind-propelled ships during the 15th century and later, they encountered sophisticated societies and markets where they could immediately exchange their goods.

During their 15th-century voyages to other parts of the world, Europeans, beginning with the Portuguese in 1415, stumbled on the African continent and saw it as a market for their products, a new field for the expansion of Christendom, a continent that could facilitate the refueling of ships on their way to the Orient in search of spices, and a springboard from which to fight the Islamic or Moorish empire, as they used to call the Arabs, through an alliance with any Christian state that might be found or created by them along the way. Once Vasco da Gama had reached India by a maritime route via the Cape of Good Hope in 1498, most of the Portuguese dreams were realized. For a long time, Africans and Europeans traded on equal terms and maintained cordial relations until the introduction of the illegitimate slave trade during the latter part of the 15th century. No longer did the Europeans respect African laws and traditions, and, through kidnapping, cunning, threats of war, and alliances with powerful kings, merchants, and chiefs, they imposed the Atlantic slave trade, as we know it, on a recalcitrant Africa.

Experts are still debating whether Africans practiced slavery and engaged in the slave trade prior to the North Atlantic slave trade that linked Europe, Africa, and America in what has been called the *triangle trade*. There seems to be a consensus that a system of bondage of mainly war captives existed on the continent prior to the 15th century but the enslaved person was not regarded or treated as chattel property. Indeed, some social scientists have avoided the term *slavery* for intra-African bondage and prefer to use the word *servility* or *servitude* to designate it. However, there also seems to be a consensus that the forced and violent bondage introduced by the Arab and Muslim kingdoms, particularly in Central Africa, differed from the New World slavery and the servility to which Africans were accustomed. The Arab slave trade involved castration of several males, forced labor, selling of victims on the open market as far away as Egypt and Turkey, trading of humans with horses, open concubinage of the captors with enslaved African women, and no freedom from bondage. Yet, some enslaved individuals eventually assumed prominent positions in the captors' armies, palaces, and societies.

The Atlantic slave trade continued until the mid-19th century, although the British and anti-slavery societies attempted to stop it during the first decade of the 19th century. The slaving activity may have taken a minimum of 50 million able-bodied Africans, thus retarding or interrupting agricultural activities and the arts, disrupting natural political developments, and, as Rodney argued, preventing several feudal kingdoms from evolving into industrialized states. Rodney wrote:[7]

> To achieve economic development, one essential condition is to maximize use of the country's labor and natural resources. Usually, that demands peaceful conditions, but there have been times in history when social groups have grown stronger by raiding their neighbors for women, cattle, and goods, because they then used the "booty" from the raids for the benefit of their own community. Slaving in Africa did not even have that redeeming value. Captives were shipped outside instead of being utilized within any given African community for creating wealth from nature.

Some historians have reported the devastation and depopulation of entire regions, especially in West Africa, and have blamed the slave trade for increased warfare and political destabilization and the shameless introduction of blatant racism into the region.

Through slavery, Africa was propelled into the European mercantilist and capitalistic systems of the time but without the benefits of economic development and control of its own resources. For a long time, the continent remained a vast reservoir of free manpower for the plantation systems of the Caribbean islands and the Americas. Internal African economic activity was determined by and evolved around the forcibly introduced slavery and slave trade. Ironically, it is interesting to note that, by and large, Europeans expressed little interest in conquering the various kingdoms and communities they encountered, even though, prior to the 19th-century, the French claimed Senegal as their possession; the Portuguese had colonized Mozambique, Angola, and Guinea-Bissau; and the British maintained their sphere of influence in the Senegambia area.

The end of the slave trade, the needs of the industrial revolution in Europe, and the nationalist phenomenon of 19th-century Europe, especially in Germany, France, Italy, and Britain, forced the Europeans to reevaluate their concept of and interest in Africa. The change of mind was facilitated by the scientific movement of the 19th century which sent hundreds of explorers to Africa, including the now famous names of Mungo Park, Savorgnan de Brazza, David Livingstone, Heinrich Barth, Richard Burton, Serpa Pinto, John Reubman, John Speke, Henry Morton Stanley, and Auguste Chevalier, among many others.

The explorers traced the sources and mouths of the major rivers and lakes in Africa, drew maps highlighting the continent's topography, exposed Africa's military and technological weaknesses, and described for the first time in greater detail the vast known and potential resources of the continent. While European statesmen saw Africa as a tool of diplomacy, nationalists viewed it as a source of national grandeur for war-torn Europe in the wake of the Napoleonic campaigns. Unfortunately for the Africans, in their portrayal of the continent and its people, "Nearly all of these men were explorers first, geographers second, natural scientists third, and humanists last."[8] While missionaries saw Africa as a place to found new missions and save the Africans from eternal fire, the business community viewed the continent as an open market, a place for future investment of surplus capital, and a source of raw materials for the industrialization of Europe. Still others, such as the misguided Darwinists, regarded Africans as savages who, incapable of governing themselves, needed whites to civilize them.

The guidelines for the partition of Africa were approved at the now infamous Berlin Conference of 1884–1885, at which 14 Western nations were represented. Insisting on the principle of effective control as proof of territorial ownership in Africa, the European powers agreed to fight the remnants of the slave trade in their territories and upheld the freedom of major Christian denominations to open missions, schools, and hospitals in any part of colonized Africa. Eventually, France and England ended up with the largest number of colonies or protectorates, about 18 each, the rest having gone to Germany, Portugal, Spain, Italy, and Belgium.

News of conquest was greeted with a violent response virtually all over Africa from the 1890s to the 1920s, especially in the French, Portuguese, and German territories; yet, the military presence of Europeans was able to overpower the Africans. By the 1920s and onward, Europeans had entrenched themselves in many strategic, productive, and temperate-climate regions of the continent. While most did not venture to live in Africa permanently, some, running away from misery at home, opted to settle in what became known as settler colonies— Southern Rhodesia, Algeria, Mozambique, Angola, Kenya, Uganda, Morocco (for enterprising Spaniards), and, of course, South Africa since 1562.

Once they had pacified the colonies through the unscrupulous use of an army, a police force, and a racist bureaucracy, the European powers introduced colonial policies that had the intended objective of making the colonies economically beneficial primarily to the mother country and the resident colonizer or settler and only secondarily to the African. This required a system of forced labor; taxation; forced growth of such cash crops as coffee, tea, tobacco, cotton, and corn by Africans; military recruitment among adult Africans; and a program of road, harbor, and railroad construction. Although the British prided themselves on using indirect rule, which attempted to govern the Africans through a semblance of African institutions on the local level, the French and Portuguese tried to transform Africans into Europeans through the policy of association and assimilation. The treatment of the African and the end result of colonization in Africa, however, were the same. All colonial powers treated Africans as sub-humans, forced them to work, and used naked force any time the Africans showed signs of rebellion.

The infrastructure that developed (roads, schools, hospitals) was primarily designed to facilitate colonization, explore the raw materials to be processed in Europe, and cement the European presence in Africa. However, African embedded resentment and nationalism, as well as external factors, would soon radically alter the prevailing colonial situation in Africa.

As political oppression accelerated, economic exploitation heightened, and cultural subjugation became unbearable under colonialism, Africans began to agitate first for equal treatment as whites and later for total independence. This occurred especially during the interwar years and immediately following World War II (1939–1945), after Africans participated in the so-called war effort. Africans returned with increased confidence that they could successfully fight the Europeans and were convinced that the argument of fighting for democracy could theoretically disarm the colonizers' justification for the their tyrannical governments in Africa.

Therefore, strengthened psychologically and politically, Africans began organizing nonpolitical associations first, such as the Kikuyu Central Association (KCA) and the Kikuyu Independent Schools Association (KISA) in Kenya during the 1920s and 1930s. They then forced the Europeans to allow them to establish political parties during the 1940s and later. Thus, the following parties emerged: the Kenya African Union (KAU) in 1944, the Rassemblement Democratique Africain (RDA) in francophone colonial Africa in 1945, the Nyasaland African National Congress (NANC) in Malawi in 1944, the Convention People's Party (CPP) in Ghana in 1948, and the National Council for Nigeria and the Cameroons (NCNC) in Nigeria in 1944. The strong internal clamoring for self-rule and independence in Africa was assisted by several external factors, including the creation of the United Nations in 1945, whose charter upheld the right of colonial peoples to self-determination, and the subsequent independence of India and Pakistan in 1947. To this one might add the fact that many influential Europeans, including businessmen, came to realize that expectations of vast resources and quick profits in Africa would go unmet and that many colonies, such as Chad, Niger, Swaziland, and Gambia would simply become a burden within an uncertain empire.

As a result of these events and African nationalist pressures, Britain was the first to accept the principle of self-government in Sub-Saharan Africa, which was realized first in the Gold Coast in 1957, when Kwame Nkrumah became the first president of the newly independent country, later to be named Ghana. Then followed Nigeria, Sierra Leone, Kenya, Malawi, Gambia, and virtually every British colony, except Southern Rhodesia, where the settler white population declared its own independence in 1965. Here, Africans, under the banners of the Zimbabwe African National Union (ZANU), led by Robert Mugabe, and the Zimbabwe African People's Union (ZAPU), led by Joshua Nkomo, waged sustained guerilla warfare that dislodged the renegade government of Ian Smith. The result was independence and majority rule under the leadership of Robert Mugabe, who became Prime Minister in 1980 and later President of the new republic.

The French attempted to resist the winds of change by offering their colonies the benefit of remaining as republics within the French multiracial empire. Consequently, in 1958, Charles de Gaulle authorized a referendum to vote for or against independence. At that time, all but Sekou Toure's Guinea opted to be part of the French empire. However, in 1960, every French colony (except Djibouti) reversed itself and declared its independence, although maintained very close ties with France through formal economic and defense treaties. Since 1954, the French had been fighting the independence movement in Algeria spearheaded by the Front National de Liberation (FNL). The war became so costly in lives and finances for France that Charles de Gaulle had to accede to the nationalist demands in 1962.

Just as for the French with their assimilation policy, the Portuguese adamantly refused to allow self-rule in Angola, Mozambique, Guinea-Bissau, Cape Verde, and São Tomé and Principe. Under these conditions, the nationalists had no choice but to resort to guerilla warfare. Thus, Angola (1956), Guinea-Bissau (1963), and Mozambique (1964) started liberation wars that lasted until 1974, when the Portuguese army overthrew Premier Marcello Caetano's government in Lisbon. As a result, by 1975, all Portuguese colonies had achieved their independence. Spain granted Equatorial Guinea independence in 1975, and also relinquished Spanish Sahara abruptly in 1975, leaving it to the machinations of Morocco, Mauritania, and Algeria, against the sentiment of the nationalists who founded a guerrilla front (called POLISARIO) in an attempt primarily to push back Morocco's invading forces.

While the former German colony of Tanganyika, which was transferred to Britain after World War II, became independent in 1964, Cameroon and Togo, split between France and Britain, achieved their independence in 1960. Former German South-West Africa, entrusted by the League of Nations to South Africa in 1918, became independent only in 1990, following a decade of guerrilla warfare waged by Sam Nujoma's South-West African People's Organization (SWAPO) against South Africa. Belgium left its colonies of Zaire and the trustee territories of Rwanda and Burundi in 1960, while Somalia achieved its independence in the same year after the two British and Italian Somali territories were unified. Of the white regimes, bastions of white supremacy in Southern Africa, Zimbabwe, as noted earlier, became independent in 1980, following 6 years of intensive guerrilla warfare. The African National Congress (ANC), assisted by international sanctions, waged a successful violent campaign against the South Africa apartheid regime during the 1970s and 1980s, making Nelson Mandela the first black president in the country in 1994. Finally, in 1993, Eritrea won its war against Ethiopia and became the 53rd independent African state, joining the many others, such as Zambia, Kenya, Comoros, Seychelles, Djibouti, Swaziland, and Lesotho, that had achieved independence after 1960.

IV. SUMMARY

As the preceding discussion demonstrates, the geographic and historical obstacles to Africa's economic development have been enormous. One can point to several factors that have slowed down Africa's progress in education, health, and economic growth. The natural geography of the continent is an almost insuperable obstacle: mountains, volcanoes, valleys, tropical diseases, poor soil, and little arable land. Ki-Zerbo concludes, in his *General History of Africa*, by stressing the fact that:[9]

> The vastness of the African continent meant that many of its peoples had little contact with peoples on the periphery until quite a late date. As long as the ecological conditions were favorable, internal development kept up a satisfactory pace as in the pre-historic West Sahara and the Nile valley of ancient Egypt. However, as the climate deteriorated, the African peoples embarked on a long period of wandering. Inter-Africa trade between areas whose agricultural produce and metals were complementary to one another led to trade with other continents, increasingly to the benefit of the latter.

The direct adverse impact of this climatic pattern on Africa's economy has not changed drastically. In fact, it appears that geographic conditions, reflected in recurrent droughts since the 1970s, floods, cyclones, soil erosion, and advance of the Sahara Desert have shifted for the worse. As one geographer commented about the interrelationship between geography and economic development: "Costs depend on soil and weather conditions; where they are unfavorable, projects are unlikely to succeed. ...Industrial development is also related to the availability of resources, notably, water, energy, and economic minerals."[10] Evidently, these are determined by climate and the forces of nature, which, in Africa, are changing constantly, eluding our ability to control our economic destiny. Added to these problems are the consequences of the slave trade, which retarded economic development for three centuries, and was followed by the colonial legacy that has inexorably tied the entire continent's infrastructure and economic policies to European capitalism. Davidson succinctly expressed this problem:[11]

> Historically, Africa's economies had been small in scale. ...There had been no industrial revolution, no reliance on the manufacture of machine-made goods, and no need for imports of goods. ...Now, in the new period of worldwide industrialism, all that was changed.... Africa had to join a world of trade and exchange that was organized by much richer countries.

So, Africa has the resources but has been unable to exploit them to the benefit of its own people.

However, external factors and geography do not account for all the historical problems the continent has experienced. Mismanagement and the enactment of wrong policies by the African leaders, whether or not they embraced the ideologies of socialism, communism, or capitalism, have contributed to the problems. Corruption, gross violations of human rights, undemocratic practices, a penchant for international parasitism or dependence, and a lack of genuine concern for the plight of the masses languishing in poverty, illiteracy, and disease are conditions whose responsibility must be squarely placed on the shoulders of the leadership.

Indeed, all natural obstacles notwithstanding, Africa has enough resources to feed its people and, if united and determined, African leaders could carry a greater voice in the world market and within the international institutions and agencies to allow them to chart their own economic future. For thousands of years before slavery, Africans had been able to control their destiny. They successfully expelled, through peaceful or violent means, the Europeans from the continent following colonialism. This proves beyond a doubt that they can assume mastery of their own destiny: their history is their best and strongest beacon.

In sum, Africa's challenges remain many and include the following: the persistent devastating impact of slavery; the pernicious legacy of almost one hundred years of colonial rule characterized by taxation without representation, forced labor, forced military and police recruitment, political oppression and repression, blatant economic and human exploitation, and cultural subjugation; a pattern of tyranny and corruption, complicated by an apparent lack of will and vision in leadership; and the absence of political unity. The many obstacles are compounded by the proliferation of local languages, the often antagonistic relationship between Islam and Christianity in several African countries, the erupting and destructive ethnic manifestations, often fuelled by petty leaders, and the absurd attachment to a multiplicity of currencies that have no international value.

Africa is justifiably known as a continent of diversity. Unfortunately, this diversity is often more constraining than liberating, more backward looking than progressive. Will Africa ever come out of its abyss? The answer has remained illusive even forty years following the achievement of independence.

DISCUSSION QUESTIONS

1. What are the major salient features of the African continent and what problems do they present for human habitation?
2. What are the physical (geographic) conditions that hinder development in Africa? Elaborate your thoughts by using the climatic zones as a basis for your answers.
3. What do you think was the impact of slavery and colonialism on African economic development?

4. What internal and external factors contributed to African nationalism and independence from colonialism?

5. Describe Africa prior to the colonial period from political, social, religious, and economical perspectives.

NOTES

[1]Hance, W. (1969) *The Geography of Africa*, New York: Columbia University Press, p. 19.

[2]Grove, A.T. (1989) *The Changing Geography of Africa*, New York: Oxford University Press, p. 18.

[3]Griffiths, I. (1984) *An Atlas of African Affairs*, London: Cambridge University Press, pp. 5–6.

[4]Stock, R. (1995) *Africa South of the Sahara: A Geographical Interpretation*, New York: Guilford Press, p. 16.

[5]Fairservis, W.A. (1962) *The Ancient Kingdoms of the Nile*, New York: A Mentor Book, p. 194.

[6]Curtin, P., Feierman, S., Thompson, L., and Vansina, J. (1989). *African History*, New York: Longman, p. 93.

[7]Rodney, W. (1972) *How Europe Underdeveloped Africa*, Dar-es-Salaam: Tanzania Publishing House, p. 108.

[8]Rotberg, R.I., Ed. (1973) *Africa and Its Explorers: Motives, Methods, and Impact*, Cambridge, MA: Harvard University Press, p. 7.

[9]Ki-zerbo. J., Ed. (1989) *General History of Africa*, Vol. I. Paris: UNESCO, p. 129.

[10]Grove, A.T. (1989) *The Changing Geography of Africa*, New York: Oxford University Press, p. 1.

[11]Davidson, B. (1994) *Modern Africa: A Social and Political History*, New York: Longman, pp. 218–219.

CHAPTER 5

Engines of Growth and Africa's Economic Performance

MARCEL FAFCHAMPS

Center for the Study of African Economics, University of Oxford, Oxford, OX 12JD, England

KEY TERMS

Agglomeration externalities	Increasing returns
Allocative efficiency	Learning by doing
Beggar your neighbor	Physical capital
Cartel	Population control
Commodity price fluctuations	Process innovation
Comparative advantage	Product innovation
Disembodied technological change	Productive resources
Embodied technological change	Schumpeterian competition
Enabling environment	Start-up costs
Engine of growth	Technological change
Human capital	Vent for surplus

I. INTRODUCTION

It is customary for people living in developed economies to treat constant economic progress as natural and self-evident. Yet, if one looks at the human record since, say, the Neolithic revolution, growth is the exception and economic stagnation is the rule. Indeed, for thousands of years prior to the industrial revolution, all regions of the earth experienced virtually no discernible change in the everyday life of their people. Empires came and went, and so did the prosperity of merchants and aristocrats in Venice, Vijayanagar, Beijing, and Timbuctu, but the livelihood of the mass of the population remained essentially the same.[1]

From an historical perspective, what is absolutely remarkable is not stagnation but the rapid and dramatic improvement in the standards of living of millions of people over the last 200 years. This is certainly true in developed countries, which have achieved unprecedented prosperity. It is also true in newly industrialized countries, which have grown at unheard of speed.[2] Compared with these outstanding performances, changes in other parts of the world—and in Africa, in particular—appear modest. But even in Sub-Saharan Africa things have evolved dramatically over the last 100 years: life expectancy has all but doubled, child mortality has been cut in half, the population has more than quadrupled with only a slight reduction in food availability, urbanization has gone from essentially nothing to one-third of the population, and standards of living have, in all likelihood, doubled over the course of this century.[3]

The growth performance of any region of the globe cannot be understood without an idea of what accounts for increased standards of living. Unless we know what fundamental economic forces can account for the diverse growth experiences of the various regions of the globe, we cannot hope to understand what happened in Africa over the last decades, what may happen in the future, and what policymakers can and should do about it.

There are many views as to what is responsible for economic growth, but little agreement as to which view best accounts for the facts. This chapter takes a fresh look at the literature. Instead of focusing on a single explanation, it examines essentially all the explanations that have been proposed to account for differences in prosperity levels between countries and regions and discusses to what extent they explain Africa's growth performance. The originality of this approach is seeking to understand the current state of the world by comparing the logical implications of different theories of growth. So doing, certain explanations can be ruled out for the simple reason that they cannot account for the facts—rapid growth in some places, stagnation in others. The outcome of the exercise is a better grasp of the determinants of economic prosperity and how they have shaped the performance of Africa. The chapter also draws important lessons for policy.

Before embarking upon the body of the chapter, the author acknowledges that understanding what is responsible for growth is far from exhausting the larger question of economic development. For instance, it is often believed that growth exacerbates income inequalities and may even have perverse effects on certain vulnerable groups.[4] To attain economic development, it is argued, one must achieve not just growth in aggregate output but also its equitable distribution among various segments of society. Yet, while it is true that the redistribution of the new prosperity generated by growth is far from automatic, there must be something to redistribute before we can talk of redistributing anything.[5] Over the last two decades, slow growth has been Africa's main problem, not the unequal distribution of increases in prosperity, which have been small by most accounts.

The question of what drives growth is often debated together with the wider issue of what conditions and policies are required for growth to take place. While not disputing that an enabling environment is required for growth to occur, the author believes that it is important to distinguish between the engine itself and the environment that makes the engine work. Indeed, it is very unlikely that one may identify what the enabling environment should look like if one does not understand what needs to be enabled. For instance, if producing more cocoa is seen as the avenue to growth, then the enabling environment is one that facilitates cocoa production—for example, roads or rail tracks to cocoa-producing areas, seed and fertilizer distribution programs, marketing infrastructure and institutions, and a harbor to export the product. In contrast, if exporting shirts is the chosen engine of growth, what needs to be facilitated is cheap urban labor, timely access to information about fashion, export finance, training on quality and packaging, etc. In both cases, whether the necessary services are likely to be supplied by private initiative or whether intervention of the state is required depends on the usual economic arguments. Examples are the presence of externalities, natural monopolies, coordination failure, credit constraints, and the like. Recent research has also emphasized the crucial role played by the institutional framework and political governance structure in which public goods are provided and private actors are allowed to operate. All of these issues are important but, for obvious space limitations, they remain beyond the scope of this chapter, which focuses exclusively on the engines themselves.[6]

This chapter is organized as follows. The discussion begins with what are called elementary engines of growth, that is, engines of growth that do not require any reorganization of production. Next is a review of engines of growth based on a static understanding of the world. Section IV discusses engines of growth that emphasize the simple accumulation of productive resources. Increasing returns and poverty traps are discussed in Section V. The role of technological change and innovation is examined in Section VI. Geographical determinants and agglomeration effects are introduced in Section VII, where the world is treated as a global economy. In each section, the relevance of each theory for Africa is discussed, together with the policy prescriptions implied by the theory.

II. ELEMENTARY ENGINES OF GROWTH

Our discussion begins by examining three elementary engines of growth: beggar your neighbor, commodity price fluctuations, and cartel formation. All three work essentially by redistributing wealth. Consequently, they cannot be regarded as ways to increase the prosperity of all and cannot account for the growth of developed economies since the mid-17th century. Yet, they have shaped events and policies for centuries in the past and continue to affect contemporary economies. They are presented first for greater contrast with the engines of growth discussed in subsequent sections which are all capable, at least in theory, of improving everyone's standard of living.

One of the most effective ways of improving one's lot is simply to impoverish someone else. Much of pre-industrial history up to Saddam Hussein's invasion of Kuwait can be understood as variations on the eternal *beggar your neighbor* principle.[7] Someone else's wealth can be taken away directly by looting and raiding, as hordes of "barbarians" have done since time immemorial, or by taxing the defeated, the golden principle on which empires rest. Wealth can also be taken away indirectly by eliminating a competitor from a profitable business. Conflicts between kingdoms and cities for the control of the trans-Saharan trade are examples of this strategy. Current efforts by industrialized nations to wrest key international markets away from each other can be seen in a similar light.

Another powerful source of windfall gains and losses is the *fluctuation of international commodity prices*. These fluctuations are particularly important for countries and regions whose export structures are highly dependent on a small number of primary exports, as is still the case in most of Africa. One major factor behind changes in commodity prices is the fluctuation of demand. If we focus on primary commodities—the most relevant category for Africa—we see that international demand follows two largely contradictory trends: increased demand for raw materials and the development of substitutes. Industrialization and rising consumption levels in developed nations require increased use of raw materials. This trend favors a rise in commodity prices over time. For example, industrialization in Europe raised the demand for vegetable oils and benefited African producers of peanuts and palm oil during the 19th century and the beginning of the 20th.[8] At the same time, improvements in production technology permits the replacement of expensive raw materials by cheaper substitutes.[9] The rubber boom that followed the rapid development of the automobile at the beginning of the century is a case in point. It generated incredible wealth in Manaus, the world's capital of rubber at the time. But the invention of a synthetic substitute led to the collapse of the rubber price and Manaus went bust. As this well-known example illustrates, the combination of the two effects makes the long-term movement of primary commodity prices difficult to predict.

The role that commodity prices play in the growth of individual developing countries has been the object of intense debate. Historically, the prices of primary commodities have not increased as quickly as one would have expected based on projections of raw material use. Although opinions diverge on this issue, many commodity prices even appear to have declined over the course of this century. As Deaton and Miller have recently shown, conventional commodity price prediction models often underestimate the role of invention and substitutes and tend to overestimate future price movements.[10]

Short of advocating *cartel formation*, there is considerable disagreement as to the policy implications to be learned from the role of commodity price fluctuations in growth. Some emphasize that betting on the right horse can work wonders and claim they can predict what commodity prices will be 10 years from now. They see nothing wrong in expanding the production of primary commodities as an engine of growth.[11] Others, best represented by the Latin American dependency theory school of the 1960s and 1970s, insist that commodity prices show a secular decline.[12] A development strategy, they argue, should not be based on increased production of primary commodities; industrialization is the only path that leads to sustainable prosperity. Still others do not see the expansion of primary exports as inherently bad but point out that making the same recommendation to all developing countries leads to a fallacy of composition: While it may be good for Ghana, Nigeria, and the Côte d'Ivoire to individually increase cocoa exports,[13] if they all do it simultaneously international prices may fall so much that they will all be worse off. This latter view, however, is but the cartel formation argument in disguise.

As is well known, international prices can be raised, even in the absence of demand shifts, through the formation of a producer cartel and other monopolistic practices. By forming a cartel and behaving like a monopolist, countries can increase their collective welfare by reducing quantities and forcing prices up. That such a strategy can generate substantial welfare gains for the countries involved is best illustrated by the OPEC cartel between the mid-1970s and the mid-1980s. When oil prices doubled in 1974 and subsequently quadrupled in 1979, oil-producing countries indeed enjoyed unprecedented prosperity, overnight reaching standards of living close to those achieved in the West.

How relevant are these three elementary engines of growth in understanding the international distribution of prosperity? Clearly, robbing wealth from someone else can improve one's lot but it cannot increase prosperity in the world as a whole. If anything, military conflicts and trade wars to control resources and commercial routes can only subtract from aggregate welfare. The formation of cartels and other monopolistic practices partake from the same approach: they benefit producers at the expense of consumers while distorting prices and thus reducing allocative efficiency. The world as a whole has interest in deterring such actions, and it does. United Nations peacekeeping activities (e.g., the Desert Storm operation) and multilateral treaties for the promotion of free trade constitute international efforts to discourage and reduce wastage generated by beggar thy neighbor policies and impediments to free trade.

Fluctuations in commodity prices cannot be seen as engines of global prosperity, either; gains for producers are losses for consumers and vice versa. These fluctuations can nevertheless have a large influence on the growth performance of individual countries. What is clear from the available evidence is that basing one's prosperity on a rise in commodity prices is extremely risky, as prices are known to fall as quickly as they rise, leading to a dramatic economic collapse when this happens.

Do elementary engines of growth help us understand the African experience? Undoubtedly. The slave trade was a source of prosperity founded on the extreme impoverishment of others. Colonialism similarly contained elements of a beggar your neighbor policy: Africans were deprived of the ownership of mineral resources and, in certain cases, of land as well. The most profitable economic activities were reserved for European settlers, and Africans were not allowed to undertake particular activities or to move freely to certain areas. African farmers were taxed either directly through head taxes or indirectly by keeping farm-gate prices artificially low. Certain colonial powers, such as Belgian Congo, went as far as restricting Africans' access to higher education. At the same time, however, colonial powers did much to increase production and develop their colonies, especially toward the end of the colonial era, so that the colonial experience is more than just a large-scale application of the beggar your neighbor approach.

Some continue to blame external interference for Africa's failures since independence. It is nevertheless difficult to find strong evidence linking the poor economic performance of Africa to plundering and looting by foreign powers, either directly or through the modern descendants of chartered companies, the multinationals. There are, indeed, very few multinationals operating in Sub-Saharan Africa, and the countries in which they operate, such as South Africa, tend to be wealthier. If anything, it is plundering and looting by African themselves—assisted or not by foreign powers—that have received much attention lately. Whatever the balance of internal and external responsibility in the African historical record, the fact remains that plundering and looting were certainly not the main engines of growth behind the extraordinary performance of nearly all newly industrialized countries in the last 50 years or so. While efforts to (mis)appropriate rents undoubtedly played a role in slowing growth in Africa, the point we want to emphasize here is that Africa as a whole cannot realistically grow by taking away from others.

Regarding price fluctuations, certain countries (Nigeria and Gabon, for instance) have been bestowed unheard of—even if temporary—wealth as the result of increases in oil prices. But, as a whole, Africa's terms of trade have deteriorated since the mid-1980s.[14] Furthermore, African countries have suffered great hardship as a result of commodity price fluctuations. The worst affected countries are those such as Nigeria for which the price of their principal export increased a lot before collapsing suddenly. It is generally accepted that commodity price fluctuations have largely contributed to Africa's problems and will continue to be a cause for concern until Africa diversifies its export base.[15]

Cartel formation and monopolistic practices have played a role in a few instances but their effect on Africa's growth has probably been minimal. For a while, African oil producers benefited from the formation of OPEC, but other African countries were hurt in the process. De Beers has a dominant position in the world market for diamonds and is known for monopolistic practices that have benefited South Africa and, possibly, other African diamond-rich countries. Producers of other primary commodities, such as coffee and cocoa, have attempted to form a cartel but failed to effectively control production. To summarize, elementary engines of growth have historically had a marked effect on the performance of African economies but they have failed to generate sustainable growth and, more often than not, have penalized Africa.

III. STATIC ENGINES OF GROWTH

We continue with models that see growth as springing from the removal of barriers to economic efficiency. We examine three basic concepts: putting idle resources to work, allocative efficiency, and comparative advantage. These concepts differ from the elementary engines of growth discussed in Section II in that a modification of the structure of production is required to generate an increase in prosperity, but they share the common feature that they are conceptually static. Most of these ideas were initially developed in the 19th century. Their current mathematical formulation still constitutes the workhorse of policy design and has been extremely influential, especially in the last decade or two, as they are at the heart of all structural adjustment programs.

The simplest static engine of growth is putting idle resources to work. According to this approach, underdevelopment manifests itself by the existence of idle resources in the economy. Growth is achieved by putting unused resources to work, hence moving the economy closer to its production possibility frontier. Unused resources can be put to work in a variety of ways. Mineral resources can be exploited and unused land can be developed and colonized by clearing unproductive vegetation, draining excess water, etc. The introduction of new crops and techniques of production such as irrigation can help employ labor resources more effectively. As a result, people are put to work who were previously underemployed because of, for instance, the seasonality of agriculture. People who earn a meager living from unproductive activities can be given a proper job. Equipment and machinery can similarly be used to their full capacity. Doing so typically requires the transformation of the organization of production, the rehabilitation of certain machines, and the provision of spare parts, fuel, and raw materials. Standard policy recommendations aiming at putting idle resources to good use also include the reduction of transportation costs so that isolated resources can find an outlet for their output.

These ideas were particularly influential during the colonial period, and colonial authorities liked to portray themselves as developing their colonies by putting idle land and labor to work. The construction of roads and railroads in Africa was seen as an outlet for idle labor, a "vent for surplus," as Myint put it,[16] and it is often seen as a major force behind the growth that took place during the early years of colonization. The same idea is behind programs to rehabilitate African countries or enterprises, such as, for instance, efforts to revamp Ghana's gold mines and cocoa farms as part of structural adjustment.

While putting idle resources to work can undeniably increase prosperity and generate growth, it is evident that it cannot do so indefinitely. Once all resources are fully employed (i.e., once the production possibility frontier has been reached), other sources of growth must be found. One such source is achieving allocative efficiency. It is widely acknowledged among economists that welfare can be raised by allocating resources to produce what people wish to consume. The question is how can an economy be producing the wrong kind of goods in the first place? After all, if consumers do not want something, there will be excess supply; if they want something that is not available, there will be excess demand. Relative prices should adjust, raising and lowering profits and hence signaling to producers that they should produce more of high-demand goods and less of goods in excess supply. Even if producers fail to respond to price signals, the economy should still adjust, albeit more slowly, as firms with low or negative profits shrink and close down, while firms with high profits expand. How, then, can allocative efficiency not eventually be achieved?

Governments are the usual suspects because they have the means and, often, the inclination to distort prices (i.e., through differential taxes, rationing, or price controls). As a result, the policy recommendation that naturally comes from focusing on allocative efficiency is to eliminate all price distortions and reduce the role of the government. One cannot but suspect that conservatives are drawn to the allocative efficiency argument not so much because they were seduced by its mathematical elegance but because they are sympathetic to its inescapable policy conclusion: Get prices right, roll back the state, and privatize. Yet, although it is clear that allocative efficiency can improve social welfare, it is difficult to see it as an important long-term engine of growth. Once allocative efficiency has been achieved, growth stops. Moreover, country estimates of welfare gains from static allocative efficiency seldom exceed a one-off increase in gross domestic product (GDP) of a few percentage points, nothing to get crazy about.[17]

A third static source of prosperity can be found in trading with others. The idea that trade can be mutually beneficial is one of the most powerful ideas in economics. It was most convincingly put forward first by Ricardo in the 19th century and has given birth to an entire body of economics—trade theory. Ricardo's argument is extremely simple: Countries should produce what they are good at, sell it abroad, and use the proceeds to import what they cannot easily produce themselves. By producing according to their comparative advantage, countries achieve a higher level of social welfare.

A question immediately arises: What could prevent an economy from taking advantage of gains from trade? Local producers, if faced with international relative prices, should realize that it is in their interest to produce more of what the world wants. As in the case of allocative efficiency, a country's failure to respect its comparative advantage is usually blamed on government's tampering with international trade, through tariffs, subsidies, foreign exchange controls, quotas, and other forms of distortions. Lack of infrastructure is also occasionally identified as a reason why the comparative advantage of a country or region is not exploited. Considerations of comparative advantage thus dictate the removal of trade distortions and the establishment of commercial infrastructures and institutions. There are strong similarities between the allocative efficiency and the comparative advantage ideas, both in the logic of their argument—reliance on price signals, static view of the world—and in their policy implications—get prices right, less state. It is therefore not surprising that they are often used simultaneously and interchangeably.

There is no doubt that static engines of growth go a long way in explaining the African experience. The vent-for-surplus idea rationalizes the success of colonial efforts to open up new areas to commercial agriculture and mining. Exploiting Africa's comparative advantage in the production of primary products (and achieving gains from trade in the process) was the primary engine of growth during the colonial era.[18] African governments' inability or unwillingness to further expand primary commodity exports after independence and other allocative inefficiencies generated by distortive government policies have been blamed for Africa's slow growth, leading some observers to call for a resumption of the colonial emphasis on Africa's static comparative advantage, which is still in the production of minerals and tropical crops.[19]

Still, it should be obvious that comparative advantage and allocative efficiency cannot be a long-term engine of growth and cannot account for the long-term growth of developed economies. Opening a new continent to trade, as was achieved by the colonization of Africa, can generate significant prosperity (particularly for those who control new trade flows), and it may take some time (e.g., 20–30 years) before new opportunities for trade have been taken advantage of.[20] But, comparative advantage must eventually run out as an engine of growth: Once all the gold and copper are being mined and all suitable land has been planted to cotton, coffee, and cocoa, comparative advantage can no longer raise social welfare.

None of the three static engines of growth discussed above—putting idle resources to work, achieving allocative efficiency, and taking advantage of gains from trade—can explain the continuous and dramatic improvement in standards of living that has taken place in the West over a long period of time. They would even be harder pressed to explain the rapid growth experiences of newly industrialized countries. Yet, these ideas, in one form or another, have had an enormous impact on policymakers, to the point where they permeate nearly all policy documents produced by donors and international organizations and constitute the intellectual backbone of all structural adjustment programs. What the above discussion makes clear is that structural adjustment cannot, by itself, be a long-term growth strategy.

IV. ACCUMULATION OF PRODUCTIVE RESOURCES

We continue our search of an explanation for economic growth and turn to ideas and models that take a dynamic view of the world. The simplest ones insist that growth is the result of an accumulation process: Output is increased, it is argued, because more productive resources are made available for production. In this section, we focus on two types of accumulable productive resources: (1) physical equipment and machinery and (2) human capital. Before doing so, we also say a few words about population.

Population growth is a somewhat tautological engine of growth: An economy that counts more workers nearly by definition produces more output. The problem, as originally emphasized by Malthus, is that some essential factors of production such as land are only available in fixed quantity. As a result, standards of living are bound to decrease as the productivity of additional workers falls. This principle thus predicts that increased population leads to negative growth per capita. The typical policy recommendation that follows from this line of argument is to reduce human fertility rates before a population increase leads to a food crisis.[21]

The Malthusian view of the world has long had a strong influence on policy circles. It nevertheless is largely contradicted by the facts. Rapid population growth in the world has not been accompanied by the kind of decrease in food availability that doomsday prophets have predicted.[22] It also fails to recognize that population growth triggers investment in infrastructure and technological innovation that may, in the long run, be beneficial.[23] Besides, developed countries did not become prosperous by reducing their population to raise returns to land per person. Population control is not a substitute for a development strategy.

A. PHYSICAL CAPITAL

A much more serious explanation for long-term growth is the accumulation of machinery and equipment, often called physical capital. It has long been recognized that the accumulation of capital is a key feature of the indus-trialization process and that it is necessary for growth to take place. As the number of pieces of machinery and equipment per worker increases, worker productivity goes up so that output per worker—and thus consumption per head—increases. This simple, commonsense observation forms the basis of what is called neoclassical growth theory.

Although more convincing than the short-term theories discussed so far, the simple accumulation of capital cannot account for long-lasting growth, either.

The reason is that too much equipment per worker saturates the workers. Think, for instance, of how many shovels a worker can use at a time. As Solow and other growth theorists have clearly demonstrated, an economy whose sole engine of growth is the accumulation of physical capital eventually stops growing; it reaches a point where the returns to an additional unit of capital fall so low that it is no longer profitable to add new equipment and machinery.[24] These ideas can easily be illustrated as follows. Let k be the stock of capital per head. Output per head y depends on the available stock of capital, i.e., $y = f(k)$. Suppose, for simplicity, that people save a constant proportion s of output and that the capital stock depreciates at a constant rate λ. The net addition to the capital stock is equal to savings minus depreciation, i.e., $\dot{k} = sf(k) - \lambda k$. Clearly, if savings is larger than depreciation, the stock of capital increases and vice versa. Now, returns to additional units of capital per worker fall as the stock of capital gets large. Formally, this means that $\partial f(k)/\partial k < 0$: the function $f(k)$ is concave. Consequently, there must be a point k^* at which $sf(k)$ intersects the line λk: at that point, savings exactly equal depreciation and growth is zero. For any capital stock above k^*, savings are insufficient to cover capital depreciation, so that the capital stock per worker decreases and growth is negative. For any capital stock below k^*, growth is positive. The economy must thus converge to k^*, at which point growth stops.[25]

Another implication of this model is that the rate at which the economy grows is higher at low levels of capital stock. The reason is that returns to the first units of capital are high. In more elaborate capital accumulation models of growth in which the assumption of a constant savings rate is relaxed, poor countries are predicted to grow even faster because high returns to capital (i.e., high interest rates) trigger high rates of saving.[26] The capital accumulation model of growth thus predicts that poor countries (i.e., countries with little capital) should grow faster than rich countries. This hardly seems to be the case.[27] The theory also predicts that countries where people are unwilling to save (i.e., where s is small) will converge to a lower k^* and will forever remain poor.[28] In this framework, if Togo is poor, it is because its people are unwilling to save enough to become rich.

Although by the reckoning of neoclassical growth economists capital accumulation alone cannot account for continuing growth in developed countries, it has been used extensively in empirical and policy-oriented work. The policy recommendation that comes out of neoclassical growth theory is to encourage savings and investment at large. In principle, the theory is indifferent as to whether the accumulation of capital is done by private individuals or by the state. In practice, however, neoclassical theory has been widely used to justify policies that favor private accumulation—for instance, by refraining from taxing returns to investment. Deviations from an exclusive focus on private investment are allowed only for large investments that have a public nature, and the typical policy recommendation is to promote the public provision or subsidization of key infrastructures.[29] The establishment of industrial parks may also be favored to reduce the cost of providing infrastructure to industries. All these recommendations naturally follow from the assumption that growth is simply due to capital accumulation, which is inconsistent because most neoclassical theorists themselves recognize that the accumulation of capital cannot by itself explain the growth of developed countries.[30]

B. HUMAN CAPITAL

Exclusive emphasis on the accumulation of physical capital has come under criticism. Some, like Schultz, have pointed out that education and skills are complementary to physical capital: New skills and higher education are required for workers to make effective use of more powerful pieces of equipment and machinery.[31] Recent empirical work has tended to confirm Schultz's claim that human capital plays an important role in growth, so much so that human capital accumulation has become the latest fad in growth theory.[32] Because people often find it difficult to borrow against future earnings, individuals may underinvest in education, thereby slowing aggregate growth. For this reason, the policy recommendations that come out of this approach revolve around promoting and subsidizing education. To the extent that firms cannot charge workers for on-the-job training, it may also be advisable to help inexperienced workers get their first job and acquire vocational skills.

Although, like physical capital, the accumulation of human capital is clearly a key ingredient of growth, it cannot any more than physical capital account for continuous and rapid improvement in standards of living. The reason is that people do not live forever, so that each generation must go back to school. Adding years of schooling subtracts from the time each worker spends in the labor force, so that there is a limit to the number of years of schooling that can profitably be accumulated in any given society.

Growth theories based on physical and human capital are implicitly based on the idea that growth is due to the accumulation of more of the same. Although neoclassical growth theory recognizes the role of technological innovation in long-term growth, it treats it as an exogenous force that bears no direct relationship with the accumulation of physical and human capital. Neoclassical models of growth, with or without human capital, all predict harmonious growth: Given enough time, and except for differences in tastes and natural resource endowments, all countries are expected to converge rapidly to the same level of well-being. The models also predict high rates of growth in poor countries, as returns to initial units of physical and human capital should, according to the theory, be very high.

Because capital accumulation is speeded up when national income and savings are higher, accumulation can be maximized by putting idle resources to work, achieving allocative efficiency, and taking advantage of gains from trade. The policy prescriptions derived from the neoclassical theory of growth are thus often combined with recommendations based on the static arguments reviewed previously. The combination of these theories offers the intellectual advantage of being internally consistent, as they all rest on the same assumptions of constant returns to scale and perfect competition. The scope for policy intervention is limited to a few areas where the market may not work perfectly: infrastructure, education, and vocational training. For the surplus, the neoclassical theory of growth provides no theoretical justification for industrial policy. Market incentives are assumed to direct investment in the most profitable activities, so that distortions of relative prices by government intervention are strongly discouraged.

At a superficial level, events in Africa appear to confirm explanations of growth based on the accumulation of productive resources. Low levels of infrastructure, physical capital, and education are often presented as explanations for Africa's plight. But Africa's failure to conform with the more fundamental predictions of the model (i.e., smooth and rapid convergence in standards of living) is not interpreted as an indictment of the theory, but rather as an indictment of Africa itself. Because the theory says that poor countries should rapidly converge to OECD (Organization for Economic Cooperation and Development), levels of per capita GDP provided that they are thrifty enough to accumulate capital and go to school, Africa's failure to grow is attributed to the "African dummy" effect. Africans are happy the way they are; they do not wish to save, go to school, and grow like, say, the Taiwanese did. Or, their governments are too stupid, or too corrupt, or both; the distortions they have introduced in their economies is what prevents them from growing.

To those familiar with the African scene, such attempts to salvage the theory at the expense of an entire continent are totally unconvincing. It is true that some Africans are too poor to save and go to school. It is also true that some African governments have launched ruinous social experiments and that many are corrupt, but not all the governments of the 50 or so African countries have been mistaken and corrupt all the time, and the great majority of Africans save and make incredible sacrifices to send their children to school. Besides, prosperous countries of today seem to forget that, not so long ago, they were quite corrupt and yet growing rapidly anyway; simply think of the United States in the first half of this century. The truth is that Africa's failure to catch up is the failure of neoclassical growth theory.

V. INCREASING RETURNS AND POVERTY TRAPS

An alternative to neoclassical theory is to drop the assumption of constant returns to scale and to acknowledge the existence of increasing returns. Authors who have taken this approach have been able to show that, under certain circumstances, an economy may be stuck in a poverty trap.[33] Because consumers are poor, the argument goes, market demand is small and benefits from increasing returns cannot be achieved. Optimal-size plants cannot function at full capacity and productivity remains low. In this section, we scrutinize these arguments more in detail.

A. INCREASING RETURNS TO SCALE

Marshall, the father of neoclassical economic theory, was the first to formalize the concept of increasing returns internal to the firm, what he called increasing returns to scale. Some things, he argued, are cheaper to produce in large numbers. Marshall recognized that the existence of increasing returns is incompatible with perfect competition because firms are likely to be large and to act strategically. For one thing, increasing returns to scale tend to advantage established firms. To see why, suppose a firm already produces something in large numbers. Its cost of production is low. Now consider a newcomer without an established market who can initially produce and sell, say, a smaller quantity. Because its costs are higher than those of the established firm, the newcomer is at a disadvantage. If forced to sell at the same price as the established firm, its profit will be lower, possibly negative, and it may fail to expand or even survive.

In the presence of increasing returns to scale, small, new producers in underdeveloped countries are expected to face serious difficulties when they try to compete with established firms in the developed world. Partisans of this view argue that a start-up car manufacturer in Africa, for instance, would find it extremely difficult to go up against the General Motors and Toyotas of this world. Extrapolating this idea to the level of an entire economy, a country that has no established industries may hesitate to initiate industrialization if it is forced to compete with developed nations. If it tries anyway, chances are it will fail. Undeveloped countries, the argument goes, may thus be trapped in their underdevelopment. Only a massive investment program or "big push" may prove sufficient to prop the economy above the minimum economic threshold below which it cannot compete with established economies.[34]

The argument has been refined in many different ways. One school of thought, represented most vividly by the Economic Commission for Latin America in the 1960s and 1970s, advocated an import substitution strategy to palliate what was perceived to be unfair competition from established firms in the West.[35] The idea was that, by protecting their domestic market from international competition, developing countries would help their infant industries grow and become more competitive. Import substitution strategies were widely adopted in Africa in the 1960s and 1970s but they failed to deliver sustainable industrialization.[36] Some argued that the failure of import substitution is due to the fact that most African countries are too small and their people too poor. While an import substitution strategy may work for large countries such as India, Brazil, and Nigeria, it could achieve little in most of Africa because African domestic markets are too narrow; consequently, local firms are unable to reduce their average cost sufficiently to be internationally competitive. For this reason, some see African economic integration as a way to establish protection for domestic industries at the regional level and thus to salvage the import substitution idea.

B. Start-Up Costs and Learning by Doing

A variant of the increasing returns idea insists that it is not so much returns to scale in everyday production that are problematic, but rather the existence of the large sunk costs necessarily to initiate production. Think, for instance, of the enormous costs of developing a new computer chip or of setting up a network of car dealerships. Even if the production of a car or chip were characterized by constant returns to scale, the existence of large sunk costs in production or marketing would be sufficient to discourage many potential entrants, particularly from poor countries. A related idea is that, over time, a firm and its workers get better at producing something and can produce it more cheaply (i.e., learning by doing).[37] Learning by doing may also be present in marketing, product design, industrial organization, etc.

The typical policy implication that follows from the existence of start-up costs and learning by doing is to subsidize new investment, e.g., through tax holiday or subsidized credit. It may also be useful to subsidize exports and to protect the domestic market for a while—that is, until infant industries can compensate their initial disadvantage. That these ideas are pervasive can be seen in the fact that virtually all developing (and developed) countries have some form of investment tax break in their investment code, and many have experimented with various forms of trade protection and promotion.

These policy implications have nevertheless come under virulent attack from neoclassical economists, to the point that one may talk of a "war of religion." The truth is that neither side has genuinely tried to assess whether or not start-up costs and learning by doing are an impediment to investment in underdeveloped countries. Each side of this debate has tended to stack up hastily collected evidence in its favor and to dismiss as erroneous and biased any evidence collected by the other side. As a result, little scientific progress has been made.

A bit of common sense may, however, come to the rescue. It is true that setting up a business is difficult; every business person will tell you that. But, if established firms had such a strong advantage over newcomers, we would observe very few newcomers even in developed economies where competition with established firms is most fierce. Yet, thousands of new firms pop up every day. On the other hand, if it was easy to successfully challenge established firms, we should observe very few old enterprises. Yet, we do. The situation must therefore be an intermediate one in which established firms are at an advantage but can successfully be challenged.

Drawing further from what we can observe in developed economies, we note that there are differences across industries: While there are few new entries in airplane manufacturing, there is a much larger turnover of enterprises in, say, small retail outlets and restaurants. One should therefore refrain from generalizing. The potential usefulness of infant industry protection is likely to vary drastically across sectors of economic activity. Finally, casual observation suggests that, at least in certain industries, innovation appears to be a prerequisite for successfully challenging an established firm. Challengers often come up with a new product, or a new way of selling it, so that they do not operate with the same average cost curve as existing firms, but with a lower one. Viewing firms' cost curves as static may thus be misleading, as it ignores the role of innovation. We revisit this issue further later.

C. Gains from Specialization and Other Spillovers

Other authors have indicated that it is not so much increasing returns and sunk costs at the level of individual firms that matter, but rather symbiotic relations between firms. Since Adam Smith's pin factory parable, economists have been aware of the existence of gains from specialization. As markets expand, tasks previously carried out jointly get separated and become undertaken by specialized firms or individuals. Specialization enables these firms and individuals to capture learning-by-doing effects; they become very good at what they do.

Firms that operate in an economy with lots of specialized providers of goods and services can subcontract these activities to outsiders and focus on their main business. Just picture all the industrial services that are available in a large U.S. city: subcontractors for technical parts and inputs; financial services and stock brokers; commodity brokers; wholesale and retail services; warehousing and transport; legal, technical, and commercial advising; auditing; product design; repair and maintenance; safety and security; publishing and media; advertising and public relations; communications; and utilities, to name a few. Whenever these specialized goods and services are not available, firms must produce them themselves. Not only is this a source of distraction for the management, it also raises average production costs in the economy because gains from specialization are not captured.

Other sources of spillover come from the existence of an experienced and diversified labor force. In large developed economies, it is easier for individual firms to identify and hire workers who are already familiar with their own equipment and procedures. Workers acquire skills and experience that they take with them to subsequent jobs, thereby indirectly benefiting their new employer. In contrast, firms operating in undeveloped countries must make do with inexperienced workers who are unfamiliar with their equipment and mode of organization. They may even encounter problems with work ethics (e.g., absenteeism, pilferage). The resources they spend training and supervising workers add to their production costs.

Gains from specialization and other spillovers are examples of pecuniary externalities, that is, of cost advantages firms enjoy from operating in a larger, more sophisticated economy. They are externalities because individual firms do not capture the full benefit of the cost advantages they generate for others. An employer who trains a machine operator does not, for instance, capture all the return to his investment, as the worker can cash in his acquired job experience by joining another firm at higher pay. They are called pecuniary because they operate through market transactions, that is, via the purchase of goods and services and the hiring of workers. The typical policy recommendations that follow from the existence of spillover effects among industrial and service firms are not very different from the "big push" argument: A critical mass must be achieved for gains from specialization and labor market externalities to materialize.[38] To achieve it, it may be necessary to subsidize industry.

Some economists, following the work of Hirschman, argue that spillover effects are stronger within certain groups of industries.[39] Using data on what firms buy from and sell to each other, which they call backward and forward linkages, they claim they can actually identify where spillover effects are strongest and what clusters of industries have the strongest spillovers. Based on evidence of backward and forward linkages, they recommend that policy support be targeted to those clusters of industries that are closely linked, instead of sprinkling support thinly over all industries. Once a viable industrial cluster has been established, these authors recommend moving on to another one. Industrial policy is perceived as an essential part of development planning, and optimal sequencing is part of industrial policy.

Needless to say, not everybody agrees with these views, even among those who insist on the necessity of supporting infant industries. Targeting, sequencing, and fine tuning in general—usually known as industrial policy—are seen by many as too good to be true. Even strong believers in spillover effects such as Jacobs point out that nobody has the information required to identify where spillovers are strongest, and that the linkages between industries that are apparent in input–output matrices only scratch the surface and miss many decisive yet imperceptible interactions.[40] In spite of these critiques, many governments, including that of Japan over the last 50 years or so, have explicitly targeted specific groups of industries, and have claimed to sequence their targeting in such a manner as to move up the scale of industrial sophistication over time. Detractors argue that these efforts were essentially futile and, in the end, counterproductive.[41] The debate continues unabated.

To summarize, the models and theories discussed in this section present convincing arguments that it is difficult getting started on the path of industrialization and growth, much more difficult than neoclassical growth theory makes it sound. Yet, although these arguments have been among the most hotly debated in the development and growth literature, they are strictly speaking not about the engines of growth themselves. The focus of the debate is rather on the catching-up process. All authors in this controversy implicitly agree that capital accumulation is the key to increased prosperity.

How relevant is the debate to understanding the African experience? The existence of spillover effects has most probably played an important part in explaining why Africa has found it difficult to join the world economy as an equal partner. Evidence from structural adjustment experiments, for instance, suggests that opening Africa to garment imports exposes domestic industries to unbearable competition from low-cost producers in East and Southeast Asia.[42] On the other hand, industrial protection in Africa does not appear to have helped infant industries to grow up and compete in international markets. The poverty trap is certainly there, but the medicine the doctor ordered does not seem to be working. Could the ailment have been misdiagnosed?

VI. TECHNOLOGICAL CHANGE AND INNOVATION

Technological change has long been recognized as an essential ingredient of growth. It is clear to almost everyone that standards of living in developed countries could not have increased the way they have over the last 200 years if it had not been for technological change. There is little doubt that it is the scientific revolution—that is, the application of science to technology not only in industry, but also in agriculture, medicine, and services—that is responsible for the remarkable achievements of the last 200 years.

If technological change is the most important engine of growth, economic development then can be seen as a modernization process, that is, as an historical transformation by which an undeveloped economy joins the scientific era. Technology transfer becomes the main requirement for this transformation to take place. The role of policy is then to speed up the transfer. The rapidity with which a country develops is attributed to the speed with which an economy absorbs modern technology and ideas. Failure to grow is interpreted as an inability to remove obstacles to progress and an unwillingness to join the rest of the world in celebrating the triumph of technology. Places that do not grow are perceived as being marginalized, as being left by the wayside of global modernization.

Although most economists acknowledge the role of technology in growth, they diverge in what they see as the critical mechanism behind the invention process. They also give different interpretations to the relationship between economic forces and technological change. These differences shape the role they recognize for government in facilitating technology transfer and modernization.

A. EMBODIED TECHNOLOGICAL CHANGE

Perhaps the most commonly held view of technological change is to associate it with particular pieces of equipment or machinery (e.g., the steam engine or the textile mill). Technological change is then said to be embodied in physical capital. In this case, new technologies can only be accessed by accumulating capital. This implies that the accumulation of physical capital is the royal path to growth, not so much because more of the same equipment makes workers more productive, as neoclassical models implicitly assume, but because the new equipment is more productive than the old. Technological change also makes it possible for workers to use larger and more powerful pieces of equipment. Piling up shovels on a single worker, for instance, does not increase labor productivity, but switching from shovels to a bulldozer does. Without the invention of bulldozers, the accumulation of capital does not go very far; little growth can be achieved by accumulating shovels alone.

Not only does technological change increase the productivity of labor, but it can also increase the productivity of capital. To see why, consider the evolution in personal computers. One can buy today a piece of office equipment that is many times more powerful than what the same amount of money would have bought 5, 10, or 15 years ago. As a result, university professors, say, can increase their output $f(k)$ without changing their computer budget k; progress in computer technology shifts $f(k)$ upward.

One does not have to be an economist to see that there is a lot of truth to the idea that many technological innovations are embedded in physical capital. From the point of view of a developing country, the issue of technology transfer then becomes one of importing up-to-date equipment and machinery. An immediate logical implication is that governments that want to speed up growth should facilitate technology transfer by subsidizing imports of machinery and equipment.[43] Furthermore, the adoption of modern methods of production usually requires a new organization of the production process (e.g., larger firms or different shop floor arrangements). Reorganization may have to be repeated to take advantage of everchanging technologies. This idea has been used to argue that growth can only be achieved by private firms because they are more flexible and thus more efficient at constantly reorganizing themselves.

Using modern equipment and machinery often requires better trained workers. Human capital accumulation is thus a complement to physical capital and is required to access new technologies. Although primary and secondary education seldom provides vocational skills that are immediately applicable on the factory floor, they foster a modern outlook and make workers more disciplined and adaptable. It is therefore not surprising that numerous studies have shown that there exists a positive relationship between economic performance and education.[44] Indeed, a country could not grow for long if it ran short of educated manpower. Although this evidence has led many to conclude that primary and secondary education should be the primary focus of government policy, it should be clear that an educated workforce is essentially useless if it is not combined with modern equipment and machinery.

B. New Consumer Products

Not all technological change takes the form of new capital equipment. Some innovations translate into new consumer products, such as the automobile or the television. These new products are occasionally used as production inputs and thus constitute cases of embodied technological change as well, but new consumer items make a separately identifiable contribution to improved standards of living. Try to imagine life without automobiles or telephones.

An immediate policy implication is that undeveloped countries can improve the welfare of their population by acquiring new products invented elsewhere. They can import them already made or copy them through reverse engineering and produce them locally.[45] Copying raises delicate copyright issues that we will not go into. What is obvious, however, is that the vested interests of developed countries where most of the inventing is done differ from those of industrializing countries where the copying is done. Most of Africa, however, has not yet reached the point where the copying by local manufacturers of products developed elsewhere has become a bone of contention with Western countries.

It is now increasingly recognized that a significant share of the welfare gains from new and improved products is not counted in GDP statistics. Think of home computing, for instance. Home computers are much more powerful today than 15 years ago, and the enjoyment one gets from them has undeniably increased. Because home computer prices have fallen, this increased welfare is not reflected in GDP growth. Similarly, when African consumers buy imported electronics, their enjoyment is not counted as development, yet it is their way of partaking in the global increase in standards of living. The same thing can be said of drugs and medical services. Their constant improvement is not counted in standard indicators of growth; yet, they make a very significant contribution to human welfare, as evidenced by increased life expectancy and the like. There is, thus, an important dimension of African modernization that does not appear in the disappointing GDP growth performance of the continent: new consumer products.

C. KNOWLEDGE

Not all technological change is embedded in new capital equipment or new consumer products. Some also take the form of public or private knowledge. Private knowledge such as know-how or patents typically belongs to firms in developed countries and is not directly accessible by firms elsewhere.[46] Knowledge can also be public and nonexcludable. Scientific knowledge is perhaps the best example of publicly accessible knowledge. Even at the height of the cold war, Russian and American scientists continued to publish results from their medical, biological, and physics research in professional journals. Any African scholar with access to a good library can read about the latest scientific discoveries.

The problem is that few Africans have a level of technical expertise sufficient to use information published in academic journals for generating technological innovations. Only laboratories and research institutes outfitted with modern equipment can turn publicly available scientific knowledge into tangible products or processes. Other forms of publicly available information similarly require equipment to access it. One cannot, for instance, access one of the most exciting technological innovations of the last few years, the Internet, without a computer and communication equipment.

To the extent that the accumulation of knowledge is an essential factor behind the ever increasing prosperity of advanced economies, it is unlikely that poor countries can attain commensurate levels of prosperity without tapping into the same stock of knowledge. However, unlike advanced economies that cannot grow without generating new knowledge, poor countries can grow simply by applying existing knowledge to their own economy. In other words, they can grow by catching up with more advanced countries. As is clear, catching up does not necessitate the generation of new knowledge; it simply requires the adoption of existing knowledge and its adaptation to local conditions. Typical policy recommendations for filling the knowledge gap emphasize subsidizing local research, sending students and scientists abroad for study, focusing on the local adaptation of fundamental research performed elsewhere to save on research costs, and favoring joint research with developed countries.[47] Grants of information-related equipment are also frequent. If the private knowledge of multinationals is essential for catching up, developing countries also have to attract investment by such firms, either directly or through joint venture agreements.

D. INNOVATION AND SCHUMPETERIAN COMPETITION

So far, we have treated technological change as manna from heaven and discussed it as if the only question is how to transfer it to developing countries as quickly as possible. Some economists, however, take a less benign view of technology. It is not so much that they have a different conception of what constitutes technological change, but they insist that what matters is the process by which new scientific knowledge is transformed into new products and techniques of production.

The most prominent thinker in this school of thought is Schumpeter.[48] According to his view of the world, firms compete with each other not so much through costs and prices, as portrayed in neoclassical theory, but through product and process innovation. In a Schumpeterian world, private invention is the driving force behind technological change. Process innovation (reducing production costs) provides a cost advantage to the inventor; product innovation (inventing a new product) procures a temporary monopoly. Schumpeterian economists propose a dynamic vision of the economy in which individual innovation initially generates rents for innovators. These rents progressively erode over time as innovations are copied by other firms. Firms find themselves on a treadmill: In order to stay ahead of the competition, they must constantly innovate.[49] It is this process of constructive destruction that Schumpeter presents as the driving force behind growth and development and what he identifies as the mark of our time.

The Schumpeterian view of the world differs widely from the harmonious vision of neoclassical economics. In a dynamic world where products and processes change constantly, what is crucial is not to be at the point where marginal cost equals marginal revenue, but rather to keep innovating and stay ahead. Moreover, competition through innovation is virulent and potentially wasteful. Indeed, firms may overdevelop new brands and designs in order to differentiate their products and lure consumers (e.g., too many different brands of cars, breakfast cereals, and pharmaceutical products). Yet, according to a Schumpeterian view of the world, tampering with this process is a bad idea; reducing innovation rents can only discourage research and development and thus slow down growth. Unbridled capitalism, they argue, is the only economic system that can deliver maximum innovation, and is the system a country must choose if it wishes to stay ahead of other nations. The typical policy recommendation that comes out of this vision of the world is to encourage and protect innovation through patent laws and the promotion of free enterprise.

Schumpeterian economics also recognizes a role for entrepreneurs; the future of the Third World is seen to depend on the quality and imagination of its business class. Entrepreneurs are conceived of as modern-day heroes to be grown, like rice plants, in nurseries before being transplanted in the real world. African governments are advised to nurture local business talents irrespective of their ethnic origin. Policies to weaken European or Asian business interests in Africa are seen as damaging because they subtract from the local entrepreneurship capital. At the same time, racial and ethnic discrimination is seen as counterproductive because it reduces the pool of potential talents from which tomorrow's entrepreneurs are drawn.[50]

Although Schumpeter was strongly opposed to any kind of government intervention, his thinking has convinced many that competition through innovation can be wasteful, that it generates excessive rents, and that its most detrimental effects should be mitigated. Efforts by the World Health Organization to draw up a list of essential pharmaceutical products, for instance, can be seen as an attempt to minimize the costs associated with excessive product diversification. Actions by countries such as India and the former U.S.S.R. to limit the number of car types allowed on their soil can similarly be seen as an effort to countervail what is perceived as superfluous diversity.

E. Assessment

There is wide agreement among economists that technological change is essential for development and growth. To the extent that technological innovations are embodied in equipment and machinery, the accumulation of physical capital is a prerequisite for growth. Because sophisticated equipment can only be operated by skilled and educated manpower, modern capital can only be put to good use if the labor force is well trained. Neoclassical economists are thus right to emphasize physical and human capital accumulation in the growth process, but they are right for the wrong reason: What matters the most is not the quantity of capital *per se* but the technology that is embodied in it. Similarly, primary and secondary education *per se* generate nothing if they are not combined with sophisticated equipment and machinery. Furthermore, neoclassical theory misses out on certain crucial dimensions of technology, such as product innovation and disembodied knowledge, and it ignores what motivates firms to innovate.

Taking a closer look at technology helps one realize not only that governments can help the transfer of technology but also that the transfer process is fraught with difficulties. On the one hand, the temptation exists to disseminate knowledge and know-how as widely as possible to speed up the catching-up process. On the other, Schumpeter argues, the absence of protection for innovators can only deter innovation. Some believe that a fine-tuning approach to development is feasible. Copying should be allowed early on, when little true innovation is done locally. Patent laws could be enforced more vigorously later on, once indigenous firms themselves have begun to innovate. This approach appears to be the one Taiwan and China have taken.

How do these concepts apply to Africa? First, it is obvious to even the most casual observer that, except for a few isolated cases, Africa is not making use of the most advanced methods of production available in the world. This is true not only in manufacturing but also in agriculture, trade, banking, transportation, education, and government services. The scientific revolution is taking hold on the African continent, as progress in infant mortality and life expectancy demonstrate, but the rate at which productive activities are modernized remains slow. Africa's inability to apply much of existing scientific knowledge to production is certainly a tragedy for the millions of Africans who continue living in poverty, but it also represents great promise for the future: Should Africa finally tap into the opportunities opened by science, growth could be rapid and improvements in standards of living could be realized virtually overnight. What, then, hinders the modernization of Africa?

The reasons why Africa is not keeping up with modern methods of production are numerous, but they appear to have little to do with the absence of protection for domestic innovation and the lack of Schumpeterian entrepreneurs. Several factors are at work, most of which have been correctly identified by the theories that we discussed earlier. Because a major portion of technological change is embodied in equipment and machinery, Africa's inability to accumulate infrastructures and physical capital fast enough means that its access to technological progress is *de facto* restricted. This is why, some argue, Africa must first export more primary products to generate the foreign exchange required for purchasing modern equipment abroad.

Because vocational skills are required to take advantage of new machinery and methods of production, Africa is hurt by its lack of trained manpower, particularly in technical fields where few jobs are currently offered in which workers could accumulate technical expertise. The small size of African markets means that few specialized industrial services are provided, making Africa an unattractive place to operate in spite of low wages. This discourages foreign direct investment that could, in theory compensate for governments' inability to finance or subsidize local capital accumulation.

To summarize, many of the observations made by various strands of literature are correct in their prescriptions, but they often give the wrong reason why they should be followed. This can be very misleading. Realizing the importance of technological change and private entrepreneurship in growth can help avoid serious mistakes. For instance, the accumulation of capital and infrastructure is, *per se*, ineffective if local technological capabilities are not upgraded. Modernization strategies cannot succeed unless enough foreign exchange is generated, initially through primary commodity exports to finance imports of modern equipment and raw materials. The provision of education to large segments of the population remains a costly luxury if it is not accompanied by vocational training and an emphasis on scientific and technical skills. Enlarging markets and providing a supportive environment for business cannot bring rapid sustainable growth if it fails to attract foreign investment and technology.

VII. AGGLOMERATION EFFECTS

So far we have regarded growth and development as a process that takes place essentially within each country separately. However, certain economists such as Myrdal, Jacobs, or Perroux have long viewed growth as a global process.[51] They insist that the performance of individual parts of the world, whether countries, states, or cities, cannot be understood in isolation from what happens elsewhere. They point out that within developed countries themselves economic activity is not spread evenly. Most industries and supporting services are concentrated in a few cities clustered in industrial basins.[52] The immense majority of counties in the U.S. and other developed countries have a trade structure similar to that of developing countries: they export primary products (e.g., agricultural output, livestock, minerals, and fish) and import manufactured product and services. A few counties, mostly suburban neighborhoods, export labor. Others, such as military bases, live from transfers from the rest of the nation. A tiny fraction of all counties export manufactured products and services to the rest of the country.

The geographical division of labor that exists within industrialized nations is not too different from what prevails in the world as a whole. A few developed countries are responsible for the bulk of manufacturing and service exports, while the rest specialize in primary exports. This analogy has inspired several authors to suggest that certain economic activities have a tendency to cluster geographically and that this tendency is reflected in the international patterns of trade.[53] Spatial clustering is attributed to a variety of agglomeration effects due to proximity. Positive feedbacks between firms may take the form of information contagion.[54] They may also result from pecuniary externalities discussed in Section IV: the local provision of specialized industrial services and the local availability of a pool of qualified workers.[55]

If location externalities are important, the poverty trap arguments discussed in Section IV must be revisited in a new light. Once a city or region of the world has built a sufficiently large and efficient industrial base, pecuniary externalities among industries and supporting services put other undeveloped cities or regions at a disadvantage. Fortunately for newcomers, industrial clusters sooner or later become overcrowded; higher land prices and wages drive up costs and eventually erode the gains from pecuniary externalities.[56] When this happens, there is a window of opportunity for newcomers.

The logic of the positive feedback argument nevertheless suggests that relocated industries are likely to cluster again elsewhere. At each window of opportunity, only a small number of newcomers can successfully industrialize. The gradual spread of modern economic activity across the world is thus not smooth. Instead, it proceeds from cluster to cluster, a bit like the spread of industries from Japan to Taiwan, Korea, Singapore, and Hong Kong; from there to Thailand, Malaysia, and Indonesia; and then from there to mainland China and Vietnam, before they might reach other shores in the future. A similar process has been at work within Europe. England industrialized first, followed by Belgium, then Germany, followed in succession by France, Holland, Scandinavia, Russia, northern Italy, Israel, and northern Spain. The process is now spreading to Greece, Turkey, Central and Eastern Europe, and North Africa (Morocco, Tunisia, Egypt).[57]

Geographical economy arguments naturally lead to their own set of policy recommendations. If countries and regions develop one at a time, developing countries are like "pretty maids all in a row;" only the prettiest will marry the millionaire. To lure foreign investment and capture agglomeration effects, governments must put together support infrastructures and commit themselves to a pro-business attitude. This can be achieved by setting up export processing zones and other industrial parks, unveiling tempting investment codes, and promising the best tax holiday on the block. Positive advertising is part of the game, as infomercials in the *Financial Times* and the *Economist* regularly remind us. Announcing one's intention loudly and lavishly is also a way of attracting attention. Even if the time has not yet come for the next cluster of industrial activity to focus in one's country, it is possible to prepare oneself for the next window of opportunity by making sure that the local workforce is well trained, by setting up the basic infrastructure, and by building up international links with the research and business establishment.

Economic geography arguments add to our understanding of Africa's performance. Historically Africa has been penalized by its geographical isolation and paucity of navigable rivers.[58] Advances in global communication and information technology and the reduced importance of sea transport in favor of air transport are likely to change the situation. Still, the absence of African NIC means that the geographical emulation process that has characterized other parts of the world has not yet started in Africa. The fact that the most prosperous economy south of the Sahara, South Africa, was until recently isolated from its neighbors by its abhorrent political system certainly did not help. On the bright side, patterns of geographical expansion elsewhere are likely to be replicated on the African continent. If economic growth indeed spreads by geographical convection, as the works of Ciccone and Hummels seem to suggest, all we really need to get things started is for a couple African NICs to take off and sustain double-digit growth for a decade or so.[59] Half a dozen countries are good candidates to foot that bill and in fact the process may already be underway.[60] The situation is still extremely fragile, however, and temporary setbacks are not only possible but likely. This makes picking winners essentially impossible.

VIII. SUMMARY

There are many views as to what is at the foundation of economic development and growth. Each of these views has some intuitive appeal and provides useful insights. Each also comes with a different set of policy recommendations. Can we ever figure out which of all these different arguments is true and which is not? Probably not; each of them contains an element of truth. It is unlikely that these different views could be integrated in a single model of the world. Such a model would indeed be too complicated to be useful. In fact, it would be nearly as messy as the real world itself! All we can realistically hope to accomplish is to combine these views at an intuitive level and use the insights they provide to guide policy.

A few key ideas emerge from the literature. My own assessment of these ideas is as follows. Economic development is a process of modernization by which scientific principles are applied to the production of goods and services. It began with the industrial revolution in England and progressively spread from there. As more and more countries, a few at a time, achieve OECD levels of development, more and more resources are spent in the world turning science into progress. Because the frontiers of knowledge and technology are being pushed back by an ever-increasing number of countries sharing the results of their research, growth in advanced countries speeds up; it is indeed faster now, over the long run, than it has ever been in the last 200 years.[61]

The way by which poor countries can achieve standards of living comparable to those of rich countries is through catching up. Catching up is a process distinct from growth in developed countries. The key to catching up is to copy and absorb technological improvements invented elsewhere and to emulate advanced economies.[62] Due to agglomeration effects and pecuniary externalities, not all countries and regions can catch up at the same time. In addition, catching up seems to take place mostly by convection; geographical and ethnic proximity largely dictates who takes off next. In this respect, Africa is penalized by its isolation.

Given that economic activity is getting ever more mobile, competition among candidates for industrialization means that investors are attracted to locations that provide the best environment. As a result, a rapid inflation seems to have taken place in the requirements that make a location attractive. While 50 years ago Japan might have lured American investors with cheap and docile labor, today's investors expect much more. The quality of the service proposed to potential investors now includes good governance and market institutions in addition to infrastructures and tax holidays. As in soccer, the nature of the game evolves over the years. Growth strategies that would have been successful in the 1960s now fail to score.

Rapid growth is typically based on industrialization.[63] This is because industries and the services that support them are the forms of economic activities that benefit the most from agglomeration effects and modernization.[64] Returns to agglomeration in manufacturing are thus responsible for cross-country differences in trade patterns but also in growth performance. Because the potential for technological improvement is limited in primary exports but strong in industry and services, geographical locations that specialize in the former stagnate while the latter prosper.[65]

A geographical approach to international patterns of industrialization thus suggests that undeveloped countries or regions can attract internationally mobile capital and skills only to the extent that congestion drives production costs up in advanced regions.[66] Given that industrialization is characterized by increasing returns and gains from specialization, not all undeveloped regions can industrialize at the same time: if a newly industrialized country has begun penetrating export markets, it gains a first mover advantage compared to other undeveloped countries. If the above interpretation is correct, absence of industrialization is the normal outcome, and catching up is the exception. Although more empirical work is required to ensure this interpretation is valid, it is worth pointing out that, historically, a lack of industrialization and modernization has indeed been the norm for the overwhelming majority of the world's population, Africa included.

Poor countries unable to attract foreign capital to finance rapid industrialization can nevertheless harness some of the engines of growth listed in this chapter, such as allocative efficiency, the production and export of primary commodities, and the import of manufactures. Becoming an efficient primary producer can generate growth for a while, but it is bound to run out of steam. Moreover, the well-being of primary producers remains sensitive to variations in commodity prices and the accumulation of external debt that invariably follows external terms of trade shocks. Primary producers nevertheless benefit from product innovation (e.g., new vaccines) in ways that are not adequately captured in standard measures of growth and welfare.

There is hope, however, because, as the gap between developed and stagnating countries keeps growing, there is more to catch up on and catching up, when it happens, takes place at an increasingly rapid pace.[67] Furthermore, the recent experience of Asian NICs indicates that things can change unexpectedly and rapidly.

Based on this understanding of the processes at work in the world today, there is room for cautious hope concerning Africa.

In terms of policy advice, there is a violent contradiction between the neoclassical view of the world, which privileges a *laissez-faire* approach to government, and arguments based on increasing returns and pecuniary externalities, which recognize a role for industrial policy. This conflict has dominated the debate about Africa, the reasons for its lackluster performance, its economic future, and the role of structural adjustment. The contradictory policy recommendations that are peddled by each side of the debate are not dictated by scientific observation but rather are derived from different theoretical assumptions and opposing philosophical views of the world. For that reason, the debate is essentially a sterile and confusing one. The author suspects that Africa will take off before the debate is resolved, and when it happens each side will claim Africa's performance was best predicted by their model, as has been the case for East Asian NICs.

DISCUSSION QUESTIONS

1. Can a country increase its welfare by reducing that of others? Give examples and counter-examples.
2. Can a beggar your neighbor policy explain the relative economic performance of Africa and the United States? Justify your answer.
3. Immediately after the colonization of Africa, colonial powers built numerous roads and railways. Apart from military considerations, what might have justified these massive and costly investments?
4. Structural adjustment programs seek to help countries realize their comparative advantage by improving allocative efficiency. Is structural adjustment a strategy for economic growth? Discuss.
5. In a famous article estimating a neoclassical growth model, Barro concludes that all countries are currently converging to standards of living compatible with their saving rate and investment in education. Barro also finds a significant and negative African "dummy." He interprets this result as implying that Africa is intrinsically inimical to growth, a situation he and others have blamed on political corruption and inappropriate governance. Discuss Barro's view.
6. Is population control a prerequisite for growth? Discuss.
7. Is the accumulation of capital essential for growth? Explain.
8. What is the role of human capital in the growth process of poor countries? What policy implications do you draw from your analysis? Should Africa invest in human capital or rather invest in other things, such as infrastructure and utilities?

9. Does the existence of increasing returns to scale, start-up costs, and learning by doing penalize African firms? Explain.

10. Dependency theorists argue that poor countries can only industrialize by closing their market to foreign competition. What implicit assumptions underlie this approach? What are the assumed engines of growth and obstacles to development? How relevant is this approach for Africa today?

11. Many regional preferential trade agreements have been initiated in Africa since independence, with little effect. What was the economic rationale behind many of these agreements and why have they failed?

12. Some argue that multinationals are bad for poor countries, others that they are beneficial. Present arguments for and against and draw your own conclusions.

13. Industrial policy sometimes includes the targeting certain industries. What rationale is behind targeting? Discuss.

14. Technology transfer is often cited as necessary for growth. Discuss various methods by which technology can be transferred to poor countries.

15. Are patent laws and international treaties on copyright infringements good or bad for growth? For catching up? Explain.

16. Are local entrepreneurs important for growth? Discuss.

17. Economic geographers point out that industrial activity is heavily concentrated across space, not only across countries but also within developed economies. What factors are responsible for spatial concentration? What does this imply for regional and international patterns of trade and specialization? What does this imply for the future of Africa?

NOTES

[1]Braudel, F. (1986) *Civilization and Capitalism*, New York; Harper & Row; Pritchett, L. (1997) "Divergence, Big Time," *Journal of Economic Perspectives*, 11(3): 3–17.

[2]Maddison, A. (1982) *Phases of Capitalist Development*, London: Oxford University Press; The World Bank, *Accelerated Development in Sub-Saharan Africa: An Agenda for Action*.

[3]Hopkins, A.G. (1973) *An Economic History of West Africa*, London: Longman Group.

[4]Kuznets, S. (1955) "Economic Growth and Income Inequality," *American Economic Review*, 55(1): 1–28, Kanbur, R. (1997) *Income Distribution and Development*, Washington, D.C.: The World Bank.

[5]Dollar, D. and Kraay, A. (2000) *Growth Is Good for the Poor*, Washington, D.C.: Development Research Group, World Bank.

[6]For a more detailed discussion, the reader is referred, for instance, to Mkandawire, T. and Soludo, C. (1998) *African Perspectives on Structural Adjustment: Our Continent Our Future*, Nairobi, Kenya: African World Press (an IDRC-CODESIRA pubication); Elbadawi, I. and Schmidt-Hebbel, K. (1998) "Instability and Growth in the World," *Journal of African Economies*, 7(Suppl. 2): 116–168; Oyejide, A. (1998) "Trade Policy and Regional Integration in the Development Context: Emerging Patterns, Issues, and Lessons for Sub-Saharan Africa," *Journal of African Economies*, 7(Suppl .1): 108–145; Collier, P.

and Gunning, J.W. (1999) "Explaining African Economic Performance," *Journal of Economic Literature*, 37(1): 64–111.

[7] See, for example, Maddison, A. (1982) *Phases of Capitalist Development*, London: Oxford University Press.

[8] See, for example, Hopkins, A.G. (1973) *An Economic History of West Africa*, London: Longman Group.

[9] See for example, the excellent description of how technological improvements in synthetic pesticides has affected the market for Kenyan pyrethrum (a natural pesticide) in Winter-Nelson, A.E. (1992) "Marketing Boards and Market Power: The Case of Konyary Pyrethrum," unpublished Ph.D. thesis, Stanford University.

[10] Deaton, A. and Miller, R. (1996) "International Commodity Prices, Macroeconomic Performance, and Politics in Sub-Saharan Africa," *Journal of African Economies*, 5(3): 99–191.

[11] See, for example, "The World Bank Accelerated Development in Sub-Saharan Africa: An Agenda for Action," Washington, D.C., 1981.

[12] See for example, Prebisch, R. (1963) *Towards a Dynamic Development Policy for Latin America*, New York: United Nations.

[13] Together, these three countries account for most of cocoa production in the world.

[14] Humphreys, C. and Jaeger, W. (1989) *Africa's Adjustment and Growth in the 1980s*, Washington, D.C.: World Bank and United Nations Development Program.

[15] See, for example, Collier, P. and Gunning, J.W. (1999) "Explaining African Economic Performance," *Journal of Economic Literature*, 37(1): 64–111.

[16] Myint, H. (1958) "The 'Classical Theory' of International Trade and the Underdeveloped Countries," *Economic Journal*, 68:317–337; also see Hopkins, A. G. (1973) *An Economic History of West Africa*, London: Longman Group.

[17] See, for example, Dervis, K., de Melo, J., and Robinson, S. (1982) *General Equilibrium Models For Development Policy*, Washington, D.C.: World Bank.

[18] See, for example, the Steel reference in Note 11; World Bank (1981) *Accelerated Development in Sub-Saharan Africa: An Agenda for Action*, Washington, D.C.: World Bank (also known as the Berg report).

[19] See, for example, Steel, W.F. and Evans, J.W. (1981) *Industrialization in Sub-Saharan Africa*, Washington, D.C.: World Bank.

[20] See, for example, Hopkins, A.G. (1973) *An Economic History of West Africa*, London: Longman Group.

[21] Ehrlich, P.R. (1968) *The Population Bomb*, New York: Ballantine Books.

[22] Bailey, R. (1995) *The True State of the Planet*, New York: The Free Press.

[23] Boserup, E. (1965) *The Conditions of Agricultural Growth*, Chicago, IL: Aldine.

[24] Solow, R.M. (1956) "A Contribution to the Theory of Economic Growth," *Quarterly Journal of Economics*, 70:65–94, Lucas, R.E. (1988) "One the Mechanics of Economic Development," *Journal of Monetary Economics*, 22: 3–42.

[25] To be technically correct, convergence to a constant steady state requires that, in the limit, returns to labor fall sufficiently close to zero. Jones and Manuelli (1990), for instance, constructed a capital accumulation model of neverending growth in which marginal returns to labor are bounded from below; see Jones, L.E. and Manuelli, R. (1990) " A Convex Model of Equilibrium Growth: Theory and Policy Implications," *Journal of Political Economics*, 98(5): 1008–1038.

[26] King, R.G. and Rebelo, S.T. (1993) "Transitional Dynamics and Economic Growth in the Neoclassical Model," *American Economic Review*, 83(4): 908–931.

[27] See, for example, Pritchett, L. (1997) "Divergence, Big Time," *Journal of Economic Perspectives*, 11(3): 3–17.

[28] See, for example, the Lucas reference in Note 24; Jones, L.E. and Manuelli, R. (1990) "A Convex Model of Equilibrium Growth: Theory and Policy Implications," *Journal of Political Economics*, 98(5): 1008–1038.

[29]Policy intervention is justified by the public good nature of most large infrastructures. Whenever discriminatory pricing is not feasible or is costly to administer, the builder of the public infrastructure may indeed be unable to capture all the economic rents generated by the investment. This results in under investment in infrastructure, even if there are no other distortions in the incentives to invest.

[30]See, for example, Solow, R.M. (1956) "A Contribution to the Theory of Economic Growth," *Quarterly Journal of Economics*, 70:65–94.

[31]Schultz, T.W. (1961) "Investment in Human Capital," *American Economic Review*, 61(1): 1–17.

[32]Barro, R.J. (1991) "Economic Growth in a Cross-Section of Countries," *Quarterly Journal of Economics*, 106(2): 407–443; Mankiw, N.G., Romer, D., and Weil, D.N. (1992) "A Contribution to the Empirics of Economic Growth," *Quarterly Journal of Economics*, 107: 407–437.

[33]Nurkse, R.(1953) *Problems of Capital Formation in Underdeveloped Countries*, New York: Oxford University Press; Murphy, K.M., Shleifer, A., and Vishny, R.W. (1998) "Industrialization and the Big Push," *Journal of Political Economics*, 97(5): 1003–1026.

[34]Rosenstein-Rodan, P. (1943) "Problems of Industrialization in Eastern and South-Eastern Europe," *Economic Journal*, June.

[35]Prebisch, R. (1963) Towards a Dynamic Development Policy for Latin America, New York: United Nations.

[36]Steel, W.F. and Evans, J.W. (1981) *Industrialization in Sub-Saharan Africa*, Washington D.C.: World Bank.

[37]Stokey, N.L. (1988) "Learning by Doing and the Introduction of New Goods," *Journal of Political Economics*, 96(4): 701–717, Young, A. (1991) "Learning by Doing and the Dynamic Effects of International Trade," *Quarterly Journal of Economics*, May: 369–405.

[38]Rostow, W.W. (1956) "The Take-Off into Self-Sustained Growth," *Economics Journal*, 261: 25–48.

[39]Hirschman, A.O. (1958) *The Strategy of Economic Development*, New Haven, CN: Yale University Press.

[40]Jacobs, J. (1969) *The Economy of Cities*, New York: Random House; Jacobs, J. (1984) *Cities and the Wealth of Nations*, New York: Random House.

[41]See, for example, World Bank (1993) The East Asian Miracle: Economic Growth and Public Policy, New York: OVP.

[42]Steel, W.F. and Webster, L.M. (1991) *Small Enterprises Under Adjustment in Ghana*, Technical Paper No. 138, Industry and Finance Series, Washington, D.C.; World Bank.

[43]This view does not entirely go unchallenged, however. Some economists have argued that modern pieces of equipment and machinery designed in developed economies are not appropriate for developing countries because they are not adapted to their relative scarcities of capital and labor. Switching from the shovel to the bulldozer is too much of a jump, they argue. More appropriate technologies are needed that recognize the relative cheapness of labor in poor countries and allow for intermediate amounts of capital per worker k. They recommend that governments and donors should subsidize the search for technologies that are appropriate for undeveloped countries. Although the idea sounds appealing, the payoffs to this type of research are uncertain. For one thing, many intermediate technologies were already developed 100 years ago, when the capital labor ratio in the West was lower (e.g., the ox plow, the horse carriage, or the water mill). It is not necessary to invent them again; all one has to do is dig for old blueprints. Second, much intermediate technology is already available for sale. Many African manufacturers, for instance, use second- or third-hand equipment purchased from the West or from other Third World countries that are a little bit more advanced than themselves. Although antiquated pieces of equipment tend to break down often and are difficult to service, they are nevertheless sufficiently productive to discourage the production of new outdated equipment. This makes the development and manufacturing of intermediate technology quite problematic.

[44]See, for example, Mankiw, N.G., Romer, D., and Weil, D.N. (1992) "A Contribution to the Empirics of Economic Growth," *Quarterly Journal of Economics*, 107: 407–437; Barro, R.J. (1991) "Economic Growth in a Cross-Section of Countries," *Quarterly Journal of Economic*, 106(2): 407–443.

[45]Grossman, G.M. and Helpman, E. (1991) "Quality Ladders and Product Cycles," *Quarterly Journal of Economics*, 106: 557–586.

[46]Romer, P.M. (1986) "Increasing Returns and Long-Run Growth," *Journal of Political Economy*, 94(5): 1002–1037; Romer, P.M. (1990) "Endogenous Technological Change," *Journal of Political Economy*, 98(5, pt.2): S71–102.

[47]High levels of training need not, by themselves, do the trick. Unless properly funded research institutions are created locally, scientists sent abroad to upgrade their skills often find it both more profitable and more fulfilling to seek employment in the research establishment of developed countries.

[48]Schumpeter, J.A. (1961) *The Theory of Economic Development*, Cambridge, MA: Harvard University Press.

[49]See, for example, Nelson and Winter (1982), Grossman, G.M. and Helpman, E. (1991) "Quality Ladders and Product Cycles," *Quarterly Journal of Economics*, 106: 557–586; Romer, P.M.(1990) "Endogenous Technological Change," *Journal of Political Economy*, 98(5, pt.2): S71–102; Aghion and Howitt (1992) "A Model of Growth Through Creative Destruction," *Econometrica*, 60(2): 323–351; Aghion and Howitt (1998) *Endogenous Growth Theory*, Cambridge, MA: MIT Press.

[50]Fafchamps, M. (2000) "Ethnicity and Credit in African Manufacturing," *Journal of Development Economics*, 61: 205–235.

[51]Myrdal, G. (1957) *Economic Theory and Under-Developed Regions*, London: Gerald Duckworth and Co.; Jacobs, J. (1984) *Cities and the Wealth of Nations*, New York: Random House; Perroux, F. (1962) *L'Economie des Jeunes Nations*, Paris: Presses Universitaires de France.

[52]Krugman, P.R. (1991) "Increasing Returns and Economic Geography," *Journal of Political Economics*, 99(3): 483–499.

[53]See, for example, Krugman, P.R. (1991) "Increasing Returns and Economic Geography," *Journal of Political Economics*, 99(3): 483–499; Young, A. (1991) "Learning by Doing and the Dynamic Effects of International Trade," *Quarterly Journal of Economics*, May: 369–405.

[54]Arthur, W.B. (1990) "Silicon Valley's Locational Clusters: When Do Increasing Returns Imply Monopoly?," *Mathematical Social Sciences*, 19: 235–251.

[55]Rodriguez-Clare, A. (1996) "The Division of Labor and Economic Development," *Journal of Developmental Economics*, 49: 3–32; Ciccone, A. and Matsuyama, K. (1996) "Start-Up Costs and Pecuniary Externalities as Barriers to Economic Development," *Journal of Developmental Economics*, 49(1): 33–59.

[56]Fafchamps, M. (1997) "Mobile Capital, Location Externalities, and Industrialization," *Journal of Comparative Economics*.

[57]Morris, C.T. and Adelman, I. (1988) *Comparative Patterns of Economic Development, 1850–1914*, Baltimore, MD: Johns Hopkins University Press.

[58]See, for example, Braudel, F. (1986) *Civilization and Capitalism*, New York: Harper & Row; Hopkins, A.G. (1973) *An Economic History of West Africa*, London: Longman Group.

[59]Ciccone, A. and Matsuyama, K. (1996) "Start-Up Costs and Pecuniary Externalities as Barriers to Economic Development," *Journal of Developmental Economics*, 49(1): 33–59; Hummels, D. (1995) *Global Income Clustering and Trade in Intermediate Goods*, Ann Arbor, MI: University of Michigan.

[60]Biggs, T., Moody, G., Leewen, J.V., and White, E. (1994) *Africa Can Compete! Export Opportunities and Challenges in Garments and Home Products in the U.S. Market*, Washington, D.C.: World Bank.

[61]Romer, P. M. (1986) "Increasing Returns and Long-Run Growth," *Journal of Political Economy*, 94(5): 1002–1037.

[62]Gerschenkron, A. (1962) *Economic Backwardness in Historical Perspective*, Cambridge, MA: Belknap Press.

[63]In the context of this chapter, industrialization should be understood to include modern services.

[64]Although the process of development is often described as one of industrialization, the distinction between industry, agriculture and services is misleading: what matters is the adoption of modern

techniques of production. The prospects for increasing output through modernization differ across sectors, however. Although the productivity of agriculture and other primary sectors can be improved through investment and innovation, manufacturing and certain types of services are where the use of modern techniques of production yields the highest payoff, if only because there are no immobile factors of production.

[65]Young, A. (1991) "Learning by Doing and the Dynamic Effects of International Trade," *Quarterly Journal of Economics*, May: 106(2): 369–405.

[66]Fafchamps, M. (1997) "Mobile Capital, Location Externalities, and Industrialization," *Journal of Comparative Economics*.

[67]Fafchamps, M. (1997) "Mobile Capital, Location Externalities, and Industrialization," *Journal of Comparative Economics*, 25: 345–365.

Population

JACOB ADETUNJI*

*United States Agency for International Development, Bureau for Global Health,
Washington, D.C. 20523*

KEY TERMS

Acquired Immune Deficiency
  Syndrome (AIDS)
Contraception
Contraceptive prevalence rate
Demographic bonus/dividend
Demographic transitions theory
Hidden unemployment/disguised
  unemployment
Human Immunodeficiency Virus (HIV)
Internal migration
International migration
Low-level equilibrium population
  trap/Malthusian Population Trap
Malthusian perspective

Maternal and child health
Migration
Mortality
Neo-Malthusian perspective
Population density
Population policies
Proximate determinants
Rural–rural migration
Rural–urban migration
Seasonal migration
Sub-fecundity
Total Fertility Rate (TFR)
Unemployment rate
Urbanization

I. INTRODUCTION

The question about whether or not rapid population growth results in
economic underdevelopment has generated much debate by scholars over the
past 200 years. Some scholars say it does, while others say it does not. Those
who say that population is a cause of economic underdevelopment and poverty
are known as "traditionalists," or population pessimists, while those who
believe otherwise are known as "revisionists." The revisionists consist of those
who argue that rapid population growth,[8] could be beneficial to economic
growth—the population optimists—and those who believe that population

*Views and opinions expressed in this chapter are those of the author and should not be interpreted
as representing those of USAID.

growth is a neutral factor in economic development (the population neutralism group). The view that dominates the population-economic development debate seems to have shifted over the past 60 years or so. This chapter focuses specifically on how the debate relates to Africa, which is the region with the highest rate of population growth and lowest level of economic development. The question is whether or not Africa's economic development results from its rapid population growth. To address this question, we begin by considering both the possible empirical correlations as well as theoretical issues. Historical trends in African population as well as reasons for Africa's high population growth rates are discussed.

A. EMPIRICAL CORRELATIONS

Empirical observations suggest the coexistence of high population growth rates and low levels of economic development in Africa, especially the region below the Sahara. For example, Africa's population grew at an annual rate of 2.6% in the 1960s, 2.9% in the 1970s, and 3.0% in the 1980s. From 1990 to 1995, the growth rate was still 2.9% per annum, but it declined to 2.4% in 2001. In spite of this decline, Africa's population still grows at twice the rate for the world.[1] Most countries in the region have population growth rates above 2% (see column 3 of Table 6.1).

However, in terms of economic performance, Africa, particularly Sub-Saharan Africa, is also one of the poorest and weakest performing regions of the world. The estimated gross national product (GNP) per capita for the year 2000 was $670, compared with $2130 in Asia and $3880 in Latin America and the Caribbean. The growth rate of the GNP per capita in Africa has been poor: 2.9% per annum between 1965 and 1973, declining to 0.1% per annum from 1973–1980, and falling again at a dismal rate of −2.8% between 1980 and 1987. For Sub-Saharan Africa, the situation is even worse. The region contains 32 of the 47 countries classified by the World Bank as least developed, and the change in GDP between 1992 and 2000 was estimated at 2.7%, which was below the population growth rate.[2] While Africa's population was growing at an annual rate of 2.9% between the 1960s and 1980s, GNP per capita grew at a low rate of 1.9% per annum between 1965 and 1983. Given this scenario, it is difficult for the region to see any real improvement in the quality of life. In fact, countries with high fertility rates in the region also happen to be among the poorest. For example, Chad has one of the highest fertility rates in Africa (see Table 6.1) and its GNP per capita of about $230 in 2000 was one of the lowest in the world. At the other end of the spectrum is Algeria, with a total fertility rate of 3.8 and a GNP per capita of $1550, suggesting that fertility is lower in richer countries. Consequently, many people tend to link Africa's slow economic development to the rapid population growth. The correlation between per capita gross national income (using purchasing power

TABLE 6.1 Population Size, Natural Increase, Total Fertility Rate, and Life Expectancy at Birth for Selected African Countries (2000)

	Population Size (in millions)[a]	Annual Natural Increase (%)	Total Fertility Rate	Life Expectancy at Birth (years)
Algeria	31.5	2.4	3.8	69
Botswana	1.6	1.6	4.1	44
Cameroon	15.4	2.6	5.2	55
Chad	8.0	3.3	6.6	48
Comoros	0.6	2.8	5.1	59
Cote d'Ivoire	16.0	2.2	5.2	47
Egypt	68.3	2.0	3.3	65
Ethiopia	64.1	2.4	6.7	46
Gabon	1.2	2.2	5.4	52
Ghana	19.5	2.4	4.5	58
Mauritius	1.2	1.1	2.0	70
Mozambique	19.1	2.2	5.6	40
Nigeria	123.3	2.8	6.0	52
Senegal	9.5	2.8	5.7	52
Uganda	23.3	2.9	6.9	42
Zambia	9.6	2.0	6.1	37
Zimbabwe	11.3	1.0	4.0	40

[a]These are estimates from the Population Reference Bureau (2000) for mid-2000.

parity of U.S. dollars) and total fertility rate in 45 African countries that have requisite data (see Population Reference Bureau, 2001) was −0.78, suggesting that about 61% of the variation in GNP per capita in the table could be explained by variations in the levels of fertility. Thus, at an aggregate level, higher gross national income is associated with lower levels of fertility.

B. THEORETICAL FACTORS

The second set of reasons for why people believe that population and economic growth in Africa are related derives from long-standing theoretical developments, the most important of which was the work of Malthus, known as the *Malthusian perspective*. The basic tenet of Malthus' theory was that the effect of population growth on economic prosperity is negative. His perspective centers on the relationship between population growth and food supply. Simply, population growth is seen as a cause of poverty and misery. He saw a self-regulating mechanism explaining population fluctuations. Human beings tend to reproduce to the limits that can be supported by their environment. Above that, positive checks move in and create a new equilibrium. These positive checks include war, famine, and pestilence. There is a tendency for population of a country, unless checked by dwindling food supplies, to grow at a geometric rate, doubling every

30–40 years. At the same time, food supply, because of diminishing returns to the fixed factor (land), can only progress at an arithmetical rate. Because food supply cannot keep pace with population growth, per capita food consumption would decrease, leading to famine or disease. In modern economic terms, this is called the *low-level equilibrium population trap* or the *Malthusian population trap*. It is a vicious cycle of economic growth leading to high population growth, which mops up the economic gains and eventually leads to poverty and positive checks, followed by another cycle of economic progress, population growth, and so on. According to Malthus, the only way to avoid this low-level equilibrium is through checks and restraints.

In *neo-Malthusian perspective*, poor nations could not rise above their subsistence levels unless they adopt "preventive" checks (or birth control) before positive checks (starvation, diseases, wars) serve as the restraining force. This view was made popular in the second half of the 20th century by well-known neo-Malthusian writers such as Paul Ehrlich and Hardin.[3,4] The main criticism of Malthus is that he did not take into account or foresee how effects of technology could alter the relationship of humans with the land and the productive capacity of the land. The population of the world at the time of Malthus was just about a billion people. He probably could not imagine that the world would support 6 billion people at the current living standards. However, while it is true that technological advances have increased the productive capacity of land and made life easier, most people in many parts of Africa still live as subsistence farmers who have benefited little from the technological innovations. Therefore, there remains a potential threat of Africa being unable to feed its population. A large number of people in Sub-Saharan Africa still depend on foreign food aid. In 2001, about 18 million people in East Africa relied on food assistance because of both natural and man-made emergencies. The Food and Agricultural Organization estimated that total cereal production in Africa declined from 114.5 million tons in 1998 to 110 in 2000 (*Food Outlook*, 2001), and cereal import increased from 41.6 to 44.9 million tons.

Apart from the Malthusian and neo-Malthusian perspectives, other scholars have viewed the relationship between population growth and economic development as positive. These are the population optimists. The most important among them are Boserup and Simon. The contention of Boserup is that population growth could spur technological innovation.[5] Although in the short run, population growth may depress labor productivity, it may in the long run encourage technological progress. Boserup found that the likelihood of technological advances increases in response to increasing population density.[5] Higher population density leads to increased intensity of labor use. This raises the pay-off from an innovation. Higher population density leads, all things being equal, to lower per capita income, which raises the utility gain from an innovation. Population growth and the resulting urbanization create new problems regarding organization of food production and transportation. Methods of food production that use vast land space with periods of fallowing are a consequence of low population density. However, as population density increases, a short-run drop in productivity occurs that arises from diminishing returns to labor. In the long run, the population-density-induced urbanization would spark technological innovation.

Separation of the short-term effects of rapid population growth is itself instructive because short- and long-term effects may not be the same. Usually, the short-run consequences of high population growth may be negative, but the long-run effect may be positive.[33] Although Simon argues that slow population growth alone cannot cause economic growth, it does not mean that its excessive growth cannot create short-term negative consequences.[7] The point that Simon is trying to make, however, is that if A does not cause B, then there is no causal relationship between the two variables. He summarized existing statistical analyses and other studies to show that population growth or density is not the reason for lack of economic development in the less developed world. Rather, it is a nation's political and economic systems that are the real culprits.[7]

In sum, both the empirical observations as well as the theoretical developments suggest that a relationship exists between population growth in Africa and the levels of economic development. They also suggest that there is more than one side to the population–economic development interrelations and that perhaps no universal law inexorably links population growth to economic underdevelopment. Nevertheless, rapid and uncontrolled population growth usually constitutes a drag on the wheels of economic progress and that effect is most severe in resource-scarce settings such as in most parts of Africa.

In the sections that follow, a broad overview of historical trends in African population in relation to human welfare is first presented, followed by a discussion of fertility, mortality, and migration, which are the three factors that determine how fast a population grows and how it is distributed by age and in space. Each of these three factors could affect and be affected by economic growth. To properly understand the interaction between population growth and economic development in Africa, it is necessary to understand the interactions between the components and economic development. Therefore, each of these components of population growth is discussed separately in the chapter.

II. ELEMENTS OF AFRICAN POPULATION GROWTH

This section discusses trends in African population size and growth rates over the past several centuries, as well as fertility, mortality, and migration, which are the components of population change in the region. The relationships between these components of population change and economic development are also discussed.

A. AFRICAN POPULATION TRENDS AND HUMAN WELFARE

Like all other regions of the world, the size of the African population in the past was small and its growth rate was minimal. Although nobody knows precisely how large the population of Africa was in the past, some conjectural estimates suggest that its share of the world population has fluctuated over time. About 1000 years ago (1000 A.D.), about 15.5% (or 39 million) of the 253 million people in the world resided in Africa. This proportion was estimated to have increased to about 19% (87 million) by 1500 A.D. This suggests that Africa gained 48 million people in 500 years, an average of 96,000 per year, or an annual growth rate of 0.16%. Thereafter, Africa's share of the world's population declined to about 8.3% in 1850 before increasing to 13% in the year 2000.[9] The decline between the 17th and 19th centuries has been attributed to factors such as European contact with Africa and the subsequent exportation of their diseases to the region, the trans-Atlantic slave trade, and the transitional population growth in Europe.

The estimated population of Africa in 2001 was 820 million (Population Reference Bureau, 2001). This suggests an increase of 733 million people in the 501 years between 1500 and 2001, an average gain of 1.46 million per year, which represents an annual growth rate of 0.45%. However, as mentioned earlier, African population grew at an average rate of 3.0% in the 1980s and 2.9% in the 1990s. Between 2000 and 2001 alone, the African population increased by 20 million people, or 2.4% in spite of the scourge of HIV/AIDS in several countries of the region. Thus, African population growth rates were mostly low in the past and have increased considerably in recent times. If the current growth rate remains constant, the African population would double within the next 30 years. That possibility itself is worrisome, particularly because the region's population has more than doubled from 402 million in 1975 to 820 million in 2001.[17] Nobody knows what the social, economic and environmental consequences of having 1.6 billion people in Africa would be.

Although empirical correlations now link population growth to negative economic development, this link seems to be recent. The relationship between welfare and population or household size seems to have changed from positive to negative as societies progress from traditional agrarian to modern economies. In a traditional, mostly agrarian society, which is still characteristic of much of Africa, standards of living are low and mortality levels are high. Because very few children survive, those having many of them are considered blessed. Households with many children tend to be those with more wealth. Of course, in an agrarian setting, those who have a large number of children are likely to benefit from the cheap labor supplied by their children compared with other families with few members. Thus, wealth and population size tend to be correlated, at least at the household level.

This apparently counterintuitive relationship was what John Caldwell, the famous Australia-born demographer, observed early in his work in Africa. He noticed that most of the elite group members he encountered were from large families, rather than from small families of the Western style. He found that large numbers of children per household did not lead to poverty in Africa. Rather, small families were least desired because people associated them with such negative characteristics as below normal fecundity.[10]

To explain the phenomenon, Caldwell proposed that, with intergenerational wealth flows (i.e., in any pretransitional setting in history, whether Africa or elsewhere), children are a source of benefit to their parents. They are a source of income and support for parents throughout life, and their costs to parents are minimal. Therefore, wealth flows from children to parents. However, as a society becomes more modern, for example, because of increases in schooling and the movement away from traditional occupations, the amount of support that parents receive from their children diminishes, gradually leading to a reversal in the direction of wealth flow. Whenever this direction of wealth flows reverses from parents to children, fertility will decline.

At the community level, in the past, there were several advantages to having a large and rapidly growing population. This was because larger population sizes often translated to larger numbers of able-bodied men and thus larger armies. In eras of such "competitive fertility," communities with the resources were able to expand their wealth and influence during wars and inter-group conflicts, which were common in those days.[11] It is only in modern times that the relationship between community wealth and family size has reversed. Those with high incomes today now tend to have fewer children than those in the low-income categories. In fact, the whole argument of linking population to poverty would sound absurd to many African agrarian societies of the early 20th century, where children were equated with prosperity and wealth. However, there has been a rapid change in population size and means to wealth over the past century in Africa.

III. FERTILITY LEVELS AND ECONOMIC DEVELOPMENT

One of the distinguishing factors of African fertility is that it is among the highest in the world (Fig. 6.1). By the year 2000, the total fertility rate in Africa was estimated to be 5.3, which is much higher than the rate in other regions of the world. Another distinguishing factor of African fertility is that its decline has been slow; it has remained high even when other developing world regions were experiencing rapid fertility declines in the 1970s and 1980s. One of the reasons for the rapid population growth in Africa in the second half of the 20th century was a high fertility rate. Although many observers believe that fertility is the

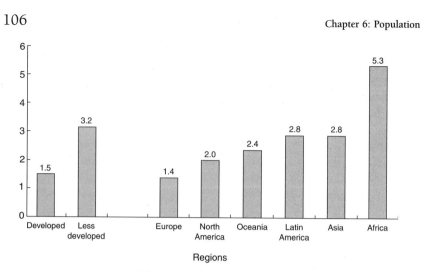

FIGURE 6.1   Total fertility rates in various regions of the world (2000).

main reason for Africa's rapid population growth rates, demographers know that population growth is the product of interactions among fertility, mortality, and migration. While it is true that fertility is high in Africa (Figure 6.1), this has been the case in most parts of the region for a long time. Nevertheless, high fertility in the past did not lead to a rapid population growth until the second half of the 20th century because mortality rates were also high. The rapid population growth of the past 50 years happened because of the rapid decline in mortality rate from the end of World War II, which was not accompanied by a corresponding decline in fertility. This type of population growth is referred to as transitional growth in demographic transition theory.

For example, in the 1980s, total fertility rates exceeding 8 children per woman were observed in countries such as Malawi, Rwanda, Ethiopia, and Angola.[12] In the early 1990s, the average total fertility rate (TFR) for Africa was still about 6 children per woman.[13] The TFR for Africa in 2001 was estimated at 5.2; and 5.6 for Sub-Saharan Africa, which is twice the global rate of 2.8 (Population Reference Bureau, 2001). Consequently, many studies have focused on explanations for the high fertility regime in the region. The explanations are usually of two types: those relating to general background factors and those relating to the proximate or intermediate determinants.

The general background factors include levels of education, religion, place of residence, and wealth or income. Although fertility varies according to these factors, their linkage to fertility is indirect. For example, we know that women with low levels of education tend to have high levels of fertility and that urban dwellers usually have lower levels of fertility than rural dwellers, but there is little about going to school or living in cities that determines the actual number of children one has. Rather, it is how education or urban residence affects the intermediate or proximate determinants that will actually determine the effects on fertility levels. The proximate determinants, therefore, have a direct link to the actual process of reproduction.

Earlier analysis of the intermediate variables by Davis and Blake identified 11 of them.[14] These were later refined to four proximate determinants (marriage, abortion, contraception, and postpartum infecundability).[15] These four proximate determinants are believed to be key factors explaining the actual fertility levels of a population. For example, if women with low levels of education end up with higher fertility rates it is usually because they marry early and therefore have long years of exposure to the risk of having children. Women with low levels of education are also less likely to use effective contraceptive methods, and many of them may end up with large numbers of unwanted and mistimed births.

One of the major analyses of the proximate determinants of fertility in Sub-Saharan Africa was performed by Jolly and Gribble and it shows that contraceptive use, marriage, and postpartum infecundability are the major proximate determinants operating in the region.[16] The role of abortion could not be determined because of the absence of requisite data. In several African countries, women marry at relatively young ages. The median age at first marriage in the region is between 18 and 19 years (Table 6.2), and between 83 and 97% of all women marry by age 25. Once married, most women spend most of their reproductive years in marital unions. Of course, marrying at a very young age may mean that women are not able to complete their schooling or have sufficient

TABLE 6.2   Median Age at Marriage and the Proportion Marrying by Age 25 Among Selected African Countries

Countries (Year of Survey)	Proportion Never Married	Proportion Married by Age 25	Median Age at Marriage Among Women at Ages		
			30–34	40–44	45–49
Cameroon (1998)	5.5	88.8	17.2	16.9	16.4
Chad (1997)	0.7	97.5	15.9	15.6	15.6
Comoros (1996)	8.8	81.7	18.4	17.5	17.6
Cote d'Ivoire (1994)	5.2	86.7	18.1	18.2	17.9
Egypt (1995)	5.5	83.0	19.4	19.0	18.0
Ghana (1998)	4.1	86.1	18.7	18.7	18.7
Kenya (1998)	6.4	85.9	19.2	18.2	18.4
Mozambique (1997)	3.3	91.2	17.4	16.9	17.0
Nigeria (1990)	2.9	91.2	16.3	16.8	17.3
Senegal (1997)	6.3	87.6	17.4	16.7	16.7
Uganda (1995)	2.8	92.2	17.3	17.0	17.3
Zambia (1996)	4.1	90.9	17.9	17.4	16.8
Zimbabwe (1994)	3.5	89.6	18.7	18.9	18.9

Source: Demographic and Health Surveys data.

TABLE 6.3   Proportion of Currently Married Women Using Methods of Contraception
in Selected African Countries that have Participated in Demographic and Health Surveys

Country (Year of Survey)	Contraceptive Method (%)		
	Any Method	Any Modern Method	Not Currently Using
Cameroon (1998)	19.3	7.1	80.7
Chad (1997)	4.1	1.2	95.9
Comoros (1996)	21.0	11.4	79.0
Cote d'Ivoire (1994)	11.4	4.3	88.6
Egypt (2000)	56.1	53.9	43.9
Ethiopia (2000)	8.1	6.3	91.9
Ghana (1998)	22.0	13.3	78.0
Kenya (1998)	39.0	31.5	61.0
Mozambique (1997)	5.6	5.1	94.4
Nigeria (1999)	15.3	8.6	84.7
Senegal (1997)	12.9	7.0	89.2
Uganda (1995)	14.8	7.8	85.2
Zambia (1996)	25.9	14.4	74.1
Zimbabwe (1999)	53.5	50.4	46.5

Source: Demographic and Health Surveys data.

career preparation. Low education means low opportunity cost of their time. Because childbearing is time intensive, women with low educational attainment tend to have more children than their highly educated counterparts.

Concerning contraceptive effects on fertility, available evidence shows that the proportion of women using contraception in Africa, although it has increased in recent years, is still low compared to other developing regions. According to recent estimates only about one-quarter of all married women in Africa were current users of at least one method of contraception. In Sub-Saharan Africa, the proportion was only 19% compared to 70% in Latin America and the Caribbean and 62% in Asia. When we look at individual countries in Africa, contraceptive prevalence rates vary more widely (see Table 6.3). In Chad, only 4% of the married women used any method of contraception in 1997, compared to 55% in Egypt. In settings where women do not use effective method of contraception, excess fertility is common; that is, many women continue to have children when they want no more.[1]

A. Does Fertility Affect African Economic Development?

Although it has been suggested earlier in this chapter that in the past large household size was seen as beneficial in Africa, in modern Africa there might be a trend toward a reversal in the direction of intergenerational wealth flows. In modern Africa of today, particularly in urban areas, if two individuals or households with similar incomes have different numbers of children (e.g., if one household has two children and the other has five or six), the household with higher fertility levels might be at a disadvantage and may lag behind in many ways, at least in the short run. If this same analogy were extended to countries, the logical conclusion would be that higher fertility rates impede economic progress. Although individuals are not the same as nations, high fertility tends to affect a nation much the same way, and large numbers of children affect resources at the households. However, these effects may be in the short run and may not be enough to hinder economic growth.

At the individual level, there are specific ways in which high fertility rates could hamper economic growth in the short run, such as the effect on savings. Both at individual and community levels, having large numbers of young children may impede the level of savings. Low savings rates affect domestic investment, which has impact on economic growth. At the macro levels, high-fertility countries have to make initial investments in providing adequate maternal and child health, schooling, and education and in job creation to absorb school graduates. This could become difficult if these expenses for maternal and child care and basic education keep increasing every year, thereby diverting critical resources from the capital investment necessary to create jobs for school graduates. Therefore, high fertility rates might impede economic growth through reduction in savings, high youth dependency ratios, and diversion of scarce investment resources into areas that have no immediate returns. For example, between 1980 and 1993, domestic savings in Africa declined from 27% of GDP to 15% and domestic investment declined from 24–16%. Within the same period, the youth dependency rate remained stable (about 43–44%). For Africa to see appreciable improvements in living standards of its people, the rate of economic growth needs to consistently be higher than the rate of population growth over a long period of time. This has not been happening in the region over the past quarter of a century or so. Therefore, economic development still eludes the region. Although there is no guarantee than reduction in fertility rate is a sure way to achieve economic development, experts now agree that slow population growth could buy a country the time needed to make necessary capital investment to stimulate economic development.

In fact, if African countries have low levels of fertility, they could benefit from a phenomenon known as *demographic bonus* or demographic dividend, which further serves as an impetus to rapid economic growth. A country with a rapidly declining fertility gets this demographic bonus when it is experiencing declining youth dependency burden, an increasing workforce of educated young people who are able to save and usually have fewer children. The country saves by providing social services for fewer children, and is not yet saddled with the burden of old-age dependency. In Asia, it has been suggested that this demographic bonus explained a large proportion of the GDP per capital growth since 1975.[19] Therefore, there are numerous advantages in taking control of the rate of population growth in Africa.

B. EFFORTS TO REDUCE FERTILITY LEVELS IN AFRICA

There have been direct and indirect efforts to reduce fertility in Africa. Direct efforts often take the form of organized family planning programs. These programs encourage couples plan the number and timing of their births, and they provide men and women with access to effective, acceptable and affordable contraception. Family planning programs are generally organized and financed by African government and nongovernmental organizations, but often with significant international assistance. For example, the U.S. Agency for International Development (USAID), which is one of the largest bilateral donors in the area of population in the world, has been helping meet the unmet contraceptive needs in the region. Between 1983 and 1991, USAID increased its annual population budget dedicated to Africa from $21.6 million to $128 million. Similarly, the funds from the United Nations Population Fund (UNFPA) increased from $16.9 million to $55 million over the same period (see National Research Council, 1993a:10). Between 1996 and 2000, USAID spent a total of $544 million on population assistance to the region (USAID, 2001). In 1998 alone, a total of $469 million (or 28%) of donor assistance for population activities went to Sub-Saharan Africa. These efforts have yielded some fruit. For example, while only nine countries had family planning programs in 1975, today, almost all countries have one. Contraceptive prevalence rates have increased in several countries and fertility levels have started to decline, even though the rate of fertility decline is still slow. The contraceptive prevalence rates among married women in Africa increased from 20% in 1993 to about 26% in 2001.[22]

There are indirect efforts directed at reducing fertility levels and promoting socioeconomic development. They include the promotion of education especially of girls, and encouragement for countries to formulate and implement population policies. Evidence from the literature suggests that educated women tend to prefer small family size, use effective contraceptives, and consequently have lower fertility levels than their counterparts with little or no education. Moreover, the longer girls stay in school, the later their age at marriage and childbearing. Education itself is an investment in human capital development of a country, which has other benefits such as improved survival chances among children and better health for the whole household.[10] Another set of activities focus on increasing the spacing among children through the encouragement of prolonged breastfeeding practices. In terms of population policies, many more African countries now see population growth as a problem and are making efforts to control it than was the case just 25 years ago. For example, in 1976, only 23% of African governments expressed a desire to lower population growth rate, compared to 57% in 1996. Similarly, while only 23% wanted to lower their country's fertility rates in 1976, the proportion was 66% in 1996 (United Nations, 1998).

IV. MORTALITY

Mortality, which focuses on the means by which those who exit the population is another component of population change that must be examined in relation to economic development in Africa. It is an indirect indicator of health in a population, and under-five mortality levels often reflect the level of socio-economic development. Globally, mortality levels, whether indicated by life expectancy at birth or by age-specific measures such as infant mortality rates, are worst in poor settings such as Africa and best in the rich countries. For example, the estimated life expectancy at birth for Africa in 2001 was 54 years compared to 64 years for all less-developed countries, 71 years for Latin America and the Caribbean, and 67 years for Asia. The last column of Table 6.1 shows life expectancy among selected African countries. It shows that even within Africa, there are wide differences in life expectancy; the difference between the highest (70 years in Mauritius) and the lowest (37 years in Zambia) is 33 years. Moreover, although Sub-Saharan Africa contributed 22% of the world live births in 1999, it contributed 32% of infant deaths, 35% of child deaths, and 37% of maternal deaths.[23]

In general, mortality levels are highest where income and living standards are lowest. The question that arises is whether mortality levels have any effects on economic development. The answer is that they do.[21] When the risk of mortality is high, people tend to have short time horizon, which affects the motivation to save for the future. High mortality risks among children also translate to high fertility, which in turn translates to high youth dependency burden and low savings rate. Low savings would affect capital accumulation and hence economic growth. As has been shown, economic progress in most African countries has been poor for the past two or three decades. These poor economic growth rates have affected the ability of governments to provide basic health services needed by the population. They also have affected people's income and hence consumption patterns, living conditions, etc., all of which affect the well-being of the population. To assess the effects of the economic reversals on the welfare of African people, a thorough investigation was carried out by the Population Committee of the U.S. National Research Council.[25] The study concluded that the economic reversals had far-reaching demographic consequences in the region. However, the effects seemed greatest in countries that depended on earnings from the export of a few primary commodities. In the particular case of under-five mortality, the effect was clearest in Ghana and Nigeria.

However, the relationship between mortality and economic development is bidirectional. Poor health, which is indirectly reflected by high mortality rates or low life expectancy at birth, also affects economic growth. A good example of how poor health and untimely death affects economic development in contemporary Africa is the case of HIV/AIDS. Sub-Saharan Africa has the highest prevalence of human immunodeficiency virus (HIV) and acquired immune deficiency syndrome (AIDS). About 25 million (or 70%) of the 36 million people living with HIV/AIDS in the year 2000 were in Sub-Saharan Africa. Note that Africa has only 13% of the world population. According to figures from the United Nations Joint Program on AIDS (UNAIDS), in some countries in Africa, the prevalence among adults ages 15–49 is between 20 and 30%. Because there is no cure yet for AIDS, these people are likely to die within the next 10 years, and an overwhelming majority of them are in the prime productive and reproductive ages. To date, more than 14 million people have died of AIDS and HIV-related diseases in the region. The social, economic, and demographic ramifications of decimating such a large proportion of the adult population are numerous. Consequently, HIV/AIDS is now considered both a developmental as well as demographic challenge for the region.[26]

Existing models on the economic impact of the epidemic suggest that it operates mainly through the effects of HIV/AIDS on savings and human capital development. The prevalence rate of HIV/AIDS is highest among adolescents and adults (between ages 15 and 49), people who represent the cream of the productive work force in any society and who are better able to provide economic support to both the young and the elderly. As HIV/AIDS decimates its victims, it digs a hole in the human capital resources of the society. Worse still, the prevalence of HIV/AIDS is also highest among the most educated urban people in Africa, which is the opposite of the situation in Europe and North America.

Businesses are affected in various ways because of the high prevalence of HIV/AIDS in several African countries. For example, HIV infection and AIDS lead to low productivity because those who are infected lose work days, and those providing care to infected relatives come to work tired and worn out and are unable to produce at optimal levels during the day. When workers die of HIV/AIDS-related problems, gifts and condolence visits take work days away from workers, and considerable resources are required to find replacement workers which usually increases the cost of production. In the interim, productivity suffers. In a sugar estate in Kenya, increased HIV/AIDS-related absenteeism led to a loss of 8000 days of work between 1995 and 1997, resulting in a 50% drop in the ratio of processed sugar recovered from cane between 1994 and 1997.[27] In six specific companies in four countries, it has been estimated that AIDS costs $50–300 per worker and that 52% of these were related to absenteeism.[28]

All of these effects have implications for the national economy. A World Bank estimate suggests that, if HIV prevalence had not reached the high prevalence level of about 8.6% among adult population in 1999, Africa's income per capita would have grown nearly three times as much as the actual 0.4% per annum recorded between 1990 and 1997.[29] In spite of the lackluster performance of the African economy and the high level of indebtedness, at a recent summit in Abuja, Nigeria, African heads of government committed themselves to allocating a target of 15% of their annual budgets to the health sector as a demonstration of their resolve to deal the with the HIV/AIDS problem in the continent.[30]

At the household level, the effects of losing breadwinners to HIV/AIDS are huge and most agonizing after protracted illness has led to spending family resources and savings on cures that failed. The resulting deaths often lead to increases in AIDS orphans and female- and (at times) child-headed households, a situation that increases vulnerability to the risk of poverty. Children under such conditions have poor school enrollment rates and low educational attainment, leading to low incomes, which further weaken their capacity to avoid HIV infection. It is estimated that of the about 13.2 million AIDS orphans now in the world, 95% of them are in Sub-Saharan Africa.

V. MIGRATION

The third component of population change to examine is migration, which focuses on how human population is distributed in a geographic space. In general, human population movement usually occurs in response to opportunities provided in the area of destination ("pull" factors) or adverse conditions existing in the area of origin ("push" factors). The opportunities that people respond to as they make their decisions about migration as well as the choices of destination are predominantly economic.[31] Therefore, there is a connection between economic growth and migration. Economic growth tends to create new jobs, which in turn tends to attract new migrants, nationally or internationally. Migrants themselves are also highly motivated people who bring much dynamism and needed skills into their areas of destination. This is because migration is most likely among the educated, the skilled, the young (people in their most productive ages), and the healthy. Thus, human capital resource represented by migrants is enormous. The peak age for internal migrants in Africa is 20–24.[32] The downside is that this pattern of migration can deprive rural areas of needed youth, brainpower, and dynamism.

Migration could be internal or international. Internal migration occurs within the boundaries of a country and could be rural–urban, rural–rural, seasonal, etc. Although much migration occurs between rural areas of Africa, a large proportion of African migration is from rural to urban areas. Thus, migration itself encourages urban growth, and the proportion of the African population residing in urban areas over the past several decades has increased. For example, while only 23% of Africans resided in urban areas in 1970, the proportion had increased to 37% in 1998.[33] In 1970, no urban center had over 8 million people; by 1998, Lagos (Nigeria) had an estimated population of 12 million and was the 10th largest city in the world.[34] Historically, cities have often been centers of economic growth, innovation, and civilization. However, one distinction between urbanization in the West and in Africa is that urbanization usually followed industrialization in the West, while it tends to proceed without industrialization in Africa.[32] Consequently, a large proportion of African urban residents are poor, and youth unemployment is usually high.

African governments are aware of the importance of cities as centers of excellence and innovation and of youthful energy and creativity, and they are deliberately creating more of such centers of growth through their development plans. For example, Nigeria has been creating more states so that their capitals will generate new jobs and serve as destinations of migration. This is supposed to ease the pressure on the dominant cities, which were quickly becoming overcrowded, accompanied by the attendant evils of high crime rates, etc.

Apart from internal migration, Africa has participated in international migration. Although the largest proportion of international migrants in Africa are refugees who crossed international boundaries, a significant amount of Africans cross the borders of their countries to work in other countries, both within Africa or beyond. The most economically significant international migration is that of highly skilled manpower leaving the continent. Many educated and bright minds have migrated to the West in response to the poor economic situation in their home countries. This is known as the "brain drain." In 1987, the United Nations Conference on Trade and Development (cited in Russell, 1993) estimated that 30% (about 70,000) of Africa's high-level manpower stock (defined by education and skill level as managerial/administrative, professional, and technical manpower) officially resided in the European Community. This figure, which does not include those who migrate to North America, could be highly underestimated. Between 1987 and 1989 alone, more than 110,000 Nigerians were estimated to have taken jobs abroad.[36] Remittances from these people are important to the economies of their countries of origin. If these people return, they may become agents of change and facilitators of technological transfers to their countries of origin. However, several African countries, particularly those that have experienced sharp reversals in economic growth, have lost a high proportion of their manpower to international migration in the most unprecedented level of brain drain that the continent has witnessed.

There are social and economic reasons for the brain drain. Social reasons include political instability and repression by corrupt regimes. However, declines in economic prospects, poor living standards, and decay in basic infrastructures are the major reasons for the brain drain in most parts of Africa in recent times. Most highly educated people leave the region and take up jobs in other regions of the world in response to economic opportunities or are pushed to leave by a declining quality of life or income. Consequently, several African countries, particularly those that have experienced sharp reversals in economic growth, have lost a high proportion of their manpower to brain drain. When this happens, in many cases the quality of training received by students often declines as experienced trainers, professors, professionals, and managers leave the system for the greener grass abroad. If care is not taken, this process can have adverse consequences on economic growth in countries of origin.

A. Population Growth, Labor Force, and Unemployment

Unemployment is measured by the *unemployment rate*, which is defined as the ratio of the unemployed to the labor force expressed as a percentage. In other words, the unemployment rate is the percentage of the labor force that is unemployed:

$$\text{Unemployment rate (\%)} = (\text{number unemployed/labor force}) \times 100$$

In Africa, the number of people who want to work increases at 2% each year. The majority of the work force is employed in agriculture, and the labor force is characterized by low wages, large wage differentials, rapid growth of labor supply, and underutilization of the existing labor supply. Although rapid population growth rate may not always lead to unemployment, whenever the rate of population growth (supply of labor) exceeds that of economic growth (which generates the demand for labor), unemployment rates increase.

As has been indicated earlier in the chapter, the rate of population growth has been much higher than the rate of economic growth in most African countries over the past three decades. Consequently, an economic crisis manifests in high unemployment among graduates, hidden unemployment, or disguised unemployment in most economies of the region. There are different types of unemployed or underutilized labor, usually referred to as disguised unemployment. The openly unemployed are usually 15–24 years of age and urban educated. The visibly active but underutilized are neither unemployed nor underemployed but have found visible means of marking time. Many people have less than full-time jobs in agriculture or in the public sector, while others engage in nonemployment activities, especially education or household chores, as a second choice.

Persistent high levels of unemployment present many problems. Because the population structure of the region is bottom heavy (meaning that the proportion of children under the age of 15 is very large), the dependency burden is worsened and demand is higher for social services such as education and healthcare services for children, which takes attention away from the capital investments necessary to stimulate economic growth, at least in the short run.

The problem of unemployment and labor underutilization has a demand side and a supply side. The supply side is more difficult to deal with and is mostly a long-run issue. Consequently, in the short run, policy must focus on the demand side. Policies to reduce unemployment include population policies, policies to discourage rural–urban migration, adoption of appropriate technology, policies to reduce factor price distortions, and educational policies. Unless this problem of unemployment is solved, the benefits of the demographic bonus, which is to be derived from declines in youth dependency burden and rise in educated workforce, can in fact be wasted.

Two different approaches could be used to deal with the problem of unemployment: The first is to stimulate output, especially in relatively high-productivity and high-wage sectors of the economy. The second is to try to increase the amount of labor used to produce a given amount of output. This means focusing on labor-intensive approaches to create labor-intensive systems as opposed to capital-intensive systems. To do this, policy must aim at altering prices and creating incentives for substitution of capital with labor and developing labor-dependent technologies. Economic growth translates to increased employment. In the final analysis, the most effective policy to reduce unemployment is a growth-oriented policy.

VII. SUMMARY

Until a few centuries ago, the whole world was characterized by slow population growth resulting from high levels of mortality and high rates of fertility. However, in the 20th century, the world witnessed an unprecedented growth in population resulting from a rapid decline in mortality rates. The same century witnessed an unprecedented economic growth. Thus, the story of the 20th century, on the aggregate levels, seems to be one in which population growth correlated with a rapid economic expansion. Although Africa participated in the economic expansion, its rates of population growth seem to outweigh its rates of economic expansion. Consequently, while other regions of the world are overcoming problems of rapid population growth and are making rapid progress in economic growth, Africa, particularly the area below the Sahara, seems to have lagged behind both in population control and in economic growth.

In this chapter, the discussion of the link between population growth and economic development has covered both the empirical association between the two variables as well as the theoretical debates that tend to provide justification for the association in Africa. Available information on this subject suggests that rapid population growth requires that substantial mount of resources—human and material—be devoted to providing basic health and social services. This could hinder savings and capital investment, which would eventually slow economic growth, at least in the short run. When population growth eventually is brought under control and slows, especially through fertility control, some resources that have been tied up in caring for the young will be freed.

Overall, the relationship between population growth and poor economic performance is most obvious among poor nations, which applies to a majority of African nations. The correlation between GNP per capita and population growth rate in the region is high and statistically significant. The prevailing view now is that rapid population growth acts as a break, an obstacle in the way of economic development. While rapid population growth alone may not be able to halt economic progress, its existence is able to slow the rate of growth. Thus, limiting population growth is seen as buying time for a country to break out of the Malthusian trap.

Population has a nontrivial contribution to economic progress in every society, including those of Africa. While low population growth alone is not enough to spur economic growth, high population growth rates could slow the pace of economic progress and improvement in people's quality of life. The commonly held view among many population analysts now is that population control can buy for a country the essential time needed for economic growth. It is rare nowadays to blame poor economic performance on high population growth rates alone. Therefore, while it is important to keep growth rate under control, that effort alone will not bring about rapid economic development in any poor African country.

DISCUSSION QUESTIONS

1. How important is the contribution of population growth to economic development prospects in Africa?
2. Interpret the wealth flows hypothesis in regard to fertility behavior in Africa.
3. What is the major difference between the Malthusian and neo-Malthusian perspectives?
4. It has been said that population has a nontrivial effect on economic development; why is it that the population effects are greatest in poor settings?
5. How important is the HIV/AIDS epidemic to the population and economic growth in Africa?
6. Describe the relationships among population growth, labor force growth, and unemployment in African countries.
7. Outline the efforts undertaken so far to control fertility in Africa.

NOTES

[1]Population Reference Bureau (2001) *2001 World Population Data Sheet*, Washington, D.C.

[2]Sparks, D. (2001) "Economic Trends in Africa South of the Sahara, 2000," in *Africa South of the Sahara 2001*, London: Europa Publications, pp. 11–19.

[3]Ehrlich, P. (1971) *The Population Bomb*, London: Pan Books.

[4]Hardin, G. (1968) "The Tragedy of the Commons," *Science*, 162(3859): 1243–1248.

[5]Boserup, E. (1965) *The Conditions of Agricultural Growth*, London: Allen and Unwin.

[7]Simon, J. (1989) "On Aggregate Empirical Studies Relating Population Variables To Economic Development," *Population and Development Review*, 15(2): 323–332.

[8]Kelley, A.C. (2001) "The Population Debate in Historical Perspective: Revisionism Revised," in N. Birdsall, A.C. Kelley, and S.W. Sinding (Eds.) *Population Matters: Demographic Change, Economic Growth, and Poverty in the Developing World*, pp. 24–54, Oxford: Oxford University Press.

[9]Weeks, J.R. (1999) *Population: An Introduction to Concepts and Issues*, 7th ed., Belmont, CA: Wadsworth.

[10]Caldwell, J.C. (1982) "The Wealth Flows Theory of Fertility Decline," In C. Hohn and R. Mackensen, Eds., *Determinants of Fertility Trends: Theories Re-examined*. Liege, Belgium: Ordina Editions. pp. 169–188.

[11]Furedi, F. (1997) *Population and Development: A Critical Introduction*, New York: St. Martin's Press.

[12]Cohen, B. (1993) "Fertility Levels, Differentials and Trends," in *Demographic Change in Sub-Saharan Africa*, K.A. Foote, K.H. Hill, and L.G. Martin, Eds., Washington, D.C.: National Academy Press, pp. 8–67. Table 2-1.

[13]The demographic transition theory states that all human populations move from a pretransitional stage of high fertility, high mortality, and low population growth rates through a period of high population growth rates resulting from a decline in mortality without a corresponding decline in fertility rates. Thereafter, both fertility and mortality rates decline to low levels, thereby resulting in another period of low population growth rates.

[14]Davis, K. and Blake, J. (1956) "Social Structure and Fertility: An Analytic Framework," *Economic Development and Cultural Change*, 4(3), 211–235.

[15]Bongaarts, J. (1982) "The Fertility-Inhibiting Effects of the Intermediate Variables," *Studies in Family Planning*, 13(6–7): 179–189.

[15a]Bongaarts, J. and Potter, R.G. (1983). *Fertility, Biology, and Behavior: An Analysis of the Proximate Determinants*, New York: Academic Press.

[16]Jolly, C. and Gribble, J. (1993) The Proximate Determinants of Fertility, in K.A. Foote, K.H. Hill, and L.G. Martin, Eds., *Demographic Change in Sub-Saharan Africa*, Washington, D.C. National Academy Press, pp. 68–116.

[17]Population Reference Bureau (1976) *World Population Growth and Response*, Washington, D.C.: Population Reference Bureau.

[18]Abou-Stait, F. (1994) "The Population Debate in Relation to Development: The Case of Sub-Saharan Africa," *Egypt Population and Family Planning Review*, 28(2): 139–161.

[19]Williamson, J.G. (2001) "Demographic Change, Economic Growth, and Inequality," in N. Birdsall, A.C. Kelley, and S.W. Sinding (Eds.) *Population Matters: Demographic Change, Economic Growth, and Poverty in the Developing World*, pp. 106–136, Oxford: Oxford University Press.

[20]National Research Council (1993a) *Demographic Effects of Economic Reversals in Sub-Saharan Africa*, Washington, D.C.: National Academy Press, pp. 10.

[21]Bloom, D. and Canning, D. (2001) "Cumulative Causality, Economic Growth and Demographic Transition," in N. Birdsall, A.C. Kelley, and S.W. Sinding (Eds.) *Population Matters: Demographic Change, Economic Growth, and Poverty in the Developing World*, pp. 165–197, Oxford: Oxford University Press.

[22]United Nations (2000b) *Levels and Trends of Contraceptive Use as Assessed in 1998*, New York: United Nations.

[23]Ross, J., Stover, J., and Willard, A. (1999) *Profiles for Family Planning and Reproductive Health Programs*, Glastonbury, CT: The Futures Group International.

[25]National Research Council (1993b) *Factors Affecting Contraceptive Use in Sub-Saharan Africa*, Washington, D.C.: National Academy Press.

[26]Adeyi, O., Hecht, R., Njobvu, E., and Soucat, A. (2001). *AIDS, Poverty Reduction and Debt Relief*, Joint United Nations Programme on HIV/AIDS (UNAIDS), Geneva.

[27]UNAIDS (2000) *AIDS Epidemic Update: December 2000*, Geneva: United Nations Joint Program on AIDS/World Health Organization.

[28]Economic Commission for Africa (1999) *Africa's Population and Development Bulletin*, June–July, Addis Ababa: ECA, pp. 15.

[29]World Bank (2000).

[30]Abuja Declaration on HIV/AIDS, Tuberculosis and Other Related Infectious Diseases, resulting from African Summit on HIV/AIDS, April 24–27, 2001 (http://www.oau-uoa.org/afrsummit).

[31]Adepoju, A. (1990), "State of the Art Review of Migration in Africa," in *Conference on the Role of Migration in African Development: Issues and Policies for the '90s*, Vol. 1, Dakar: Union for African Population Studies, pp. 3–41.

[32]Oucho, J. and Gould, W.T.S. (1993) "Internal Migration, Urbanization and Population Distribution," in K.A. Foote, K.H. Hill, and L.G. Martin, Eds., *Demographic Change in Sub-Saharan Africa*, Washington, D.C.: National Academy Press, pp. 257–296.

[33]United Nations (2000a) *World Population Monitoring 1999: Population Growth, Structure and Distribution*, New York: United Nations, pp. 69, 73.

[34]United Nations (1990), p.73.

[36]Adegbola, O. (1990) "Demographic Effects of Economic Crisis in Nigeria: The Brain Drain Component," paper presented at the Conference on the Role of Migration in African Development: Issues and Policies for the '90s, Union for African Population Studies, Nairobi.

[37]Food and Agricultural Organization, *Food Outlook*, No. 2, April 2001.

[39]USAID (2001) *Overview of USAID Population Assistance FY 2000*, Washington, D.C.: PHNI for USAID.

[40]Caldwell, J.C. (1979) "Education as a Factor in Mortality Decline: An Examination of the Nigerian Data," *Population Studies*, 33(3), 395–413.

CHAPTER 7

Poverty and Development

NICK VINK AND NORMA TREGURTHA

Department of Agricultural Economics, University of Stellenbosch, Matieland 7602, Stellenbosch, South Africa

KEY TERMS

Alienation or exclusion
Beneficiaries
Capabilities
Causes of underdevelopment:
  obstacles to growth, missing
  production factors, vicious cycles
Demographic features
"Doing" and "being": being adequately
  nourished, being literate, leading a long
  and healthy life, and avoiding homelessness
Entitlements
Household infrastructure index
Human development

Human development Index
Income supplements
Means of development
Minimum wage
Modernization
Neoclassical or orthodox
  development paradigm
Nutritional status
Objectives of development
Population census
Poverty levels
Production function

I. INTRODUCTION

In everyday language we all have some understanding of poverty and of what it means to be poor. However, when it comes to the scientific measurement of poverty, what is implicit in everyday language has to be made explicit. The capability model of Sen[1] provides an appropriate conceptual framework for such measurement. In Sen's view, poverty is not simply a question of having too little money; rather, it is about living a life devoid of economic, social, and political choice. It is clear from their rhetoric and from the kinds of policy instruments for poverty alleviation that they endorse that the major development agencies and aid donors also support such a multivariate interpretation of poverty at an ideological level. However, at the methodological level there is still a tendency to measure poverty indirectly in terms of private current incomes (or private consumption expenditures). The ready availability of income data and of statistical techniques to calculate poverty lines, minimum living levels, and poverty head count ratios has encouraged the institutional acceptance of this ideological–methodological incongruence.[2]

Analysts in South Africa have not fared any better, and most of the empirical work on poverty measurement has also utilized the indirect poverty line method.[3] Therefore, the purpose of this chapter is to illustrate how these basic choices or capabilities can be accounted for in the measurement of poverty to ensure a more policy relevant understanding of the plight of poor people. This will be accomplished through a case study of farm workers on commercial farms in South Africa. While some readers will regard their plight as atypical of Africa, those who are concerned with the poor in this part of the world are aware that this community of workers is no more and no less than another piece in the mosaic of poverty that afflicts the continent.

For this reason the chapter starts with a literature review to substantiate the capability model of poverty and to highlight the importance of defining and measuring poverty in a composite way. This is followed by a brief discussion of data sources and methodology and then by a case study.

II. DEVELOPMENT AND POVERTY: THE EARLY DEBATE

The way we choose to measure poverty tells us much about the way we interpret the concept. Given that poverty is normally understood in relation to a specific development paradigm, a point of departure for this analysis is an understanding of development. Until the 1980s development studies was conventionally supported by the so-called neoclassical or orthodox development paradigm, namely the growth model. Within the context of this paradigm, an economy that afforded its citizens a high level of personal income was considered developed, while an economy whose per capita gross domestic product (GDP) was relatively low was considered undeveloped and poor. Thus, the *values* underlying this paradigm described the "good life" in terms of the consumption of goods and services: The "good" society was defined as one that provides a high level of material wealth for its citizens. The success *criterion* this supported was the highest rate of GNP growth per capita possible, although this later became subject to distributional constraints.

It is against this core value that Sen, economist and Nobel Prize winner, launched his critique of the neoclassical development model. He offered three arguments as to why a person or country's level of development cannot be measured in terms of commodity possession or income. The **first** point he made has to do with the fact that commodities, as such, have no real value. Rather, their value is derived from "what they do for people, or rather what people can do with these goods and services."[4] Opulence, income, and "stuff" are said to have instrumental rather than intrinsic value. They are the means and not the end of well-being or development. To equate development with commodity possession is to overlook this critical distinction.

Sen's second argument questions the link between commodity possession— "being well off"—and well-being. He claims that this link is conflicting and fragile,[5] weakened by what is labeled the "interpersonal variability argument."[6] This argument is best illustrated with the help of an example. Two people, Dick and Jane, both have the same level of income. In terms of the commodity approach, Dick and Jane enjoy a similar level of well-being. However, Dick is handicapped and both his overall health and mobility are less than those of Jane. Given this, is it still possible to assume that these two people enjoy a similar level of well-being? Sen argues no. To enjoy a life of good health and mobility, Dick needs more resources than Jane does. It therefore follows that, with the same resources as Jane, Dick achieves lower levels of well-being. Thus, the ability to convert commodities into well-being varies interpersonally, and to equate opulence with well-being is to ignore this important distinction.

Sen's **third** criticism of the "opulence as well-being approach" extends the interpersonal variability argument to a societal level. Assume, for example, that community participation is an important aspect of well-being. Sen[7] explains that access to a telephone and television are necessary for this type of participation for the urban American, while for the rural African they are not. Thus, for the American to achieve the same level of well-being as the African requires more commodities. The commodity requirements for well-being are thus culturally and historically bound. This essentially renders transcultural, -regional, and -national income or opulence comparisons useless.

Having rejected the conventional approach to development, Sen sets about to argue that when assessing a person's quality of life, the focus has to be on the "doings and being," or capabilities that make up that life. Certain of these capabilities play a fundamental or basic role in determining the quality of life. Satisfying them up to a certain critical level is a necessary, although not sufficient, condition for living a valuable life. Sen regarded being adequately nourished, leading a long and healthy life, being literate, and avoiding homelessness as basic capabilities.[8]

Sen defines poverty in terms of "basic capability failure." To be poor is not only about having insufficient income, it is also about being malnourished, being unhealthy, being illiterate, and being homeless. Income remains important, but it is of instrumental and not intrinsic value.[9] While the ability to achieve certain basic capabilities such as being well nourished depends on a person's command over goods and services (i.e., on income), the relationship between low income and capability failure is not normally direct. Experience shows that this relationship can be parametrically variable between different communities and even between different families and different individuals.[10] To focus only on income is, therefore, to ignore this variability. In this fashion, Sen introduced the era of human development of the 1990s and beyond. This philosophy has been taken up and reflected in much of the development and poverty reduction work being undertaken by the United Nations Development Program (UNDP) and the World Bank.

III. DEVELOPMENT AND POVERTY: HUMAN DEVELOPMENT

The human development approach to development and poverty is based on two separate but related strands of development thought. The **first** of these originates from an eclectic body of development research loosely termed *social exclusion theory* which identifies important themes that the neoclassical development approach failed to reflect in its theoretical and methodological structure and are primarily a response to the inherent limitations of the neoclassical model in identifying who or what the process of development marginalizes.

The **second** strand of the human development approach is the capability approach formulated and refined by Sen. This approach establishes the philosophical and theoretical foundations of human development. More specifically, it clarifies the question: "What is well-being, how do we measure it, and how is it linked to development and poverty?"

A. SOCIAL EXCLUSION THEORY

Contra-modernization, as Beukes prefers to call social exclusion theory, is a range of fragmented theories joined by a shared belief that the content of development (its meaning and purpose) is more important than its form.[11] These diverse views or approaches converge around the theme of alienation or exclusion, and its adherents focus on giving voice or drawing attention to those whom development processes have left out.

The topic of development and alienation was sparked in the 1970s by a series of international conferences and publications. The Declaration of Cocoyoc[12] and a report prepared by the Dag Hammerskjöld Foundation for the United Nations emphasized how the process of development induced alienation and marginalization of people and the environment. As signs of these trends were also evident in developed countries, the development goal of high mass consumption was fundamentally flawed. The Hammerskjöld Report was aptly titled *What Now—Another Development*.[13] More specifically this view claimed that the benefits of development, and implicitly its costs, were not evenly distributed. Sectors and sections of societies were left behind or left out. These include the so-called beneficiaries of development: people's cultures, women, the environment, and rural areas.[14] If poverty is to be addressed, these issues must be reflected in the analysis and critically engaged to ensure the inclusivity of the development process as well as to reshape the social processes by which people come to be excluded.

B. THE CAPABILITY APPROACH OF SEN

Social exclusion theory is essentially a critique of the values, methodology, and strategy of neoclassical development economics and on its own does not offer an alternative conceptual framework. Such a framework is found in the work of Sen,[15] who integrated these ideas into a single conceptual framework. For Sen, the measure of a developed society is the extent to which it empowers its citizenry to "live and act in certain valuable ways."[16] Consequently, development must focus on removing the constraints or barriers that inhibit people from achieving a worthwhile life. Development must "emancipate people from the forced reality to live less or be less"[17] and focus on improving their overall level of well-being. There is nothing original or radical about seeing well-being in terms of the capability to function Sen shows how traces of his capability approach can be found in the work of Aristotle, Smith, and Marx.

The primary focus of well-being has to be the life that people are living. While goods and services available in an economy may enhance the lives people live, to concentrate on them is to neglect what is more important—people. Well-being has to be concerned with what people can or cannot do, can or cannot be. These "being" and "doings"[18] are called functionings.

Functionings represent different aspects of the state of a person. They either can be activities such as working, resting, and loving or are states of existence such as being employed, being well rested, or being loved. Functionings can also be viewed in a hierarchical manner. They can vary from rudimentary, such as being well nourished, to more complex, such as being able to command self-respect:[19]

> It is on the basis of these functionings that an evaluation of a person's well-being is possible. The claim is that the functionings make up a person's being, and an evaluation of a person's well-being has to take the form of an assessment of these constitutive elements.

Closely connected to functionings is the idea of the capability to function. The capability to function is the various functioning combinations that a person can achieve, the entire set of doings and beings that are possible. More formally put, a capability set can be defined as the set of alternative functioning vectors within a person's reach.[20]

Sen explains the importance of the distinction between functionings and capabilities by using the example of two people who are starving, Jack and Jill. Superficially, because they "enjoy" the same functioning achievement of starving, it can be argued that they have the same level of well-being. But, Jill is a hunger striker who could be well nourished should she choose, while Jack is a refugee and has no choice but to starve. Clearly, Jill's well-being is higher than Jack's, even though they both have the same functioning achievement of starving.

A functioning is an achievement, whereas a capability is the achievement alternative, the "is" stands for the "possible." Capabilities are possible options or choices open to a person, possible functionings from which to choose. The hunger striker chooses to starve, but she also has the opportunity to be well nourished. The refugee faces only starvation.[21] Clearly, they do not enjoy the same level of well-being. The hunger striker enjoys a degree of choice the refugee does not: She has the additional functioning of choosing.

Within this capability framework, Sen contends that development occurs when an increase in freedom (choice) is brought about via an expansion of valuable capabilities. Furthermore, people or households are deemed poor when they lack access to basic capabilities, not if their incomes fall below a certain level. Income streams are not, however, totally excluded from the analysis of poverty levels, as Sen states that entitlements (or livelihoods) are central to well-being, development, and poverty because they generate capabilities. Not all capabilities are generated by commodities (livelihoods); however, many basic capabilities such as being well nourished depend on people's command of goods and services. Resources or entitlements generate capabilities, while the nature and extent of this relationship is circumscribed by factors such as demographic characteristics and location.

To summarize, the human development approach as a theoretical construct to poverty assessment is grounded in the work of Sen and supported by the work done on social exclusion theories. If human development is defined as an increase in the capability level of a community and poverty as basic capability failure, social exclusion theories provide insight into what types of capabilities are important and which social groups are more likely to experience capabilities failure (i.e., more likely to be poor).

C. Measuring Poverty

Unlike the gross national product (GNP) per capita development indicator of the orthodox development paradigm, measuring well-being in a more plural way has always created problems. The first alternative measures to per capita

GNP were introduced in the late 1970s (e.g., the Physical Quality of Life Index [PQLI] which combined statistics on infant mortality, literacy, and life expectancy to render a cross-country comparative development index.[22] More recently, the Human Development Index (HDI) of the United Nations Development Program (UNDP) has garnered significant academic and political interest. The HDI incorporates three important dimensions of human development: longevity, knowledge, and living standards. By assimilating data on average life expectancy, literacy levels, and income, these three dimensions are converted into a single numeric, an internationally or interregionally comparable index.[23]

Although it is a much richer development measure than an economic growth statistic, the HDI still fails to capture the complexity of the development process. It omits the important question of human rights and the issue of sustainability, two important failings of GNP. It also confines itself to only two capabilities: health and education. Furthermore, it still includes an explicit monetary measure of income.

If human development theory continually reiterates the importance of understanding well-being in a complex and plural way, the question arises as to the usefulness of such an index. Streeten points out that when such composite indices are compared with per capita GNP, they reinforce the shortcomings of the latter.[24] A human development index is therefore only a summary tool. It is not a substitute for a more thorough account of well-being. Its merits and failings should be interpreted with this in mind.

This problem is compounded in the case of farm workers in South Africa because the evidence shows that available income and expenditure data are not reliable indicators of their real income levels or their ability to achieve certain basic capabilities. This is largely because:

- Farm workers receive a significant proportion of their wages in in-kind payments. It is difficult for both employers and employees to translate these into a cash equivalent.
- In many cases, it is more costly for rural people to translate income into capabilities. For example, if a farm worker is to purchase high school education for her child, she has to consider the cost of either transport or alternative accommodation arrangements in addition to the cost of the schooling, because South Africa high schools are geographically concentrated in urban centers.

When measuring the poverty status of farm workers it is, therefore, even more important than usual to do so on the basis of their achieved basic capabilities rather than merely their income. For this reason a human development poverty profile highlighting farm workers achieved capabilities will be constructed.

IV. THE MEASUREMENT OF POVERTY: FARM WORKERS IN SOUTH AFRICA

A. Data Sources

The case study provided in this chapter draws on several datasets collected by Statistics South Africa over the past 5 years. The single most important of these is the 1996 population census refereed to in the text as Census 96. Aside from Census 96, employment and income data from the 1996 Agricultural Survey were also used, as well as data from the October Household Survey series. None of these datasets contains information on the nutritional status of South African farm workers; this information was gleaned from the 1999 National Food Consumption Survey commissioned by the country's Department of Health.

B. Locating Farm Workers within the South African Labor Market and Agricultural Economy

South Africa is the single largest economy in Africa, contributing $162,212 million or 30% to the GNP of the continent.[25] While South Africa is relatively prosperous in African terms, the country is beset by a host of structural economic problems such as poor economic growth, high levels of unemployment, and an extremely skewed distribution of skills, wealth, and income, a distribution that keenly follows existing racial, gender, and spatial divisions.

In 1996, the South African population was estimated at 41 million people, grouped in 9.1 million households. Spatially, these individuals and households are concentrated in certain provinces such as Gauteng and KwaZulu-Natal, as well as in the urban areas[26] of the country.

Both formal unemployment (at more than a third of the total labor force for the country as a whole) and the proportion of the working-age population that is formally employed (the labor absorption rate, or LAR) are measured. This structural feature, which implies that a large proportion of the working-age population have to find their livelihoods in the informal economy, is common to many developing countries. The Western Cape has the lowest unemployment rate and the highest LAR. In contrast, 46% of the Northern Province's working population are unemployed, and fewer than one in four adults has a formal sector job.

Of the 9.5 million South Africans employed in the formal economy, 86% classified themselves as an "employee." The remaining workers are self-employed (7%), are employed in a family business (2.1%), or are themselves employers (4.3%). The tertiary sectors of the economy provide the bulk of the country's jobs.

However, the absolute size of these sectors obscures the importance of the primary sectors as a job provider. Collectively, the primary sectors (agriculture, hunting, forestry, fisheries, and mining) employ 1.2 million people, while the manufacturing sector employs about 942,000. Agriculture and hunting provide 640,000 jobs, or more than 7% of South Africa's formal employment, while contributing less than 5% of GDP. The provincial distribution shows that these agricultural jobs are concentrated in certain provinces, with 50% of farm workers employed in the Western Cape (20%), the Free State (15%), and KwaZulu Natal (15%). Data from the 1996 *Agricultural Survey* suggest a similar absolute and relative distribution of workers across provinces when compared with Census 96.

Looking at the distribution of agricultural employment on a provincial basis ignores the considerable intraprovincial concentration. On a magisterial district level, 20% of all South African farm workers are found in 10 of the country's 354 magisterial districts (2.8%), with the majority of these located in the Western Cape and KwaZulu Natal coastal areas, where they are mainly employed by the deciduous fruit and sugar-cane industries, respectively.

The 1996 Agricultural Survey makes a distinction between regular workers and seasonal and casual workers. Seasonal and casual workers are grouped together and defined as occasional or day laborers. This category includes sheep shearers, reapers, and fruit pickers. Not included under casual and seasonal workers in the 1996 Agricultural Survey are labor contractors and their employees. In 1999, a postal survey carried out by the National Department of Agriculture (NDA) reported that contract workers accounted for an increasing proportion of the agricultural labor force. In 1996/1997, 21% of farm workers were employed by labor contractors, a figure that apparently had increased to 25% in 1998/99. The provincial ratio of regular to casual employees is shown in Figure 7.1. This ratio shows considerable inter-provincial variation.

It is important to note that the farm workers identified in the previous analysis are all employed by the country's commercial agricultural sector. A distinction is normally drawn between this sector and the country's homeland or developing agricultural sector. The commercial sector is characterized by large, owner-operated, capital-intensive farming units that account for 90% of the value-added agricultural production and who own 86% of all agricultural land. In contrast, the developing, homeland agricultural consists of a large number of small-scale, resource-poor farmers engaged in subsistence production under communal tenure. These homeland areas were created in 1959 by the apartheid government in an attempt to form national self-governing units for the country's eight largest ethnic communities. The objective of this policy was to control the free movement of black South Africans into the urban or white areas of the country and to relocate and confine any African considered "redundant" to these remote areas. Practically, this policy meant that able-bodied men were permitted to work as migrant labourers in the mines and on commercial farms in the white areas, while women

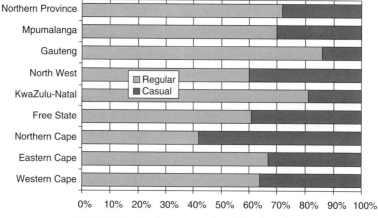

FIGURE 7.1   Regular and casual agricultural workers.

and the aged were expected to eke out a living in these over-crowded homeland areas. While in the late 1980s this system of control effectively broke down, the legacy of the homelands continues to present policymakers with a development challenge. There is much evidence to suggest that the poverty level of this segment of the rural population is equal to that of farm workers; however, the structural causes differ significantly, thus they have been excluded from the analysis.[27]

C. Demographic Features of South African Farm Workers

The objective of this poverty profile is to reflect the absolute and relative poverty status of farm workers in South Africa. It begins with a demographic overview of farm workers that looks specifically at the following variables: gender, age, nationality, and household size and structure. The second part of the profile looks at farm worker capabilities, covering among others nutritional status, education levels, and access to housing and household services. The profile is concluded by a discussion of farm worker income levels and livelihoods.

In this analysis the position of farm workers is compared with the following labor reference groups:

- *Other (urban)*—This group consists of all employees working in other sectors of the economy and who work in urban areas. Official South African statistics define urban areas as being those areas that lie within the boundaries of formally declared towns, cities, or metropolitan areas.
- *Other (non-urban)*—This group consists of all employees working in other sectors of the economy and who work in non-urban areas. An area of the

country is designated non-urban (rural) if it falls outside the boundaries of formally declared towns, cities, or metropolitan areas.

- *Unemployed (urban)*—This group consists of all people who were classified in the census as being unemployed and living in urban areas. By unemployed is meant that these people (1) did not work 7 days prior to the interview, and (2) want to work and are available to start work within 4 weeks after the interview.
- *Unemployed (non-urban)*—This group consists of all people who were classified in the census as being unemployed and living in non-urban areas. By unemployed is meant that these people (1) did not work 7 days prior to the interview, and (2) want to work and are available to start within 4 weeks after the interview.

1. Gender

As can be seen in Figure 7.2, 70% of all agricultural workers are male. This distribution reflects a strong male bias, especially when compared with other employees working in the economy. These data also show that women in both urban and non-urban areas bear a disproportionate share of the country's unemployment burden.

2. Age

Compared with other employees in the country, farm workers are relatively young. Figure 7.3 shows this distribution, which reveals that the youth (people

FIGURE 7.2   Gender and farm employment.

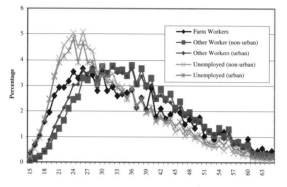

FIGURE 7.3   The age distribution of farmworkers aged 15–65.

ages between 15 and 19) are more likely to be among the unemployed in both
the urban and non-urban areas of the country.

3. Household Size and Structure

The average household size for farm workers is relatively small, as more than
60% of farm workers live in households containing 4 or fewer members. This
small household size may well be an artificial construct, as the on-farm housing
provided on most commercial farms is normally restricted to farm workers and
their dependent children. The larger average household size of the unemployed
in South Africa, 5.8 members, highlights the importance of family and community
networks as a form of social security.

When looking at the relationship of farm workers to the household head, more
than 80% were either the head of the household or were the partner of the

TABLE 7.1   Relationship to Household Head

	Farm Workers	Other (Urban)	Other (Non-Urban)	Unemployed (Urban)	Unemployed (Non-Urban)
Head of household	62.76	54.16	55.52	26.45	31.51
Husband/wife/partner	15.36	21.08	17.90	22.01	14.37
Son/daughter	10.64	13.48	16.23	31.71	37.45
Brother/sister	2.04	2.80	2.72	7.49	5.43
Father/mother	0.50	0.55	1.41	0.66	1.33
Grandparent	0.06	0.06	0.11	0.17	0.27
Grandchild	0.66	0.71	0.98	3.48	3.67
Other relative	2.16	2.72	2.15	5.77	4.66
Non-related person	5.81	4.44	2.99	2.25	1.30

Source: Census 96.

household head. Table 7.1 specifies this relationship. It is interesting to note the extent to which unemployed South Africans rely on their parental household for support.

4. Nationality

Census 96 found that the overwhelming majority of farm workers were South African citizens, and that less than 3% were foreign nationals mainly originating from other Southern African counties. Geographically, these foreign workers were concentrated in the provinces forming the country's northern border, namely the Northern Province (39%) and Mpumalanga (24%).

D. HUMAN CAPABILITIES OF SOUTH AFRICAN FARM WORKERS

This part of the chapter assesses farm worker poverty levels by looking at their absolute and relative basic capability levels. In determining which capabilities to include as part of any well-being or human development assessment, Sen argues that the choice depends on the values present in a society as well as on the motivation or objective of the assessment.[28] When it comes to the measurement of poverty (a special case of the measurement of well-being), Sen is more prescriptive and, as discussed previously, singles out the following basic capabilities as being important: being adequately nourished, leading a long and healthy life, being educated (or literate), and avoiding homelessness.[29] For the purposes of this study, the following capabilities will be explored in some depth and revisited in the next section, which looks at the relationship between income and capability achievement.

- Nutritional status
- Access to housing and household services
- Education and literacy levels

Note the omission of health status from the list due to the lack of a farm worker dataset detailing their health status and access to medical services.

1. Nutritional Status of Children Living on Commercial Farms

Household surveys such as Census 96 and the October Household Survey tend to be general and rarely collect detailed information on the nutritional status of a population. With respect to farm workers, this information gap has been fill by the recently published National Food Consumption Survey (NFCS) (2000).

TABLE 7.2   The Anthropometric Status of Children Ages 1–9 years by Area of Residence

	% of Sample	Stunting[a] (Height/Age)	Underweight[a] (Weight/Age)	Wasting[a] (Weight/Height)
Commercial farms	11	30.6	18.1	4.2
Formal urban	39	16.0	7.8	2.6
Informal urban	11	19.3	7.6	2.1
Former homeland areas	39	25.3	11.3	5.1
Average	100	21.6	10.3	3.7

[a]Standard deviation, −2.
Source: National Food Consumption Survey (2000).

The NFCS measured the nutritional status of children ages 1–9 using a variety of methods and disaggregated the data by area of residence. Note that while the data presented here specifically pertain to the children of farm workers, it is assumed that this information is indicative of the nutritional status of the farm worker household in general.

The anthropometric status of South African children ages 1–9 is shown in Table 7.2. The prevalence of moderate to severely stunting, underweight, and wasting (progressively more severe signs of malnutrition) was measured as being more than −2 standard deviations from the median measurements of the reference population. As can be seen from the table, children living on commercial farms in South Africa are most likely to be stunted and underweight; only children in the former homeland areas had a higher prevalence of wasting. Almost 1 in 3 children on commercial farms is stunted, 1 in 5 is underweight, and 1 in 25 displays the symptoms of wasting.

An alternative way of gauging access to food, and thus nutrition, is to adopt a qualitative approach by administering, for example, a hunger scale questionnaire. The caregivers of the children who took part in the NFCS survey were requested to complete such a questionnaire. Briefly, respondents were asked a series of questions[30] on their level of household food security. When more than five of the eight questions were answered in the affirmative, this indicated a food shortage problem. A "yes" score of between one and four indicated that the household was at "risk of hunger," while a negative response for each of the eight questions denoted a food-secure household. Table 7.3 shows the results of this hunger risk survey. As can be seen, urban households with a member employed in the formal economy experience the most food security. Only one in four children on commercial farms is food secure, and almost a third are at risk of hunger. Nevertheless, by these measures, children on commercial farms are better off than children from other rural and informal sector households. While fewer farm children experience hunger than the national average, the difference is small;

TABLE 7.3 Hunger Risk Classification in Children Ages 1–9 by Area of Residence

	Food Secure	At Risk of Hunger	Experience Hunger
Commercial farms	23	29	48
Formal urban	40	23	37
Informal urban	21	18	61
Former homeland areas	11	23	66
Average	25	23	52

Source: National Food Consumption Survey (2000).

more than half (52%) of South Africa's children experience hunger, and 48% of those on farms share this tragedy.

2. Access to Housing and Household Services

The data displayed in Figure 7.3 show that more than 65% of all farm workers live in a formal dwelling, which is a higher proportion than for other non-urban employees. This difference can probably be explained by the fact that most farm workers live on the farms in houses provided for them by their employers. Detailed analysis of Census 96 data shows the following:

- Farm workers appear better off than other non-urban workers with respect to the availability of on-site piped water (59% versus 38%). However, the availability of piped water on-site in the urban areas of the country is considerably higher compared to the non-urban areas. This is illustrated by the fact that 76% of unemployed residents in urban areas have access to piped water on-site compared with only 18% of the non-urban unemployed.
- In the case of the provision of electricity (measured in terms of using electricity for lighting), farm workers and other non-urban workers have identical access levels (44%). In contrast, urban workers are much better off, with 82% making use of electricity for lighting. As was the case with direct water provision, when it comes to electricity access, the non-urban unemployed lags the most (25%).
- In the case of adequate sanitation (measure with respect to the availability of a chemical or flush toilet in a dwelling), the same water and energy provision access pattern could be discerned. That is, farm workers were better off than other non-urban workers (27% versus 18%) but lagged behind the urban unemployed (67%).
- Few adults in the non-urban areas of the country have access to a telephone in their own homes. Moreover, a significant proportion of

non-urban people indicated that they had no access to any form of telecommunications. Fewer than 10% of farm workers have access to a phone in their dwelling while 23% indicated they had no access to any telephone at all.

Access to specific household services on an individual basis, however, does not provide a clear picture of the general trends in access for different types of households. To address this need, Statistics South Africa has developed a summary development index, using the data from Census 96, called the Household Infrastructure Index. This index, as the name implies, examines a household's access to different categories of infrastructure.[31] This index was used as the basis to develop the access to housing and services index presented here. Seen in Table 7.4, this index, which ranges between 0 and 100, is the arithmetic mean of the individual components listed. A person who lives in a formal dwelling and has access to electricity for lighting, a flush or chemical toilet, and a telephone in his dwelling scores 100, while a person with access to none of the above scores 0.

As can be seen in Table 7.4, urban employed individuals are considerably better off than their non-urban and unemployed counterparts. Furthermore, a strong urban bias exists with respect to service provision, as the unemployed in urban areas are better off than individuals working in non-urban areas. While non-urban individuals have similar access levels, farm workers are marginally better off than other employed non-urban households and significantly better off than the non-urban unemployed. This difference can be explained by the fact that many of the household services farm workers have access to are, for the most part, provided by their employers as part of their service contract.

While the average access to housing and services index for farm workers is 35.5%, this figure shows considerable variation on a magisterial district basis. Few magisterial districts scored an average in excess of 60, with most of these being in the Western Cape and in Gauteng province.

TABLE 7.4   Housing and Services: A Summary Index

	Farm Workers	Other Workers (Urban)	Other Workers (Non-Urban)	Unemployed (Urban)	Unemployed (Non-Urban)
Formal housing	69.72	79.06	64.80	62.63	44.56
Electricity for lights	44.60	81.76	47.05	66.56	25.18
Tap water inside	27.05	82.41	20.02	67.05	67.06
Flush or chemical toilet	26.73	71.96	23.41	49.58	6.12
Phone in dwelling or cellphone	9.06	51.06	10.17	23.99	1.63
Average	35.43	73.25	33.09	53.96	28.91

Source: Calculations based on Census 96.

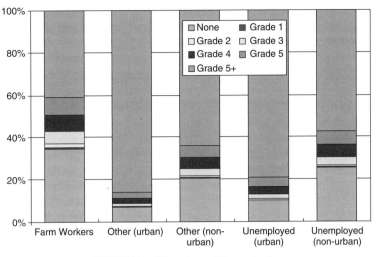

FIGURE 7.4   Education and literacy levels.

3. Education and Literacy Rates

Literacy can be measured in a variety of ways. In this case, it is defined as the percentage of the population over the age of 13 who have completed the first 5 years of education. The data in Figure 7.4 show that farm workers have the lowest rates of literacy in the country when compared with all other labor groups. Moreover, a significant proportion of farm workers (33%) indicated that they had no formal education whatsoever.

Changes in literacy levels can be measured by means of the average number of school years completed by age group. The data confirm that the average level of education is generally higher for younger South Africans (<40 years). However, this age differential is lower for farm workers than for any of the other groups, including the non-urban unemployed. One implication of this absolute and relative discrepancy is that agricultural employers place no economic value on education, given that the unemployed non-urban population has higher education levels compared to farm workers. A more likely explanation could be the localized character of agricultural labor markets that impedes its proper functioning. A survey conducted in 1997 among South African wine-grape farmers found, for example, that in most cases farmers employed workers recruited through the network of relatives and friends of workers already working on the farm.[32]

The extent to which the literacy rate and education level of farm workers and their families can be improved depends on their access to education services. From the mid-1950s to the mid-1990s, the education of farm workers was governed by the Bantu Education Act. This act allowed commercial farmers to set-up and run small schools on their property, thus providing rudimentary education in the rural areas and thereby ensuring an adequate labor supply through discouraging the urbanization of farm workers and their families. While the new South African political dispensation saw the governance and finance of these schools revert to the state, many of the inherent characteristics of these old-style farm schools such as multilevel classes, an absence of basic infrastructures, and high dropout rates continue to plague the country's rural education system. In addition, most of these schools provide only primary school education; very few extend beyond grade 7. For example, in 1996, only 3% of the farm schools in the Western Cape extended beyond grade 7, and none went beyond grade 9. Surveys among various Western Cape farm communities have found that the absence of a school in the immediate vicinity together with economic factors were the main reasons why such a high proportion of farm children do not continue with secondary education.[33]

E. Farm Worker Wage and Income Levels

The 1996 Agricultural Survey found that the average cash wage paid to regular and casual workers in agriculture was R419 per month.[34] At current prices, this translates into an average of U.S. $2.30 per day, which is not much higher than the popular "dollar a day" definition of poverty. At a provincial level there is also considerable variation. Workers in Gauteng were paid an average of R790 per month, while those in the Free State and Northern Province received R407 and R416 per month, respectively.

Aside from a cash wage, workers receive additional income under the heading of "other remuneration." Included in this category is the value of free housing and grazing provided to farm workers and contributions to the Workmen's Compensation Fund and Unemployment Insurance Fund made by farmers. Contributions to pension and medical funds are also included under "other remuneration" as well as in-kind payments received by them. Under "payments-in-kind" the following items are specified: the value of rations such as maize flour, slaughter animals, meat, fish, milk, wine, bread coffee, sugar, tobacco, clothing, shoes, transport, training, medicine provided to farm workers, and medical expenses paid on their behalf. While cash wages paid varied considerably across the provinces in the survey, the "other remuneration" paid to farm workers was fairly constant in absolute terms, averaging 20% of total remuneration.

Average wage data hide the distribution of wages. This is a particular problem in agriculture, where the distribution of wages consists of a clustering of workers at low levels of wages and a distinct tailing off at the upper end of the distribution. Data from the October Household Survey show that this phenomenon is most pronounced in South Africa in the case of agriculture, where the mean wage rate per worker was calculated at R3.57 per hour and the median at

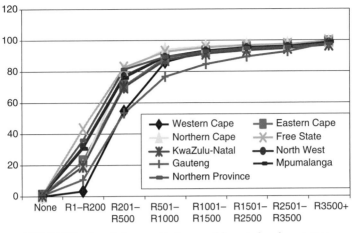

FIGURE 7.5 Cumulative monthly income of farm workers by province.

only R1.68. Assuming a 48-hour work week, this translated into a monthly average wage of R648.53 and a median wage of R322.56. This means that 50% of all farm workers are earning R322.56 per month or less.

The cumulative monthly income distribution for full-time farm workers can be seen in Figure 7.5. Data in Figure 7.5 show that 20% of farm workers earn between R0 and R200 per month, 70% earn between R0 and R500 per month, and 87% earn less than R1000 per month. The gender income distribution is skewed.

The provincial distribution of the wage categories also shows some variation. As can be seen in Figure 7.5, workers in Gauteng and the Western Cape earn the highest wages while workers in the Free State earn the lowest. Further, the data in Table 7.5 reflect the wage distribution by industry. Farm workers and domestic workers earn the lowest wages while the financial services and electricity sector workers are paid the highest.

V. INCOME AND CAPABILITIES

The evidence raised in this chapter is clear: Most South African farm workers live in circumstances of absolute poverty. Moreover, when their standard of living is compared to that of other urban and non-urban workers, their relative poverty is also evident. Some form of policy intervention is therefore needed to redress the situation. Whether intervention is successful will depend on the extent to which the capabilities of these workers are improved.

Calculations based on the data presented here show that there is a clear correlation between farm worker income categories and their access to housing and

TABLE 7.5   Mean and Median Hourly Wages by Industry (1997)

Industry	Mean (Rand)	Median (Rand)	Median as % Mean	Agriculture as % of sector
Agriculture	3.57	1.68	47	100.00
Mining	11.95	7.67	64	29.87
Manufacturing	13.07	8.73	67	27.31
Electricity	16.08	11.11	69	22.21
Construction	9.83	6.39	65	36.32
Trade	10.77	7.07	66	33.15
Transport	14.37	10.16	71	24.84
Finance	18.26	11.46	63	19.55
Services	17.87	13.85	78	19.97
Domestic	4.10	2.60	63	87.10

household services, as well as between income and literacy levels. Thus, it seems as if policies such as a minimum wage or an income supplement aimed at increasing the incomes of farm workers in South Africa will at the same time improve their capabilities. Yet, this may not be the case, for a number of potential reasons:

- Income supplements may end up in the hands of male workers, whose spending patterns are different than those of women. Improvement of capabilities requires investment in nutrition, education, health, etc., those rather than in consumer goods.
- A minimum wage that is set too high may benefit those who are able to retain employment but will harm those who become unemployed. As the latter is more likely to include vulnerable groups such as women, youth, and non-South African workers, there is a limit to the extent to which a minimum wage can be used to take people out of poverty.

This latter effect can be illustrated by means of an example of the potential effect of a countrywide minimum wage of R200 per month. The analysis is done with reference to Table 7.6, where there is a comparison between the primary demographic characteristics of workers earning below R200 per month and those earning above R200 per month, together with the average for all farm workers. The demographic characteristics of the unemployed are also included to assess the degree of difficulty these workers will encounter in trying to re-enter the job market.

Table 7.6 shows that women, youth, and non-South African farm workers are the most vulnerable to unemployment. For example, the table shows that comparatively more women earn less than R200 per month in relation to the total farm worker population. Women in the economy also bear a disproportionate share of the unemployment burden. Table 7.6 also shows the extent to which younger farm workers, those ages 15–34, earn the least. This is of particular concern

TABLE 7.6 Comparative Demographic Profile

	<R200 (%)	R200+ (%)	Farm Workers (%)	Unemployed (%)
Gender				
Male	59.5	73.6	69.4	43.7
Female	40.5	26.4	30.6	56.3
Cumulative Age				
15–19	8.2	4.8	5.7	6.2
20–24	25.6	19.5	21.1	27.6
25–29	40.8	36.8	37.8	48.6
30–34	54.1	52.1	52.6	64.8
35–39	65.5	64.9	65.0	77.0
40–44	75.1	75.8	75.6	85.7
45–49	83.4	84.6	84.3	91.8
50–54	89.6	90.7	90.4	95.6
55–59	94.4	95.3	95.1	98.1
60–64	97.3	98.0	97.8	99.2
65+	100.0	100.0	100.0	100.0
Nationality				
South Africa	94.8	97.8	97.0	99.5
Southern Africa	5.1	2.1	2.9	0.4
Other	0.1	0.1	0.1	0.1

Source: Census 96.

given the high national unemployment rate among the youth. Non-South African farm workers are also relatively more vulnerable.

Related to the introduction of a minimum wage and potential unemployment effects is the real impact or consequence of losing your job if you are a farm worker, given that many of the basic capabilities to which farm workers have access, such as housing and household services, are contingent on their continued employment status. Thus, to lose your job is to lose your home. In 1997, in an attempt to decouple this relationship, the government introduced the Extension of Security of Tenure Act (ESTA). The essence of this legislation is that it grants occupiers of rural land (i.e., farm workers) earning less the R5000 per month security of tenure. Review of the impact of this legislation suggests that there is compelling evidence that this legislation together with other agricultural labor legislation introduced over the same period has had the unintended result of encouraging farmers to shed labor and become more mechanized.[35]

VI. SUMMARY

The purpose in this chapter is to illustrate how these basic choices or capabilities can be accounted for in the measurement of poverty to ensure a more policy relevant understanding of the plight of poor people. This is accomplished through a case study of farm workers on commercial farms in South Africa.

Poverty is not simply having too little money; rather, it is about living a life without choices. While aid agencies also support this interpretation, they still tend to measure poverty indirectly in terms of incomes or expenditures. The availability of income data and of techniques to calculate poverty lines, minimum living levels, and poverty headcount ratios has encouraged the acceptance of this incongruence.

The standard of living of these workers is low, in absolute terms and relative to other urban and non-urban workers. Some form of policy intervention is necessary as redress, while success will depend on the extent to which the capabilities of these workers are improved. As the analysis shows a strong correlation between income categories and access to housing and household services, as well as between income and literacy levels, it seems as if a minimum wage or an income supplement will at the same time improve capabilities. Yet, this may not be the case, because:

- Income supplements may go to male workers, whose spending differs from women. Improving capabilities requires investment in nutrition, education, health, etc., rather than in consumer goods.
- A minimum wage that is set too high may benefit those in employment but will harm those who become unemployed, mainly women, youth, and foreign workers.

DISCUSSION QUESTIONS

1. Contrast different views of the definition and causes of poverty.
2. In this chapter it is argued that there exists incongruence between conceptual models of development and the available methods for the measurement of poverty. Do you agree with this argument? Explain your answer.
3. Contrast Sen's capabilities approach with neoclassical development theories in terms of their value assumptions, criteria for measuring development performance, the mechanisms of development and development strategies.
4. Do you agree with Sachs when he argues that "The idea of development stands today like a ruin in the intellectual landscape. . . . It's high time to set about the archaeology of this idea and uncover its foundations . . . to see it for what it is: an outdated monument to an immodest era"?
5. Name some examples of entitlements or capabilities other than income that allow poor people to manage their poverty status.

6. To what extent do development indicators such as the Physical Quality of Life Index (PQLI) and the Human Development Index differ from GNP per capita measures? Discuss differences in both the content of each measure as well as their conceptual bases.

7. The statement is made in this chapter that in many cases it is more costly for rural people to translate income into capabilities, and an example is given of the cost of providing education for children. Provide three more examples of this "rural premium" in translating income into capabilities.

8. Review the methodology used in this chapter to establish the level of poverty of children in South Africa.

9. Discuss how the provision of adequate sanitation, electricity, and a telephone rather than a higher income can make rural people less poor. (Hint: Each of these capabilities can lead to less poverty because it makes it easier to get access to employment and hence to income. Yet, each of them can lead to a reduction in poverty in its own right.)

10. Discuss the role of gender in determining spending patterns among poor rural people.

NOTES

[1]Sen, A. (1983) "Poor, Relatively Speaking," *Oxford Economic Papers*, 35(2), 153–169.

[2]Boltvinik, J. (1999) *Poverty Measurement Methods: An Overview*, SEPED Series on Poverty Reduction, New York: United Nations Development Project.

[3]See for instance, May, J., Carter, M., and Posel, D. (1995) *The Composition and Persistence of Poverty in Rural South Africa: An Entitlements Approach*, Policy Paper No 15, Johannesburg: Land and Agriculture Policy Centre; Leibbrandt, M. and Woolard, I. (1999). "A Comparison of Poverty in South Africa's Nine Provinces,". *Development Southern Africa*, 16(1): 28–54.

[4]Sen, A. (1984) "Goods and People," in A. Sen, Ed., *Resource, Values and Development*, Oxford: Basil Blackwell, p. 510.

[5]Sen, A. (1987) "The Standard of Living, Lecture 1: Concepts and Critiques," in G. Hawthorn, Ed., *The Standard of Living: The Tanner Lectures, Clare Hall, Cambridge 1985*, Boston, MA: Cambridge University Press, p. 15.

[6]Crocker, D. (1992) "Functioning and Capability: The Foundations of Sen's and Nussbaum's Developmant Ethic," *Political Theory*, 20(4), p. 591.

[7]Sen, A. (1992) *Inequality Reexamined*, Oxford: Claredon Press; Sen, A. (1995). "Food, Economics and Entitlements," in Dreze, J., Sen, A., and Hussain, A., Eds., *The Political Economy of Hunger*, Vol. III, Oxford: Claredon Press.

[8]Laderchi, C. (1999) *The Many Dimensions of Deprivation In Peru: Theoretical Debates and Empirical Evidence*, Working Paper 29 QEHWP29, Oxford: Queen Elizabeth House.

[9]Sen, A. (1984) "Goods and People," in A. Sen, Ed., *Resource, Values and Development*, Oxford: Basil Blackwell, p. 510.

[10]Ladrechi, C. (1999) *The Many Dimensions of Deprivation in Peru: Theoretical Debates and Empirical Evidence*, Working Paper 29, QEHWP29, Oxford: Queen Elizabeth House, p. 8.

[11]Beukes, E.P (1989) "Theories of Economic Development: An Overview and Some Implications," in J.K. Coetzee, Ed., *Development is for People*, Johannesburg: Southern Book Publishers, p. 225;

Van Zyl, J.C. (1995) *Needs-Based Development Strategy and the RDP: Some Broad Issues*, Johannesburg: DBSA.

[12]A statement issued at the conclusion of the Patterns of Resource Use, Environment and Development Strategies seminar hosted by the United Nations bodies in 1971.

[13]Hettne, B. (1995) *Development Theory and the Three Worlds*, 2nd ed., Essex, U.K.: Longman.

[14]These beneficiaries of development were obtained from the following sources: Goulet, D. (1995). "Participation in Development: New Avenues," in V.K. Pillai and L.W. Shannon, Eds., *Developing Areas: A Book of Readings and Research*, Oxford, Berg Publishers, p. 316; Korten, D.C. (1984) "People-Centred Development: Towards Framework," in D.C. Korten and R. Klauss, Eds., "*People-Centred Development: Contribution Towards Theory and Planning Frameworks*, West HartFord, CT: Kumarian Press, p. 300; Marglin, S. (1990) "Towards the Decolonisation of the Mind," in F. Apffel-Marglin and S. Marglin, Eds., *Dominating Knowledge: Development, Culture and Resistance*, Oxford: Claredon Press, p. 15; Verhelst, T. (1990) *No Life Without Roots: Culture and Development*, London: Zed Books, p. 160; Glover, J. (1995) "The Research Programme of Development Ethics," in M. Nussbaum and J. Glover, Eds., *Women, Culture and Development. A Study of Human Capabilities*, Oxford: Claredon Press; Hettne, B. (1995), *Development Theory and the Three Worlds*, 2nd ed., Essex, U.K: Longman; Jaquette, J. (1990) "Gender and Justice in Economic Development," in I. Tinker, Ed., *Persistent Inequalities: Women and World Development*, New York: Oxford University Press; The World Conservation Strategy (IUCN, 1981); Bruntland Commission (1987) *Our Common Future*; Saraceno, E., (1994) "Recent Trends in Rural Development and Their Conceptualisation," *Journal of Rural Studies*, 10(4): 321–330; Staatz, J.M. and Eicher, C.K. (1998) "Agricultural Development Ideas in Historical Perspective," in C.K. Eicher and J.M. Staatz, Eds., *International Agricultural Development*, 3rd ed., Baltimore, MD: John Hopkins University Press.

[15]Information used in this section was obtained from Sen's various publications including Sen, A. (1984) "Goods and People," in A. Sen, Ed., *Resource, Values and Development*, Oxford: Basil Blackwell, p. 510; Sen, A. (1985) "Well-Being, Agency and Freedom: The Dewey Lectures 1984," *The Journal of Philosophy*, 72(4): 197; Sen, A. (1987) "The Standard of Living, Lecture 1: Concepts and Critiques," in G. Hawthorn, Ed., *The Standard of Living: The Tanner Lectures, Clare Hall, Cambridge 1985*, Boston, MA: Cambridge University Press, pp. 15, 37; Sen, A. (1988) "The Concept of Development," in H. Chenery and T.N. Srinivasan, Eds., *Handbook of Development Economics*, Vol. 1, Amsterdam: North Holland, p. 15; Sen, A. (1989) "Development as Capability Expansion," *Journal of Development Planning*, 17: 41–58; Sen, A. (1989) "Development as Capability Expansion," *Journal of Development Planning*, 17: 44; Sen, A. (1992) *Inequality Reexamined*, Oxford: Claredon Press; Sen, A. (1983) "Poor, Relatively Speaking," *Oxford Economic Papers*, 35(2), 153–169; Sen, A. (1995) "Food, Economics and Entitlements," in Dreze, J., Sen, A., and Hussain, A., Eds., *The Political Economy of Hunger*, Vol. III, Oxford: Claredon Press, p. 63.

[16]Sen, A. (1984) "Goods and People," in A. Sen, Ed., *Resource, Values and Development*, Oxford: Basil Blackwell, p. 510.

[17]Sen, A. (1988) "The Concept of Development," in H. Chenery and T. N. Srinivasan, Eds., *Handbook of Development Economics*, Vol. 1, Amsterdam: North Holland, p. 15.

[18]Sen, A. (1988) "The Concept of Development," in H. Chenery and T. N. Srinivasan, Eds., *Handbook of Development Economics*, Vol. 1, Amsterdam: North Holland, p. 15.

[19]Sen, A. (1989) "Development as Capability Expansion," *Journal of Development Planning*, 17: 44.

[20]Sen, A. (1992) *Inequality Reexamined*, Oxford: Claredon Press.

[21]Boltvinik, J. (1999) *Poverty Measurement Methods: An Overview*, SEPED Series on Poverty Reduction, New York: United Nations Development Project.

[22]Boltvinik, J. (1999) *Poverty Measurement Methods: An Overview*, SEPED Series on Poverty Reduction, New York: United Nations Development Project; Miles, I. (1992) "Social Indicators for Real-Life Economics," in P. Ekins and M. Max-Neef, Eds., *Real Life Economics: Understanding Wealth Creation*, London: Routledge.

[23]UNDP (1993) *Human Development Report 1993*, New York: Oxford University Press.

[24]Streeten, P. (1994) "Human Development: Means and Ends," *American Economic Review: Papers and Proceedings*, 84(2): 232–237.

[25]World Bank (2000) *World Development Report 2000*, New York: Oxford University Press.

[26]Here an urban area is defined as an area that has been legally proclaimed to be urban. This distinction is problematic, as people living in large informal settlements are classified as nonurban. This especially affects the rate of urbanization in provinces such as the Northern Province and the Eastern Cape.

[27]World Bank (1994) "South African Agriculture: Structure, Performance and Options for the Future," in *Informal Discussion Papers on Aspects of the Economy of South Africa*, Washington, D.C.: World Bank.

[28]Sen A. (1998), "Development as Capability Expansion," *Journal of Development Planning*, 17, 41–58.

[29]Ladrechi, C. (1999) p. 8.

[30]The eight questions asked are as follows: (1) Does your household ever run out of money to buy food? (2) Do you ever rely on a limited number of foods to feed your children because you are running out of money to buy food for a meal? (3) Do you ever cut the size of meals or skip them because there is not enough money for food? (4) Do you ever eat less than you should because there is not enough money for food? (5) Do your children ever eat less than you feel they should because there is not enough money for food? (6) Do your children ever say they are hungry because there is not enough food in the house? (7) Do you ever cut the size of your children's meals or do they ever skip meals because there is not enough money to buy food? (8) Do any of your children ever go to bed hungry because there is not enough money to buy food?

[31]The components of this index include: Living in formal housing; access to electricity for lighting; tap water inside the dwelling; a flush or chemical toilet; a telephone in the dwelling or a cellular phone; refuse removal at least 1 a week; the level of education of the household head; and monthly household expenditure.

[32]Sen, A. (1987) "The Standard of Living, Lecture 1: Concepts and Critiques," in G. Hawthorn, Ed., *The Standard of Living: The Tanner Lectures, Clare Hall, Cambridge 1985*, Boston, MA: Cambridge University Press, p. 15.

[33]Vink, N. and Tregurtha, N. (1999). *Spatial Guidelines for Infrastructure, Investment and Development: Rural Issues Theme Paper*, report to the CIU, Office of the President.

[34]The exchange rate has moved from roughly US$1 = South African Rand (R) 6.00 to US$1 = R10.00 since 1996.

[35]Vink, N., Kirsten, J., and Tregurtha, N. (1999) *Job Shedding in South African Agriculture*, a background paper prepared for the Agricultural Job Summit, National Department of Agriculture, October.

PART **III**

Critical Issues

Implications of Ethnic Diversity*

PAUL COLLIER

The World Bank, Washington, D.C. 20433

KEY TERMS

Civil war

Diasporas

Dictatorships

Dysfunctional politics

ELF index (index of ethno-linguistic fractionalization)

Ethnic diversity

Ethnic dominance

Ethnic hatreds

Ethnicity

Fractionalization

Fragmented societies

Multiethnic societies

Nation building

Nationalism

OECD countries

Victimization of minorities

I. INTRODUCTION

Nation building has been seen as the decline of ethnic or local loyalties and their replacement by allegiance to a nation. The new states of the developing world have not often gone through this process: People identify more strongly with their kin group, ethnic group, or religious group than with the nation. The power of such subnational identities is commonly regarded as a curse. Societies divided by ethnicity are seen as less likely to reach cooperative solutions and more likely to victimize minorities.

The most serious charge leveled against ethnic differentiation is that it is the prime cause of violent civil conflict. The evidence seems to bear this out. The developing countries are more ethnically diverse than the OECD societies, and they suffer a much higher incidence of civil war. Among developing countries, Africa is more ethnically diverse than other regions and it has the highest incidence of civil war, a phenomenon often interpreted as the post-colonial re-emergence of ancestral ethnic hatreds. Ethnic conflicts in developing countries have become a major policy concern to OECD governments, triggering both humanitarian

*This chapter is reproduced with permission from Blackwell publishers.
See the rest of footnote * in the Notes section at the end of the chapter.

and military interventions. In addition to the massive military and financial interventions in the former Yugoslavia, during the 1990s Belgium, Britain, France, and the United States all dispatched troops to African conflicts. Such policy interventions were partly motivated by the manifestly debilitating consequences of civil war for the society in which it occurs. However, there was probably also an element of self-interest. Civil wars have social repercussions far beyond the boundaries of the affected state. Refugees create waves of migration, and the diasporas are often drawn into the conflict. Indeed, many civil wars have a penumbra of illegal migration and drug trafficking, which directly affect OECD societies.

Ethnic differentiation has also come to be seen as detrimental to economic management. Easterly and Levine report that ethnic diversity reduces the rate of economic growth.[1] They explain this in terms of a hypothesized effect of diversity upon political choices. Diverse societies are alleged to find it more difficult to reach cooperative solutions and to be more likely to waste resources in distributional struggles. The economic consequences of such allegedly dysfunctional politics are claimed to be huge. Easterly and Levine attribute Africa's present poverty predominantly to its unusually high ethnic diversity. The title of their article, "Africa's Growth Tragedy: Policies and Ethnic Divisions," aptly summarizes the proposition: Ethnic divisions are responsible for economic policies which are so impoverishing as to be tragic. As with civil war, impoverishment casts a long shadow: OECD governments attempt to remedy it through aid programs, motivated both by compassion and by fear of the social and political consequences of bordering on regions of extreme poverty.

These two detrimental effects of ethnic differentiation can be nested. Civil war can be viewed as the extreme manifestation of the more general phenomenon of dysfunctional politics. The underlying propositions are that ethnic divisions make cooperation more difficult and victimization more likely.

If strong subnational ethnic identification is indeed dysfunctional, then there appear to be two solutions. Governments could engage in the sort of virulent nationalism that Europe used in its own building of national identities. The obvious danger in this process is that it risks international conflict, as happened in Europe. Alternatively, governments could accede to the demand for ethnic self-determination, creating many new states. This solution gained momentum during the 1990s although it has some evident limitations. In this paper, I argue that neither of these solutions is necessary because the premises on which they are based are false. With a few specific exceptions, ethnic diversity neither increases the risk of civil war nor reduces economic growth. Multiethnic societies can usually be socially and economically fully viable.

Section II presents the current state of knowledge as far as what is meant by ethnic identity and why it is thought to be dysfunctional. Sections III and IV venture beyond the literature. Section III investigates how ethnic politics might affect economic performance, deriving predictions from theories of political choice and testing them on global data. Section IV turns to the causes of large-scale violence and investigates how ethnic differentiation might affect civil conflict. Building on new theories of conflict that stress the importance of the budget constraint faced by the rebel organization, Section IV tests three predictions on global data. Section V draws out some implications for policy. Ethnic diversity is not "guilty as charged." It does not usually cause slower growth, and it does not usually cause civil war. The international community may need to rethink its current tolerant approach to secession.

II. WHAT DO WE KNOW AND WHAT ARE THE GAPS?

How does ethnicity sometimes come to be the basis for social and political identity? Ethnicity as a basis for identity is a social rather than a physiological phenomenon. As a *cultural* phenomenon, ethnicity is nevertheless highly persistent: people choose to pass on their culture by marrying within their own group.[2] However, as a *political* phenomenon, ethnic identity is considerably more fluid. This is indeed implied by "nation building"—in Europe, perceptions of identity changed during the 18th and 19th century from being, say, Scottish or Breton to being British or French. The process is recounted for 18th-century Britain in *Britons: Forging the Nation* and for 19th-century France in *Peasants into Frenchmen*.[3] Currently, in much of the developing world the most powerful levels of social identity are neither the nation nor the region, but the kin group and the tribe. One of the developments in New Institutional Economics has been to reinterpret kin groups not as primitive emotional bonds but as efficient responses to problems of information and contract enforcement in traditional economies. Posner[4] brilliantly shows why kinship was (and remains) such an efficient basis for collective action. Basing group membership upon kinship provides clear rules of lifetime membership, thereby overcoming the standard problems of adverse selection. Kinship also provides high observability of behavior: The involvement and gossip of relatives ensure that the group is well informed about antisocial behavior, and this discourages moral hazard. Kin groups are thus well placed both to enforce bilateral contracts among members and to provide group-level insurance or defense, anchored on a robust web of reciprocal obligations. The value of kin groups applies in a variety of contexts: Posner's original application was to high-risk agriculture, but Greif shows their value in medieval long distance trade, and Biggs *et al.* show their value in manufacturing.[5] On this view, kin groups are efficient responses to the information and contract enforcement problems of market economies. An implication is that a society composed of multiple kin groups is more efficient than a homogenous, but atomized, society. Kin groups do not divide a preexisting whole, but rather aggregate an atomized society into groups large enough to reap the gains from collective action.

While the basis of social identity in developing countries may usually be the kin group, effective political groupings are too large to be based upon social interaction, and so must be based upon an *imagined* shared identity.[6] Where collective action is already based upon ties of blood as in kin groups, it is easy to conjure up imagined larger blood-related political groupings. For example, in Africa the advent of colonialism created opportunities for large political groupings to secure economic advantages. Kin groups invented tradition as they amalgamated into large tribes, although in practice language seems to have been the main basis for tribal agglomeration. The three main tribal groupings in Nigeria (Yoruba, Ibo, and Hausa-Fulani) appear to date from the 19th century, while the currently dominant Kenyan tribe, the Kalenjin, dates back only to the 1940s. This process of amalgamation is continuing. Posner shows how African tribes have formed durable political alliances, so that societies are considerably less fractionalized politically than implied by tribal identity.[7] Modern ethnic political loyalties thus start from reciprocal economic obligations within a kin group, extend to an imagined community of shared interest within a tribe, and often extend to alliances with other tribes to form a political party.

Given that in many societies ethnicity, real or imagined, is the basis for social and political identity, what are its consequences? To research these issues empirically, social scientists need a quantitative measure of how societies differ with respect to the extent of ethnic differentiation. The most widely used measure is the index of ethno-linguistic fractionalization (ELF). Homogenous societies are scored zero, and the theoretical maximum of 100 would be reached if each person belonged to a distinct group. The observed range is from 0 to 93. This measure has some serious problems. Posner describes some substantial inaccuracies.[8] Further, representation by a single number can lose critical information. We might expect that victimization arises in societies in which one or more minorities face a majority, while an inability to cooperate arises in societies in which there are many groups, none with a majority, yet the ELF index cannot distinguish between them. These two circumstances are termed *dominance* and *fragmentation*, and the following discussion will show that they have significantly different consequences. Examples of societies with ethnic politics in which there is a majority ethnic group and one or more ethnic minorities are Malaysia, Belgium, Northern Ireland, Canada, South Africa, and Rwanda. In these societies, the fear of ethnic politics is that it will lead to the permanent exclusion of other groups and discrimination against them. However, most societies are characterized by neither ethnic dominance nor homogeneity, but by fragmentation.

Recent literature suggests that kin groups may also create substantial problems of cooperation between members of different groups. Four studies in ascending order of size and complexity of organization are considered here. Miguel has studied school boards in different areas of Kenya.[9] He shows that to function effectively, the boards need to be able to enforce obligations within the community—for example, the duty to make financial contributions to the school. He finds that those boards which are ethnically diverse are less able to do this, as board members are less willing to criticize someone from their own ethnic group in front of members from other groups. Alesina *et al.* investigated a larger type of community and a more general decision, namely city government in the United States.[10] They found that the more ethnically diverse the electorate, the worse the productivity of public expenditure. They suggest that diversity increases the problems of collective action because more of the benefits are external to the group. Garg and Collier analyzed the effect of ethnic diversity in the Ghanaian labor market. They also found that ethnic diversity had consequences that must have been highly problematic. Controlling for other characteristics, workers from whichever tribe was locally the largest were commanding a substantial wage premium. This was explained in terms of the power of kin group patronage in promotions, with larger groups having disproportionate power. The highest level of organization and generality of decision is that analyzed by Easterly and Levine.[10] Here the adverse consequence is on the national growth rate, and the inferred mechanism is poor national economic policy. Easterly and Levine infer that ethnic diversity makes political cooperation more difficult. Thus, at various sizes of organization, ethnic diversity appears to make cooperation more difficult.

However, there is also counterevidence. Although Miguel convincingly establishes why ethnic diversity is dysfunctional within a Kenyan school board, the explanation cannot account for the other examples of the costs of diversity. In the school boards, diversity nullifies the cooperation that can otherwise be achieved by kin groups. Diversity only takes the society back to the noncooperative outcome of atomistic homogeneity. Obviously, this cannot be the explanation for Easterly and Levine's result that ethnically diverse societies grow less rapidly than ethnically homogenous societies.

It turns out that the ethnical diversity of cities analyzed by Alesina *et al.* are characterized by dominance, not fragmentation. Thus, the costs of diversity they found might only occur in conditions of dominance. If so, this would be an important qualification, unlike U.S. cities, most ethnically diverse countries are characterized by fragmentation rather than dominance. The author's own study with Garg distinguished between the public sector and the private sector and found that in the public sector the patronage-induced wage premium for the locally largest tribe was 25%, whereas in the private sector it was zero. This was interpreted as suggesting that in the private sector competition forces firms to curb the patronage power of kin groups, so that ethnic diversity is only a problem for public sector organizations. Recall that both the Miguel and Alesina *et al.* studies were of public sector organizations. Easterly and Levine simply use the ELF score as a measure of ethnic diversity and do not distinguish between dominance and fragmentation so, again, potentially all the costs of diversity could be due to dominance. Further, as argued by Arcand *et al.*, if the adverse effect of ethnic diversity works through poor policy choice, then once policy choices are added to the Easterly and Levine growth regression the negative coefficient upon ethnic diversity should diminish.[11] They added a range of macroeconomic policies to the regression and showed that the coefficient on ethnic diversity does not diminish. Thus, rather than amounting to a unified critique of ethnic diversity, the literature may simply show that it can have negative effects in particular circumstances. Perhaps ethnic diversity is damaging if it takes the form of dominance; perhaps it is damaging in the public sector. A more nuanced analysis seems to be required.

Another study considers an altogether darker supposed consequence of ethnic diversity, not as an impediment to cooperation, but as an incitement to victimization and civil war. Horowitz shows that ethnic identity is often accompanied by hostility to other groups. The problem of victimization of minorities, such as Jews in Europe and the Tutsi in Rwanda, has been extensively analyzed, most notably through the Minorities at Risk project. Emminghaus *et al.* conclude that "the formation of cultural identities about primordial sentiments without the parallel or subsequent development of civil identities has led to primordial violence in today's world."[12] However, both political science and economics have countervailing theories, which argue that ethnic hatred does not provide a good explanation for large-scale violent conflict. Two distinguished political scientists, Fearon and Laitin,[13] analyzed the Minorities at Risk data and roundly rejected both cultural differences and the degree of cultural and economic discrimination against minorities as explanations for episodes of major violence. Similarly, Bates[13] finds that while political *protest* is more common in ethnically diverse societies, political *violence* is less common. He concludes, "It is diversity, not homogeneity that lowers the risk of conflict." Economists have also developed a countervailing theory of civil war. Starting with the pioneering work of Grossman,[13] they have focused upon the budget constraint for rebellion: trying to identify the circumstances in which rebellion is financially profitable. In Grossman's work, the very rationale for rebellion is financial: rebels are indistinguishable from criminal bandits. More recently, in the author's own work, the motivation for rebellion is allowed to be more general, but financial and military viability are treated as important constraints. The core of the analysis is the differential ability of rebel organizations to raise finance, depending upon the opportunities for predation of primary commodity exports and for the taxation of diasporas. The predicted effects of ethnic diversity depend upon whether it takes the form of dominance or fragmentation. Dominance (one ethnic group in a permanent majority) may well produce victimization and so increase the risk of rebellion. Fragmentation, however, is predicted to make rebellion more difficult because to be militarily viable a rebel organization must maintain cohesion. If diversity reduces organizational cohesion, rebel recruitment is more problematic in diverse societies. Thus, in diverse societies, even if people hate each other more than in homogenous societies, they are less able to translate hatred into large-scale organized violence. Here, the "ethnic hatred" and economic theories of the causes of conflict radically diverge in a testable way. The author's empirical work has attempted to test these rival theories on a comprehensive dataset of civil wars between 1960 and 1999.[13] The research has shown that, whereas ethnic dominance indeed doubles the risk of civil war, fragmentation significantly *reduces* the risk. Thus, as with the literature on ethnic diversity and cooperation, the case against diversity is less robust and less general than might appear at first sight.

III. DOES ETHNIC DIVERSITY CAUSE DYSFUNCTIONAL POLITICS?

If democratic politics is dysfunctional in ethnically diverse societies, then an implication might be that ethnically diverse societies need a strong leader above politics to avoid these pressures. This argument is beloved of third world dictators: Their ethnically diverse societies need them.

The discussion now compares the effect of ethnic politics in democracy and dictatorship. This requires a counterfactual, how political choices are made in the absence of ethnic loyalties. Unsurprisingly, modern theories of political choice seldom yield unambiguous predictions. Even something as basic as the relative efficacy of dictatorship and democracy turns out to be *a priori* ambiguous, a result consistent with the empirical literature. The argument will be that usually the introduction of party loyalties based on ethnicity does not substantially change outcomes, but that in two specific circumstances it is likely to have significant negative effects.

A. Effect of Ethnic Diversity in Democracies

To analyze the democratic political process, it is useful to contrast two commonly used approaches to legislative decision-taking. One is the process originally analyzed by Downs (1957),[14] in which voter preferences are distributed only over a single issue, such as the rate of taxation, so that these preferences can be arrayed along a left–right spectrum. In the second, voters have preferences over multiple issues. Potentially, ethnic politics can take place within either of these systems.

1. Single-Issue Politics

Single-issue politics is a good point of embarkation. We will assume that the government is constrained so that all electors must benefit equally from the provision of a public good financed out of taxation such that the single issue is to choose the rate of taxation. Electors have different preferences because they differ by income: High-income voters will prefer a low income tax rate, and low-income voters will prefer a high income tax rate.

In the absence of identity politics, Downs' model produces a clear result. Parties compete to form a minimum winning coalition, and the winner is the party that attracts the support of the median voter. Thus, the tax rate will be set at that rate preferred by someone with median income (although this need not be socially optimal). Now introduce ethnic politics. Each ethnic group has its own political party, supported by all members of the group. What happens depends upon whether income differences are related to ethnic differences. First, suppose that the two are unrelated: The distribution of income is the same for each ethnic group. In this case, ethnic politics does not change the median voter outcome, although the process by which democracy reaches the tax rate decision is different. With ethnic politics the important democratic process is that which is internal to each party. Regardless of which ethnic party is in power, with internal democracy each party will represent the median voter within its ethnic group. By assumption, all of these median voters have the same interests. Hence, ethnic politics makes no difference to political decisions regardless of whether diversity takes the form of fragmentation or dominance.

Now consider the other extreme, where incomes differ so much between ethnic groups that all the members of the richest group are richer than all the members of the next group, and so on (income is lexicographic in ethnicity). The ethnic party that contains the voter with the median economic interest now becomes the pivotal party, able to determine the government. However, this pivotal ethnic party need not maximize the well-being of the voter with the median economic interest. This voter is already locked into supporting the party by virtue of his or her ethnic identity. Hence, if the party is internally democratic, it will be driven to maximize the well-being of the voter who is at the median of the party rather than at the median of the electorate as a whole. Whether this difference is important depends upon the nature of ethnic diversity. If there is fragmentation then the median voter within the pivotal party is likely to have interests very close to those of the median elector. If, however, there is ethnic dominance then the divergence may be greater. Consider, for example, a stylized version of South African politics in which the black party holds 65% of the vote, with whites and Asians having higher incomes than blacks. Now, ethnic politics delivers policies that maximize the well-being of the 33rd percentile as opposed to the 50th percentile with ethnicity-free politics. However, paradoxically, as ethnic dominance increases, the divergence diminishes. If the dominant ethnic group has 90% of the electorate, then its party maximizes the interests of around the 46th percentile.

To summarize, in single-issue politics ethnic politics is scarcely alarming. If ethnic identities are unrelated to economic interests ethnic politics has no effect. Even when ethnic identity is strongly correlated with economic interest, ethnic politics makes surprisingly little difference. When diversity takes the form of fragmentation ethnic politics will normally have only a negligible effect. When it takes the form of ethnic dominance, it will only have a substantial effect if the dominant group has a small plurality, and if, at the same time, there is a large difference between the income of this group and other groups.

2. Multi-Issue Politics

Single-issue politics is not, however, a very illuminating window on the political process. Now consider an extreme form of multi-issue politics, namely the distribution of expenditure. Instead of the good financed out of taxation being a public good that benefits all electors equally, suppose that it benefits only the electors of the constituency in which it is located. Further, suppose that the taxation necessary to finance it has disincentive effects and so reduces the growth rate of the economy. The higher the public expenditure, the lower the growth. The political process must now decide on the pattern of public expenditure bearing in mind the resulting taxation. In the absence of identity politics, political parties (if they exist at all), will be weak. Legislators depend for their survival on their ability to deliver expenditures to local voters, rather than on party loyalties. In general, games such as this have no "core": there is no equilibrium and the likely outcome is therefore instability.[15] The political system continues to try to build a minimum winning coalition that captures all the benefits of public expenditure for its own members. However, no such coalition can persist. Any group that assembles 51% support can always be supplanted by some other alliance. Hence, majorities keep forming and breaking up. As Drazen[16] notes: "Indeterminacy in general ... is seen as perhaps the major defect of majority voting as a choice mechanism." However, whichever group is temporarily in power has an incentive to sacrifice overall growth for redistribution to its own supporters. It consequently chooses a high tax rate in order to benefit from the resulting expenditures. Each group only benefits temporarily from the expenditures, but because the tax rate is sustained, there is a continuous sacrifice of growth.

Now introduce identity politics. First consider the consequences of exogenous party loyalties in the case of fragmentation: No ethnic group constitutes a majority.

Because unstable minimum winning coalitions inflict costs on most or all groups in society, there are mutual gains from cooperation if only a bargain can be negotiated and enforced. Because the game is played repeatedly, if there were only two players (the leaders of two political parties), there would be no dilemma; in a two-person repeated game both players come to deploy a tit-for-tat strategy, and this enforces cooperation. A reasonable presumption is that the more players in the game, the less likely it is that legislators can escape from the dilemma, although Drazen shows that this need not be the case in sufficiently complex models of political bargaining.[17] If legislators are grouped into strong parties that can discipline their behavior and so enforce agreements, the number of players is reduced and cooperation may become easier. This suggests that in a parliamentary system the presence of exogenously given party identity, on whatever basis, is useful. If the alternative to ethnic politics is parties that are too weak to control legislators, ethnic identity might be an improvement. However, comparing among societies all of which have ethnic politics, the more ethnically fractionalized the society, and hence the greater number of political parties, the more difficult it might be to arrive at the cooperative solution. Thus, differentiation into, say, three equal parties may be an improvement upon homogeneity, but differentiation into 30 parties would be worse.

Now consider identity politics in the circumstances of ethnic dominance. Suppose, as before, that there is ethnic politics in South Africa with one ethnic group holding a majority of 65%. If the group holds together it can now capture 100% of the expenditures and so does very well. Ethnic identity may be sufficiently strong to enforce cohesion on the dominant ethnic group, producing a stable winning coalition, although the group would be inefficiently large. If it could do so without losing cohesion, the party of the dominant ethnic group would slim down to representing just 51% of the electorate, conferring larger benefits on its remaining members. Assuming that an ethnic party is only able to keep a stable political majority by including its entire ethnic group, then an interesting paradox follows. A dominant ethnic group will do more damage to growth the smaller is its majority. For example, a group with only just over 50% of the electorate is indeed a minimum winning coalition and so, in the example in Appendix A, will set the tax rate at 33%. By contrast, if the dominant ethnic group constitutes 90% of the electorate and all are represented by the same party, it will choose to set the tax rate at under 5%. Redistribution is not worth the costs because the minority is too small to be worth exploiting. While ethnic politics in the context of ethnic dominance is liable to produce discrimination against the minority, this is obviously not specific to ethnicity as a basis for political identity. Any system in which electoral allegiance is based on identity will have the same tendency if one party has a permanent majority.

To summarize, inserting ethnic parties into democratic systems generates the following propositions. In the (probably unusual) circumstances of single-issue politics, ethnic fragmentation will not have large effects. Ethnic dominance may have moderately large effects, but there will be no systematic effect on growth. In the (more usual) circumstances of multi-issue politics, without identity politics the expectation is of instability due to the lack of an equilibrium. Ethnic dominance confers durable power on a winning coalition which then has an incentive to sacrifice growth for redistribution, although the incentive is weaker than for a *minimum* winning coalition. Limited ethnic fragmentation facilitates cooperative outcomes that avoid or reduce the costs of unstable minimum winning coalitions. However, the greater the extent of ethnic fragmentation, the more difficult it is to reach a cooperative solution.

3. Differences in the Role of Identity Politics

Before turning to econometric testing of these propositions it is useful to "ground truth" them against the differing role of identity politics in the democracies of America, Europe, and Africa. American political allegiance, at least at the national level, is not strongly related to identity: Many voters are willing to switch between parties based on current interests. In Europe, political allegiance is more influenced by identity, with the basis for identity being class, religion, language, or history rather than ethnicity. Because European electors tend to have these exogenous loyalties to parties and the party leaders control candidate nominations, parties are much stronger than in America, with party leaderships controlling how legislators vote. In Africa, party identification is normally ethnic except where such identification is deliberately suppressed.

The above analysis of multi-issue politics would predict that in America the weakness of parties due to the absence of identity politics would produce unstable minimum winning coalitions. This is not borne out in American experience. Instead of congressional voting being characterized by minimum winning coalitions of changing composition, most spending votes are supported by large majorities, the phenomenon being known as "pork barrel" politics. A large body of theory has developed to explain this behavior.[18] The argument is that changing minimum winning coalitions would be highly disadvantageous for the legislators. Periodically, they would be unable to provide any benefits to their local electors and so would risk being defeated. Legislators have therefore evolved a pattern of behavior in which each legislator is given equal powers over the agenda. Specifically, each has the power of proposing an expenditure that benefits his locality. Legislators may devise benefits which are complex non-monetary transfers, thereby making it more difficult for voters to understand the true costs and beneficiaries.[19] Proposals are log-rolled, an implicit norm of deference among legislators amounting to "I'll scratch your back if you'll scratch mine." While this is good for legislators, it is not good for the economy. The projects must be paid for and so, as with minimum winning coalitions, the outcome is that expenditures are too high. The problem is that there is no process for internalizing the externalities of the taxes needed to pay for the expenditures, analogous to the restaurant bill problem; if a group of people agree to share the bill, they all have an incentive to over-eat. Hence, pork-barrel log-rolling results in inefficient reductions in growth. To counter this, the American constitution gives veto powers to the President.

Evidently, the practical problem in democratic politics appears to be pork-barrel log-rolling rather than unstable minimum winning coalitions. Potentially, however, exogenous strong parties can again reduce the problem. Party leaders internalize the negative fiscal externalities of pork-barrel politics. Empowered by stable voter allegiance they can cooperate to rein in log-rolling and so improve economic performance.

The European parliamentary system, being more characterized by identity politics, is therefore predicted to have less of a problem with log-rolling. Further, the huge variation within European politics in the number of parties provides a test of the proposition that fragmentation will reduce the durability of inter-party cooperation. Both of these propositions find empirical support. Schofield shows that within Europe variation in the number of parties (associated with whether or not there is proportional representation) is associated with a shorter life of governing coalitions.[20] However, he argues that the effect is too weak to constitute a substantial problem.

Recent democratizations in Africa provide an unusual opportunity to see what happens when ethnic politics is suppressed. There are currently two experiments in which a party contest previously based on ethnicity was purged of ethnic identity. In the 1960s, both Ugandan and Nigerian political parties were ethnically based with legislator voting following these party lines. After a period of dictatorship, democracy has been reestablished but with a constitutional changes that suppress the old parties. In Uganda, legislators are elected to parliament but are not allowed to campaign except as individuals; there are no parties. In Nigeria, two new political parties were imposed by the departing military government, each with requirements to be multiethnic. The result to date has been a dramatic confirmation of Weingast's theory that weak parties produce legislative log-rolling. As in America, both legislatures have had a strong universalist, pro-expenditure bias.

B. DICTATORSHIP

We now turn from democracy to dictatorship. With or without ethnic parties, democracy is unlikely to reach the hypothetical social planning optimum. An all-powerful, all-knowing dictator could *be* the social planner, for example, overcoming the restaurant bill problem. However, even the benevolent social planning dictator is in practice not all knowing. Indeed, he will lack much information revealed through democratic processes and so miss opportunities for mutually beneficial political deals. Hence, *a priori*, it is ambiguous whether benevolent dictatorships are more or less efficient than democracy. More fundamentally, there is no particular reason why a dictator should have this objective. Olsen argues that, in the absence of democratic checks, rules will tend to abrogate property rights.[21] Indeed, because they lack the power to bind themselves, even benevolent dictators face a classic time-consistency problem in which potential investors cannot infer from current benevolence that future policy will not become predatory. Empirical studies of the effect of dictatorship on economic performance have generally failed to find a clear effect, suggesting that the scope for a social planner to outperform democracy roughly offsets the scope for dictators to be more predatory than elected politicians.[22]

The theoretical literature on dictatorship has not previously analyzed the effect of ethnic diversity. A useful starting place is to consider the power base of the dictator. A benevolent dictator who succeeds in realizing the gains of social planning may be sufficiently popular not to need military support. Was Lee Kwan Yew a dictator of Singapore or an astonishingly successful politician? The following discussion treats benevolent dictators as random acts of God, distributed without relation to ethnic diversity and focuses on those dictators who do not take the social planning route to the maintenance of power. They must rely upon an army. In Section II, it was suggested that rebel military organizations need cohesion and so must avoid the impediments to cooperation introduced by recruiting across ethnic boundaries. Self-serving dictatorships are analogous to rebel organizations and face the same constraint. Further, in ethnically diverse societies, kinship or tribal loyalties are likely to be useful in maintaining military cohesion. Currently, the most spectacular example of the use of kinship by a dictator is surely Saddam Hussein's control over the Iraqi military, with key positions dominated by his own Tikriti clan. The pattern is widespread; either dictators shape the army around their own ethnic identities (as with Saddam Hussein), or, perhaps more commonly, an army which is already ethnically distinctive produces a coup leader from its ranks (as with Idi Amin in Uganda). This relationship between ethnic cohesion and the power base of dictatorship has the important implication that *the more ethnically fractionalized the society, the narrower the maximum military support base of the dictatorship*. In turn, unless this is offset by other differences, this lower maximum will imply that on average predatory dictatorships will have narrower support bases the more ethnically fractionalized is the society. Note that the relationship only holds on average. One exception is that even in an ethnically homogenous society a dictatorship may choose to build a support base that is socially very narrow, as in Duvalier's Haiti. A second is that a highly fractionalized society may happen to have a dictatorship based on its largest ethnic group, whereas a relatively unfractionalized society may have a dictatorship based on its smallest ethnic group, the latter being smaller than the former.

The size of the military support base is important because in practice dictators are not individually all powerful. A dictator who failed to satisfy the material aspirations of his military support base would be replaced by an internal coup. For example, the Nigerian military replaced its dictator on several occasions while maintaining the same ethnic power base. An approximation to this state of affairs is to characterize the dictator as the elected leader but on a franchise confined to his own ethnic group. The military power of the ethnic group confers on it the power to determine policy. The outcome expected then follows from the above analysis of ethnic dominance in the context of multi-issue politics. As in that case, the government is free to redistribute in favor of the ruling ethnic group. The key difference is that now the winning coalition need not constitute a majority of the population. Far from trying to make such discrimination discreet, as Coate and Morris suggest happens in democracies, the dictator needs to demonstrate his favoritism as visibly as possible. The threat he faces is not national voter anger at the cost of patronage but an internal coup from within the group he needs to favor. He must locate infrastructure in the locality of his ethnic group, and he must skew public employment to those members of his group who come to the capital for jobs. For example, during the time of President Kenyatta, a Kikuyu, the main Kikuyu city grew very rapidly at the expense of non-Kikuyu cities such as Kisumu and Mombasa. When President Moi took over, he built a new international airport in the small town that was the heartland of his own minor tribe, the Kalenjin. Over the years, employment in the post office, the part of the public sector most intensive in unskilled labor, has become dominated by the Kalenjin.

Recall from the previous analysis that the costs of ethnic dominance are predicted to *decrease* with the size of the dominant group. The smaller the group, the stronger the incentive for it to choose redistribution to itself at the expense of growth to the economy as a whole. In the context of democracy, this rising cost as the size of the group diminishes was checked by the barrier of 50%: Below this level, the group is not in power. However, in dictatorship, there is no such barrier. Remarkably small ethnic groups have always been able to retain military power. In 11th-century England and Southern Italy the Norman ethnic group seized and maintained power to their own advantage despite constituting only some 2% of the population. In 20th-century Burundi and South Africa ethnic minorities of less than 20% of the population did likewise.

Such narrow winning coalitions would have a much stronger incentive to sacrifice growth than the larger winning coalitions in democracies, and this leads to a clear prediction: *Dictatorship will tend to be more detrimental to growth the more ethnically fractionalized is the society.*

C. Testable Hypotheses

We now bring together the testable propositions on the effects of ethnic differentiation in democracy and dictatorship to see whether they are supported by econometric evidence. The likely effects of ethnic diversity in different political systems are summarized in Table 8.1. The presumption that ethnic politics is damaging regardless of the political system is not supported by the theories discussed above. Rather, ethnic diversity is predicted to be damaging in particular circumstances, namely dominance and dictatorship. Other than in these circumstances theory does not provide a clear prediction. Ethnic politics may facilitate the internalization of externalities lacking when party leaders cannot control legislators. However, ethnicity may simply substitute for some other basis for stable voter allegiance, as with the class identity politics common in Europe, or other features of the constitution may compensate for the effects of weak parties.

In societies characterized by ethnic dominance, the government has both the power and the incentive to trade off redistribution at the expense of growth. Whether the system is democratic or dictatorial will make no difference if the

TABLE 8.1 Ethnicity and the Political Process: A Summary

	Ethnic Fragmentation	Ethnic Dominance	Homogeneity
Single-issue democracy	Similar to the median voter outcome	Fairly similar to the median voter outcome	Two parties: median voter outcome Multiple parties: close to median voter outcome
Multi-issue democracy	Ethnic parties may reduce the economic costs of instability or log-rolling (like PR)	Stable winning coalition uses its power to choose redistribution at the expense of growth	Instability or log-rolling: both result in choice of redistribution at the expense of growth
Benevolent dictatorship	Better or worse than democracy	Better or worse than democracy	Better or worse than democracy
Predatory dictatorship	Strong preference for redistribution at the expense of growth	Moderate preference for redistribution at the expense of growth; identical to multi-issue democracy if the same group is in power	Mild preference for redistribution at the expense of growth

same group is in power, but the dictatorship will be radically worse if it permits a minority to maintain power. In democracy, the problem diminishes the larger the ethnic majority and if there is single-issue politics.

In ethnically fragmented societies, predatory dictatorships will be highly damaging, with narrow groups exploiting their power at the expense of overall growth. In ethnically homogenous societies, predatory dictatorships may be just as narrowly based and hence just as damaging, but they will tend to be less narrowly based. Outside the context of dictatorship, ethnic fragmentation does not appear likely to produce markedly worse politics than ethnic homogeneity, and indeed the political system might work better.

D. EMPIRICALLY TESTING THE HYPOTHESES

These analytic predictions are empirically testable using the conventional Barro–Lee dataset, which includes all countries for which sufficient data are available. The data are arranged so that the dependent variable is the growth rate for a country over the period 1960–1990. Explanatory variables help to control for non-policy influences on growth, such as whether a country is landlocked, but policies are excluded as explanatory variables because these are the result of the political process.

First, the effects of ethnic diversity were tested. Recall that the Easterly and Levine proposition is that ethnic diversity is directly detrimental because it produces bad political decisions. Previously, it has been argued that this is not sufficiently nuanced; in democracies, the effects of ethnic politics are likely to be small and ambiguously signed, whereas in dictatorships ethnic loyalties are liable to intensify predatory behavior. This more nuanced proposition is tested against that of Easterly and Levine by interacting the measure of ethnic diversity (ELF) with a measure of political rights. This interaction term is highly significant and large.[23] Ethnic diversity has no adverse effects on growth in fully democratic societies but reduces growth by up to three percentage points in dictatorships.

The effects of ethnic dominance were also tested. Recall that, unlike in the case of ethnic fragmentation, ethnic dominance was predicted to reduce growth regardless of the political system. The magnitude of this negative effect is predicted to diminish with the size of the dominant group. This effect can be approximated by introducing a dummy variable that takes the value of unity over a particular size range of the largest ethnic group. Various ranges were evaluated. For example, it may be that a group is able to control national policy even if its share of the population is slightly less 50%. Conversely, a group with 95% of the population may find that the benefits of exploiting the minority are outweighed by the costs. It was found that for all possible values the sign of the ethnic dominance dummy is negative but the effect is at its maximum and the significance level is highest for the range 45–60%. This regression provides some weak support for the hypothesis that ethnic dominance is detrimental to the growth process. Societies with such a dominant ethnic group on average lose over half a percentage point of the growth rate. The effect is only statistically significant at 18%, far below conventional levels. However, the results are still of some interest. The significance level measures how often we would get this result by chance were we drawing a sample of 102 countries randomly from a much larger population of countries. In fact, 102 countries is quite close to being the entire population. Thus, we should conclude that on average countries with ethnic dominance had quite substantially slower per capita growth, but that there was considerable variation around this average. The inclusion of ethnic dominance does not alter the coefficient on the interaction of ethnic diversity and the political system, or its level of significance.

To conclude, both theoretical reasons and empirical evidence support three propositions on the effect of ethnic differentiation on political outcomes. The most important proposition is the negative one that in democracies, except in circumstances of dominance, ethnic diversity does not significantly adversely affect economic performance. Contrary to the apparent implications of Easterly and Levine and Alesina *et al.*, ethnic diversity, in general, therefore, is not problematic for economic policy. The second proposition is that ethnically diverse societies are peculiarly ill suited to dictatorship. This is precisely contrary to the self-justifying arguments of third-world dictators. The third proposition is that ethnic dominance is likely to worsen economic performance, regardless of the political system. The empirical evidence for this proposition is weaker. Further, most ethnically diverse societies are not characterized by dominance. Taken together, these propositions evidently do not amount to a condemnation of ethnic diversity.

Recall that the microeconomics literature on ethnicity in organizations has found some quite substantial negative effects. At least within the public sector, there was disturbing evidence that ethnic diversity is detrimental to performance. Evidently, this does not scale up to worse overall national economic performance. Perhaps this is because the effects on public sector performance are too small to show up in aggregate performance. Alternatively, it may be because worse performance in the public sector is offset by enhanced performance in the private sector. The New Institutional Economics perspective is after all that kin groups enhance the economic performance of the group. Possibly, in the public sector the benefit for the group is the capture of rents (as in Ghana), whereas in the private sector it is enhanced productivity.

To test the proposition that ethnic diversity is detrimental in the public sector but advantageous in the private sector, we need to be able to distinguish factor productivity in the two sectors; a convenient new dataset is that of Collier *et al.*,[24] who built estimates of public and private capital stocks for 58 countries and estimated an aggregate production function. Their analysis is unrelated to ethnic diversity, as it investigates the effect of capital flight, but it can easily be adapted to our purpose here. Their production function explains GDP in terms of the public and private capital stocks and labor. Although it is estimated as a cross-section using period averages for 1980–1989, country fixed effects are included, being derived from a generalized method of moments growth model for 1960–1995.[25] For 56 of these countries, data are available on the extent of ethnic diversity, and so for this sample it is possible to investigate whether ethnic diversity raises the productivity of private capital and lowers the productivity of public capital. Testing for this requires the addition of two interaction terms to the production function, one for ethnic diversity and the private capital stock and the other for ethnic diversity and the public capital stock.

Details of the variables and the method are given in Collier et al.[26] The following observations can be made. The addition of the two interaction terms is jointly significant at the 10% level: ethnic diversity does significantly change the productivity of capital. Further, the signs of the two interaction terms differ: Societies that are diverse have a higher productivity of private capital than those that are homogenous, but they have a lower productivity of public capital. Upon testing for whether the coefficients on the two interaction terms are significantly different from each other, they narrowly failed the test. There is a 15.8% risk that ethnic diversity does not differentially affect the productivity of public and private capital. Nevertheless, the balance of probabilities is sufficiently strongly in favor of a difference that it is worth investigating the size of the differential effects implied by the coefficients. In this sample, the mean of ethnic diversity as measured by ELF is 47 and the standard deviation is 30. Next, Collier et al. compared the productivity of capital among countries one standard deviation above and below the mean—that is, with ELF values of 17 and 77, respectively. The productivity of each type of capital now depends upon the net effect of the interaction term and the direct effect. The productivity of public capital is 10% lower in the ethnically diverse society (77) than in the ethnically more homogenous society (17). By contrast, the productivity of private capital is 5% higher in the ethnically diverse society than in the more homogenous society. These orders of magnitude are neither too large to be credible nor so small as to be without interest. Further, because the private capital stock is usually larger than the public capital stock, differential effects of this magnitude would in aggregate approximately offset each other, hence being consistent with the previous result that in democratic societies diversity does not have an adverse effect on aggregate economic performance.

Before considering the implications further, we turn to the effect of diversity on the risk of civil conflict. Even if diversity is normally unproblematic for the economy, it might sometimes be disastrous for the society.

IV. DOES ETHNIC DIVERSITY CAUSE CIVIL WAR?

While popular discussion of the cause of civil conflict focuses upon the motivations of the rebels, it can be more revealing to focus on how rebellion is organized and financed, in effect, emphasizing the budget constraint rather than preferences as an explanation for variation in behavior. The basic theoretical idea is presented, followed by discussion of the econometric evidence that supports this model over alternative accounts that emphasize rebel grievances. Taking the theoretical results as a baseline, I then investigate how ethnicity affects the risk of conflict through three routes.

A. The Financing of Rebellion

The basic theoretical analysis treats the motivation for rebellion as exogenous. In effect, let us assume that in all societies there are some groups keen to further their objectives through organized large-scale violence and what determines whether this happens is the feasibility of maintaining a military organization opposed to the government but on its territory.

A rebel organization must be able to defend itself from government forces. This military survival constraint depends partly upon geography and partly upon the ability of the government to finance defense expenditures. The constraint determines the minimum size of rebellion that is viable, and, in turn, this affects the cost of rebellion. The larger a rebel organization must be to survive militarily, the more demanding the financing requirements. The other component of the cost of rebellion is the ease or difficulty of recruitment of rebel labor. While the size of the government army can be assumed to be in steady state, the rebel organization is wholly dependent upon current recruitment and so is disproportionately sensitive to the current tightness of the labor market. Hence, the costs of rebel recruitment are assumed to be increasing both in per capita income and in the rate of growth. The ability to rebel, then, depends upon the available sources of finance. In the basic model, the source of rebel finance is predation of primary commodity exports. These activities are assumed to be particularly vulnerable in view of their location-specific rents and their long transport routes to ports. Hence, the basic predictions of the analysis are that the risks of rebellion will be increases in primary commodity dependence and decreases in per capita income and the rate of growth.[27]

Although this abstracts from the motivation for rebellion, the conditions under which a rebellion is financially viable are also those under which it is financially attractive. Hence, a more cynical interpretation of this, and the supporting econometric evidence discussed later, is to see finance as *motivating* rather than merely *enabling* rebellion. The econometric evidence cannot discriminate between the two interpretations, but case study evidence sometimes points strongly to finance as a motivation. For example, during the civil war in Sierra Leone, the predation of the diamond fields by the RUF rebel organization could be interpreted as either enabling or motivating. However, during the peace negotiations, the rebel leader rejected the offer of the vice presidency, insisting additionally upon being Chairman of the Council of Mineral Resources. Such behavior is difficult to interpret as other than revealing motivation. Those rebellions that appear least related to financial motivation are ethnic liberation secession movements. However, even here the underlying motivation may often be the capture of primary commodity rents.

The financial rationale for secession on the part of rich districts was first modelled analytically by Buchanan and Faith.[28] Their insight can usefully be linked to Anderson's notion that political communities must be "imagined." The population of a district that initially imagines itself as belonging to the larger nation can reimagine itself as a distinct political community once natural resources are discovered. Because ethnic groups, like natural resources, are also geographically concentrated, the resulting political community may be broadly coincident with some ethnic group. Thus, the creation of a political community for the control of a region's natural resources may also create a political community for the ethnic group.

Three of the following five examples are related to oil discoveries and price shocks. In Zaire, copper and diamonds are concentrated in the southeast. The secessionist Katanga movement was formed in this region shortly after independence. In Nigeria, the oil discoveries of the 1960s were also concentrated in the southeast. The secessionist Biafra movement was formed in this region in 1967. In the United Kingdom, the oil discoveries were concentrated off the shores of Scotland. The secessionist Scottish National Party, after years of negligible electoral support, suddenly broke through in 1974, months after oil became valuable due to the hike in the oil price. In Indonesia, the oil discoveries were concentrated on the outer islands, notably Aceh, with a per capita GDP triple the national average. The secessionist Merdeka Aceh movement was formed in 1979 by a local businessman. In Ethiopia, the richest region was the coastal belt, which had been industrialized by the Italians; Eritrea had a per capita GDP double the national average. In 1951, the Eritrean population voted for federation with Ethiopia (suggesting that at that stage it was not an imagined nation), but a decade later the Ethiopian government dissolved the Federation and drastically reduced fiscal autonomy. The Eritrean Liberation Front was formed shortly after this dissolution. Four of these five new political communities went on to mount secessionist civil wars. In such situations, although the conflict takes on the appearance of a demand for ethnic liberation, ethnicity is secondary to geography. For example, the Eritrean secession aggregated nine different ethno-linguistic groups into a common political community while splitting the Tigrini ethno-linguistic group between Eritrea and Ethiopia. Hence, what appears to be a demand for ethnic liberation based on a primordial sense of identity, may more reasonably be interpreted as a root attempt to control lucrative primary commodities that has created the ethnic identity as a by-product.

B. QUANTITATIVE EMPIRICAL EVIDENCE

Collier and Hoeffler[29] have tested this model against alternative explanations of conflict based on the intensity of objective grievance. The dataset covers 161 countries over the period 1960–1999, arranged into 5-year subperiods, giving a total of 1288 potential observations. In 73 of these observations a civil war broke out. Here, a civil war is defined, as is conventional in the conflict literature, as a conflict between a government and an identifiable non-government organization which takes place on the territory of the government and causes at least 1000 combat-related deaths. We then try to explain why conflict erupted in these 73 instances but not in the other 1215 instances. Our methodology is that of logit regressions, with the risk being explained by the characteristics in the preceding 5-year period. We then use non-nested tests to compare the model with alternatives in which both ethnicity and various measures of grievance are included. The basic model performs surprisingly well, with around 30% of the variance explained and all variables significant with the expected signs and survives a battery of robustness tests.

The effects of primary commodity dependence are very powerful. Comparing two societies with otherwise mean characteristics, the risk of conflict is less than 1% if the society has no primary commodity exports, whereas it is 23% if such exports constitute a quarter of GDP. Nor is this simply a cross-section association. When the regression is run as a fixed-effects panel, so that the only variation in primary commodity export dependence is over time, the relationship remains the same. An increase in primary commodity dependence increases the risk of conflict.

The importance of primary commodities in conflict has recently been recognized outside the research community. The Nongovernmental Organization (NGO) Global Witness has conducted a campaign against "conflict diamonds," highlighting their role in the conflicts of Angola and Sierra Leone. De Beers, the world's largest diamond company, has ceased to purchase diamonds on the open market and has proposed a plan to tighten regulation of the market. With Antwerp as the world's major trading centre for diamonds, Europe is critical for the effective implementation of this plan. The objective is to create a substantial discount in the price rebel movements receive for diamonds, thereby squeezing them financially. A second primary commodity now recognized as central to rebellion is cocaine. For example, cocaine generates around $500 million annually for the FARC rebel movement in Colombia. Because OECD governments have persuaded developing country governments to make production illegal, they have created a demand for territory which is not under government control. Rebels supply such territory to drug growers in exchange for payment.[30]

Whereas primary commodity exports are thus important risk factors, some grievances widely assumed to fuel conflict appear to be unimportant. Neither the degree of income inequality nor the degree of political rights is significant, and their inclusion in the model is rejected by non-nested tests. There is some evidence from Europe that income inequality increases voter support for "revolutionary" propositions, but evidently such support does not translate into large-scale organized killing.[31] The unimportance of grievance variables strengthens the argument that large-scale organized killing is dependent upon the unusual circumstances that produce organizational feasibility more than upon motivation. Indeed, the only variables which non-nested tests show must be added to the basic model are three measures of ethnic and religious diversity.

Ethnicity enters the model in three ways. First, ethnic dominance might be a sufficiently compelling grievance factor that it affects the risk of conflict. The previous section discussed why with dominance there is both the ability and the incentive for the majority to exploit the minority. The structural permanence of this condition, and the inability of democracy to resolve it, may make organized violence more likely. In the simple theory of Section III, dominance abruptly becomes a problem once the group exceeds 50% of the electorate. This is also the point of maximum incentive to exploit. Thereafter, exploitation diminishes as the share of the majority group increases. In testing the effect of dominance on conflict risk, Collier and Hoeffler followed the same procedure as for its effects on economic performance, introducing a dummy variable that takes the value unity if the largest ethnic group is in a particular size range, the range being determined by experiment. They also tested this specification against a variable that simply measures the share of the population constituted by the largest ethnic group. So defined, societies with ethnic dominance have around double the risk of civil war of other societies. This is consistent with the theory that in this range majorities have both the ability and the incentive to exploit minorities. Evidently, given this structural problem, it is arbitrary whether the rebel group is drawn from the minority, as in Sri Lanka, or whether the minority preemptively controls the government but faces rebellion from within the majority, as in Burundi. While the model thus finds evidence that ethnic dominance is problematic, the scale of the effect should be kept in perspective. The effect of ethnic dominance can, according to the model, be fully offset for the mean country by reducing dependence upon primary commodities from 16% of GDP to 11%.

The second way by which ethnic diversity enters the model is through fragmentation. Recall that the rebel organization is assumed to need cohesion and for this must avoid recruiting across boundaries of identity. Societies fragmented by ethnicity or indeed by other types of identity thus pose greater problems for rebel organizations. A possible example of this is Irian Jaya in Indonesia. This province is dependent upon primary commodity exports, and over the past 30 years many small groups have attempted to mount armed opposition to rule from Indonesia. However, none of these groups succeeded in building a viable rebel organization of any scale. A likely reason for this is that Irian Jaya is so astonishingly ethnically fragmented, with some 450 distinct language groups; the groups simply cannot cohere into a military organization. In principle, the same effect would be generated by religious fractionalization as by ethnic fractionalization. Societies divided by both ethnicity and religion would potentially be even more protected from rebellion if the religious divisions were cross-cutting over the ethnic divisions. A society equally divided into e ethnic groups and r religious groups, with religion cross cutting ethnicity, would be divided into $e \cdot r$ distinct cells. Good data are available on the composition of societies according to religion, but unfortunately such data cannot be related to ethnic divisions. At one extreme, ethnic and religious divisions might be coincident, and at the other they may be perfectly cross cutting, so the empirical testing must allow for these possibilities. To incorporate the effects of religious fractionalization, Collier and Hoeffler built a measure of religious fractionalization (RF) precisely corresponding to the index of ethno-linguistic fractionalization.[32]

One possibility is that both ethnic diversity and religious diversity matter but that there is no interaction effect. To test for this, both measures were introduced into the logit regression. At the other extreme, only the interaction effect might matter. The interaction effect can be measured by constructing an index of social fractionalization which proxies the concept $e \cdot r$. The interaction term is approximately the product of the two measures of diversity, $ELF \cdot RF$. However, in the case of religious homogeneity and ethnic diversity, the measure of social fractionalization should collapse to the measure of ethnic diversity rather than to zero (and conversely, if there is religious diversity but ethnic homogeneity). To allow for this, Collier and Hoeffler measured the index of social fractionalization as the interaction term $ELF \cdot RF$ plus whichever is the maximum of ELF and RF. In practice, this is a very minor modification and the measure of social fractionalization performs virtually identically whether it is defined in this way or more simply as $ELF \cdot RF$. The interaction effect, social fractionalization, dominates the direct effects of religious and ethnic diversity. Indeed, once social fractionalization is included, neither direct effect is significant. Thus, ethnic and religious divisions are apparently usually cross-cutting. Not only does social fractionalization dominate the direct effects, it is highly significant with a *negative* sign and is a large effect. Hence, the risk of civil war is *lower* in societies fractionalized by ethnicity and religion. Such societies might well have higher levels of hatred, but this does not usually translate into large-scale organized killing.

This effect of ethnic and religious diversity also accounts for why so many civil wars *appear* to be caused by ethnic or religious hatreds. Most societies are to some degree diverse. Where rebellions occur in such societies, the organizational constraint of cohesion will tend to confine recruitment to a single cell of the ethno-religious matrix. Rebellion will be *patterned* by ethnicity and religion even if it is not *caused* by ethnic and religious differences. A good example of this process is the recent violent attempted coup d'etat in Fiji.[33] The demands of the coup leader, George Speight, were ostensibly entirely related to ethnic power. He claimed to want a transfer of power from the Indian part of the population to the aboriginal group. However, beneath this apparent instance of ethnically motivated political violence was a quite different story. Fiji has the world's largest plantations of mahogany. Indeed, it is estimated as supplying two-thirds of the entire world market, thus constituting the single most important asset in Fiji. In 1998, the government began the process of putting out to tender the management contract for the mahogany plantations. Two companies were shortlisted: the Common-wealth Development Corporation (CDC) and a private American company. The American company hired a local businessman as its representative, none other than George Speight. Eventually, the government awarded the contract to the CDC. Shortly after losing the contract, Speight launched his coup. The loss of the contract by an American company to the Commonwealth Development Corporation evidently did not provide a very robust basis for a popular political uprising against a democratic government. Speight indeed loudly denied that the motivation was the loss of the mahogany contract. Instead, as noted above, he chose ethnicity as his rallying cry: The government happened to be drawn from a predominantly Indian party, whereas Speight was not Indian. In short, the conflict was ethnically *patterned*, but not ethnically *caused*.

Taken together, the effects of ethnic dominance and cross-cutting fractiona-lization produce a broadly nonmonotonic relationship between the number of ethnic groups and the risk of conflict. Moving from one to two groups almost inevitably switches the society into ethnic dominance. Usually, this is not fully offset by the benign effect of the increased fractionalization, so the society overall becomes more at risk. Moving from two to many groups almost inevitably switches the society back out of ethnic dominance and gradually increases fragmentation, making the society safer than were it homogenous.

The third way by which ethnic diversity enters the model is through diasporas living in Europe and America. Although the basic model considers only primary commodity predation as a source of rebel finance, an obvious extension is to consider financial contributions from diasporas living in high-income countries. Angustures and Pascal (1996)[34] provide a chilling series of case studies showing how such diasporas are currently organized by rebel movements to finance conflict. This role of diasporas has a long history. For example, Irish-Americans assisted the secession of Eire from the United Kingdom, Jewish-Americans assisted the secession of Israel, Eritreans in Europe and America were the main source of finance for the secession of Eritrea from Ethiopia, and currently Tamils in Canada are financing the attempt of the Tamil Tigers to secede from Sri Lanka. Collier and Hoeffler investigated the effect of diasporas more formally by using data on diasporas in the United States. The size of the diaspora for, say, Somalia was measured as the number of people born in Somalia but resident in the United States, relative to the resident population of Somalia. Because civil war increases emigration, a large diaspora might simply proxy previous conflict. In order to control for this, a migration model was estimated based upon income differences and time lags; in all cases where there had been a civil war, the actual diaspora population in America subsequent to the outbreak of the conflict was replaced with a predicted population based on the counterfactual of continued peace. Both with and without this correction, the larger the diaspora, the greater the risk of conflict. The risk applied, however, only in post-conflict situations. Post-conflict, countries temporarily have a very high risk of further conflict. This is not spuriously due to an omitted variable; a dummy variable for whether a country has had a previous conflict is insignificant. Rather, conflict generates risks, which gradually fade again. The effect of diasporas is significantly and substantially to slow down the rate at which these risks fade. Large diasporas appear to keep conflicts alive. This is consistent both with the case study evidence and with theory. Diasporas in OECD economies have the income to finance rebel organizations, often have romantic attachments to their ethnic identity to counter the anomie they experience in their host societies, and do not suffer the consequences of the violence they finance. They are consequently often more extreme than the populations they purport to defend.

In order to tap the potential that a diaspora offers, a rebel organization needs to sell ethnic vengeance. Hence, rebellions need to generate a discourse of ethnic hatred. Thus, in most societies not only will rebellions be organized along ethnic lines, but they will also be justified in terms of ethnic grievance and supported by ethnic diasporas. It is unsurprising that in these circumstances ethnic diversity will appear to cause violent conflict. Nevertheless, these appearances are entirely consistent with the big brute fact that ethnic diversity usually makes a society safer. Whether societies suffer an outbreak of civil war is determined more by the financial and military opportunities for rebellion than by ethnic hatreds or other objective grievances.

V. POLICY IMPLICATIONS

We start with two charges that are widely made against societies in which ethnicity is the basis for social identity. Ethnically differentiated societies would find cooperation difficult and victimization of minorities easy. The inability to cooperate would manifest itself in dysfunctional politics and consequently worse economic performance. The tendency to victimization of minorities would manifest itself as dysfunctional societies beset by violent civil conflict. Such sweeping charges are not justified either theoretically or empirically. As a first approximation, ethnically diverse democracies do not have worse economic performance and are actually safer than homogenous societies.

The fallacious popular orthodoxy that ethnically diverse societies are unviable is directly reflected in current policy towards multiethnic societies. Despair has encouraged radical social and political engineering, involving population movements and intricate border redesign and secession, in order to achieve ethnically less diverse, and hence supposedly more viable, states. The trend to secession since the end of the Cold War, much of it violent, has been remarkable: Eritrea, Slovakia, Slovenia, Croatia, Macedonia, Bosnia, Chechnya, Quebec, Belgium, Kosovo, Montenegro, the Western Sahara, East Timor, Somaliland, Aceh, and the Niger Delta are all recent examples of completed, incipient, or potential creation of small ethnic states. The author has argued that such secessions are often at root economic rather than ethnic. The patina of legitimacy associated with ethnic historicism and political grievance should disguise neither the tendency of secessionist violence to be concentrated in regions well endowed with primary commodities, nor the absence of a statistical relationship with inequality and political oppression. Secessionist states would probably be *more*, rather than less prone to conflict. It is self-evident that as the number of countries increases so does the risk of *international* war. For example, the secession of Eritrea from Ethiopia has not brought peace but rather reclassified a conflict from a civil war to an international war, bringing with it a severe cost escalation as both parties are now able to field an airforce. However, the more telling point is that such states are also liable to be more prone to *civil* conflict.

First, if endowments of primary commodities tend to be the basis for secession, the resulting states would be more dependent upon primary commodities than if they were part of larger political entities. As an approximation, each extra percentage point of dependence upon primary commodities raises the risk of conflict by one percentage point. Second, secessionist states would have less ethnic heterogeneity. Recall that, contrary to popular perception, this would increase the risk of conflict. Third, as secessions occur from ethnically fragmented states, the residual state is liable to switch from ethnic fragmentation to ethnic dominance. The secessionist state is also more likely to be characterized by ethnic dominance than by ethnic homogeneity. On average, this doubles the risk of conflict. Such a process occurred in the former Yugoslavia. The secession of Slovenia (with international support) created the precedent for the secession of Croatia, which in turn converted the Yugoslav state from being ethnically fragmented to a Serb majority. The Serb government thereby acquired the power to discriminate in favor of its own supporters. Thus, the main policy implication is perhaps that the international community has a stronger interest than is currently recognized in the preservation of large, multiethnic societies such as Russia, Indonesia, and Nigeria.

Because primary commodity dependence increases the risk of conflict, which in ethnically diverse societies then becomes organized on ethnic lines, a further implication is the desirability of export diversification. In Africa, dependence on primary commodities has actually increased over the past 30 years and this may have contributed to the region's rising incidence of conflict. By contrast, over the same period other developing regions have on average sharply reduced primary commodity dependence and some of this difference is presumably attributable to economic policy.

While popular opinion has greatly exaggerated the difficulties faced by ethnically diverse societies, the author has argued that diversity does create some problems. At the level of the individual organization, ethnic identity sometimes enhances cooperation and sometimes impedes it. Ethnic group identity is interpreted by institutional economics as an endogenous response to the need for cooperation, and evidence from both households and businesses illustrates that ethnicity can be useful in enforcing reciprocity. However, in the public sector, there is evidence that ethnically differentiated organizations encounter problems. Thus, a third policy issue is how best to respond to the problem of public sector performance in ethnically diverse societies. Two approaches that are not exclusive follow. Ethnic employment patronage in the public sector can be countered by greater transparency in hiring and promotion, perhaps reinforced by targets and quota protection for minorities. In developed countries most large organizations now have such explicit policies to safeguard minorities. Thus, established procedures are known to be effective and could be implemented in the public sectors of ethnically diverse societies. An additional approach is to accept that the public sector may be relatively less effective in diverse societies than in homogenous societies, so that the boundary between public and private activity should be drawn somewhat differently.

At the level of aggregate economic performance there is an important exception to the general proposition that ethnic diversity is not a problem. Dictatorships are an average substantially more damaging in ethnically diverse societies than in homogenous societies. Hence, a fourth policy implication is the need for democratization in those ethnically diverse societies which are currently dictatorships. Encouraging democratization is partly simply a matter of the climate of opinion. If the claim by dictators that they are the alternative to chaos is called into question, then their hold on power is weakened; however, it is also a policy choice for OECD governments. For many years, Western governments actively propped up dictators.

A fifth policy implication concerns societies characterized by ethnic dominance. There is a theoretical argument and some weak supporting evidence that such countries have worse economic performance. By itself this would not constitute a sufficient basis for policy intervention. However, there is stronger evidence that ethnic dominance increases the risk of violent civil conflict. Taken together, this suggests a need for better protection of minority rights in societies with ethnic majorities. In developing countries, the struggle for democracy has generally taken the form of empowering the majority against an elite, whether colonial or domestic military. Rights to equal treatment, individual or group, now need to be incorporated into the popular conception of democracy. The recent European Union concern to include protection of minorities as a condition for the continued inclusion of the Austrian government is a powerful practical instance of this redefinition.

A final policy issue, particularly pertinent for European governments, is the role of ethnic diasporas living in Europe and the United States in promoting violent conflict and separatist movements in their countries of origin. Individual OECD governments are somewhat reluctant to police the external activities of diaspora organizations; often these organizations have some influence in host country political parties. Because of the collective nature of the benefits, contrasted with the individual incidence of the costs, OECD governments need to coordinate their policy towards diasporas. International policy coordination is usually difficult and is only worthwhile if the benefits are substantial. It would, however, be ironic if the peaceful, prosperous, and increasingly multiethnic societies of the OECD inadvertently financed the break-up of developing countries into violent and impoverished ethnic theme parks.

VI. SUMMARY

Ethnically differentiated societies are often regarded as dysfunctional, with poor economic performance and a high risk of violent civil conflict. The author argues that this perception is not well founded. *Dominance*, in which one group constitutes a majority, is distinguished from *fractionalization*, in which there are many small groups. In terms of overall economic performance, both theoretically and empirically, fractionalization is normally unproblematic in democracies, although it can be damaging in dictatorships. Fractionalized societies have worse public sector performance, but this is offset by better private sector performance. Societies characterized by dominance are in principle likely to have worse economic performance, but empirically the effect is weak. In terms of the risk of civil war, both theoretically and empirically, fractionalization actually makes societies safer, while dominance increases the risk of conflict. A policy implication is that fractionalized societies are viable and secession should be discouraged.

DISCUSSION QUESTIONS

1. Why do OECD countries get involved in African conflicts? Why do diasporas finance conflict?
2. What is the relationship between sources of finance such as primary commodity exports and rebellion and conflict? What are the effects of primary commodity dependence on the risk of conflict? Illustrate your answers.
3. What is the difference between dominance and fractionalization in ethnically diverse societies and how do they affect economic performance and the likelihood of conflict?
4. Compare and contrast the consequences of ethnic diversity as outlined by the author with those found in literature exemplified by Easterly and Levine (1997).
5. In looking at the relationship between ethnic diversity and dysfunctional politics the author uses two approaches to analyze the democratic political process. Provide a detailed discussion of these two approaches.
6. Based on your understanding of the arguments presented in this chapter, to what extent can we really generalize about many of the outcomes in multiethnic societies? Justify your answer.
7. Using the evidence presented in this chapter, present arguments to counter the prevailing view that ethnically differentiated societies are often dysfunctional, with poor economic performance and high risk of violent conflict.
8. What are the major policy implications of ethnic diversity and conflict in Africa?

NOTES

[*] Reproduced with permission from Blackwell Publishers. To view the complete paper, please consult Collier, Paul (2000) *Economic Policy*. The findings, interpretations, and conclusions expressed in this paper are entirely those of the author. They do not necessarily represent the view of the World Bank, its Executive Directors, or the countries they represent. I would like to thank the editors, a referee, and *Economic Policy* commentators for suggestions. I would also like to acknowledge the work of Anke Hoeffler on the regressions reported in the Appendices. Those Appendices, drawn from Collier and Hoeffler (2000), are joint work. The dataset on civil wars has been built by Anke Hoeffler and Nick Sambanis. I have also benefited from written comments by Nat Colletta, Macartan Humphreys, and Michael Ross and from a seminar presentation at CERDI, Universite d'Auvergne.

[1] Easterly, W. and Levine, R. (1997) "Africa's Growth Tragedy: Policies and Ethnic Divisions," *Quarterly Journal of Economics*, 112(4), 1203–1250.

[2] Bisin, A. and Verdier, T. (2000) "Beyond the Melting Pot: Cultural Transmission, Marriage and the Evolution of Ethnic and Religious Traits," *Quarterly Journal of Economics*, 115(3), 955–988.

[3]Colley, L. (1992) *Britons: Forging the Nation*, New Haven, CT: Yale University Press; Weber, E. (1975) *Peasants into Frenchmen*, Stanford, CA: Stanford University Press.

[4]Posner, R.A. (1980) "A Theory of Primitive Society with Special Reference to Law," *Journal of Law and Economics*, 23(1), 1–53.

[5]Greif, A. (1992) "Institutions and International Trade: Lessons from the Commercial Revolution," *American Economic Review*; Biggs, T., Raturi, M., and Srivastava, P. (1996) *Enforcement of Contracts in an African Credit Market*, RPED discussion paper, Washington, D.C.: World Bank.

[6]Anderson, B. (1983) *Imagined Communities*, London: Verso.

[7]Posner, R.A. (1980) "A Theory of Primitive Society with Special Reference to Law," *Journal of Law and Economics*.

[8]Posner, D.N. (1999) *Ethnic Fractionalization in Africa*, Los Angeles: Dept. of Political Science, UCLA.

[9]Miguel, T. (1999) *Ethnic Diversity and School Funding in Kenya*, Boston, MA: Dept. of Economics, Harvard University.

[10]Alesina, A., Baqir, R., and Easterly, W. (1999) "Public Goods and Ethnic Divisions," *Quarterly Journal of Economics*, 114(4), 1243–1284; Collier, P. and Garg, A. (1999) "On Kin Groups and Wages in the Ghanaian Labor Market," *Oxford Bulletin of Economics and Statistics*, 61(2), 133–151; Easterly, W. and Levine, R. (1997) "Africa's Growth Tragedy: Politics and Ethnic Divisions," *Quarterly Journal of Economics*, 112(4), 1203–1250.

[11]Arcand, J.-L., Guillaumont, P., and Guillaumont, S. (2000) "How To Make a Tragedy: On The Alleged Effect of Ethnicity on Growth," *Journal of International Development*.

[12]Horowitz, D. (1985) *Ethnic Groups in Conflict*, Berkeley: University of California Press; Gurr, T.R. (1993) *Minorities at Risk: A Global View of Ethnopolitical Conflicts*, Washington, D.C.: U.S. Institute of Peace; Emminghaus, W., Kimmel, P., and Stewart, E. (1998) "Primal Violence Illuminating Culture's Dark Side," in E. Weiner, Ed., *The Handbook of Inter-Ethnic Coexistence*, New York: Continuum Publishing, p. 140.

[13]Fearon, J.D. and Laitin, D.D. (1999) *Weak States, Rough Terrain, and Large-Scale Ethnic Violence Since 1945*, Stanford, CA: Dept. of Political Science, Stanford University; Bates, R. (1999) *Ethnicity, Capital Formation and Conflict*, Social Capital Initiative Working Paper 12, Washington, D.C.: World Bank, p. 31; Grossman, H.I. (1991) "A General Equilibrium Model of Insurrections," *American Economic Review*, 81(4), 912–921; Collier, P. (2000a) "Ethnicity, Politics and Economic Performance," *Economics and Politics*, 12(3), 225–245; Collier, P. (2000b) "Rebellion as a Quasi-Criminal Activity," *Journal of Conflict Resolution*; Hoeffler, A. (1998) "Econometric Studies of Growth, Convergence and Conflicts," D. Phil. thesis, London: University of Oxford; Collier, P. and Hoeffler, A. (1998) "On the Economic Causes of Civil War," *Oxford Economic Papers*; Collier, P. and Hoeffler, A. (2000) *Greed and Grievance in Civil War*, Policy Research Working Paper 2355, Washington D.C.: World Bank.

[14]Downs, A. (1957) *An Economic Theory of Democracy*, New York: Harper & Row.

[15]Inman, R.P. and Rubinfeld, D.R. (1997) "The Political Economy of Federalism," in D. Mueller, Ed., *Perspectives on Public Choice*, Cambridge, MA: Cambridge University Press.

[16]Drazen, A. (2000) *Political Economy in Macroeconomics*, Princeton, NJ: Princeton University Press, pp. 71–72.

[17]Hardin, R. (1997) "Economic Theories of the State," in D. Mueller, Ed., *Perspectives on Public Choice*, Cambridge, MA: Cambridge University Press; Drazen, A. (2000) *Political Economy in Macroeconomics*, Princeton, NJ: Princeton University Press, pp. 71–72.

[18]See, for example, Weingast, B. (1979) "A Rational Choice Perspective on Congressional Norms," *American Journal of Political Science*, 23(2), 245–262.

[19]Coate, S. and Morris, S. (1995) "On the Form of Transfers to Special Interests," *Journal of Political Economy*, 103(6), 1210–1235.

[20]Schofield, N. (1997) "Multiparty Electoral Politics," in D. Mueller, Ed., *Perspectives on Public Choice*, Cambridge, MA: Cambridge University Press.

[21]Olson, M. (1991) "Autocracy, Democracy and Prosperity," in R. Zeckhauser, Ed., *Strategy and Choice*, Cambridge MA: MIT Press.

[22]Benabou, R. (1996) "Inequality and Growth," in B. Bernanke and J. Rotemberg, Eds., *NBER Macroeconomics Annual*, Cambridge MA: MIT Press.

[23]The baseline result is from Collier (2000a), which discusses the sources of variables and shows that the result is robust to a range of alternative specifications and dominates any direct effects of political rights and ethnic diversity. The new sample adds eight countries for which data were not previously available. Further results available from the author show that no other size of group comes as close to being significant, and that the addition of an interaction term between this dummy variable and political rights is completely insignificant.

[24]Collier, P., Hoeffler, A., and Pattillo, C. (2001) "Flight Capital as a Portfolio Choice," *World Bank Economic Review*, 15(1), 55–80.

[25]Hoeffler, A. (1998) "Economic Studies of Growth, Convergence and Conflicts, Ph.D. thesis, London: University of Oxford.

[26]For instance, the estimation of the capital stocks is described in Appendix IV in Collier *et al.* (2001), and Appendix I describes the production function. Hoeffler (1998) generates the country fixed effects. Taking an example, the productivity of public capital in a country with ELF = 17 is thus $0.192 + (0.487/17) = 0.221$, whereas with ELF = 77 productivity would be 0.198. Similarly, the productivity of private capital with the two different values of ELF would be 0.426 and 0.448.

[27]For a formal analysis, see Collier, P. (2000) "Rebellion as a Quasi-Criminal Activity," *Journal of Conflict Resolution*, 44(6), 839–853. Empirically, Collier and Hoeffler (2000) found that the risk of conflict increases strongly in the share of primary commodity exports until the latter are around 26% of GDP, beyond which risk diminishes.

[28]Buchanan, J.M. and Faith, R.L. (1987) "Secession and the Limits of Taxation: Towards a Theory of Internal Exit," *American Economic Review*, 77(5), 1023–1031.

[29]Collier and Hoeffler (1998), "On Economic Causes of Civil War," *Oxford Economic Papers*," 50(4), 563–573; "Greed and Grievance in Civil War," Development Research Group, The World Bank, Mimeo.

[30]Brito, D.L. and Intriligator, M.D. (1992) "Narco-Traffic and Guerrilla Warfare: A New Symbiosis," *Defence Economics*.

[31]MacCulloch, R. (1999) *What Makes a Revolution*, Working Paper B24, Bonn: Center for European Integration Studies.

[32]For details see Collier and Hoeffler (2000).

[33]Frank, R. (2000) "Fiji Mahogany Fuels Latest Resource Battle in Troubled Region," *The Wall Street Journal*, September 13, p. A1.

[34]Angoustures, A. and Pascal, V. (1996) "Diasporas et Financement des Conflicts," in F. Jean, and J.-C. Rufin, Eds., *Economie des Guerres Civiles*, Paris: Hachette.

CHAPTER 9

Health and Economic Development

MARIO J. AZEVEDO

Department of African American and African Studies, University of North Carolina,
Charlotte, North Carolina 28223

KEY TERMS

Diarrhea
Disability-Adjusted Life Years (DALYs)
Ecosystem
Epidemiology
Guinea worm disease
Health
HIV/AIDS
Infant mortality rate
Infectious versus chronic diseases
International Monetary Fund (IMF)
Life expectancy at birth
Literacy
Malaria

Malnutrition
Material mortality ratio
Measles
Onchocerciasis
Polio
Primary Health Care (PHC)
Schistosomiasis
Sub-Saharan Africa
Trypanosomiasis
WHO
World Bank
Yellow fever

I. INTRODUCTION

The issue of interdependence between the state of a community's or nation's economic progress and the health of its people is slowly coming to prominence among scholars, international agency decision-makers, and financial under-writers of projects in developing countries. The focus of this chapter is the state of Africa's health care and its impact on the economic welfare of the continent. Within this general context, such issues as the impact of colonial legacy on the structure of health care, the nature of health policies on the continent, post-independence leaders' initiatives on health care, and the impact of international donors and multinational financial and business corporations, as well as climatic factors are discussed. Essentially, Africa's environmental disease factor is overwhelming the continent, as the health and economic conditions of Africans are getting worse than they were during the early years of independence. Recently, international financial agencies and several multinational corporations have exerted pressure on the African states that has endangered the lives and well-being of the Africans in their unscrupulous pursuit of profit and the political and economic hegemony over a seemingly powerless continent led by generally unconcerned, weak, and disunited autocrats.

As a result, Africa's healthcare system is in total disarray and unable to cope with the old and newly emerging diseases that are having an unprecedented negative impact on Africans' ability to work and improve the living standards of their predominantly young population. For the sake of completeness and clarity, it seems appropriate at this juncture to alert the reader that the United Nations defines health as "a state of complete physical, mental, and social well-being and not merely the absence of disease or infirmity." According to many epidemiologists, however, this definition ought to include the existence of conditions that promote "fulfilling and satisfying lives." To many Africans, this concept of health is out of reach because there is no day in their lives that does not bring affliction.

II. ECOLOGY AND THE EPIDEMIOLOGICAL FACTOR

In contrast to the Western world, the African continent suffers less from deadly chronic diseases than from infectious and parasitic illnesses that decimate millions of Africans, especially the young, the old, and women. While infectious are acute and sudden diseases caused by viruses, bacteria, and fungi, chronic diseases, such as cancer and cardiovascular ailments, are slower and at times less painful at the onset but in the long run they are often deadlier than the infectious diseases. With about 80% of its land mass located within the tropics, Africa has experienced endemic and pandemic disease eruptions over the past 150 years. In fact, when Africans seem to be winning the battle against some types of diseases, as is the case with smallpox, eradicated in 1977, new and reemerging diseases cause Africa to move one step forward and two steps backward, as the case of today's HIV/AIDS crisis illustrates. What are the major killer diseases in Africa as the world enters the 21st century? The following section is a general overview of the illnesses that affect the continent, especially Sub-Saharan Africa, given that each country's sociophysical ecology has its own unique disease pattern.

Of all the maladies, malaria is the most widespread and most deadly infectious tropical disease in Africa. Malaria is caused by four species of the protozoa (parasite) genus, *Plasmodium*: *P. falciparum* being the most widespread in Africa. It is transmitted from human to human by the Anopheles mosquito and is characterized by chills, fever, anemia, and an enlarged spleen in the patient. Even though several experiments have been conducted in an effort to prevent infections, no vaccine is yet available. However, chloroquine or a combination of quinine, perymethamine, and sulfones constitute effective treatment. Worldwide, malaria yearly infects 300 million people, of whom 90% (270 million) are found in Africa. It is estimated that malaria kills between 500,000 and 1.2 million people in Africa, mostly children ages less than 5 years. Discounting unreported cases, experts estimate that, in the course of a year, an African gets an average of 300 infectious mosquito bites, at times affecting about 80% of the population, as is the case in Kenya.[1] Schistosomiasis, bilharzia, or bilharziasis, which is transmitted through water snails, causes liver, urinary, and intestinal damage. It affects 140 million people in Africa, with an unknown high attending death rate. Experts note that the building of water projects such as dams in Africa for economic development have unwittingly increased the snail population that infects humans when the latter come in contact with them in the waters.

Notwithstanding the fact that the effective and safe Enders vaccine has been available since 1962, measles, an endemic, infectious, and skin disease transmitted through direct contact with droplets spread from the nose or throat out of a paramyxovirus-infected person, kills thousands of children less than 3 years old. Figures on death rates from diarrhea are unfortunately unavailable in Africa (proving, as experts have noted, the sorry state of the African healthcare system). Yet, recurrent epidemics of the disease on the continent are well known throughout the world. Affecting children primarily, diarrhea frequently occurs (up to five times a day) in the form of watery stools that at times contain pus, mucus, blood (dysentery), and excessive amounts of fat. When untreated, diarrhea leads to dehydration, electrolyte imbalance (e.g., lack of potassium, calcium, phosphates, and magnesium), and death. In fact, it is estimated that a child less than 5 years old faces five times the risk of having diarrhea per year, a 10% probability of getting it in a given year, and a 14% probability of dying from it. The harmful effect of diarrhea is that it accounts for 25% of the other infant illnesses and is the cause of 15% of children's hospital visits each year. Unfortunately, World Health Organization (WHO) studies also indicate that 37% of all diarrheal bouts in the world occur in Sub-Saharan Africa, where only one-half of the affected children receive oral rehydration therapy (ORT), as opposed to 70% of children living in North Africa and Asia.[2]

The incidence of tuberculosis (TB) accelerated during the colonial period as a result of increased intercommunication, forced labor settlements, work in the mines and factories, and overcrowded conditions in urban areas. Tuberculosis is an infectious ailment caused by an acid-fast bacillus called *Mycobacterium tuberculosis*, usually transmitted to the lungs through inhalation or ingestion of infected droplets. Symptoms include chest pain, inflammation of lung membranes, loss of appetite, weight loss, fever, night sweats, coughing up of sputum with pus, and shortness of breath. Although there is an effective vaccine against it, about 171 million people are still affected in Africa, and out of 1.4 million new cases in 1990, for example, 600,000 people died.[3] Of course, the re-emergence of TB worldwide and the resistance of *Mycobacterium* to old drugs make the case the more ominous for Africa. Since the advent of HIV/AIDS, for example, the incidence of tuberculosis has skyrocketed by 140% in Burundi and 180% in Malawi, just to name some of the most affected countries in Africa.

In regard to TB, pneumonia, bronchitis, and other diseases of the respiratory system, the grave conditions in Africa should not be underestimated. Experts hold the view that an African child faces at least 10 infectious respiratory ailments (IRAs) each year and has a 25% probability of getting one some day. Apparently, IRAs are responsible for 55–60% of children's diseases and for 17% of their visits to healthcare facilities. Indeed, although vaccines against many IRAs are available, 20% of children's deaths in Africa are attributed to infectious respiratory diseases.[4] Yellow fever and poliomyelitis are also deadly ailments. Carried by a mosquito as the vector, yellow fever causes headaches, fever, liver disease, vomiting, and bleeding in the patient. Poliomyelitis (or simply polio) is a viral disease transmitted from person to person that can cause paralysis, accompanied by severe cases of irritation of the brain membranes or meninges, resulting in pain and stiffness in the victim's back.

However, both of these diseases are preventable through vaccine. Lymphatic filariasis, which can cause elephantiasis, affects 90 million people worldwide but mainly in Africa and Asia. (Elephantiasis is the enlargement and hardening of the lower body from blockage of lymphatic ducts caused by parasitic worms.) Onchocerciasis, or river blindness, is a disease caused by a black fly that lays eggs and worms under the human skin, affecting the eyes through irritation, and can sometimes lead to blindness. River blindness infects 17 million people worldwide, but mostly in Africa. Again, many of these diseases, including river blindness, could be either eliminated altogether or contained through massive immunization campaigns and other preventive programs. Trypanosomiasis, or sleeping sickness, another deadly disease of the tropics, is carried by the tsetse fly, and it affects some 25,000 people in Africa. Leprosy is caused by *Mycobacterium leprae*; symptoms include skin lesions, eye inflammation, destruction of nose cartilage and bone, testicle atrophy, and at times blindness, although it rarely leads to death and is not as infectious as it was once thought to be. Leprosy affects thousands of Africans, especially in the warmest tropical climates of the continent, and is considered to be one of the most "abominable" afflictions a family can endure.

Acquired immunodeficiency syndrome (AIDS), of course, has emerged as the most frightening infectious, heterosexually transmitted disease in Africa, particularly in Central and East Africa. AIDS is caused by the human immunodeficiency virus (HIV), which is transmitted sexually and through body fluids and essentially attacks, weakens, and eventually destroys the human immune-cell system.

In 1996, WHO estimated that 10 million Africans were HIV positive, up from 3 million in 1992; however the most recent figures claim that, in the large urban areas of East and Central Africa, 25–30% of people between the ages of 15 and 49 years are infected.[5] It is also noted that in Kenya, for example, one in 18 adults and 8% of people of this age in Uganda have HIV; 10% of the population in Zimbabwe and 18% of 15- to 49-year-olds in Botswana carry the deadly virus.[6] Alemayehu asserts that as much as 25% of the Sub-Saharan African population is infected with HIV.[7] In terms of economic impact, tuberculosis and HIV/AIDS are hitting Africans at their most productive stage in life, between 15 and 49 years of age, and decimating teachers (four a day in Côte d'Ivoire), government officials, intellectuals, and the wealthy as well, all of whom are indispensable if Africa is to live up to its potential. The situation in Africa is so alarming that the U.N. Security Council held an extraordinary unprecedented session on HIV/AIDS in Africa in New York on January 10, 2000, chaired by U.S. Vice President Al Gore. The world learned from the session's frank discussions that, to date, "... almost 14 million people in Sub-Saharan Africa have died from the disease, with a staggering 23 million Africans—70 percent of the world total—currently infected."[8] Since 1980, 13.7 million Africans have died from the disease, at the rate of 10 per minute in 1999, or about 5500 a day.

In toto, parasitic and infectious diseases killed at least 4.25 million people in Africa during the mid-1980s alone.[9] The emergency of new viral diseases, such as Ebola/Marburg and AIDS, and the reemergence of tuberculosis as a concomitant to AIDS, as well as the resistance of mosquitoes to common drugs (due to mutations and humans' overuse of hitherto effective drugs) cast a cloud on the survival of the African continent as a whole. In general, the leading death causes in Africa are infectious and parasitic diseases (41.5%); diseases of the circulatory (blood and lymphatic body fluids) system (10.7%); malignant neoplasm or tumors that affect surrounding tissues and spread through the bloodstream (8.9%); prenatal and neonatal diseases (7.9%); and external factors of mortality such as automobile accidents, land mines, deaths from war, and injuries leading to death (7.9%). Indeed, political instability resulting in war affects some 165 million Africans annually, almost a third of Sub-Saharan Africa alone (even though AIDS has already killed 10 times as many Africans as wars and violent conflicts during the post-independence period). Unfortunately, about 90% of the victims of war in Sub-Saharan Africa have been civilians and not the military forces that wage war.[10] Prenatal, infectious, and parasitic diseases altogether are responsible for 75% of infant deaths in Africa.

A. Measurement of Health

Health standards can be measured by such indicators as infant mortality rates (measured by the number of deaths among children under the age of 1 per 1000

TABLE 9.1   Life Expectancy Years in Sub-Saharan
Africa by Region

Region	Male	Female
East	48.6	51.2
West	49.9	52.9
Central	50.6	53.8
Southern	62.1	67.9

Source: Ishikawa, K. (1999) Nation Building and
Development Assistance in Africa, Tokyo: Macmillan,
p. 70.

live births in a given year), public health expenditure, population-per-physician ratio (or population-per-nurse ratio), immunization rates, population with access to safe water, life expectancy at birth, and child and maternal mortality. Life expectancy at birth (or the average number of years a newborn would live if mortality rates at the time of birth and throughout his/her life would remain the same) is one of the best measures of the health status of a population and its healthcare system. Currently, in Africa, the low life expectancy rates at birth are still alarming, as they stand at least 20 points below those of the industrialized countries, as shown in Table 9.1.

Southern Africa has been more fortunate in life expectancy at birth than other parts of Sub-Saharan Africa. However, this gain will soon be wiped out by the prevalence and high incidence of AIDS in Zimbabwe, Zambia, Malawi, South Africa, and Botswana.

Maternal deaths are another major health problem the continent has to contend with every year. Of the 500,000 annual worldwide maternal deaths resulting from pregnancy complications estimated by WHO, one-third of them (about 170,000) occur in Africa. In certain communities, maternal death ratios (measured per 100,000 women) reach as high as 1000/100,000. Turschen notes that, "Maternal mortality is the health indicator that displays the greatest differential between developed and developing countries. The lifetime risk of death during pregnancy and childbirth is 500 times higher for African women than women in industrial countries."[11]

The risks that African women face during pregnancy and childbirth are well known and are not difficult to address. They include poor nutrition, illiteracy and ignorance, lower social status, discrimination, and inadequate maternal health-care services, such as family planning (the introduction of which African men are still resisting). In addition, adds Nasah et al., women experience "feelings of powerlessness, fear, social taboos [such as some society's proscription against the consumption of eggs and fish during pregnancy], and other factors resulting from illnesses and discriminatory practices [that place women as second-class

TABLE 9.2   Disease and Injury Incidences by Gender (1990)

Female Population	Percent (%)	Male Population	Percent (%)
Malaria	11	Injuries	13
Respiratory ailments	11	Respiratory ailments	11
Diarrheal illnesses	10	Malaria	11
Infant diseases	9	Diarrheal diseases	10
HIV/AIDS	6	Infant diseases	10
Perinatal ailments	6	Perinatal ailments	9
Maternal ailments	6	HIV/AIDS	6
Injuries	6	Tuberculosis	5
Tuberculosis	4	Various sexually	2
Various sexually	3	transmitted diseases	
transmitted diseases		Other causes	23
Other causes	28		

Source: Banque Mondiale (1994) Pour une meilleure Afrique: les lecons de l'experience, Washington, D.C.: World Bank, p. 23.

citizens]. They are trapped in circumstances from which there is little hope of escape."[12]

Table 9.2 provides a general idea of disease and injury incidences by gender for Africa by level of severity in 1990. It appears that males suffer more injuries, more perinatal ailments (more likely as infants), and more TB cases, but females experience maternal diseases, more sexually transmitted disease (STD) incidences, and more deaths from other causes.

III. AFRICA'S COMMITMENT TO HEALTH CARE

During the colonial era, health care in Africa was concentrated in the major towns and was designed primarily to meet the needs of the European population—settlers, administrators, and soldiers. A few health centers were built in the rural areas. Where epidemics of such diseases as trypansomiasis, influenza, meningitis, and smallpox were endangering the lives of Europeans and preventing economic development, colonial governments supported eradication campaigns, as occurred in French Equatorial Africa and French West Africa and in colonies such as Mozambique, in the then Tete District, near Moatize, and undertook vegetation clearance. Quite often, the few physicians were military personnel. Very little training was afforded Africans, except at the rank of auxiliaries to doctors and as nurses and hospital janitors. It is generally acknowledged today that colonialism carried with it the curse of new diseases and epidemics, such as syphilis, smallpox, meningitis (caused by a bacterial infection that inflames the membranes of the brain and the spinal cord; symptoms include fever, stiff neck, nausea, and skin rash), and influenza (e.g., the Spanish influenza of 1918–1920 being one such case), and contributed to the accelerated spread of those infectious diseases that were local or endemic to certain areas.

At independence, every new government in Africa turned its attention to providing the basic health services to all people, including the rural masses. This included creating more hospitals and providing the rural areas with accessible healthcare facilities. Unfortunately, while fewer resources were provided for training medical personnel (such as "foot doctors") for the rural regions, no effort was made to integrate traditional healers into the biomedical field. In fact, the new initiative "...did not explicitly address broader issues related to health development, such as the provision of safe water and the improvement of agricultural productivity."[13] Only after 1976 was there a concerted effort on the part of the new African leaders to tackle the issue of basic health issues and the obstacles to wellness, embedded in the concept of primary health care, which focuses primarily on preventive rather than curative medicine. It is in this context that virtually every African state embraced the United Nations recommendations on primary health care (PHC) enunciated at Alma Atta (Kazakhastan) in 1978. The espoused PHC recommendations were designed to provide "health care for all" by the year 2000, implying that health care was a right for all rather than a privilege of a few wealthy citizens.

In essence, the conference recommended universal children's immunization, sanitation, safe water, health education, and community involvement in healthcare decisions and implementation. This was followed by several other recommendations such as those approved at the Bamako (Mali) initiative conference in 1987, which focused on "costs related to mother and child health (MCH)" and the sell of "essential drugs in health facilities." The Bamako initiative further insisted that, due to cost considerations, "the most important interaction within the community—the interface—would no longer be at the village level, but at the level of the peripheral dispensary."[14] Every African country pledged to implement the 1978 Alma Atta and the Bamako initiatives. Yet, most leaders simply paid lip service to the recommendations. At the time, only minor differences were discernible within the ideological spectrum of the newly independent African states. Among the so-called capitalist states—Nigeria, Kenya, Cameroon, Senegal, and Malawi, for example—that believed in free market forces, emphasis was placed on providing basic health services in both urban and rural areas but with much latitude for private healthcare institutions. Those states believed that the same opportunities for basic healthcare, including PHC, should be provided to every citizen and that the more complex and costly care ought to be left to individual choice. Therefore, the system favored the elite and the wealthy class.

The few truly socialist states (Tanzania, Kenya, Zambia, and Ghana, during Kwame Nkrumah's leadership) that espoused the state's active intervention in the economic sector to correct and minimize wealth inequalities, attempted seriously to redress the imbalance of the colonial healthcare system. Indeed, they made strides to provide the rural areas with basic health care, engaging the state in economic enterprises; enacting reforms that would create new hospitals, healthcare centers, and dispensaries; and training new medical personnel willing to leave the city. Thus, in Zambia, for example, health facilities doubled, while in Tanzania, the number of health facilities jumped from 1754 in 1972 to 2892 in 1976. More were provided after Alma Atta. These socialist states were also the first ones to advocate and incorporate the knowledge and contribution of traditional medicine into modern biomedicine, notwithstanding the objections of the Western-trained African and expatriate doctors. The now-defunct Afro-Marxist governments of Angola, Mozambique, Guinea-Bissau, Zimbabwe, Ethiopia, Benin, Congo (Brazzaville), Burkina Faso (then Upper Volta), and Madagascar attempted nationalization of all institutions, thus eliminating altogether private practice in the health sector. Their aim was to eliminate any disparity between urban and rural healthcare facilities and opportunities and that both the "reactionary bourgeoisie" (soon to be eliminated, Marxists had vowed) and the masses would have the same access to medical care. Whether the wishes were sincere or not, political instability in all Marxist states thwarted their policy and, in the end, their healthcare systems turned out to be worse than those of the capitalist states they derided as anti-poor.

All ideological differences notwithstanding, the major characteristics and policies of the colonial healthcare system remained virtually intact in post-independence Africa. Comparing the three ideological spectra, Stock and Anayinam note:[15]

> African capitalist states have tended to allocate comparatively small proportions of their budgets to health, and to spend most of their health allocation on urban, curative medicine. The pronounced class biases in access to health care are accentuated by the rapid growth in private sector health care. Populist socialist states have given priority to rural health care and have shown more openness toward non-technological medicine, particularly the primary health care approach, and traditional medicine, than the capitalist states. While some progress was made toward a reallocation of resources toward rural needs and preventive care, urban curative medicine has continued to absorb a disproportionate share of resources. The revolutionary Afro-Marxist states have attempted to restructure their health systems within the larger context of social and economic transformation. While their achievements have been noteworthy, they have fallen far short of objectives.

Malnutrition is currently a major problem in Africa. Malnutrition (or any disorder resulting from an imbalanced diet or improper food intake) and undernutrition (resulting from eating too little, below the required quantify of food, often not differentiated from malnutrition) are also continental problems.

A combination of malnutrition and disease in Sub-Saharan Africa is estimated to account for 210/1000 deaths among children under 5 in West Africa, 171/1000 in East Africa, 169/1000 in Central Africa, and 129/1000 in Southern Africa. In fact, malnutrition and its sequelae seem to account for 4 million deaths a year among children below the age of 5. Experts tell us that, in Africa, the average daily food consumption is only 85% of the daily United Nations' recommended dosage. Alemayehu alleges that, even though per capita calorie (energy content in food when oxidized in the body) intake in Sub-Saharan Africa rose by about 10%—from 2124 in 1977 to 2337 in 1993, it is expected to be only 2170 (compared to 3470 in developed countries) by the year 2010. Malnutrition certainly implies the inability to maintain a strong immune system and a propensity to mental and physical retardation when it occurs at an early age. Undernutrition (lack of sufficient food intake) during the 1980s seems to have affected 175 million people, compared to 94 million during the 1970s. During a third presidential gathering dedicated to the management of science and technology in Africa, held in Kampala in July 1995, the heads of state and government agreed that "basic food and nutritional security have the priority of priorities in Africa," once they realized that, by the year 2000, Africa was expected to produce "less than 75 percent of its food requirements, ...if the current trend continues." As a result, they pledged to work toward a "10-year multisectoral program of action aimed at achieving food and nutritional security." As expected, no discernible outcomes have resulted from such solemn promises. The same old pledges were made in Libreville, Gabon, in January 2000, when 21 African heads of state vowed to reduce by half the level of poverty in Africa by the year 2015.

The preceding remarks are not intended to deny that Africa has made progress in the health sector. As noted earlier, facilities doubled in most countries, and physicians began to be trained on a larger scale, decreasing the ratio of population per physician from 33,390:1 in 1965 to 23,610:1 in 1984 and 18,488:1 (6504 per nurse) in 1990, according to U.N. Development Program (UNDP) statistics.[16] By 1980, so many healthcare facilities had been built that 50% of the African population lived less than one hour (of walking) away from a healthcare clinic, healthcare center, or a hospital. In Zimbabwe, in the aftermath of independence in 1980, the motto was "No Zimbabwean should walk more than 10 miles to the nearest healthcare center," which turned out to be the case, at least for the densely populated areas of the country. By 1986, just 6 years into independence, Zimbabwe had built 163 new rural healthcare clinics, upgraded the existing 450 rural healthcare facilities, and ended segregation in healthcare provision.[17]

Furthermore, average annual budget allocations for healthcare increased from 0.7% of the GNP in 1960 to an average of 2.4% of the GDP by 1990. Another sign of improvement has been the increased number of Africans who have access to healthcare (64% for 1985–1991), safe water (56%), and sanitation (41%) during the 1988–1991 period. For rural versus urban areas, following are the figures for 1985–1995:[18]

1. Access to healthcare services: 50% rural versus 81% urban.
2. Safe water: 35% rural versus 63% urban.
3. Sanitation: 30% rural versus 56% urban.

More significantly, during the 1990–1994 period, 64% of 1-year-olds had been immunized against tuberculosis and 51% against measles. Prior to its civil war, Mozambique was commended by WHO for the success of its immunization campaign against smallpox, measles, and tetanus (a bacterial disease that affects the nervous system and is marked by muscular spasms and rigidity, especially the jaw, fever, and headache). The campaign in Mozambique had reached 90% of the people, along with doubling in the number of nurses (only 1258 during the 1960s) and hospitals beds (only 11,200 in 1960) through the allocation of 6–7% of its annual budget to health.[19]

Even the current low life expectancy at birth is an improvement over 1960, when it was only 43 years. Since 1976, the UNDP, the World Bank, and other international agencies, through the Special Program for Research in Tropical Medicine, have been working toward the development of a "multi-drug therapy" against leprosy in Africa and are in the process of testing several potential vaccines against schistosomiasis and malaria and developing new diagnoses and vector control schemes that will make a difference in the lives of many Africans. Furthermore, expanded immunization campaigns, such as the Expanded Campaign on Immunization (EPI) sponsored by the United Nations, are being undertaken and projects to provide better access to safe water and sanitation are underway. WHO and international underwriters have put in place several strategies designed to eradicate certain infectious diseases such as malaria and polio. The WHO Roll-Back Malaria Program, the Malaria Control Strategy (1992), the Medicines for Malaria Venture, and the Multinational Initiative on Malaria (1997), are all steps that should have a measurable impact on the number one African children's killer disease. In fact, WHO predicts that, by the year 2007, measles, polio, leprosy, and Guinea worm will be eradicated just as smallpox was in 1977. The fight against onchocerciasis is producing positive results, especially in Burkina Faso, where in certain areas along the Volta River the fly density is receding, and new villages are springing up. In decades past, as the experts tell us, no villages could be seen 20 miles from the banks of the river.

Yet, several observers predict a healthcare disaster for Africa. Alemayehu notes: "In short, using social and economic meters, the average African's standard of living was worse than it has been in the 1960s and 1970s, and by 1994, close to 60% of the African population was under the poverty line."[20] Progress in infant mortality notwithstanding, the pace of improvement has been slow compared to other developing regions of the world. For example, close to 24% of the children under 5 would die in Africa in 1960, whereas in China the rate of infant mortality was almost the same, about 22%. Yet, by 1990, China's infant mortality had dropped to 4%, while that of Africa had been reduced only to 17%.[21]

Falola and Ityavyar stress the fact that, "No matter how health is defined, in Africa the state of health care delivery is in crisis." Echoing this sad reality, Pearce shows the increasing health disparity between Western and African populations and the health inequalities among segments of African populations:[22]

> These inequalities can be traced to the complex of economic, political, and family relationships existing between the interacting segments. Thus morbidity and mortality patterns remain rooted in the problem of poverty, while the volume of each remains high for all but a few privileged groups.

Public health services are disintegrating and pathogens are mutating everywhere in Africa, leaving behind outbreaks of typhoid and cholera with little hope that the private market will serve more than the urban elite. Typhoid is a bacterial infection, usually from *Salmonella typhi* found in water, food, and milk, and is marked by high fever, mental confusion, cough, watery diarrhea, and rash. Cholera is a bacterial infection of the small intestine with symptoms such as diarrhea, vomiting, muscular cramps, and dehydration or lack of water in the body.[23] Indeed, it is estimated that, during the mid-1990s, expenditures in Africa dropped, on the average, by 5 percent for social programs, 11 percent for production, and 22 percent for infrastructure [roads, bridges, and facilities, for example, all critical for healthcare distribution and access] in thirty-seven countries. In addition, the rate of inflation was running at 23.4% during the 1980–1991 period, with a per capita gross domestic product (GDP) of approximately $350 a year. It is safe to assume, therefore, that during the first decade of the 21st century, conditions will not change drastically for the better. Also, given the precarious financial situation, foreign assistance to Africa's healthcare sector rose to almost $5.0 billion in 1990, representing about 10.4% (with ranges between 3.4% and 48.4%, depending on countries) of the total budget for the healthcare sector.[24] The end of the Cold War, however, has slowly marginalized the African continent, slowing down the level of overall assistance coming from the international community.

Commenting on the current health situation in Africa, Mburu observed that, "The major hindrance to the formulation of more effective health systems would appear to be the value systems of the elite groups and agencies and the structures these produce."[25] The challenge on modern health care practice, in Mburu's view, is to design systems that are not only fair and just to all but efficient and effective. It is said that just a minimum of further improvement in Africa's water systems would prove to be a tremendous boost toward the elimination of many preventable diseases and deaths, because water is such an important conduit for infectious disease transmission that it is indirectly responsible for a large number of ailments and deaths in Africa (and elsewhere), but particularly in Sub-Saharan Africa, where most of the water is not chemically treated and where the absence of clean indoor latrines is common. Six or more general exposure routes can be identified:

1. Water-borne diseases (watershed and water-related insect vectors or carriers) result from ingestion of microorganism-contaminated water, as is the case with many intestinal ailments, such as typhoid, cholera, and infective hepatitis (inflammation of the liver with symptoms such as enlarged liver, clay-colored stools, dark urine, loss of appetite, yellow skin or jaundice).

2. Water-contact diseases occur through direct contact with pathogens present in water (as is the case with Guinea worm and schistosomiasis), contracted from swimming or wading in snail-infected water. Proper disposal of human and animal feces is one preventive measure.

3. Water-insect-related diseases are infections in the form of malaria and yellow fever (mosquitoes thrive in wet conditions). Prevention requires elimination of the vectors, avoiding contact with them, and drainage of ponds, pools, and water containers left in the open.

4. Water-wash diseases occur as a result of water scarcity, which has an adverse impact on personal hygiene and washing. Examples of resulting diseases include trachoma (infectious eye disease that causes inflammation of adenoid tissue), shigellosis (a type of diarrhea caused by a rod-shaped bacteria of the genus *Shigella*), and conjunctivitis (or inflammation of the conjunctiva).

5. Refuse-related infections attract insects and rodents (mosquitoes, flies, rats, mice, and worms).

6. Finally, especially in the Third World, housing-related infections stem from airborne particles and domestic animals. They include tuberculosis, whooping cough, or pertussis (an acute infectious disease transmitted through coughing or sneezing or through objects in contact with the patient; marked by loud whooping breath taken in, usually in children under the age of 4 years), various respiratory ailments, ticks, and lice.[26]

Political instability continues to create violence on the continent, contributing to unemployment estimated to be 20–50% labor migration, abandonment of family, and the spread of diseases. Indeed, soldiers are some of the greatest vectors and carriers of infectious diseases. Consequently, few analysts are optimistic about the continent's economic future, despite infusions of loans by the International Monetary Fund (IMF) and the World Bank. Several economists attribute the growing healthcare problems to these two international financial institutions and others. In fact, through their structural adjustment programs (SAPs), they have succeeded in forcing about 33 African countries to retrench social program spending by as much as 13% and have imposed the institutionalization of a user fee and advocated reliance of health care on private agencies as the best response to the crisis. The major victims of the new recovery programs have been the millions of already impoverished Africans. Among these, children and women are worse off, as, indeed, Africa has seen what some call the "feminization" of poverty.[27]

The World Bank and several financial institutions blame African leaders for the slow improvement in the status of health care on the continent. They point out that African statesmen had an opportunity to do something 30 years ago when they embraced the concept of primary health care and prevention. Unfortunately, they seldom "proceeded to enact the institutional and financial changes needed to achieve the objectives." Instead, notes the West, "they have focused on the expensive curative health and hospital services that deplete funds in the ministries of health for the benefit of a small segment of their populations."[28] Although such criticism is often well placed and justified, the same institutions, along with the IMF and the World Bank, tell African heads of state and government that the state must only play the role of first in line, while naively expecting it to determine the cost-effective approaches to health and "encouraging and facilitating the activities of both public and private [health care] providers." This role, however, continue the policy directives of the World Bank, does not mean that the state "ought to be the main health care services provider."[29]

The reality is quite different, however. As Turschen and others have poignantly argued, only a government, and not a private agency or charity, can meaningfully tackle community (rather than individual) and statewide health problems by undertaking the necessary steps, such as quarantining people and allaying unwarranted epidemiological concerns. Only a state can negotiate effectively, through diplomacy, on issues such as international remedies and border travel restrictions and precautions. Also, in Africa, only the state has the capacity to establish *ad hoc* efficient research laboratories and to deploy national and international personnel through the ministries of health, information, and foreign affairs, as was the case with the Ebola virus outbreak (of unknown and deadly cause, transmitted through an infected person's blood or body fluids and characterized by fever, headache, vomiting, diarrhea, rash, and blood out of several body openings, killing 90% of the victims in a less than a week), in former Zaire and the Marburg viral epidemic (similar to Ebola) in Sudan a few years ago.

Shepherd's study showed that the countries that accepted the SAPs saw their social welfare budgets fall from 16.3% in 1970 to 12.2% in 1988 for education and from 6.3 to 4.7% for healthcare during the same period. In contrast, the non-adjusting countries kept their budget intact and some raised it to 16% for education, while maintaining the health care at 5% of the "total budgetary expenditures."[30] Furthermore, Shepherd adds, in the adjusting countries, there was a lower survival rate for children during the 1980s, especially in the rural areas, as fewer and more expensive drugs were available to the poor. In such countries, calorie intake decreased from an average of 2225 per person per day in 1965 (85% of the recommended intake) to 2148 calories in 1988. In contrast, in non-adjusting countries, calorie intake rose from 1916 in 1965 to 2271 in 1988.

It is ironic that the developing world and its financial institutions reproach Africa for spending too much on social welfare, including education and health, when, in fact, they spend much more on health care per person per year. For example, while some European countries spent $300 per person on drugs in 1996 and Americans spent $1600 during the same period, in most of the Third World the amount was about $5 per person, $1 per person in Africa.[31] For total health care, while developed countries spent about $41 per person (about 50 times more than in the developing world), Africa's spending was only $14 per person in 1996. It is also an irony of life that, even though the population of the Third World represents over 75% of humanity, it consumes less than 20% of the world's pharmaceuticals. Yet, experts note that about 60% of the developing world has no regular access to drugs. Turschen sarcastically adds that Africa's health policies are now being determined and dictated not by Africans or their health professionals and the World Health Organization, but by international corporations, the IMF, the U.S. Agency for International Development, and financial underwriters and accountants in Western capitals. He goes on to note that corporations are now giving ultimatums to African governments to "roll-back tax-supported state services and mandated benefits—in effect to disband public services, deregulate labor, and lower their tax bills," before they will invest their financial resources. They are determined to see that health care is relegated to charity and non-governmental organizations (NGOs), under the wrong premise that private organizations are necessarily more efficient, more effective, and more generous than governments.

As a result, thousands of African workers in the public and private sectors have either lost their jobs or seen their wages slashed to the bare bone to conform to IMF and the World Bank structural adjustment programs. Even though some privatization schemes have been heralded as a success, in some cases they have been a disaster. In Burkina Faso, for example, enterprise privatization mandated by the IMF and the World Bank seems to have resulted in the loss of 1200 jobs by 1996, according to labor union leaders, while 54 privatized enterprises in Benin, Burkina Faso, Ghana, Togo, and Zambia are said to have cut employment down by 15% 3 months into the process in 1996. In Sudan, the Federation of Workers accused the government of forcing 40,000 people out of the job market since introduction of privatization in 1992.[32]

With privatization, it is said that government's ability to finance health care and education, the most important foundations of a good life, has thus been reduced to a minimum in the so-called adjusting countries. Privatization has been the principal commandment of the IMF and the World Bank bible. Pharmaceuticals (corporations that make or sell drugs), on the other hand, continue to raise the prices of their drugs and refuse to dispense them if African governments attempt to roll the prices back when people cannot afford to buy them. In fact, with support from the United States at first, the AIDS pharmaceutical industry in South Africa took its own government to court in 1988 when the latter tried to force it to lower its prices by "the mandatory licensing of some of the medication and 'parallel importing' others from low-cost manufacturers in India." AIDS is a very profitable disease for pharmaceuticals. Just note that Uganda alone would have to spend $24 billion a year to treat its 2 million people who are HIV positive. Economists estimate that this figure is 12 times higher than the country's annual budget.

Even though international funding for AIDS in Africa has increased over the years, donors' contributions have fallen far shorter than the United Nations expected. At the dawn of the millennium, all funding combined totaled only $160 million per year, when the needed assistance was estimated at $1.5–$3.0 billion annually. The Bill and Melinda Gates Foundation contributed $57 million in early April 2000, but the funds were specifically earmarked for AIDS prevention and education programs in Botswana, Ghana, Tanzania, and Uganda. In March 2000, Ted Turner's U.N. donation for HIV/AIDS programs in Mozambique and Zimbabwe totaled $6 million, boosted by $500,000 from the M-A-C funds for AIDS awareness programs in Africa. However, the largest private sector donation—$100 million for the Africa-specific AIDS virus strain known as HIV-1C—came from the Bristol-Myers Squibb Company in 2001 to benefit Lesotho, Namibia, South Africa, and Swaziland.[33] Unfortunately, more money going to AIDS means less money to combat other diseases.

IV. DISEASE AND ECONOMIC SECURITY

The disease toll on economic productivity is only now being addressed. Preliminary studies estimate that, at present, the rate of disability-adjusted life years (DALYs) lost per 1000 population between the ages of 15 and 45 years in Southern Africa is 575 per 1000, whereas for the industrialized world it is only 111 years per 1000.[34] In 1990, 69.5% of total DALYs lost in Africa came from communicable, maternal, perinatal, and nutritional causes, representing about one-third of the world total. It is estimated that 2020 will be an epidemiological transition year and that communicable diseases will be on the rise from the 19% DALYs lost in 1990 to 32% in 2020, coupled with an increase in injury DALYs lost from 15% in 1990 to 28% in 2020.[35] As a result, costs from inability to work, absenteeism, and tardiness due to ill health run into the millions of dollars every year. Yet, in the midst of the crisis, multinationals are reneging on their obligations and "transferring the costs of sickness and death benefits to workers and especially women."[36] The imposed cuts on health are being implemented at the worst health period in the history of the continent. The economic crisis is still upon Africa, while old and new infectious diseases are on the rise. In addition, the so-called diseases of affluence are, unfortunately, on the rise as well, caused by high intake of salt, fat, tobacco, and alcohol; by automobile accidents; and by pollution of the ecosystem (or the ecological community and its harmonious interaction with the environment), including the dumping of toxic (poisonous) waste by Western countries on the African soil and subsoil. Indeed, "Cardiovascular disease, degenerative (weakening) diseases, and cancer," as Stephenson notes, now account for 23.9% of all fatalities in Africa, and are predicted to reach 58.1% "as the population ages, further taxing health-care systems."[37]

Specific and detailed studies on the interdependence between health and economic development are rare. In fact, by 1995, only about eight important studies had been conducted to measure the economic toll of disease in Africa. Following is a paraphrased, translated summary of such studies extrapolated from the Banque Mondiale report. Four of the studies conducted in 1993 focused on countries where adult illnesses are high, including Côte d'Ivoire, Ghana, and Mauritania. In Côte d'Ivoire, it was found that, during the month prior to the study, 24% of the adult workforce had been ill or injured, of whom 15% had stopped working that season. The affected individuals lost an average of 9 days of work, and their medical treatment measured in dollars represented about 11% of their monthly income. The World Bank estimated that, if these costs were added to the adjustments from other segments of the population, the impact of the diseases would have amounted to 15% of the GDP.[38]

Malaria studies in Rwanda, Burkina Faso, Togo, and Congo (Brazzaville) revealed a loss of 12 days on average, just for one case of malarial bout, in direct and indirect costs. Overall, the economic loss from the disease was estimated to have been $800 million in 1987 and was projected to rise to $1.7 billion by 1995, which would have been about 0.6% of Africa's GDP in 1987. This figure was projected to reach 1.0% of the GDP by 1995, an amount that would have surpassed the annual budget of most African countries in mid-1980. In 1987, the Guinea worm disease (caused by a long subcutaneous parasitic worm in humans and other animals) is said to have temporarily disabled 2.5 million Nigerians. It was determined that, in one region, the worm was the factor in the reduction of rice production, contributing also to a reduction in the value of production of this staple by $50 million. Combating the worm effectively would have cost more than resuming rice production during a 4-year period. Onchocerciasis, or river blindness, as noted elsewhere in the chapter, and malaria have prevented many people from moving to and exploiting otherwise fertile lands. Apparently, trypanosomiasis or sleeping sickness prevents one-third of the African continent's soil from hosting cattle while at the same time exacerbating the problems of a deficiency of protein (organic nitrogen compounds in living cells that carry carbon, nitrogen, hydrogen, oxygen, sulfur, phosphorous, iron, iodine). Of course, river blindness has depopulated riverbanks in Nigeria, Niger, Ghana, Cameroon, Burkina Faso, and other regions in Africa. Simultaneously, malaria and trypanosomiasis prevent migration and settlement of areas yet unexplored in Uganda. The ravages of the AIDS epidemic have been discussed elsewhere in this chapter. Suffice it to note here that, where AIDS strikes, households have to liquidate their savings and their productive assets to pay medical bills and funerals. This, anthropologists note, is hard on widows, who normally do not have inheritance rights in many parts of Africa. Due to poverty and people's lower incomes, virtually no African can afford the benefit of the multi-drug therapy that has prolonged the lives of so many AIDS patients in the United States and the Western world.

In Tanzania and Uganda, as well as in Zimbabwe, it is already clear that absenteeism and the death of adults are retarding economic growth. Zimbabwe has instituted a special national tax to be used for AIDS treatment. In West Africa, on the one hand, households affected by the disease sell their assets to pay healthcare bills and maintain a modicum of their normal consumption level. In areas with onchocerciasis, on the other hand, people have been using bridewealth to pay for medical treatment. It has also been noted in Côte d'Ivoire, for example, that the average cost to the household, when illness strikes, is higher than the salary of a full-time worker receiving the minimum local wages. This condition forces households to sell their livestock in order to survive. A study of coastal Kenya also suggests that one-fourth of the land sells are motivated by the economic ravages brought about by illness and injury. In Sudan, a study of 250 smith families struck by malaria and schistosomiasis (bilharzia) showed that the healthy family members abandoned their own occupations to attend to the needs of the ill relatives and maintain an accepted level of production.

The same has been observed among malaria-stricken individuals: the steady decrease in working days as a result of illness is partly compensated by the work of other family members. Furthermore, in the urban areas, employers experiencing high rates of absenteeism due to employees' health problems lose the benefits of large-scale production. The World Bank's summary ends by pointing out that further improvement in the healthcare sector in Africa could increase economic productivity, especially of family households, by reducing healthcare costs and minimizing the pressures of taking care of sick relatives. Employers would likewise benefit by the reduction in absences of employees "who have the experience and possess essential qualifications."[39]

Experience has shown that improved health conditions improve economic productivity, while higher incomes (as in the developed world) contribute to better health and higher life expectancy at birth. Interestingly, in this context, the change is more dramatic among the poor than among the wealthy segment of the population. It is estimated also that one-third of the impact of economic growth on life expectancy operates through poverty alleviation and the remaining two-thirds through increased public spending on health. Pannenborg notes that:[40]

> ... An increase of 1 percent in income per capita would lower infant mortality by one death per thousand in countries averaging 100/1000 IMR (infant mortality rate). If that 1 percent gain in income were used to promote basic education, literacy rates would rise by 20 percent.

High literacy rates lead to higher health awareness, better standards of hygiene and sanitation, and fewer deaths. At present, Africa's overall adult literacy is around 45%, still favoring males over females by a ratio of 3:1. Although this is not a chapter focusing on education, let it be known that studies have demonstrated that, each time a mother adds one year of education to her life, there is a corresponding 8% decline in childhood mortality. Data from more than 100 countries collected during the 1960s and 1970s have also shown that "moving from 0 percent to 100 percent adult literacy would—ceteris paribus— increase life expectancy at birth by about twenty years, and reduce infant mortality by about 100–130 deaths per thousand live births."[41]

Of course, there is a relatively major difference in the gross national product (GNP) per capita in African countries and quality healthcare delivery; the more endowed experience better health conditions when healthcare outcome indicators are assessed. The World Bank has divided Sub-Saharan African countries into lowest income (with an average per capita GNP of less than US$300), low-income (with per capita GNP between $300 and $765), and middle-income (with incomes greater than $765) countries. The lowest income countries include Burkina Faso, Burundi, Chad, Congo Democratic Republic, Eritrea, Ethiopia, Guinea-Bissau, Liberia, Madagascar, Malawi, Mali, Mozambique, Niger, Nigeria, Rwanda, Sierra Leone, Somalia, Tanzania, and Uganda. The low-income countries include Angola, Benin, Cameroon, Central African Republic (CAR), Comoros, Côte d'Ivoire, Equatorial Guinea, the Gambia, Lesotho, Ghana, Guinea, Kenya, Mauritania, São Tomé and Principe, Senegal, Sudan, Togo, Zambia, and Zimbabwe. The middle-income countries are made up of Botswana, Cape Verde, Congo, Djibouti, Gabon, Namibia, Mauritius, Seychelles, South Africa, and Swaziland. Table 9.3 indicates healthcare performances on various health outcome indicators based on the World Bank's classification. A definition of low-birth weight baby (LBWB) may clarify the table. A LBWB is an infant who weighs less than 2500 grams immediately following birth.

The table certainly indicates that if—ceteris paribus—budget allocations to health are reasonable, higher income societies tend to do much better than others, even in Africa. It is no secret, as well, that the adverse impact of disease and high mortality rates on economic conditions is increased by high rates of population growth in Africa, resulting from centuries-old, welcome, high traditional fertility

TABLE 9.3   Health Outcome Indicators in Africa by Income Group Classification (1990–1996)

	Health Indicator	Lowest	Low	Middle	All of Africa
1.	Infant mortality rate (/1000 live births)	102	81	55	92
2.	Under-5 mortality rate (/1000 live births, 1995)	173	125	74	151
3.	Male life expectancy (years, 1995)	48	52	60	50
4.	Female life expectancy (years, 1995)	51	55	65	54
5.	Male adult mortality (/1000 men, 15–60 years, 1995	467	416	326	448
6.	Female adult mortality (/1000 women, 15–60 years 1995)	389	357	253	376
7.	Years of potential life lost (/1000 population, 1995)	106	67	40	89
8.	Crude birth rate (/1000 population, 1995)	45	39	31.5	42
9.	Crude death rate (/1000 population, 1995)	16	12	9	14
10.	Total fertility rate (children, 1995)	6.3	5.4	3.4	5.8
11.	Maternal mortality (/1000 live births, 1990–1995)	1015	606	277	822
12.	Adolescent fertility rate (/1000 girls, 15–19 years, 1995)	153	119	78	137
13.	Low-birth weight babies (%, 1990–1995)	16	15	—	16
14.	Childhood underweight (%, 1990–1995)	38	38	11	32
15.	Childhood stunting (%, 1990–1995)	44	31	23	39
16.	Childhood wasting (%, 1990–1995)	8	8	8	8

Source: Peters, D. et al. (1999) Health Expenditures, Services and Outcomes in Africa: Basic Data and Cross-National Comparisons 1990–1996, Washington, D.C.: World Bank, p. 17.

rates (the number of births per 1000 women ages 15–44 in a given population over a certain period of time). During the last decades, such countries as Cameroon, Côte d'Ivoire, Kenya, Zimbabwe, Egypt, Botswana, and Mozambique (prior to its civil war, 1977–1992), had population growth rates as high as 4% per year, with women having an average of 6.7 births, "probably achieved after 10 pregnancies."[42] Such fertility rates are harmful to women's health and are also not in sync with the continent's rate of economic growth and productivity, which, overall, has been less than 2% per year over the last two decades.

It is also noteworthy to point out that the international debt, which amounted to $345.2 billion in 1998 ($230.1 billion for Southern Africa alone), will continue to disrupt progress in the healthcare sector. It has been estimated that, in 1994, the average repayment of the debt was about $43 per person in Africa, contrasted to $35 per capita allocated for education and health. Under these circumstances, it is difficult to dispute the claim that "Africa's share of the world's poor will grow from 30 to 40% by the year 2000, overtaking Asia," while "Sub-Saharan Africa accounts for only 10% of the world's 5.6 billion people (52% of them in Asia)."[43] Obviously, under such conditions, the health prospects of the continent are indeed very grim. AIDS alone is costing Africa $393 per person per year, a financial burden that no African country can sustain indefinitely, when, according to some accounts, the average expense per person is as low as $24. In fact, in 1993, the UNDP estimated that Africa had already spent $30 billion on HIV/AIDS in direct or indirectly related costs.[44] An increase in AIDS sequelae, such as tuberculosis, makes one wonder what will become of Africa healthwise during the next decade.

As prenatal and perinatal mortality increases, the number of orphans in Sub-Saharan Africa will also increase from the estimated 1.1–1.6 million in 1992, further stretching African expenditures to their limit. Garrett notes that, as a result of mothers' deaths, "Hope had to rest with the children of Africa, the continent's next generation of potential bankers, lawyers, economists, farmers, business financiers, and planners. But studies in Zambia, Zaire, and Malawi revealed that many AIDS orphans died shortly after their mothers' demises, even though the children were not themselves infected."[45] During the 1990s, about 10.4% (or $4.8 billion) of the total health expenditure came from foreign assistance, at a ratio of $2.45 per capita per year. It appears, however, that no matter how much international assistance the continent will receive in the future, leaders will not be able to stamp out the health crisis the continent faces, unless they take drastic measures. As international travel continues to swell and overcrowding in the cities accelerates (over 51% of Zambians, for example, now live in the cities), the spread of infectious diseases is bound to expand. Scientists also claim that, if global warming is real, and El Nino and La Nina are intermittent phenomena, Africa will not fair well and its people's disease quagmire may worsen.

Epidemiologists caution that, as lower altitudes of our troposphere become warmer, insect vectors such as mosquitoes, house and river flies, tsetse flies, and moths will climb up to higher altitudes and latitudes, thus far the safest havens for many Africans living in the highlands of Ethiopia, Eritrea, Kenya, Mozambique, Zimbabwe, South Africa, Malawi, and parts of West Africa, in countries such as Cameroon and Gabon, rendering the African ecosystem more dangerous to human habitation. Africa's generally hot climate and its pattern of dry and wet seasons make survival difficult in many areas of the continent. Experience has demonstrated that the most infectious diseases strike harder during the rainy season, precisely when food provisions are lowest and malarial infestation highest. It is estimated that in the tropical rainforest and the savanna infected malarial bites are twice as frequent as in Africa's mountains and the Sahel.[46]

V. SUMMARY

In order for Africa to stamp out the current health and healthcare crisis and uplift its economic conditions, it must first rethink its priorities. It seems clear that privatization of health care will not solve the healthcare problem in Africa. If one agrees with the United Nations that health care is a right of every individual rather than a privilege and that epidemiological occurrences that affect a community rather than isolated individuals are turning into a global rather than a local problem, only an organization such as the state can muster the resources to ensure and monitor fairness and equity in healthcare services, mobilize international assistance, and set research laboratories to study the ecosystem and its impact on people, with private health enterprise and NGOs assisting in the process. As such, therefore, African governments should not abdicate their role and ought to resist any decisions made abroad that will leave their people poorer and sicker.

Adequate provision of inexpensive essential drugs also ought to be a major concern to health officials in Africa. Studies conducted in several countries in Africa note the absolute absence of essential drugs in healthcare clinics and centers. When drugs are available, quite often they are damaged during transportation, are not refrigerated properly, or have expired altogether (even though they are still being used).[47]

Overall, the focus in Africa should be on primary health care, for the simple reason that epidemiological studies have proven that, economically, prevention is less costly and more effective than treatment (secondary and tertiary health care) both in lives and monetary terms. Immunization, safe water, and sanitation for all ought to be among the most urgent priorities, along with the active participation of the community, especially in Africa, where cultural traditions and beliefs related to health and disease are extremely resilient. Indeed, as social scientists have stressed recently, all medical systems and their theories on disease etiology (cause) are culture systems, thus community involvement is a *sine qua non* in healthcare success. Some experts even claim, as Airhihenbuwa does, that, "Among the approaches to health education/promotion and disease prevention, the self-empowerment method is believed to be more encompassing and more effective than preventive-medical or radical-political approaches."[48] In this context, it is encouraging to see that African governments, including those that considered traditional medicine to be superstitious and ignorance based, are now enlisting the knowledge and practice of traditional healers and traditional birth attendants, most of whom were seen as "quack doctors" and charlatans during the colonial period and the two decades following independence. Obviously, maternal health should be totally integrated into the primary healthcare system because most maternal deaths that have such an adverse impact on children's health are preventable.

A major debate is raging among healthcare professionals as to whether the fight against diseases in Africa should be selective (as suggested by the international financial institutions and, according to some, the U.S. Agency for International Development, USAID) or be all encompassing, a position favored by most Third World physicians. The selective approach seems to be ill based, because old and new epidemics appear and re-emerge, at times with unprecedented virulence. Should, in those instances, health resources be shifted immediately to the new diseases to the detriment of older endemic maladies? The answer seems to lie in an all-out fight, on all fronts, against the entire disease environment. Unfortunately, only the adoption of a strong primary healthcare program has a chance of achieving the intended results against both infectious and chronic diseases.

Finally, there is no dichotomy or trichotomy among illiteracy (lack of education and ignorance), poverty, and illness. The three go hand-in-hand. Therefore, in order to eliminate disease and improve people's livelihood, it appears that governments in Africa must spend a large portion of their scarce resources not to procure arms but to provide educational opportunities for all, especially women, by fighting poverty to create better living conditions (through jobs, reasonable salaries and wages, and better housing). Unfortunately, again, all these frontline campaigns will be lost if feeding the people is not the priority of priorities on the continent. The Latin dictum, *mens sana in corpore sano* ("a sound mind in a sound body") appears to be more important to Africa today than ever before.

DISCUSSION QUESTIONS

1. What are the most deadly diseases in Africa today and what accounts for their prevalence on the continent?
2. What is meant by primary health care and why is it generally thought to be the best approach to health care in developing countries?
3. Describe and analyze the role the IMF and the World Bank have played in Africa and explain why many Africanists are having second thoughts about their influence on health policies on the continent.
4. What do you think are the factors that have to be taken into account in order to improve the state of health in Africa today? What is the relationship between education and health and between income and health?
5. Why is it that the health of African women is much more in peril than that of African males?
6. What do you think will be the impact of old, emerging, and re-emerging diseases on economic development in Africa? Which diseases do you think are more threatening to Africa's future and why?
7. Summarize the progress that Africa has made in the health sector during the last four decades. Could African leaders have done more? Explain. How do you assess the future of the continent regarding health?

NOTES

[1] Ishikawa, K. (1999) *Nation Building and Development Assistance in Africa*, Tokyo: Macmillan.
[2] Banque Mondiale (1994) *Pour une meilleure Afrique: les lecons de l'experience*, Washington, D.C.: World Bank, p. 18.

[3]Ishikawa, K. (1999) *Nation Building and Development Assistance in Africa*, Tokyo: Macmillan, p. 72.

[4]Banque Mondiale (1994) *Pour une meilleure Afrique: les lecons de l'experience*, Washington, D.C.: World Bank, p. 20.

[5]Alemayehu, M. (2000) *Industrializing Africa: Development Options and Challenges for the 21st Century*, Trenton, NJ: Africa World Press, p. 235.

[6]Ishikawa, K. (1999) *Nation Building and Development Assistance in Africa*, Tokyo: Macmillan, p. 71.

[7]Alemayehu, M. (2000) *Industrializing Africa: Development Options and Challenges for the 21st Century*, Trenton, NJ: Africa World Press, pp. 28–29.

[8](2000) "Aids in Africa," *Africa Recovery*, 14(1): 24 UN document.

[9]Turschen, M. (1999) *Privatizing Health*, New Brunswick, NJ: Rutgers University Press, p. 9.

[10]Turschen, M. (1999) *Privatizing Health*, New Brunswick, NJ: Rutgers University Press, p. 9.

[11]Turschen, M. (1999) *Privatizing Health*, New Brunswick, NJ: Rutgers University Press, p. 19.

[12]Nasah, B.T., Mati, J.K.G., and Kasonde, J.M. (1994) *Contemporary Issues in Maternal Health Care in Africa*, Toronto: Toronto University Press, p. xiii.

[13]Stock, R. and Anyinam, C. (1992) "National Governments and Health Services in Africa," in T. Falola and D. Ityavyar, Eds., *The Political Economy of Health in Africa*, Africa Series No. 60, Athens, OH: University Monographs, pp. 217–246.

[14]Charbot, J., Harmeijer, J.W., and Streetfland, P.H., Eds. (1995) *African Primary Health Care in Times of Economic Turbulence*, Amsterdam: Royal Tropical Institute, p. 101.

[15]Stock, R. and Anyinam, C. (1992) "National Governments and Health Services in Africa," in T. Falola and D. Ityavyar, Eds., *The Political Economy of Health in Africa*, Africa Series No. 60, Athens, OH: University Monographs, p. 239.

[16]Alemayehu, M. (2000) *Industrializing Africa: Development Options and Challenges for the 21st Century*, Trenton, NJ: Africa World Press, pp. 28, 29.

[17]Rasmussen, R. and Rubert, S.C. (1990) *Historical Development of Zimbabwe*, Metuchen, NJ: Scarecrow Press, pp. 121–122.

[18]Alemayehu, M. (2000) *Industrializing Africa: Development Options and Challenges for the 21st Century*, Trenton, NJ: Africa World Press, p. 28.

[19]Azevedo, M.J. (1991) *Historical Development of Chad*, Metuchen, NJ: Scarecrow Press, p. 73.

[20]Alemayehu, M. (2000) *Industrializing Africa: Development Options and Challenges for the 21st Century*, Trenton, NJ: Africa World Press, p. 21.

[21]Pennenborg, O. (1995) "An Economic and Financial Look at Health in Low- and Middle-Income Countries," in K. van de Velden, J.K.S. van Ginneken, J.P. Velema, F.B. de Walle, and J.H. van Wijnen, Eds., *Health Matters: Public Health in North–South Perspective*, Amsterdam: Royal Tropical Institute, pp. 43–62.

[22]Falola, T. and Ityavyar, D., Eds. (1992) *The Political Economy of Health in Africa*, Africa Series No. 60, Athens, OH: University Monographs, p. 3; Pearce, T.O. (1992) "Health Inequalities in Africa," in T. Falola and D. Ityavyar, Eds., *The Political Economy of Health in Africa*, Africa Series No. 60, Athens, OH: University Monographs, pp. 184–216.

[23]Turschen, M. (1999) *Privatizing Health*, New Brunswick, NJ: Rutgers University Press.

[24]Stephenson, M. (1997) "Health Care," in *Encyclopedia of Africa South of the Sahara*, Vol. 2, New York: Scribners' Sons, pp. 288–293.

[25]Mburu (1992), pp. 103–104.

[26]Moeller, D. (1997) *Environmental Health*, Cambridge, MA: Harvard University Press, p. 131; van Wijk-Sijbesma, C. and deWalle, F.B. (1995) "Environmental Hygiene and Human Health," in K. van de Velden, J.K.S. van Ginneken, J.P. Velema, F.B. de Walle, and J.H. van Wijnen, Eds., *Health Matters: Public Health in North–South Perspective*, Amsterdam: Royal Tropical Institute, pp. 103–115.

[27]Turschen, M. (1999) *Privatizing Health*, New Brunswick, NJ: Rutgers University Press, p. 13.

[28]Banque Mondiale (1994) *Pour une meilleure Afrique: les lecons de l'experience*, Washington, D.C.: World Bank, p. 4.

[29]Banque Mondiale (1994) *Pour une meilleure Afrique: les lecons de l'experience*, Washington, D.C.: World Bank, p. 11.

[30]Shepherd, G. and Karamo, N.M., Eds. (1994) *Economic Justice in Africa: Adjustments and Sustainable Development*, Westport, CO: Greenwood Press, p. 85.

[31]Turschen, M. (1999) *Privatizing Health*, New Brunswick, NJ: Rutgers University Press, p. 130.

[32]United Nations (2000) "AIDS in Africa," *Africa Recovery*, 14(1), 12–14.

[33]United Nations (2000) "AIDS in Africa," *Africa Recovery*, 4(3), 24–25.

[34]Stephenson, M. (1997) "Health Care," in *Encyclopedia of Africa South of the Sahara*, Vol. 2, New York: Scribners' Sons, pp. 289.

[35]Peters, D., Kandola, K., Elmendorf, A.E., and Chellaraj, G. (1999) *Health Expenditures, Services, and Outcomes in Africa: Basic Data and Cross-National Comparisons: 1990–1996*, Washington, D.C.: World Bank, p. 3.

[36]Turschen, M. (1999) *Privatizing Health*, New Brunswick, NJ: Rutgers University Press, p. 115.

[37]Stephenson, M. (1997) "Health Care," in *Encyclopedia of Africa South of the Sahara*, Vol. 2, New York: Scribners' Sons, p. 289.

[38]Banque Mondiale (1994) *Pour une meilleure Afrique: les lecons de l'experience*, Washington, D.C.: World Bank, pp. 29–33.

[39]Banque Mondiale (1994) *Pour une meilleure Afrique: les lecons de l'experience*, Washington, D.C.: World Bank, pp. 30–33.

[40]Pannenborg, O. (1994) "An Economic and Financial Look at Health in Low and Middle Income Countries," *Health Matters: Public Health in North-South Perspective*, Amsterdam: Royal Tropical Institute, p. 51.

[41]Pannenborg, O. (1995) "An Economic and Financial Look at Health in Low and Middle-Income Countries," *Health Matters: Public Health in North-South Perspective*, Amsterdam: Royal Tropical Institute, pp. 43–62.

[42]Kwast, B.E. (1995) "Maternity Care in Developing Countries," in K. van de Velden, J.K.S. van Ginneken, J.P. Velema, F.B. de Walle, and J.H. van Wijnen, Eds., *Health Matters: Public Health in North–South Perspective*, Amsterdam: Royal Tropical Institute, pp. 175–183.

[43]Turschen, M. (1999) *Privatizing Health*, New Brunswick, NJ: Rutgers University Press, p. 21.

[44]Stephenson, M. (1997) "Health Care," in *Encyclopedia of Africa South of the Sahara*, Vol. 2, New York: Scribners' Sons, p. 289; Garrett, L. (1995) *The Coming Plague: Newly Emerging Diseases in a World Out of Balance*, New York: Penguin Books, p. 527.

[45]Pages 486–487 in the Garrett reference in Note 44.

[46]Banque Mondiale (1994) *Pour une meilleure Afrique: les lecons de l'experience*, Washington, D.C.: World Bank, p. 15.

[47]See WHO (1994) *Project on Health Systems Research for the Southern African Region*, Vol. 1, Harare, Zimbabwe: World Health Organization, pp. 69–88.

[48]Airhihenbuwa (1995) *Health and Culture: Beyond the Western Paradigm*, London: Safe Publications, p. 26.

CHAPTER 10

Education

MARIO J. AZEVEDO
Department of African American and African Studies, University of North Carolina, Charlotte, North Carolina 28223

EMMANUEL NNADOZIE
Department of Economics, Truman State University, Kirksville, Missouri 63501

KEY TERMS

Adult literacy	Literacy rates
Brain drain	Primary school enrollment rates
Education	Public education expenditure
Education for development	School-leavers
Educational attainment	Secondary school enrollment rates
Educational widening	Self-reliance
Educational deepening	Southern Africa
Human capital	Sub-Saharan Africa
Human capital formation	Tertiary education
Human resources	Universal and compulsory education
Illiteracy rates	Youth literacy

I. INTRODUCTION

In post-colonial Africa, education has been advanced by governments as a right of every African citizen. This fundamental tenet explains why primary education is universal, compulsory, and free in almost all of Africa. The same does not apply to secondary education, however, for which parents are asked to pay tuition. In contrast, university or tertiary education (higher learning beyond secondary or high school) is generally free, although students are often compelled to secure government loans to supplement their financial assistance.

This chapter discusses the state of education in Africa, especially in Sub-Saharan Africa, and examines the relationship between education and economic development, with an eye toward improving people's living standards and ending

African Economic Development

or containing poverty, ignorance, and ill health. It concludes by noting that African leaders and educators have failed in this area for several reasons: inappropriate training of its graduates; the persistence of outmoded and Eurocentric curricula; lack of adequate funds; corruption and mismanagement; gender, regional, and ethnic inequalities; political instability; and the demands of the International Monetary Fund.

The primary focus in this chapter is Western-introduced education, or modern education (as opposed to traditional and Islamic education), which has been accepted everywhere on the continent. Because Africa South of the Sahara is the main region targeted in the chapter, very little is said about Islamic and traditional educational systems, both of which are briefly mentioned only in the conclusion.

How a country is faring in the education of its citizenry can be measured by the adult literacy or illiteracy rates, primary school enrollment rates, secondary enrollment, tertiary enrollment, male and female enrollment rates of children reaching grade 5, achievements and contributions of the graduates to society, and public education expenditure. Better education involves increases in primary, secondary, and tertiary school enrollments and adequate financial support for education.

II. EVOLUTION AND TRANSFORMATION OF EDUCATION IN AFRICA

A. EDUCATION NEGLECT IN COLONIAL AFRICA

In a formal conference at Addis Ababa in 1965, African leaders agreed that expanded education would greatly contribute to Africa's economic development and to better health conditions for their people. As a result of that consensus, Africa's leaders have spent millions of dollars to make education free and compulsory. This was in sharp contrast to the aims and realities of colonial education. During the colonial era, the vast majority of Africans were deliberately excluded from the school system to prevent them from challenging the political and social conditions created by colonialism. As a result, at the time of independence, few African colonies had a university-level institution that could become the nucleus for a National University.

The earliest institutions of higher learning included Fourah Bay College in Sierra Leone (1827); the University of Algiers (1879); the University of Rwanda-Burundi (1955); the University College of Ibadan (1948); the Kumasi College of Technology in the Gold Coast, later named Ghana (1951); the University of Dakar in Senegal (1957); the University of Makerere in Uganda (1950); the Catholic University of Louvanium in Zaire (1954); and the State University at Elizabethville in Zaire (1956). In Mozambique, by contrast, a university education became available to a few only in 1964. Even by the standards of the time, these institutions, in spite of the fact that some were affiliated with European universities, were no more than glorified high schools, with virtually none of the laboratory equipment, books, and facilities required for rigorous university training. The few Africans who completed university education as lawyers (in Ghana and Sierra Leone, for instance) and teachers were trained in Europe and often acquired an elitist and European outlook on life. Some developed a sense of superiority and seemed to look down on their fellow Africans.

These conditions were true regardless of whether the colonial policy was indirect rule (Britain), assimilation (France and Portugal), or paternalism (Belgium). In fact, everywhere in colonial Africa from the 1890s to the 1920s, missionaries, whose primary purpose was to impart Christian doctrine, pioneered the education of Africans. This implied teaching basic reading and writing to enable Africans to read and understand the Bible and to serve as catechists, clerks, teachers, and language interpreters. Only during the 1930s and onward did the school curriculum change to include secular subjects, a change that was sparked by colonial governments' establishment of their own primary schools for the privileged few Africans, at first. However, in both missionary and colonial state schools, the curriculum emphasis was the same: basic reading, writing, arithmetic, and preparation for 'semiskilled labor' required by trading centers for carpentery, masonry, smithing, shoe repairing, and driving. Students had to pay for their own education.

Where secondary and tertiary schools were available, the curriculum was entirely Eurocentric. There were, of course, subtle differences between the education goals of the major colonial powers. Whereas France attempted to provide an education that would transform the African into a Frenchman, forcing the assimilated Africans to speak French, the British wished to adapt education to the "mentality, aptitudes, occupations, and traditions of the various peoples." Yet, "while higher education in the British colonies was largely the development of academic intellectuals, some measure of professionalization and vocational education was introduced by the French."[1] Overall, as one expert noted, the objective of colonial education was to prepare the Africans to be "efficient drawers of water and hewers of wood for the white masters."[2] Davidson aptly put it this way: "Knowledge is the way to understanding, and understanding is the way to power. The colonial systems blocked each of these ways. The systems were there to keep power for the colonial rulers."[3]

Within the colonial setting, taxes paid by the Africans were primarily used for the education of children of white settlers and colonial agents, the most flagrant example being Southern Rhodesia (when Apartheid South Africa is left out of the equation), as Table 10.1 illustrates.

It is quite clear that colonial education did very little too late to prepare Africans to assume economic and political roles during the post-colonial period. This educational neglect had serious implications for the development of Africa's human resource capacity.

TABLE 10.1 Rhodesia's Colonial Expenditures in Education by Race

Year	White Pupils	Percentage of Total	African Pupils	Percentage of Total	Grant Total
1909	$1,048,052	99.72	$3,000	0.28	$1,051,052
1919	1,855,300	98.83	22,000	1.17	1,877,300
1929	4,587,032	97.01	141,740	2.99	4,728,772
1939	7,354,208	97.30	204,212	2.7	7,558,420
1949	32,361,140	96.49	1,178,524	0.35	33,539,664

Source: Mungazi, D. (1998) Colonial Education for Africans: George Stark's Policy in Zimbabwe, New York: Praeger.

B. THE POST-INDEPENDENCE PERIOD

The neglect of African education in most colonies was such that at the time of independence only 10% of the population could read and write. In Zaire, not a single African held a doctorate or a law degree or had received medical training in June 1960. Since 1960, however, each African country, including the poorest ones such as Burkina Faso, Niger, Chad, and Swaziland, have built institutions of higher learning and technical schools of their own to provide much-needed skills to the younger generations. Nigeria, for example, with only one university college (in Ibadan) in 1960, now has some 50 state and federal universities.

Between 1960 and 1980, Africa's primary school population increased by more than 40% although today college education is still available only to a relatively small number of high school graduates. Even on this level, however, the number enrolled in Sub-Saharan Africa alone jumped from 17,000 in 1960 to 150,000 in 1980. At the general tertiary level, enrollment jumped from 185,000 students in 1960 to 1,366,000 in 1980.[4] Primary, secondary, and tertiary enrollments altogether more than doubled, rising from 17.8 million to 37.6 million in 44 countries between 1960 and 1972.[5] During the same period, expansion of facilities doubled at all levels (creating 16 million new primary school seats between 1960 and 1972), while technical and professional instruction accelerated, accompanied by some effort to Africanize the curriculum.[6]

The enrollment figures for primary and secondary schools in Africa from 1949 to 1993, as illustrated by the seven countries in Table 10.2 provide an idea of the enrollment changes that have occurred on the continent (population increases must be taken into account).

Notwithstanding such increases in enrollment, major problems remain to be solved. First, since independence, the total school-age population has been increasing at a faster rate than the population itself and the continent's economic

TABLE 10.2　Number of Children in Selected Africa Countries (in thousands) in Primary and Secondary Schools (1949–1993)

Year	Chad Pr	Chad Se	Nigeria Pr	Nigeria Se	Ghana Pr	Ghana Se	Angola Pr	Angola Se	Kenya Pr	Kenya Se	Cameroon Pr	Cameroon Se	Côte d'Ivoire Pr	Côte d'Ivoire Se
1949	—	—	3.1	0.1	212	66	11	2.2	326	6.0	128	1.1	28	1.1
1959	540	1.1	21	0.7	503	177	104	6.5	720	18	435	9.3	200	8.4
1969	162	8.5	84	5.6	976	474	385	37	1282	115	888	48	464	53
1979	—	—	233	—	1296	597	—	240	3698	377	1303	154	954	172
1989	492	60	344	681	1703	793	1041	155	5389	641	1946	367	1405	334
1993	542	69	414	89	2122	—	—	—	5643	616	—	—	1554	445

Source: Mitchell, B.R. (1998) International Historical Statistics: Africa, Asia, Oceania (1750–1993), New York: Macmillan, pp. 966–979.
Pr: Primary; Se: Secondary.

growth. Indeed, if improving enrollment numbers becomes the primary target of the African leaders, as it has been over the years, the cost of education will be staggering and may very well create massive resource shifts from other sectors of the economy, thereby contributing to underdevelopment and defeating the original goal they set for themselves at Addis Ababa in 1965.

Second, there are still significant regional, ethnic, and gender imbalances that must be seriously addressed. During the colonial period, some ethnic groups (the Igbo of Nigeria, the Kikuyu of Kenya, the Sara of Chad, for example), certain geographical areas (cities and towns), and male children in general had better educational opportunities than others. This trend has not been drastically reversed in most African countries. For instance, female adult literacy, as a percent of male literacy, is only 75% in Senegal and 85% in Kenya.

Third, the post-colonial school curriculum continues to be patterned after that of Europe in both former British and French colonies, never truly adapting itself to local African needs. Yet, even though a high percentage of students from many countries, who are enrolled in African Virtual University are studying computer-related subjects, nursing, and other areas with practical applications, most university students in Africa have tended to concentrate unevenly in the social sciences and the humanities. This imbalance makes it difficult for African countries to have an adequate supply of human resources that have the know-how and technical skills to contribute to national development.

III. EDUCATION AND DEVELOPMENT IN AFRICA

In Africa and elsewhere education plays an important role in economic growth and economic development. This is why the colonial neglect of education in

Africa and post-colonial imbalances have had serious consequences on Africa's economic development prospects. The contributions of such economists as Schultz, Becker, Denison, and Weisbrod, among others, help us understand the role that education plays in economic growth.[7] These authors agree that education is important for economic growth and essential for development; education increases productivity (output per unit of input) because educated workers are more efficient than uneducated workers. Education serves as a force for socialization, training human resources or human capital, and improving incomes and productivity.

A. ECONOMIC THEORY OF EDUCATION AND GROWTH

The role of education in economic development is often couched in terms of the *theory of human capital*. Generally, investments that improve human capital come by way of schooling, learning on the job, advances in health, and information about the economy. According to Schultz, the concept of labor force man-hours worked must take into account the improvements in the capabilities of workers.[8] We can use cost–benefit analysis and comparative rates of return to establish the human capital theory. In looking at the overall benefits of education, we must focus on both the private and social rates of returns, so we look at both the private costs and benefits and social costs and benefits.

Costs and benefits play a key role in the individual's (or family's) decision about whether or not to invest in education. The principal monetary costs to the student are tuition, books, supplies, and the income foregone. The principal monetary benefit to the student is the increase in lifetime income that will accrue as a result of completing a certain level of education. There are other benefits that cannot be easily estimated in monetary terms, including better fringe benefits and working conditions, improved health, ability to make better choices, an increased rate of return from saving, and positive intergenerational effects.

We cannot focus, however, only on the monetary rewards that education provides to the individual who obtains an education; we must also look at the benefits that accrue to society, the so-called social benefits. What are the nature and magnitude of the benefits of education? It is difficult to set a value, in monetary terms, on the magnitude of these benefits. The main problem one faces in calculating the private rate of return to education is predicting how the structure of earnings will change.

In general, we can theorize that education contributes to economic development in Africa because it builds human capital and enables workers to improve their productivity, thereby contributing to overall economic growth and human welfare. Education improves human resource and human capital formation, as well as the productivity of labor because workers improve their productivity by learning new skills and perfecting old ones. Further, education helps to improve the nutrition, health, and social well-being of individuals and contributes to the improvement of social conditions and quality of life. Because development equals growth plus improvement in quality of life, education contributes directly and indirectly to economic development. Education correlates positively with per capita income and life expectancy and negatively with infant mortality and fertility rates.

Just as investment in physical infrastructure leads to the formation of physical capital, investment in education leads to the formation of human capital either for the individual or for the society. Hence, the impact of education can be felt at the micro, macro, and societal levels. At the micro level, the impact is on the individual—improving earnings, for instance. At the macro level, the impact is at the level of the aggregate economy—that is, individual and social levels. In this case, there is ample evidence to show that education has a significant impact on economic growth. At the social level, we are concerned with mostly nonmonetary *externalities* often called *nonmarket effects*. Education generates external benefits. This is why subsidies are used as a means of promoting access. The extent to which subsidies actually provide greater access is questionable, given that higher rather than lower income individuals might benefit from such subsidies if they are unfairly distributed, which seems to be the pattern in many African countries. Quite often, assistance designed to alleviate the misery of the lower tier of society ends up in the hands of the wealthy and government officials.

B. Education's Role in Economic Growth and Development

In discussing the role that education plays in the economic development of African countries, we need to look at the benefits of education and human resource improvement. Likewise, we need to look at education's impact on economic growth. This is because of the more obvious and direct linkage between education and growth and the fact that there could be no development without growth in African countries. Many economists have concluded that improvements in the quality of human resources are one of the major sources of economic development, which is different from pure economic growth, which is evidenced by more buildings, more social establishments, and more vehicles but no accompanying reduction in poverty and illiteracy. For instance, Gapinski found labor growth dominance over capital in the economic growth of African countries and shows that the marginal productivity of education is highest in Algeria, Mozambique, Nigeria, and South Africa.[9]

C. Macroeconomic Impact of Education

One can illustrate the impact of education on development and its relationship with other social variables by using the following simple mathematical model:

$$Y = F(L, K, N, E, T)$$

In this model, the concepts of output and inflow are critical. Output or national product Y, which also corresponds to the *production possibilities curve*, during a given period of time depends on the inflows of labor (L), capital (K), natural resources (N), entrepreneurship (E), and technology (T). This technical relationship between input and output is also known as the *production function*.

We could assume that L represents a number of labor units in which a skilled person is more than one unit. More realistically, L stands for a list of skills, together with the number of individuals possessing each skill available during the unit of time. Skill levels depend on education and training. L represents the labor input and labor flows, as determined by the size and skill of the African labor force. Labor force is one of the factors that African countries have in abundance. However, for labor to be a significant resource it must be of good quality, and this is what is scarce in Africa. The only way to improve the skill of labor is by increasing and improving educational and training opportunities. Another important human resource variable is entrepreneurship (E), or the risk-bearers and innovators who coordinate other resources. Like labor, entrepreneurship depends heavily but not solely on education and training.

Technology (T), which consists of the technical knowledge of the production of goods and services, determines how effectively and efficiently the different factors are utilized and depends on education. Technologies are the skills, knowledge, and procedures necessary for producing goods and services. Technology or technical knowledge connotes the practical arts, ranging from hunting, fishing, and agriculture through manufacturing, communication, and medicine. Technical knowledge can be a direct production input, as labor in our production function, or a variable affecting the relationships among inputs L, K, N, and E and output Y. For instance, a farmer who possesses mechanized farming technology (knowledge of how to use tractors and plows and harrows) will cultivate more acreage and produce more output per unit of time than a farmer who possess only the know-how to use hoes and shovels. Hence, technology increases acreage cultivated by each farmer in a given time period.

From this perspective, increased technical knowledge decreases inputs per unit of output. That is, it increases productivity. To increase output (Y), African countries must increase or improve all or some of the variables on the right-hand side of the equation. Because three of the key variables depend on education, we can see how a well-educated population can contribute to economic growth in an African country. It is therefore important that African countries improve the quality of education and increase educational attainment among the population. Often, there is need to choose between *educational widening* and *education deepening*. Educational deepening refers to using people with more schooling to do jobs that previously were done by less-educated people. Clearly, African governments must choose between building more educational institutions, as the multiplicity of universities in Nigeria illustrates, as opposed to deepening or strengthening and improving the effectiveness of existing institutions. When the private rate of return to education is much higher than the social rate of return, then it is not economically efficient to expand education to the point of fully satisfying private demand.

IV. EDUCATION AND FUTURE ECONOMIC GROWTH IN AFRICA

We can illustrate the future growth potential of an African country's present educational decisions by means of the *production possibilities concept*. An African country's current choice of positions on its production possibilities curve determines among other variables the future location of that curve. Suppose that panels A and B of Fig. 10.1 show the current choices of two countries, Procrastica and Realistica, each of which produces only two goods—education and consumer goods. We assume fixed technology, fixed resources, and full employment. In each of the graphs, we have designated the two axes as education—an important ingredient of economic growth that improves the quality of human resources—and pure consumer goods, such as clothing, luxury items, etc. The production possibilities curve shows the limits of a country's

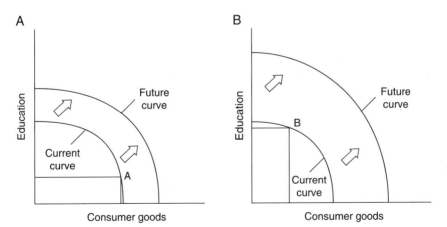

FIGURE 10.1   (A) Procrastica's production possibilities, current choices, and future growth. (B) Realistica's production possibilities, current choices, and future growth.

growth at time t. For a country to grow, it must shift its production possibilities frontier to the right, through such things as resource increase (improvement).

Suppose that the two economies of Procrastica and Realistica are identical in every respect expect one: Procrastica's current choice of positions (point A in Fig. 1A) on its production possibilities curve strongly favors consumer goods rather than education. In contrast, Realistica has a high priority for education in its current choices, as shown by point B in Fig. 1B. Assuming all else constant, we can expect the future production possibilities of Realistica to shift farther to the right than those of Procrastica. By channeling more resources into education relative to consumer goods, Realistica achieves more economic growth.

A. EDUCATION, INCOME, AND OTHER BENEFITS

Education and income tend to move in the same direction, as Fig. 10.2 illustrates. Does higher income lead to higher educational attainment or does better educational attainment lead to higher incomes? The direction of causation between income and education is not quite certain. The scatterplot (Fig. 10.2) shows that a significant number of African countries have both low income and high illiteracy rates. Also, from the scatterplot, we can see that African countries with higher incomes have lower literacy rates and vice versa. For instance, with per capita income of $202, Niger has one of the highest illiteracy rates in Africa,

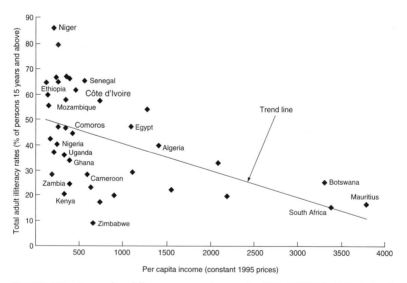

FIGURE 10.2   Scatterplot of illiteracy rates and per capita GNP. (1999 World Bank data.)

whereas Mauritius with per capita income of $3796 has an illiteracy rate of 17%, one of the lowest in Africa. Likewise, Botswana and South Africa, which have per capita incomes in excess of $3000, have illiteracy rates of less than 30%. In contrast, the majority of the countries with $500 or less per capita income have over 40% illiteracy rates. The exceptions are Zimbabwe, which is a low-income country with high literacy rates, and Algeria, a lower middle-income country with 40% illiteracy rate.

Spending on education has been inefficient in many African countries because dropout rates are high. For the student's family, the main *implicit* cost of secondary education in most African countries is the earnings or work at home foregone while the student attends school. In manpower planning, one estimates gross national product (GNP) growth, then the sectoral structure of output, then employment by sector, then employment by occupational category, and then the corresponding educational requirements.

Education, women in the labor force, urbanization, and income equality are negatively correlated with fertility. According to Psacharopoulos, education increases the opportunity cost of a woman not staying in the labor force.[10] Also,[11]

> As the pillars of family life, educated women are better able to institute good child and family care and to manage these appropriately. Child survival, the success of children in school, nutritional status are all better assured in homes, in which the mothers and the sisters have had the benefit of good education. *Improving the education of women and girls is therefore a very important means of ensuring future all-round development of families, communities, and nations.*

When people are educated, they become more aware of opportunities that exist outside their immediate environment and they may migrate. They are also likely to make better choices when it comes to health.

Education addresses the problem of imbalance between the stock of human and non-human capital. Also, education enables a country to produce more technologically sophisticated goods.[12] Whereas education affects economic growth positively, a lack of educated workers may affect economic growth negatively. Hence, "literacy is not only of value to the individual possessing it and to employees but also is of value to others."[13]

From the literature on the economic effects of education we can draw the following general conclusions:

1. African countries often have higher rates of return for education than for investment in physical capital.
2. Investing in basic education yields a higher return to society than spending at other levels. Primary education provides the highest rates of return, at least before universal primary education.
3. Social returns to investment in education in Africa are greater for primary education and least for university education.

4. Psacharopoulos shows that, in Africa, education contributes over 15% to economic growth compared to less than 10% in Europe and North America. The rates of return to education tend to flatten or even decline as countries become more developed.[14]

5. The greater the extent of schooling, the higher the level of income and the faster the rise in earnings. The amount of schooling is temporally positively related to earnings before it levels off or declines after age 40. The larger the amount of schooling, the slower the rate of attainment of maximum income, which leads to higher retirement earnings.

6. Education systems in nearly all African countries are managed poorly and administered inefficiently: "There continues to be a mismatch between curricular emphases and orientations on the one hand and labor market needs on the other."[15]

V. EDUCATIONAL CRISIS IN AFRICA

Many African leaders are keenly aware of the imbalances and cost of improving educational outcomes in Africa. Yet, it appears now that the euphoria of the 1960s is disappearing, and many experts claim that there is an education crisis virtually everywhere in Africa today, "a state of disarray" that is heading for total disintegration.[16] As one analyst stated, "It is evident that educational opportunities in Africa are neither equitably distributed among different regions and sections of the population, nor are they evenly utilized."[17] Sub-Saharan Africa's enrollment ratios by gender and region in primary and secondary school have improved but gender imbalances are still high (see Table 10.3).

The rate of dropouts, especially among girls in Sub-Saharan Africa, remains too high among students in grade 1, a period generally following 6 years of schooling. Such factors as cultural traditions, family labor needs, and financial constraints exacerbate the dropout rates, especially among women.

The highest repeat rates are found in Gabon, the Republic of Congo, Chad, Madagascar, Mozambique, Benin, Togo, Guinea, Cote d'Ivoire, Eritrea, and

TABLE 10.3   Regional Literacy Ratios by Gender in Africa (1990)

Region	Males	Females
East Africa	71	43
Southern Africa	78	63
Central Africa	64	40
West Africa	49	24

Source: Ishikawa, K. (1999) *Nation Building and Development Assistance in Africa*, New York: St. Martin's Press.

Lesotho, with rates as high as 20 and 33%. Among the most successful, the following countries stand out: Zambia (2.8%), Botswana (3.3%), Egypt (6.5%), Ethiopia (7.8%), and Rwanda (7.6%).[18]

Figures on primary school girls' enrollment in certain countries give cause for serious concern: Somalia, 8%; Mali, 14%; Guinea, 15%; Burkina Faso, 20%; and Uganda, 38%.[19] Overall, then, adult literacy rates are skewed highly in favor of men when one compares regional ratios in Sub-Saharan Africa for 1990.

With regard to patterns of female education in Africa, Egypt, Libya, Lesotho, The Republic of Congo, Eritrea, Botswana, South Africa, Namibia, Mauritius, Madagascar, Zambia, and Zimbabwe have relatively high percentages of female enrollment in primary school, ranging from 48 to 100%. However, in secondary school, with the clear exceptions of Botswana, Namibia, Mauritius, and South Africa (all in the 50th percentile), virtually every percentage falls dramatically into the 30s and lower in the cases of Chad (1.3%), Burkina Faso (3.4%), Ethiopia (9%), Eritrea (15%), and Cote d'Ivoire (15%). Adult illiteracy for females is worse in Niger, Burkina Faso, Burundi, Gambia, Guinea, Mali, Mauritania, Mozambique, Senegal, and Somalia, where the percentages range between 77 and 91%.[20]

Again, we may reiterate that the reasons for the imbalance are many, but cultural traditions, lack of adequate resources and facilities, and weak determination on the part of the leadership adequately explain the neglect of female children. Higher education is for very few, so female enrollment is relatively negligible, in some cases as low as 3% or less, as is the case of Lesotho (which has a female enrollment of 99% in primary school), Madagascar, Botswana, and Zambia. Zimbabwe's 15% is one of the highest in Sub-Saharan Africa.

Weighted literacy rates on the continent have risen dramatically, relatively speaking, over the last two decades, from 38% in 1981 to 45% in 1984 and 52% in 1991. But, as one education expert noted, "This progress, however, is marred by the increase in the absolute number of illiterates," which was projected to increase from 132 million in 1980 to 147 million by mid-2000 in Sub-Saharan Africa alone.[21] In fact, the rate of enrollment declined because of economic and political instability during the 1980s. Between 1965 and 1970, enrollment increased by 5.6% and during the 1970–1980 period by 8%, only to decline to a 2.8% increase during the 1980s. In addition, a "gross enrollment ratio of school-aged children at the primary level declined almost 71% by the mid-1990s compared to about 81% in the mid-1980s."[22]

VI. EDUCATIONAL POLICY IN AFRICA

In Addis Ababa in 1965, African leaders pledged to ensure that 30% of the secondary school-age and 6% of the tertiary-age population would have a chance to go to school. But, unexpected demographic growth, political unrest and war, and economic crises dashed these hopes and aspirations. As some analysts note, even by 1985, only 61% of school-age children were in primary school and, "although 61% of the adult population was estimated to be illiterate in 1980 compared to 81% in 1960, the absolute number of illiterates in the continent was thought to have risen from 124 million to 156 million."[23]

As alluded to earlier, a major problem for Africa is that the continent has, at present, the highest birth rate in the world, about 43 per 1000, and its population, currently estimated at over 750 million, doubles every 25 years or so. Furthermore, 50% of the population is under the age of 15. The implications are that, in Africa, it will be impossible to achieve universal, compulsory, and free education, despite the fact that, in 1996, the Organization of African Unity (OAU) proclaimed the 1997–2006 period as the Education Decade for Africa. Table 10.4 gives an idea of educational expenditures in African countries.

From Table 10.4, one can detect that public expenditures in education have ranged recently from 0.9 to 9%. Namibia, Lesotho, South Africa, and Tunisia are at the highest percentile (7–9%), followed by Kenya and Congo Republic (6%), and Malawi, Algeria, Mauritania, Cote d'Ivoire, and Morocco (5%). At the bottom of the list one finds Nigeria (most recently), Zambia, Chad, Burkina Faso, Eritrea, Guinea, Madagascar, and Mali ranging between 0.9 and 1.5%. The remainder spend only between 2 and 4.5%. Comparative figures for the year 1988 give us an idea of the actual expenditures on education per person in U.S. $ for the world in 1988:[24]

Africa (except North Africa)	$16.00
Asia	$68.00
Latin America and the Caribbean	$90.00
Arab States	$134.00
Developed countries	$769.00

It is clear that Africa has a long way to go, if it is going to have as many educated citizens as the rest of the world, including even Asia and Latin America.

Given its strategic importance to national economic development, one would expect a significant investment in education by African governments. Yet, the reality is strikingly different, as the figures presented in this section indicate. Indeed, lack of funds has been a major setback for Africa's educational systems during the last two decades. In Sub-Saharan Africa, gross domestic product (GDP) allocations for education, which was 5.1% in 1980 rose to only 5.7% by 1992, and in many countries, the percentage shrank dramatically to 2.7% in Zambia in 1991, 3.1% in Ghana in 1980, 5.7% in Liberia in 1980, 1.7% in Nigeria in 1993, and 1.3% in Sierra Leone in 1989. Ironically, the countries that accepted the structural adjustment program of the International Monetary Fund (IMF) and the World Bank, which deem universal primary education in Africa unrealistic, seem to have

TABLE 10.4 Africa's Recent Public Education Expenditure as a Percentage of the GNP (1980 and 1997)

Country	1980 (%)	1997 (%)
Algeria	7.8	5.1
Angola	—	—
Burkina Faso	2.2	1.5
Burundi	3.4	4.0
Cameroon	3.8	—
Central African Republic	—	—
Chad	—	1.7
Congo (Democratic Republic of)	2.6	—
Congo Republic	7.0	6.1
Cote d'Ivoire	7.2	5.1
Egypt	5.7	4.8
Eritrea	—	1.8
Ethiopia	3.1	4.0
Gabon	2.7	2.9
Ghana	3.1	4.2
Guinea	—	1.9
Guinea-Bissau	—	—
Kenya	6.8	6.5
Lesotho	5.1	8.4
Libya	3.4	—
Madagascar	4.4	1.9
Malawi	3.4	5.4
Mali	3.7	2.2
Mauritania	—	5.1
Mauritius	5.3	4.6
Morocco	6.1	5.0
Mozambique	3.1	—
Namibia	1.5	9.1
Niger	3.2	2.3
Nigeria	6.4	0.7
Rwanda	2.7	—
Senegal	—	3.7
Sierra Leone	3.5	—
South Africa	—	—
Sudan	4.3	0.9
Tanzania	—	—
Togo	5.6	4.5
Tunisia	5.4	7.7
Uganda	1.3	2.6
Zambia	4.5	2.2
Zimbabwe	5.3	—

Source: World Bank (2000) *World Development Indicators*, Washington, D.C.: World Bank, pp. 70–72.

suffered more than the nonadjusting ones. Zimbabwe's refusal to accept structural readjustment in some measure explains the high levels of literacy and low incomes, to which must be added mismanagement and chronic maldistribution of resources. Thus, 19 adjusting African countries' expenditures on health and education, as percentages of total expenditures, declined from 16.3% in 1970, 16.3% in 1975, and 14.0% in 1980 to 12.6% in 1985 and 12.2% in 1990. In contrast, in 12 nonadjusting countries the percentage of expenditures on education and health increased from 19.2% in 1970, 16.2% in 1975, and 17.0% in 1980 to 17.0% in 1985 and 18.5% in 1988. Whereas in adjusting countries expenditures on education represented about 4.0% of the GNP/GDP prior to adjustment (1970–1980), this figure dropped to 3.5% for the 1970–1988 period, following introduction of adjustment programs.[25] In nonadjusting countries, in contrast, the numbers rose from 4.5% in 1975, 3.9% in 1975, and 4.9% in 1980 to 5.3% in 1985 and 5.7% in 1988. More recent figures (Table 10.5) show that, during the mid-1990s, illiteracy in Africa remained high.

Given an equal chance, female African children do as well as, if not better than, male children. However, as they advance in age and in grade, their problems are magnified by family demands and space, sexual advances (which result often in pregnancies), early marriages, contraction of sexually transmitted infections and diseases, and eventual withdrawals from school.

Despite the tremendous expansion that followed independence, African educational systems have also been criticized for a lack of adequate facilities.

TABLE 10.5   Illiteracy Rate in Africa (1995)

County	Percentage (%)	Country	Percentage (%)
Angola	51.0	South Africa	18.2
Botswana	30.2	Swaziland	23.3
Chad (1993)	86.5	Sudan	49.4
Djibouti	53.8	Morocco	43.3
Cameroon	36.6	Togo	48.3
Cote d'Ivoire	59.9	Gabon	36.8
Niger	79.1	Ethiopia	64.5
Ghana	35.5	Liberia	61.7
Zimbabwe	14.9	Madagascar (Democratic Republic of)	54.3
Zambia	21.8	Congo	22.7
Guinea-Bissau	64.1	Congo Republic	25.1
Mauritania	62.3'	Algeria	38.4
Mauritius	17.1	Equatorial Guinea	21.5
Mali	69.0	Burundi	62.2
Mozambique	59.9	Rwanda	39.5

Source: United Nations (1999) *Statistical Yearbook*, New York: United Nations, p. 72.

Today, many universities are languishing with no space to accommodate student classrooms or to store outdated and or new books. In Ghanaian universities, for example, dormitory rooms that were designed to accommodate two students may house as many as five students or more. In Nigeria, certain universities have had to schedule separate hours and days for different schools or faculties in their use of library resources. To this is added the problem of university closings linked to political instability or student unrest and a lack of access to the new information technology.

Indeed, wars in Mozambique, Rwanda, Angola, Chad, Somalia, Sierra Leone, Liberia, Burundi, Congo, and Guinea-Bissau, for example, have had a detrimental impact on education. In these countries, schools have been either destroyed or indefinitely closed during civil unrest and war. In Cameroon, Ghana, Kenya, Nigeria, Zimbabwe, and Congo, just to give a few examples, autocratic presidents and military dictators have closed institutions of higher learning at will, whenever there has been student unrest based on political and economic (loans and scholarships) grievances. Denial of university funds has also been one way the African leadership has dealt with dissenting students and faculty. This inhospitable educational environment has created massive brain drain across Africa, especially during the 1980s and 1990s. In fact, a significant number of professors at African universities would relocate abroad, if they had the opportunity. The African brain drain causes:

- Loss of highly skilled workers who would have otherwise contributed to economic growth
- Human capital loss and loss of capital invested in training these people
- Reduction in the capacity of African countries to train a new generation of professionals
- Dependence on expensive expatriates to replace qualified Africans who have gone overseas

Overall, brain drain causes a net gain to the recipient developed countries and a net loss to Africa.

Given all the problematic trends outlined here, the goal of reaching universal primary education targeted for 2020 is in serious jeopardy because educational expenditures are often misdirected (bureaucratic structures and accompanying salaries are two examples) and books, teacher salaries, and essential school materials are neglected, thus lowering the quality of education. One analyst estimates that, to meet the 2020 goal, African governments would have to add a minimum of U.S. $5 per pupil to the current public expenditures to enhance quality and guarantee adequacy of teaching materials.[26]

One major criticism leveled against African educational systems, especially at the university level, is that they are too often irrelevant to Africa's needs and therefore have little impact on economic development. The irrelevance is first detected not only in the fact that students are allowed to flock into the social sciences and the humanities but that the curriculum is still patterned after that of Europe or North America. This trend was strongly encouraged by the United States in the 1960s through the Rockefeller initiatives in the social sciences when Africa's newer universities adopted the American model rather than the Oxbridge model. Not only is there a shortage of students in agriculture, science, engineering, and in the technical fields, as the United Nations Economic Commission for Africa has pointed out, but there is also inadequate training to meet the challenge of rapid transition from a traditional economy to an industrial one and to solve newer development problems.

In sum, it has been suggested that African education is not "development oriented," as the experts have put it, and that Africa has not focused on education or embraced the concept of education for development.[27] In this context, some claim, post-independence African education is no better than the much-despised colonial education of yester years. One education expert has said:[28]

> Despite the phenomenal expansion of educational systems, there is a widespread feeling that the qualitative aspects of education have not received enough attention. With reference to Africa, it is felt that educational institutions are producing academic robots—or to use Leopold Senghor's famous terminology, "photographic negatives"— of the British, French, and Belgian colonial rulers.

African universities have taken on the trappings of Western universities and have become "enclaves" within their countries, while lacking such necessary "accompaniments as adequate buildings, facilities, and maintenance funds."[29] No wonder it is said that African universities not only do not help create conditions for employment but also produce graduates who cannot find employment because they do not have the relevant qualifications for the desperate needs of the continent:[30]

> Evidently, there are those who emphasize education for self-reliance and those who advocate education for development. There is no reason why the two must be mutually exclusive. It is widely accepted today that one's income increases with every extra year of schooling. It is also generally accepted today that one of the roles of education is making the individual "more productive in the market place." Yet, this goal cannot be achieved unless the education dispensed is relevant to the country's present and potential market forces. As some analysts note, "If school-leavers [graduates] are unable to find work for which they have been trained, the resources invested in them will have been at least partially wasted."

Sensing the devastating economic conditions in Southern Africa, Mungazi and Walker argue that the educational system here must be radically modified so that it can help find solutions to the pressing problems of "national development."[31] Jolly and others, a long time ago, had already advocated that economists have definitely proven the relationship between education (literacy, knowledge, relevant skills) and economic growth, as exemplified in developed countries, where the expansion of the labor force and physical capital have resulted in large measure from education and training.[32] Africa is urged to take this reality into account as it prepares to face new challenges that can further lower its people's already lowest standard of living in the world.

Whether the universities can actually solve all economic problems a given African country faces is a different issue, but it is suggested that universities should be at the forefront, assessing national needs, foreseeing new problems, suggesting viable solutions, and providing the necessary training to implement them, with the ultimate aim of creating jobs and alleviating poverty, disease, and ignorance. In the words of Leonor, school solutions must, minimally, "speed up or intensify the economic conditions."[33] Otherwise, there will be no explicit connection between education and economic development.

Understandably, one reason why school-leavers, or graduates, abandon their villages and prefer to stay in the city is the failure of the educational system to prepare them to meet the rural needs from which they came. Not adequately prepared in skills or *spirit* to readapt to rural life, the school-leavers not only do not find jobs outside the urban areas but also believe that physical work and a rural life are only for the illiterate. Ironically, South Africa's poor whites have expressed similar sentiments. The government response, in addition to the color bar, was a major investment in rural and vocational/technical education for whites in the 1920s and 1930s. Thus, Leonor expressed the problem that Tanzania experienced in this respect some time ago:[34]

> ... There is evidence that the school-leavers were also village-leavers. The school-leavers migrated to towns and cities, keeping the density of literate and educated workers constantly low in the villages, despite the massive reforms and expansion of the primary school system.

As the world knows, these symptoms are aggravated by corruption and mismanagement throughout Africa.[35] It appears that the French adage, *plus ca change plus c'est la meme chose* ("the more things change, the more they remain the same"), is applicable to education in Africa. The worst part, however, is that it is changing for the worse. It is all the more astonishing that so many dedicated teachers can be found in both rural and urban areas, and that genuinely significant scholarship is produced in many African universities.

VII. POLICY IMPLICATIONS

The preceding discussion shows that, despite the tangible advances Africa has made in the sector of education, much more needs to be done to make the educational system work more effectively and more efficiently. The principal policy implication of the foregoing discussions is that African countries must improve their *educational attainment* (encompassing mean years of schooling and adult literacy) to raise the living standards in terms of higher incomes and better paying jobs and should devote greater attention to cultural and humanistic values. Writing on "The Great Conversation Revisited," in the *Guide to the Great Books of the Western World*, Adler differentiated between the "goods of the body" and the "goods of the mind." According to him, the goods of the body are food and drink, sleep, clothing, and shelter; the goods of the mind are information, knowledge, understanding, and wisdom. The goods of the body, if we are to believe Adler, "are the goods we need because they are indispensable for sustaining life." In Adler's opinion, "To be without them in sufficient quantity is a life threatening deprivation. To possess them is not only necessary, but also a source of pleasure and enjoyment." In contrast, Adler concludes that the goods of the mind enable us not only to live but to live well and at a higher level, in addition to providing pleasure and enjoyment.[36]

Africa must consider the goods of the body and mind as basic human needs to which every African is entitled as a basic human right. Because the goods of the mind are the prerequisite for unleashing the productive prowess of the people, African leaders must pay particular attention to them. The most important thing is to understand the need to focus on *technical education* first and then on *liberal education*, because technical education will provide, according to Adler, the "economic base that will make universal liberal education possible."[37]

Above all, African leaders and educators need to rethink their curricular priorities and focus on finding training opportunities that reflect the economic and social needs of their people. Education for education's sake has its merits, but the pressing conditions in Africa make it imperative that education for development be one of the greatest motivating forces, along with self-reliance and political maturity, the latter designed to create a greater sense of nationhood in countries that are plagued with ethnic fragmentation.

Leaders and educators ought to take a lesson from traditional education in Africa, which has been described by many as "intrinsically functional," as Fafunwa notes.[38] Traditionally, people viewed education not as an end in itself, separate from society and community, but as a means to help youngsters grow and become productive members of society. In this sense, traditional education has met society's traditional needs. To that end, as Fafunwa (whom we paraphrase below) explains, traditional education trained youngsters in three areas: (1) agricultural occupations, such as fishing, farming, animal care, and animal rearing; (2) trades and crafts, such as weaving, smelting, drumming, smithing, soapmaking, carpeting, singing, wine-tapping, pottery making, dyeing, and hair platting; (3) professions, such as priesthood, medicine, justice (police, messengers, judges), hunting, military, chieftaincy, and kingship. In a sense, this was education for self-reliance, economic development, and community building.

Although Islamic schools or *madrasas* are not widespread in Sub-Saharan Africa, especially below the equator, and their curriculum is limited, their objective is clear—to train Muslims to meet the needs of their changing communities. Their education is also, in a true sense, functional and utilitarian, as they prepare their students for contemporary employment, as do the secular schools, although Islam is an intrinsic part of the curriculum. Secular Africa could also take inspiration from such institutions to make its Western-oriented educational system more relevant, with an eye toward social and economic development that will improve its people's living standards, utilizing with the utmost efficiency the natural resources with which the continent is highly endowed. Finally, African countries must harness the new information and communications technologies (ICTs) with a view to achieving sustainable development by developing relevant strategies and policies in education.

VIII. SUMMARY

Education contributes directly and indirectly to economic development by improving human capital, productivity of labor, economic growth, and human and social welfare. This is why the skill level of the labor force is important in determining the role that human resources play in economic growth, not the size of the labor force. Human capital was not developed in colonial Africa because the colonial authorities provided highly insufficient educational resources and left Africans largely uneducated. Colonial economies were geared toward primary production, and skilled workers were not needed—in addition to the potential political dangers of an educated work force. Like the colonial educational system, the post-colonial African educational systems have been inadequate and have had difficulty in adapting to the development needs of the African people.

In sum, Africa needs to provide more funds for its educational endeavors, on the premise that literacy is one of the major solutions to human problems. African leaders need to eliminate the educational gender gap, because the benefits of one educated woman, given the crucial roles she plays in society, are immense. In addition, each African country must adapt its curriculum to its people's economic and social needs so that its entire educational system not only liberates the mind and combats ignorance, poverty, and ill health but also contributes directly and measurably to sustained and sustainable economic development.

DISCUSSION QUESTIONS

1. Compare and contrast colonial and post-independence education in Africa.
2. How does education contribute to economic development in Africa?
3. What are the economic and noneconomic benefits of education in Africa?

4. Using the production possibilities concept, describe how an African country's future growth depends on current choices in terms of investment in education.
5. African countries that have higher incomes tend to have lower illiteracy rates. Discuss.
6. What has been the major criticism leveled against the educational system in Africa today? Do you agree? Why or why not?
7. What are the prerequisites for the implementation of a sound universal, compulsory, and free education?
8. Given the scarcity of resources, do you think that Africans should try to focus primarily on primary education or on secondary and tertiary education for its citizens? Develop your ideas with examples from other continents.

NOTES

[1]Fafunwa, A.B. and Aisiku, J.U. (1982) *Education in Africa: A Comparative Survey*, London: Allen & Unwin, p. 25.

[2]Mungazi, D. (1991) *Colonial Education for Africans: George Stark's Policy in Zimbabwe*, New York: Praeger, p. xix.

[3]Davidson, B. (1994) *Modern Africa*, London: Oxford University Press, p. 184.

[4]Nwomonoh, J. (1998) *Education and Development in Africa: A Contemporary Survey*, London: International Scholars Publications, p. xii.

[5]Davidson, B. (1994) *Modern Africa*, London: Oxford University Press, p. 186.

[6]Datta, A. (1984) *Education and Society: A Sociology of African Education*, New York: St. Martin's Press, p. 44.

[7]In 1962, Theodore W. Schultz, Gary Becker, Edward E. Denison, and Burton A. Weisbrod contributed articles to *The Journal of Political Economy* on the socioeconomic impact of education and the relationship between education, investment in human capital, and economic growth.

[8]Schulz, T.W. (1962) "Reflections on Investment in Man," *The Journal of Political Economy*, 70(5, part 2): 1–8.

[9]Gapinski, J.H. (1996) "Economic Growth and its Components in African Nations," *Journal of Developing Areas*, 30: 525–548.

[10]Psacharopoulos, G. (1984) "The Contribution of Education to Economic Growth: International Comparisons," In J.W. Kendrick, Ed., *International Comparisons of Productivity and Causes of the Slowdown*, New York: Ballinger, pp. 335–360.

[11]UNESCO (2001) "Education of Girls and Women Beyond Access," *Education*, http://www.unesco.org/ education/primary/access.shtml.

[12]Meier, G.M. and Rauch, J.E. (2000) *Leading Issues in Economic Development*, New York: Oxford University Press.

[13]Weisbrod, B.A. (1962) "Education and Investment in Human Capital," *The Journal of Political Economy*, 70(5, part 2): 119.

[14]Psacharopoulos, G. (1984) "The Contribution of Education to Economic Growth: International Comparisons," In J.W. Kendrick, Ed., *International Comparisons of Productivity and Causes of the Slowdown*, New York: Ballinger, pp. 335–360.

[15]UNESCO (1996) *Analysis, Agendas, and Priorities for Education in Africa: A Review of Externally Initiated, Commissioned, and Supported Studies of Education in Africa, 1990–1994*, summary prepared for UNESCO, Working Group Lead Agency.

[16]Nwomonoh, J. (1998) *Education and Development in Africa: A Contemporary Survey*, London: International Scholars Publications, p. xii.

[17]Datta, A. (1984) *Education and Society: A Sociology of African Education*, New York: St. Martin's Press, p. 145.

[18]World Bank (2000) *World Development Indicators*, Washington, D.C.: World Bank, pp. 78–80.

[19]Ishikawa, D. (1991) Ishikawa, K. (1999) *Nation Building and Development in Africa: A Comparative Survey*, New York: St. Martin's Press, p. 59.

[20]Ness, I. and Ciment, J. (1999) *The Encyclopedia of Global Population and Demographics*, Vol. 1 and 2, Armonk, NY: M.E. Sharpe.

[21]Alemayehu, M. (2000) *Industrializing Africa: Development Options and Challenges for the 21st Century*, Trenton, NJ: Africa World Press, p. 27.

[22]Alemayehu, M. (2000) *Industrializing Africa: Development Options and Challenges for the 21st Century*, Trenton, NJ: Africa World Press, p. 26.

[23]Bray, M., Clarke, P.B., and and Stephens, D. (1988) *Education and Society in Africa*, London: Edward Arnold, p. 170.

[24]Third World Institute (1996) *A Third World Guide 1995/96*, London: OXFAM.

[25]Tiesen, J.K. (1994) "A Study of the Effects of Structural Adjustment on Education and Health in Africa," In G.W. Stepherd and N.M. Karamo, Eds., *Economic Justice in Africa: Adjustment and Sustainable Development*, London: Greenwood Press, pp. 92–93.

[26]Tiesen, J.K. (1994) "A Study of the Effects of Structural Adjustment on Education and Health in Africa," In G.W. Stepherd and N.M. Karamo, Eds., *Economic Justice in Africa: Adjustment and Sustainable Development*, London: Greenwood Press, p. 100.

[27]Fafunwa, A.B. and Aisiku, J.U. (1982) *Education in Africa: A Comparative Survey*, London: Allen & Unwin, pp. 257–259.

[28]Nwomonoh, J. (1998) *Education and Development in Africa: A Contemporary Survey*, London: International Scholars Publications, p. 20.

[29]Nwomonoh, J. (1998) *Education and Development in Africa: A Contemporary Survey*, London: International Scholars Publications, pp. 12–13.

[30]Bray, M., Clarke, P.B., and and Stephens, D. (1988) *Education and Society in Africa*, London: Edward Arnold, p. 36.

[31]Mungazi, D. (1991) *Colonial Education for Africans: George Stark's Policy in Zimbabwe*, New York: Praeger, p. xix; Dickson, A., Mungazi, D., and Walker, L.K. (1997) *Education Reform and the Transformatin of Southern Africa*, Westport, CT: Praeger.

[32]Jolly, R. (1969) *Planning Education for Economic Development*, Nairobi: East Africa Publishing House, p. XV.

[33]Leonor, M. (1998) *Unemployment, Schooling, and Training in Developing Countries*, London: Croom Helm, pp. 46–47.

[34]Leonor, M.D. (1985) p. 265.

[35]Rwomire, A. (1998) "Education and Development: African Perspectives," in Nwomonoh, J. (1998) *Education and Development in Africa: A Contemporary Survey*, London: International Scholars Publications, pp. 2–23.

[36]Adler, M.E. (1994) *Great Books of the Western World*, Chicago: Encyclopedia Britannica, 24.

[37]Adler, M.E. (1994) *Great Books of the Western World*, Chicago: Encyclopedia Britannica, 55.

[38]Fafunwa, A.B. and Aisiku, J.U. (1982) *Education in Africa: A Comparative Survey*, London: Allen & Unwin, p. 15.

CHAPTER 11

Democracy and Development

John J. Quinn

Department of Political Science, Truman State University, Kirksville, Missouri 63501

KEY TERMS

Bourgeoisie
Civil society
Consolidated democracies
Currency overvaluation
Economic determinism
Economic reform
Economically irrational
Electorialism
Established democracies
Fiscal imbalance
Fragment of democracy
Free/partially free/not free
Freedom House Index
Gemeinschaft/ Gesellschaft
Interest groups
International Monetary Fund
Inward-oriented policies
Legitimacy
Mode of production

Modernization theory
Multiparty regimes
Neomodernization theory
Overseas development assistance (ODA)
Operationalization
Patronage
Pluralism
Political liberalization
Principle democrats
Process democrats
Proletariat
Rents
Secularization
Societal prerequisites/democracy
Structural adjustment
Structural explanations
Transitions
World Bank

I. INTRODUCTION

For both economists and political scientists, the relationship between democracy and development represents an interesting and intriguing question. Though it has been a much-studied issue, even the direction of causation is still much in debate: Does development lead to democracy, or does democracy promote development? Or both? The literature supports both sides. This chapter offers a basic overview of some of the debates concerning the relationship between development and democracy. It examines the debate sequentially from both sides of the issue: What effect does development have on democracy, and what effect does democracy have on development? The chapter first examines competing definitions of democracy, followed by a discussion of the school of thought regarding how development impacts democracy. The history of democracy in the region is examined, and the likelihood that democracy can survive in Sub-Saharan Africa is assessed. Next, the chapter examines the question of how democracy impacts development and whether or not democratic, or quasi-democratic, regimes in the subregion have performed differently than non-democratic ones in the economic realm. This question is explored in both the pre- and post-cold war periods. The preliminary findings are that established democracies have, on average, better macroeconomic policies and outcomes than new democracies, and that, on average, the freer the country, the better the policies. In the post-cold war era, the established democracies continue to do better than other countries. However, a comparison between new electoral democracies and non-democracies produces mixed results, as both do well in certain economic policy arenas. The new electoral democracies seem to have more growth and higher incomes than do more authoritarian regimes, though they have worse fiscal balances. The paradox appears to be solved with outside sources of capital explaining the better performance for the new electoral democracies. The chapter then concludes by discussing the inherent fragility, yet seeming inevitability, of these new democracies.

II. DEFINITIONS OF DEMOCRACY

To discuss the relationship between democracy and development, we need definitions of each. Because the majority of this book concerns itself with the idea of development, we will not cover a definition here, though we do discuss the following question: What is democracy? This question is actually quite difficult to answer because the idea of democracy is a multidimensional, multifaceted one. Nonetheless, many feel that there are two basic schools of thought concerning democracy: *process democrats*, who look to see if the leaders were elected in free and fair elections, and *principle democrats*, who look to the rights of individuals and the level of inclusion of minority groups to assess the level of democracy. In a similar distinction, Lijphart refers to the most important ways of viewing democracy as *majoritarian* and *consensual polities*.[1] For majoritarian polities, the dominant idea of democracy is that the majority rule, whereas the dominant idea of consensual polities is that all groups have some say in the establishment of policies and that their rights are protected against the majority.

Such competing and overlapping views necessarily lead to contending definitions of how best to capture the idea of democracy. One of the early attempts to represent democracy was made by Schumpeter, who wrote: "The democratic method is that institutional arrangement for arriving at political decisions in which individuals acquire the power to decide by means of a competitive struggle for the people's vote." Similarly, Huntington defined democracy as "a twentieth century political system as democratic to the extent that most powerful collective decision makers are selected through fair, honest, and periodic elections in which candidates freely compete for votes in which virtually all the adult population is eligible to vote."[2] The procedural approach to democracy has recently been called *electorialism*. That is to say, leaders can be chosen for office without *all* the attendant rights to which people in advanced democracies are accustomed. One possible measure of electorialism is to determine whether or not different political parties compete for power in free and fair elections, or if the country can be called a *multiparty regime*. Dahl tried to bridge this distinction by suggesting the idea of *polyarchy*, whereby a complex index of rights, as well as processes, is incorporated into a single measure.[3] He distinguishes between democracy as an ideal type and polyarchy by which two qualities are met: public contestations and the right to participate. Several authors have offered the term *consolidated democracy* to indicate either deep democracy or one unlikely to revert to authoritarianism. In this regard, Huntington suggests that a two-turnover rule would be a rigorous decision rule.

Perhaps the most widely used index for democracy is the *Freedom House Index*, which, like polyarchy, measures various subcomponents of political and civil freedoms and then ranks them from one to seven, where seven is completely authoritarian and one completely free. Although it is an interval-level variable, the scholars at Freedom House overlay an ordinal step function and label countries with averaged political and civil freedoms between 1 and 2.5 as free, those with averages between 3 and 5.5 as partially free, and those with an average score of 5.5 to 7 as not free. As such, the index can be used as either an interval level variable or an ordinal one.

III. THE RELATIONSHIP BETWEEN DEVELOPMENT AND DEMOCRACY

A. THE IMPACT OF DEVELOPMENT ON DEMOCRACY

On the one hand, many feel that the level of economic development of a country helps determine its political regime type. Four dominant approaches help us to determine the effects of development on democracy: modernization, neomodernization, civil society, and structural.

B. MODERNIZATION THEORY

The first, *modernization theory*, emerged soon after World War II to explain how countries would develop outside of a communist paradigm. It held that countries with higher per capita gross domestic product (GDP), higher levels of education, more urban dwellers, more unions, higher levels of education, and other indices of more modern society also had more demands from society for political inclusion. According to Lipset,[3a] such countries are more likely to institute democratic regimes as a result of these social pressures over time. Thus, according to this approach, as authoritarian countries prosper they are more and more likely to produce the *societal prerequisites for democracy* and thereby become democratic. Modernization theory was bolstered by significant empirical support. Bollen and Jackman, for example, showed that there is a high correlation between levels of per capita GDP and democracy.[4]

Within modernization theory, one can usefully divide the concept into three dominant approaches: sociological, economical, and political. First, from a cultural/sociological perspective, Tonnies argued that all societies move from a *Gemeinschaft* to a *Gesellschaft* society. Gemeinschaft societies are characterized by a community, family, geographic solidarity, blood, religious association, and rank through ascriptive characteristics.[5] Gesellschaft societies are more purposeful and are based more on common interests, unbundled communities, secular association, and rank through merit. The movement from less modern to more modern society is called *secularization*. Similarly, Parsons[5a] argued that the movement to modern society included the movement from ascription to merit, from particularism to universalism, and from functionally diffuse institutions to functionally specific ones. In an economic approach, Beers[5b] saw modernization as arising from interdependence, which results in increases in differentiation (or division of labor), increases in scale, and interactions between both specialization and scale. Finally, Coleman characterized political modernization as increases in differentiation, equality, and capacity. The criterion of equality was sometimes attacked as overly normative, though it did seem to reflect the development of democracies in the most advanced countries.

Modernization theory soon came under attack from several quarters and lost center stage as a paradigm for studying developing countries. An early critic of the modernization paradigm was Huntington, who argued that the presumed linear relationship between incomes and levels of democracy was inaccurate. He held that as less-modern countries became more modern, their existing institutions— the very ones that upheld stability—would become undone faster than new, more complex institutions could be constructed. This called into question the assumption of modernization theory that there was a relatively easy and direct path to democracy through economic development. Thus, for Huntington, modernization was more likely to result in political decay than political progress in newly developing countries. As such, he held that stability was the key variable of interest for these countries. Here, the creation of strong institutions, such as the military or strong single parties, became essential elements for stability. For Huntington, institutions varied along four poles of comparison: adaptability versus rigidity; complexity versus simplicity; autonomy versus subordination; and coherence versus disunity.

Other criticisms of modernization theory centered upon the "American-centric" nature of the paradigm. As countries appeared to be more and more like the United States (e.g., they hold elections, have interest groups, have mass political parties, have free and fair voting), they were deemed more and more "modern." Finally, with the reversals of democracies in the late 1960s and 1970s, especially in Africa and Latin America, the seeming inevitability of democracy being the necessary outcome of economic development was called into question. Authoritarian government seemed to be compatible with the development process, especially in the Far East.

C. THE NEOMODERNIZATION THEORY

Recently, however, modernization theory, or *neomodernization theory*, is making a return, though with more nuance. This renewal is, in part, due to the resurgence of democratic regimes surfacing in the wake of the fall of the Berlin Wall. Once again, waves of countries in Latin America, the Far East, Eastern Europe, and Sub-Saharan Africa are making the transition to democracy. Przeworski and Limongi have shown that the relationship between income growth and democracy is more complex than previously thought.[6] They argue that, according to traditional modernization theory, when any political regime collapses, the type of system installed thereafter would be best predicted by the level of development of the country. Instead, they found that countries were equally likely to implement either authoritarian or democratic systems following a regime collapse, at all levels of economic development.

However, according to their study, where income (their measure of economic development) plays its most important role is in the durability of different regimes: democratic regimes are robust at high levels of income and fragile at low ones. For example, democratic regimes in which per capita incomes were under $2000 were quite likely to collapse during economic downturns (and then be replaced with either a new democratic regime or an authoritarian one). In fact, they found that the likely durability of democratic regimes at this average level of income was 9 years. Nonetheless, these democracies could prove to be as durable as authoritarian countries, as long as they experienced increasing economic growth. For countries between $2000 and $6000, they found democratic regimes to average 20 years. For countries above $6000 per capita, no democratic regime has ever collapsed.

They also part company with the traditional modernization theory by arguing that the level of economic development does not predict which regime type will be instituted following the collapse of a previous regime; they are equally likely to be installed in each of these income categories. Instead, they found that the higher the per capita incomes in the country in which democracy is instituted, the more likely it is to survive. Furthermore, economic downturns are the most detrimental to democratic regimes with low per capita incomes. By contrast, authoritarian regimes can be vulnerable even at high incomes, especially with the death of the leader. Therefore, the positive correlation between development and democracy is due to the fragility of democracies at low income levels combined with its durability at high levels, as well as the inevitable attrition of authoritarian regimes at high income levels. Nonetheless, Przeworski and Limongi hold that even the poorest countries can maintain democratic systems as long as they have economic growth.

Finally, in reviewing the literature of concerning the relationship between development and democracy, Geddes holds that the relationship between incomes and democracy may be more usefully described with a logit function, where the probability of authoritarianism is high for lower incomes and the probability of democracy is high for higher incomes. At intermediate income levels, great variability exists.[7] This finding bolsters the neomodernization paradigm.

D. The Civil Society Theory

Similar to modernization theory, *civil society* theory holds that there are societal preconditions, or requirements, for democracy or transitions to democracy to take hold. Specifically concerning democratization in Africa, many argue that those countries that have a stronger civil society will be better positioned to become more democratic. Civil society includes a general body of private voluntary associations (e.g., student groups, chambers of commerce, labor unions, women's groups, church groups) that do not derive their power or legitimacy from the state. It is held that where civil society is strong, and a tradition of such organizations exists, a country is more likely to become democratic because civil society can act "as a sphere of action that is independent of the state and that is capable—precisely for this reason—of energizing resistance to a tyrannical regime."[8] As such, countries with more voluntary organizations that have institutional depth are better candidates for democratic transition and, once a transition has taken place, are less likely to fall back into authoritarianism. Thus, the civil society paradigm is similar to the pluralist one, but it holds that various interest groups are combined into a societal *gestalt* that can be mobilized for political liberalization or against tyranny. But, also like *pluralism*, this approach assumes that these groups have independent power from the state and that political outcomes can, and ought to be, attributed to the power of self-interested actors.

E. The Structural Explanation

Unlike either modernization or neomodernization theory, *structural explanations* for the relationship between democracy and development tend to involve class analysis and/or the strength of a business class. Karl Marx, the founder of *economic determinism*, analyzed the nature of class conflict to understand history and politics. According to this view, the political systems of countries and their relevant class structures are determined by their economies, or their predominant "mode of production." For Marx, economics provided the foundation, or substructure, for the political superstructure. Democratic systems emerged out of capitalist systems. Under the previous feudal period (in Europe), monarchy was the appropriate political superstructure for the agrarian economic substructure. In capitalism, the *bourgeoisie* (a class of business people) exploited the *proletariat* (a class of workers) through a state characterized by a bourgeois democratic system.

Moore, also a class analyst, found that only countries with a bourgeoisie that was independent of the state had democratic systems. He holds that democracy is most likely to emerge under conditions of a strong capitalist impulse, where the state is dependent on a bourgeoisie for its revenue. Under these circumstances, the bourgeoisie can extract the concession of a parliament from the ruling elite in exchange for the government's ability to increase taxes.[9] From his analysis emerged the famous aphorism: "No bourgeoisie, no democracy." Anderson has argued that the "Absolutist State" in Europe had its genesis in the crown's ability to gain access to revenue without depending on, or compromising with, the bourgeoisie or other nobles. In Spain, the crown had access to American bullion; in the case of Sweden, the crown owned tin mines. In each case, the monarchy procured funds for the state and its military (which was usually mercenary) without the full cooperation of the bourgeoisie.[10] Thus, early authoritarian systems were marked by political elite independence from a bourgeois class.

Similarly, although not a class analyst, Lindblom has demonstrated that democracies have emerged only in market economies—not in all of them, but only in them. He demonstrated that the form of government known as *polyarchy* (his and Dahl's measure of democracy) has existed only where there have been strong and independent market forces (i.e., a property-owning bourgeoisie). Additionally, Przeworski has argued that democracy is most likely to emerge where a bourgeoisie—with divided interests—has emerged.[11] Specifically for Africa, Quinn has shown that from 1966 to 1986, no country has had long-lasting multiparty regimes where the state held a majority stake in either the largest export sector or most capital-intensive industries.[12] This majority state ownership would necessarily reduce the political elites' reliance upon a domestic bourgeoisie for its revenues. Thus, where the political elites had control over most of the productive sector, a unity of political and economic power militated in favor of a monopoly of power in the hands of a one-party (or military) system.

In another structural approach to the understanding of multiparty democracy, Hodder-Williams has argued that multiparty democracy can only survive "where two conditions are met: opposition to the national government must be accepted as legitimate and there must be channels for acquiring wealth and status outside the patronage of government."[13] Thus, a broad societal consensus of what is an acceptable form of rule can underpin the chances of a successful democracy.

A final view of the emergence of democracy does not examine a particular country's level of development; rather, it examines the international roles of ideas and legitimacy. According to Huntington, the international legitimacy of democracy is necessary for the "third wave" of democracy to continue. Moreover, with few exceptions, more and more of the international community clearly see democracy as the best form of government. With the end of the Cold War, the United States, France, and the United Kingdom have announced that overseas development assistance (ODA) would be tied to political liberalization.[14] The spread of elections and the liberalization of political systems in Eastern Europe, the Far East, Latin America, and Sub-Saharan Africa bodes well for the eventual political liberalization of the subcontinent. In fact, Fukuyama[14a] has declared that we are now at the *end of political history*, with liberal democracy as the only viable form of government with universal legitimacy.

III. THE LEGACY OF DEMOCRACY IN AFRICA

As one would expect from the previous discussion, Africa has not been known as a bastion of democracy—quite the contrary. Political regimes have been characterized as neopatrimonial, personal, and military. Even countries that have had more politically inclusive systems have mostly been one-party systems. Nonetheless, there have been two movements toward democratization in Africa: during the decolonization period and the recent wave of democratization beginning in 1989.

A. THE COLONIAL ORIGINS OF NON-DEMOCRATIC AFRICA

During the colonial period, the economy of a typical black African state consisted of three levels: Europeans and Americans at the top holding the large industries, Asians in the middle doing much of the wholesale and retail trading, and Africans at the bottom continuing in farming, market trading, and rudimentary services.[15]

At decolonization, no African bourgeois class existed, nor did one emerge in the ensuing few decades in many countries. In many countries that followed a capitalist path, many of the most productive economic sectors remained in the hands of foreigners, therefore in the hands of a foreign, bourgeois class. In many other countries that followed a socialist or state-led path to development, the newly independent states passed laws that transferred assets to the state in an attempt to diminish the economic power of the former colonial power or foreign business interests generally. Toward that end, political elites *nationalized* industries, especially the large extractive ones. In Tanzania, Guinea, and Ghana, nearly all industries and firms were acquired by the state. In other countries, such as Zaire, Zambia, and Nigeria, their dominant export sectors became majority or 100% state-owned. In those countries with significant nationalizations, the political class came to control the greatest wealth-generating engines, which gave them access to sources of revenue unattached to private owners who might one day mobilize against taxation or for greater political inclusion. Thus, the ruling elites in many countries came to be independent of a class of private property owners for revenue and did not need to grant them an independent parliament. In those states where the most significant owners of industry were foreign, this powerful group of individuals would be more interested in property rights than agitating for democratic institutions or more political inclusion, which they already obtained in their home country.

B. DECOLONIZATION AND EMERGENCE OF REPRESENTATIVE DEMOCRACIES

During the period of decolonization (following the end of World War II and until the early 1960s), most of the former colonial powers tried to quickly establish a form of representative democracy in their colonies, despite their history of authoritarian control within the colonies. Few of the multiparty political institutions designed by the departing colonial powers were durable; within less than a decade, most multiparty electoral systems were displaced by one- or no-party systems (read: military). Of the 15 former French colonies, the 14 former British colonies, and the 3 former Belgian colonies, only the former British colonies of the Gambia, Botswana, and Mauritius maintained multiparty polities through 1989 (excluding the white minorityrule polities of Rhodesia and South Africa which had also been British colonies).[16] Not surprisingly, none of the Portuguese colonies inherited multiparty electoral institutions (as the Portuguese had been under authoritarian control until 1975).

During the period from independence until the fall of the Berlin Wall, however, several countries did attempt to transition to multiparty regimes, such as Senegal, Ghana, and Nigeria. Senegal, in 1974, did institute some party competition, though the Senghor's *Parti Socialist* maintained a majority in the assembly as well as the presidency until very recently. Nonetheless, Senegal did have minority party representation in its national assembly from that point forward. Ghana tried twice during this first period to move away from military rule. The first experiment in democratic rule began when the military regime allowed for a transfer of power. Dr. Kofi Busia and his party, the Progress Party (PP), won 105 of 140 seats. Busia became prime minister on October 1, 1969. The return to military rule came when Busia's regime was overthrown amid economic difficulties on in January of 1972. The second experiment in democratic elections began with the elections of 1979. Elections were contested by five parties, but Dr. Hilla Limann of the People's National Party (PNP) was elected as president and took office on September 24, 1979. The second experiment in popularly elected government ended a bit over one year later, on December 31, 1981, when Rawlings seized power through his second putsch. The national assembly was dissolved, the constitution abolished, and political parties banned.

Nigeria, as well, experimented with democracy during the cold war, though it had more years under multiparty regimes than did Ghana. Nigeria had two periods of democratic rule. The First Republic ran from 1960–1966, and the Second Republic lasted from 1979–1983. Both ended in coups, which were considered to be widely accepted at the times.

According to Freedom House, prior to 1989 only three countries (i.e., Botswana, the Gambia, and Mauritius) had been considered to be free (average scores of under 2.5 for both their political and civil right indices). In addition, Freedom House calculated that there were 17 partially free countries, with scores between 3 and 5.5; 25 countries were shown to have averages above 5.5 for political and civil rights in the region prior to 1989.

From decolonization through 1989, most countries were characterized by one-party systems or military rule. Tanzania, Guinea, Congo, and other socialist/Afro-Marxist regimes had one-party states as a matter of ideology. Senegal (until 1974) and Cote d'Ivoire also featured one-party states (either *de facto* or *de jure*), though not due directly to socialist ideology. Many leaders argued that multiparty regimes would lead to a fragmentation along ethnic lines. Other countries were better known for military rule: Burundi, Nigeria, and Sierra Leone are notable examples. Many of the francophone countries which had *coup d'états* formalized them into one-party systems afterwards. Togo and Zaire (now the Democratic Republic of Congo) both fit this pattern.

The beginning of the second wave of democratization was coincident with the fall of the Berlin Wall, though direct causation is a matter of dispute. Beginning with the National Conference in Benin, which intentionally paralleled the French national assembly of 1789, many countries in Sub-Saharan Africa have experienced significant political liberalization. Between 1989 and 1991, over 21 countries changed constitutions and political practices to allow greater participation within their countries. During the entire decade of the 1990s, 42 of 50 countries held elections, though not all could be deemed "free and fair." For example, only 10 of these elections resulted in a change of government; Zambia, Togo, and Senegal are examples. Others, such as Kenya and Gabon, have held elections in which the incumbents have won the office of president. Nonetheless, these latter countries were listed by Freedom House as party free (Gabon) or not free (Kenya) for the years 1990–2000. Most recently, Africa's most populous country, Nigeria held elections in 1999, leading to civilian rule once again. Moreover, South Africa, nearly at the same time, held its second multiracial general elections.

Despite the inconsistencies in the fairness of elections, the citizens of countries in Sub-Saharan Africa enjoy more political and civil rights than they did 20 years ago. According to Freedom House numbers, between 1989 and 2000 nearly all countries had increases in both political and civil rights. Averaging these scores from 1989 and 2000, we find that eight countries are now considered to be free (up from two): Benin, Botswana, Cape Verde, Mali, Mauritius, Namibia, São Tomé and Principe, and South Africa. Malawi was also considered to be free from 1994 onward. According to these calculations, 22 countries are coded as partly free (up from 17) and only 18 are considered to be not free (down from 25). The prior benchmark was an average of countries from 1972–1989.[17]

IV. WHAT DOES THE FUTURE HOLD FOR DEMOCRACY IN AFRICA?

Using the above theoretical discussion concerning how democracy arises, we can try to assess the strength and durability of democracy in the region. First, that there have been so few democracies is not surprising given that none of the four approaches examining the relationship between development and democracy would see conditions in Sub-Saharan Africa as propitious for democracy. According to modernization theory, Sub-Saharan Africa should have, or have had, few democracies. At independence, the region featured very low levels of per capita income, weak indigenous bourgeois classes, low percentages of urban dwellers, and low literacy rates. For example, the 1965 per capita income for the region as a whole was $895 (adjusted for 1985 dollar values) and the median per capita income was $726. Excluding South Africa, the range was from a low of $290 for Ethiopia and a high of $2589 for Gabon. Moreover, only about 41% of school-age children were enrolled in primary schools, and urban dwellers accounted for less than 15% of the population.

Recently, statistics still indicate low levels of economic development for the region. For example, per capita incomes remain quite low. In 1998, the average per capita income was only $513. In the same year, most of the new electoral democracies averaged very low levels of per capita incomes: Benin, $380; Mali, $250; and Zambia, $330. Of the other democracies, only Botswana, Mauritius, Namibia, the Seychelles, and South Africa had per capita incomes above $2000, the level where democracies are likely to last 20 years. Nonetheless, primary school enrollment is up (77% by 1994–1996), as is the percentage of people living in cities (32.3% in 1997). Should Przeworski and Limongi be right, then most of these new democracies can survive only as long as they continue to grow.

Moreover, the structural aspects of the economy did not bode well for democracy at the time of independence. In fact, Sub-Saharan Africa still has not seen the creation of a strong indigenous bourgeois class (or business class) that is independent of the state, such as was the case in Europe.

Furthermore, compared to other regions of the world, Sub-Saharan Africa has not had a tradition of a strong civil society. In fact, the African state has been described as predatory, overexpanded, neopatrimonial, personal, and military. As such, leaders have often been wary of allowing any truly independent organizations to arise. Even institutional elements of the state are kept weak under personal and neopatrimonial rule. In Zaire, now the Democratic Republic of the Congo, Mobutu adapted a quasi-corporatist approach to society whereby all important civic organizations became wings of the official political party. For example, even the Boy Scouts were attached to the JMPR (the youth wing of the *Movement Populaire de la Revolution*, which was the only political party of the country). However, with the rise of opposition parties, popular protests, and more vocal student and workers' groups, the civil society in Sub-Saharan Africa may be on the rise, though civil society was not met with a warm embrace for most of the post-colonial period.

In other regions and at other times, farmers could help form an important element of civil society; however, this has not usually been the case in Sub-Saharan Africa. Although large farmers or cattle owners have been influential in a few countries, such as Kenya and Botswana, most of Africa's farmers are peasants who face large *collective action costs* for political organization. They tend to be poorly educated, have no access to their own media, often speak different languages from one another, and often live far away from each other. Such a group of individuals faces very high costs to organize political action and is, thus, ill suited to mount an effective challenge to government policy. In fact, many have attributed the antiagricultural policies frequently found in Sub-Saharan Africa to be a consequence of the political weakness of this sector. Therefore, this group, which represents a majority of the population in most African countries, is unlikely to form the base of either an independent property-owning class or a strong element of civil society. This is not to say that a large land-owning class usually or necessarily promotes a democratic state; rather, this class could possibly function as a "fragment of democracy" as its power is derived primarily outside of the state sphere.

Next, following Hodder-Williams' discussion of the two preconditions for democracy, we can see that neither one has been widespread within the region. The first condition (i.e., accepting opposition to the government as legitimate) was very much in question in the early years of independence. Leaders such as Sekou Toure of Guinea and Julius Nyerere of Tanzania considered a competitive political party system to be an anathema for nation building that could plunge their countries into ethnic division and war. Even in current Uganda, the people voted in 2000 for the continuation of their "non-party" system. All members of the legislature belong to the "Movement," which appears to mirror a one-party system. However, in this system, parties may not hold conventions or rallies or support a slate of candidates for office. Nonetheless, with the wave of elections in the region since 1989, opposition parties seem to be more and more common and therefore acceptable. Also, recent events in Zimbabwe (the imprisoning of opposition members, death threats against members of the judiciary, and the invasions of farms and businesses, all condoned by the government) show how even one of the most developed countries in the region can have no acceptance of the opposition as legitimate by state leaders.

The second condition (i.e., having channels for acquiring wealth outside of the state) is undermined when political outcomes determine access to economic resources. This has generally been the case where neopatrimonial states have been established; it is even more the case where such states own the most productive sectors of the economy. In countries such as Tanzania, Ghana, and Guinea, the state nationalized all large industries. In Nigeria, Zambia, and Zaire, the state took a majority share of the largest export sector (oil for Nigeria and copper for Zambia and Zaire). Moreover, more state-owned economic activity occurs in Africa than in any other developing region. For example, in 1991, state-owned activity accounted for 18% in Africa, 10.5% in Asia, and 9.1% in Latin America.[18] If one examines nonagricultural activity, then the African state share increases to 21.6%, compared to 14% for Asia and 10% for Latin America. Finally, the state takes up much of the available credit in Africa, 17.1%, compared to 10.1% in Asia and 10% in Latin America.

The only source for optimism vis-á-vis maintaining democracies in the region comes from the worldwide legitimacy of democracy in the post-cold war era. As Huntington would argue, this is a growing influence on all countries in the world. With few exceptions, more and more of the international community clearly sees democracy as the best form of government. As discussed above, the United States, France, and the United Kingdom have tied ODA to political liberalization. Moreover, democracy and elections have spread to Eastern Europe, parts of the Far East, Latin America, and Sub-Saharan Africa.

In sum, from a modernization, neomodernization, civil society, or structuralist perspective, the social, economic, and structural preconditions for democracy in the region are quite weak. Only the international legitimacy of democracy seems to militate in favor of the creation and maintenance of democratic regimes in the region. This international legitimacy can be bolstered by the delegitimacy of the prior regimes—most of the authoritarian regimes were associated with economic downturns, corruption, and mismanagement. As such, the new democratic elites may not be held responsible for current economic difficulties in the short term. This may give them a honeymoon period in which to conduct the most difficult reforms that are needed in the region. Also, if citizens in the new democracies blame the previous regime for the difficulties, as well as the policy regimes that they followed, protests may not form against reforms that are seen as painful, yet unavoidable. Third, World Bank and IMF conditionality comes with money attached which may grease the wheels of governments enough to forestall a breakdown or complete economic collapse, should the various economic difficulties come to head.

The conditions on the ground are not promising for the new democracies. According to the modernization theory, few should be in existence. According to the neomodernization paradigm, they are fragile and require economic growth to take root, as most have per capita incomes well below $2000. The civil society argument must also see that these nascent democracies are fragile, especially compared with the rest of the word. Finally, the structural argument concerning the requirement of a strong and independent business class would also hold that these new governments have a very weak foundation upon which this type of government can be built. Only the legitimacy of democracy itself seems to augur well for the maintenance of the new electoral democracies.

V. DEMOCRACY'S IMPACT ON DEVELOPMENT

On the other hand, thinkers as far back as Alexis de Tocqueville have held that democratic regimes perform differently than do other types. For example, Tocqueville wrote that democracy would push many talented individuals out of government service and into trade and manufactures. More recently, Sklar[18a] has argued that democracy is developmental (i.e., leads to development). He argues that the core principle of democracy is accountability. Accountability can be vertical (i.e., from ruler to ruled), as in voting. Moreover, it can be horizontal (i.e., from institution to institution), such as in the division between the executive, legislative, and judicial branches in the American system. Sklar holds that any institution or idea that increases either horizontal or vertical accountability is, therefore, a *fragment of democracy*. These fragments are developmental insofar as they promote or deepen other fragments. An example might be a free press that could help keep an independent judiciary independent, and vice versa, or free and fair elections could keep politicians from ignoring court orders, and so on. As such, development here has a political meaning as well as an economic one. Finally, in the later portion of this chapter, the links between democracy and policy outcomes are explored.

However, here we narrow the question from development, broadly, to economic policies, more narrowly. Do countries with electoral choice, or more democratic accountability, perform better economically than do more authoritarian systems? A significant and large literature has emerged on the question of the ability of democratic regimes to implement difficult economic reforms. Two schools of thought are evident. On the one hand, many think that political liberalization can have a positive impact on economic policies. These thinkers, for example, hold that this is the only means of dislodging the old political and economic elites who prosper from the distortionary policies criticized by the World Bank and IMF. As many analysts have pointed out, these polices are used to bolster the ruling elite and are thus quite politically expedient. With continued inward-oriented policies, especially in Sub-Saharan Africa, the political elites maintain control over the distribution of import licences and scarce currency as well as the power associated with monopolies. This gives incumbent political elites an incentive not to reform because they will lose their power over the old patronage networks that consists of economic rents distributed on a political basis. Should there be both economic and political competition, this type of system will crumble and the current incumbents will lose power. In order to forestall this inevitability, some political elites may intentionally thwart reforms. Thus, many feel that political reforms must precede economic reform because the authoritarian governments in Sub-Saharan Africa have been too corrupt for too long. Political openness is held as the primary means of reversing the fortunes of the region. Here, political openness allows for the natural entrepreneurial spirit that had been squelched under authoritarianism to be released and to follow its own inclination—that is, to release the invisible hand of the market through political liberalization. Thus, political liberalization will help decentralize many political and economic decisions, which in turn will promote growth.

The other school of thought holds that having political reforms precede economic ones places the latter in jeopardy. With this view, when politicians are held accountable to voters, it makes the implementation of painful, and politically unpopular, reforms unlikely. Those that lose economically from these policies may organize politically to reverse or thwart their implementation. Therefore, the policies more likely to be passed are not only populist ones that placate the majority of voters, but also are likely to may harm the economy in the medium to long run. Therefore, such countries are less likely to privatize state-owned companies, layoff government workers, reduce pay, or implement fee-for-service in education and healthcare, all because there would be a backlash by voters. Moreover, interest groups that are better organized will benefit from economic policies that allow them to make profits, despite the overall effects on the country as a whole. One example would be continued protection of markets for domestic producers of import substitution industries, such as batteries, footwear, and textiles. By contrast, this school of thought holds that authoritarian countries may be better able to implement difficult austerity measures as they are less beholden to the lobbying of interest groups and are better able to ignore domestic discontent. In Latin America, for example, many have held that "Bureaucratic Authoritarianism" was that region's response for similar conditions, (i.e., the need to implement unpopular reforms led to the repression of labor and the rule of an authoritarian technocratic elite with the aid of the military).

Nonetheless, the empirical records to date are mixed. A common empirical finding throughout the developing world is that authoritarian countries are no more successful at implementing policies than are established democracies. However, new democracies have been shown to be worse at implementing reforms requiring austerity. By extension, the regimes that have the most difficulty implementing reforms are newly established democracies. The question now is whether or not these findings hold in Sub-Saharan Africa.

VI. TESTING THE RELATIONSHIP BETWEEN DEMOCRACY AND DEVELOPMENT

To explore this question in the domain of Sub-Saharan Africa, we must use a looser definition of democracy than many would like. We will consider countries holding regular elections for office and having minority party representation in the legislature as "multiparty regimes." This is our first *operationalization* (definition precise enough for numbers to be assigned to concepts) for the idea of democracy. Under this definition, prior to the post-cold war shifts, only five countries could qualify: Botswana, Mauritius, the Gambia (prior to 1994), Senegal (after 1974), and Zimbabwe. We will also use a second criterion for democracy: the Freedom House Index. Here, countries with average measures of political and civil rights between 1 and 3.49 are considered free; those with indices between 3.5 and 5.49 are partially free; and those countries with average indices of 5.5 or higher are considered to be not free.

We will examine seven very different economic policies and outcomes to see if countries which have held elections or had higher levels of political and civil freedoms have performed better than those which have not. The first period is from 1985–1989. The countries considered to be multiparty regimes, or to have higher levels of freedom, were all established democracies for at least a decade. The second period, after the great increase in the number of democracies, is from 1990–1995. This will tell us if the longer term trends found in the region are the same for the recently democratized countries undergoing simultaneous political and economic liberalization.

The economic categories to be included are these: per capita GDP (1989), average growth of real GDP, gross domestic savings rates, level of currency overvaluation, levels of inflation, illiteracy rates, financial balances, and total debt as a percentage of GDP.[19] The data are averages of 1985–1989 where possible; otherwise, they are for single years within this frame. Each of these is a common index of responsible, or sound, economic management. Per capita GDP measures wealth; change in GDP measures growth; gross domestic savings reflect planning for the future; the level of currency overvaluation measures price distortions or management of price distortions; levels of inflation measure sound monetary and banking policies; financial balances indicate trade and fiscal balances; illiteracy levels reveal investment in the citizens (or lack thereof); and debt as a percentage of GDP measures economic balance or prudence. None of the categories by itself can tell the whole story, but a composite of these indices should be indicative of economic performance.

Examining the differences in average economic performance, it is clear from Table 11.1 that the multiparty regimes had better average scores on these indicators than their authoritarian brethren in every category. On average, they were richer, grew faster, saved more, had positive fiscal balances, and had lower levels of inflation, currency overvaluation, illiteracy, and levels of debt. Nonetheless, the multiparty regimes had quite a bit of variance in both GDP per capita, average growth levels, and levels of literacy. However, there was less variance in the outcomes for currency overvaluation, inflation, fiscal balance, and the debt burden (levels of debt divided by GDP). Given the very wide levels of variance in these categories, ANOVA results are significant only for GDP and growth of GDP at the 10% level (the usual accepted limit is 5% or lower). Thus, though the averages for the categories are quite different, they are not statistically significant.

Next, we examine to see if these trends are continued with the Freedom House operationalization where the emphasis is on rights and merely not elections and parties (though these are included in part of the measure). This comparison is presented in Table 11.2.

TABLE 11.1 Multiparty Regimes versus Non-Multiparty Regimes.[20] (Average of 1985–1989 Unless Otherwise Indicated)

Multiparty	GDP (1989)	Change in GDP	Savings (%)	Overvaluation (Non-CFA) (%)	Inflation (%)	Fiscal Balance	Illiteracy (1985) (%)	Debt as Percent GDP (1986) (%)
Yes								
X	2286	5.66	20.72	1.192	10.4	1.08	46.6	41.77
N	5	5	5	4	5	5	5	4
SD	2202	3.33	15.36	0.238	9.06	8.63	26.5	18.63
No								
X	1188	3.21	7.4	11.15	16.2	−1.06	55.6	62.26
N	29	32	34	20	27	28	26	22
SD	993	2.75	17.53	33.56	31.9	10.86	18.2	40.14
p value	0.07[a]	0.08[a]	0.14	0.61	0.69	0.63	0.35	0.33

[a]Significant at $\alpha = 0.10$.
Note: X = mean; N = sample size; SD = standard deviation; p value = probability value (describes the exact significance level associated with the statistical result). GDP is in U.S. dollars (million).

TABLE 11.2 Free versus Partially Free versus Not Free.[21] (Average of 1985–1989 Unless Otherwise Indicated)

Multiparty	GDP (1989)	Change in GDP	Savings (%)	Currency Overvaluation (%)	Inflation (%)	Fiscal Balance	Illiteracy (1985) (%)	Debt as Percent GDP (1986) (%)
Free								
X	4156	9.1	33.75	1.15	7.4	6.35	23.5	33.9
N	2	2	2	2	2	2	2	2
SD	2769	1.989	11.67	0.17	2.97	11.53	9.19	3.677
Partially free								
X	1152.3	3.77	8.26	16.518	29.75	−2.23	45.45	49.37
N	11	12	12	10	12	10	11	9
SD	761.6	1.757	25.1	47.5	43.7	6.95	18.4	40.1
Not free								
X	1122.7	2.95	8.59	1.97	6.15	−0.79	62.9	66.74
N	19	19	22	8	17	20	18	14
SD	1030.8	3.05	10.92	0.881	10.68	12.02	15.1	38.8
p value	0.002[a]	0.01[a]	0.14	0.64	0.10[b]	0.59	0.002[a]	0.389

[a]Significant at $\alpha = 0.05$.
[b]Significant at $\alpha = 0.10$.
Note: X = mean; N = sample size; SD = standard deviation; p value = probability value (describes the exact significance level associated with the statistical result). GDP is in U.S. dollars (millions).

As we can see from Table 11.2, the countries considered to be free had average scores in these indicators that were better than either the partially free and not-free countries in nearly every category. On average, they had higher incomes, grew faster, and had greater levels of savings. Moreover, they had lower levels of every other category: currency overvaluation, fiscal balance, illiteracy, and debt as a percentage of GDP. The only economic outcome that was matched or exceeded by the less-free countries was that not-free countries had lower average inflation. However, because so few countries are in the free category, we should be cautious not to overgeneralize.

The partially free countries outperformed the not-free countries, but only in certain categories. For example, the partially free countries had higher GDPs and grew faster, though not by much. Moreover, the partially free countries had lower levels of illiteracy and debt burden along with higher levels of currency overvaluation, inflation, and worse levels of fiscal balance. Finally, the partially free countries were nearly identical in gross domestic savings rates to the not-free. The partly free countries also experienced more variance in savings, currency overvaluation, inflation, illiteracy, and levels of debt.

For the contrasts across all three categories, GDP, change in GDP, inflation, and literacy rates were significantly different, using a 10% rejection level. Moreover, GDP, change in GDP, and literacy rates were significant at a 95% level of confidence. Thus, for many countries, the category to which a country belongs is a strong predictor of certain policy differences.

From both operationalizations of democracy, it appears clear that in the later 1980s, the multiparty democratic countries had better economic policies and outcomes than did their more authoritarian cousins, especially in per capita GDP and growth. Because these countries have all had democratic institutions for at least a decade, it seems safe to conclude that established multiparty regimes in the region have had better economic outcomes than countries without minority party representation. Even among countries with more freedoms, the more established multiparty regimes performed better economically: They had slightly higher GDP and growth as well as lower levels of illiteracy and debt. However, the more authoritarian countries had better inflation, currency overvaluation, and fiscal balance levels. Nonetheless, we must exercise some care in interpreting the results as only four of the categories were statistically significant.

VII. THE RECENT ECONOMIC PERFORMANCE OF DEMOCRACIES IN SUB-SAHARAN AFRICA

Now the question presents itself: Do these trends hold under conditions of simultaneous economic and political restructuring? To answer this question, we will follow the above process and test different economic outcomes in Sub-Saharan Africa. Once again, there will be two operationalizations of democracy: elections and political freedom. The first will look at established multiparty regimes, recently emerged multiparty regimes, and non-democratic regimes.[22a]

TABLE 11.3 Established Multiparty versus New Multiparty Regimes versus Non-Multiparty Regimes (Average of 1990–1996 Unless Otherwise Indicated)

Multiparty	GDP 1997	Change in GDP	Savings (%)	Currency Overvaluation (%)	Inflation (%)	Fiscal Balance	Illiteracy (1995) (%)	Debt as Percent GDP (1995) (%)
Established								
X	1602	3.16	17.12	1.1075	11.9	−1.64	38.0	71.98
N	5	5	5	4	5	5	5	5
SD	1532	1.83	11.25	0.076	8.42	5.27	24.5	41.71
New								
X	916	2.22	3.4	1.19	23.46	−4.40	44.4	189.9
N	10	12	13	6	10	11	10	10
SD	1833	1.707	14.9	0.212	29.17	3.947	22.0	124.2
No								
X	623	2.03	11.52	1.354	13.69	−4.52	44.27	146.2
N	14	16	13	8	13	13	15	12
SD	876	3.34	10.78	0.364	13.2	2.78	16.86	81.7
p value	0.434	0.71	0.09[a]	0.33	0.44	0.32	0.81	0.10[a]

[a]Significant at $\alpha = 0.10$.

Note: X = mean; N = sample size; SD = standard deviation; p value = probability value (describes the exact significance level associated with the statistical result). GDP is in U.S. dollars (millions).

The second operationalization will be the same as before: the average of countries' political and civil freedoms from 1990–1996. As a result, we do not test, directly, the implementation of economic reform as such, rather we test the same economic policies and outcomes as before. These are held to be both the means and ends of economic reform.[22] (see Table 11.3).

Just looking at the overall averages, it appears that the established democracies have outperformed both the new electoral democracies (New) and the authoritarian countries (No) in almost every measure. On average, established democracies had higher incomes, grew faster, had more gross domestic savings, and had better fiscal balance (though all were in the red for this period). Moreover, they had lower rates or levels of currency overvaluation, inflation, illiteracy, and levels of debt (as percent of GDP). The new electoral democracy also grew slightly more quickly and had higher levels of GDP than did non-democratic countries. Nonetheless, they underperformed greatly vis-à-vis the non-democracies in three areas: savings, inflation, and debt. If these numbers are indicative, new democracies are more likely to go into debt, have less savings, and have higher levels of inflation. Each of these allows for a shifting of fiscal burdens from now to a later period. Dissaving rarely results in economic collapse in the short term, though the long-term continuation of these policies would eventually undermine the economy. However, despite the lower levels of investment

TABLE 11.4   Free versus Partially Free versus Not Free (Average of 1990–1996 Unless Otherwise Indicated)

Multiparty	GDP (1997)	Change in GDP	Savings (%)	Currency Overvaluation (%)	Inflation (%)	Fiscal Balance	Illiteracy (1995) (%)	Debt as Percent GDP (1995) (%)
Free								
X	1998	4.36	17.46	1.09	9.78	−2.68	36.7	55.7
N	5	5	5	3	4	5	3	3
SD	1329	0.716	10.00	0.04	2.88	6.01	23.7	47.9
Partially free								
X	1060.5	1.91	9.85	1.25	19.66	−4.73	44.3	166.1
N	19	19	19	9	17	18	18	16
SD	1717	1.41	13.87	0.361	24.15	3.414	21.8	117.04
Not free								
X	337.3	0.815	5.13	1.256	13.95	−3.29	43.62	146.7
N	11	13	14	10	11	12	13	10
SD	174.2	4.818	9.617	0.195	10.2	2.86	15.3	53.9
p value	0.09[a]	0.10[a]	0.15	0.66	0.56	0.42	0.82	0.20

[a]Significant at $\alpha = 0.10$.
Note: X = mean; N = sample size; SD = standard deviation; p value = probability value (describes the exact significance level associated with the statistical result). GDP is in U.S. dollars (millions).

as well as higher levels of debt and inflation, they still grew somewhat faster than did the non-democracies. Perhaps more importantly, they did no worse than authoritarian regimes and certainly were not significantly worse off.

Moreover, the new electoral democracies had higher variance in nearly every category relative to the non-democracies. Only in currency overvaluation and growth of GDP did they have less variance. As such, the experience of these countries contains quite a bit of heterogeneity. In fact, the analysis of variance was predictive at a 10% rejection rate for only two variables: debt and savings. Thus, higher averages is no guarantee of higher performance for any particular country in question. The question now is whether these results are limited to the operationalization. To see this, we must examine Table 11.4.

Table 11.4 shows results similar to those of Table 11.3, though the categories, which are significant, are different. Just looking at the overall means, free countries outperformed the other two types of countries in every category. Though all were in the red for these years (at least on average), the free countries were less out of fiscal balance. Moreover, they grew faster, maintained their lead in GDP per capita,[23] and had higher levels of savings. Furthermore, they had lower levels of debt, inflation, currency overvaluation, and illiteracy than did the other two.

The partially free countries, many of which are recent electoral democracies, show the same volatility as in the previous operationalization. Nonetheless, they grew faster, had higher per capita GDPs, and had higher savings rates than did the not-free countries. However, they had levels of illiteracy and currency

TABLE 11.5   Total Per Capita Inflows of Capital and Foreign Direct Investment (1992–1996)

			Established versus New versus Non-Multiparty Regimes				
Multiparty	Capital[a]	FDI		Capital	FDI		Capital	FDI
Established								
X	61.92	147.4	New	158.98	51.2	Authoritarian	77.27	123.8
N	5	5		13	13		16	16
SD	12.79	213.2		171.5	130.3		91.27	272.8
p value	0.16	0.59						
			Free versus Partially Free versus Not free					
Free								
X	101.4	158.3	Partially free	110.37	143.96	Not free	65.383	23.74
N	5	5		19	19		15	14
SD	62.6	208.6		137.6	269.5		48.2	32.2
p value	0.51	0.22						

Note: X = mean; N = sample size; SD = standard deviation; p value = probability value (describes the exact significance level associated with the statistical result); FDI = foreign direct investment.
[a]In U.S. dollars (millions).

overvaluation comparable to the not-free countries.[24] Nonetheless, compared to the other categories, they had higher levels of debt, higher levels of inflation, more negative fiscal balances, and lower levels of savings. Moreover, these three categories contained much variance for these types of countries, which indicates an uneven experience in dealing with each. As such, only two categories were significant in an ANOVA analysis: GDP per capita and growth of GDP, though only at 10%.

Given these unexpected differences, inflows of money were examined to see if they could explain the higher debts and faster savings. Comparing the per capita inflow of overseas development assistance (ODA), loans from international financial institutions (IFIs) such as the World Bank and IMF, as well as foreign direct investment (FDI), these mixed results now seem clearer.[25]

As we can see from Table 11.5, and examining only the averages, the countries most likely to be in transition are receiving the highest inflow of capital, though from a variety of sources. It appears that the new democracies are receiving ODA, grants, and loans at higher rates than the other two groups. However, the newly established democracies seem to obtain less FDI than either the established democracies or the authoritarian countries. As businessmen often require predictability in investment decisions, this is logical. This may also explain the difference between new electoral democracies and partially free countries. Investors may well prefer less-authoritarian regimes in which to do business, though they may prefer even more a predictable environment. Thus, the continued growth of these newly emerging democracies, or partially free, countries may well depend upon international sources of loans, grants, and investment. However, given the great variance within the categories, the p value for the ANOVA is not significant. Given the limited nature of our examination of the issues involved in African development, other rival hypotheses were considered to be even distributed throughout the sample;[26] nonetheless, some partial explanations seem to emerge from this exercise.

VIII. WHAT HAS BEEN THE EFFECT OF DEMOCRACY ON DEVELOPMENT IN AFRICA?

We have analyzed the literature and some data concerning the effects of democracy on development. It seems that those countries that do manage to become established democracies may outperform their more authoritarian cousins in the medium to long run. On average, the established democracies have had higher per capita GDPs, higher growth in GDP, higher levels of gross domestic savings, lower debts relative to GDP, lower rates of inflation, better fiscal balance, lower illiteracy rates, and lower levels of currency overvaluation. Also, it seems that they also had higher than average capital inflows through FDI. However, the new electoral democracies seem to obtain higher levels of capital than do the other two categories. Most of this, however, seems to be in the form of loans and grants, and not private investment, which is often held to be more dynamic for the economy.

Moreover, these newly established democracies may see higher levels of growth and higher incomes, but they may also see more debt, more inflation, worse fiscal balance, and lower domestic savings. However, should these new regimes survive for a decade or so, the numbers suggest that these trends will stabilize and they will continue to grow and prosper, as did the established democracies prior to 1989. Nonetheless, it is difficult to reconcile fiscal imbalance, debt, and inflation with growth, but perhaps the productive energy of a people with greater freedoms may be greater than the sum of their economic policies.

Given the great diversity of the region, the differences in the categories, though sometimes large, often were not significant. Because so many other factors go into GDP and GDP growth, conclusions drawn from one variable are only so indicative, however important that variable is. As those who follow the region know, Africa faces daunting challenges in creating the conditions to promote long-term sustainable development. Therefore, given the great variance in the numbers, we can expect new electoral democracies to have a wide variety of experience. On average, they may outperform less politically open countries in the region, though one cannot make these claims with high levels of statistical certainty. Though only mild inferences can be drawn given the weak statistical claims, it is clear that the *new democracies have not been worse off than similar, authoritarian countries*, as some have argued would be the case. Nonetheless, new democracies seem to do at least as well, if not better, than more authoritarian countries, on average. Finally, authoritarian countries in Africa can look forward to stable policies but lower growth and lower incomes, at least those that can maintain peace. War-torn countries rarely outperform others.

IX. SUMMARY

Does development lead to democracy or does democracy lead to development? This piece cannot answer that question other than to show that the evidence supports both sides. It is possible, as well, that both are true. More developed countries are more likely to become democratic, which, in turn, leads to higher levels of growth and development. It may be a virtuous cycle which is most likely to happen above certain levels of development. Democracy may release the hidden talents and efforts of the citizens of the country and may have its best effects at higher levels of development. Even at low levels of development, some fragments of democracy can bolster other fragments of democracy. An independent judiciary can help keep elections free and fair, and a free press can help expose attempts to undermine the independent judiciary, and so on.

Moreover, there is an unexamined normative question that often is ignored in these discussions. Even if democracies grow less quickly than do authoritarian systems (and this has not been illustrated to be the case in Sub-Saharan Africa), one must ask which system leads to a better life as understood in non-economic criteria. Freedom to choose your leaders, freedom to participate in the policy decisions of your country, freedom from arbitrary arrest—freedom to have most basic political and civil rights—such rights can be seen as good in-and-of themselves. The search for the "good life" should not be completely ignored, despite the requirement to enter into the normative realm of human existence.

Nonetheless, whether or not democracy leads to development and whether or not democracy is good in and of itself, few alternatives seem available to countries in Sub-Saharan Africa. Authoritarianism in the region has not led to rapid and sustainable development, quite the contrary. Moreover, international norms and financial aid from international donors, both bilateral and multilateral, are being tied to the process of political liberalization and good governance. The fruits of development which may or may not be created by this transition to democracy will be produced and ripen in the decades to come, but the initial evidence appears to be that democracies can exist at low levels of development and that new democracies, even in simultaneous transitions, do no worse than authoritarian systems. In the long run, however, democracies will probably be more developed than the countries that remained on the authoritarian path, and all developing countries will, one day, be democratic.

DISCUSSION QUESTIONS

1. What is the relationship between development and democracy? What would modernization thinkers say? Neomodernization proponents? Structuralists? Civil society thinkers?
2. What are the three major approaches for modernization theory?
3. Is Huntington's analysis a strong critique of modernization theory?
4. Do democracies have policies that are systematically different than non-democracies? Does it matter how long they have been democracies?
5. What do Barrington Moore, Charles Lindblom, and Adam Przeworski have in common?
6. What are the differences between process democrats and principle democrats?
7. What is an electoral democracy?
8. What does it mean for a democracy to be consolidated?
9. How likely is it that the recent democracies in Sub-Saharan Africa can become consolidated? What would the modernization theoriests say? The neomodernizationists? The structuralists? What would Fukuyama say?
10. As of the writing of this chapter, how many African countries were democratic? Does it matter if we use an electoral operationalization or one based upon right?
11. What types of countries get more aid? Which type gets more FDI?
12. What are the real prospects for African democracies? Tie into analytical sections from other chapters.

NOTES

[1]Lijphart, A. (1991) "Majority Rule in Theory and Practice: The Tenacity of a Flawed Paradigm." *International Social Science Journal*, 43: 483–493.

[2]Schumpeter, J.A. (1942) *Capitalism, Socialism and Democracy*, New York: Harper & Brothers, p. 269; Huntington, S. (1991) *The Third Wave: Democratization in the Late Twentieth Century*, Norman, OK: Oklahoma University Press, pp. 6–7.

[3]See, for example, Dahl, R.A. (1971) *Polyarchy: Participation and Opposition*, New Haven: Yale University Press.

[3a]Lipset, S. (March 1959) "Some Social Requisites of Democracy: Economic Development and Political Legitimacy," *American Political Science Review*, 53, 69–105.

[4]Though they set out to determine the relationship between democracy and income inequality, their most notable findings were the relationship between incomes and democracy. See Bollen, K. and Jackman, R.W. (1985) "Political Democracy and the Size Distribution of Income," *American Sociological Review* 50(4): 438–457; see also Vanhanen, T. (1997) *Prospects of Democracy: A Study of 172 Countries*, New York: Routledge.

[5]See Tonnies, F. (1940) *Fundamental Concepts of Sociology, Gemeinschaft and Gesellschaft*, (translated and supplemented by Charles P. Loomis), New York: American Book Company.

[5a]Parsons, T. (1951) *The Social System*, Glenco, IL: Free Press.

[5b]Beer, S.H., Ed. (1973) "Modern Political Development," *Patterns of Government: The Political Systems of Europe*, New York: McGraw-Hill, 54–70.

[6]Przeworski, A. and Limongi, F. (1997) "Modernization: Theories and Facts," *World Politics*, 49: 155–183.

[7]Geddes, B. (1999) What Do We Know About Democratization After Twenty Years?" *Annual Reviews Political Science*, 2: 115–144. Arat also argues that the relationship is not linear; see Arat, Z.F. (1988) "Democracy and Economic Development: Modernization Theory Revisited," *Comparative Politics*, October: 21–36.

[8]Foley, M.W. and Edwards, B. (1996) "The Paradox of Civil Society," *The Journal of Democracy*, 7(3): 38–52.

[9]Moore, B. Jr. (1996) *Social Origins of Dictatorship and Democracy: Lord and Peasant in the Making of the Modern World*, Boston: Beacon Press.

[10]Anderson, P. (1974) *Lineages of the Absolutist State*, New York: Verso.

[11]Lindblom, C.E. (1977) *Politics and Markets: The World's Political-Economic Systems*, New York: Basic Books. For the origins of the term, see Dahl, R.A. and Charles E. Lindblom, C.E. (1953) *Politics, Economics, and Welfare*, New York: Harper & Brothers; also see Przeworski, A. (1991) *Democracy and the Market: Political and Economic Reforms in Eastern Europe and Latin America*, Cambridge, MA: Cambridge University Press.

[12]Quinn, J.J. (1999) "The Managerial Bourgeoisie: Capital Accumulation, Development, and Democracy," in *Postimperialism and World Politics*, Sklar, R.L. and Becker, D.G., eds., Westport, CT: Praeger, 219–252.

[13]Hodder-Williams, R. (1984) *An Introduction to the Politics of Tropical Africa*, London: George Allen & Unwin, p. 120.

[14]For analysis of ODA in Africa, see Lancaster, C. (1999) *Aid to Africa: So Much to Do, So Little Done*, Chicago: University of Chicago Press.

[14a]Fukuyama, F. (1992) *The End of History and the Last Man*, New York: The Free Press.

[15]Rood, L.L. (1976) "Nationalisation and Indigenisation in Africa," *Journal of Modern African Studies*, 14(2): 428.

[16]The Gambia's multiparty regime was toppled in a military coup on July 23, 1994. Unlike the last *coup d'etat* in Gambia (1981), Senegal did not intervene to reverse it.

[17]Freedom House, www.freedomhouse.org.

[18]World Bank (1995) *Bureaucrats in Business: The Economics and Politics of Government Ownership*, New York: Oxford University Press, Table A1.

[18a]Sklar, R.L. (October 1987) "Developmental Democracy," *Comparative Studies in Society and History*, 29(4), 686–714.

[19]Unless otherwise indicated, these data come from World Bank (1997) *African Development Indicators 1997*, Washington, D.C.: World Bank. For change in GDP, see Table 2–1, p. 17; for savings, see Table 2–11, p. 27; for currency overvaluation,* see Table 3–8, p. 51; for inflation, see Table 3–3, p. 46; for fiscal balance, see Table 7–1, p. 189; for levels of illiteracy, see Table 13–13, p. 341. For levels of debt, see World Bank (1986) *World Development Report 1986*, Washington, D.C.: World Bank, Table 17, p. 212. GDP numbers come from the Penn Tables; see http://datacentre2.chass. utoronto.ca/pwt/. *Only non-CFA countries are included for currency overvaluation numbers, as the leaders could not raise them unilaterally; thus, Benin, Burkina Faso, Cameroon, CAR, Chad, Comoros, Congo, Cote d'Ivoire, Equatorial Guinea, Gabon, Mali, Niger, Senegal, and Togo are excluded.

[20]Countries included as multiparty regimes are Botswana, the Gambia, Mauritius, Senegal, and Zimbabwe. South Africa is excluded. Benin, Burkina Faso, Burundi, Cameroon, Cape Verde, CAR,

Congo, Cote d'Ivoire, Democratic Republic of the Congo, Djibouti, Equatorial Guinea, Gabon, Ghana, Guinea-Bissau, Kenya, Lesotho, Madagascar, Malawi, Mali, Mauritania, Niger, Nigeria, Rwanda, São Tomé and Principe, Seychelles, Somalia, Swaziland, Tanzania, Togo, Uganda, and Zambia are not multiparty regimes.

[21] The countries are averaged from 1985 to 1989. The countries listed as free are Botswana and Mauritius. Countries listed as partially free are Cote d'Ivoire, Gambia, Kenya, Lesotho, Madagascar, Nigeria, South Africa, Swaziland, Uganda, Zambia, and Zimbabwe. Countries listed as not free are Benin, Burkina Faso, Burundi, Cameroon, Cape Verde, CAR, Comoros, Congo, Democratic Republic of Congo, Djibouti, Equatorial Guinea, Gabon, Ghana, Guinea, Guinea-Bissau, Malawi, Mali, Mauritania, Niger, Rwanda, Seychelles, Tanzania, and Togo.

[22] Unless otherwise indicated, these data come from World Bank (1997) *African Development Indicators 1997*, Washington, D.C.: World Bank. For per capita GDP, see Table 1, pp. 6–7; for change in GDP, see Table 2–1, p. 17; for savings, see Table 2–11, p. 27; for currency overvaluation,* see Table 3–8, p. 51; for inflation, see Table 3–3, p. 46; for fiscal balance, see Table 7–1, p. 189; for levels of illiteracy, see Table 13–13, p. 341; for levels of debt Table 6–26, p. 180. *Only non-CFA countries are included for currency overvaluation numbers as the leaders could not raise them unilaterally; thus, Benin, Burkina Faso, Cameroon, CAR, Chad, Comoros, Congo, Cote d'Ivoire, Equatorial Guinea, Gabon, Mali, Niger, Senegal, and Togo are excluded.

[22a] Following operationalization in N. van de Walle, (October 1999) "Economic Return in Democratizing Africa," *Comparative Politics*, 21–41. Established countries include Botswana, The Gambia (prior to 1989), Mauritius, Senegal, and Zimbabwe. New democracies are Benin, Cape Verde, CAR Congo (B), Guinea Bissau, Lesotho, Madagascar, Malawi, Mali, Niger, Sao Tome, Seychelles, and Zambia. Authoritarian countries are Burkina Faso, Cameroon, Comoros, Congo (K), Côte d'Ivoire, Equatorial Guinea, Gabon, Ghana, Guinea, Kenya, Mauritania, Nigeria, Swaziland, Tanzania, Togo, and Uganda, South Africa, Samolia, Ruwanda, Namibia, Eritrea, and Burundi as per his operationalization.

[23] The deflators for 1985–1989 and 1990–1996 were different, so the numbers cannot be compared directly across time units.

[24] By this time, countries with IMF standby agreements, or World Bank structural adjustment programs were forbidden from having high levels of currency overvaluation as a matter of conditionality.

[25] Data for FDI and capital inflows are from the Organization for Economic Cooperation and Development (1997) *Geographical Distributions of Financial Flows to Aid Recipients*, Paris: OECD Publications.

[26] Thus, other, pressing social, economic, and political issues have been ignored and are assumed to be independent of regime type. Problems with refugees, collapsing states, HIV/AIDS, high transportation and communication costs, etc., are all important constraints on development and have to be faced independently from the policies or regime types discussed here. Moreover, some may swap institutional effects if not dealt with.

CHAPTER 12

Political Instability*

KWABENA GYIMAH-BREMPONG

Department of Economics, University of South Florida, Tampa, Florida 33620

KEY TERMS

Bi-directional causal relationships
Direct growth effects of PI
Disembodied technical change
Economic development
Economic growth
Elite political instability
Embodied technical change
Executive instability
Human capital
Indirect growth effects of PI

Institutions
Inter-temporal growth effects
Investment
Panel data
Physical capital
Political instability (PI)
Political system
Principal components
Research and development (R&D)
Simultaneous equations

I. INTRODUCTION

Since independence, most Sub-Saharan African countries have experienced declines in all measure of economic performance.[1] According to the World Bank's *World Development Report 1999/2000*, between 1980 and 1990, the average growth rate of aggregate gross domestic product (GDP) in Sub-Saharan Africa was 1.8% compared to 4.0% for all developing countries (excluding China and India). From 1990 to 1998, the comparable growth rates were 2.1% and 3.6% for Africa and all developing countries, respectively. With Africa's population growing at the rate of about 3.5% during the earlier period, it is clear that income per capita declined during this time period. Indeed, the same source shows that per capita private consumption in Sub-Saharan Africa decreased by an average of 2.1% per year during the 1980s and 1990s. According to the United Nations Development Program (UNDP) Human Development Report 1999, Sub-Saharan Africa is the region with the lowest human development index, 0.463, far below the average for all developing

*This chapter has benefited from the comments of several anonymous referees and I thank them; however, I am solely responsible for any remaining errors.

regions of the world. More important is the fact that Sub-Saharan Africa lags behind the rest of the world in *improvements* in the quality of life for its citizens.

Accompanying this poor record of economic performance has been a high degree of political instability.[2] Currently, there are more than 15 full-scale cross-border and internal wars going on in the world, with most of them on the African continent.[3] These are in addition to numerous politically unstable events that are internal to countries throughout the continent; examples include internal conflicts in Sudan, Liberia, Uganda, Angola, the Democratic Republic of Congo (formerly known as Zaire), and Sierra Leone, as well as ethnic and religious strifes (Nigeria, for example). Besides the generally poor record of political stability and economic stagnation, there is a high degree of variation in economic performance and political stability across countries in this part of the developing world. For example, there are politically stable and good economic performers such as Botswana and Mauritius at one end of the spectrum and politically unstable countries with a poor economic performance record, such as the Democratic Republic of Congo, Liberia, Sierra Leone, and Sudan. Despite these observations and the fact that several theoretical analyses have argued that institutional weakness is at the core of slow economic development in less developed countries (LDCs),[4] empirical growth studies have, until recently, generally neglected institutional factors such as political stability and have focused on the quantities and quality of inputs in determining the pace of economic growth. This neglect has occurred in spite of the argument of endogenous growth theory that economic policy is an important determinant of long-term economic growth. If the institutional environment is important in determining the pace of economic growth and an unstable political environment may prevent LDCs from successfully embarking on sustained economic growth, then excluding it from empirical studies of economic growth may result in biased estimates.

To what extent is economic development in African countries influenced by political instability (PI)? If PI affects economic development, what is the mechanism through which it impacts economic development? Does economic development have any impact on PI or is the relationship between PI and economic development a unidirectional one, with PI affecting economic development but not the other way around? How does one define and empirically measure political instability? This chapter discusses the relationship between PI and economic development in Africa. It then uses time-series cross-national data, a simultaneous equations model, and a dynamic panel estimation method to empirically investigate the effects of PI on economic development in Sub-Saharan Africa. While a few studies have included PI in their analyses of economic growth, they have generally treated PI as exogenous. However, empirical evidence from the political science literature and recent economic studies suggest that, at least in Sub-Saharan Africa, poor economic performance has a direct impact on PI, implying that PI is determined in part by economic performance.[5] Additionally, given the uncertainty generated by PI, I hypothesize that investment is endogenously determined by PI as well as other variables. The use of panel data to estimate the relationship between PI and economic development has advantages over the use of either cross-national or times-series data alone to investigate such relationships. Because institutions affect the productivity of existing resources, using panel data allows the researcher to treat each country as it were using a different production function. The use of panel data in estimation also allows the researcher to account for country heterogeneity on account of institutional change in the development process.

Economic development is a multifaceted concept that aims at improving the living standards and range of choices available to a majority of citizens in a country. It encompasses improvements in the physical quality of life, freedom from servitude, and the freedom to choose. Economic development, as defined here, is too broad to be adequately captured in any particular study, let alone in one chapter of a book. In this chapter, I focus on the relationship between political instability and economic growth, which is a quantitative concept, rather than economic development, which is a qualitative concept. I proxy economic development by the annual growth rate of real per capita GDP in a country. I recognize that the two concepts are different. However, I also note that economic growth is a necessary condition for sustained economic development. While a more comprehensive proxy of development would consider improvement in the quality of life, no index is available for most countries for any reasonable period of time that allows me to empirically study the development impact of PI, except the growth of real GDP.[6] Because I proxy development with economic growth, the policy conclusions that flow from the relationship between economic growth and political instability should therefore be considered as *necessary but not sufficient* conditions for economic development in Sub-Saharan Africa.

This chapter differs from previous studies of the relationship between PI and economic growth in several ways. First, I provide a systematic economic framework within which to explore the issue of simultaneity in the relationship between PI and economic growth and establish the direction of causation, something that single-equation models using cross-national data cannot do.[7] Second, the estimation of a multiple equation model allows me to explore both the direct and indirect channels through which PI affects economic growth. Third, I develop a more comprehensive measure of PI than the narrowly defined elite PI that has been used in earlier research, permitting the measurement of the impacts of other forms of political instability on economic development in Sub-Saharan Africa. Fourth, lagged values of PI are included to measure the intertemporal relationship between PI and economic growth. Fifth, I use a principal components method to develop a more comprehensive measure of political instability in this study than has been used before. Finally, the use of panel estimation techniques allows correction for correlated country effects with regressors as well as exploring the dynamics of the PI/growth relationship. I hope the results of my study will shed further light on the relationship between PI and economic growth in LDCs.

The rest of the chapter is organized as follows. Following this introduction, in Section II I discuss the effects of institutions on economic growth and the concepts of PI and how it may affect economic growth, as well as providing a brief review of previous studies. In Section III, I discuss the mechanisms through which PI can affect economic growth. Section IV provides a three-equation augmented production function growth model that endogenizes investment in physical capital and political instability. Section V discusses the data used to estimate the model, while Section VI presents and discusses the statistical results as well as policy implications. Section VII summarizes and concludes the paper. The Appendix presents a brief introduction to the dynamic General Method of Moments (GMM) panel estimator I use to estimate the model.

II. INSTITUTIONS AND ECONOMIC DEVELOPMENT

A. INSTITUTIONS DEFINED

Neoclassical growth theory has stressed the importance of savings and capital accumulation together with exogenously determined technical progress as the sources of economic growth. Endogenous growth theory argues that in addition to the accumulation of capital, technical progress is not exogenous but is planned and produced through research and development (R&D) efforts. However, both neoclassical and endogenous growth theories assume that the environment within which capital and technology are accumulated (institutions, generally) are available, efficient, and stable over time to allow development to take place. The effectiveness of policy formulation and implementation depends on the effectiveness of institutions.

What do we mean by institutions? Institutions are many and varied and encompass several things. The definition a researcher adopts will therefore depend on what aspect of institutions the researcher wants to emphasize. This chapter adopts the definition of institutions provided by Bardhan who defines institutions as:[8]

> ... the social rules, conventions and other elements of the structural framework of social interaction.

These institutions can be informal, such as social capital and norms or formal legal rules such as laws ensuring individual liberties, property rights, and the enforcement of contracts. Capital (both physical and human) accumulation and technical progress require an institutional framework which provides and guarantees incentives for those who sacrifice present consumption to accumulate capital and develop technology. Until recently, most of the economic growth literature had assumed that institutions were at best neutral and hence assumed away. Yet, the institutional school of thought has made a strong point that institutions do matter in determining not only the pace, but also the character of economic development. Institutions are not static; they are dynamic as they change to meet the changing needs of social development.

A major institution that is central to the development process is the political system. A stable political system with a strong and efficient judiciary that provides secure property rights and predictable ways of changing laws will not only accumulate human and physical capital efficiently as well as increase investment in R&D, but it will also lead to increased productivity of existing resources, hence economic growth.[9] Societies with such stable institutions provide an environment for entrepreneurs, students, and workers to be forward looking, an environment that encourages increased savings and investment. Mauro and Gyimah-Brempong and Munoz de Camacho[10] argue that political instability leads to decreased investment in human capital, hence a reduction in long term economic growth. This is in part because stable and efficient institutions result in low transactions costs and increase the flow of information generally. This is the essence of the institutional approach to economic development.[11]

Economic institutions that foster economic growth can only function effectively in a well functioning and stable political system. To foster economic growth, not only will the political system have to be efficient, but it also has to be stable. An unstable political system is not likely to be an efficient one because such a system will not be able to generate the necessary consensus to make necessary but sometimes painful reforms for long-term development. By stability, I do not imply that the political system is rigid, unchanging, and stagnant. Political stability here is used to mean that the political system changes in a predictable way that is acceptable to majority of citizens. A predictable change in the political system that is supported by the majority of citizens through a participatory process is likely to be accepted by the citizenry at large.

An unstable political system is one that changes in an unpredictable way, that generates uncertainty about social and economic relations, and in which the incumbent government loses its authority to govern. An unstable political system is likely to produce a government that does not respect the rights of the majority, whose authority, in turn, is not respected by the majority of citizens and therefore not able to govern effectively. In part, this may result from the fact that an unstable political system is not likely to produce a government that is representative of the aspirations of the majority of citizens. Therefore, an unstable political system is likely to change the nature of interactions among citizens in a country in ways that discourage long-term economic growth. This means that an unstable political system is not able to provide the institutional framework that is conducive to the accumulation of human and physical capital as well as the development of technical progress.

B. CONCEPTS OF POLITICAL INSTABILITY

A central concept in this chapter is the concept of political instability so I briefly discuss it here from an economist's perspective, as opposed to that of a political scientist's. My discussion of the concept of PI may therefore not be consistent with the way political scientists define the concept. PI has been defined in different ways by different researchers. Some researchers have defined political instability as rapid changes in governments before scheduled elections. I do not consider this political instability, as what is changing is the *executive* rather than the *political* system. So long as there is a mechanism in place that ensures the smooth transfer of executive power to an incoming executive through constitutional means, there is political stability no matter how often the government changes. For example, countries such as Japan and Italy have stable political systems but may have an unstable executive system. I note that this way of changing government does not change the political system itself or the nature of interactions among people and organizations. The political science literature and most of the economic growth literature that includes elements of political instability in their studies have defined PI as the overthrow of an incumbent government through extra constitutional mechanisms—for example, through coups d'état. Others have defined PI to include other forms of political violence, such as political assassinations. While these incidents of political violence could lead to PI (hence, negative impact on economic growth), they are not the only manifestations of PI. Several social and political events may change the political system and the relationship among social institutions without necessarily changing the incumbent government. It must be noted that changing the political system is not a necessary condition for political instability. A high *probability of change* of the political system through unconstitutional means is itself unstable.[12] For this reason, the concept of political instability needs to be broadened to include executive instability as well as other politically unstable events that might have an impact on economic growth.

Morrison and Stevenson recognize three kinds of PI: elite, communal, and mass.[13] Elite PI involves the removal or attempted removal of a country's political leadership through extra-constitutional means. These incidents include successful and unsuccessful coups d'état, assassination of heads of states, and plots. Elite PI may or may not involve violence. Communal PI involves efforts by a communal groups (ethnic, religious, or territorial) to sever its relationship with the present polity through unconstitutional means. Communal events include civil wars, secessionist movements, rebellions, and religious and ethnic violence. Communal PI is usually accompanied by violence. Mass PI is an attack on the national political system by a mass group with the purpose of overthrowing the current government or changing its relationship with the current political system. The objective of mass PI is not to break away from the polity but to secure more political autonomy and/or privileges within the present polity. Unlike communal PI, mass PI is organized not along ethnic/religious lines but around a well-defined objective. Anyone who believes in that objective can participate in the mass movement without regard to ethnicity or religious affiliation. Riots, revolutions, political assassinations, and politically motivated strikes are examples of mass PI events. It is clear from these examples that mass PI is associated with violence. I note that not all violent mass behaviors can be characterized as mass PI events; to be characterized as such, a mass event should be aimed at the political system. A labor strike for better working conditions or common crimes and mass murders do not qualify as mass PI.

The forgoing discussion implies that the concept of political instability is much broader than the elite PI that has hitherto been used in the growth/PI literature by economists and political scientists. Mass and communal PI could bring about more uncertainty and undermine government authority than elite PI. Elite PI only changes the executive and those in high political positions but does not change or undermine the political system itself. In this regard, elite PI is less likely to have a lasting impact on economic development than other forms of PI. Elite PI is likely to be of short duration with short-lived growth effects, while mass and communal PI are likely to persist for long periods of time and have long-term impact on economic growth. I attempt to provide a broad measure of PI that encompasses all three elements of PI in this chapter.

I define political instability as situations, activities, or patterns of political behavior that threaten to change or actually change the political system in a nonconstitutional way. These politically unstable events often bring about sudden radical changes in property rights laws and the rules governing business conduct as well as social relationships. The key attribute of PI, as defined here, is that it generates uncertainties about the stability of the existing political system and/or government and this uncertainty negatively impacts the authority and effectiveness of governing institutions, the judiciary included. Often, this change is accompanied by counteracting forces to reverse the change or by those who demand that the changes go further than it already has. This situation often leads to policy paralysis. In this framework, PI need not involve a change in government or take a violent form. For example, acts of secession or prolonged antigovernment demonstrations could result in PI without causing the incumbent government to fall from power. On the other hand, there could be changes in government (e.g., through the ballot) without PI. Because of this, only nonconstitutional changes in government are included in my measure of political instability. In this sense, my definition of PI differs from the definition adopted by other researchers, such as Deaton and Miller, who have used changes in government, constitutional or otherwise, as their measure of political instability.[14] Most previous research has narrowly focused on elite political instability and measured it as the occurrence of coups d'état, plots, political assassinations, or purges. However, elite instability is not the only form of PI that may influence economic growth. The definition of PI adopted here is, however, broad enough to include a wide range of politically unstable events, including elite, communal, and mass PI, that could affect economic performance in a country.

Fedderke and Klitgaard make a distinction between regime-threatening political instability and non-regime-threatening political instability.[15] Regime-threatening PI include events such coups d'état, constitutional change, and revolutions that are aimed at the overthrow of the incumbent regime. Non-regime-threatening PI events include strikes, riots, and crises aimed not at changing the incumbent regime but at wrestling some concessions from the incumbent government or political system. My definition of PI encompasses both regime-threatening and non-regime-threatening PI. Fedderke and Klitgaard also find that a PI is not simply correlated with the economic growth rate, but the direction of causation runs both ways—economic growth rate and the level of income affect PI while PI also affect economic growth rate. The authors also conclude that PI is multifaceted and is correlated with other socio-economic and cultural variables. Their regime-threatening PI is similar to Morrison's elite PI, while their non-regime-threatening PI is similar to Morrison's mass and communal PI.

C. Previous Studies

The literature on the relationship between institutions and economic development is growing rapidly. In this section, I only mention a few of the studies that investigate the effects of political instability on economic performance rather than the effect of institutions generally on economic performance. I do so in order to focus on the topic of interest—the effects of PI on economic development. I make only occasional reference to those studies that investigate the effects of institutions generally on economic performance, as necessary. In a study that included PI as a determinant of economic growth in LDCs, McGowan and Johnson found a negative correlation between economic growth and political instability in Sub-Saharan Africa although they did not report any significance tests.[16] However, by analyzing the relationship between PI and growth within a political science framework, the paper failed to control for the widely acknowledged economic factors that influence economic growth in LDCs. Fosu used cross-national data and a single equation model to investigate the effects of PI on economic growth in Sub-Saharan Africa over the

1960–1986 period and found a significantly negative direct relationship between PI and economic growth after controlling for other economic variables.[17] Separate single-equation estimates of the relationship between PI and capital and exports failed to provide statistically significant support for the hypothesis that PI indirectly decreases economic growth through reductions in capital accumulation and exports. The failure to confirm this intuitive hypothesis may be attributed to the use of separate single equations to evaluate the question, a problem rectified by the use of simultaneous equations modeling.

Recent research on the relationship between property rights and economic growth argues that political instability induces governments to refrain from legal reforms that strengthen property rights, and this lack of strong property rights protection leads to lower economic growth in LDCs.[18] Mbaku investigates the effects of PI on economic growth and the Physical Quality of Life Index (PQLI) in African countries. Assuming that there is unidirectional causation of PI on growth and development, he finds that PI has no statistically significant effect on economic growth in Sub-Saharan Africa. However, he found that PI has a negative and statistically significant impact on the physical quality of life in African countries. Alexander and Hansen have investigated the effects of PI, export instability, and investment instability on economic growth in African countries. They find that, after accounting for both investment and export instability, PI still has a significantly negative effect on economic growth rate in Sub-Saharan African countries. There is another mechanism through which PI can negatively affect economic growth in LDCs. Besides the direct effect PI has on the output through reduction in factor productivity or indirectly through the reduction on resource accumulation. Edwards and Tabellini have argued that PI weakens a government, making it difficult, if not impossible, for the government to develop and implement necessary economic policy reforms for long-term economic growth. Because of political weakness resulting from PI, governments are likely to implement policies that encourage rent-seeking activities as a means of survival. This leads, at best, to policy paralysis and, at worst, to bad economic policies, hence economic stagnation. Devereaux and Wen argue that PI induces incumbent governments to leave fewer assets to their successors, thereby forcing them to raise taxes on capital.[19] The expected high tax on capital induces capital flight, low investment, and slow economic growth. A number of African economic experts have used single-equation models and cross-national data to estimate the neoclassical growth model that emphasizes the convergence hypothesis.[20] They generally find that political instability has negative effects on economic growth rate. These studies primarily use a subset of politically unstable events as their measure of PI.

The studies reviewed above assume that the relationship between economic growth and PI is unidirectional—PI affects economic growth but is not affected by economic growth. The assumption that PI is exogenous is however inconsistent with the political science literature dealing with coups d'état and other manifestations of political instability in LDCs as well as the recent excellent papers by Fedderke and Klitgaard and Fedderke *et al.* While there is no consensus as to whether slow economic growth causes political instability or rapid economic growth is destabilizing, there is a general agreement that PI is influenced by economic performance. Londregan and Poole used a two-equation model and time-series cross-national data to investigate the relationship between economic growth and coups d'état.[21] They concluded that the probability of a coup d'état is significantly affected by past and present income growth, but that coups d'état have no significant impact on income growth. This despite the fact that they concluded that coups d'état and economic growth cannot be treated as exogenous variables in their model. While their approach represents a first effort at addressing the issue of simultaneity, their growth equation does not include any economic variables other than past growth rate and the level of per capita income. This of course raises important questions about possible incorrect model specification leading to a downward bias of the impact that political instability has on economic growth.

A few studies have used simultaneous equations models to investigate the relationship between PI and economic growth and found a negative relationship between the two; however, they measure PI narrowly as elite PI. Besides, none of these studies has investigated the indirect effect PI has on economic growth through reduced investment. Fedderke and Klitgaard estimate the effect of political rights and other institutional factors on economic growth. Allowing for simultaneity between economic growth and political rights, they find that there is, generally, a positive correlation between economic growth and political rights. They find, however, that the strength of this association depends on what other variables are included in the growth equation or what variables are used as instruments for political rights. They also find that political instability is strongly associated with such socioeconomic variables as political rights and institutional efficiency. Gyimah-Brempong and Traynor find that PI has negative impacts on savings and investment in Sub-Saharan Africa but did not extend the analysis to growth effects. Gyimah-Brempong and Munoz de Camacho find that in addition to negative effects on human capital formation, PI has a negative effect on economic growth in Latin America through decreased factor productivity.[22] None of these papers used a dynamic panel estimation method in the analyses.

Recently, a number of studies have used panel data and panel estimation methodology to estimate the neoclassical growth model.[23] These studies conclude that previous studies employing single-equation models have produced biased and inconsistent estimates of the growth/PI relationship because they do not take into account the endogeniety of some of the regressors as well as the correlation between fixed country effects and some of the right-hand-side variables. They generally confirm the convergence hypothesis and conclude that the speed of convergence is much faster than has been calculated by previous studies employing single equations and cross-national data. However, these studies, like most empirical growth models before them, emphasize the convergence hypothesis and, as such, pay scant attention to the role of political instability in economic growth, when it is included at all as an explanatory variable. This chapter, on the other hand, focuses on the effects of political instability on economic growth in Sub-Saharan Africa.

III. THEORETICAL ISSUES

A. POLITICAL INSTABILITY AND ECONOMIC GROWTH

There are several possible mechanisms through which political instability can affect economic growth in a negative way. The relationship between political instability and economic growth could be direct as well as indirect, simple as well as complex. I posit that, because PI affects the interactions among individuals and organizations in a negative way, thus increasing transactions cost, it will affect economic growth directly by reducing the productivity of existing resources. Because it increases uncertainty, PI affects economic growth indirectly through decreased accumulation of resources and slow technical progress.[24] PI is likely to lead to corruption, proliferation of rules and regulations, confusion, misallocation of public resources, and bureaucratic inefficiency.

Among the important determinants of long-term economic growth are capital accumulation (both physical and human) and technical progress. Investment in both physical and human capital requires sacrifices in the current period in order to increase productive capacity, leading to higher output in the future. This requires long-term planning, and assurances that the benefit that comes from such sacrifices can be reaped in the future. Technical progress is characterized as *embodied* or *disembodied*. Embodied technical progress refers to new technologies embodied in new machines or products while disembodied technical progress refers to technical change not associated with any particular equipment or product but with new knowledge or process. The endogenous growth literature suggests that technical progress, embodied as well as disembodied, is the result of investment in research and development efforts. Therefore, like increases in physical and human capital, technical progress requires savings and investment, or sacrifice in the current period. Investors will be willing to sacrifice, risk their capital while looking at a long-term horizon, and invest if they are sure that their property rights will be protected, that there will be a stable environment, and that an efficient and impartial judiciary will protect their investments and returns on such investment. Unfortunately political instability is usually accompanied by abridgement of property rights laws as well as increased uncertainty about returns on investment and the general business environment.

This leads to reduced investment in physical and human capital and in research and development. More important, political instability leads to the flight of both financial and human capital from countries that are experiencing such instability.

There is another mechanism through which political instability can negatively affect economic growth in LDCs besides the direct effect PI has on the output from existing resources or indirectly through the reduction on resource accumulation—inability to develop and implement necessary policy changes. Edwards and Tabellini have argued that political instability weakens a government, making it difficult if not impossible, for the government to develop and implement necessary economic policy reforms for long-term economic growth. Because of political weakness resulting from political instability, governments are likely to implement policies that encourage rent-seeking activities as a means of survival. This leads to economic stagnation. Devereaux and Wen argue that PI induces incumbent governments to leave fewer assets to their successors, thereby forcing them to raise taxes on capital. The expected high tax on capital induces capital flight, low investment, and slow economic growth.[25] Governments may also resort to borrowing from the domestic private sector, foreign sources, or the central bank to cover recurrent expenditures because of their inability to raise the necessary revenue through taxation. This results in debt overhand that burdens the economy.[26]

Another mechanism through which political instability may affect economic growth is the impact on income distribution and allocation of government expenditures. Taxation may be skewed toward the politically powerful group even though such a tax system leads to inefficient allocation of resources and a reduction in economic efficiency. For example, the tax system may be skewed in favor of nonproductive activities (such as imports of luxury consumer goods) at the expense of productive activities such as investment if high-income consumers have the political power to threaten bringing down the incumbent government. In the same way, public expenditures may be allocated to benefit political allies rather than in a way that will be in the interest of long-term growth of the economy. A classic example in African countries of such an expenditure pattern is the increased allocation of public expenditures toward defense and other security spending at the expense of education and health care even though most of these countries are not engaged in any external or internal war. The result of such public sector allocation priorities is that public capital is neglected and therefore not able to complement the efforts of the private sector to generate economic growth. For example, in most African countries, a large proportion of agricultural output perishes because of lack of roads linking farms to urban markets. The effect of such public expenditure and tax pattern is to distort resource allocation through increased rent-seeking activities, resulting in a reduction in the productivity of existing resources.

B. Issues of Simultaneity

The foregoing arguments imply that PI can have negative impacts on economic growth directly through a reduction in the productivity of existing resources as well as reducing the accumulation of productive resources and retarding technical progress. However, the relationship between PI and economic growth is not likely to be a unidirectional one. While PI affects economic growth in a negative way, there is evidence that poor economic growth performance has a negative effect on political stability. It is reasonable to expect that poor economic performance increases the clamor to change the incumbent government or political system. In developed countries with well-established institutional processes for changing governments, this dissatisfaction manifest itself through the election of a new government or reforms of the economic and political systems. In Sub-Saharan Africa where, until very recently, there has been very little chance of changing an incumbent government or political system through formal processes, frustration with poor economic performance has manifested in politically unstable events such as coups d'état, riots, and secessionist movements. Theoretical as well as empirical evidence from the political science literature and recent economic studies support this proposition. Indeed, this is one of the central arguments of the literature on coups d'état. Casual empirical evidence in African countries suggests that most politically unstable events in African countries are preceded by periods of poor economic performance or are precipitated by some policy changes that impose short-term economic hardships on some powerful interest groups. Looking at a cross section of African countries, countries with poor economic performance (such as Sudan, Ethiopia, Chad, Central African Republic, Ghana, and the Democratic Republic of Congo, formerly known as Zaire) tend to be the countries with the most unstable political systems while countries with relatively good economic performance records tend to be those with relatively stable political systems (for example, Botswana, Gabon, and Mauritius). Longitudinal evidence also indicates that stable political systems in countries are threatened in the face of poor economic performance (Côte d'Iviore, a former beacon of political stability in Africa, is the latest example). The implication of these observations is that one cannot treat PI as an exogenous variable; hence, one has to model PI if one is to understand the relationship between PI and economic performance.

Political instability, therefore, can be viewed as a function of, among other things, economic performance in a country. While political scientists and a few economists have argued that rapid economic growth generally has a significantly positive impact on political stability, economists generally, on the other hand, have argued that political instability has a deleterious effect on economic growth. In most empirical research, political scientists treat economic growth as exogenous while economists treat PI as exogenous. The question of whether or not PI and economic growth are jointly endogenous is a testable hypothesis. Therefore, in modeling the relationship between PI and growth, I combine these two strands of the PI/growth literature and treat PI and economic growth as jointly endogenous. In addition to economic performance, PI is influenced by the role the military plays in civil society, the structure and representativeness of the legislative body, and the type of head of state in the country, all variables that must be considered when modeling political instability in a country.

IV. ECONOMETRIC ANALYSIS AND RESULTS

This section provides an empirical specification of the relationships among economic growth rate, investment in physical capital, and political instability to illustrate the relationship discussed above. Data from a sample of African countries are used to estimate the model, and the results of the estimates are discussed. I try as much as possible to make the three-equation simultaneous model as simple as possible without pretending that the model is a comprehensive one. (The three-equation model estimated and variable definitions appear in the Appendix in this chapter.) Because the equations are standard growth

TABLE 12.1   Summary Statistics of Data

Variable	Mean	Standard Deviation
g (%)	2.942	6.774
k (%)	21.125	10.760
PI	−0.00009	0.999
y	485.727	569.696
l	2.761	1.437
mil	3.080	3.352
pres	0.084	0.293
frac	0.083	0.193
gen	0.0782	0.414
lgsl	1.419	0.897
m (%)	41.272	24.758
s (%)	6.975	19.436
rds (%)	42.26	39.15
$\dot{x}$	6.224	28.513
elite	−0.000005	1.00002

[a]g, growth rate of GDP; k, investment; PI, political instability; y, per capita GDP; l, growth rate of labor; mil, military role; pres, president; frac, fractionalization; gen, general; lgsl, legislative selection process; m, imports/GDP ratio; s, savings rate; rds, real foreign debt service/GDP ratio; $\dot{x}$, growth rate of exports; and elite, ?
Note: N = 546; means reported here are unweighted averages.

equations modified to account for the endogeniety of PI and investment, I only present outlines of the model. Details of the model can be found in the references.

Summary statistics of the data are presented in Table 12.1. As the standard errors indicate, there is a wide variation in the value of the variables across countries and through time, with the data showing relatively high and variable levels of political instability as well as low average rates of economic growth during the sample period. With aggregate GDP growing at 2.942%, on average, and population growing as 2.76% per annum, the gross domestic product (GDP) per capita, on average, stagnated in Sub-Saharan Africa during the sample period. The model is estimated with annual data which may be influenced by cyclical movements.

V. STATISTICAL RESULTS

The three-equation simultaneous equations model is estimated with data from 39 countries over a 14-year period. In panel estimation, consistent estimation of the structural coefficients depends crucially on the stochastic properties of the error terms, particularly whether they are correlated with the regressors and whether the error terms are serially correlated. As argued above, the error term in (4) has a country-specific component, a time-specific component, and an idiosyncratic component. If the right-hand-side (RHS) variables are orthogonal to μ_{it}, a generalized least squares (GLS) estimator, also known as the random effects (RE) estimator, can be used to obtain consistent estimates of the coefficients. On the other hand, if the RHS variables are strictly exogenous with respect to ν_{it} but not to α_{it}, a within-group estimator, also known as the fixed effects (FE) estimator, will be consistent. In my model, there is no reason to believe that either condition will hold, as there are endogenous regressors as well as lagged dependent variables as regressors. Besides the endogeniety of some of the RHS variables, the inclusion of lagged endogenous variables in the PI and k equations implies that the orthogonality condition will not be satisfied even for the FE estimator, whether it is estimated in levels or in differences. An estimator that is capable of taking care of these problems is therefore needed.

An estimator that produces consistent estimates in the presence of correlated fixed effects as well as endogenous regressors is the dynamic panel data (DPD) estimator proposed by Arellano and Bond.[27] The DPD estimator is a generalized method of moments (GMM) estimator which uses all lagged endogenous variables as well as exogenous variables as instruments in a differenced equation to achieve efficiency in estimation. The DPD estimator is used to estimate the system of equations presented in Eq. (4) in the Appendix. I estimate the model in difference of the variables and lag the variables twice to ensure that there is no autocorrelation among the error terms, as the presence of autocorrelation will lead to inconsistent estimates. Because consistency of estimates depends on a lack of autocorrelation, I test for autocorrelation as well as the suitability of the instruments used.

A. COEFFICIENT ESTIMATES

Table 12.2 presents the estimates of the dynamic GMM estimator. Column 2 presents estimates of the growth equation; column 3, the estimates of the investment equation; and column 4, the estimates for the PI equation. Asymptotic t statistics calculated from heteroskedastic consistent standard errors associated with the GMM estimator are reported in parentheses. The table also presents statistics for the Sargan test of over-identifying restrictions, which is a joint test of model specification and appropriateness of the instrument vector; test statistics for first- and second-order serial correlation (m_2 statistics) test; and the Hausman exogeneity test. In addition, Table 12.2 also presents Wald test statistics to test for the significance of a subset of regressors. As the estimates indicate, the model goodness-of-fit statistics are relatively strong. In all three equations, I reject the null hypothesis that the variation in the dependent variables cannot be explained by the variation in all of the independent variables at $\alpha = 0.01$ or better as indicated by the x^2 statistics of the joint test of significance.

Before discussing the coefficient estimates and their growth implications, I discuss some specification tests, because the validity of the results depends upon the consistency of the dynamic GMM estimator used. In the analysis, the key moment condition I exploit is lack of serial correlation among the error terms. The test statistics show the absence of first- or second-order serial correlation. The Sargan test for over-identifying restrictions also indicate that the model is correctly specified, that the restrictions are correct, and that the set of instruments used to estimate the equations are the correct set of instruments. The Hausman test of the null hypothesis of the exogeneity of all regressors is soundly rejected for all equations. This implies that both the FE and RE estimators would produce inconsistent estimates. The Wald tests indicate that all the tested variables (in parentheses) are significantly different from zero at conventional levels.

I now turn to a discussion of the coefficient estimates from the dynamic GMM estimator. In the growth equation presented in column 2, k and l have positive coefficients as expected but only that of k is significantly different from zero at $\alpha = 0.01$ while that of l is significant at $\alpha = 0.05$.[28] The positive coefficient of these variables indicate that they are normal inputs into the growth process. The fact that the coefficient of l is less than unity is consistent with the

TABLE 12.2   Dynamic Panel GMM Estimates of Model Coefficients Estimates

Variable	Estimate of Growth Equation (g)	Estimate of Investment Equation (k)	Estimate of PI Equation
g	—	0.1203 (3.1136)	−0.0385 (2.5508)
k	0.2453 (2.9076)	—	—
k_{t-1}	—	0.2598 (10.621)	—
PI	−0.1013 (2.0843)	−0.2053 (1.8032)	—
Pi_{t-1}	—	−0.9619 (2.2637)	0.1786 (4.5931)
$\dot{x}$	0.0552 (6.3759)	—	—
l	0.8541 (1.6965)	—	—
y_{t-1}	· −0.0018 (1.3088)	—	0.0022 (2.7303)
s	—	0.5971 (16.1072)	—
m	—	0.6191 (37.7909)	—
rds	—	−0.2223 (4.9794)	—
mil	—	—	0.0886 (1.0769)
$lgsl$	—	—	−0.2647 (4.1091)
$frac$	—	—	0.4118 (1.6774)
Joint test for significance	39.059 (5)	4200.72 (6)	76.940 (6)
Sargan test	12.305 (19)	21.973 (18)	16.303 (19)
First-order serial correlation	1.050	1.007	1.217
Second-order serial correlation	0.591	0.371	0.427
Hausman exogeniety test	95.6989	76.9745	399.023
Wald test	16.342 (PI)	23.72 (PI, PI_{t-1})	13.021 (g)

[a]g, growth rate of GDP; k, investment; PI, political instability; $\dot{x}$, growth rate of exports; l, growth rate of labor; y, per capita GDP; s, savings rate; m, imports/GDP ratio; rds, real foreign debt service/GDP ratio; mil, military role; $lgsl$, legislative selection process; and $frac$, fractionalization.
Note: Absolute value of asymptotic t-statistics in parentheses.

neoclassical hypothesis that increased population growth decreases the growth of per capita income. The coefficient of x is positive and significantly different from zero at $\alpha = 0.01$ as expected. This result is consistent with those of researchers who find a positive relationship between export growth and economic growth in LDCs. The coefficient of y_0 is negative as expected but is insignificant at conventional levels. There is some evidence of the convergence hypothesis; however, the evidence is very weak, as the coefficient of y_0 barely missed significance at the 0.10 level. PI has a negative coefficient as expected and is significantly different from zero at $\alpha = 0.05$ or better in the growth equation. A one-standard-deviation increase in political instability directly decreases economic growth in Sub-Saharan Africa by 0.10 percentage point. This is a relatively large effect given that the average growth rate of aggregate GDP in Sub-Saharan Africa during the sample period was only 2.9%. This implies that political instability has a significant negative impact on economic growth in Sub-Saharan Africa after controlling for other factors that affect economic growth in a system of equation models. The result is qualitatively similar to the results of other researchers who have explored the relationship between PI and growth. The coefficient estimates indicate that PI negatively affects economic growth through decreased factor productivity.

In the PI equation, g has a negative coefficient that is significantly different from zero at $\alpha = 0.01$, implying that all things equal, good economic performance increases political stability in Sub-Saharan Africa, a result that is consistent with the political science literature and the results obtained in many other studies.[29] A 1% increase in economic growth rate decreases political instability by 0.04 standard deviation. An alternative way to state this result is that economic deterioration leads to political instability in Sub-Saharan Africa. The implications of the negative coefficient of g in the PI equation is that governments, democratic as well as autocratic, can achieve political stability with improved economic performance. The coefficient of $lgsl$ is negative, relatively large, and significantly different from zero at the 0.01 level of significance. An open legislative selection process, therefore, reduces political instability. Both $frac$ and mil have positive coefficients but only that of $frac$ is significantly different from zero at $\alpha = 0.05$, indicating that fractionalization of the legislative body increases political instability in Sub-Saharan Africa. PI_{t-1} has a positive and statistically significant coefficient, suggesting that Sub-Saharan African countries that experience political instability tend to develop a "culture of political instability," a result that is consistent with the results of previous research. The negative and significant coefficient of PI in the growth equation together with the negative and statistically significant coefficient of g in the PI equation are compatible with the hypothesis of simultaneity in the relationship between PI and economic growth.

In the investment (k) equation, the coefficients of g, m, and s are positive as expected, and are significantly different from zero at $\alpha = 0.01$. The large positive and significant coefficient of m indicates that import capacity is a very important determinant of investment in Sub-Saharan Africa. The coefficient of rds is negative and significant at $\alpha = 0.01$ as expected. This is an indication that external debt overhang decreases the investment rate in Sub-Saharan Africa. The coefficient of k_{t-1} is positive and significantly different from zero at $\alpha = 0.01$. This indicates that last period's investment is positively correlated with investment in the current period. The coefficients of PI and k_{t-1} are both negative, relatively large, and significantly different form zero at $\alpha = 0.05$ or better. These significantly negative coefficients imply that political instability has deleterious effects on investment both contemporaneously as well as with a lag. A one standard deviation increase in political instability decreases investment rate by 0.21 percentage point contemporaneously. Investment in the current year is also decreased by 0.9619 percentage points as a result of one standard deviation increase in PI in the previous year. This negative and statistically significant coefficient of current and lagged PI in combination with the positive and significant estimate of the coefficient for k in the growth equation indicates that PI negatively influences growth indirectly through investment. This result is consistent with the hypothesis that PI impacts economic growth through investment by altering incentives through changes in property rights and rules governing business conduct, increasing uncertainty about the outcome of investment decisions, and increases in capital taxation.

The estimates presented in Table 12.2 indicate that PI negatively affects economic growth in two ways: directly and in the current period through a reduction in output as well as indirectly and over time through its impact on present and future levels of investment. The total current period effect of PI on economic growth, as shown earlier, is given as $dg/dPI = \alpha_5 + \alpha_1\gamma_2$, which is -0.1517, made up of -0.1013 direct effects and -0.0504 indirect effects through reduced investment, while the one-period lag effect is $dg/dPI_{t-1} = \alpha_1\gamma_3 + \alpha_5\beta_8$, which is equal to -0.253, a much larger effect than the current period effect. This is a very significant effect given the poor growth record of Sub-Saharan African countries. The lagged growth effect of PI implies that an increase in PI in an earlier period has a negative and significant impact on economic growth in the current period through reduced investment, making the PI effects on growth longer lasting than the direct contemporaneous effect estimated by earlier researchers. The lagged effect arises from two sources: a decrease in investment and subsequent negative impact on growth, and through additional episodes of PI in the future generated by the current episode of PI leading to further economic deterioration. The implied direct PI growth elasticity for the current period, calculated at the means of the variables is -0.056. Failure to estimate a dynamic structural model would imply missing this lagged effect of PI on economic growth. This implies that studies that do not account for this indirect effect may seriously underestimate the effects of PI on economic growth in Sub-Saharan Africa and, more importantly, miss the mechanisms through which PI affects economic growth. The intertemporal nature of the investment effects of PI implies that the growth effect will be magnified over time.

It is possible that the annual data used to estimate the model are subject to cyclical movements, making my results dependent solely on the cyclical movements in the data. It is also possible that the annual data do not adequately capture political instability because institutions change slowly. To investigate this possibility the model was re-estimated using 3-year averages of the data. With 14 years of data for each country, averaging over 3 years provided 5 years of data for each country. Taking first differences and lagging the difference variables by one period yielded a total of 117 observations (39 countries over 3 years) to estimate the model. Coefficient estimates, together with regression statistics, are presented in Table 12.3. The regression statistics, as well as test statistics, indicate that the model fits the data relatively well. In the growth equation, the coefficients of k, $\dot{x}$, and l, are positive as expected but only those of k and $\dot{x}$ are significant at conventional levels. The coefficient of y_0 is negative as expected but is statistically insignificant. The coefficient of PI is negative as expected, relatively large, and significantly different from zero at $\alpha = 0.01$, indicating that political instability has a directly negative impact on economic growth in the current period in Sub-Saharan Africa. In the investment equation, the coefficients of g, k_{t-1}, s, and m are positive as expected and all are significantly different from zero at $\alpha = 0.05$ or better. The coefficients of PI, PI_{t-1} and rds are negative and significantly different from zero at $\alpha = 0.01$. This implies that investment in current period is negatively affected by PI in the current period as well as political instability in the previous period. In the PI equation, the coefficients of PI_{t-1} and $frac$ are positive and significant at $\alpha = 0.05$, while those of g and $lgsl$ are negative and significant at $\alpha = 0.01$. The coefficients of y_{t-1} and mil are insignificant. The estimates in Table 12.3 imply that changing the time frame of the analysis does not qualitatively change the results.

TABLE 12.3 Dynamic Panel GMM Estimates of Model: Averaged Data Coefficient Estimates

Variable	Estimate of Growth Equation (g)	Estimate of Investment Equation (k)	Estimate of PI Equation
g	—	0.0898 (2.346)	−0.0071 (2.722)
k	0.2710 (2.484)	—	—
k_{t-1}	—	0.4062 (2.299)	—
PI	−0.2270 (2.662)	−0.6949 (1.948)	—
PI_{t-1}	—	−0.6033 (2.345)	0.3733 (3.761)
$\dot{x}$	0.0048 (1.4300)	—	—
l	0.6138 (1.4300)	—	—
y_{t-1}	−0.0068 (1.3680)	—	−0.0001 (0.519)
s	—	0.4148 (3.856)	—
m	—	0.4475 (7.766)	—
rds	—	−0.7534 (2.744)	—
mil	—	—	−0.0356 (1.128)
$lgsl$	—	—	−0.3067 (2.612)
$frac$	—	—	1.5939 (2.9748)
Joint test for significance	52.133 (5)	897.298 (7)	65.903 (6)
Sargan test	6.504 (19)	6.903 (10)	6.461 (10)
First-order serial correlation	0.0607	0.087	0.308
Second-order serial correlation	56.297	0.087	0.308
Hausman exogeneity test	8.255 (PI)	68.9745	89.683
Wald test		13.89 (PI, PI_{t-1})	6.216 (g)

[a] g, growth rate of GDP; k, investment; PI, political instability; $\dot{x}$, growth rate of exports; l, growth rate of labor; y, per capita GDP; s, savings rate; m, imports/GDP ratio; rds, real foreign debt service/GDP ratio; mil, military role; $lgsl$, legislative selection process; and $frac$, fractionalization.
Note: Absolute value of asymptotic t-statistics in parentheses.

The growth effect of PI in the current year from the estimates presented in Table 12.3 is -0.4153 divided into -0.227 direct effect and -0.188 indirect effect through reduced investment. The total intertemporal effect of PI on economic growth calculated from these estimates is -0.2398. These estimates are relatively large, given that the average growth rate of aggregate GDP in the sample period was only 2.9%. The results presented in Table 12.3 are qualitatively the same as those presented in Table 12.2. In both tables, PI has a negative and statistically significant effect on growth directly and indirectly through decreased investment. In both tables, PI has an intertemporal effect on growth through decreased investment in addition to the current year effects. The only major difference between the results presented in the two tables is that the estimates using the 3-year averages are quantitatively larger in absolute magnitude than those based on annual data. The conclusion drawn from a comparison of the estimates in the two tables is that there is no qualitative difference in the results, whether using annual data or the 3-year averaged data, hence the results are not being driven by cyclical variation in the data.

How do the results presented here differ from the results of earlier researchers who either have treated PI as exogenous or have not employed the dynamic panel estimator? To investigate this question, I estimate a single-equation growth equation allowing for fixed effects and a 3SLS version of the structural model and compare the results to the estimates presented in Table 12.2. Table 12.4 presents the 3SLS estimates. Column 2 of Table 12.4 presents the estimates for the g equation; column 3, estimates for the k equation; and column 4, the estimates for the PI equation. All the 3SLS coefficient estimates in all equations, except that of PI_{t-1} in the investment equation, have the expected signs but the coefficients of l in the growth equation and gen and $pres$ in the PI equation are statistically insignificant. The coefficient of PI_{t-1} in the investment equation is positive, relatively large, and significantly different from zero at $\alpha = 0.05$. This is contrary to expectation and different from the results in Tables 12.2 and 12.3. In addition to the wrong sign of the coefficient of PI_{t-1} in the investment equation, the coefficient of PI in the growth equation implies that a one-standard-deviation increase in PI decreases growth rate by about 1.35 percentage points. The total growth effect of a one-standard-deviation increase in PI is -1.709 in the current period and -0.313 in the next period. These estimates are far larger than those estimated from the DPD estimator. Given the average annual growth rate of 2.9% during the sample period, these effects are likely to be overestimates of the growth effects of PI. Single-equation estimates show that the coefficient of PI is negative and significant. The estimates indicate that a one-standard-deviation increase in PI decreases growth rate by 0.65 percentage point, estimates that are larger in absolute magnitude than the total growth effect calculated from the dynamic GMM estimates in Table 12.2.

TABLE 12.4   3SLS Estimates of Economic Growth in Sub-Saharan Africa

Variable	Coefficient Estimates g	k	PI
g	—	0.0299 (2.040)	0.0595 (6.315)
k	0.1173 (3.661)	—	—
k_{t-1}	—	0.5172 (15.867)	—
PI	−1.2182 (2.1247)	−4.1868 (3.661)	—
PI_{t-1}	—	1.2258 (2.553)	0.3745 (8.764)
$\dot{x}$	0.0687 (7.209)	—	—
l	0.1652 (0.4315)	—	—
y_{t-1}	−0.0012 (2.178)	—	−0.0002 (2.369)
m	—	0.1473 (8.437)	—
s	—	0.0707 (3.802)	—
rds	—	−0.1996 (2.610)	—
mil	—	—	0.0194 (1.668)
$pres$	—	—	0.0248 (0.170)
gen	—	—	−0.1229 (1.169)
$frac$	—	—	0.3658 (1.983)
$lgsl$	—	—	−0.0392 (2.518)
N	546	546	546
R^2	0.1598	0.6821	0.2041
DW	1.9161	2.011	2.089

[a]g, growth rate of GDP; k, investment; PI, political instability; $\dot{x}$, growth rate of exports; l, growth rate of labor; y, per capita GDP; m, imports/GDP ratio; s, savings rate; rds, real foreign debt service/GDP ratio; mil, military role; $pres$, presidential; gen, general; $frac$, fractionalization; and $lgsl$, legislative selection process.

Note: Absolute value of t-statistics is given in parentheses.

Earlier researchers have used elite PI as the measure of political instability in their empirical analyses. To what extent do the results from the broad measure of PI differ from the results based on elite PI? For the purposes of comparison, I re-estimate the dynamic GMM model replacing the broad measure of PI with an elite PI index (based on successful and attempted coups, revolutions, and plots) that have been used in most studies. The new estimates are qualitatively similar to those presented in Table 12.2. As in the previous estimate in Table 12.2, the coefficients of k, $\dot{x}$, and l are positive and statistically significant. The coefficient of PI in the new equation is statistically insignificant. In the k equation, all coefficients have the expected signs and a large number of them are statistically significant. The coefficient of PI is also insignificant in the investment equation although it has the expected sign. In the PI equation, almost all coefficients have the expected signs; the only exceptions being those of PI_{t-1} and mil although neither is statistically significant.

Except in a few cases, both sets of coefficient estimates have the same signs. However, the coefficients of the new equation are generally less precisely estimated than their counterparts in Table 12.2. There are also some marked differences between the two sets of estimates. The coefficient of elite PI in the growth and investment equations are statistically insignificant while the coefficient of the broader measure of PI in these equations is negative and statistically significant. This suggests that elite PI has no statistically significant direct impact on economic growth or investment in the current period while the broader measure of PI has a statistically significant negative growth impact. The only impact elite PI has on growth is its lagged effect through reduced investment on physical capital. This may explain why research that uses cross-national data based on single-equation models and measure PI as elite PI has produced mixed results. It is clear that elite PI cannot capture all the growth effects the broad measure of PI used in this study is able to capture. This may result from the fact that economic agents discount changes in executives that do not change or threaten to change the political system. The more comprehensive measure of PI, on the other hand, reflects instability in political and social institutions that is likely to lead to both short-term and long-term economic stagnation. This economic effect is likely to be more widespread and long-lasting. The implication is that a comprehensive measure of PI is more capable of capturing the deleterious effect it has on economic growth than elite PI. Note that the growth effect of PI estimated in this study does not take into consideration the possible negative effect that PI may have on human capital formation. This implies that the evidence presented in this study should be considered as lower bounds of the effects of PI on economic growth in African countries.

VI. POLICY IMPLICATIONS

The findings that PI affects economic growth both directly and indirectly through reduced investment in the current period as well as over time have implications for economic development in LDCs. If political instability has a negative impact on economic growth, then it should be considered an integral part of economic development policy formulation and implementation. At the least, policymakers should make sure that economic policy does not disrupt political stability. For example, structural adjustment programs imposed by the International Monetary Fund (IMF) and the World Bank may create short-run hardships which in turn may increase political instability and ultimately have negative impact on short-run economic growth. These programs may also lead to long-term economic stagnation if they lead to frequent policy reversals and loss of credibility in policy implementation. On the other hand, failure to carry out the necessary economic reforms will create long-term economic stagnation and worsen and prolong political instability. An implication from the results of this chapter is that these programs may best be accomplished if they are accompanied by efforts to elicit political support for them. Alternatively, economic reforms can be linked to political reforms to reduce uncertainty about political stability, which is necessary for the successful implementation of economic policies. This can reduce the likelihood that resources will be misallocated to doomed development efforts. After all, good policies are useless unless they are effectively implemented, but effective implementation of policies may not be possible without political stability. Fortunately, the World Bank, the IMF, and other multilateral development agencies are painfully, but gradually, learning this lesson.

Another policy implication flowing from the results is that it is in the best interest of all governments (democratic or autocratic) to promote economic growth and development as a way of ensuring political stability. Governments and political systems that provide good economic performance can "buy" the goodwill of the citizenry. Bill Clinton's 1992 presidential campaign mantra of "It's the economy, stupid" is as true in African countries as it is in the United States. A cursory look at all the civil strife going on in African countries reveals that they are all fights over dwindling economic bases.[30] The implication is that a nation cannot achieve political stability in the presence of sustained economic retardation. Perhaps Kwame Nkrumah's famous dictum, "Seek ye first the political kingdom and all other things shall be added unto thee," should be changed to: "Seek ye first the economic kingdom and the political kingdom shall be yours."

The results indicate that simultaneous equation models using dynamic panel estimation methodology provide insights into the channels through which political instability affects economic growth. For example, the estimates indicate that, while the direct effect of PI on economic growth is statistically significant, PI has a statistically significant negative indirect and intertemporal effect on economic growth through reduction in capital accumulation. Simultaneous-equation models appear to be useful tools in uncovering the indirect mechanisms through which PI affects economic growth. More important, dynamic panel estimation methods allow the researcher to account for fixed effects and endogeniety of regressors, as well as explore the dynamic nature of the political instability/growth relationship. The results also show that economic stagnation, leads to political instability which in turn leads to economic stagnation, a bidirectional causal relationship between PI and economic growth. The results of this study also imply that a more comprehensive measure of PI which includes non-elite PI events such as riots and politically motivated strikes will more completely capture the relationship between PI and economic growth in LDCs than the elite political instability events that have been used in previous research. The growth effect of elite PI is likely to be narrow and short lived compared to the effects of the broad measure of PI used in this study.

VII. SUMMARY

This chapter uses a simultaneous-equation model, cross-national time-series data, and a dynamic panel estimating methodology to investigate the effects of political instability on economic growth in Sub-Saharan Africa. Using a more comprehensive measure of political instability than has been used in earlier studies, I confirm the findings of studies that indicate that political instability has a negative and statistically significant effect on economic growth in Sub-Saharan Africa. Moreover, the estimates presented here provide evidence that political instability affects economic growth directly as well as indirectly through a reduction in capital formation. Using 3-year averages of the data to estimate the model indicates that the results are not driven by cyclical movements in the data. I am also able to confirm both the conclusions by political scientists and economists who have investigated the PI/growth relationship. I find that there is a bidirectional causal relationship between political instability and economic growth; slow economic growth causes political instability, which in turn leads to further economic stagnation. The implication of this result is that economic policymakers in Sub-Saharan African should consider the impact of policy changes on political stability when formulating and implementing economic policy. Better still, economic policy could be combined with policies designed to increase political stability. Additionally, I have developed a measure of political instability using a principal-components approach which is not arbitrarily weighted and is developed independent of the growth model. This broader measure of political instability is better able to capture the effects of PI on economic growth and investment than the elite PI that has been used by other researchers.

DISCUSSION QUESTIONS

1. What are institutions and how do effectively functioning institutions promote economic growth?
2. Explain why clearly defined guarantees of property rights are important for long-term economic growth.
3. Identify and discuss three key determinants of economic growth.
4. What is the difference between political instability and executive instability and how might each affect economic growth?
5. Identify and discuss three channels through which political instability affects economic growth.
6. Distinguish between embodied and disembodied technical progress.
7. Explain why political instability should be considered an endogenous variable in a growth equation.

8. According to the results presented in this chapter, is the effect of political instability on investment limited to the current period? How does the time path of the PI effects on investment affect long-term economic growth?

9. Suppose you are the President of Anahg, a country that has had bouts of political instability in the past, and you go to the IMF for a desperately needed loan. The IMF imposes certain conditions (such as the elimination of subsidies on bread) for granting the loan. You are aware that implementing these conditions could lead to serious urban riots, yet not going for the loan could create economic stagnation and riots. Discuss possible strategies you could use to resolve this problem.

APPENDIX

GROWTH EQUATION

I use an augmented production function framework to investigate the relationship between political instability and economic growth in Sub-Saharan Africa. I model economic growth as a function of the growth rates of capital, labor, and exports.[31] As many economists have argued, economic growth is directly influenced by production losses created by PI, which is included as an additional explanatory variable.[32] I expect this output loss (and decreased economic growth) even if PI has no impact on investment. Additionally, initial per capita real GDP is included to test the convergence hypothesis. The growth equation I estimate is given as follows:[33]

$$g = \alpha_0 + \alpha_1 k + \alpha_2 l + \alpha_3 \dot{x} + \alpha_5 y_0 + \alpha_5 \text{PI} + e \tag{1}$$

where g is the growth rate of GDP, l is the growth rate of labor, k is investment, $\dot{x}$ is the growth rate of exports, PI is political instability, y_0 is initial per capita real GDP, and e is a stochastic error term. Because k is a normal input, I expect its coefficient to be positive. In neoclassical growth theory, an increase in population growth is expected to decrease the growth rate of per capita GDP, all thing equal. However, because the growth rate of aggregate GDP is the dependent variable in this model, I expect the coefficient of l to be positive in the growth equation. Since the economic growth of nations in Sub-Saharan Africa has historically varied positively with exports, α_3 is expected to be positive. As discussed earlier, PI is expected to directly disrupt the production process (apart from indirectly disrupting growth through a reduction in investment as detailed below) and is therefore expected to have a negative coefficient. The coefficient of y_0 is expected to be negative in accordance with the convergence hypothesis.

Recent empirical growth literature include a range of variables, such as the quality of the bureaucracy and corruption, to reflect the quality of the policy environment. These variables are highly correlated with PI.[34] I therefore assume that PI also reflects the policy environment in African countries and do not include any other additional variables to reflect the policy environment.

PI EQUATION

As discussed earlier, there are reasons to question the assumption that PI is exogenous in the growth equation. Following the political science literature, I represent PI as a function of economic growth, the strength of the military's role in civil society (mil), the legislative selection process ($lgsl$), the type of head of state ($pres$, gen), the level of economic development proxied by per capita real GDP, and the extent of fractionalization in the polity ($frac$). Formally, the PI equation is given as:

$$PI = \beta_0 + \beta_1 g + \beta_2 mil + \beta_3 frac + \beta_4 pres + \beta_5 gen + \beta_6 \lg sl + \beta_7 PI_{t-1} + \mu \tag{2}$$

where μ is a stochastic error term and all other variables are as defined above. The political science literature suggests that the military tends to intervene in politics when it has a strong, high-profile role in society. This may be because the military sees itself as the arbiter between competing interest groups in the country or because it sees an easy opportunity to seize power. The coefficient for mil is therefore expected to be positive in the PI equation, and $frac$ is expected to have a positive coefficient as increased fractionalization may either create opportunities for military involvement in political matters or create greater frustration and uncertainty among the public in the polity and generate politically unstable events. Both $pres$ and gen are dummy variables, representing constitutionally elected and military heads of state, respectively (monarchy is the excluded category). The coefficients of $pres$ and gen cannot be signed a priori as their signs will depend upon how they affect PI relative to that of a monarchy. On average the more democratic and open the legislative selection process is, the lower the PI will be, all things equal. Fedderke and Klitgaard find that the level of development is positively associated with political stability, all things equal.[35] I therefore expect the coefficient of y_{t-1} to be positive in the PI equation. The faster economic growth is, the lower the PI will be, all things equal. Therefore, the coefficient of g is expected to be negative in the PI equation. I have included a lagged value of PI based on the hypothesis that countries that experience political instability develop an intertemporal "culture of political instability."[36] If this hypothesis is correct, I expect the coefficient of PI_{t-1} to be positive. I have included per capita real GDP to test whether political instability is correlated with level of development.

INVESTMENT EQUATION

Political instability can affect economic growth in two ways: directly by reducing the output of existing resources and indirectly by reducing the availability (or growth) of inputs, such as capital. Investment in capital requires long-term planning and guarantees of property rights. Drastic and frequent changes in property rights laws and rules governing repatriation of profits, as well as the increased uncertainty that often accompanies political instability make long-term planning impossible. In Sub-Saharan Africa, the drastic increase in the "brain drain" in the last two decades has been attributed in part to political instability.[37] This implies that investment is, in part, determined by PI and the savings rate (s). The expected negative impact of PI on investment is consisted with the model developed by Ozler and Roderick, Devereaux and Wen, and Gyimah-Brempong and Traynor.[38] I write the investment equation as:

$$k = \gamma_0 + \gamma_1 g + \gamma_2 PI + \gamma_3 PI_{t-1} + \gamma_4 m + \gamma_5 rds + \gamma_6 s + \gamma_7 k_{t-1} + \varepsilon \qquad (3)$$

where m is the imports/GDP ratio, rds is the real foreign debt service/GDP ratio, s is the savings ratio, ε is a stochastic error term, and all other variables are as defined above. I expect the coefficients of g and s to be positive. In Sub-Saharan Africa, where almost all investment goods are imported, investment is constrained by import capacity, so a relaxation of that constraint will increase investment assuming that the composition of imports at the margin does not change dramatically toward consumer goods. I therefore expect the coefficient of m to be positive. High foreign debt constrains investment because of the need to divert resources which would otherwise have gone for investment to service external debt. Therefore the coefficient of rds is expected to be negative. I have included k_{t-1} in the investment equation to investigate the dynamic nature of investment in Sub-Saharan Africa.

The system of equations I estimate is given as follows:

$$g_{it} = \alpha_0 + \alpha_1 k_{it} + \alpha_2 l_{it} + \alpha_3 \dot{x}_{it} + \alpha_4 y_0 + \alpha_5 PI_{it} + e_{it}$$

$$k_{it} = \gamma_0 + \gamma_1 g_{it} + \gamma_2 PI_{it} + \gamma_4 m_{it} + \gamma_5 rds_{it} + \gamma_6 s_{it} + \gamma_7 k_{i,t-1} + \varepsilon_{it}$$

$$PI_{it} = \beta_0 + \beta_1 g_{it} + \beta_2 mil_{it} + \beta_3 frac_{it} + \beta_4 pres_{it} + \beta_5 gen_{it} + \beta_6 lgsl_{it}$$
$$+ \beta_7 y_{i,t-1} + \beta_8 PI_{i,t-1} + \mu_{it}$$

From the model presented here, the total current period effect of a one-standard-deviation change in PI on economic growth (dg/dPI) is the sum of the direct and indirect current periods effects, given as:

$$dg/dPI_{t-1} = (\partial g/\partial k)(\partial k/\partial PI_{t-1}) + (\partial g/\partial PI)(\partial PI/\partial PI_{t-1}) = \alpha_5 + \alpha_1\gamma_2$$

Thus, the model allows for the fact that the direct effect of PI on growth may only be a partial determinant of the overall relationship between PI and growth. Additionally, the one-period intertemporal impact of PI on growth is represented by:

$$dg/dPI = \partial g/\partial PI + (\partial g/\partial k)(\partial k/\partial PI) = \alpha_1 y_3 + \alpha_5\beta_8$$

This intertemporal impact shows the effects of PI on economic growth one year after the occurrence of PI. Alternatively, one can interpret this as the effects of earlier episodes of political instability on economic growth in the current period. Note that the relationship between PI and growth does not represent the usual multiplier effect; it simply displays the total effect that PI has an economic growth, regardless of the source of variation in PI.

DATA

The endogenous variables in the model are g, PI, and k. I measure g as the annual growth rate of aggregate real GDP in a country, and following Ram and others, I measure k as the investment/GDP ratio.[39] There is no simple way to measure PI. For one thing, my notion of PI is multidimensional, taking such diverse forms as political assassinations, secession movements guerrilla warfare, coups d'état, and purges. For another, these events can occur with different degrees of frequency in different countries at different times. For example, there may be more coups d'état in one country than another but there may be more guerrilla attacks in the second country than the first. The traditional approach to measuring political instability in the extant political science and economics literature is to create a political instability index by assigning arbitrary weights to various politically unstable events. The resulting political instability index reflects the subjective evaluations of political events of the researcher and is therefore not the kind of objective measure that would be better suited for research on political instability and economic growth, such as this one. Moreover most of these PI indices do not include the effects of "less serious" politically unstable events as they use only elite PI events.

Because the many different politically unstable events that make up PI in this analysis are likely to be highly correlated, I measure PI as a single weighted index of politically unstable events in a country during a single calendar year. In an effort to measure political instability in a less arbitrary manner than those developed for previous research, the principal-components method is used to create a weighting mechanism for PI. This method creates a variable that is weighted such that it maximizes the correlation between itself and the individual politically unstable events, thus creating a single representative measure of political instability.[40] This means that instead of arbitrarily assigning weights to create the PI index, the principal-components methodology creates the weights from the data. In calculating this index, I normalize the variable so the resulting principal components indicate the deviation of PI from its mean; in effect, the PIs are standardized z scores. The use of the principal-components method for the development of a measure of PI allows for the use of a statistically determined variable in the analysis which, although not based on economic and political science theory, is free from the potentially arbitrary hands of the researcher in its development. I note that this approach to calculating PI is similar to the method employed by Gupta.[41] While my approach to calculating PI solves the problem of arbitrarily assigning weights to the various politically unstable events, like all statistical methods, it could create another problem; it is not clear which specific events are important for policy purposes. Second, it is possible that my measure of PI may not reflect what it was theoretically intended to measure.

Variables used in the construction of this broad index of political instability are successful and attempted coups d'état, guerrilla warfare, secession movements, political assassinations, revolutions, riots, major government crises, purges, constitutional crises, large-scale antigovernment demonstrations, politically motivated strikes, constitutional changes, and plots. These variables are those that have been used by researchers to reflect various forms of PI. I note that this measure of PI encompasses Morrison's elite, mass, and communal PI as well as Fedderke and Klitgaard's regime-threatening and non-regime-threatening PI. In addition to this broad measure of PI, I also create an index of elite political instability using principal components methodology and use the resulting PI measure to re-estimate the model. I do so in order to compare the estimates using elite PI events with those using the more comprehensive measure detailed above to see if the index used makes a difference in the results in light of the fact that previous research have focused mainly on elite PI. The events used to create the elite PI index are a subset of the politically unstable events used to create the broader index of PI consisting of successful and attempted coups, revolutions, and plots.

To capture a nation's import ability, I measure m as the import/GDP ratio; rds is measured as the ratio of external debt service to GDP; y is measured as real per capita GDP; and y_0 is real per capita GDP in a country in period $t - 5$. It is difficult to quantify the role the military plays in society. However, as the political science literature suggests, the extent of military involvement in civilian societies can be captured by the amount of resources the military commands in the society. I therefore measure mil as the number of military personnel per thousand in the population; $frac$ is the party fractionalization index as defined by Rae and is measured as $frac = 1 - \Sigma_{i=1}^{m}(t_i)^2$, where t_i is the proportion of members of the legislature associated with the ith political party.[42] $lgsl$ is a scale variable that equals 0 if no legislature exists; 1, for a non-elected legislature; and 2, for a legislature that is elected either directly or indirectly. *pres* is a dichotomous variable that equals 1 for a constitutionally elected head of state; zero, otherwise. *gen* is a dummy variable that equals 1 if the head of state is either a military leader or a civilian imposed by the military; zero, otherwise. The excluded category is monarchy so the effects of *pres* and *gen* on PI are relative to that of a monarchy. I measure $\dot{x}$ as the annual growth rate of real export earnings of a country.

Data for the calculation of the sociopolitical variables (PI, *frac*, *pres*, *gen*, *lgsl*) were obtained from Arthur S. Banks, Cross-National Time-Series Data Archives, 1993, Center for Social Analysis, State University of New York at Binghamton, New York, while the economic data (g, l, k, m, $\dot{x}$, s, y, and *rds*) were obtained from the World Bank's *World Development Indicators 1995* and *African Economic Indicators 1992* (Washington, D.C., World Bank Publications). Data for *mil* were obtained from the Arms Control and Disarmament Agency (ACDA) and the World Military Expenditures and Arms Transfers, (various years). The data consist of annual observations for the 1975–1990 period for 39 Sub-Saharan African countries.[43] The choice of sample countries and periods of coverage was constrained by the availability and completeness of data.

ESTIMATING METHOD

The system of equations to be estimated can be written in a compact format as:

$$\Gamma y + X'\beta + \mu = 0 \qquad (4)$$

where y, β, and μ are the vectors of endogenous variables, coefficients to be estimated, and stochastic error terms, respectively, and X is a matrix of exogenous variables. The error term in Eq. (4) consists of a country-specific component, a time component, and white noise. Formally, the error term is $\mu_{it} = \alpha_i + \lambda_t + v_{it}$, where α_i is the country-specific component, λ_t is the time-specific component, and v_{it} is white noise, assumed to have zero mean with a constant finite variance. There is reason to expect that $E(\alpha_i) \neq 0$ and the same can be said of λ_t. In general, α_i and λ_t will be correlated with the regressors in the equation. This implies that, for this model, it is likely that $E(X'\mu) \neq 0$; hence, the orthogonality condition necessary to produce consistent estimates is not likely to be present.

NOTES

[*]This chapter has benefited from the comments of several anonymous referees, and I thank them for these comments; however, I am solely responsible for any remaining errors.

[1]See, for example, World Bank (1984) *Towards a Sustained Development in Sub-Saharan Africa: A Joint Program for Action*, Washington, D.C.: World Bank Publications; African Development Bank (2000) *African Development Report 2000*, London: Oxford University Press.

[2]See McGowan, P. and Johnson, T.H. (1984) "African Military Coups d'Etat and Underdevelopment: A Quantitative Historical Analysis," *Journal of Modern African Studies*, 22(4), 633–666; Wells, K. (1992) "South Africa Violence Wounds Economy," *The Wall Street Journal*, September 30.

[3]Stockholm International Peace Research Institute (2000) *SIPRI Yearbook 2000*, London: Oxford University Press.

[4]For example, see Powelson, J.P. (1972) *Institutions of Economic Growth*, Princeton, NJ: Princeton University Press; Scully, G.W. (1988) "The Institutional Framework and Economic Development," *Journal of Political Economy*, 96(3), 652–662; North, D.C. (1990) *Institutions, Institutional Change, and Economic Performance*, New York: Cambridge University Press; Hirschman, A.O. (1956) *A Strategy of Economic Development*, New Haven, CT: Yale University Press; Williamson, O. (1985) *The Economic Institutions of Capitalism* New York: Free Press; Wells, K. (1992) "South Africa Violence Wounds Economy," *The Wall Street Journal*, September 30; Kuznets, S. (1966) *Modern Economic Growth: Rate, Structure, and Spread*, New Haven, CT: Yale University Press; and other political science literature referenced in the text.

[5]Fedderke, J. and Klitgaard, R. (1998) "Economic Growth and Social Indicators: An Exploratory Analysis," *Economic Development and Cultural Change*, 46(3), 455–489; Gyimah-Brempong K. and Traynor, T.L. (1999) "Political Instability, Investment, and Economic Growth in Sub-Saharan Africa," *Journal of African Economies*, 8(1), 52–86.

[6]The Physical Quality of Life Index (PQLI) developed by the United Nations Development Program (UNDP) may be a better measure of development than per capita income; however, such data are not available over any extended period of time for any country. I also note that, in general, there is a positive relationship between per capita income and the PQLI so income levels and growth rate can be considered reasonable proxies for development.

[7]See Fosu, A.K. (1992) "Political Instability and Economic Growth: Evidence from Sub-Saharan Africa," *Economic Development and Cultural Change*, 40(2), 823–841; Londregan, J.B. and Poole, K.T. (1990) "Poverty: The Coup Trap, and Seizure of Executive Power," *World Politics*, 42(2), 151–193; McGowan, P. and Johnson, T.H. (1984) "African Military Coups d'Etat and Underdevelopment: A Quantitative Historical Analysis," *Journal of Modern African Studies*, 22(4), 633–666; Barro, R.J. (1991) "Economic Growth of Cross Section of Countries," *Quarterly Journal of Economics*, 106, 407–433; Svenson, J. (1998) "Investment, Property Rights and Political Instability: Theory and Empirical Evidence," *European Economic Review*, 42(7), 1317–1341; Knack, S. and Keefer, P. (1995) "Institutions and Economic Performance: Cross-Country Tests Using Alternative Institutional Measures," *Economics and Politics*, 7, 207–227.

[8]Bardhan, P. (1989) *The Economic Theory of Agrarian Institutions*, New York: Oxford University Press.

[9]World Bank (1997) *World Development Report 1997*, New York: Oxford University Press.

[10]Mauro, P. (1995) "Corruption and Growth," *The Quarterly Journal of Economics*, 110(3), 681–712; Gyimah-Brempong K. and Munoz de Camacho, S. (1998) "Political Instability, Investment, Human Capital, and Economic Growth in Latin America," *Journal of Developing Areas*, 32(4), 449–466.

[11]North, D.C. (1990) *Institutions, Institutional Change, and Economic Performance*, New York: Cambridge University Press; Williamson, O. (1985) *The Economic Institutions of Capitalism* New York: Free Press.

[12]I thank an anonymous referee for making this point to me.

[13]Morrison, D.G. and Stevenson, H.M. (1971), "Political Instability in Independent Black Africa: More Dimensions of Conflict Behavior Within Nations," *The Journal of Conflict Resolution*, 15(3), 347–368.

[14]Deaton, A. and Miller, R. (1995) "International Commodity Prices, Macroeconomic Performance, and Politics in Sub-Saharan Africa," *Princeton Studies in International Finance*, No. 79, December.

[15]Fedderke, J. and Klitgaard, R. (1998) "Economic Growth and Social Indicators: An Exploratory Analysis," *Economic Development and Cultural Change*, 46(3), 455–489.

[16]McGowan, P. and Johnson, T.H. (1984) "African Military Coups d'Etat and Underdevelopment: A Quantitative Historical Analysis," *Journal of Modern African Studies*, 22(4), 633–666.

[17]Fosu, A.K. (1992) "Political Instability and Economic Growth: Evidence from Sub-Saharan Africa," *Economic Development and Cultural Change*, 40(2), 823–841.

[18]See Svenson, J. (1998) "Investment, Property Rights and Political Instability: Theory and Empirical Evidence," *European Economic Review*, 42(7), 1317–1341; Knack, S. and Keefer, P. (1995) "Institutions and Economic Performance: Cross-Country Tests Using Alternative Institutional Measures," *Economics and Politics*, 7, 207–227; Besley, T. (1995) "Property Rights and Investment Incentive: Theory and Evidence from Ghana," *Journal of Political Economy*, 103(5), 903–937; among others.

[19]Mbaku, J.M. (1992) "Political Instability and Economic Development in Sub-Saharan Africa: Further Evidence," *The Review of Black Political Economy*, Spring, 39–53; Alexander, W.R.J. and Hansen, P. (1998) "Government, Exports, Instability, and Economic Growth in Sub-Saharan Africa," *The South African Journal of Economics*, 66(4), 492–511; Edwards, S. and Tabellini, G. (1991) *Political Instability, Political Weakness, and Inflation: An Empirical Analysis*, Working Paper No. 3721, Cambridge, MA: National Bureau of Economic Research (NBER); Devereux, M. and Wen, J.F. (1996) *Political Uncertainty, Capital Taxation and Growth* (mimeo), University of British Columbia.

[20]Barro, R.J. (1991) "Economic Growth of Cross Section of Countries," *Quarterly Journal of Economics*, 106, 407–433; Renelt and Levine (1991) "A Sensitivity Analysis of Cross-Country Regressions," *American Economic Review*, 82(4), 942–963; Collier, P. and Gunning, J.W. (1999) "Explaining African Economic Performance," *Journal of Economic Literature*, 37(1), 64–111; Collier, P. and Gunning, J.W. (1995) "War, Peace, and Private Portfolios," *World Development*, 23, 233–241; Deaton, A. and Miller, R. (1995) *International Commodity Prices, Macroeconomic Performance, and Politics in Sub-Saharan Africa*, Princeton Studies in International Finance, No. 79, December; Easterly, W. and Levine, R. (1997) "Africa's Growth Tragedy: Policies and Ethnic Divisions," *Quarterly Journal of Economics*, 112(4), 1203–1250; Sachs, J.D. and Warner, A.M. (1997) "Fundamental Sources of Long-Run Growth," *American Economic Review Papers and Proceedings*, 87, 184–188; Sachs, J. and Warner, A.M. (1997) "Sources of Slow Growth in African Economies," *Journal of African Economies*, 6, 335–376.

[21]Fedderke, J. and Klitgaard, R. (1998) "Economic Growth and Social Indicators: An Exploratory Analysis," *Economic Development and Cultural Change*, 46(3), 455–489; Fedderke J., de Kadt, R.H., and Luiz, J.M. (2001) "Indicators of Political Liberty, Property Rights and Political Instability in South Africa: 1935–97," *International Review of Law and Economics*, 21(1), 103–134. See also McGowan, P. and Johnson, T.H. (1984) "African Military Coups d'Etat and Underdevelopment: A Quantitative Historical Analysis," *Journal of Modern African Studies*, 22(4), 633–666; Johnson, T., Skater, R.O., and McGowan, P. (1984) "Explaining African Coups d'Etat, 1960–1982," *American Political Science Review*, 78, 622-640; Londregan, J.B. and Poole, K.T. (1990) "Poverty: The Coup Trap, and Seizure of Executive Power," *World Politics*, 42(2), 151–193; Fedderke, J. and Klitgaard, R. (1998) "Economic Growth and Social Indicators: An Exploratory Analysis," *Economic Development and Cultural Change*, 46(3), 455–489; Fedderke J., de Kadt, R.H., and Luiz, J.M. (2001) "Indicators of Political Liberty, Property Rights and Political Instability in South Africa: 1935–97," *International Review of Law and Economics*, 21(1), 103–134; Jenkins, C.J. and Kpososwa, A.J. (1990) "Explaining Military Coups d'état: Black Africa 1957–1984," *American Sociological Review*, 55(6), 861–875; O'Kane, R. (1981) "A Probabilistic Approach to the Causes of Coups d'Etat," *British Journal of Political Science*, 11, 287–308; O'Kane, R. (1983) "Towards an Examination of the General Causes of Coups d'Etat," *European Journal of Political Research*, 11, 27–44; Jackman, R. (1978) "The Predictability of Coups d'état: A Model with African Data," *American Political Review*, 72, 1263–1275; Olson, M. (1963) "Rapid Growth as a Destabilizing Force," *Journal of Economic History*, 23(4), 529–552.

[22]Gyimah-Brempong and Traynor (1999) *Journal of African Economics*, 8(1), 52–86; Gyimah-Brempong K. and Munoz de Camacho, S. (1998) "Political Instability, Investment, Human Capital, and Economic Growth in Latin America," *Journal of Developing Areas*, 32(4), 449–466.

[23]Knight, M., Loayza, N., and Villanueva, D. (1993) "Testing the Neoclassical Theory of Economic Growth: A Panel Data Approach," *IMF Staff Papers*, 40(3), 512–541; Islam (1995); Caselli F.G., and Lefort, F. (1996) "Reopening the Convergence Debate: A New Look at Cross-Country Growth Empiries," *Journal of Economic Growth*, 1, 363–389.

[24]While it is possible that increased uncertainty about future earnings could lead to increased investment (see, for example, Dixit, A. and Pindyck, R. (1994) *Investment Under Uncertainty*, Princeton, NJ: Princeton University Press), PI not only increases uncertainty of future earnings but also increases uncertainty about ownership of property, as the chances of unlawful appropriation of businesses increase with increased political instability.

[25]Edwards, S. and Tabellini, G. (1991) *Political Instability, Political Weakness, and Inflation: An Empirical Analysis*, Working Paper No. 3721, Cambridge, MA: National Bureau of Economic Research (NBER); Devereux, M. and Wen, J.F. (1996) *Political Uncertainty, Capital Taxation and Growth* (mimeo), University of British Columbia.

[26]Alesina, A. and Perotti, R. (1994) "The Political Economy of Growth: A Survey of the Literature," *The World Bank Economic Review*, 8(30), 351–371; Alesina, A. and Tabellini, G. (1990) "A Positive Theory of Fiscal Deficits and Government Debt," *The Review of Economic Studies*, 57(3), 403–414; Cukierman, A., Edwards, S., and Tabellini, G. (1992) "Seigniorage and Political Instability," *The American Economic Review*, 82(3), 537–555.

[27]Arellano, M. and Bond, S. (1991) "Some Tests of Specification for Panel Data: Monte Carlo Evidence and Application to Employment Equations," *Review of Economic Studies*, 58, 277–297; Arellano, M., and Bond, S. (1988) *Dynamic Panel Data Estimation Using DPD: A Guide for Users*, Working Paper No. 88/45, London: Institute for Fiscal Studies (IFS).

[28]In the cases where a definite sign for the parameter estimate is hypothesized, a one-tailed *t*-test was conducted; otherwise, two-tailed *t*-tests were used.

[29]Alesina, A. and Perotti, R. (1994) "The Political Economy of Growth: A Survey of the Literature," *The World Bank Economic Review*, 8(30), 351–371; Alesina A., Perotti, P., and Tavares, J. (1998) "The Political Economy of Fiscal Adjustments," Londregan, J.B. and Poole, K.T. (1990) "Poverty: The Coup Trap, and Seizure of Executive Power," *World Politics*, 42(2), 151–193; Fedderke, J. and Klitgaard, R. (1998) "Economic Growth and Social Indicators: An Exploratory Analysis," *Economic Development and Cultural Change*, 46(3), 455–489; Gyimah-Brempong K. and Traynor, T.L. (1999) "Political Instability, Investment, and Economic Growth in Sub-Saharan Africa," *Journal of African Economies*, 8(1), 52–86.

[30]Collier, P. (2000) "Rebellion as a Quasi Criminal Activity" *Journal of Conflict Resolution*, 44(6), 839–853. provides an excellent review of the economic causes of civil wars.

[31]See Feder, G. (1983) "On Exports and Economic Growth," *Journal of Development Economics*, 12, 59–73; Krueger, A.O. (1980) "Trade Policy as an Input to Development," *American Economic Review Papers and Proceedings*, 70, 288–292; Balassa, B. (1978) "Exports and Economic Growth: Further Evidence," *Journal of Development Economics*, 5, 181–189; Ram, R. (1987) "Exports and Economic Growth in Developing Countries: Evidence from Time-Series and Cross-Section Data," *Economic Development and Cultural Change*, 36(1), 51–72.

[32]Fosu, A.K. (1992) "Political Instability and Economic Growth: Evidence from Sub-Saharan Africa," *Economic Development and Cultural Change*, 40(2), 823–841; Barro, R.J. (1991) "Economic Growth of Cross Section of Countries," *Quarterly Journal of Economics*, 106, 407–433; Gyimah-Brempong and Traynor (1996) "Political Instability and Savings in Less Developed Countries: Evidence from Sub-Saharan Africa," *Journal of Development Studies*, 32(5), 695–714; Gyimah-Brempong K. and Traynor, T.L. (1999) "Political Instability, Investment, and Economic Growth in Sub-Saharan Africa," *Journal of African Economies*, 8(1), 52–86; Fedderke, J. and Klitgaard, R. (1998) "Economic

Growth and Social Indicators: An Exploratory Analysis," *Economic Development and Cultural Change*, 46(3), 455–489.

[33]Recent growth models include the stock of human capital as a determinant of economic growth. The data series available on education (to proxy human capital) covers only a few African countries for the time frame under consideration; therefore, human capital cannot be included as a regressor in the growth equation being estimated.

[34]Fedderke, J. and Klitgaard, R. (1998) "Economic Growth and Social Indicators: An Exploratory Analysis," *Economic Development and Cultural Change*, 46(3), 455–489; Fedderke J., de Kadt, R.H., and Luiz, J.M. (2001) "Indicators of Political Liberty, Property Rights and Political Instability in South Africa: 1935–97," *International Review of Law and Economics*, 21(1), 103–134.

[35]Fedderke, J. and Klitgaard, R. (1998) "Economic Growth and Social Indicators: An Exploratory Analysis," *Economic Development and Cultural Change*, 46(3), 455–489.

[36]See Londregan, J.B. and Poole, K.T. (1990) "Poverty: The Coup Trap, and Seizure of Executive Power," *World Politics*, 42(2), 151–193.

[37]Apraku (1991).

[38]Ozler, S. and Roderik, D. (1992) "External Shocks, Politics, and Private Investment: Some Theory and Empirical Evidence," *Journal of Development Economics*, 39, 141–162; Devereux, M. and Wen, J.F. (1996) *Political Uncertainty, Capital Taxation and Growth* (mimeo), University of British Columbia; Gyimah-Brempong and Traynor (1996) "Political Instability and Savings in Less Developed Countries: Evidence from Sub-Saharan Africa," *Journal of Development Studies*, 32(5), 695–714.

[39]Ram, R. (1987) "Exports and Economic Growth in Developing Countries: Evidence from Time-Series and Cross-Section Data," *Economic Development and Cultural Change*, 36(1), 51–72; Balassa, B. (1978) "Exports and Economic Growth: Further Evidence," *Journal of Development Economics*, 5, 181–189.

[40]Using principal components creates a composite variable that has the highest possible correlation with the individual events of political instability. This is accomplished by choosing the vector of weights, b, which maximize the variance of $b'b'x$ subject to $b'b = 1$. See G. Dunteman, G. (1984) *Multivariate Analysis*, Beverly Hills, CA: Sage Publications, for a review of the principal-components methodology.

[41]Gupta, D. (1990) *Economics of Political Violence*, New York: Praeger Publications.

[42]Rae, D. (1968) "A Note on the Fractionalization of Some European Party Systems," *Comparative Political Studies*, 1, 413–418. See also Fedderke J., de Kadt, R.H., and Luiz, J.M. (2001) "Indicators of Political Liberty, Property Rights and Political Instability in South Africa: 1935–97," *International Review of Law and Economics*, 21(1), 103–134, for an alternative measurement of party fractionalization.

[43]The countries in the sample are Benin, Botswana, Burkina Faso, Burundi, Cameroon, Cape Verde, Central African Republic, Chad, Comoros, the Republic of Congo, Côte d'Iviore, Ethiopia, Gabon, Gambia, Ghana, Guinea, Kenya, Lesotho, Liberia, Madagascar, Malawi, Mali, Mauritania, Mauritius, Mozambique, Niger, Nigeria, Rwanda, Senegal, Sierra Leone, Somalia, Sudan, Swaziland, Tanzania, Togo, Uganda, Zaire (also known as the Democratic Republic of Congo), Zambia, and Zimbabwe.

CHAPTER 13

Inequality and Conflict[1]

E. WAYNE NAFZIGER

Department of Economics, Kansas State University, Manhattan, Kansas 66506

KEY TERMS

Commodity terms of trade	Negative real interest rate
Complex humanitarian emergencies	Parastatal enterprises
Conflict tradition	Patronage
Debt service	Predatory rule
Economic regression	Relative deprivation
Gini coefficient	Rent seeking
GNP per capita in international dollars (I$)	State failure
Kleptocracy	Trade balance
Legitimacy	Warlord
Military centrality	

I. INTRODUCTION

Economic development and deadly political violence interact in two ways: Economic factors contribute to conflict, while conflict has an adverse effect on economic growth and average material welfare. About 20% of Africans live in countries seriously disrupted by war or state violence. The cost of conflict includes refugee flows, increased military spending, damage to transport and communication, reduction in trade and investment, and diversion of resources from development. The World Bank estimates that a civil war in an African country lowers its GDP per capita by 2.2 percentage points annually.[2]

This chapter, however, focuses on how economic factors affect complex humanitarian emergencies, comprising a human-made crisis in which large numbers of people die and suffer from war, physical violence (often by the state), and refugee displacement. The complexity of the crisis results from its multidimensionality, politicization, and persistence.[3] "Economic" here refers to political economy, which not only includes economic analysis but also examines the interests of political leaders and policymakers who make economic decisions, as well as the interests of members of the population who are affected by these decisions. Emergencies in Africa includes the four horsemen of the apocalypse, or humanitarian emergencies: war, disease, hunger, and displacement.

Prunier contends that for a 3-month period, the 800,000 estimated deaths (11% of the population) from genocide in Rwanda from April to July 1994 represented perhaps the highest non-natural casualty rate in history.[4] Other emergencies in the 1980s and 1990s (identified by 2000 or more dying and refugees crossing international boundaries as a result of war, internal conflict, or state violence during at least one year) include Algeria, Angola, Burundi, Chad, Congo (Brazzaville), Congo (Kinshasa), Guinea-Bissau, Eritrea, Ethiopia, Liberia, Mozambique, Sierra Leone, Somalia, South Africa, Sudan, and Uganda.

Auvinen and Nafziger have analyzed econometrically the relationship between humanitarian emergencies and their hypothesized sources, based on annual data from Africa and other developing countries from 1980–1995.[5] Their analysis indicates that stagnation and decline in real gross domestic product (GDP), high income inequality, a high ratio of military expenditures to national income, a tradition of violent conflict, and slow growth in average food production are sources of emergencies.[6] In addition, the study found that countries that failed to adjust to chronic external deficits were more vulnerable to humanitarian emergencies.

The findings are by and large consistent for three measures of the dependent variable and whether we use ordinary least squares (OLS), generalized least squares (GLS, or Prais–Winsten), two-stage least squares, fixed and random effects, tobit, or probit models. Humanitarian emergencies are most robustly associated with slow or negative economic growth, a low level of economic development, military centrality, and a tradition of violent conflict.

II. STAGNATION AND DECLINE IN INCOMES

The next several sections discuss the major sources of humanitarian emergencies in Africa. Emergencies are found only in low- and middle-income (that is, developing) countries,[7] suggesting a threshold above which emergencies do not occur. Moreover, these emergencies are more likely to occur in countries experiencing stagnation and decline in real GDP, which affects relative deprivation—people's perception of social injustice based upon a discrepancy between goods and conditions they expect and those they can get or keep. This deprivation often results from vertical (class) or horizontal (regional or communal) inequality, where people's incomes or conditions are related to those of others within society. This deprivation spurs social discontent, which provides motivation for collective violence.[8] Among the various components of emergencies, war and violence have major catalytic roles, adding to social disruption and political instability, undermining economic activity, spreading hunger and disease, and fueling refugee flows. Tangible and salient factors such as a marked deterioration of living conditions, especially during a period of high expectations, are more likely to produce sociopolitical discontent that may be mobilized into political violence.

Only a portion of violence results from insurgent action. In fact, the policies of governing elites are at the root of most deadly political violence, including not only genocide but also structural violence.[9] Slow or negative growth puts more pressure on ruling elites, reducing the number of allies and clients they can support, undermining the legitimacy of the regime, and increasing the probability of regime turnover. To forestall threats to the regime, political elites frequently use repression to suppress discontent or capture a greater share of the majority's shrinking surplus. These repressive policies may entail acts of direct violence against, or withholding food and other supplies from, politically disobedient groups, as in Sudan in the 1980s.

Stagnation and decline in incomes exacerbate the feeling of relative deprivation. Slow or negative growth puts ruling coalitions on the horns of a dilemma. Ruling elites can expand rent-seeking opportunities for existing political elites, contributing to further economic stagnation that can threaten the legitimacy of the regime and future stability. Or they can reduce the number of allies and clients they support, risking opposition by those no longer sharing in the benefits of rule. Either strategy to manage power, in the midst of economic crises, can exacerbate the potential for repression and insurgency and, ultimately, humanitarian emergencies.

Because economic deceleration or collapse can disrupt ruling coalitions and exacerbate mass discontent, we should not be surprised that, since 1980, African countries have been more vulnerable to political violence and humanitarian emergencies. This increase in intrastate political conflict and humanitarian emergencies in Africa in the last two decades of the 20th century and initial years of the 21st century is linked to its negative growth record in the 1970s and 1980s and virtual stagnation in the 1990s. Indeed Sub-Saharan Africa GDP per capita was lower in the late 1990s than it was at the end of the 1960s.[10]

In the Sub-Saharan Africa, falling average incomes and growing political consciousness added pressures on national leaders, whose responses usually have been not only anti-egalitarian but also anti-growth by depressing returns to small farmers, appropriating peasant surplus for parastatal industry, building parastatal enterprises beyond management capacity, and using these inefficient firms to give benefits to clients. Regime survival in a politically fragile system required expanding patronage to marshal elite support, at the expense of economic growth.[11] Spurring peasant production through market prices and exchange rates would have interfered with state leaders' ability to build political support, especially in cities.

Africa's economic crisis in the 1980s and early 1990s originated from its inability to adjust to the 1973–1974 oil shock, exacerbated by a credit cycle in which states overborrowed at negative real interest rates in the mid- to late 1970s, but faced high positive rates during debt servicing or loan renewal in the 1980s. African leaders' statist economic policies during the 1970s and early 1980s emphasized detailed state planning, expansion of government-owned enterprises, heavy-industry development, and government intervention in exchange rates and agricultural pricing. These policies contributed to economic regression and growing poverty (especially in rural areas) and inequality. The political elites used the state to pursue economic policies that supported their interests at the expense of Africa's poor and working classes.

This stagnation and decline contributed to political decay in the 1980s and early 1990s in such countries as Nigeria, Sierra Leone, Zaire, and Liberia. Ethnic and regional competition for the bounties of the state gave way to a predatory state. Predatory rule involves a personalistic regime ruling through coercion, material inducement, and personality politics, tending to degrade the institutional foundations of the economy and state. In some predatory states, the ruling elite and their clients "use their positions and access to resources to plunder the national economy through graft, corruption, and extortion, and to participate in private business activities."[12] Ake contends that, "Instead of being a public force, the state in Africa tends to be privatized, that is, appropriated to the service of private interests by the dominant faction of the elite."[13] People use funds at the disposal of the state for systematic corruption, from petty survival venality at the lower echelons of government to kleptocracy at the top.

Humanitarian crises are more likely to occur in societies where the state is weak and venal and thus subject to extensive rent seeking, "an omnipresent policy to obtain private benefit from public action and resources."[14] Cause and effect between state failure and rent seeking are not always clear. State failure need not necessarily result from the incapacity of public institutions. Instead, while "state failure can harm a great number of people, it can also benefit others,"[15] especially governing elites and their allies. These elites may not benefit from avoiding political decay through nurturing free entry and the rule of law and reducing corruption and exploitation. Instead political leaders may gain more from extensive unproductive, profit-seeking activities in a political system they control than from long-term efforts to build a well-functioning state in which economic progress and democratic institutions flourish. These activities tend to be pervasive in countries that have abundant mineral exports (for example, diamonds and petroleum), such as Sierra Leone, Angola, Congo, and Liberia, while predatory economic behavior is less viable in mineral-export-poor economies such as Ghana and Tanzania.

The majority of countries with humanitarian emergencies have experienced several years (or even decades) of negative or stagnant growth, where growth refers to real growth in gross national product (GNP) or GDP per capita. Virtually all emergencies in Africa in the 1990s (except Chad; see list in Section I) were preceded by slow or negative economic growth.

Contemporary humanitarian disaster in Africa is rarely episodic but is usually the culmination of longer term politico-economic decay over a period of a decade or more. Negative growth interacts with political predation in a downward spiral, a spiral seen in African countries such as Angola, Ethiopia, Sudan, Somalia, Liberia, Sierra Leone, and Zaire (the Democratic Republic of Congo). The metaphor is not that of steadily climbing a mountain to the summit of high material welfare and ethnic harmony, but of Sisyphus trying to push a huge rock uphill, where every slip could mean backsliding or even plunging to the abyss below.

The causes and accompaniments of economic stagnation or decline vary enormously. In Africa, a major factor contributing to the explosion of humanitarian emergencies is worsening international conditions. Sudden external shocks and long-term deterioration in the international economic position can contribute to stagnation or precipitous slumps. Abrupt shocks may include large shifts in terms of trade, falling development assistance, and interest-rate shocks (factors frequently observed in the early 1980s and 1990s), while protracted deterioration may include a long-run decline in commodity terms of trade, rising foreign protection, or the gradual exclusion from international capital markets and flows of foreign direct investment. For example, during its slow and negative per capita growth, Sub-Saharan Africa experienced declining commodity terms of trade (price index of exports divided by the price index of imports)—a fall of 52% from 1970–1992 (or 38% from 1980–1992). Sub-Saharan Africa's income terms of trade or export purchasing power (the commodity terms of trade times export volume) declined 46% from 1970–1992 (or 29% from 1980–1992). This substantial fall in export purchasing power and material levels of living made the region more vulnerable to political crises.[16] While the distributive effects can vary, and some of the countries affected have been able to adjust, the depressive effect of these trends on weak states and economies, especially those difficult to restructure, are largely unavoidable.

III. FAILURE OF ADJUSTMENT TO CHRONIC EXTERNAL DEFICITS

Economic stagnation, frequently accompanied by chronic trade deficits and growing external debt, intensifies the need for economic adjustment and stabilization. A persistent external disequilibrium has costs whether countries adjust or not. But nonadjustment has the greater cost;[17] the longer the disequilibrium, the greater is the social damage and the more painful the adjustment.

More than a decade of slow growth, rising borrowing costs, reduced concessional aid, a mounting debt crisis, and the increased economic liberalism of donors and international financial institutions compelled African elites to change their strategies during the 1980s and 1990s. Widespread economic liberalization and adjustment provided chances for challenging existing elites, threatening their positions and contributing to increased opportunistic rent seeking and overt repression. Cuts in spending reduced the funds to distribute to clients and required greater military and police support to remain in power.

IV. THE FAILURE OF AGRICULTURAL DEVELOPMENT

Agriculture is a major component of GDP in low-income countries and a major influence on the rest of the economy through its contribution to food supplies, foreign exchange, labor supply, capital transfer, and markets. Frequently the failure of food and agricultural development is a key element of a protracted stagnation or decline and rising social tensions. In several Sub-Saharan countries, agricultural stagnation is associated with slow technological and institutional modernization, unfavorable government policies and factor market distortions, and obsolete agrarian structures. Declining rural productivity contributes not only to increased dog-eat-dog contention among severely impoverished rural populations, but also spurs rural-urban migration, increasing urban unemployment, underemployment, and political discontent, which contribute to humanitarian emergencies.

Our econometric work, including a test of lags and leads, suggests that slow growth of food production per capita was a source of humanitarian emergencies (an even stronger relationship than the reverse chain from emergencies to slow food growth). We can illustrate the relationship between food availability and humanitarian emergencies in Sub-Saharan Africa. Africa's food crisis since the 1960s has made it especially vulnerable to humanitarian emergencies. Declining real household income (through falling income or rising food prices among low-income households) reduces household food availability, decreasing nutrient intake, increasing malnutrition, and increasing disease and mortality (especially among infants and children).

From 1962–1989, food output per capita grew at an annual rate of 0.5% in developing countries, 0.3% in developed countries, and 0.4% overall, but declined 0.8% in Sub-Saharan Africa, meaning that food production there grew more slowly than the population. (The data are calculated using a 5-year moving average to smooth out weather fluctuations.) Food production per person increased from 1962–1989 in all world regions except Sub-Saharan Africa (Fig. 13.1).

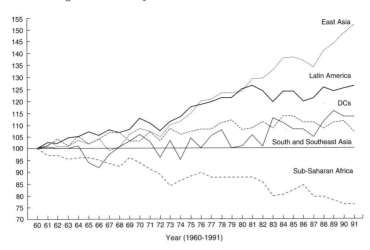

FIGURE 13.1 Growth in food production per capita, 1960–1991 (1960 = 100). DCs = developed countries. (From Nafziger, E.W. (1997) *The Economics of Developing Countries*, 3rd ed., Upper Saddle River, NJ: Prentice-Hall, p. 176. with permission)

Africa's daily calorie consumption per capita in 1989–2116 (the same as in the early 1960s and less than the 2197 of the mid-1970s)—was 92% of the requirement estimated by the United Nations Food and Agriculture Organization (FAO); calorie consumption in all other regions exceeded the FAO figure. Africa's food security index was low (and falling since the 1960s), not only because of large food deficits but also because of fluctuations in domestic output and foreign-exchange reserves, as well as declining foreign food aid. In 1989, the Economic Commission for Africa Executive Director Adebayo Adedeji spoke of "the humiliation it has brought to Africa in having to go round with the begging bowl for food aid."[18]

Illustrative of the enormity of Sub-Saharan Africa's difference from other developing countries is that while Sub-Saharan Africa and India both produced 50 million tons of foodgrains in 1960, in 1988 India produced 150 million tons (after the Green Revolution and other farm technological improvements), and Sub-Saharan Africa (with faster population growth) had stagnated at little more than 50 million tons. India's yield per hectare increased by 2.4% yearly, while Sub-Saharan Africa's yield grew at a negligible annual rate of 0.1%. Thus, Sub-Saharan Africa, which was on parity with India in 1960, produced only about one-third of Indian output in 1988.[19]

Additionally, increasing population density on cultivable land has already exacerbated conflict and humanitarian disaster in low-income Africa. Population pressure on land contributed to the diaspora from the Eastern Region to the rest of Nigeria in the one to two decades before the 1967–1970 civil war. The East had a 1963 population density of 1088/km^2 compared to the entire country's 404/km^2. Contemporary Rwanda and Burundi, with only 5 and 6% respectively, of their population living in urban areas, have a population density of 1295/km^2. This is about the same as Italy (1298), which is 67% urban, and exceeds the population density in France (717), which is 74% urban. While parts of Asia have also faced high agrarian population densities, more rapid economic growth, with its accompanying expansion of employment in industry and services, has generally reduced the political salience of these pressures.

V. INCOME INEQUALITY

The vulnerability of populations suffering deprivation from humanitarian emergencies is exacerbated by high income inequality. Alesina and Perotti's cross-section study of 71 developing countries for the years 1960 to 1985 found that income inequality, by fueling social discontent, increases sociopolitical instability, as measured by deaths in domestic disturbances and assassinations (per million population) and coups (both successful and unsuccessful). Severe social tensions leading to complex humanitarian emergencies may also arise under conditions of positive (even rapid) growth and expanding resource availability.[20] High inequality can contribute to the immiseration or absolute deprivation of portions of the population, even with growth. Absolute deprivation during substantial growth was experienced, for instance, by Igbo political elites, dominant in Nigeria's Eastern Region in 1964–1965. The East lost oil tax revenues from a change in its regional allocation by the federal government, which ceased distributing mineral export revenues to regional governments.

Moreover, through consumption levels demonstrated by the relatively well-off, high-income concentration increases the perception of relative deprivation by substantial sections of the population, even when these do not experience absolute deprivation. The risk of political disintegration increases with a surge of income disparities by class, region, and community, especially when the population views these disparities as lacking any justification. Class and communal (regional, ethnic, and religious) differences often overlap with economic disparities, exacerbating perceived grievances and potential strife.

The trends and policies leading to high income inequality may be summarized as follows:

- Historical legacies of discrimination (such as colonialism, apartheid, failed past policies, and so forth), are often sources of such inequality. Affluent classes and dominant ethnic communities use the advantages accumulated in the past—for example, access to capital, information, mobility, superior education and training, and privileged access to licenses and concessions from government—to start enterprises, buy farms, and obtain government jobs in disproportionate numbers. Less affluent and influential groups are underrepresented in entrepreneurial activity, investment, and employment. Moreover, even if current policies no longer discriminate against a particular social group, large differentials in the initial distribution of assets and opportunities lead, through market forces, to growth patterns characterized by large, and rising, inequalities. The failure to rectify initial inequalities may therefore, over time, contribute to increasing conflict.

- Government policies in distributing land and other assets and the benefits of public expenditure and differential burdens of taxation affect political and social cohesion. Included are policies that contribute to differential regional, communal, and generational opportunities in employment (especially in government), education, and the armed forces; the effects of these opportunities on regional, ethnic, and generational grievances; and the influence of these grievances on social mobilization and political protest. Another policy instrument is differential access of classes and communities during periods of major expansion of asset acquisition, such as indigenization, privatization, or outright expropriation.
- Growing regional inequality and limited regional economic integration, associated with economic enclaves, can exacerbate ethnic and regional competition and conflict.

Regional factors contributing to conflict include educational and employment differentials, revenue allocation, and language discrimination, which disadvantages minority language communities. Examples include the struggle for petroleum tax revenues and employment in the civil service and modern sector in Nigeria in the early to mid-1960s, and the conflict between Hutu and Tutsi for control of the state and access to employment in Burundi and Rwanda.

The following examples of Nigeria and South Africa illustrate how discriminatory government policies cause economic inequality, fuel social discontent, and lead to political conflict and emergencies. These dynamics may occur even when either the nation's real per capita GDP is growing, as in Nigeria, or when the disadvantaged group's economic position is improving, as for non-white South Africans from the 1970s through the early 1990s.

A. NIGERIA: INCREASED ELITE INEQUALITY DURING RAPID GROWTH

Although humanitarian disasters rarely occur in high-income countries, should we not expect some instances where developing countries are split asunder into a humanitarian crisis from conflict over the potential for abundant resources and rapid economic growth? Yes, this can happen, as illustrated by the Nigerian–Biafran war (1967–1970), in which perhaps 4 million people died from hunger and other war-related causes and several million people were displaced. The war was fought for control of Nigeria's rich resources, especially oil, but in the mid-1960s political elites from the Eastern Region (subsequently Biafra) expected economic loss amid rapid Nigerian economic growth. Election fraud and manipulation during Nigeria's 1964–1965 elections undermined the previous roles of Igbos, the dominant ethnic group in the Eastern Region, in the federal coalition. The East, which produced two-thirds of Nigeria's petroleum, lost profits and tax revenues from oil under a change in the formula for revenue allocation. Moreover, Igbo and other Eastern ethnic groups were losing the battle for key positions in the federal civil service and modern sector of Lagos and had fled from business and high-level employment in the politically dominant North. Thus, Igbo political elites, government employees, and émigré business people experienced not only relative but also absolute economic decline.

The Nigerian civil war followed a period of 3% real annual growth in GDP per capita from fiscal years 1958/59 to 1965/66; petroleum expansion led the way, but industrial and agricultural growth were also steady. Moreover, in the mid- to late 1960s, Nigeria's regional elites foresaw some of the growth potential of the subsequent decade. Thus, despite the massive resource diversion and destruction, GDP per head fell only 4% yearly during the war. In addition, Nigeria's oil-fueled real economic growth per capita accelerated after the war to 8% yearly from fiscal years 1969/70 to 1978/79 (at 1974/75 prices, a year of high oil prices, thus moderately overstating growth for the period).[21]

B. South Africa: Inequality Under Apartheid

South Africa, where 3750 people were killed in internal repression and resistance in 1993, according to the International Federation of Red Cross and Red Crescent Society's *World Disasters Report*, demonstrates that, if the perceived inequality is sufficiently grave, even improved material welfare for the disadvantaged group does not guarantee the absence of conflict. South Africa's real GDP per capita stagnated from the early 1970s through the early 1990s. However, per capita incomes of the white population fell, while the per capita incomes of the black population increased, at least from the mid-1960s to the mid-1970s and even through 1980. Still, a survey conducted in 1988 demonstrated that only a very small proportion of a nationwide sample of the black population was satisfied with various dimensions of their lives. More importantly, the results showed a deterioration of over 40% in blacks' perceived life satisfaction as compared with a survey in 1983. Why did grievances and dissatisfaction among the black population rise as its average income increased?

The political exclusion of blacks by the apartheid regime doubtless accounts for a great deal of the generalized dissatisfaction, but the role of income differentials should not be discounted, either. To blacks, the increase in income during the previous two decades was insufficient, considering the substantial discrepancies in favor of the white population. In 1992, the GDP per capita of black, Asian, and mixed-race South Africa was I$ (international dollars, or U.S. dollars adjusted for purchasing power) 1710, about the same as Senegal's I$1680, and in excess of I$1116 for Africa as a whole. Yet this low income for 36.1 million non-white South Africans stood in stark contrast to that of 7.3 million whites: I$14,920 income per capita, a figure higher than New Zealand's I$13,970. Moreover, the collapse of the growth of non-white incomes in the 1980s and early 1990s increased feelings of relative deprivation.

South Africa's Gini coefficient of income concentration was 0.65, with the top 10% of the population receiving more than 50% of the national income, while the bottom 40% received less than one-tenth. This made South Africa, alongside Mexico and Brazil, one of the countries with the most unequal distribution of income in the world, and exacerbated mistrust in the non-white population. Moreover, life expectancy was 52 years for blacks, 62 for Asians and mixed races, and 74 for whites compared to 54 for Africa as a whole, while the adult literacy rate was 67% for non-whites and 85% for whites.[22]

It was not difficult for the African National Congress (ANC) to mobilize the masses against the apartheid regime as the perceived source of inequality. Both inequality and the emergency resulted from the actions of the regime, which dug its own grave by a conscious policy of discrimination against the majority of the population. Even the destructive political conflict of 1990–1994 between the ANC and the Inkatha Freedom Party was directly manipulated and fueled by the regime in its effort to maintain power. The South African case illustrates how economic inequality, combined with authoritarian structures and rules of governance, contributes to conflict and resistance.

High income inequality can be a source of conflict in both rapidly and slowly growing countries. However, once a population is dissatisfied with income discrepancies and social discrimination, as the non-white majority was in white-ruled South Africa, the rising expectations associated with incremental reductions in poverty and inequality may actually spur the revolt, conflict, and state hostile action that exacerbates the probability of deadly political violence.

VI. MILITARY CENTRALITY

Military centrality, as indicated by the ratio of military expenditure to GNP, contributes to humanitarian emergencies through several alternative dynamics.

On the one hand, military resources are used to support authoritarian political structures, which generate desperate action and military response by the opposition; under political deprivation and in the absence of political mechanisms to settle grievances, full-scale rebellion becomes more likely. Alternatively, a strong military may overthrow either a democratic or an authoritarian regime, which may lead to political instability and humanitarian crises. Powerful armed forces constitute a constant threat to civilian regimes in less-developed countries. Particularly during economic austerity, they are afraid to cut back military spending. Furthermore, they may strengthen the military to stave off threats from the opposition. This, in turn, entails heavy socio-economic costs for the population, inducing further discontent and increasing the risk of rebellion. In very poor countries, increasing budget allocations for the military may produce downright starvation and destitution.

VII. CONFLICT TRADITION

Citizens adapt to a certain, acceptable level of violence through the cultural experience of violence. A tradition of intensive political violence makes societies more susceptible to war and humanitarian emergencies. Countries with a history of mass political mobilization for conflict, such as Burundi and Rwanda, are likely to be more susceptible to conflict in complex humanitarian emergencies than other, historically more peaceful countries. Conflict tradition is an indicator of stress, strain, and the legitimacy of political violence.[23]

VIII. COMPETITION FOR MINERAL RESOURCES

The struggle for control over minerals and other natural resources is an important sources of conflict. Reno indicates that in Angola, Sierra Leone, Liberia, and Congo (Kinshasa), rulers and warlords use exclusive contracts with foreign firms for diamonds and other minerals to "regularize" sources of revenue in lieu of a government agency to collect taxes.[24]

After the fall in aid after the cold war, Sierra Leone was more susceptible to pressures for liberalization and adjustment from the International Monetary Fund (IMF) and the World Bank. In 1991, the IMF, the World Bank, and bilateral creditors offered loans and debt rescheduling worth $625 million, about 80% of GNP, if Sierra Leone reduced government expenditure and employment. In response, Freetown heeded the World Bank's advice to use private operators to run state services for a profit.[25] However, privatization did not eliminate the pressures of clients demanding payoffs, but merely shifted the arena to the private sector. Sierra Leone's ruling elites, needing new ways of exercising power, relied on foreign firms to consolidate power and stave off threats from political rivals. In the 1990s, Sierra Leonean heads of state have relied on exclusive contracts with foreign firms for diamond mining to "regularize" revenue, foreign mercenaries and advisors to replace the national army in providing security, and foreign contractors (sometimes the same mining or security firms) to provide other state services. In the process, rulers found it advantageous to "destroy state agencies, to 'cleanse' them of politically threatening patrimonial hangers-on and use violence to extract resources from people under their control."[26]

In Liberia, Charles Taylor used external commercial networks (foreign firms), some a legacy of the Samuel Doe regime of the late 1980s, to amass power over Liberia and, at times, the eastern periphery of Sierra Leone. Taylor's territory had its own currency and banking system, telecommunications network, airfields, and export trade (in diamonds, timber, gold, and farm products) to support arms imports, as well as (until 1993) a deepwater port. For Taylor, a warlord during most of the 1990s before being elected Liberia's president in 1997, controlling territory by building a patronage network was easier than building a state and its bureaucracy.

Even Zaire's President Mobutu Sese Seko (1965–1997), like other hard-pressed rulers in weak African states, mimicked "the 'warlord' logic characteristic of many of [his] non-state rivals."[27] But, with the shrinking patronage base from foreign aid and investment, to prevent a coup by newly marginalized groups in the army or bureaucracy Mobutu, similar to rulers in other retrenching African states, needed to reconfigure his political authority. In this situation, foreign firms and contractors served as a new source of patronage networks. However, indigenous commercial interests that profit from the new rules are not independent capitalists with interests distinct from those of the state. As Reno points out, "Those who do not take part in accumulation on the ruler's terms are punished."[28] Mobutu weathered the collapse of the state bureaucracy but fell because his strategy of milking state assets had reached a limit, seriously weakening the patronage system. In 1997, his forces fell to the Alliance des Forces Democratique pour la Liberation (AFDL) of Laurent Kabila, the president of the Democratic Republic of Congo until being assassinated in 2001.

State failure, as in Sierra Leone, Liberia, and Zaire, increases vulnerability to war and humanitarian emergencies. Yet, in a weak or failed state, some rulers, warlords, and traders are more likely to profit from war and violence than peace. Indeed, as Väyrynen argues, war, political violence, and state failure do not result from the incapacity of public institutions but from the fact that rulers, warlords, and their clients benefit from the harm thereby befalling a substantial share of the population.[29]

IX. CONCLUSION

The chapter examines the extent to which various factors explain a dependent variable, humanitarian emergencies, comprising multidimensional crises characterized by warfare, state violence, and refugee displacement in Africa. Humanitarian emergencies are directly associated with the Gini index of income concentration, military centrality as defined by military expenditure as a percentage of GNP, conflict tradition, and the abundance of mineral exports, and inversely associated with GDP growth, GNP per capita, food output growth, and external adjustment.

Economic decline leads to relative deprivation or the perception by influential social groups of injustice arising from a growing discrepancy between goods and conditions they expect and those they can get or keep. Relative deprivation spurs social discontent, which provides motivation for potential collective violence. Poor economic performance undermines the legitimacy of a regime, increasing the probability of regime turnover. Political elites use repression to forestall threats to the regime and capture a greater share of the majority's shrinking surplus. Repression and economic discrimination trigger further discontent and socio-political mobilization on the part of the groups affected, worsening the humanitarian crisis. Protracted economic stagnation increases the probability of population displacement, hunger, and disease. Protracted stagnation also spurs elites to expropriate the assets and resources of weaker communities violently.

Because low average income, slow economic growth, and high income inequality are important contributors to emergencies, African states, with the support of the international community, must strengthen and restructure the political economy of poor, economically stagnant, and inegalitarian countries. The major changes African governments need to make are economic and political institutional changes: the development of a legal system, enhanced financial institutions, increased taxing capacity, greater investment in basic education and other forms of social capital, well-functioning resource and exchange markets, programs to target weaker segments of the population, and democratic institutions that accommodate and co-opt the country's various ethnic and regional communities. Institutional and infrastructural development increases the productivity of private investment and public spending and enhances the effectiveness of governance.

Industrialized countries and international agencies bear substantial responsibility for modifying the international economic order to enhance economic growth and adjustment. Africa and other developing regions can demand greater consideration of their economic interests within present international economic and political institutions. The interests of the Third World can generally be served by its enhanced flexibility and self-determination in designing paths toward adjustment and liberalization; a shift in the goals and openness of the IMF and World Bank; the restructuring of the international economic system for trade and capital flows; the opening of rich countries' markets; more technological transfer by foreign companies, bilateral donors, and international agencies; a greater coherence of aid programs; and increased international funding to reduce food crises, directly help the poor, ameliorate external shocks, and write down debt burdens.

Because the policies of governing elites are at the root of most humanitarian emergencies, and because usually some powerful factions in society benefit from emergencies, there may be a number of countries vulnerable to emergencies not amenable to political economy solutions. Yet a large number of countries vulnerable to emergencies have the will to change. Thus, there is a substantial scope for international, national, and nongovernmental economic and political actors to coordinate their long-term policies to reduce Africa's vulnerability to humanitarian emergencies.

DISCUSSION QUESTIONS

1. What are the economic factors that contribute to Africa's substantial vulnerability to deadly political violence?
2. How does land and income inequality contribute to political conflict in Africa?
3. How does deadly political violence affect economic development in Africa?
4. Is ethnicity a factor contributing to political conflict or is an increase in ethnic identity a result of intensified political conflict?
5. What are some of the reasons for Sub-Saharan Africa's poor record in recent years regarding the growth in food output per person?
6. How are economic regression, chronic external deficits, macroeconomic adjustment failure, and political instability related to each other?
7. Is a high ratio of military spending to GNP more likely to be a cause or an effect of political instability?
8. To what extent are international economic and political factors contributors to war and state violence?
9. In what instances might ethnic communities or economic groups benefit from war? What strategies might African countries or the international community use to reduce the benefits of war to communities or economic groups?

10. What can African leaders do to reduce the probability of war and state violence?

11. What can industrial countries and international agencies do to reduce the probability of humanitarian emergencies in Africa?

NOTES

[1]This chapter is based on joint work with Juha Auvinen, University of Helsinki.

[2]World Bank (2000) *Can Africa Claim the 21st Century?*, Washington, D.C.: World Bank, pp. 57–59.

[3]Väyrynen, R. (2000) "Complex Humanitarian Emergencies: Concepts and Issues," in E.W. Nafziger, F. Stewart, and R. Väyrynen, Eds., *War, Hunger, and Displacement: The Origins of Humanitarian Emergencies*, Vol. 1, Queen Elizabeth House in Development Economics and UNU/WIDER Studies in Development Economics, Oxford: Oxford University Press, pp. 43–89.

[4]Prunier, G. (1995) *The Rwanda Crisis, 1959–1994: History of a Genocide*, London: Hurst & Co., pp. 264–265.

[5]Auvinen, J. and Nafziger, E.W. (1999) "Sources of Humanitarian Emergencies," *Journal of Conflict Resolution*, 43(3), 267–290.

[6]We introduced the growth of food production per capita in lieu of GDP growth in both OLS and GLS models. A test of lags and leads indicated that slow food production growth is conducive to wars rather than vice versa.

[7]Developing countries include all low- and middle-income countries with more than 1 million people, as indicated by the World Bank in *World Development Report 1996* (New York: Oxford University Press, 1996, pp. 188–189). The World Bank divides countries into four groups on the basis of per capita GNP. In 1994, these categories were low-income countries (less than $750), lower-middle-income countries ($750–$2900), upper-middle-income countries ($2900–$8500), and high-income countries (more than $8500). While the margin of error is substantial and the boundary between categories rises each year with inflation, few countries shifted categories between 1974 and 1994. See Nafziger, E.W. (1997) *The Economics of Developing Countries*, 3rd ed., Upper Saddle River, NJ: Prentice-Hall, pp. 9–37.

[8]The concept of "relative deprivation" is from Gurr, T.R. (1970) *Why Men Rebel*, Princeton, NJ: Princeton University Press. For a discussion of vertical and horizontal inequality, see Stewart, F. (2000) "The Root Causes of Humanitarian Emergencies," in E.W. Nafziger, F. Stewart, and R. Väyrynen, Eds., *War, Hunger, and Displacement: The Origins of Humanitarian Emergencies*, Vol. 1, Queen Elizabeth House in Development Economics and UNU/WIDER Studies in Development Economics, Oxford: Oxford University Press, p. 16.

[9]Galtung, J. (1971) "A Structural Theory of Imperialism," *Journal of Peace Research*, 9(2), 81–118.

[10]World Bank (2000) *Can Africa Claim the 21st Century?*, Washington, D.C.: World Bank, p. 1.

[11]Nafziger, E.W. (1988) *Inequality in Africa: Political Elites, Proletariat, Peasants, and the Poor*, Cambridge, U.K.: Cambridge University Press. See also Ake, C. (1996) *Democracy and Development in Africa*, Washington, D.C.: Brookings Institution, pp. 1, 18. This contention is reinforced by Ake, who stated that, for Africa, "the problem is not so much that development has failed as that it was never really on the agenda in the first place. ...[W]ith independence African leaders were in no position to pursue development; they were too engrossed in the struggle for survival."

[12]Holsti, K.J. (2000) "Political Causes," in E.W. Nafziger, F. Stewart, and R. Väyrynen, Eds., *War, Hunger, and Displacement: The Origins of Humanitarian Emergencies*, Vol. 1, Queen Elizabeth House in Development Economics and UNU/WIDER Studies in Development Economics, Oxford: Oxford University Press, p. 251.

[13] Ake, C. (1996) *Democracy and Development in Africa*, Washington, D.C.: Brookings Institution, p. 42.

[14] Väyrynen, R. (2000) "Weak States and Humanitarian Emergencies: Failure, Predation, and Rent-Seeking," in E.W. Nafziger, F. Stewart, and R. Väyrynen, Eds., *War, Hunger, and Displacement: The Origins of Humanitarian Emergencies*, Vol. 2, Queen Elizabeth House in Development Economics and UNU/WIDER Studies in Development Economics, Oxford: Oxford University Press, p. 440.

[15] Väyrynen, R. (2000) "Weak States and Humanitarian Emergencies: Failure, Predation, and Rent-Seeking," in E.W. Nafziger, F. Stewart, and R. Väyrynen, Eds., *War, Hunger, and Displacement: The Origins of Humanitarian Emergencies*, Vol. 2, Queen Elizabeth House in Development Economics and UNU/WIDER Studies in Development Economics, Oxford: Oxford University Press, p. 442.

[16] Nafziger, E.W. (1993) *The Debt Crisis in Africa*, Baltimore, MD: Johns Hopkins University Press, pp. 67–71.

[17] A major contributor to non-adjustment is the distortion to both internationally and domestically traded goods from an overvalued domestic currency. For a discussion of the political economy of African governments' resistance to exchange-rate adjustment, see Nafziger, E.W. (1988) *Inequality in Africa: Political Elites, Proletariat, Peasants, and the Poor*, Cambridge, U.K.: Cambridge University Press, pp. 150–160.

[18] Adedeji, A. (1989) *Towards a Dynamic African Economy: Selected Speeches and Lectures, 1975–1986*, London: Frank Cass, p. 2.

[19] Singer, H. (1990) "The Role of Food Aid," in J. Pickett and H. Singer, Eds., *Towards Economic Recovery in Sub-Saharan Africa*, London: Routledge, pp. 178–181.

[20] Alesina, A. and Perotti, R. (1996) "Income Distribution, Political Instability, and Investment," *European Economic Review*, 40(6), 1203–1228.

[21] Nafziger, E.W. (1983) *The Economics of Political Instability: The Nigerian–Biafran War*, Boulder CO: Westview Press.

[22] See Nafziger, E.W. (1997) *The Economics of Developing Countries*, 3rd ed., Upper Saddle River, NJ: Prentice-Hall, p. 32; Auvinen, J. and Kivimäki, T. (1997) *Towards More Effective Preventive Diplomacy: Lessons from Conflict Transformation in South Africa*, Working Paper No. 4, Series C, University of Lapland: Faculty of Social Sciences, pp. 9–10, 16–17; Schlemmer, L. (1994) "Sustainable Development for South Africa: Proposition and Scenarios for Debate," in H. Giliomee and L. Schlemmer, Eds., *The Bold Experiment: South Africa's New Democracy*, Halfway House, South Africa: Southern Books, pp. 99–111; Esterhuyse, W. (1992) "Scenarios for South Africa: Instability and Violence or Negotiated Transition?," *Long Range Planning*, 25(3), 21–26.

[23] Gurr, T.R. (1970) *Why Men Rebel*, Princeton, NJ: Princeton University Press, pp. 155–192; Gurr, T.R. and Duvall, R. (1973) "Civil Conflict in the 1960s: A Reciprocal Theoretical System with Parameter Estimates," *Comparative Political Studies*, 6, 157.

[24] Reno, W. (1996) "Ironies of Post-Cold War Structural Adjustment in Sierra Leone," *Review of African Political Economy (ROAPE)*, March (no. 67), 7–8, 12; Reno, W. (1998) *Warlord Politics and African States*, Boulder, CO: Lynne Rienner; Reno, W. (2000) "Liberia and Sierra Leone: The Competition for Patronage in Resource-Rich Economies," in E.W. Nafziger, F. Stewart, and R. Väyrynen, Eds., *War, Hunger, and Displacement: The Origins of Humanitarian Emergencies*, Vol. 2, Queen Elizabeth House in Development Economics and UNU/WIDER Studies in Development Economics, Oxford: Oxford University Press, pp. 231–259.

[25] World Bank (1994) *World Development Report 1994*, New York: Oxford University Press, pp. 22–51.

[26] Reno, W. (1995) "Reinvention of an African Patrimonial State: Charles Taylor's Liberia," *Third World Quarterly*, 16(1), 111; includes quotation from Reno, W. (1996) "Ironies of Post-Cold War Structural Adjustment in Sierra Leone," *Review of African Political Economy (ROAPE)*, March (no. 67), 7–8, 12.

[27] Reno, W. (1996) "Ironies of Post-Cold War Structural Adjustment in Sierra Leone," *Review of African Political Economy (ROAPE)*, March (no. 67), 7–8, 12.

[28]Reno, W. (1996) "Ironies of Post-Cold War Structural Adjustment in Sierra Leone," *Review of African Political Economy (ROAPE)*, March (no. 67), 16.

[29]Väyrynen, R. (2000) "Weak States and Humanitarian Emergencies: Failure, Predation, and Rent-seeking," in E.W. Nafziger, F. Stewart, and R. Väyrynen, Eds., *War, Hunger, and Displacement: The Origins of Humanitarian Emergencies*, Vol. 2, Queen Elizabeth House in Development Economics and UNU/WIDER Studies in Development Economics, Oxford: Oxford University Press, pp. 437–479.

CHAPTER 14

Corruption and Economic Development

JOHN MUKUM MBAKU

Department of Economics, Weber State University, Ogden, Utah 84408

KEY TERMS

Benefit-enhancing corruption
Benefit-reducing corruption
Bribe
Bureaucratic bottlenecks
Bureaucratic corruption
Clientelism
Cost-enhancing corruption
Cost-reducing corruption
Expansive corruption
Extra-legal compensation
Incentive structures
Moral hazard

Nepotism
Patrimonialism
Personalistic rule
Political corruption
Political opportunism
Political prostitution
Property rights regimes
Rent seeking
Restrictive corruption
Shirking
Societal, legal, market, and political
    strategies for corruption cleanups

I. INTRODUCTION

As recent scandals in Italy, the United States, South Korea, the Russian Federation, Indonesia, Japan, Israel, and many other countries have shown, corruption is a universal problem—affecting the economies of both developed and developing societies. However, given that this is a book on African development, the emphasis in this chapter will be on corruption in the African economies. Each year, Transparency International (TI), a Berlin-based civil society organization, releases a corruption perceptions index (CPI), which ranks countries based on how investors/entrepreneurs, political and risk analysts, and the general public around the world perceive levels of corruption in various countries. The index ranges between zero (0 meaning highly corrupt) and ten (10 meaning highly clean). The data for the 1999 CPI are presented in Table 14.1.

African Economic Development
Copyright © 2003, Elsevier Science (USA). All rights reserved.

TABLE 14.1   The Transparency International Corruption Perceptions Index (CPI)

Country Rank	Country	1999 CPI Score	Standard Deviation	Surveys Used
1	Denmark	10.0	0.8	9
2	Finland	9.8	0.5	10
3	New Zealand	9.4	0.8	9
	Sweden	9.4	0.6	10
5	Canada	9.2	0.5	10
	Iceland	9.2	1.2	6
7	Singapore	9.1	0.9	12
8	Netherlands	9.0	0.5	10
9	Norway	8.9	0.8	9
	Switzerland	8.9	0.6	11
11	Luxembourg	8.8	0.9	8
12	Australia	8.7	0.7	8
13	United Kingdom	8.7	0.5	11
14	Germany	8.0	0.5	10
15	Hong Kong	7.7	1.6	13
	Ireland	7.7	1.9	10
17	Austria	7.6	0.8	11
18	United States	7.5	0.8	10
19	Chile	6.9	1.0	9
20	Israel	6.8	1.3	9
21	Portugal	6.7	1.0	10
22	France	6.6	1.0	10
	Spain	6.6	0.7	10
24	Botswana	6.1	1.7	4
25	Japan	6.0	1.6	12
	Slovenia	6.0	1.3	6
27	Estonia	5.7	1.2	7
28	Taiwan	5.6	0.9	12
29	Belgium	5.3	1.3	9
	Namibia	5.3	0.9	3
31	Hungary	5.2	1.1	13
32	Costa Rica	5.1	1.5	7
	Malaysia	5.1	0.5	12
34	South Africa	5.0	0.8	12
	Tunisia	5.0	1.9	3
36	Greece	4.9	1.7	9
	Mauritius	4.9	0.7	4
38	Italy	4.7	0.6	10
39	Czech Republic	4.6	0.8	12
40	Peru	4.5	0.8	6
41	Jordan	4.4	0.8	6
	Uruguay	4.4	0.9	3
43	Mongolia	4.3	1.0	3
44	Poland	4.2	0.8	12

(*Continues*)

TABLE 14.1   (*Continued*)

Country Rank	Country	1999 CPI Score	Standard Deviation	Surveys Used
45	Brazil	4.1	0.8	11
	Malawi	4.1	0.5	4
	Morocco	4.1	1.7	4
	Zimbabwe	4.1	1.4	9
49	El Salvador	3.9	1.9	9
50	Jamaica	3.8	0.4	3
	Lithuania	3.8	0.5	6
	South Korea	3.8	0.9	13
53	Slovak Republic	3.7	1.5	9
54	Philippines	3.6	1.4	12
	Turkey	3.6	1.0	10
56	Mozambique	3.5	2.2	3
	Zambia	3.5	1.5	4
58	Belarus	3.4	1.4	6
	China	3.4	0.7	11
	Latvia	3.4	1.3	7
	Mexico	3.4	0.5	9
	Senegal	3.4	0.8	3
63	Bulgaria	3.3	1.4	8
	Egypt	3.3	0.6	5
	Ghana	3.3	1.0	4
	Macedonia	3.3	1.2	5
	Romania	3.3	1.0	6
68	Guatemala	3.2	2.5	3
	Thailand	3.2	0.7	12
70	Nicaragua	3.1	2.5	3
71	Argentina	3.0	0.8	10
72	Colombia	2.9	0.5	11
	India	2.9	0.6	14
74	Croatia	2.7	0.9	5
75	Côte d'Ivoire	2.6	1.0	4
	Moldova	2.6	0.8	5
	Ukraine	2.6	1.4	10
	Venezuela	2.6	0.8	9
	Vietnam	2.6	0.5	8
80	Armenia	2.5	0.4	4
	Bolivia	2.5	1.1	6
82	Ecuador	2.4	1.3	4
	Russian Federation	2.4	1.0	13
84	Albania	2.3	0.3	5
	Georgia	2.3	0.7	4
	Kazakhstan	2.3	1.3	5
87	Kyrgyz Republic	2.2	0.4	4
	Pakistan	2.2	0.7	3
	Uganda	2.2	0.7	5

(*Continues*)

TABLE 14.1 (*Continued*)

Country Rank	Country	1999 CPI Score	Standard Deviation	Surveys Used
90	Kenya	2.0	0.5	4
	Paraguay	2.0	0.8	4
	Yugoslavia	2.0	1.1	6
93	Tanzania	1.9	1.1	4
94	Honduras	1.8	0.5	3
	Uzbekistan	1.8	0.4	4
96	Azerbaijan	1.7	0.6	5
	Indonesia	1.7	0.9	12
98	Nigeria	1.6	0.8	5
99	Cameroon	1.5	0.5	4

Source: Transparency International 1999 Corruption Perceptions Index, (Berlin: Transparency International, http://www.transparency.de/documents/cpi/index.html.

Notes: The rank relates solely to the results drawn from a number of surveys and reflects only the perceptions of the business people (more than 770 senior executives at major companies, chartered accountants, chambers of commerce, major commercial banks, and law firms) that participated in the surveys. The number of surveys used had to be at least three for a country to be included in the 1999 CPI. The standard deviation indicates the differences in the values of the sources: The greater the standard deviation, the greater the differences of perceptions of a country among the sources. Additional information on the index can be found at the website provided.

As can be seen from the data, corruption is a worldwide phenomenon, not one unique to the continent of Africa. Although the data show that, of the ten most corrupt countries in the world in 1999, as perceived by the international investment community, four of them were in Africa (Cameroon, Nigeria, Tanzania, and Kenya), the continent also had as many as five countries represented among the 40 "cleanest" countries in the world that year. Thus, while corruption is a serious development problem for most of the countries in the continent, several countries, notably Botswana, Mauritius, Namibia, Tunisia, and South Africa, are making significant progress in fighting this scourge.

Since the 1960s, scholars have debated the effects of corruption on Africa's *post-independence* economies. Two schools of thought have emerged from these debates. One school argues that corruption encourages bureaucratic inefficiency, stunts entrepreneurship, and discourages wealth creation. According to the other school, corruption "greases" the wheels of an African bureaucracy that is traditionally rigid, unresponsive, and hostile to the private sector and makes it more flexible and responsive to the needs of the entrepreneurial class. This second school argues that corruption can help remove *bottlenecks* in the civil service and improve its efficiency and, consequently, its ability to effectively direct economic development.

Recent studies have been unable to find any evidence to support the claim that corruption improves the participation of the business community in public policy formulation and implementation.[1] In addition, other studies have determined that the negative effects of corruption far outweigh its positive or efficiency enhancing properties.[2] Since independence, African civil servants and politicians have viewed corruption as an important vehicle for self-enrichment.[3] The argument that corruption can improve the relationship between the country's civil service and its entrepreneurial class or that it can make the bureaucracy more flexible and thus more responsive to the needs of the private sector is not informed by the available evidence from the continent. Corruption, as it was in the 1960s, remains an important constraint to wealth creation and, as a consequence, human progress in Africa.

Briefly, corruption has several negative effects on African economic development. First, it provides the *incumbent* leaders the incentive to resist change. Consequently, corruption threatens to:

1. Derail grassroots efforts to provide African countries with more effective governance structures and resource allocation systems that enhance the creation of wealth.
2. Reverse many of the democratic gains that have been made in the continent since the end of the Cold War.
3. Make it extremely difficult for the African countries to develop and sustain viable and effective economic infrastructures.

Second, in those African countries in which corruption has become quite pervasive, the cost of *public goods and services* is highly inflated, usually to provide additional income for the individuals whose job it is to serve the public. Third, corruption increases the burden of the public sector on the people. In several countries throughout the continent, citizens must bear the costs of an extremely bloated, inefficient, wasteful, and parasitic civil service. Fourth, corruption and other forms of *political opportunism* (e.g., rent seeking) can demoralize the bureaucracy, generate significant amounts of distrust throughout the civil service, and negatively impact the ability of the society to efficiently utilize its skilled labor resources. For example, in making promotion decisions or delegating power, the manager of a government department may not choose the most qualified, competent, productive, or skilled subordinate but may prefer to appoint the person who is most likely to use the new position to extort the most corruption (or extra-legal) income for the department. Fifth, if corruption becomes pervasive, the ability of the government to develop and sustain a professional, competent, and efficient bureaucracy is compromised. Sixth, corruption can encourage the under-utilization of a nation's skilled and educated labor resources. For example, highly skilled individuals seeking work in the public sector may lie about their education and training in order to qualify for jobs for which they are actually over-qualified but which significantly improve their opportunities for corrupt enrichment. Seventh, corruption can significantly distort international trade and the flow of investment. In fact, opportunistic civil servants, determined to use their public positions as vehicles for corrupt enrichment, can frustrate the efforts of foreign investors to penetrate the domestic economy. Such behavior, on the part of civil servants, continues to deprive the African people of critical resources for development. Eighth, corruption can discourage domestic investment and encourage outward migration of capital (and skilled labor resources) to "cleaner" and more stable economies—that is, those with low levels of corruption and more predictable rules. Finally, as argued by Bardhan, corruption can severely stunt innovation and subsequently prevent the introduction of new goods and technologies.[4]

Several strategies have been used to deal with pervasive corruption in Africa. Unfortunately, none has had any *long-term* effect on corruption control in these countries. The most effective way to deal with corruption is to first examine the *rules* that regulate sociopolitical interaction in the society. The rules determine the *incentive structures* faced by traders and how they behave and relate to other participants in the market. Thus, to adequately deal with corruption, one must begin with a modification of market incentive structures, which in the case of the African countries implies state reconstruction to provide accountable, transparent, and participatory governance structures and resource allocation systems that guarantee *economic freedoms* (e.g., the right of individuals to freely engage in exchange and contracting) and enhance entrepreneurship and wealth creation. Unfortunately, the *institutional arrangements* that the African countries adopted at independence endowed states with almost unlimited power to intervene in economic activities and thus enhanced the ability of the post-independence leaders to engage in political opportunism. As a consequence, public policy in many African countries came to be pervaded by corruption, rent seeking, and other forms of opportunism. What Africans need today are institutional reforms to provide themselves with *constitutionally limited governments* and resource allocation systems that guarantee economic freedoms, thus enhancing entrepreneurship and wealth creation. If the appropriate incentive structures are provided, corruption will eventually become a less attractive option for self-enrichment. On the other hand, the appropriate incentive structures should enhance investment and wealth creation, allowing each African economy to secure the resources that it needs to deal more effectively with poverty and deprivation in the new century and beyond.

II. DEFINING AND EXPLAINING CORRUPTION IN AFRICA

Definitions for corruption usually contain two important elements: *perform-ance of a public duty* and *deviations from the rules that regulate the activities of civil servants.* Thus, a public servant can be said to be corrupt if in the performance of his duties he sacrifices the interests of the principal (the people) for his own. Corruption, then, can be seen as "a departure from the norms of modern bureaucracy."[5]

Africans see corruption in more practical terms: the theft of public resources by civil servants; embezzlement; illegal extraction of income from state enterprises; nepotism; favoring relatives, friends, and those who are able to pay bribes in the distribution of public goods and services, employment in the civil service, etc.; abuse of one's public office in an effort to extract benefits for the officeholder and his relatives, friends, and supporters; capricious and selective enforcement of state regulations in an effort to benefit the enforcer or regulator; differential treatment of business owners in the expectation of a bribe from the owner of the enterprise that is enjoying the preferential treatment; and illegal taxation of private economic effort with benefits accruing to the bureaucrat.

Usually, the civil servant's compensation is made up of the salary paid by the state and legal or illegal income obtained through participation in outside activities. Mbaku argues that, "If bureaucrats are able to earn more income from external sources (e.g., from interest groups seeking government transfers or relief from government regulation) than from their regular employment, they may pay more attention to the demands of interest groups than to the needs of society as a whole."[6] Thus, in a highly regulated economy, bureaucrats may spend a significant part of their time and effort helping business owners evade the rules and thus minimize the burden of government regulation on their enterprises. In exchange, of course, the bureaucrat is rewarded with extra-legal income.

In 1964, Leff argued that "[c]orruption is an extra-legal institution used by individuals or groups to gain influence over the actions of the bureaucracy."[7] He stated further that, "If the government has erred in its decision, the course made possible by corruption may well be the better one."[8] Leff is one of several scholars who advanced the argument, beginning in the 1960s, that corruption could be used to improve the participation of historically deprived and excluded individuals and communities in political and economic markets. Unfortunately, the evidence, although circumstantial, has since indicated that corruption has not been able to improve effective participation of these groups in the economic and political systems of their countries. For example, Cameroon and Nigeria are perceived by the international investment community to be among the most corrupt nations in the world today. Yet, in these countries, minority ethnic groups continue to be denied effective participation in governance. In fact, in Cameroon, the minority Anglophones are so angry at their systematic exclusion from economic and political participation during most of the post-independence period that they now want to secede and form their own sovereign nation. In Nigeria, ethnic minorities in the Delta Region continue to battle the federal government, often violently, for increased control of their natural resources.

In addition, corruption enhances the ability of inefficient enterprises to remain in business indefinitely. In the last several years, the survival of business enterprises in many African countries has come to be determined not by competition and managerial expertise but by how well their owners manipulate the political system through payment of bribes to civil servants and politicians.

Joseph Nye provides a broad definition for corruption when he argues that it is:[9]

> ...behavior which deviates from the formal duties of a public role because of private-regarding (personal, close family, private clique) pecuniary or status gains; or violates rules against the exercise of certain types of private-regarding influence. This includes such behavior as bribery (use of a reward to pervert the judgement of a person in a position of trust); nepotism (bestowal of patronage by reason of ascriptive relationship rather than merit); and misappropriation (illegal appropriation of public resources for private-regarding uses).

This chapter, however, places significant emphasis on bureaucratic corruption because it is considered the most prevalent and damaging to wealth creation in the continent and hence economic development.

Four categories of corruption are usually identified in the literature. The first type is called *cost-reducing* corruption, in which civil servants attempt to lower the costs imposed on a business enterprise by state regulations below their normal levels. Usually, the taxes owed the state by a business are either eliminated or lowered significantly. In addition, the regulator (i.e., the civil servant) can exempt a business from compliance with certain government regulations. In exchange, the owner of the affected business shares the cost savings generated with the bureaucrat based on a prearranged formula. *Cost-enhancing* corruption is the second type of corruption. In many African economies, civil servants who control stocks of public goods may attempt to extract rents from potential consumers either by demanding payment (in the case of goods that are supposed to be free to consumers) or by charging a price that is greater than the ceiling or government imposed price. Quite often, the price charged by the opportunistic bureaucrat approximates the free market price for the good or service. Additionally, civil servants whose job it is to issue permits or licenses for entrepreneurs to enter economic sectors closed by state regulations (e.g., import, export, or production licenses) may also attempt to appropriate part of the monopoly profit that the license owner is expected to earn. Finally, the civil servant can use the state's coercive power to illegally seize private property (e.g., through illegal taxation) for his personal use. The third form of corruption is called *benefit enhancing*. In the process of performing their duties, civil servants can allow more public benefits to accrue to individuals or groups than are legally due to the affected parties. In exchange, the recipients share the additional benefits with the bureaucrats based on prior arrangements. This is a very popular form of corruption in post-independence Africa. It allows the incumbent to transfer resources to government supporters and those who possess enough violence potential to threaten regime stability (e.g., military elites). The final type of corruption is called *benefit-reducing* corruption. Here, civil servants illegally appropriate public benefits due to private citizens or groups for their own use. The director of a public pension program, for example, can delay the transmission of retirement benefits to retirees, allow the money to stay in the bank and earn interest, and subsequently appropriate the accrued earnings for his own benefit. In many African countries where civil servants have more information about public benefits programs than most citizens, this type of corruption is relatively easy to undertake.[10]

It is important to recognize that private citizens also contribute to the culture of corruption in Africa, for without the supply of bribes by private enterprise owners and individuals seeking government favors, corruption would be limited to nepotism, illegal taxation, and misappropriation of public resources by civil servants. Payments made to civil servants by business owners in order to obtain preferential treatment for their enterprises and also to gain access to sectors of the economy that have been closed by state regulations represent the most important sources of extra-legal income to civil servants and, thus, of corruption in the continent. Through these activities, the private sector contributes significantly to corruption in the continent. State regulations place enormous transaction costs on entrepreneurial activities and force business owners to engage in corrupt activities in an effort to minimize these costs and their effects on profitability. In addition, intervention creates rents which are competed for through the political system. Groups and individuals may bribe civil servants, whose job it is to distribute the rents, in an effort to maximize their share of the rents.

The literature distinguishes between *bureaucratic* and *political* corruption. While the former is used by civil servants to raise their compensation levels above and beyond the legal limit, the latter is employed by politicians to capture and hold leadership positions in the country's political system. Political corruption is also used by incumbents to help them continue to maintain a monopoly on power and the allocation of resources. Activities associated with political corruption include vote-rigging, registration of unqualified voters, buying and selling of votes, and the falsification of election results. Bureaucratic corruption may not necessarily have a political dimension; it is directed primarily at helping the civil servant (the corrupted) enrich himself and provide benefits for the entrepreneur (the corrupter). The process imposes significant costs on society at large.

III. WHAT ARE THE CAUSES OF CORRUPTION IN AFRICA?

In this section, we briefly examine what the literature on development in Africa has to say about the causes of corruption in the continent. Researchers have identified several structural factors that are said to contribute significantly to corruption in Africa. One such factor is the "soft state," which is said to be characterized by citizens who have a "weak or diffuse sense of national interest" and do not have "a commitment to public service."[11] The absence of an efficient and professional civil service, and of competent civil servants, has been cited as being an important contributor to corruption in the continent. It is argued that most African civil servants view public service as an opportunity to generate income for themselves and their families and friends. Consequently, instead of designing and implementing programs to enhance the national welfare, civil servants promote perverse economic policies which generate benefits for them but impose significant costs on society. Public policies are not chosen based on their potential to contribute to the common good, but on their ability to generate benefits for the incumbent and members of the ruling coalition. Eventually, the government ceases to provide citizens with public goods and to protect them and becomes an instrument for private capital accumulation. Such an approach to public policy is illustrated very well by Nigeria's several post-civil-war military governments. The country's public security network, which many Nigerians believed would be utilized to enforce laws against theft, illegal appropriation of public resources, fraud, embezzlement, and other forms of opportunism, either functions very inefficiently or does not function at all. In fact, since the late 1960s, this and other state structures have been converted into instruments for the enrichment of ruling elites and other politically dominant groups.

Nigeria is not the only country in Africa in which state institutions are being used by individuals and groups as instruments of plunder. In apartheid South Africa, state structures were used very effectively to extract benefits from the economy for the white minority while subjecting the black majority to a life of poverty and deprivation.[12] In seeking to maximize their personal objectives instead of performing the jobs for which they were hired, many post-independence African elites came to represent an important constraint to economic growth and development. Throughout the continent, elites constantly subvert national rules, promote perverse economic programs, and engage in other activities that benefit them but impose significant development costs on society. In the process, they stunt growth and marginalize many groups and communities.

The second determinant of corruption in Africa, according to the literature, is inefficiency and incompetence in the civil service. Each country needs a competent, efficient, and professional civil service as a necessary condition for sustainable economic growth and development. The bureaucracy must be responsive to the needs of the entrepreneurial class in order to enhance and facilitate innovation and productivity in the economy. In addition, the civil service should be able to deliver public goods and services to the population equitably and efficiently. Implicit in this is the fact that hiring into the civil service should be based on merit and not on political considerations. A civil service that consists of incompetent, unprofessional, and inefficient workers can severely damage the country's growth and development prospects. In many countries in the continent, a significant number of those in the top echelons of the civil service are political appointees with strong connections to the incumbent government. These individuals owe their jobs and allegiance to the ruling coalition and not to the people they are supposed to serve. As a consequence, the people have no effective way to discipline poorly performing and opportunistic civil servants.

African civil servants are also notorious for promoting policies that allow them to earn extra-legal income but impose significant costs on society. However, it is important to note that the tendency for African bureaucrats to promote perverse economic policies is not unique to them. Research carried out by *public choice* economists has shown that the tendency for individuals (in both public and private sectors) to maximize their self-interest is universal.[13] African countries are unique in that their laws and institutions have made it relatively easy for civil servants to engage in opportunism to maximize their self-interest.

The third factor listed in the literature as contributing to corruption in Africa is chronic poverty and severe inequalities in the distribution of income and wealth. Today, Africa is the poorest region of the world. It is also one among several regions of the world in which income and wealth are concentrated in the hands of a few individuals and groups. In a study completed in 1972, Adebayo determined that the ratio of the salary of the highest to the lowest paid civil servant in Nigeria was about 30:1. Since he completed that study in 1972, the gap has widened substantially as most of the income generated within Nigeria continues to accrue primarily to a group of politically well-connected households. The emergence of the military, after the civil war, as an important factor in resource allocation has had a significant negative impact on income and wealth distribution in the country. The military has dominated public policy during most of Nigeria's existence as a sovereign nation. As a result, the armed forces continue to receive a disproportionate share of national income.[14]

In a study of Zaire in 1979, the World Bank determined that nearly 92% of state employees were not able to meet their subsistence needs (e.g., clothing, food, and shelter) with their legal salaries. Even with state subsidies on food, many of the people who resided in the urban areas were still unable to feed themselves and their families. The situation that the World Bank found in Zaire in 1979 was not unique. Throughout the continent, there are large numbers of so-called working poor—individuals who hold different types of jobs in the urban periphery but earn too little to support themselves and their (usually extended) families. Many of these individuals are likely to participate in corrupt activities willingly in order to secure the additional income that they need to buy food, shelter, and other necessities of life. The small group of individuals who control the political system and the allocation of resources (i.e., top civil servants and

TABLE 14.2　Distribution of Income or Consumption in Selected African Countries

	Percentage Share of Income or Consumption						
Country	Lowest 10%	Lowest 20%	Second 20%	Third 20%	Fourth 20%	Highest 20%	Highest 10%
Côte d'Ivoire (1988)	2.8	6.8	11.2	15.8	22.2	44.1	28.5
Egypt (1991)	3.9	8.7	12.5	16.3	21.4	41.1	26.7
Ghana (1992)	3.4	7.9	12.0	16.1	21.8	42.2	27.3
Guinea (1991)	0.9	3.0	8.3	14.6	23.9	50.2	31.7
Guinea-Bissau (1991)	0.5	2.1	6.5	12.0	20.6	58.9	42.4
Kenya (1992)	1.2	3.4	6.7	10.7	17.0	62.1	47.7
Madagascar (1993)	2.3	5.8	9.9	14.0	20.3	50.0	34.9
Mauritania (1988)	0.7	3.6	10.3	16.2	23.0	46.5	30.4
Morocco (1990/1991)	2.8	6.6	10.5	15.0	21.7	46.3	30.5
Niger (1992)	3.0	7.5	11.8	15.5	21.1	44.1	29.3
Nigeria (1992/1993)	1.3	4.0	8.9	14.4	23.4	49.4	31.4
Rwanda (1983/1985)	4.2	9.7	13.2	16.5	21.6	39.1	24.2
Senegal (1991)	1.4	3.5	7.0	11.6	19.3	58.6	42.8
Sierra Leone (1989)	0.5	1.1	2.0	9.8	23.7	63.4	43.6
South Africa (1993)	1.4	3.3	5.8	9.8	17.7	63.3	47.3
Tanzania (1993)	2.9	6.9	10.9	15.3	21.5	45.4	30.2
Tunisia (1990)	2.3	5.9	10.4	15.3	22.1	46.3	30.7
Uganda (1992)	3.0	6.8	10.3	14.4	20.4	48.1	33.4
Zambia (1993)	1.5	3.9	8.0	13.8	23.8	50.4	31.3
Zimbabwe (1990)	1.8	4.0	6.3	10.0	17.4	62.3	46.9

Source: World Bank (1999) *World Development Report, 1998/1999*, New York: Oxford University Press, pp. 198–199.

other members of the ruling coalition—in Cameroon, these "super-civil servants" include judges, senior military officers, officers in the customs and excise department, and directors of the security forces) continue to live luxuriously, thanks to corruption and the promotion of perverse economic programs.[15] The data in Table 14.2 provide information on the distribution of income or consumption in selected African countries (those for which data were available). In Nigeria, for example, the richest 10% of the population received more than one-third of the income while the poorest 10% received as little as 1.3%. Of course, there are several factors (e.g., educational and skills levels, labor mobility, culture, discrimination, luck, etc.) that can have a significant impact on the earnings ability of an individual and subsequently on income distribution within a country. However, corruption, which usually distorts market incentive structures, is an important contributing factor.

In many countries in the continent, certain civil servants (especially those with little or no political influence) are often not paid for several months. Failure to pay teachers and university professors on time is quite common in Nigeria, Cameroon, and many other African countries. It is not uncommon for university professors to wait up to 6 months for their pay. It has been argued that workers faced with such unpredictable working conditions are likely to actively seek and participate in corrupt activities in an effort to secure income for their basic needs.

African culture is the fourth factor which the literature lists as a major contributor to corruption in the continent. It is argued that corruption in Africa arises from the existence of *defective cultural norms* within societies. According to some scholars, corruption arises from the clash between Africa's traditional cultural values and the norms that were brought from abroad with political, industrial, and economic development (i.e., modernization).[16] From this perspective, one can argue that corruption is a cost that each country must bear as it seeks to transform itself politically, economically, and industrially.

In most traditional societies, the rights of the individual are usually made subordinate to those of the extended family, tribe, religious group, or even society. Thus, loyalty to the group is considered more important than individual rights or accountability. These *particularistic attachments* are quite strong in African societies and are said to contribute significantly to corruption. For example, a successful government employee is expected to share the benefits of his office with members of his extended family. This approach to corruption posits that the civil servant may engage in corrupt activities in order to meet his obligations to members of his group. Those who reside in the urban centers must be able to earn enough money to meet the needs of their immediate family and also provide for their extended family members back in the village. Young people who come to the urban area in search of opportunities for education and economic advancement are usually without the means to survive in the harsh urban environment. However, "relatives" who had preceded them in migration and are now productively employed must provide assistance to the new arrivals. Such help includes food, lodging, and other necessities of life. These culturally related pressures, according to many scholars, can force the civil servant to engage in corruption.

One can find fault with almost all of the four determinants of corruption provided in the extant literature and discussed briefly above. For example, the argument that corruption is due to defective cultural norms is quite weak considering the fact that many societies outside Africa have the same or similar norms but do not suffer from equivalent levels of venality. In addition, one can also question why corruption was not as widespread during the colonial period as it is today. Africans certainly did not suddenly discover their cultural norms after independence. It is important to note that incentive structures, not cultural norms, determine a society's propensity to engage in corrupt activities. Quite often, existing incentive structures create opportunities for corruption and provide an environment in which even honest and highly ethical individuals are forced to engage in corruption in order to survive.

Regarding whether the African state is "soft," Fatton argued in 1989 that the perception of the African state as a "weak, factionalized, and ineffective bureaucratic apparatus that consistently fails both to improve its authority and to serve the general interest" is flawed because it assumes that a "hard" state is necessarily more efficient and promotes the national welfare.[17] The literature's argument that corruption in the continent is caused by the disparity in the earnings of high-level public servants and low-level bureaucrats forces one to ask the question: Will narrowing the income gap lead to less corruption?

IV. A NEW WAY TO LOOK AT CORRUPTION: THE PUBLIC CHOICE PERSPECTIVE

During the last several years, economists, dissatisfied with these explanations for corruption in the continent, have started to look at corruption from the *public choice perspective* and seek alternative approaches to explain its pervasiveness in the continent. Corruption is seen as post-constitutional opportunism, aimed at producing benefits for an individual or group at the expense of the rest of society. Usually, the scope and extent of corruption in a country are determined primarily by the country's institutional arrangements and not necessarily by the character of its bureaucrats and politicians. Once the constitution has been adopted and the apparatus of government established, there is an incentive for individuals and groups to capture the government and use its redistributive powers to effect wealth and income transfers in their favor. Such behavior can be undertaken in both democratic and non-democratic societies. Every political choice made in a country usually has distributional effects. Individuals participating in political markets have preferences about these distributional effects and about public policy outcomes. As a result, some individuals and groups within the society are willing to expend resources to influence these outcomes. The process through which individuals or groups expend resources to affect distributional outcomes is called *rent seeking*.[18]

Bureaucrats, whose job it is to devise and implement public policies may attempt to maximize their own objectives at the expense of serving society effectively. There exists a strong incentive for civil servants to become engaged in opportunism to promote their own interests instead of performing the duties for which they were hired. The desire by civil servants to maximize their own objectives and the effort by private interest groups to subvert the rules to generate benefits for themselves create opportunities for corruption. For example, an importer who is interested in securing a lucrative import license may pay bribes to a bureaucrat at the trade ministry in order to (1) get the permit, and (2) make sure that the bureau protects his new monopoly rights by not issuing additional permits to entrepreneurs from his jurisdiction or area of operation. Civil servants at the trade ministry "earn" extra-legal income for themselves, the importer receiving the permit earns monopoly profits, but the society loses. One must note here that without intervention by the state (through trade regulation) to create the license, the importer will have no incentive to bribe the bureaucrat at the trade ministry. Of course, prospective importers can lobby or bribe the government to pass laws creating the scarcity. The latter process is also rent seeking.

Government regulatory activities usually impose significant transaction costs on business owners and affect profitability. To minimize these regulation-related costs, entrepreneurs often seek the help of the bureaucracy, whose job it is to enforce the laws. Usually, a bribe is paid to the civil servant by the owner of a business in an effort to receive preferential treatment and minimize the burden of state regulations on his operations. Public choice scholars argue, then, that bureaucratic corruption is directly related to the scope and extent of state intervention in market processes. Bureaucrats demand bribes and business owners supply them. The market for this transaction is created by state regulatory activities. Effective control of corruption, thus, must be based on institutional reforms to constrain the ability of the state to intervene in private exchange and create artificial scarcities.

V. THE ONE-PARTY POLITICAL SYSTEM AND CORRUPTION IN AFRICA

At independence, Africans had to decide whether to retain the political and economic systems inherited from the colonial government or design new ones to meet their needs. Many of the erstwhile African leaders (e.g., Julius K. Nyerere of Tanzania, Siaka Stevens of Sierra Leone, and Ahmadou Ahidjo of Cameroon) argued that "tribalism" was a major development problem and that it was necessary to have a political system that could bring together competitive ethnic groups and provide the appropriate environment for peaceful coexistence and sustainable development. Many of these leaders also argued that the institutions they had inherited from the colonial state were not appropriate for their new societies. However, instead of engaging the people in a national debate on *state reconstruction*, they undertook opportunistic reforms that enhanced their ability to monopolize power and the allocation of resources.[19] They argued that what their countries needed were *unitary political systems* with strong central governments which could keep competitive ethnic cleavages together. Through amendments to the independence constitutions, passage of restrictive statutes, and the use of the state's (greatly enhanced) coercive apparatus to prevent entry (of competitive elites) into political markets, the new leaders made it virtually impossible for competitors to come to power through legal means. The head of state came to monopolize and dominate both political power and the allocation of resources. Multiparty democracy, as practiced by several Western countries, was believed to be a vehicle for the politicization of ethnic or tribal cleavages and subsequently an important constraint to national integration and economic development.

The option chosen by many of these elites was the one-party political system with a strong central government, with little or no *devolution of power* to the regional and local political jurisdictions. This approach to civil–state relations, however, paved the way for the emergence of the *all-encompassing national state structure*, which would later become an important constraint to economic and political development. Specifically, the one-party political system adopted by many African countries at independence created several political societies that were to become major obstacles to economic growth and development. Among these are *personalistic rule*, in which incumbent politicians use public resources to purchase loyalty and thus continue to maintain a monopoly on political power and the supply of legislation; *patrimonialism*, a political system in which incumbents use governmental structures as instruments for their personal enrichment; *rent seeking*, which involves the expending of resources to capture transfers created by government intervention in the economy; and *bureaucratic corruption*.[20]

During most of the post-independence period in Africa, political economy has been characterized by: (1) high levels of poverty and deprivation; (2) endemic political violence, including destructive ethnic conflict; (3) bureaucratic and political corruption; (4) suffocation of civil society; (5) unmanageable external debts; (6) economic and political decay; (7) military opportunism (e.g., coups d'état); and (8) continued dependence on the European economies. In addition to the fact that the one-party political system has failed to provide Africans with the appropriate structures for peaceful coexistence and genuine development, it has not produced any significant improvements in the living conditions of the majority of the people. However, the one-party state has enhanced the ability of ruling elites to engage in corrupt enrichment. An important outcome of this approach to governance has been the emergence of corruption as a *pervasive institution* in post-independence society.[21]

Throughout most of post-1960s Africa, public resources were devoted to the development of structures to help the ruling elite plunder the economy for its own benefit. As a result, institutions of state coercion such as the military and the police were strengthened. Although many African governments allocated significant portions of their budgets to the military and other institutions of state coercion, very few resources were spent on education and the development of human capital, health care, economic infrastructures, communications, power generation, and other areas vital to development and popular participation. By the late 1970s, governmental structures in many African countries were no longer instruments for the enhancement of peaceful coexistence and sustainable development, but had been converted into tools for the private capital accumulation activities of the members of the incumbent government. What emerged was a corrupt, exploitative, patrimonial system that was characterized by relatively high levels of political opportunism, especially corruption and rent seeking. There were, of course, exceptions. Notable among them are Mauritius and Botswana.[22]

We have argued above that the one-party political system, adopted by many African countries shortly after independence, bankrupted these societies and contributed significantly to increased levels of corruption and rent seeking. It is important to caution, however, that the introduction of a multiparty system in a country may not necessarily lead to improvements in the allocation of resources and governance. In fact, since the late 1980s, multiparty political systems have been introduced in several African countries (e.g., Cameroon, Zambia, Malawi, Kenya, Zimbabwe, and Ghana). Yet, levels of venality and public malfeasance remain quite high in these countries.

In many countries throughout the continent, a significant number of these new parties have turned out to be vehicles for ethnic groups to participate in the political competition for resources. Most of the leaders of these political organizations are not interested in proper transformation of existing laws and institutions but are eager to use the transition for self-enrichment. In Cameroon, for example, after failing to capture the government during elections in 1992 and 1997, many opposition leaders (e.g., Bello Bouba of the Union nationale pour la démocratie et progrès [UNDP]) eagerly sought and accepted high-paying positions in the Cameroon People's Democratic Movement-led government. In exchange, these opposition elites helped the incumbent government maintain the façade of a competitive political system in Cameroon. The most important reason why political competition has failed to have a significant impact on corruption in these countries is that no effort has been made to reconstruct the post-colonial state to provide society with institutional arrangements that adequately constrain the exercise of government agency and thus minimize the ability of civil servants, to engage in corruption, for example. As supported by the data presented in Table 14.1, the "cleanest" countries (those with relatively low levels of corruption) are those that practice competitive politics within an environment that is characterized by laws and institutions that place significant constraints on the government, enhance entrepreneurial activities, guarantee economic freedoms and make it relatively difficult for public servants to engage in opportunistic behaviors. Examples include Botswana, Namibia, South Africa, and Mauritius.

VI. STATISM AND CORRUPTION IN AFRICA

The second issue to be resolved by Africans after independence was the choice of a development model, one that could enhance rapid economic growth to provide the state with enough wealth to confront massive poverty and deprivation. The *market-centered* resource allocation systems inherited from the colonial state were regarded by many of the new African leaders as significant constraints to economic growth and development. In fact, several of these leaders blamed the *market system* for the severe inequalities in the distribution of wealth that existed in their respective countries. As a result, many of them chose a development model that emphasized state control of resource allocation and the minimization of the functions of the market system.[23] *Statism* was supposed to provide the state with the wherewithal to deal more effectively with poverty in the post-independence society. Unfortunately, excessive regulation of private exchange and state ownership of productive resources have encouraged, enabled, and enhanced nepotism and bureaucratic and political corruption and have significantly constrained the development of viable political and economic infrastructures.[24]

Since the late 1980s, Africans have been struggling to transform their societies socially, economically and politically in an effort to introduce new dispensations that can adequately constrain the government and enhance the ability of entrepreneurs to create the wealth that these societies need to deal with poverty. Part of the effort to improve macroeconomic performance has involved attempts to deal more effectively with corruption and improve the efficiency and professionalism of the bureaucracy. In this chapter, we shall examine corruption in Africa and seek to advance the *public choice approach* as the most effective and sustainable way to control corruption in the continent. It will be argued that a sustainable corruption cleanup program can only be designed and implemented if policymakers place corruption in its right context. One must understand that bureaucratic corruption is *opportunistic behavior* which is related to the scope and extent of government regulation of private economic activities. State reconstruction—through democratic (bottom-up, participatory, inclusive, and people driven) constitution making to establish and sustain participatory, accountable, and transparent governance structures and economic systems that guarantee economic freedoms—is the only way to deal effectively with corruption and other forms of political opportunism.

VII. THE IMPACT OF CORRUPTION ON THE AFRICAN ECONOMIES

Significant research has been done to determine the effects of corruption on the African economies.[25] On the one hand, several scholars argue that corruption is a major constraint to development in the continent; on the other, it is argued that corruption can enhance economic growth and development. The enhancement school believes that corruption can "grease" the wheels of what is essentially a rigid and unresponsive bureaucracy and make it more responsive to the needs of the entrepreneurial class. According to researchers Bayley, Nye, and Leff, corruption has both harmful and beneficial effects for economic growth and development.[26] First, corruption can advance economic growth by channeling scarce capital resources to the economy's most enterprising individuals. Second, corruption can provide access to the government to individuals who ordinarily would not be served by the bureaucracy. It has also been argued that corruption can provide resources that can be utilized to minimize conflict between the bureaucracy and the nation's political leaders. A closer relationship between the two groups should improve the efficiency of the civil service and enhance its ability to design and implement national development plans. Third, corruption can get rid of important bottlenecks in the civil service and subsequently improve efficiency, flexibility, and responsiveness in the delivery of public goods and services and in the implementation of state regulations.

Most of these propositions, however, have not been supported by research. Although available research consists primarily of country case studies which cannot be generalized to the continent, these studies cover most of the major economies in Sub-Saharan Africa (e.g., Cameroon, Nigeria, Ghana, Zaire, Zambia, Ethiopia, Kenya, and Botswana).[27] For example, LeVine's study of Ghana determined that the bulk of the resources derived from corruption were invested overseas or utilized in the importation of luxury goods.[28] In those instances in which corruption-related income was invested in domestic projects, the latter did not produce any visible benefits for the local people. Windfalls from petroleum made Nigeria a very rich country in the late 1970s. Unfortunately, along with this wealth came significantly high levels of bureaucratic corruption. Most of the illegally appropriated resources were not devoted to domestic investment activities but were sent abroad, primarily to Western Europe and North America to provide retirement positions for the crooks who had deprived Nigerians of the opportunity to improve their livelihood. The government also squandered part of the oil windfall on providing privileges (which included free or subsidized housing, health care, luxury cars, vacations, and other amenities) for a bloated, parasitic, inefficient, and corrupt civil service.[29] Thus, despite the relatively large earnings from the export of petroleum, most people in Nigeria are actually worse off now than they were when the country gained independence in 1960.[30] Most of the resources generated from the sale of oil were squandered through corruption.

The second proposition has not been supported by research, either. For example, there is no evidence to support the argument that access to the government for historically marginalized groups has been improved by the institution of corruption. What corruption has achieved is to enrich a few individuals and groups, and help the incumbent continue to monopolize power and the allocation of resources.[31] In the last several years, corruption has been useful in helping the ruling elites maintain a monopoly on power. Thus, despite increased poverty and deprivation, many African societies have continued to exhibit a significant level of political stability, thanks to corruption. Stability of this kind has been achieved at a very high economic and social cost: suffocation of civil society, high public debt levels, mass poverty, very high levels of material deprivation, environmental degradation, increased marginalization of children and women, and crumbling economic infrastructures. In several African countries, national institutions such as the courts, the police, and the civil service have been compromised by corruption and are no longer able to perform their functions properly. Unfortunately, civil society, which is still suffering from many years of abuse by the state, is unable to provide the leadership to move these countries forward. It is no wonder that in some African countries, multilateral organizations such as the International Monetary Fund (IMF) and the World Bank have become *de facto* policymakers. Fortunately, there appears to be some hope—post-apartheid South Africa, Mauritius, Botswana and a few other African countries have relatively strong and emerging civil societies and viable institutions that are quite able, with varying degrees of success, to check the abuse of government agency.

Can bureaucratic bottlenecks be removed by corruption and the system made more efficient, and responsive to the needs of the business class? It is important to note that most of the rigidities found in several of the bureaucracies in Africa are imposed intentionally by civil servants who expect to extort bribes from the private sector when they want them removed. Bureaucratic roadblocks increase the transaction costs faced by businesses and, in addition, reduce firm efficiency. In order to minimize such costs on their operations, business owners are willing to pay bribes to civil servants. Unless comprehensive reforms are undertaken (and the ability of civil servants to introduce such rigidities effectively constrained), ambitious and opportunistic civil servants are most likely to institutionalize these rigidities and transform them into a permanent source of extra-legal compensation for themselves. Through such institutionalization, corruption will become a permanent constraint to entrepreneurial activities and the creation of wealth. We must, therefore, emphasize here that corruption is not an efficient and sustainable way to remove bottlenecks from the bureaucracy. To make the civil service more efficient and responsive to investors requires reforms to develop institutions that are transparent and accountable to the public.

In a study conducted in 1992, Osterfeld argued that in economies that are heavily regulated, one can find two types of corruption. He called the first one *expansive corruption* and argued that it involves activities that significantly improve and enhance the competitiveness of markets. The second type, which he called *restrictive corruption*, limits avenues for socially beneficial exchange. According to Osterfeld, restrictive corruption promotes the redistribution of income in favor of certain individuals and groups and thus, exacerbates inequalities in income and wealth distribution.[32] He argues further that most corruption falls in the restrictive category and involves the misappropriation of public resources for private uses and the misuse of one's public office for personal gain. He also stated that bureaucratic corruption constrains economic growth because it distorts market incentives and hinders the proper functioning of markets. Like other members of the enhancement school of corruption, however, Osterfeld believes that expansive corruption can improve economic development by eliminating from the bureaucracy important bottlenecks and making the latter more responsive to the needs of the business class. For example, he argues that providing the proper officials (e.g., judges, high-ranking civil servants, etc.) with bribes can minimize the burden or harmful effects of state regulations on one's enterprise and thus improve the participation of citizens in national development.

Although certain kinds of corruption may indeed have a *few* economic and political benefits, the institution in general imposes severe transaction costs on business activities; distorts market incentives and subsequently discourages investment in productive effort, thus negatively affecting long-term economic growth and development; allows inefficient enterprises to remain in business indefinitely, consuming scarce resources and earning only meager returns; compromises the civil service and renders it incapable of performing its duties; destroys the effectiveness of public institutions (e.g., the judiciary and the police); and alienates the people from their leaders. Civil servants who anticipate making a lot of money from corruption can intentionally distort state policies (e.g., artificially create information asymmetries) in order to provide themselves with opportunities to benefit financially.

Corruption increases, in a significant way, the costs of supporting the state bureaucracy. Taxpayers are forced to underwrite what is essentially a bloated, highly inefficient, and severely wasteful public institution. In addition, corruption forces citizens to pay more for public goods, and in return receive relatively poor and inferior quality and service. For example, in many African countries, individuals who go to public hospitals for treatment must pay twice for what are often inferior and poor quality services: once as taxpayers and then again in the form of bribes to hospital personnel. Consequently, in many of these countries, only individuals who have the resources to pay bribes have adequate access to public goods and services. The illegal charges imposed on demanders of public goods by the bureaucracy prevent many poor people from having effective access to goods and services that are either supposed to be free or highly subsidized.

Corruption can demoralize and destroy the civil service. It generates distrust throughout the system and significantly affects the utilization of labor resources. For example, in making assignments, senior officials may not favor qualified individuals (that is, those who can perform the job well) but those who are able to utilize the position or assignment effectively to generate extra-legal income for themselves and their superiors. In an effort to maximize revenues from corruption, department heads may base their recruitment and promotion decisions on the applicant's potential to extort bribes from the private sector rather than on merit (that is, ability to perform the job). Consequently, the civil service can easily become overwhelmed with mediocre talent. Because the ability to pay bribes, loyalty to the boss, and political connections, not efficiency, professionalism, and merit, determine whether an individual gains promotion, junior officers may refrain from constructively criticizing their superiors. In 1983, Szeftel determined that many Zambian junior civil servants evaluated state parastatals improperly in order to avoid offending their bosses. Instead of employing generally accepted or standard methodologies, they relied on variables preferred by their superiors. Most of them simply provided their bosses with what they believed their supervisors wanted to hear instead of results produced by research. Such an approach to project analysis usually results in the implementation of perverse economic programs.[33]

In a study conducted in 1961, McMullan argued that a society's institutional arrangements can place some individuals and groups at a competitive disadvantage and make them candidates for corruption. An important role of institutional reforms is to produce laws and institutions that minimize the number of individuals and groups that are placed at a competitive disadvantage. Additionally, well designed laws and institutions should constrain the abuse of public authority by civil servants and other state officials.[34]

VIII. TRADITIONAL CORRUPTION CLEANUP STRATEGIES

Until recently, the control of corruption was limited to four strategies: *societal, legal, market,* and *political.*[35] The societal approach searches for a common standard of morality which can be used to determine if behavior is corrupt. Members of society are expected to be vigilant and look out for individuals who stray from the generally accepted standard of morality. In addition, education of the public about corruption is emphasized, making it easier for individuals to identify and report corrupt behaviors.

Legal strategies for corruption control are supposed to work through the activities of the courts, police, media, and members of society. First, the law defines the responsibilities of civil servants and constrains them in the performance of their jobs. Second, the law defines what constitutes corrupt behavior. Third, members of society are encouraged to remain vigilant and report suspected cases of corruption to the police, whose job it is to investigate such reports and submit their findings to the appropriate judiciary officers. The latter are expected to judge and punish the guilty according to the law. The press is expected to play an important part; it can investigate and expose incidents of corruption and serve as a check on the behavior of civil servants and other public employees who are likely to engage in corrupt activities. Special commissions of inquiry or special prosecutors can be chosen to investigate evidence that points to large-scale corruption and pave the way for prosecution by the courts.

Market strategies for corruption control are based on the argument that there is a relationship between market structure and the incidence of corruption. Government intervention in the marketplace creates opportunities for individuals to engage in corruption. The remedy prescribed is less government intervention in private exchange and greater reliance on markets for the allocation of resources. This advise has two problems: first, it emphasizes the manipulation of outcomes within a given set of rules instead of changing the rules to guarantee the appropriate outcomes. Second, the problem is not with the market, but with the incentive system that exists in the market or the rules that regulate the behavior of market participants. Rules define the incentive structure and consequently determine the outcomes. Thus, greater reliance on markets for the allocation of resources without changing the incentive structure faced by market participants will have little effect on outcomes. To minimize corruption, then, the rules that regulate sociopolitical interaction in a country must be reformed in order to limit the ability of civil servants to engage in opportunism. If the incentive structure is flawed, it is near impossible to significantly alter the expected outcomes. Any hope of obtaining significantly different outcomes must be based on a consideration of the rules themselves with a view to changing them. In other words, there has to be modifications of the incentive structure through rules change.[36]

Political strategies for controlling corruption emphasize governmental decentralization. The argument is that corruption arises from the concentration of political power at the center and in the hands of a few individuals. Thus, a process which improves citizen access to the political process will significantly reduce levels of corruption in the country. Under this approach, dealing effectively with corruption should begin with political liberalization and the subsequent improvement of opportunities for citizens to participate in governance. Those who are in favor of administrative reforms as a way of reducing the incidence of corruption recommend that civil service compensation rates be increased in order to reduce the chances that a public employee will engage in corrupt activities as a way to subsidize his earnings.

Corruption control programs in many African countries have often been motivated by *political exigency* instead of a genuine interest to improve bureaucratic efficiency and macroeconomic performance. In fact, in many instances, post-coup commissions of inquiry have usually worked to discredit the ousted regime and help the incoming elites gain recognition and legitimacy. Little effort is made to achieve the kind of structural change that will minimize corruption and other types of opportunism. A new or incumbent leader faced with an economic crisis and a challenge from competing elites may initiate a campaign to control corruption within his government in an attempt to direct attention away from the country's impending problems and the state's inability or unwillingness to deal effectively with these problems.

The corruption control strategies described above suffer from many shortcomings. One of these is very critical: Success of these strategies depends on the effectiveness and professionalism of existing *counteracting agencies* (e.g., the police, the judiciary, the press, etc.), for success and assume that these institutions are properly constrained by the law and as a result are free of corruption. First, few African countries have an independent press that can contribute significantly to the exposure of corruption. Second, most African judiciaries are not independent of the incumbent government; instead, judicial officers serve at the pleasure of the head of state and usually owe their job to the president and the party in power. As a result, they are not free of government manipulation. Third, many of these agencies are pervaded by high levels of corruption. Thus, a corruption control program backed by these agencies is not likely to be effective. An effective corruption control program calls for the selection of appropriate new rules which will (1) properly constrain the state and those who work within it, and (2) provide the foundation for the design of new and more effective counteracting institutions (e.g., an independent judiciary, a professional civil service, a free press; etc.) to enforce compliance to the rules.[37]

IX. RULES, INSTITUTIONS, AND THE PUBLIC CHOICE APPROACH TO CORRUPTION CONTROL

In 1985, Brennan and Buchanan argued that rules matter and determine the way individuals and organizations behave. Rules determine the incentive structures faced by market participants—in both political and economic markets. Thus, the behavior of civil servants and the entrepreneurs who bribe them can only be effectively examined within the context of the existing set of rules. Without a clear understanding of the laws and institutions of a country, an attempt to analyze corruption in that country would not yield policy-relevant information. To design an effective corruption control program, one must take into consideration the impact of existing laws on the behavior of market participants (voters, politicians, civil servants, entrepreneurs, and organized interest groups). Exactly what do rules do? According to Brennan and Buchanan, they determine the interaction of individuals with each other; provide a means for the resolution of conflict; provide information, allowing individuals to anticipate the behavior of other market participants; and impose constraints on the behavior of individuals, as well as on that of organizations (including public institutions) within society. In performing their duties, for example, the police and judiciary officers are constrained by the law.[38]

Institutions determine the incentive structures for each society, helping to shape the behavior of individuals participating in political and economic markets. As a consequence, institutions determine outcomes from markets and other forms of socio-political interaction. Thus, any attempt to affect outcomes must involve a change in the structure of incentives. For example, to increase productivity, innovation, and the efficient and productive use of resources, it is necessary to change the incentive structure to one that minimizes opportunism and enhances the ability of entrepreneurs to engage in wealth production.[39]

Rules can be explicit (e.g., a written constitution) or implicit (e.g., custom and tradition). Within a given set of rules, corruption can be seen as opportunistic behavior on the part of individuals or groups to generate extra-legal benefits for themselves at the expense of society. Accordingly, corruption can be seen as part of the problem of *constitutional maintenance*, which must be handled effectively only through reform of existing rules. Here, *opportunism* is defined as behaviors designed to improve the welfare of an individual at the expense of that of other citizens and includes activities such as shirking, adverse selection, moral hazard, corruption, and free riding.[40]

In an effort to improve our appreciation for the role rules play in determining market outcomes, one can refer to the "tragedy of the commons," the Hardin example about the overexploitation of "common" property. Suppose existing rules mandate that land be owned communally with open access; overgrazing is likely to be an outcome. Contrary to claims by some observers, overgrazing is not a result of market failure but a problem that arises from the rules (in this case, the existing property rights regimes, which are part of the society's institutional arrangements) that define market incentives and consequently the behavior of market participants. Given the existing rules, utility maximization by farmers will lead to overexploitation. Policing, a method quite common in most countries, will not yield the outcomes desired by society—that is, efficient allocation of the resource, land. According to Hanna, Folke, and Mäler, "The 'tragedy of the commons' is an environmental outcome that results from an inadequate specification of property rights to environmental services."[41] Most problems with overexploitation of natural resources are caused by "incomplete, inconsistent, or unenforced property rights regimes."[42] To deal effectively with the problem of overexploitation of environmental resources, first, society must have complete, consistent, and well-specified property rights regimes (i.e., an effective set of rules). Second, society should have institutions (e.g., an independent judiciary) that can effectively enforce the rules. What are property rights? These are a subset of a nation's institutional arrangements "which structure [market] incentives and shape human interactions."[43] Because, as stated earlier, the rules determine the incentive system faced by market participants, and consequently the latter's behavior and the expected outcomes, corruption, then, can be seen as an outcome from a market that is defined by a given incentive structure, and of course, an existing set of rules. To affect or change the market outcome requires modifications of the incentive structure through changes in existing rules.

If existing rules make corruption highly lucrative, efforts to control it would not be effective unless they include a negotiated change of the rules resulting in the alteration of the existing incentive structure. Suppose, as a result of rules adopted earlier, rent seeking, instead of managerial expertise and competition, becomes the primary determinant of firm profitability. Then entrepreneurs will devote most of their time and resources to rent seeking instead of engaging in the production and distribution of goods and services. Using the police to prevent entrepreneurs from taking advantage of highly rewarding rent-seeking opportunities would likely not succeed, especially if members of the police force are themselves corrupt. The problem is not market failure but distorted incentives provided by existing rules. The appropriate procedure for dealing effectively with rent seeking and other opportunistic behaviors, including corruption, is to reform the rules of the game and alter the incentive structures.

Public choice theory views the control of corruption and other forms of opportunism as part of the problem of constitutional maintenance. Even if the rules chosen are efficient (that is, they generate mutual gains for all members of society), opportunism would still be a problem for the post-constitutional society. To make sure that opportunism is minimized in the post-contractual society requires an effective enforcement system to force cooperation and compliance. Unfortunately, third-party enforcement of constitutional rules is usually unreliable, inefficient, and not particularly viable. It has been suggested that the judiciary system and the police be given the job of enforcing the constitutional rules. Unfortunately, in most countries these institutions are subject to manipulation by interest groups. In addition, in the majority of the African countries these institutions are not properly constrained by the law, are pervaded by high levels of corruption, and do not enjoy any degree of independence. Currently, national judiciary systems and the police in these countries do not appear to be appropriate instruments for corruption control and effective enforcement of the constitutional rules.[44]

In recent years, researchers have developed a theory of constitutional maintenance, whose main objective is to find ways to minimize opportunism in the post-constitutional society.[45] It is argued that opportunities for rent seeking and other opportunistic behaviors can be eliminated from the post-constitutional society by making the constitution *self-enforcing*. One way to achieve this is to make certain that the post-constitutional society is made competitive. First, there must be a devolution of political power in favor of local, regional, or provincial jurisdictions. That is, power should not be concentrated in the center; some political functions should be performed at the local level in order to bring government closer to the people. For example, decisions that deal with the production and distribution of public goods are made more efficiently if those who actually consume the goods are effectively represented or allowed more input into the making of the decisions. Individuals at the local level have more time-and-place information about conditions in their environment and know more about their tastes and preferences than civil servants in the center. It is economically more sensible to allow production and distribution of public goods to be undertaken at the local level where demand and supply conditions can be determined with greater levels of accuracy. Second, national political space should be divided into as many political jurisdictions as possible, and these units allowed to compete with each other for the organization and distribution of public goods. Third, individuals should be granted the right to migrate between political jurisdictions. This implies the establishment of some form of *constitutional federalism* with a large number of political units, making it difficult for the government to coerce citizens. Such a political arrangement enhances the ability of citizens to migrate freely and at relatively low cost to competitive political jurisdictions within the country. The ability of an individual to exit freely and at low cost minimizes coercive action by local governmental units. A local government would be unable to pursue perverse economic policies for fear of losing taxpayers to jurisdictions with more investment-friendly policies or more attractive fiscal packages. Fourth, the power of the state to intervene in private exchange (that is, to interfere with or abrogate economic freedoms) should be constitutionally constrained. Most opportunism in post-independence Africa has been made possible by the fact that the constitutions adopted by the African countries at independence endowed most governments with almost unlimited power to intervene in private exchange. Perhaps, most important is the fact that many of these governments have been able to engage almost indiscriminately in the redistribution of income and wealth. Political coalitions that captured the apparatus of government after independence rarely used these discretionary powers to benefit the people; instead they used them to redistribute income and wealth in their favor, resulting in increased social inequality. Many deprived and locked-out individuals and groups were forced to either turn to violence or bribery to gain access to markets. The results have been a cycle of political violence and corruption that has become endemic to many African societies. If government redistributive powers are restricted constitutionally, then interest groups would not invest as much in rent seeking and the government will be less likely to enact fiscally discriminatory legislation.

The right of individuals to freely engage in exchange and contract (that is, economic freedom) is an important determinant of economic growth. State restrictions on economic freedoms provide opportunities for civil servants to extract extra-legal income for themselves through corruption. However, such restrictions impose severe costs on society and stunt economic growth. It is important that economic freedoms are guaranteed constitutionally in order to prevent politicians from abrogating them through ordinary legislation. In response to lobbying from interest groups, the government can place restrictions on economic freedoms and as a result promote policies that grant privileges to certain groups and individuals, but reduce the national welfare. To prevent the state from interfering with economic freedoms and creating opportunities for rent seeking and other opportunistic behaviors, the individual's ability to engage in exchange and contract should be guaranteed by the constitution.[46]

X. PRODUCING THE SELF-ENFORCING CONSTITUTION

As already mentioned above, the most effective way to make a country's constitution self-enforcing is to introduce and sustain competition in the economic and political markets in the post-constitutional society. In addition, there should be a significant devolution of power in favor of local, regional, and provincial units. In order to make political space competitive, the polity should be divided into as many autonomous political jurisdictions as possible and the right of citizens to migrate freely between political units guaranteed by the constitution. Usually, this implies the establishment of some form of constitutional federalism. Wiseman argues that a federal system with many autonomous political jurisdictions, each with a constitutionally guaranteed level of autonomy, should effectively constrain the ability of governments, at all levels, to exploit citizens.[47] Federalist constitutions of this type appear to embody the kind of diversity and pluralism that is characteristic of African societies.[48]

A constitutional arrangement of the type described above should enhance the ability of citizens to escape exploitative governmental jurisdictions, making it much more difficult for civil servants and politicians to be exploitative. If individuals within the society can migrate freely and at relatively low cost, to competitive political jurisdictions, then the ability of governmental units to oppress their citizens will be severely diminished.[49]

Being able to migrate freely is very important to the maintenance and proper functioning of voluntary agreements, such as those that we are proposing for the African countries. One, however, must realize that internal migration can be quite costly. Congleton argues that because most political jurisdictions are geographical, exit implies that the individual has abandoned his previous geographic residence in favor of another one.[50] The process can involve significant economic and social costs. For Africans, migration may involve the abandonment of one's geographic residence, as well as critical ethnic and family affiliations.

The greater the costs of exiting political jurisdictions, the easier it is for governments to be oppressive. The creation of many political jurisdictions within the polity, however, should reduce the geographic or physical distance associated with exit and subsequently lower the cost of migration. In addition, the existence of a large number of political jurisdictions should reduce the possibility that the individual would actually have to radically change his or her lifestyle. As Congleton has argued, in the case where one can choose from several political jurisdictions, exit can be viewed as a change of neighborhood without significantly altering one's lifestyle.[51] Under such circumstances, the individual can actually retain his job and continue to have relatively easy access to friends and family. Congleton concludes by stating that "the smaller the governmental jurisdictions are, the *more* likely it is that affiliated individuals receive positive net benefits from local governments."[52]

The public choice theory's approach to construction of the self-enforcing constitution is based, partially, on the work of Wicksell.[53] Several years ago, Wicksell suggested what he believed was a more effective way to constrain the legislature and minimize its ability to engage in political opportunism. He suggested that membership in each legislative chamber be based on proportional representation and that lawmakers be subjected to a rule of approximate unanimity instead of majoritarianism. He argued further that if the legislature is required to secure consensual or supramajority approval of *all* its members (e.g., 75% of its membership) before laws (especially those dealing with income redistribution) are enacted, then interest groups will find it very difficult to subvert the rules to their advantage. Such a supramajority rule can minimize rent seeking, rent extraction, and the enactment of fiscally discriminatory laws—those that redistribute income and wealth in favor of one group.[54]

The above discussion points to the adoption of highly decentralized federalist structures as a way to minimize opportunism, including corruption in the African countries. The actual mix of institutions, however, must be determined by the relevant stakeholder groups during constitution making, as they have access to the time-and-place information required. While a highly decentralized governmental system is more responsive to the interests and values of both large (i.e., dominant) and small ethnic groups, unless the right to migrate is constitutionally protected, such a system would degenerate into a series of small unitary governments, with each one monopolizing political space in its geographic region and burdened with the problems of centralized governance.

XI. CHALLENGES TO CONSTITUTIONALISM IN AFRICA TODAY

Some individuals are likely to argue that the type of constitutionalism and state reconstruction that can provide African societies with accountable, transparent, and participatory governance structures can only be undertaken, at least at this time, in societies with characteristics and traits that are not now present in Africa. For example, they would argue that currently in Africa the ability of the ordinary citizen to make choices is constrained significantly by political and economic monopolies, limited information, and an absence of trust in the national laws and institutions, as well in the country's leaders. Africans, these critics argue, are subjected to a form of "bounded rationality."[55]

In the West, the management of modern institutions requires complex information. Individuals who manage these institutions (e.g., bureaucrats and business executives) are expected to have acquired the highly technical skills needed to understand and appreciate the complexities of these organizations. Additionally, these managers are constrained by stakeholder groups who understand their rights, are willing to enforce these rights, and have the facilities to do so. Of course, it is assumed that each society has a properly functioning educational system to educate both managers and the relevant stakeholders and provide them with the necessary skills; a mass media to expose any corruption and other forms of opportunism on the part of managers (including bureau chiefs); and systems that enhance the ability of the managers to have access to the information that they need to manage their organizations effectively.

What is the situation that currently obtains in Africa? First, most of the laws and institutions that currently exist in the African countries are based on those imposed on the colonies by the European colonialists and managed by a foreign economic and political class with values alien to those of the indigenous peoples. These colonial institutions were despotic, exploitative, and designed not to enhance African welfare but to help the Europeans maximize their objectives in the colonies. As a consequence, managers of these colonial institutions usually did not reveal to Africans the true nature of their activities. Second, at independence, there did not exist in many of the new countries an indigenous managerial and entrepreneurial class, as colonial authorities had intentionally stunted their development. Third, many of these countries did not have an independent media. Finally, most Africans were considered illiterate. According to these critics, "Neither effective management nor democratic control is possible under such circumstances."[56]

It is a truism that the absence of properly functioning mass media structures has made it relatively difficult for Africans to remain informed about the operation of their governments. However, it is important to recognize that the absence of *modern* media structures such as television and radio stations, as well as newspapers and magazines, in many African countries does not necessarily mean that the people are in the dark about the goings-on in their societies. In fact, such an analysis completely ignores traditional forms of communication or information transmission. For example, during the reign of Ahmadou Ahidjo in Cameroon (1961–1982), the country had no television and the mass media was reduced to a public radio station and one or two newspapers owned and controlled by the government. These media structures only reported "news" cleared by state authorities. In addition, foreign newspapers and magazines were heavily censored. However, Cameroonians, using informal and traditional structures, were able to keep themselves informed of developments in government. In addition to underground newspapers, "rumor mills" provided relatively accurate information about such things as corruption and public malfeasance. During the pro-democracy riots of the late 1980s and early to mid-1990s, "sidewalk" radio and other informal communication structures were utilized very effectively to coordinate demonstrations, provide information about government policies toward democratization, and generally increase national awareness about the changes that were taking place in the global political environment at the time.

It is true that literacy is an important determinant of a society's ability to practice democratic governance. Most data on literacy in Africa, however, usually refer to the ability of Africans to read and write some European language (e.g., French or English). In most of West Africa, while a significant portion of those who live in the rural areas are not literate in either French or English, they can communicate relatively well across ethnic groups in *pidgin English*. In fact, the latter is an important medium for a significant amount of the music that is produced and distributed throughout the region. Since the reintroduction of multiparty politics in Cameroon, for example, several opposition leaders have used pidgin English effectively to communicate with a population that is largely "illiterate." Ni John Fru Ndi, Chairman of Cameroon's most important opposition political party, the Social Democratic Front (SDF), is not fluent in French, one of the country's national languages. However, he has communicated very effectively with Cameroonians through pidgin English. During the 1992 presidential election, he addressed large crowds and received questions from them in pidgin. Unfortunately, all of these Cameroonians, the majority of whom have not studied either English or French, would be considered illiterate and therefore incapable of participating fully and effectively in democratic discourse.

Today, fax machines, cellphones, and the Internet have changed the ability of African governments to control the media. In Cameroon, Liberia, Sierra Leone, and several other countries, journalists who have been forced underground by government censors are no longer able to print and distribute their papers but have not gone out of business. Many of them maintain websites from which they publish their papers almost without interruption. Unfortunately, most of these Internet-based newspapers are read primarily by people outside the continent because most Africans cannot afford the resources needed to gain access to the Internet.

The availability of skilled and competent managers is a necessary but not sufficient condition for the efficient management of political and economic markets. Unless each society is provided with the appropriate incentive structures, individuals are likely to engage in opportunistic behaviors in an effort to extract benefits for themselves. Thus, even if African countries are able to secure the necessary skilled manpower, development and effective governance are not likely to be the outcome in the absence of the appropriate institutional environment.

Will rational self-interest be able to drive constitution making and provide Africans with viable institutional arrangements? We have argued in this chapter that most people's behavior is governed by self-interest and that, given the opportunity, they are most likely to behave opportunistically to advance that self-interest even if doing so reduces the welfare of others or imposes significant costs on the rest of society. Democratic constitution making, as argued by public choice theorists, provides society with institutional arrangements that prevent individuals from engaging in corruption, rent seeking, and other forms of opportunism. However, will self-interested Africans be willing to engage in state reconstruction to provide governance structures that will constrain their ability to engage in, for example, corruption? Given existing institutional arrangements in most African countries today, any attempt to introduce a new dispensation (even if it promises to minimize corruption and allocate resources more efficiently) will be opposed by incumbents who now benefit from the *status quo*. However, as the overthrow of apartheid in South Africa and several dictatorships in the continent shows, it is possible for grassroots organizations to overcome opposition from entrenched groups and engage the people in democratic constitution making.

XII. SUMMARY AND CONCLUSION

The primary purpose of this chapter was to examine corruption in Africa and seek to show why traditional approaches to corruption control have not been successful in ridding the continent's economies of endemic corruption. Societal, legal, market, and political strategies have traditionally been used to control corruption in Africa. Each one of these strategies represents an attempt to manipulate outcomes within a given set of rules and assumes the existence of efficient and effective counteracting institutions. If existing rules provide incentive systems that encourage opportunistic behaviors, including corruption, the only effective way to control corruption is to change the rules and subsequently the incentive structure. An attempt to manipulate outcomes (e.g., through policing) while leaving the rules (and, by implication, the incentive structure) constant will fail to produce the efficient outcomes desired by society. If the police force is not properly constrained by the law and is pervaded by corruption, it is unlikely to serve as an effective instrument for corruption control. Thus, proper corruption cleanup requires institutional reforms that result in a change in the incentive structure to guarantee the outcomes desired by society.

Corruption can be seen as an outcome determined by the incentive structure of a market, which itself is determined by the rules within which the market functions. A proper normative evaluation of such an outcome can only be done after the analyst has understood the rules (and incentive structure) that generate the outcome. In other words, to understand why individuals and groups within a society participate in corruption, it is necessary to study the rules that regulate sociopolitical interaction. Because these rules determine the incentive structures and consequently how individuals behave and relate to each other, they also determine the outcomes generated in each market. Therefore, effective corruption control should not involve efforts to manipulate outcomes within a given set of rules; an effective corruption control system must begin with a modification of the incentive structure (that is, rules reform). Undertaking the latter will allow society to select and adopt new rules that generate (through the appropriate incentive structure) the outcomes desired by society. Given the fact that the rules determine the incentive system that will prevail in markets in the post-constitutional society, members of society can effectively impose the outcomes that they desire through a negotiated design of rules. For example, the problems of agro-ecological degradation and overexploitation of environmental resources can be minimized through the establishment of complete, consistent, and well-enforced property rights regimes.

Given the incentive systems provided by the rules that exist in most African countries today, corruption is an important and inevitable outcome. Using traditional strategies to force a change in this outcome is not likely to succeed as evidenced by nearly 40 years of post-independence efforts to control corruption in the continent. An effective way to control corruption is to undertake institutional reforms that seek to modify the incentive structure and force markets to produce the outcomes desired by society. Thus, African countries seeking to eliminate this important development constraint from their societies should engage in state reconstruction through democratic constitution making to provide themselves with appropriate institutional arrangements, and by implication, incentive structures that minimize corruption and other forms of political opportunism.

DISCUSSION QUESTIONS

1. What is a constitutionally limited government? How important is such a political arrangement to corruption control?
2. What were some of the arguments advanced by African leaders shortly after independence in favor of the one-party political system? Were these legitimate political, social, and economic concerns?
3. Why, according to the author, has corruption become so pervasive in post-independence Africa?

4. Name and discuss ways that indigenous entrepreneurs have dealt with potentially ruinous government regulations in the African economies?

5. Briefly examine the argument that corruption can enhance bureaucratic performance, improve popular participation, and generally advance development in Africa.

6. Name and discuss the four categories of corruption identified in the literature.

7. Distinguish between *political* and *bureaucratic* corruption.

8. What are some benefits of corruption to an incumbent government?

9. What, according to this chapter, are the main causes of corruption in Africa?

10. Briefly examine corruption in Africa from the *public choice perspective*.

11. Examine Osterfeld's two types of corruption.

12. Name the four traditional strategies used to control corruption in Africa. Critique them. Why have these strategies not been successful in reducing levels of corruption in the African economies during the last several years?

13. Why must an effective corruption control system begin with a modification of the incentive structure faced by market participants?

NOTES

[1]See, for example, Mbaku, J.M. (1998) "Improving African Participation in the Global Economy: The Role of Economic Freedom," *Business and the Contemporary World*, 10(2), 297–338; Mbaku, J.M. (2000) *Bureaucratic and Political Corruption in Africa: The Public Choice Perspective*, Malabar, FL: Krieger; Rose-Ackerman, S. (1997) *Corruption and Government: Causes, Consequences, and Reform*, Cambridge, U.K.: Cambridge University Press; Elliott, K.A., Ed. (1997) *Corruption and the Global Economy*, Washington, D.C.: Institute for International Economics; Kligaard, R. (1991) *Controlling Corruption*, Berkeley, CA: University of California Press.

[2]For an-indepth treatment of this issue, see Bardhan, P. (1997) "Corruption and Development: A Review of the Issues," *Journal of Economic Literature*, 35(3), 1320–1346. Also see Kaufmann, D. and Wei, S.-J. (1999) *Does "Grease Money" Speed Up the Wheels of Commerce?*, Policy Research Paper No. 2254, Washington, D.C.: World Bank.

[3]Bardhan, P. (1997) "Corruption and Development: A Review of the Issues," *Journal of Economic Literature*, 35(3), 1329, argues that in many developing countries, including those in Africa, "corruption is perceived to be so pervasive and endemic that it is unlikely to have good net effects..."

[4]Bardhan, P. (1997) "Corruption and Development: A Review of the Issues," *Journal of Economic Literature*, 35(3), 1328.

[5]Alam, M.S. (1989) "Anatomy of Corruption: An Approach to the Political Economy of Underdevelopment," *The American Journal of Economics and Sociology*, 48(4), 442.

[6]Mbaku, J.M. (1992) "Bureaucratic Corruption as Rent-Seeking Behavior," *Konjunturpolitik (Berlin)*, 38(4), 247.

[7]Leff, N.H. (1964) "Economic Development Through Bureaucratic Corruption," *American Behavioral Scientist*, 8(3), 8.

[8]Leff, N.H. (1964) "Economic Development Through Bureaucratic Corruption," *American Behavioral Scientist*, 8(3), 11.

[9]Nye, J.S. (1967) "Corruption and Political Development: A Cost-Benefit Analysis," *American Political Science Review*, 61(2), 419.

[10]Alam, M.S. (1989) "Anatomy of Corruption: An Approach to the Political Economy of Underdevelopment," *The American Journal of Economics and Sociology*, 48(4), 442.

[11]Gould, D.J. and Mukendi, T.B. (1989) "Bureaucratic Corruption in Africa: Causes, Consequences and Remedies," *International Journal of Public Administration*, 13(3), 431.

[12]Mbaku, J.M. (1993) "Markets and the Economic Origins of Apartheid in South Africa," *The Indian Journal of Social Science*, 6(2), 139–158.

[13]Gwartney, J.D. and Wagner, R.E. (1988) "Public Choice and the Conduct of Representative Government," in J.D. Gwartney and R.E. Wagner, Eds., *Public Choice and Constitutional Economics*, Greenwich, CT: JAI Press.

[14]Adebayo, A. (1972) "Formulating Administrative Reform Strategies in Africa," *Quarterly Journal of Administration* (Nigeria), 6, 223–244; Adekson, J.B. (1981) *Nigeria in Search of a Stable Civil–Military System*, Boulder, CO: Westview, pp. 71–72.

[15]World Bank (1979) *Zaire: Current Economic Situation and Constraints*, Washington, D.C.: World Bank.

[16]Jabbra, J.G. (1976) "Bureaucratic Corruption in the Third World: Causes and Remedies," *Indian Journal of Public Administration*, 22, 673–691; Merton, R.K. (1976) *Sociological Ambivalence and Other Essays*, New York: Macmillan.

[17]Fatton, R. Jr. (1989) "The State of African Studies and the Studies of the African State: The Theoretical Softness of the 'Soft State'," *Journal of Asian and African Studies*, 24(3–4), 170–187.

[18]Tullock, G. (1967) "The Welfare Costs of Tariffs, Monopolies and Theft," *Western Economic Journal*, 5(3), 224–232. For an early effort to explain corruption in Africa from a public choice perspective, see Mbaku, J.M. (1992) "Bureaucratic Corruption as Rent-Seeking Behavior," *Konjunturpolitik* (Berlin), 38(4), 247–265.

[19]De Lusignan, G. (1969) *French Speaking Africa Since Independence*, London: Pall Mall; LeVine, V.T. (1997) "The Fall and Rise of Constitutionalism in West Africa," *The Journal of Modern African Studies*, 35(2), 181–206.

[20]Bates, R.H. (1994) "The Impulse to Reform in Africa," in J. A. Wildner, Ed., *Economic Change and Political Liberalization in Sub-Saharan Africa*, Baltimore, MD: The Johns Hopkins University Press.

[21]Mbaku, J.M. (1997) *Institutions and Reform in Africa: The Public Choice Perspective*, Westport, CT: Praeger.

[22]See Mbaku, J.M. (1997) *Institutions and Reform in Africa: The Public Choice Perspective*, Westport, CT: Praeger, for a review of the literature.

[23]See, for example, Decalo, S. (1992) "The Process, Prospects and Constraints of Democratization in Africa," *African Affairs*, 9(362), 7–35; Nyerere, J. (1966) *Freedom and Unity*, Dar-es-Salaam: Oxford University Press.

[24]See, for example, Bates, R.H. (1981) *Markets and States in Tropical Africa*, Berkeley, CA: University of California.

[25]LeVine, V.T. (1975) *Political Corruption: The Ghanaian Case*, Stanford, CA: Hoover Institution; Jua, N. (1998) "Cameroon: Jump-starting an Economic Crisis," in J.M. Mbaku, Ed., *Corruption and the Crisis of Institutional Reforms in Africa*, Lewiston, NY: The Edwin Mellen Press. Hope, K.R., Sr. and Chikulo, B.C., Eds. (2000) *Corruption and Development in Africa: Lessons from Country Case Studies*, London: Macmillan; Gould, D.J. (1980) *Bureaucratic Corruption and Underdevelopment in the Third World: The Case of Zaire*, New York: Pergamon Press; Madunagu, E. (1983) *Nigeria: The Economy and the People*, London: New Beacon Books.

[26]See Nye, J.S. (1967) "Corruption and Political Development: A Cost–Benefit Analysis," *The American Political Science Review*, 61(2), 417–427; Leff, N.H. (1964) "Economic Development Through

Bureaucratic Corruption," *American Behavioral Scientist*, 8(3), 8–14; Bayley, D.H. (1996) "The Effects of Corruption in a Developing Nation," *The Western Political Quarterly*, 19(4), 719–732.

[27]See, e.g., Jua (1998), in Note 25; Gould, D.J. (1980) *Bureaucratic Corruption and Underdevelopment in the Third World: The Case of Zaire*, New York: Pergamon Press; LeVine, V.T. (1975) *Political Corruption: The Ghanaian Case*, Stanford, CA: Hoover Institution; Hope, K.R., Sr. and Chikulo, B.C., Eds. (2000) *Corruption and Development in Africa: Lessons from Country Case Studies*, London: Macmillan; Madunagu, E. (1983) *Nigeria: The Economy and the People*, London: New Beacon Books.

[28]LeVine, V.T. (1975) *Political Corruption: The Ghanaian Case*, Stanford, CA: Hover Institution.

[29]See, for example, Madunagu, E. (1983) *Nigeria: The Economy and the People*, London: New Beacon Books; Ihonvbere, J.O. and Ekekwe, E. (1988) "Dependent Capitalism, Structural Adjustment and Democratic Possibilities in Nigeria's Third Republic," *Afrika Spectrum*, 23, 273–291.

[30]World Bank (1998) *African Development Indicators, 1998/99*, Washington, D.C.: World Bank.

[31]See, for example, Mbaku, J.M. (1994) "Military Coups as Rent-Seeking Behavior," *Journal of Political and Military Sociology*, 22, 241–284; UNDP (1990) *Human Development Report 1990*, New York: Oxford University Press; UNDP (1995) *Human Development Report 1995*, New York: Oxford University Press.

[32]Osterfeld, D. (1992) *Prosperity Versus Planning: How Government Stifles Economic Growth*, New York: Oxford University Press, pp. 204–218.

[33]Szeftel, M. (1983) "Corruption and the Spoils System in Zambia," in M. Clarke, Ed., *Corruption: Causes, Consequences and Control*, New York: St. Martin's Press.

[34]McMullan, M. (1961) "A Theory of Corruption," *Sociological Review*, 9(6), 21–47.

[35]Gillespie, K. and Okruhlik, G. (1991) "The Political Dimensions of Corruption Cleanups: A Framework for Analysis," *Comparative Politics*, 24(1), 80.

[36]See, for example, Bardhan, P. (1997) "Corruption and Development: A Review of the Issues," *Journal of Economic Literature*, 35(3), 1330. Also see Buchanan, J.M. (1991) *Constitutional Economics*, Oxford: Basil Blackwell.

[37]See Mbaku, J.M. (1997) *Institutions and Reform in Africa: The Public Choice Perspective*, Westport, CT: Praeger, for a review of the literature.

[38]Brennan, G. and Buchanan, J.M. (1985) *The Reason of Rules: Constitutional Political Economy*, Cambridge, U.K.: Cambridge University Press.

[39]North, D.C. (1990) *Institutions, Institutional Change and Economic Performance*, Cambridge, U.K.: Cambridge University Press.

[40]Ostrom, E., Schroeder, L., and Wynne, S. (1993) *Institutional Incentives and Sustainable Development: Infrastructure Policies in Perspective*, Boulder, CO: Westview.

[41]Hanna, S., Folke, C., and Mäler, K.-G. (1995) "Property Rights and Environmental Resources," in S. Hanna and M. Munasinghe, Eds., *Property Rights and the Environment: Social and Ecological Issues*, Washington, D.C.: World Bank, p. 15.

[42]Hanna, S., Folke, C., and Mäler, K.-G. (1995) "Property Rights and Environmental Resources," in S. Hanna and M. Munasinghe, Eds., *Property Rights and the Environment: Social and Ecological Issues*, Washington, D.C.: World Bank, p. 15.

[43]Hanna, S., Folke, C., and Mäler, K.-G. (1995) "Property Rights and Environmental Resources," in S. Hanna and M. Munasinghe, Eds., *Property Rights and the Environment: Social and Ecological Issues*, Washington, D.C.: World Bank, p. 17.

[44]Gwartney, J.D. and Wagner, R.E. (1988) "Public Choice and the Conduct of Representative Government," in J.D. Gwartney and R.E. Wagner, Eds., *Public Choice and Constitutional Economics*, Greenwich, CT: JAI Press. It must be noted that a few countries (e.g., Botswana, Mauritius, and South Africa) do have relatively viable judiciary systems. In these countries, the judiciary, like other institutions, is well constrained by the national constitution, and as a consequence performs its duties with a significant level of efficiency.

[45]See, for example, Anderson, T.L. and Hill, P.J. (1986) "Constraining the Transfer Society: Constitutional and Moral Dimensions," *Cato Journal*, 6(1), 317–339.

[46]Gwartney, J.D., Lawson, R., and Block, W., Eds. (1996) *Economic Freedom of the World: 1975–1995*, Vancouver: The Fraser Institute.

[47]Wiseman, J. (1990) "Principles of Political Economy: An Outline Proposal, Illustrated by Application to Fiscal Federalism," *Constitutional Political Economy*, 2(1), 121–122.

[48]Wildavsky, A. (1990) "A Double Security: Federalism as Competition," *Cato Journal*, 10, 39–58; Mbaku, J.M. (1997) *Institutions and Reform in Africa: The Public Choice Perspective*, Westport, CT: Praeger; Mbaku, J.M. (1998) "Constitutional Engineering and the Transition to Democracy in Post-Cold War Africa," *The Independent Review*, 2(4), 501–517.

[49]Anderson, T.L. and Hill, P.J. (1986) "Constraining the Transfer Society: Constitutional and Moral Dimensions," *Cato Journal*, 6, 317–339; Congleton, R.D. (1994) "Constitutional Federalism and Decentralization: A Second Best Solution," *Economia Delle Scelte Pubbliche (Italy)*, 11(1), 15–29.

[50]Congleton, R.D. (1994) "Constitutional Federalism and Decentralization: A Second Best Solution," *Economia Delle Scelte Pubbliche (Italy)*, 11(1), 15–29.

[51]Congleton, R.D. (1994) "Constitutional Federalism and Decentralization: A Second Best Solution," *Economia Delle Scelte Pubbliche (Italy)*, 11(1), 15–29.

[52]Congleton, R.D. (1994) "Constitutional Federalism and Decentralization: A Second Best Solution," *Economia Delle Scelte Pubbliche (Italy)*, 11(1), 18.

[53]Wicksell, K. (1967) "A New Principle of Just Taxation [originally published in 1896]," in R.A. Musgrave and A. T. Peacock, Eds., *Classics in the Theory of Public Finance*, New York: St. Martin's Press.

[54]Gwartney, J.D. and Wagner, R.E. (1988) "Public Choice and the Conduct of Representative Government," in J.D. Gwartney and R.E. Wagner, Eds., *Public Choice and Constitutional Economics*, Greenwich, CT: JAI Press.

[55]Brett, E.A. (1995) "Institutional Theory and Social Change in Uganda," in J. Harriss, J. Hunter, and C.M. Lewis, Eds. (1995) *The New Institutional Economics and Third World Development*, London: Routledge, p. 203.

[56]Brett, E.A. (1995) "Institutional Theory and Social Change in Uganda," in J. Harriss, J. Hunter, and C.M. Lewis, Eds. (1995) *The New Institutional Economics and Third World Development*, London: Routledge, p. 204.

PART IV

Sector Analyses

Land Tenure, Agriculture, and Economic Development

Nii O. Tackie, Arthur Siaway, and Ntam Baharanyi

Department of Agriculture Sciences, Tuskegee University, Tuskegee, Alabama 36088

KEY TERMS

Agricultural development	Exchange rate
Agricultural growth	Foreign exchange
Agricultural productivity	Gross domestic product (GDP)
Communal land tenure	Land tenure
Debt servicing	Land tenure reform
Economic development	

I. INTRODUCTION

Economic development cannot occur in a vacuum. Certain things, such as sustained economic growth, good physical infrastructure, efficient land tenure system, good public management system, good education system, and good health system, must exist as economic development occurs. To pursue a discussion on land tenure, agriculture, and economic development in Africa, the issues and factors that impact them need to be reasonably addressed. The discussion in this chapter is an attempt to pinpoint the key issues and suggest approaches that can help improve or solve these issues.

II. LAND TENURE AND ECONOMIC DEVELOPMENT

Land tenure is a very important agrarian issue in many African countries. It is likely that the land tenure systems must undergo some changes if agricultural growth and improvement in the lives of the people are to occur. Land tenure is

African Economic Development

a set of rights that determines who owns land and therefore has rights to use land and how it will be used. In general, land tenure is based both on customary and statutory law. In Africa, land tenure has ramifications in such areas as marriage, inheritance, sale, mortgage, size of farming operation, water, pasture use, and tenancy. Of extreme importance also is that land tenure directs access to productive resources on land, influences income and employment opportunities in rural areas, and impacts wealth and status in the community.[1] Because land tenure gives individuals or groups control of and/or access to the use of land, it is appropriate to distinguish between *control* and *access*. Control of land is the command an individual has over land and is based on possession or ownership; access to land means a person is able to make use of the land without necessarily owning the land. A sharecropper has access but a land-owner has both control and access.[2]

Land tenure systems in Africa usually fall into three major categories: communal, private or freehold, and state. Communal ownership is the most common form of land tenure in Africa. Under this system, land is collectively owned by the community, tribe, clan, or family. Any member of this group who needs a piece of land to farm seeks permission from the group head and uses only available land. Strangers use the land under specific arrangements. With the communal system, land is sometimes passed on to succeeding generations within a particular family. This occurs when the patriarch has been farming the piece of land for years. Passing of land from one generation to the next usually involves inheritance, where men of one generation transfer land to men of the next generation. This transfer of land may be done while the male parent or head is alive, in which case the adult son gets a piece of household land when he marries. If the head of the family dies, the household land is divided among sons or male heirs. (Daughters or females usually do not inherit land, an issue that will be addressed later in the chapter.) In Ghana, for example, types of land acquisition for farming under the communal land tenure system include family, gifts, first till (farming a tract of unused communal land on a first-come, first-served basis), sharecropping, rent, and purchase. Private or freehold ownership is when the individual owns the land and has the right to farm whatever he or she wants to farm on the land within the confines of regulations in the area. Under state ownership, government acquires land through legislation or other means in the "interest" of the state.[3]

Bruce mentions eight issues related to communal land tenure systems in Africa: land use and conservation; security of tenure and investment; exclusivity of tenure and farm management; efficiency in resource allocation; land-secured credit; fragmentation and subdivision of holdings; the tenure needs of women farmers; and person/land ratios, population mobility, and citizenship. These are briefly discussed below, except gender and land tenure, a topic discussed in more detail later because of the importance of the subject.[4]

A. Land Use and Conservation

Shifting cultivation, a once common farming practice in Africa, is losing ground due to population pressure. As a result of this change in land use, farmers have had to use their farm land more often and in so doing quickly degrade the land in terms of fertility. Technologies to improve land fertility will have to be adopted along with changes in land use. An example of such technology is agroforestry where trees and food crops are grown on the same land. In this case, the farmer derives the usual benefits of the food crop and, at the same time, conserves soil fertility, in addition to gaining a new source of cash income as old trees are harvested and sold.

B. Security of Tenure and Investment

Farmers will be more inclined to make long-term investments in land if they believe the land is secure. Generally, in Africa, security of tenure is short; therefore, farmers make less long-term investments on the land they farm. Insecurity of tenure may result from abuse of power by traditional land administrators, ineffectiveness of traditional leaders in enforcing land tenure rules, competition between ethnic groups, inappropriate land acquisition by new powerful elite, seizure of land by the government without compensation, and granting of concessions by the government without due regard to prevailing laws.

C. Exclusivity of Tenure and Farm Management

The traditional farmer may lack the power to make management decisions about his farm due to the nature of communal land tenure rules. An example of such a situation may be if rules require a farmer to allow community cattle to graze on the farm after harvest. The farmer cannot fence off the land or grow trees that may tie up the land for a long time. Such rules and regulations discourage farmer innovation.

D. Efficiency in Resource Allocation

The criticism that land allocation in Africa is not efficient is unfounded. Indigenous mechanisms are in place that allow unused land to be made available to farmers who want to use it. In fact, in Africa, individuals who have the necessary finances to buy land may not be interested in farming but instead may prefer to invest in other sectors. Thus, these individuals direct their skills and capital to these other sectors. In addition, the liquidity of assets is of little importance to a farmer who lacks the necessary assets to invest outside the agricultural sector. Apart from indigenous allocation mechanisms, the market and state are other forces affecting land allocation, though to a limited extent. Which of these allocating forces may become the dominant allocation force in the future is yet to be seen.

E. Land-Secured Credit

Bankers are generally reluctant to give credit to farmers because they lack security of tenure. This is not the only issue, but there is also the issue of creditworthiness. Most traditional farmers do not have good credit, as bankers view it, so these farmers have a difficult time obtaining loans. Legislation that makes land mortgagable or allows banks to give credit to farmers may be a step in the right direction. However, in addition, other conditions, such as the existence of rural land markets, attractive lending terms for farmers, agriculture support services, appropriate prices for recovery of investment cost, and modalities on foreclosure, must be in place to make the access to credit worthwhile.

F. Fragmentation and Subdivision of Holdings

Fragmentation and subdivision are common land tenure practices. Fragmentation entails holding different parcels of land at the same time. This may affect the productivity of a resource-low farmer because he will have to move from parcel to parcel to work with his fewer resources. If the parcels of land are wide distances apart, then he faces a real production problem. At the same time, though, this practice could serve as a risk-management tool that allows farmer access to different types of soils. Subdivision involves dividing a parcel of land into several pieces. In this case, there comes a time when further subdivision seriously affects productivity. A way around this is to allow several individuals to own a piece, or perhaps to ask for more land from the community head. Usually, fragmentation and subdivision stem from inheritance laws.

G. Person/Land Ratios, Population Mobility, and Citizenship

Land tenure rules may prevent people from moving from places of low quantities of land to places of high quantities of land. However, in certain areas of Africa (e.g., The Gambia), "strangers" have been absorbed into abundant landowning communities with little problem. It all depends on factors prevailing in a particular area.

H. Gender and Land Tenure

In most of Africa, men control the land. Women have access to the land through their husbands or male relatives. In case of death of a husband or divorce, women lose tenure rights and have to reclaim them through male sons or male relatives. It stands to reason, then, that security of tenure is even worse for women than men.[5]

There is also the issue of customary versus contemporary civil law (official law) in Africa. Most of the countries have laws on the books indicating men and women have equal rights to land. To complicate matters, these countries recognize both customary law and official law. Because both types of laws are recognized, women lose out on two fronts. First, most women marry under customary law so, in cases of land complaints or litigation, most go to local land administrators. These administrators use customary laws in their judgments which, of course, favor men. Second, when women do go to the regular courts and customary law and official law are in conflict, the courts usually rule using customary law. A typical case is demonstrated in Niger, where a Dogo man passed away. His widowed wife and three daughters could not claim his land, though the official law said they could. The deceased man's male heir used an old customary law which was also recognized by the state to win the ensuing litigation.

In addition, there is the issue of land transfer. The most common type of land transfer is through inheritance from one male relative to another, whether in patrilineal or matrilineal societies. Other forms of land transfer of less importance are borrowing, gifts, leasing, and sale. Indeed, for several reasons, such as commercialization, migration, population pressure, restructuring programs, urbanization, and HIV/AIDS, the communal land tenure system in some countries seems to be slowly disintegrating, thus making it more likely that the family and community will neglect their role of providing land use rights for their citizens. In such an atmosphere, women more than men will lose out if care is not taken.[6]

I. Other Land Tenure Issues

The communal land tenure system in Africa has been blamed by some scholars for the lack of agricultural development in the region. It has been argued that innovative farmers are prevented from having unfettered access to communal land. This may not be helpful as these farmers are more able to adjust to the continuous change of agriculture than other farmers and thereby have a greater impact on agricultural productivity. Also, because most farmers do not own land (i.e., lack security of tenure) they are reluctant to significantly improve farm land. Added to this, lenders are hesitant to give credit to such farmers because these farmers really cannot use the land as collateral.

Furthermore, it is argued, communal ownership lacks flexibility. The reason is that land is seen as an immobile commodity by innovative farmers and is nonmarketable to strangers; therefore, forward-looking innovative farmers cannot consolidate fragmented land or obtain larger tracts of land, and strangers cannot get more land for increasing agricultural production.[7] Gyasi seemed to agree with the foregoing assessment when he wrote:[8]

> Constraints on development have been associated with lack of clarity about the land allocating authorities and about boundaries; disputes; trespassing; inequitable tenancies; capitalist exploitation; lack of security for peasants, especially tenants as well as stranger or alien farmers; inability to use the community owned land as collateral for a bank loan; and customary system of inheritance, which, in certain cases, excludes females, and entails subdivisions among succeeding generations with consequential fragmentation of holdings.

Some form of land tenure reform in Africa may be necessary for agricultural development and therefore economic development in the broader sense. The premise of linking land tenure to economic development stems from the fact that many African countries depend on agriculture as the main foreign exchange earner and contributor to the gross domestic product (GDP). Most of the people, especially the rural population, are employed in agriculture. The rural people operate in land tenure systems that probably are not conducive to agricultural efficiency and growth. Therefore, if guarded land tenure reforms are put in place agricultural productivity may perhaps increase, and it is hoped that incomes will also increase, especially for those farming and in rural areas. Also, revenues for the central government could increase, and expected economic development in the form of reductions in poverty, unemployment, and inequality; improvements in education and health care; improvements in the physical infrastructure; and desired changes in institutions might possibly occur.

III. LAND TENURE REFORM

Land tenure reform may entail, among other things, dividing a large plot of land among the poor, nationalizing agricultural land and creating state-owned farms, making tenant farmers owners of the land on which they farm, preventing creditors from taking land from poor indebted farmers (though such reform undermines the purpose of using land for collateral), or consolidating small parcels of land into larger parcels. The first four reforms deal with redistribution of wealth and the last deals with economy of scale and productivity concerns.[9] The basic idea behind land tenure reforms is the concern that the existing system may be so inefficient that it is necessary to improve the allocation of land in order to enhance agricultural productivity.[10]

From a theoretical perspective, Lambert and Seligson present five land tenure reform mechanisms that can be implemented: redistributive land tenure reform, land titling and registration, land market interventions, land taxation, and land settlement schemes. The economic reasoning behind redistributive land tenure reform is the negative relationship between farm size and land productivity. On the contrary, the economic reasoning behind the remaining mechanisms is tenure security.[11] Tenure security reduces land litigation, influences efficient credit allocation of and investment in land, and encourages farmers who gain higher returns from land use to acquire more farm land for production, ultimately leading to increased productivity.[12]

In Africa, most land tenure reforms are intended to improve agricultural productivity by facilitating tenure security. The governments believe that enhancing property rights is closely linked to positive socio-economic change in society. Most have passed legislation on land transactions and property rights. In doing so, the governments declared their main goal is to facilitate economic development of their countries. Examples of countries where reform has taken place are Kenya, Ghana, Nigeria, and Zambia. In Kenya, the Swynnerton Plan of 1954 was developed for land tenure reform and ultimately to promote agricultural reform and development. However, another motive of the government of the day was to achieve political tranquility. In Ghana, Nigeria, and Zambia governments nationalized some lands in the mid-1970s, claiming economic development as motive.[13]

Land titling in Africa has been criticized for moving rights away from the group and toward an individual—the family head, a man. Women, it is argued, often lose out when land titling and registration are instituted. At the same time, however, land titling and registration offer women opportunities to buy land in the long term. Wholesale land tenure reform may not be ideal, but specific changes in land tenure rules may help agricultural productivity and development. Examples of such changes may include inheritance reform, which is a community property regime for marriage, and credit programs that would facilitate women purchasing land. In fact, Basset argues that calls for sweeping tenure changes are ill-conceived. Furthermore, he states that the notion that tenure reform is the solution to Africa's agrarian problems is not a new idea, but one that ignores critical social dynamics that strongly influence how productive resources are acquired, utilized, contested, and immobilized. Those advocating overhauling the entire communal land tenure system to make it freehold are probably not aware of the flexibility of the land tenure system in Africa.[14]

IV. EFFECTIVENESS OF LAND TENURE REFORM

The effect of land tenure reform on land-use patterns, control, and credit and investment in Africa has been quite minimal. Land tenure reform improves tenure security to some extent but does not necessarily increase agricultural productivity. The reason is that reform takes place without significant change in existing technology, among other things, leaving productivity growth virtually untouched. Land tenure reform, especially titling and registration, should be implemented as a way of enhancing tenure change spontaneously occurring.[15] Sanders and others advanced a similar argument:[16]

> If there were evidence that the indigenous land tenure systems were in fact constraining the adoption of new agricultural technologies, then there would be a need for large-scale, expensive [land tenure reform programs]. Yet, with few exceptions, land rights are not found to be a significant factor in determining investments, use of inputs, access to credit, or the productivity of land.

Furthermore, a study by Place and Migot-Adholla in Kenya found that land registration and titling had a weak impact on land rights of farmers, credit use and terms, crop yields, or concentration of land holdings. In fact, land titles were obtained for securing ownership of land and not for increasing agricultural output. Also, Basset makes similar observations for land titling and notes that even when credit was available for agriculture after land titling, recipients funneled money into off-farm investments such as children's education, charcoal production, and land speculation.[17]

In light of this, both the Global Coalition for Africa and Place and Migot-Adholla suggest that governments should institute land tenure reforms in Africa only if necessary, because the effort could be better put elsewhere, such as improving the infrastructure and market opportunities for farmers. Barrows and Roth warn that African policymakers should not be fooled into thinking that embarking on land tenure reform programs will automatically result in massive investments in agriculture and subsequent increases in productivity, thereby ultimately resulting in desired economic development.[18] In other words, broad-based land tenure reform may not be necessary for raising agricultural productivity in Africa. The question is, then, how can agricultural productivity in Africa be increased?

V. INVESTING IN AGRICULTURE TO INCREASE ITS PRODUCTIVITY

Agriculture contributes a high share (40–50%) to the GDP in many African countries; therefore, agriculture's role in economic growth and development in Africa is very important. The rural economies are also important participants in economic growth and development, as most people involved in agriculture live in rural areas.[19] There are many challenges and opportunities in agricultural production, marketing, and international trade. This section deals with the role of agriculture in economic development, selected indicators for African agriculture, and aspects of common problems and opportunities in African countries and suggests pragmatic approaches to increasing the contributions of agriculture to economic development. A brief mention is made also of the problem of political instability and its relationship to investment in agriculture.

The key roles of the agricultural sector are (1) provide food and agricultural products, (2) create employment for a large segment of the population, and (3) create income and savings that can be invested to facilitate economic development. The sector also makes other significant contributions to national economic growth such as creating demands for consumption goods and services. This implies that agricultural development can help economic development in countries that have a large agricultural base. Agricultural development is an improvement in aspects of agriculture resulting in sustained increase in overall agricultural productivity. Agricultural development means change, the altering of equilibria. The basic challenge of development is to deal continuously with shifting disequilibria in agriculture. The tenets in the process are improvements in technology, strengthening of institutions, human capital development, and investment in research.[20]

Agriculture has a primary role to play in any structural transformation of African economies because of its size. The large number of people employed in agriculture and its great potential to create savings that can be invested in nonagricultural sectors of the economy are a good reason to focus on this sector as a propeller to economic development in the region. A change in technology that increases output in the agricultural sector can substantially increase national income and hence hasten economic transformation and investment in other potentially faster-growing sectors. On the contrary, if the change in technology begins in the smaller nonagricultural sector, then it will have to take place at a higher rate than in the agricultural sector to achieve a similar effect on national income, mainly because agriculture is the largest sector in many of the countries of Africa. In addition, the diversity of the nonagricultural sector makes it quite difficult to achieve as uniform a change in technology in this sector than can occur in agriculture.[21]

Stevens and Jabara summarize the interactions between the agricultural and nonagricultural sectors as follows:[22]

1. *Contributions of agriculture to other sectors*
    1. Production of food and other agricultural products for urban domestic use and for export
    2. Supply of additional labor to nonagricultural sectors
    3. Net outflow of capital for investment in other sectors

4. Consumer demand in the agricultural sector for the goods and services produced in other sectors
2. Contributions of other sectors to agriculture
   1. Industrial production of improved farm inputs and capital equipment
   2. Demand for food and other agricultural products due to increased income and the shift of a greater proportion of the labor force to the nonagricultural sector
   3. Provision of needed infrastructure such as roads, transportation equipment, communication, education, and health

VI. SELECTED INDICATORS OF AFRICAN AGRICULTURE

Total agricultural area, arable land, arable land as a percent of agricultural area, irrigation agricultural area, and percent agricultural area irrigated from 1970–1999 are shown in Table 15.1. Agricultural area averaged a little over 1 billion hectares, ranging from 961 million to about 1.1 billion. Arable land ranged from 149 million to 178 million hectares. Arable land as a percent of agricultural area never exceeded 16% or one-sixth, over the three decades. Irrigation agricultural area increased slightly over the years, but in terms of percent of agricultural area it was very low, ranging from 0.8–1.1%.

Cereal production, meat production, growth of cereal production, growth of meat production, per capita cereal production, per capita meat production, index of per capita agriculture production, and index of per capita food production for three decades, 1970 to 1999, are shown in Table 15.2. The highest cereal production value was 125 million metric tons in 1996, and the lowest was 57 million metric tons in 1973. The highest and lowest values for meat were about 10 million metric tons in 1999 and 5 million metric tons in 1970. There was no discernable growth in cereal production from year to year, but the average annual growth rate (not shown in the table) in the 1970s was 1.4%; in the 1980s, 4.7%; and in the 1990s, 2.1%. Meat production never showed a negative growth in any year. Its average annual growth rates were 2.8% in the 1970s, 2.7% in the 1980s, and 2.3% in the 1990s. Per capita cereal production ranged from 126 kg in 1984 to 180 kg in 1974, whereas per capita meat production was approximately 14 kg for the entire period. In the 1970s, both indexes of per capita agriculture and food production were high, but a steady decline was observed into the early 1980s, when the production indexes fell to their lowest levels. After that there was a rising trend into the 1990s. Over the entire period, though, both agriculture and food production declined. The production in the 1990s was not as high as the 1970s.

TABLE 15.1   Selected Land Indicators

Year	Agricultural Area (1000 ha)	Arable Land (1000 ha)	Arable Land of Agricultural Area[a](%)	Irrigation Agricultural Area (1000 ha)	Agricultural Area Irrigated[a] (%)
1970	960,996	149,103	15.5	8,483	0.9
1971	1,062,992	150,907	14.2	8,609	0.8
1972	1,063,108	150,928	14.2	8,609	0.8
1973	1,062,638	151,210	14.2	8,809	0.8
1974	1,064,028	152,121	14.3	8,913	0.8
1975	1,065,270	153,415	14.4	9,010	0.8
1976	1,066,955	155,138	14.5	9,067	0.8
1977	1,068,370	155,981	14.6	9,123	0.9
1978	1,069,591	156,584	14.6	9,289	0.9
1979	1,070,439	157,076	14.7	9,324	0.9
1980	1,072,787	158,212	14.7	9,491	0.9
1981	1,068,672	158,858	14.9	9,631	0.9
1982	1,069,695	159,620	14.9	9,726	0.9
1983	1,071,497	160,297	15.0	9,917	0.9
1984	1,073,261	161,876	15.1	10,222	1.0
1985	1,075,828	162,836	15.1	10,331	1.0
1986	1,079,939	163,939	15.2	10,585	1.0
1987	1,083,188	165,019	15.2	10,660	1.0
1988	1,088,022	166,318	15.3	10,817	1.0
1989	1,091,735	168,149	15.4	10,986	1.0
1990	1,094,793	168,442	15.4	11,235	1.0
1991	1,096,119	169,575	15.5	11,350	1.0
1992	1,098,674	171,157	15.6	11,822	1.1
1993	1,083,618	173,658	16.0	12,318	1.1
1994	1,085,992	173,824	16.0	12,347	1.1
1995	1,089,456	176,578	16.2	12,380	1.1
1996	1,090,563	177,248	16.3	12,451	1.1
1997	1,091,001	177,720	16.3	12,458	1.1
1998	1,094,040	177,686	16.2	12,520	1.1
1999	1,093,605	177,251	16.2	12,538	1.1

[a]Values computed by authors.
Note: Data derived from FAO.

Table 15.3 shows agricultural exports, agricultural imports, growth rates for agricultural exports, growth rates for agricultural imports, and net agricultural exports. Overall, the values show both agricultural exports and imports have been increasing. Average annual growth rates (not shown in the table) for agricultural exports for the 1970s, 1980s, and 1990s were 11.2%, −0.3%, and 2.2%, respectively. Corresponding values for agricultural imports were 21.3%, 4.3%, and 1.8%. Net agricultural exports were positive for the 1970s, but negative for both the 1980s and 1990s. Over the latter decades, Africa imported more agricultural products than it exported. The highest net agricultural exports value over the period was almost $4 billion in 1973 and the lowest value was a deficit

TABLE 15.2   Selected Production Indicators

Year	Total Cereal Production (Mt)	Total Meat Production (Mt)	Cereal Production Growth Rate[a] (%)	Meat Production Growth Rate[a] (%)	Per Capita Cereal Production[a] (kg)	Per Capita Meat Production[a] (kg)	Agriculture PIN[b] per Capita (1989–1991)	Food PIN per Capita (1989–1991)
1970	60,507,494	5,006,229	—	—	169	14	113.5	110.4
1971	65,686,694	5,067,734	8.5	1.2	179	14	113.7	111.3
1972	64,676,457	5,231,266	−1.5	3.2	172	15	109.8	107.2
1973	57,542,493	5,306,587	−11.0	1.4	149	14	105.9	103.3
1974	71,313,556	5,324,114	23.9	0.3	180	14	111.2	109.3
1975	68,854,791	5,395,358	−3.4	1.3	170	13	108.4	106.7
1976	70,664,658	5,647,547	2.6	4.7	169	14	105.8	104.7
1977	66,398,082	5,905,334	−6.0	4.6	155	14	102.6	101.3
1978	69,516,489	6,222,506	4.7	5.4	158	14	102.5	101.5
1979	65,784,110	6,412,107	−5.4	3.0	145	14	100.0	99.0
1980	72,602,167	6,599,095	10.4	2.9	156	14	99.9	98.9
1981	77,560,558	6,701,079	6.8	1.5	162	14	100.0	99.4
1982	71,828,726	6,933,246	−7.4	3.5	146	14	97.4	96.7
1983	65,587,910	7,181,297	−8.7	3.6	129	14	94.4	93.6
1984	65,837,744	7,409,129	0.4	3.1	126	14	92.3	91.4
1985	83,058,439	7,555,715	26.2	2.0	155	14	96.8	96.0
1986	88,168,244	7,632,382	6.2	1.0	160	14	98.4	97.8
1987	83,455,450	7,833,200	−5.3	2.6	147	14	96.1	95.7
1988	95,187,163	8,048,478	14.1	2.7	163	14	98.9	98.6
1989	98,969,923	8,335,541	4.0	3.6	165	14	99.7	99.6
1990	92,762,230	8,587,841	−6.3	3.0	151	14	98.0	98.0
1991	104,533,854	8,812,085	12.7	2.6	166	14	102.3	102.4
1992	88,922,460	8,952,605	−14.9	1.6	137	14	97.2	97.6
1993	99,817,365	8,977,268	12.3	0.3	150	14	98.2	98.7
1994	110,810,953	9,027,389	11.0	0.6	163	13	98.2	99.1
1995	97,671,027	9,348,983	−11.9	3.6	140	13	97.3	97.8
1996	124,667,322	9,617,919	27.6	2.9	175	14	104.9	105.4
1997	110,639,581	10,051,086	−11.3	4.5	151	14	101.2	101.4
1998	115,752,733	10,272,757	4.6	2.2	154	14	102.1	102.6
1999	11,921,895	10,441,535	−3.3	1.6	146	14	101.7	102.4

[a]Values computed by authors.
[b]PIN = production index.
Note: Data derived from FAO.

of about $7 billion in 1992. Average net agricultural exports (not shown in the table) for the three periods were $2.8 billion for the 1970s, −$3.2 billion for the 1980s, and −$4.7 billion for the 1990s.

VII. THE NATURE OF THE AGRICULTURAL SECTOR

The basic structure of Africa's agriculture is dichotomous, consisting mainly of two sectors: (1) a domestic food sector, and (2) an export sector involving the

TABLE 15.3   Selected Agricultural Trade Indicators

Year	Agricultural Product Value, Exports ($1000)	Agricultural Product Value, Imports ($1000)	Agricultural Product Exports, Growth Rate[a] (%)	Agricultural Product Imports, Growth Rate[a] (%)	Net Agricultural Exports[a] ($1000)
1970	5,476,118	2,288,322	—	—	3,187,796
1971	5,361,363	2,656,808	−2.1	16.1	2,704,555
1972	6,249,060	2,885,304	16.6	8.6	3,363,756
1973	7,919,955	3,997,146	26.7	38.5	3,922,809
1974	9,905,994	6,739,381	25.1	68.6	3,166,613
1975	9,457,180	8,073,207	−4.5	19.8	1,383,973
1976	10,425,915	7,377,325	10.2	−8.6	3,048,590
1977	12,801,356	9,115,662	22.8	23.6	3,685,694
1978	12,561,322	10,812,170	−1.9	18.6	1,749,152
1979	13,513,842	11,515,453	7.6	6.5	1,998,389
1980	14,265,218	15,181,745	5.6	31.8	−916,527
1981	12,620,303	17,813,017	−11.5	17.3	−5,192,714
1982	11,343,547	15,492,657	−10.1	13.0	−4,149,110
1983	10,368,815	15,155,019	−8.6	−2.2	−4,836,204
1984	11,476,619	15,760,667	10.7	4.0	−4,284,048
1985	10,819,740	15,019,158	−5.7	−4.7	−4,199,418
1986	12,640,047	13,760,460	16.8	−8.4	−1,120,413
1987	12,083,920	13,023,164	−4.4	−5.4	−939,244
1988	11,946,088	14,654,847	−1.1	12.5	−2,708,759
1989	12,566,867	16,261,658	5.2	11.0	−3,694,791
1990	12,239,270	15,967,546	−2.6	−1.8	−3,728,276
1991	11,473,831	15,088,406	−6.2	−5.5	−3,614,575
1992	11,021,875	18,049,499	−3.9	19.6	−7,027,624
1993	10,796,678	16,681,629	−2.0	−7.6	−5,884,951
1994	13,367,516	18,251,099	23.8	9.4	−4,883,583
1995	15,202,947	21,439,555	13.7	17.5	−6,236,608
1996	16,515,675	20,566,842	8.6	−4.1	−4,051,167
1997	16,027,609	20,272,315	−3.0	−1.4	−4,244,706
1998	16,817,078	20,592,633	4.9	1.6	−3,775,555
1999	14,885,432	18,641,049	−11.5	−9.5	−3,755,617

[a]Values computed by authors.
Note: Data derived from FAO.

production of cash crops, most of which are not locally consumed. The demand for outputs from the two sectors are different. The key link between the two sectors is the shared labor both sectors depend on for production of outputs. The perceived lack of opportunities in agriculture has resulted in rural-to-urban migration by the younger generation. Many of the producers are older and illiterate and have limited resources. Sometimes younger adults who do not migrate to urban areas do not want to participate in agriculture, which creates a labor problem, especially in the peak of the growing season.

The new technologies from national and international research do not quickly reach the domestic sector mostly because effective extension systems are lacking. The market for products from the domestic food sector operates differently because usually there are few or no incentives such as price support and other forms of subsidies, which are popular in the export sector to producers. High food prices that serve as incentives for farmers are often the cause of political unrest led by vocal urban consumers. The political unrest almost always causes governments to back down on price hikes. Therefore, while the national political rhetoric usually tends to support high prices for food for producers, resource allocation to provide support for implementation of such policies is lacking. This phenomenon is known as the "food price dilemma." The low food price is an implicit tax on farmers and a subsidy for urban consumers. Also, this low food price has a negative influence on growth in output and ultimately can cause a decline in rural employment.[23] Coupled with this situation are the weak services such as marketing, credit, feeder road networks, processing plants, storage facilities, and transportation.

The economic conditions of the export sector, in some cases, are the opposite of the foregoing. When multinational corporations invest in export products, they ensure that the latest available technologies are employed, the roads to the production plants or sites are well maintained, and necessary processing facilities are provided. They provide funding for research, product development, and marketing. This notwithstanding, the small farmers also produce cash crops in the export sector, and they rely on governmental support (e.g., research, other inputs, and price support) to help them produce and market cash crops. The export sector performs relatively better in countries across Africa, probably because of the better support the sector receives. It is worthy to note, however, that the export sector sometimes faces some of the same problems the traditional sector faces. Apart from the problems mentioned above, the lack of political leadership, servicing of foreign debts, large expenditures on disease control, and the proliferation of political strife have also been blamed for the shortage of resources to redress the problems in agriculture. In fact, these problems are exacerbated by the scourge of HIV/AIDS that continues to imperil cities and agricultural villages alike in the region, thereby forcing governments to divert even more of their limited resources to treatment and containment programs.

The foregoing are challenges that African countries face today. What are the opportunities and suggested solutions to these problems? Clearly, the responsibility for increased agricultural productivity and economic development in Africa lies primarily with Africans themselves and secondarily with their sympathizers, political allies, and interested investors. Added to this, competitiveness in the international market is important. Competitiveness in agriculture for Africa depends on the international market price, World Trade Organization effectiveness, exchange rate systems in each African country, use in industrial countries of new substitutes for African materials such as rubber and cotton, level of output capacity, diversification of export products instead of sticking to the traditional products, and policies of governments to help and give incentives to farmers. The error being committed by many African countries is their apparent failure to recognize the overriding importance of agriculture. Agriculture employed about 60% of the population in 1999; it feeds the increasing urban population, can be an important source of national savings, and generates foreign exchange earnings.[24] It can, therefore, be the engine driving economic development in Africa.

The key problem areas have been listed, but what needs to be done depends on the extent to which some national efforts have already been directed at solutions. Following is a list of key areas for investment that can boost the economic development impact of agriculture in any country, especially African countries. To elevate themselves from their current development quagmire, African countries should invest in the following areas:

1. Research, extension, and targeted agricultural subsidies to facilitate the productivity of the farmer.
2. Infrastructure for development, such as roads, transportation, communication, and irrigation schemes.
3. Complementary services, such as marketing, credit for small holders, price support, granting tax advantages to new processing plants, and government buying and storing of surplus output in years of good production.
4. National foreign relations effort to garnish preferential treatments in key foreign markets for domestic products (e.g., through bilateral and multinational negotiations).
5. Expanding general and vocational/technical education to increase the literacy rate while improving labor and managerial skills.
6. Supporting the development of national capacity for economic policy analysis, especially agricultural policy analysis.
7. Creating a constitutional basis for the formation of farmers' groups and granting them special privileges (e.g., though farmer cooperatives in the United States operate as user-owned corporations, they do not pay corporate income tax like investor-owned corporations[25]).
8. Strengthening health centers and social services to reduce or eliminate the devastating effects of deadly diseases on agricultural productivity.
9. Supporting new investment partnerships between nationals and foreign financiers, especially those partnerships that are involved in the production of food staples and cash crops, by providing them special tax incentives.
10. Strengthening macroeconomic policies (e.g., exchange rate, interest rate, food prices, and other agricultural incentives) as well as investing in rural areas.[26]

Obviously most of these investments cannot be done without resources, which are already in very short supplies in many African countries. Nonetheless, the list indicates where to start and where African countries, their sympathizers, political allies, and foreign investors should focus their attention, if they want to seize the opportunities for economic growth and development of the region.

Despite the problems in Africa, there are seeds of hope and encouragement. The improvement in maize yields in Zimbabwe and Zambia are a result of concerted efforts by those countries in developing or adopting improved hybrids of the crop and passing them on to their farmers to cultivate. Similarly, the emergence of floriculture in Kenya, sustained export of coffee in the Ivory Coast, peanuts in Senegal, dairy product marketing in Kenya, cassava production for export in Nigeria, and fishery product exports from Ghana in recent years are examples of concerted investments yielding desired results.[27] National research stations in these countries play a key role in the improvement process.

A. ZIMBABWE AND ITS MAIZE SUCCESS STORY

Zimbabwe, a nation of about 12 million people in Southern Africa, has experienced dramatic success in increasing maize production. The first success came in the period from 1960 to 1980, accruing mainly to large commercial farmers, and the second occurred from 1980 to 1986, benefiting small farmers. The technical and institutional preconditions for the first maize success story were generated through large public and small private investments in four areas: (1) long-term investments in research resulting in new technology; (2) investments in schools and other training programs resulting in human capital and managerial skills development; (3) investments in infrastructure such as roads, telecommunication, dams, and irrigation; and (4) investments in farmer support services such as marketing, credit, and fertilizer and seed distribution. After many years of research, a new variety of maize, SR52, was launched in 1960. The incredible thing about SR52 was that it increased maize yield by 46% without the use of fertilizer. In the early 1970s, Zimbabwean researchers launched a series of varieties, R200, R201, and R215. These were short-season varieties that allowed farmers to have more plantings in a year. Though these varieties benefited large farmers several small farmers in the region of the large farmers gained from this breakthrough.

The second maize success story began after independence in 1980. The new government declared support for the small farmer and leveled the playing field in terms of incentives for the small farmer. Small farmers quickly embraced their new fortunes. They doubled maize production in 6 years. Indeed, the small farmers could not have achieved this improvement without technological and institutional spillovers from the efforts of previous governments and large farmers.

Today, Zimbabwe sells maize to several African countries. The maize success story in Zimbabwe has slowed down a bit because of a few problems (e.g., managerial, loan supervision, and lack of financial sustainability), but these problems are being addressed. Indeed, Zimbabwe's current challenge is to institute cost-effective marketing policies and institutions to finance and sustain its small farmer maize success story.

VIII. THE PROBLEM OF POLITICAL INSTABILITY

Another major set of problems facing African countries, in terms of agricultural productivity and economic development, is the proliferation of political strife and genocide. These problems are often engendered by greed, ethnic animosities, desires for vengeance, and high rates of illiteracy. Another factor is external interest in the vast mineral and other natural resources of the region, especially West Africa and Central Africa in recent years. Again, the economic reality is that these crises provide business opportunities for some people (i.e., gun dealers, diamond and gold importers in developed countries, and local people in the region). Military dictatorships and rebel governments that control the countries in political strife show no loyalty to the people they claim to serve. In fact, the bulk of the people suffer while the gun-wielding few benefit. These are the most formidable problems because of their economic underpinning. Investments should be directed at agriculture, not at wars and atrocities that open doors for international profiteering.

IX. SUMMARY

The land tenure system in Africa falls into three main categories but the one that receives most attention is communal land tenure. The reasons are (1) this is where most of the farming takes place, and (2) this category has been blamed for the lack of increase in agricultural productivity and hence lack of economic development in Africa. Indeed, the latter reason is not entirely founded. A solution to the land tenure problem is selective or guarded land tenure reform. Yet, land tenure reform is not the be-all and end-all to solving Africa's economic development problem. The solution may require broader actions than simply fiddling with the land tenure reform.

Agriculture has unique roles to play in African economies. It can serve as the propeller of economic growth and development. Africa's agricultural structure is made up of two sectors, the domestic food sector and the export sector. Both of these sectors have problems that need to be addressed but are confronted with resource shortages, debt servicing burden, and disease containment expenditures. Most governments have failed to effectively address sufficiently these problems. The error being committed by policymakers in economic development in African countries is their failure to recognize agriculture as the engine that could drive economic development. Agriculture employs about 60% of the population, feeds the burgeoning city populations, garnishes foreign exchange earnings, and has untapped potentials to be a reliable source of national savings. Key areas for investment focus include the infrastructure, institutions that serve farmers, and trade promotion. Another major problem to be addressed is political strife, which leads to the squandering of resources on unending wars by local leaders and profiteering by foreign arms and precious metal dealers. Nonetheless, there are bright spots in some countries where appropriately directed investments have been made; more needs to be done across the continent.

DISCUSSION QUESTIONS

1. What is land tenure? Do you think the definition provided here is adequate? Why or why not?
2. Briefly describe the categories of the land tenure system. Why is the land tenure system blamed for the lack of economic development?
3. Indicate ways by which land tenure reform can be implemented. In your opinion are these ways appropriate?
4. How can agriculture contribute to economic development in Africa?
5. Why do African countries give lip service to price support for food crop farmers, backing it up with little action?
6. What is the key link between the domestic food sector and the export sector?
7. How can Africa's agricultural problems be solved?

NOTES

[1]For another definition on land tenure see, for example, Maxwell, D. and Weibe, K. (1998) *Land Tenure and Food Security: A Review of Concepts, Evidence, and Methods,* Land Tenure Center Research Paper 129, Madison, WI: Land Tenure Center, University of Wisconsin-Madison, p. 1. A more elaborate definition can be found in Cohen, J.M. (1980) "Land Tenure and Rural Development in Africa," in R.H. Bates and M.F. Lofchie, Eds., *Agricultural Development in Africa,* New York: Praeger, p. 353.

[2]Lastarria-Cornhiel, S. (1997) "Impact of Privatization, Gender, and Property Rights in Africa," *World Development,* 25, 1317-1333. For an extensive discussion on access to land, see also Berry, S. (1993) *No Condition Is Permanent: The Social Dynamics of Agrarian Change in Sub-Saharan Africa,* Madison, WI: University of Wisconsin Press, pp. 101–134.

[3]For a detailed discourse on types of land tenure, see Global Coalition for Africa Economic Committee Document (1999) "Promoting Agricultural Productivity and Competitiveness in Sub-Saharan Africa," paper presented at Economic Committee Meeting, Nairobi, Kenya, April, 1999. A more general description is given by Daniel Maxwell, D. and Wiebe, K. (1998) *Land Tenure and Food Security: A Review of Concepts, Evidence, and Methods*, Land Tenure Research Center Research Paper 129, Madison, WI: Land Tenure Center, University of Wisconsin-Madison, p. 4; Gyasi, E.A. (1994) "The Adaptability of African Communal Land Tenure to Economic Opportunity: The Example of Land Acquisition for Oil Palm Farming in Ghana," *Africa*, 64, 391–403.

[4]Bruce, J.W. (1993) "Do Indigenous Tenure Systems Constrain Agricultural Development?," in T.J. Basset and D.E. Crummey, Eds., *Land in African Agrarian Systems*, Madison, WI: University of Wisconsin Press, pp. 35–56.

[5]Lastarria-Cornhiel, S. (1997) "Impact of Privatization, Gender, and Property Rights in Africa," *World Development*, 25, 1317–1333; Bruce, J.W. (1993) "Do Indigenous Tenure Systems Constrain Agricultural Development?," in T.J. Basset and D.E. Crummey, Eds., *Land in African Agrarian Systems*, Madison, WI: University of Wisconsin Press, pp. 35–56; du Guerny, J. and Topouzis, D. (1996) "Gender, Land and Fertility: Women's Access to Land and Security of Tenure," in *Modules on Gender, Population and Rural Development with a Focus on Land Tenure and Farming Systems*, Rome, Italy: Food and Agriculture Organization of the United Nations.

[6]Lastarria-Cornhiel, S. (1997) "Impact of Privatization, Gender, and Property Rights in Africa," *World Development*, 25, 1317–1333.

[7]A somewhat comprehensive critique of the communal land tenure system is given in Cohen, J.M. (1980) "Land Tenure and Rural Development in Africa," in R.H. Bates and M.F. Lofchie, Eds., *Agricultural Development in Africa*, New York: Praeger, pp. 354–356.

[8]Gyasi, E.A. (1994) "The Adaptability of African Communal Land Tenure to Economic Opportunity: The Example of Land Acquisition for Oil Palm Farming in Ghana," *Africa*, 64, 391–403.

[9]Foster, P. and Leathers, H.D. (1999) *The World Food Problem: Tackling the Causes of Undernutrition in the Third World*, 2nd ed., Boulder, CO: Lynne Rienner Publishers, p. 270.

[10]Addison, T. and Demery, L. (1989) "The Economics of Rural Poverty Alleviation," in S. Commander, Ed., *Structural Adjustment and Agriculture: Theory and Practice in Africa and Latin America*, London: James Curry, Ltd., p. 77.

[11]For a comprehensive dissection of theoretical concerns associated with land tenure reforms, see Lambert, V.A. and Seligson, M.A. (1997) "Asset Distribution and Access: Land Tenure Programs," in L.G. Tweeten and D.G. McClelland, Eds., *Promoting Third World Development and Food Security*, Westport, CT: Praeger, pp. 160–164.

[12]Barrows, R. and Roth, M. (1990) "Land Tenure and Investment in African Agriculture: Theory and Evidence," *The Journal of Modern African Studies*, 28, 265–297.

[13]Berry, S. (1993) *No Condition Is Permanent: The Social Dynamics of Agrarian Change in Sub-Saharan Africa*, Madison, WI: University of Wisconsin Press, pp. 124–125.

[14]Lastarria-Cornhiel, S. (1997) "Impact of Privatization, Gender, and Property Rights in Africa," *World Development*, 25, 1317–1333; Bassett, T.J. (1993) "Introduction: The Land Question and Agricultural Transformation in Sub-Saharan Africa," in T.J. Basset and D.E. Crummey, Eds., *Land in African Agrarian Systems*, Madison, WI: University of Wisconsin Press, pp. 3–31; Cohen, J.M. (1980) "Land Tenure and Rural Development in Africa," in R.H. Bates and M.F. Lofchie, Eds., *Agricultural Development in Africa*, New York: Praeger, p. 357.

[15]Barrows, R. and Roth, M. (1990) "Land Tenure and Investment in African Agriculture: Theory and Evidence," *The Journal of Modern African Studies*, 28, 256–297.

[16]Sanders, J.H., Shapiro, B.I., and Ramaswamy, S. (1996) *The Economics of Agricultural Technology in Semiarid Sub-Saharan Africa*, Baltimore, MD: The Johns Hopkins University Press, p. 153.

[17]Place, F. and Migot-Adholla, S. (1998) "The Economic Effects of Land Registration on Smaller Farms in Kenya: Evidence From Nyeri and Kakamega Districts," *Land Economics*, 74, 360–373;

Bassett, T.J. (1993) "Introduction: The Land Question and Agricultural Transformation in Sub-Saharan Africa," in T.J. Basset and D.E. Crummey, Eds., *Land in African Agrarian Systems*, Madison, WI: University of Wisconsin Press.

[18]Global Coalition for Africa Economic Committee Document (1999) "Promoting Agricultural Productivity and Competitiveness in Sub-Saharan Africa," paper presented at Economic Committee Meeting, Nairobi, Kenya, April, 1999, p. 12; Place, F. and Migot-Adholla, S. (1998) "The Economic Effects of Land Registration on Smaller Farms in Kenya: Evidence From Nyeri and Kakamega Districts," *Land Economics*, 74, 360–373; Barrows, R. and Roth, M. (1990) "Land Tenure and Investment in African Agriculture: Theory and Evidence," *The Journal of Modern African Studies*, 28, 265–297.

[19]Timmer, P. (1998) "The Macroeconomics of Food and Agriculture" in C.K. Eicher and J.M. Staaz, Eds., *International Agricultural Development*, Baltimore, MD: The John Hopkins University Press, pp. 187–211.

[20]An in-depth discussion of the role of agriculture in economic development is provided in Stevens, R.D. and Jabara, C.L. (1988) *Agricultural Development Principles: Economic Theory and Empirical Evidence*, Baltimore, MD: The Johns Hopkins University Press, pp. 31–54; Bhuduri, A. and Skarstein, R. (1997) "Introduction," in A. Bhuduri and R. Skarstein, Eds., *Economic Development and Agricultural Productivity*, Cheltenham, U.K.: Edward Elgar Publishing, pp. 1–22.

[21]Mellor, J.W. (1995) "Introduction," in J.W. Mellor, Ed., *Agriculture on the Road to Industrialization*, Baltimore, MD: The Johns Hopkins University Press, pp. 1–22.

[22]Stevens, R.D. and Cathy L. Jabara, C.L. (1988) *Agricultural Development Principles: Economic Theory and Empirical Evidence*, Baltimore, MD: The Johns Hopkins University Press, pp. 31–54.

[23]For a detailed discussion on the macroeconomic aspects of agriculture, see Timmer, P. (1998) "The Macroeconomics of Food and Agriculture," in C.K. Eicher and J.M. Staaz, Eds., *International Agricultural Development*, Baltimore, MD: The Johns Hopkins University Press, pp. 187–211.

[24]FAOSTAT (2001) Online Data, www.fao.org. Also see Global Coalition for Africa Economic Committee Document (1999) "Promoting Agricultural Productivity and Competitiveness in Sub-Saharan Africa," paper presented at Economic Committee Meeting, Nairobi, Kenya, April, 1999, pp. 2–3.

[25]For a detailed discussion of American farmer cooperatives, see Rhodes, J.V. and Dauve, J.L. (1998) *The Agricultural Marketing System*, 5th ed., Scottsdale, AZ: Holcomb Hathaway, pp. 234–248.

[26]Timmer, P. (1998) "The Macroeconomics of Food and Agriculture," in C.K. Eicher and J.M. Staaz, Eds., *International Agricultural Development*, Baltimore, MD: The Johns Hopkins University Press, pp. 187–211.

[27]For details on food marketing in Africa, see Jaffee, S. and Morton, J., Eds. (1995) *Marketing Africa's High-Value Foods: Comparative Experiences of an Emergent Private Sector*, Washington, D.C.: World Bank; Van der Laan, L.H. (1984) *The Trans-Oceanic Marketing Channel: A New Tool for Understanding Tropical Africa's Export Agriculture*, New York: The International Business Press. For a discussion on the management aspects of organizations, see Waiguchu, M.J., Tiagha, E., and Mwaura, M., Eds. (1999) *Management of Organizations in Africa: A Handbook and Reference*, Westport, CT: Quorum Books.

CHAPTER 16

Financial Markets and Economic Development

LÉONCE NDIKUMANA

Department of Economics, University of Massachusetts, Amherst, Massachusetts 01003

KEY TERMS

Banking regulation	Financial structure
Banking supervision	Foreign direct investment
Capital flight	Information asymmetry
Central bank independence	Market capitalization
Credit supply	Maturity transformation
Economic development	Non-bank financial institutions
Financial intermediation	Portfolio diversification
Financial liberalization	Saving mobilization
Financial repression	Stock market liquidity

I. INTRODUCTION

The role of financial markets in economic development continues to attract increasing attention both in academia and among policymakers. Evidence from recent empirical studies suggests that deeper, broader, and better functioning financial markets can stimulate higher economic growth.[1] Although evidence on Africa is still limited, the results from existing empirical work supports the view that financial development has a positive effect on economic growth in African countries.[2] The discussion of strategies for enhancing African economic development must therefore take into account the role of the financial sector in economic development.

This chapter reviews the theory and evidence on the links between financial development and economic activity in the context of African countries. The text is organized as follows. Section II gives a brief summary of the various functions of the financial system and the mechanisms of transmission through which financial intermediation can enhance economic activity. Section III presents stylized facts on the trends and patterns of financial development in Africa since the 1970s, discusses the size and performance of African stock markets, and summarizes the findings from existing empirical studies on the effects of financial development on economic growth in African economies. Section IV briefly discusses selected issues related to financial market development and economic development policy—namely, the role of the government in the banking industry; the role of the central bank, central bank independence, and regulatory efficiency; the structure of the financial system (i.e., stock-market-based versus bank-based); and the capital flight problem and its effects on financial intermediation. Section V concludes.

II. THE FINANCIAL SYSTEM AND REAL ECONOMIC ACTIVITY: OVERVIEW

A. FUNCTIONS OF THE FINANCIAL SYSTEM

The financial system interacts with real economic activity through its various functions by which it facilitates economic exchange. The financial system plays an important role in mobilizing funds and transforming them into assets that can better meet the needs of investors. By facilitating portfolio diversification, financial intermediaries allow savers to maximize returns to their assets and to reduce risk. Financial intermediaries transfer resources across time and space, thus allowing investors and consumers to borrow against future income and meet current needs. This enables deficit units (those whose current expenditures exceed current income) to overcome financing constraints and the difficulties arising from mismatches between income and expenditure flows. Financial institutions play an important role in easing the tension between savers' preference for liquidity and entrepreneurs' need for long-term financing. Therefore, at any given level of saving, an efficient financial system will allow for a higher level of investment by maximizing the proportion of saving that actually finances investment.[3] With an efficient financial system, resources will also be utilized more efficiently due to the ability of financial intermediaries to identify the most productive investment opportunities.

Financial systems play an important role in creating a pricing information mechanism. By providing a mechanism for appraisal of the value of firms, financial systems allow investors to make informed decisions about the allocation of their funds. Financial intermediaries can also mitigate information asymmetries that characterize market exchange. One party to a transaction often has valuable information that the other party does not have. In such circumstances, there may be unexploited exchange opportunities. In the case of a firm, information imperfections can result in suboptimal investment. When a manager cannot fully and credibly reveal information about a worthy investment project to outside investors and lenders, the firm may not be able to raise the outside funds necessary to undertake such a project.[4] In a market plagued by information imperfections, the equilibrium quantity and quality of investment will fall short of the economy's potential. Financial intermediaries can mitigate such problems by collecting information about prospective borrowers.

The financial system can enhance efficiency in the corporate sector by monitoring management and exerting corporate control.[5] Savers cannot effectively verify the quality of investment projects or the efficiency of the management. Financial intermediaries can monitor the behavior of corporate managers and foster efficient use of borrowed funds better than savers acting individually. Financial intermediaries thus fulfill the function of "delegated monitoring" by representing the interests of savers.[6] Financial markets also can improve managerial efficiency by promoting competition through effective takeover or threat of takeover although there is some disagreement as to the value-enhancing role of takeovers.

B. FINANCE AND ECONOMIC GROWTH: HISTORICAL AND ECONOMETRIC EVIDENCE

The links between financial development and economic growth are not a new theme in the economics literature. Ninety years ago, Schumpeter observed that financial markets play an important role in the growth process by channeling funds to the most efficient investors and by fostering entrepreneurial innovation.[7] Schumpeter's view was that financial development leads to economic growth. Robinson however, argued that financial development passively follows economic growth by responding to the increasing demand for funds due to economic prosperity.[7] While the debate on causality is still unsettled, existing historical and econometric evidence suggests that better functioning financial markets (i.e., markets that are able to meet the needs of savers and investors efficiently) have a positive effect on future economic growth.[8]

The economic history literature has documented cross-country and country-specific evidence that illustrates the importance of financial systems in early industrial development. Using data from 1790–1850, Rouseau and Silla find quantitative evidence to support the hypothesis that early industrial growth in the United States was prompted by finance. These authors conclude that by providing debt and equity finance to the corporate and government sectors, the financial system was critical to the modernization process, which it predated. Using data on the United States, United Kingdom, Canada, Norway, and Sweden, Rousseau and Wachtel concluded that financial intermediation was an important factor in the industrial transformation of these countries.[9] Other studies include Corosso who documented the role of early U.S. investment banking in mobilizing savings to raise capital; Cameron et al.,[10] who examined European countries, Russia, and Japan; and Haber, who compared the cases of Brazil, Mexico and the United States.[10] These studies provide evidence that supports the proposition that better functioning financial systems play an important role in economic growth.

Following the work by King and Levine, several studies have provided econometric evidence that supports the view that financial development is a potent predictor of future economic growth. The results in these studies have made significant progress in establishing that, to some extent, the causal relationship runs from financial development to economic growth.

The findings from studies based on aggregate data have been supported by studies that use disaggregated data on the industry and firm level. Using a large sample of industries from many countries, Rajan and Zingales found evidence indicating that financial development mitigates financing constraints for industries that rely most heavily on external finance. These authors found that such industries grow faster in countries with more developed financial systems. Demirgüç-Kunt and Maksimovic and Beck and Levine provide further international firm-level evidence on the positive effects of access to a well-functioning financial system on firm growth. These studies have generalized the results from the literature on the effects of financing constraints on investment initiated by Fazzari et al., who used data from the manufacturing sector of the United States.[11] Several studies have shown that the results on the links between financing constraints and investment by manufacturing firms also hold for developing countries.

It is important to reiterate that while this large amount of historical and econometric evidence suggests that financial development facilitates economic growth, this does not rule out the possibility of a causal relationship in the reverse direction. It is perfectly possible that financial systems develop in response to higher economic growth or in anticipation of future prosperity. These two causal processes are not mutually exclusive and may very well be a natural feature of the links between finance and economic growth. It is in this context that we should interpret the evidence discussed in this chapter.

III. FINANCIAL DEVELOPMENT AND ECONOMIC GROWTH IN AFRICA: AN ASSESSMENT

A. A NOTE ON THE DATA

Measuring financial development constitutes an important challenge to researchers in their efforts to assess the impact of financial intermediation on real economic activity. In measuring financial development, it would be ideal to obtain detailed information that enables us to assess how the financial system fulfills its roles of facilitating exchange, mobilizing saving, managing risk, identifying productive investment projects, and monitoring management. Such detailed information is still sparse especially in the case of developing countries.

The indicators of financial development used in empirical studies can be classified roughly in the three broad categories of monetary aggregates, stock market indicators, and structural and institutional indicators:

- *Monetary aggregates*, also referred to as "traditional measures," are the most widely used indicators because they are the most widely published in national and international datasets. The main sources of these data are the World Bank's *World Development Indicators* and the International Monetary Fund's *International Financial Statistics*. The indicators used include:
  - Conventional measures of money supply such as narrow money (M1), broad money (M2), and quasi-money (M3) scaled by the country's gross domestic product (GDP).
  - Measures of the supply of credit by banks as a share of total domestic credit or as a ratio of GDP.
  - Measures of the supply of credit to the private sector as a share of total domestic credit or as a ratio of GDP.
- *Stock market measures* include indicators of the size of the market and indicators of liquidity. The size of the stock market is measured by the number of listed companies and the capitalization of listed companies (total volume or as ratio of GDP). Stock market liquidity is measured by the value of shares traded (volume or ratio of GDP) and the turnover ratio.
- *Structural and institutional indicators* provide information that enables us to directly or indirectly assess the efficiency and sophistication of the financial systems. These indicators include:
  - Indicators of financial structure that distinguish between bank-based and stock market-based financial systems[12]
  - Indicators of banking regulation, banking ownership structure, and banking concentration, which provide information on the degree of concentration in the banking sector, the share of state-owned versus privately owned banks, and the level of regulatory restrictions in the business of banking
  - Indicators of financial liberalization, which include the degree of control of the interest rate and the degree of intervention of the state in credit allocation

In the case of African countries, recent surveys, especially those by Mehran *et al.* and Gelbard and Leite, have made a significant contribution to this area. Based on results from a survey of 38 Sub-Saharan African countries in 1997, Gelbard and Leite compiled indicators on six major aspects of financial development: (1) the market structure and competitiveness of the financial system, (2) the range of financial products available on the market, (3) the degree of financial liberalization, (4) the institutional environment under which the financial system operates, (5) the degree of integration with foreign financial markets (financial openness), and (6) the degree of sophistication of monetary policy instruments.[13] Gelbard and Leite computed indices that summarize the level of development of a country for each of the six aspects as well as a composite index that measures the overall level financial development in 1987 and 1997.[14] Countries were then classified as undeveloped, minimally developed, somewhat developed, or largely developed. The indicators compiled in by Gelbard and Leite are highly informative, not only on cross-country variations in the overall level of financial development, but also on differences in certain features of the institutional environment that are relevant for financial development. The findings from these surveys are summarized in Section III.D.

B. Financial Development: Trends and Patterns

In this section we present some stylized facts on economic performance and overall financial development using aggregate statistics based primarily on the World Bank's *World Development Indicators*. Average real income, investment, and saving have declined in the 1990s compared to the 1980s.[15] Real income, investment, and saving have declined systematically in every decade since the 1970s. For many countries, per capita real income in the 1990s was lower than in the 1970s. The data illustrate what some researchers have referred to as "growth tragedy" or "development disasters."[16] While the continent includes success stories such as Botswana, Mauritius, and Seychelles, whose income levels are high and rising, it also includes a number of disappointing cases. Even countries with vast resources such as the Democratic Republic of Congo (formerly Zaïre) and Nigeria have been unable to meet expectations due to many factors, including poor macroeconomic management and political corruption.

Since the 1980s, indicators of financial development have either stagnated or declined on average in Sub-Saharan Africa. For Sub-Saharan Africa, excluding South Africa, the average sizes of the financial system (as measured by total liquid liabilities of financial intermediaries) and credit supply were lower in the 1990s compared to the 1980s. If South Africa or North African countries (Egypt, Morocco, and Tunisia) are included, the statistics show an increase in the volume of credit supply from the 1970s to the 1990s. The data also highlight the predominant size of the South African financial system. The average ratio of bank credit to GDP for the Sub-Saharan African sample from 1990–1998 is 81% when

South Africa is included, but only 26% when it is excluded. It is primarily through the supply of credit that financial intermediation stimulates real economic activity. Therefore the decline in credit supply in Sub-Saharan Africa may be a factor for the poor economic performance of the subcontinent over the past two decades.

The aggregate indicators of financial development hide wide disparities across countries. As can be seen in Table 16.1, there is a large gap between countries with sizeable financial systems with liquid liabilities of over 40% of GDP and countries with much smaller financial systems. The countries with relatively large financial systems include North African countries (Algeria, Egypt, Morocco, and Tunisia) and some Sub-Saharan African countries such as Kenya and South Africa. These countries also have high ratios of credit supply to GDP, and most of them have experienced an increase in credit supply while credit supply declined in the majority of other Sub-Saharan African countries over the 1970–1998 period.

The diversity in financial development across the African continent is illustrated also in a high concentration of the largest banks in just a few countries. Although detailed information is sparse on this topic, the existing evidence shows that North African countries and South Africa have larger banks than other countries. Table 16.2 contains information on the 150 largest banks in Africa in 1996. The banks from three countries, Egypt, Morocco, and South Africa account for about 75% of the assets held by the 150 largest banks. Adding Tunisian banks raises the share to over 80%. Banks in these countries also account for the bulk of deposits and loans in this subsample of the African banking sector. There is a high disparity in the ratio of loans to deposits, varying from 49.9% in Nigeria to 153% in Algeria. In some countries banks seem to have large idle capacity in credit supply. It would be worth investigating what causes the large variations in the ratio of loans to deposits across countries and why banks in some countries choose to hoard cash rather than issue loans.

C. STOCK MARKET DEVELOPMENT

African stock markets are characterized by high diversity in terms of age, size, and performance. The continent counts both long-established stock markets (Egypt, South Africa, Zimbabwe) dating from the 1880s, as well as more recent ones (Table 16.3). With a market capitalization of $170 billion in 1998 (128% of GDP), the South African stock market is a giant compared to tiny markets such as Swaziland ($85 million, or 7% of GDP). Overall, the majority of African markets are still in their infancy, with a limited number of listed companies, low capitalization, and little diversity among market participants. This is the case even for markets that were established a long time ago. For example, the Egyptian

TABLE 16.1   Financial Development Indicators for African Countries (Averages by Decade), 1980–1998

Country	Overall Development[a]		Liquid liabilities (% GDP)		Credit to Private Sector (% GDP)		Credit by Banks (% GDP)	
	1987	1997	1980–1989	1990–1998	1980–1989	1990–1998	1980–1989	1990–1998
Algeria	MD	SD	71.9	47.5	54.1	13.6	82.0	54.0
Benin	MD	SD	22.3	26.5	27.7	11.0	27.4	12.0
Botswana	MD	SD	24.7	23.2	9.7	11.9	12.2	13.0
Burkina Faso			16.8	22.6	15.5	11.3	13.4	10.2
Burundi	MD	SD	17.4	19.6	10.5	16.8	24.4	23.4
Cameroon	MD	MD	21.7	17.6	27.1	13.5	25.4	23.7
Central African Republic			17.9	18.6	10.3	4.8	17.8	12.5
Chad			15.7	12.6	13.2	4.8	17.0	11.8
Congo, DRC	MD	MD	14.9	15.0	2.2	1.1	9.2	13.2
Congo, Rep.	UD	SD	17.4	17.4	20.0	10.8	25.3	22.1
Côte d'Ivoire	MD	SD	28.6	27.9	38.1	25.8	44.9	36.3
Egypt			85.6	82.6	31.7	35.9	108.4	88.7
Gabon	MD	SD	19.9	16.1	19.2	9.9	23.5	19.2
Gambia	MD	SD	24.5	24.9	19.3	10.5	41.8	6.8
Ghana	MD	LD	14.8	17.1	2.8	5.8	21.0	22.7
Kenya	MD	SD	29.0	39.3	30.1	33.1	47.4	52.9
Lesotho	UD	MD	49.8	37.8	13.2	19.0	28.8	23.9
Madagascar	MD	SD	17.0	20.3	18.5	13.7	39.6	23.0

Malawi	UD	MD	21.9	19.4	13.1	8.3	33.6	16.2
Mali	MD	SD	20.1	22.3	17.1	12.5	27.5	12.4
Mauritania	SD		21.9	21.3	27.9	31.4	34.7	31.8
Mauritius	SD	LD	49.2	72.9	25.9	43.9	55.3	61.6
Morocco	UD	SD	44.6	63.1	19.0	32.0	47.9	58.1
Mozambique	MD	SD	41.7	26.0	37.2	13.9	51.9	6.7
Niger	MD	SD	16.3	14.9	16.4	7.8	18.5	11.9
Nigeria	MD	SD	29.4	18.3	15.4	8.6	37.7	21.2
Rwanda			14.3	15.9	7.2	7.3	9.4	15.5
Senegal	MD	SD	27.1	23.0	36.1	21.1	46.9	27.8
Seychelles			31.3	52.5	12.7	14.9	35.6	73.2
Sierra Leone			18.5	12.2	4.4	3.0	30.9	42.9
South Africa	LD	LD	54.2	51.9	68.8	108.2	89.8	128.1
Sudan			28.3	16.1	10.8	3.6	32.0	13.8
Swaziland	MD	SD	31.6	30.0	20.6	21.7	16.1	4.7
Togo	MD	MD	39.5	29.5	24.3	21.7	26.2	23.8
Tunisia			45.9	47.7	49.4	52.8	56.7	57.1
Uganda	MD	SD	12.1	10.3	3.3	4.3	23.2	8.5
Zambia	MD	LD	31.7	17.8	14.8	7.5	63.2	58.8
Zimbabwe	MD	SD	24.6	23.5	20.0	31.0	42.7	49.4

[a]This is Gelbard and Leite's assessment of overall development (sample includes only Sub-Saharan African countries). The categories correspond to the four quartiles based on a composite index including six aspects of financial development: market structure, range of financial products, financial liberalization, institutional environment, openness, and monetary policy instruments. The categories are undeveloped (UD), minimally developed (MD), somewhat developed (SD), and largely developed (LD).
Sources: World Development Indicators 2000; Gelbard, E. and Leite, S.P. (1999) Measuring Financial Development in Sub-Saharan Africa, working paper 99/105, International Monetary Fund.

TABLE 16.2 The 150 Largest Banks in Africa: Deposits, Credit, and Revenue, 1996

Country	Among the 150 Largest Banks Total Assets			Share in Total Deposits		Among the 50 Largest Banks Share in Total Credit Supply		Loans/ Deposits (%)	Revenue/ Product (%)
	Million FF	% of Total	No. of Banks[a]	% of Total	No. of Banks	% of Total	No. of Banks		
South Africa	28,822	33.9	10	39.8	6	43.9	7	91.5	24.4
Egypt	22,363	26.3	21	34.6	14	27.4	15	77.5	45.4
Morocco	12,350	14.5	8	12.5	7	11.7	7	116.3	31.4
Tunisia	5,291	6.2	7	3.9	6	4.3	6	92.6	23.4
Algeria	3,679	4.3	3	1.9	1	7.0	2	152.9	3.8
Nigeria	2,014	2.4	16	1.5	3	0.9	3	49.9	55.9
Mauritius	1,355	1.6	3	0.6	1	0.4	1	51.1	49.6
Gabon	919	1.1	3	—	—	0.2	1	—	28.8
Ethiopia	863	1.0	2	1.4	1	1.4	1	83.9	66.2
Cameroon	825	0.9	3	0.4	2	—	—	—	—
Côte d'Ivoire	727	0.8	4	0.9	2	1.0	2	97.3	36.3
Namibia	715	0.8	3	0.7	2	0.8	2	94.8	31.1
Kenya	704	0.8	6	0.3	1	0.3	1	76.5	78.3
Senegal	396	0.5	5	0.2	1	—	—	—	—
Sudan	387	0.4	2	1.0	2	0.6	2	56.0	127.6
Botswana	354	0.4	2	0.2	1	—	—	—	35.5
Malawi	287	0.3	3	—	—	—	—	—	58.6
Madagascar	203	0.2	2	—	—	—	—	—	36.5
Mozambique	108	0.1	1	—	—	—	—	—	50.5

[a]The total does not add up to 150. Only countries that are represented in 50 largest banks are included in this table.

Source: "Le Classement des banques Africaines", Jeune Afrique Economie, Hors-Série, November 1998.

TABLE 16.3 Stock Markets in Sub-Saharan Africa: Some Indicators, 1990–1998[a]

Country	Year Established	Listed Companies (1998)	Market Capitalization				Capital Return (%)		Trading (1998)[b]	
			Volume		As % GDP					
			Million U.S. $ (1998)	Annual % Growth (1990–1998)	% of GDP (1998)	Annual % Growth (1990–1998)	1997	1998	Value (% GDP)	Turnover Ratio (%)
Botswana	1989	14	724	15.7	14.8	12.1	92.2	14.3	1.4	1.1
Côte d'Ivoire[c]	1976	35	1818	16.1	16.5	15.8	3.6	22.9	0.3	4.5
Egypt	1888	861	24,381	38.8	29.5	28.0	15.8	−26.6	6.1	22.3
Ghana	1989	21	1384	51.4	18.5	48.6	9.5	63.1	0.8	6.5
Kenya	1954	58	2024	20.6	17.5	16.1	−12.2	−3.5	0.7	0.3
Mauritius	1988	40	1849	27.3	44.0	20.2	−0.2	5.8	2.4	2.9
Morocco	1929	53	15,676	41.7	44.1	36.1	35.3	26.4	3.9	10.1
Namibia	1992	15	429	65.3	13.8	63.9	4.7	−46.6	0.4	2.3
Nigeria	1960	186	2887	9.7	7.0	4.8	−8.6	−20.8	0.4	5.2
South Africa	1887	668	170,252	2.7	127.6	0.5	−10.4	−27.6	43.8	30.4
Swaziland	1990	5	85	22.3	7.0	17.0	na[d]	na[d]	28.8	126
Tunisia	1969	38	2268	19.8	11.4	12.8	−29.7	5.9	0.9	0.9
Zambia	1994	8	293	148.9	8.7	151.8	103.3	−58	0.2	2.0
Zimbabwe	1896	67	1310	−7.3	20.7	−3.4	−53.1	−54.8	2.6	9.2

[a]The data for 1990 are not available for some countries. The relevant years are 1991 for Botswana and Ghana, 1992 for Namibia, and 1995 for Zambia. Countries with recently established stock markets are not included in this table: Malawi (established in 1997), Tanzania (established in 1996), and Uganda (established in 1997).

[b]1997 for Swaziland and Zambia

[c]The Abidjan Stock Exchange was officially closed in December 1997, ahead of the opening of the regional stock exchange (Bourse Régionale des Valeurs Mobilières, BRVM).

[d]Not available.

Sources: World Bank (2000) World Development Indicators 2000, Washington, D.C.: World Bank; Global Financial Data, www.globalfindata.com; MBendi Information for Africa (1998) "African Capital Market 1998," www.mbendi.co.za.

stock market was largely dormant for over 40 years following the policy shifts of the 1950s marked by the nationalization of industry and the adoption of a central planning policy.[17] The market developed substantially in the 1990s, with an increase in the number of listed companies, market capitalization, and liquidity.

The African continent has experienced a relatively fast development of equity markets over the past two decades. In 1980, Africa counted only eight active stock markets (Table 16.3), but by 1999, the number had more than doubled, up to 20. Market capitalization also expanded significantly. The newer markets have grown quickly in general, whereas the situation is more mixed among the more mature ones. Relative to GDP, stock market capitalization in Zimbabwe declined by 3.4% from 1990–1998; it increased by 0.5% in South Africa, 4.8% in Nigeria, 16% in Kenya, and 28% in Egypt over the same period. However, the observed stock market expansion has not been accompanied by any systematic improvement in economic performance (Table 16.4). Real income, domestic investment, and saving have declined or stagnated in the 1990s in the majority of countries with active stock markets, mirroring the overall poor economic performance in the continent as discussed earlier.

African stock markets are highly illiquid, with very low trading and turnover ratios. Low liquidity of stock markets has important implications for real economic activity. It is stock market liquidity, more than the size of the market, that plays an important role in facilitating long-term (illiquid) investment.[18] Therefore, low liquidity implies limited opportunities for the transformation of illiquid assets into liquid assets, which can constrain economic activity.

African stock markets are highly volatile, both in their growth rates and their rates of return. For example, after an increase by 261% from 1996 to 1997, market capitalization in Zambia declined by 58% from 1997 to 1998. The rate of return in this market dropped from 103% in 1997 to −58% in 1998. The weak economic base, high country-specific risk, and weak external position constitute important obstacles to growth and stability of African stock markets.

Despite the various structural problems faced by African stock markets, some of them are highly profitable and often rank among the most lucrative markets in the world. This illustrates the generally high returns to foreign capital in African economies. The rates of return to foreign investment in Africa are often higher than those in other developing regions. For example, in 1997, the average rate of return to U.S. foreign direct investment (FDI) was 25% in Africa compared to 16% in Asia, 12% in Latin America, and 14% in all developing countries. Two important facts about FDI in Africa are worth emphasizing. First, the aggregate volume of FDI in Africa has increased substantially over the 1990s. Annual FDI inflows to Africa, excluding South Africa, increased from an average of $1.2 billion in the 1981–1985 period to $2.9 billion for the 1986–1991 period, and $5.3 billion for the 1992–1998 period.[19]

TABLE 16.4 Some Economic Performance Indicators for African Countries with Stock Markets, 1990–1998[a]

Country	Real per Capita GDP		Gross domestic saving		Gross domestic investment		FDI as % of Gross Fixed Capital Formation	
	Value for 1998 (in 1995 U.S. $)	Annual % Growth (1990–1998)[b]	% of GDP (1998)	Annual % Growth (1990–1998)	% of GDP 1998	Annual % Growth (1990–1998)	1992	1998
Botswana	3611	1.7	21.8	–3.5	20.6	–4.6	–0.1	7.5
Côte d'Ivoire[c]	823	0.6	24.5	12.5	18.2	13.6	–29.1	15.7
Egypt	1146	2.2	15.8	–1.5	22.2	–2.8	5.3	6.1
Ghana	399	1.5	13.2	15.8	22.9	6.7	2.5	3.4
Kenya	334	–0.6	6.7	–10.1	14.4	–2.1	0.5	2.2
Mauritius	4034	3.8	24.0	–0.4	24.1	–2.6	1.7	1.3
Morocco	1388	0.4	14.7	–1.5	22.6	–1.9	6.6	4.1
Namibia	2133	0.8	18.8	3.5	19.0	–1.4	20.2	12.9
Nigeria	256	–0.3	11.8	–6.5	20.0	–2.5	26.3	12.7
South Africa	3918	–0.2	16.9	0.2	15.6	4.7	–0.2	2.5
Swaziland	1409	–0.2	19.2	0.1	12.3	0.3	33.8	35.8
Tunisia	2283	2.7	24.3	–1.5	27.5	–3.3	12.5	13.6
Zambia	388	–1.7	5.3	11.1	14.3	0.8	12.9	44.3
Zimbabwe	703	0.0	15.4	–1.2	17.2	–0.8	1.3	39.8

[a]The data for 1990 are not available for some countries. The relevant years are 1991 for Botswana and Ghana, 1992 for Namibia, and 1995 for Zambia.
[b]The annual average changes are obtained with an ordinary least squares regression of the logarithm of the relevant variable on time (a time trend).
[c]The Abidjan Stock Exchange was officially closed in December 1997, ahead of the opening of the regional stock exchange (Bourse Régionale des Valeurs Mobilières, BRVM).

Source: Author's computations from World Development Indicators 2000; FDI data are from UNCTAD's World Investment Report (1998, 2000).

The second noteworthy fact is the increasing diversification in the destination of FDI in Africa. While FDI has traditionally targeted resource-rich countries, especially oil exporters, other countries are attracting increasing attention from international investors. The share of oil exporters in total FDI in Africa declined from 70% in the 1980s to about 59% in the 1990s. Mozambique, Tanzania, Uganda, Zambia, and Zimbabwe, in particular, have experienced a substantial increase in FDI (Table 16.5 and Fig. 16.1). The evidence suggests that FDI is responsive to improvement in the macroeconomic environment through economic and institutional reform. For example, Uganda, which has made significant progress in economic reform, has attracted more FDI than neighboring Kenya. Although Kenya has a more developed financial system than Uganda, it also has a more unstable macroeconomic and political environment, which tends to discourage foreign capital.

D. STRUCTURAL AND INSTITUTIONAL INDICATORS OF FINANCIAL DEVELOPMENT

From the surveys by Mehran and Gelbard and Leite, we can draw the following conclusions about the development of financial markets in African countries over the past two decades:[20]

- *Overall development*: The structural and institutional indicators illustrate the cross-country diversity in financial development pointed out earlier using aggregate measures. The structural and institutional indicators paint a much better picture (than aggregate indicators) for the overall financial development in the continent. Based on Gelbard and Leite's overall financial development index, the number of countries in their sample that were classified as somewhat or largely developed financially grew from two (Mauritius and South Africa) in 1987 to 27 in 1997 (see Table 16.1). According to Gelbard and Leite, the countries with the most developed financial system in 1997 were Ghana, Kenya, Mauritius, Namibia, South Africa, and Zambia. However, measures of credit supply have deteriorated in some countries that are classified as largely developed or somewhat developed. This is the case for Zambia (largely developed), Nigeria, Malawi, and others (see Figure 16.2). It is important to notice that the rankings in Gelbard and Leite are relative to other African countries; they should not be interpreted as indicators of financial development from a worldwide perspective. Only Egypt, Morocco, and South Africa, which are classified among "emerging markets," can be considered as relatively developed from an international standard.

TABLE 16.5 FDI Inflows in Selected African Countries, 1986–1998 (million, constant 1995 $)

Country	1986	1987	1988	1989	1990	1991	1992	1993	1994	1995	1996	1997	1998	1999
Countries with active stock markets														
Botswana	87	138	47	47	41	−9	−2	−301	−15	70	69	98	90	111
Côte d'Ivoire	88	107	61	21	23	17	−246	92	122	268	295	440	315	277
Egypt	1516	1150	1388	1389	788	271	489	517	1301	596	623	868	1080	1491
Ghana	5	6	6	17	16	21	24	131	241	107	117	81	56	114
Kenya	41	52	0	69	61	20	6	2	4	32	13	39	42	42
Mauritius	9	21	28	40	44	20	16	16	21	19	36	54	12	49
Morocco	1	73	99	186	244	339	450	516	571	335	349	1055	330	842
Namibia	na[a]	na[a]	−2	−1	31	129	126	58	102	153	126	82	77	113
Nigeria	208	732	440	2092	631	762	955	1411	2030	1079	1558	1505	1054	1392
South Africa	−66	−91	514	1517	1883	227	−45	−20	394	1241	800	3732	563	1368
Swaziland	39	58	63	83	42	85	88	73	26	33	−61	−47	51	−4
Tunisia	78	112	71	88	80	134	560	485	586	378	343	358	672	366
Zambia	35	91	108	182	218	36	48	55	41	97	114	202	199	162
Zimbabwe	10	−38	−21	−11	−13	3	21	40	42	118	79	132	445	59
Countries without stock markets														
Angola	78	112	153	222	−360	712	307	317	176	472	177	403	1117	1803
Cameroon	24	15	78	0	−67	−16	31	5	−9	7	34	44	50	40
Congo	27	52	10	3	8	5	4	156	5	3	8	9	4	5
Gabon	137	109	155	−34	79	−59	135	−120	−104	−113	305	140	212	199
Lesotho	2	7	24	14	18	9	3	16	283	275	280	263	263	135
Mozambique	0	0	6	3	10	25	27	34	36	45	71	63	214	382
Tanzania[b]	−10	−1	5	7	−3	3	13	21	52	150	146	155	172	182
Uganda[b]	0	0	−5	−7	−16	1	3	58	91	125	117	171	211	179

[a]Not available.
[b]Stock markets recently established (1996 in Tanzania, 1997 in Uganda).
Source: UNCTAD, World Investment Reports (1992 to 2000); nominal values are deflated to real values using the U.S. PPI index (base 1995 = 100) from the International Financial Statistics Yearbook (various issues).

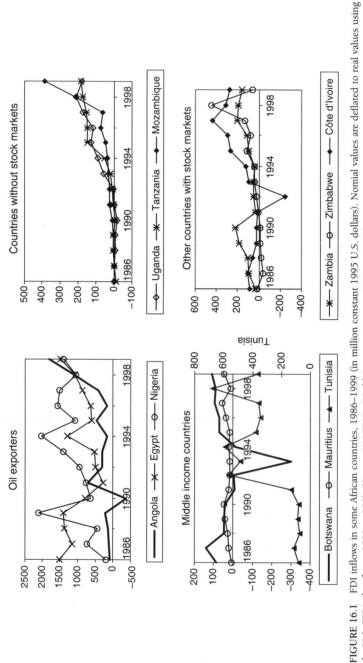

FIGURE 16.1 FDI inflows in some African countries, 1986–1999 (in million constant 1995 U.S. dollars). Nomial values are deflated to real values using the U.S. PPI index (base: 1995 = 100). (*Source:* UNCTAD, *World Investment Reports*, 1992 to 2000.)

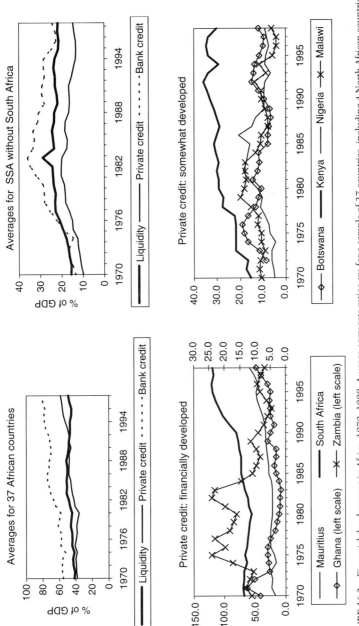

FIGURE 16.2 Financial development in Africa, 1970–1998. Average aggregate ratios are for a sample of 37 countries, including 4 North African countries (Algeria, Egypt, Morocco, and Tunisia). SSA = Sub-Saharan Africa; liquidity = liquid liabilities of financial institutions (M3% of GDP); investment = gross domestic investment (% of GDP); private credit = credit to the private sector (% of GDP). (*Sources:* World Bank (2000) *World Development Indicators 2000*, Washington, D.C.: World Bank; Gelbard, E. and Leite, S. P. (1999) *Measuring Financial Development in Sub-Saharan Africa*, working paper 99/105, International Monetary Fund.)

- *Market structure*: Ownership in the banking industry has evolved significantly from a predominantly state-controlled to a more privately owned system. In 1997, 13 out of the 38 countries in Gelbard and Leite's sample had almost complete private ownership of banks. Banks were predominantly state-owned in 10 countries in the sample, where the state accounted for at least 30% of bank loans and deposits. The banking system is still highly concentrated in the majority of Sub-Saharan African countries as indicated by the conventional Herfindahl index and the interest rate spread in the Gelbard–Leite study.

- *Performance*: The performance of the banking system has improved in some countries, but it is still low in the majority of countries. High proportions of non-performing loans illustrate the inefficiencies in the credit allocation process and in loan repayment enforcement mechanisms. The average share of non-performing loans for the 38 countries in the Gelbard–Leite sample was over 20% in 1997. Low loan repayment rates (high default rates) constitute an important handicap for the stability of the banking system and have adverse effects on the real sector. In particular, high default rates discourage lending, thereby reducing the overall supply of credit, which depresses private investment.

- *Financial products*: With the exception of South Africa, African financial systems offer a limited range of financial products. Gelbard and Leite find that bank lending is predominantly short term, government securities tend to have short maturities (less than a year in 23 countries in 1997), banks in many countries still do not issue credit cards (issued in only 15 countries in 1997), and inter-bank lending is still underdeveloped (inexistent in 8 countries in the sample in 1997).[21]

- *Banking requirements*: The institutional environment is still deficient in many countries. Table 16.6 presents some indicators of the institutional environment from the Mehran *et al.* study,[22] namely the supervisory framework (banking law and central bank autonomy), prudential regulation (bank capital ratios), the safety net (availability of deposit insurance), and the legal infrastructure. The table shows that some of the basic requirements for effective banking regulation and supervision are still inexistent in many countries. For example, many countries have no provisions for deposit insurance, and the legal infrastructure for the protection of bank performance is weak or inexistent in many countries.

The Gelbard and Leite study paints a brighter picture. According to the Gelbard–Leite indexes, in 1997 the institutional environment could be considered as reasonably supportive for financial intermediation in 23 countries, up from just 8 countries in 1987. The institutional environment index includes indicators of specific features of the legal system and the regulatory framework

TABLE 16.6 Indicators of Banking Regulation and Supervision in Selected Sub-Saharan African Countries, 1997

Country/Group	Supervisory Framework Banking Law (year)	Central Bank Autonomy	Prudential Regulation Capital Ratio (%)	Safety Net Deposit Insurance Available	Legal Infrastructure Adequate Legal Protection of Bank Performance
Angola	Draft completed	Limited	Negative to >20	na[f]	No
BCEAO[a]	1990	Average	na[f]	Under consideration	No
BEAC[b]	1992	Average	na[f]	No, agreement reached for a scheme	No
Botswana	1995	Full	19.8	No, under discussion	No, plans under way
Ethiopia	1994	Limited	4.5	No	No
Ghana	1989	Average	14.7	No	No
Kenya	1991	Partial	18	Yes	No
Lesotho	1973	Low	5	No	Yes
Madagascar	1996	Full	na[f]	No	No
Malawi	1989	Average	36.2	No	No
Mauritius	1966, 1988, 1995[c]	Full	9-10	No	Yes
Mozambique	1992	Average	13	No	n.a.
Namibia	1965	Full	>8	No	Yes
Rwanda	About to be adopted	Full	5	No	No
South Africa	Banks Act 1990, Mutual Banks Act 1993	Full	9.8	No, proposed	Yes
Swaziland	1975	Full	8	No	No
Tanzania	1991	Low	1.55	Yes	No
Uganda	1964, 1993, 1993[d]	Full	6.15	Yes	Yes[e]
Zambia	1994	Average	15	No, proposed	No
Zimbabwe	1965	Low	10.1	No	No

[a]BCEAO = Benin, Burkina Faso, Côte d'Ivoire, Mali, Niger, Senegal, Togo (and Guinea-Bissau as of 1997).
[b]BEAC = Cameroon, Central African Republic, Republic of Congo, Equatorial Guinea, and Gabon.
[c]Bank of Mauritius Act in 1966, Banking Act in 1988, and Foreign Exchange Dealers Act in 1995.
[d]Bills of Exchange Act in 1964, Bank of Uganda Statute in 1993, Financial Institutions Statute in 1993.
[e]No special legal facilities ensuring contracts performance.
[f]Not available.
Source: Mehran, H. et al. (1998) Financial Sector Development in Sub-Saharan African Countries, Occasional Paper 169, International Monetary Fund.

that facilitate financial intermediation. These features include the existence of property and creditors' rights and the ability of the judicial system to enforce such rights. Empirical studies have established a positive connection between financial development and the quality of the legal environment. The two aspects of the legal system that are most critical for financial intermediation are the quality of laws and the effectiveness of enforcement of these laws. These two aspects must exist simultaneously. The quality of a legal system determines the rights of creditors, especially in respect to the security of loans and the ability to repossess the assets of defaulting borrowers. To encourage lending, these legal rights must be both clearly defined and effectively enforced. Enforcement of the rights of creditors requires a judiciary that maintains the rule of law, low corruption, and low risk of expropriation or contract repudiation.

While visible progress was achieved over the past years, there are important institutional constraints to financial intermediation that African countries need to address. For example, the Gelbard–Leite survey reports that in 1997 the loan recovery process was difficult in as many as 28 Sub-Saharan countries, commercial legislation was inadequate in 14 countries, and there was no legislation of the use of checks in as many as 11 countries in the sample.

E. LINKING FINANCIAL DEVELOPMENT AND ECONOMIC GROWTH IN AFRICA: EXISTING EVIDENCE

Examining the linkages between financial development and economic growth requires addressing two separate but related empirical questions. The first is whether the overall development of the financial system leads to higher economic growth. The second question is to identify the channels through which financial intermediation affects economic growth.

The empirical economic growth literature has addressed the first question by relating indicators of financial development to the growth rate of real per capita income in growth models, including conventional determinants of economic growth (especially investment, human capital, and initial income). While only a handful of studies focus explicitly on Africa, the existing evidence suggests that financial development has a positive effect on economic growth. Odedokun and Spears find that aggregate measures of financial intermediation have positive and statistically significant effects on the growth rate of real per capita GDP.[23] Allen and Ndikumana found similar results in the case of the Southern African Development Community.[24] Gelbard and Leite also found evidence that suggests a positive and statistically significant link between real per capita GDP growth and their indices of financial development. They found that both the level of initial financial development and the change in the overall financial development index between 1987 and 1997 are positively and significantly related to economic growth. Their results confirm the findings from earlier studies that concluded that the initial level of financial development is an important determinant of future economic growth.[25] Gelbard and Leite also found that the changes in the indexes of financial liberalization, the institutional environment, and the array of financial products enter the growth equation positively and significantly.[26]

To address the second empirical question, researchers seek to examine how financial development affects the factors that are believed to cause economic growth. These include capital accumulation, factor productivity growth, and saving. Cross-country studies have made significant advances on this front,[27] but evidence on African countries remains limited. However, the existing evidence suggests that research in this area is promising. Ndikumana finds that financial development positively affects domestic investment. At this point, we are not aware of empirical studies that have linked financial development to factor productivity growth or saving in Africa.

IV. SELECTED ISSUES IN FINANCIAL MARKETS AND ECONOMIC DEVELOPMENT POLICY

In this section we identify and briefly discuss some important topics related to financial development and the role of financial markets in economic development. The list is by no means exhaustive nor is the discussion in any way comprehensive.

A. GOVERNMENT AND BANKING

In the early post-independence era, African governments sought to use financial development as a tool of speeding up economic growth. Governments became the main players in the creation of new financial intermediaries, including development banks and commercial banks as well as in the nationalization of commercial banks. Policymakers adopted the view that it was possible to foster economic growth by identifying growth-promoting sectors and providing subsidized credit to promote those sectors. Governments also controlled interest rates, which, in the context of high and volatile inflation, often resulted in negative real interest rates.

By the 1980s, the financial sector was experiencing the same problems of mismanagement and inefficient allocation of resources that plagued the public sector in the majority of African countries. The financial system was characterized by pervasive default on loans, especially by state-owned enterprises, which accounted for a large share of the domestic credit supply. This weakened financial intermediaries, forcing governments to inject more resources in the system in the form of subsidies to keep ailing institutions afloat. The disappointing experience of government-sponsored financial development forced countries to revise their strategies. Even though the government's presence is still significant in many countries, there is a visible trend toward more private ownership of banks. As part of the financial sector reform programs initiated in the 1980s and accelerated in the 1990s, state-owned financial institutions have been privatized or restructured to reduce the share of the government in the ownership structure, and the creation of new private banks has accelerated due to the easing of licensing requirements. One undesirable effect of liberalization in some countries has been the proliferation of small undercapitalized institutions. Moreover, the expansion of private sector participation has not resulted in a systematic increase in competition in the banking sector. Banking systems in many countries are still characterized by a high degree of concentration.

The government can foster financial development by pursuing sound macroeconomic management, especially fiscal discipline to improve macroeconomic stability, which minimizes macroeconomic uncertainty. African countries have systematically suffered from bad fiscal policies that have exacerbated the effects of external shocks, resulting in high chronic fiscal deficits. At reasonable levels, fiscal deficits have minimal adverse effects on the financial system. But, when fiscal deficits are chronically high, this increases the likelihood of monetary financing of the deficits and also forces the government to compete with private actors in the credit market. There is evidence that African countries that have made significant progress in macroeconomic and financial sector reform also have experienced improvement in economic performance and that their financial systems are improving. Uganda is often cited as an example of recent success in economic reform. The Ugandan government as well as the Bank of Uganda have progressively established a good record of credibility in policy decision making, which has promoted an environment that is conducive to private investment and growth.

The government also can enhance financial development by promoting a strong, independent, and effective legal system. The judiciary plays an important role in enforcing the constitutional protection of individual and property rights and by adjudicating commercial disputes. The benefits of an efficient judiciary include the predictability of the legal environment and the protection of investors against policy reversals. The predictability of commercial law reduces the risk associated with saving and other forward-oriented transactions both in the real sector and in the financial system. As a result, this facilitates the maturity transformation role of financial intermediaries as well as portfolio management by savers.

Legal systems in many African countries do not adequately fulfill their role of facilitating and enforcing the rules of economic exchange. Legal procedures often are excessively long, which imposes costly delays on economic actors. The lack of autonomy of the judiciary from the executive branch and from political and business interest groups results in lack of impartiality in the handling of commercial disputes. There are wide variations across African countries in the quality of law and the effectiveness of the legal system in facilitating economic exchange. To date, there are no studies on Africa that have linked these cross-country variations in the legal system to differences in financial development. It would be worthwhile to investigate the links between enforcement of investor rights and financial market development in the case of African countries.

B. The Role of the Central Bank: Independence and Regulatory Efficiency

The development of robust financial systems in African countries will necessitate the ability of central banks to exercise efficiently their functions to promote the stability of the financial system and the macroeconomy. To achieve this goal, central banks need to be endowed with an adequate level of autonomy. In principle, central bank independence serves as a restraint on government policy, especially by shielding monetary policy from fiscal indiscipline through specific rules governing government borrowing from the central bank. This enables the central bank to exercise discretionary monetary policy rather than simply being a "printing press" for the government. Central bank independence also plays an important role in establishing credibility for monetary policy, which is a key ingredient for the stability of the macro-economy. Credibility of the central bank facilitates decision making by private actors by reducing the uncertainty of the policy environment.

In most African countries the central banks have not performed well in their function as a restraint on government policy, and they have also performed poorly in their role as regulators of the banking sector. Until recently, most countries lacked the basic laws that govern the regulatory functions of the central bank, and, even when the laws existed, they were poorly enforced. This is true for national banks as well as supranational banks, as in the case of the Communauté Financière Africaine (CFA) zone, for instance. We highlight three main reasons for these weaknesses.

First, national authorities have regarded the central bank as their primary financier and have therefore been reluctant to relinquish their political leverage over monetary policy for the purpose of deficit financing. This illustrates the short-term thinking that characterizes political calculations on the part of national leaders.

The second factor is the poor institutional design of central banks starting from their creation. For example, while countries have rules on limits for government borrowing from the central bank, they rarely have statutory provisions for conditionality and sanctions in the event that those rules are violated. Moreover, the leadership of central banks (national and regional) is generally not independent of the executive branch of government. Governors of national central banks in Sub-Saharan Africa (with few exceptions, such as South Africa) usually have little or no independence from the government. This is also the case for the regional central banks in the CFA zone. For instance, the members of the boards of the two regional central banks of the CFA zone are representatives of the finance ministries of member countries and include no representatives from commercial banks. Recently, many countries have made significant advances in this area with the establishment or strengthening of banking laws to provide more independence to the central bank and a stronger prudential regulation base.[28]

The third factor is the lack of a strong private financial sector lobby.[29] An active private financial sector lobby is an important factor in fostering central bank independence especially when the formal institutional foundation is weak or inexistent. The private financial sector has an interest in central bank independence because it is a means to achieving greater price stability. Due to the inherent maturity mismatches between the assets and liabilities of financial institutions, inflation volatility is highly costly for these institutions.

The willingness of politicians to grant central bank independence depends on whether the perceived problem (or political liability) is price instability or low growth. If it is the former, governments are likely to be more inclined to relinquish control over monetary policy, whereas if it is the latter politicians may sacrifice monetary policy autonomy to the short-run benefits of expansionary monetary policy. In the long run, however, countries benefit from the macroeconomic stability that arises from monetary policy autonomy.

Before closing the discussion of central bank independence, two observations are warranted. First, while central bank independence has received the most attention, there are alternative arrangements that can be used to restrain monetary policy.[30] Examples include the adherence to a fixed exchange rate regime and membership to a monetary union. However, just as in the case of central bank independence, these alternative arrangements are effective only if there are clear rules that prevent countries from reneging on the commitment. Second, unlike what some scholars claim, having an independent central bank (or adhering to any other institutional arrangement of restraint) is not like having a free lunch. Central bank independence involves a trade-off between price stability and the ability of national authorities to respond to exogenous shocks.

Excessively rigid monetary policy can be counterproductive, as was seen in the case of CFA zone countries from the 1980s to the early 1990s. Following the collapse of commodity prices in the late 1970s, these countries suffered the "twin blows" of declining terms of trade and real appreciation of the CFA due to the appreciation of the French franc, especially vis-à-vis the dollar. In the end, while CFA zone countries enjoyed higher price stability than most other African countries, this came at the cost of a protracted recession that could have been avoided under a more flexible monetary policy and exchange rate regime.

C. DOES FINANCIAL STRUCTURE MATTER?
MARKETS VERSUS BANKS

In designing policies aimed at developing their financial systems to stimulate economic growth, African countries must address two related but distinct questions. First, what are the best strategies for fostering financial development? Second, which financial structure—bank-based or stock-market-based, or a combination of the two—is most appropriate to their national objectives and their specific economic environment? While the first question has attracted substantial attention both in academia and in policy circles, the issue of financial structure has received relatively less consideration. Nonetheless, there are good reasons for why African countries must take this issue seriously. Some of these reasons are highlighted below.

First, historical evidence suggests that a connection exists between a country's stage of development and the structure of its financial system. In the early stages of development, banks play a predominant role in financing investment in infrastructure, which stimulates the growth process. As a country reaches higher levels of income, it is expected that stock markets play an increasing role. This argument has been supported both by historical studies on industrial growth and by more recent studies using broad datasets on financial structure around the world.[31] These studies find that more developed countries tend to have relatively larger and more liquid stock markets while the financial systems of less developed countries tend to be predominantly bank based.

Second, there is a close connection between financial structure and the type of investment finance supplied by the financial system. Banks tend to specialize in debt finance, while stock markets provide equity finance. Both forms of finance are needed for private sector activity, and the economy will prosper better when both forms of finance are available.

Empirical research shows that bank loans constitute the primary source of outside funding for the corporate sector. For instance, U.S. banks provided about 62% of total outside finance for nonfinancial firms on average for the 1970–1998 period, while stock issues accounted for only 2%.[32] Banks play a predominant role in supplying both short-term and long-term credit. By providing liquidity through short-term credit that can be used to finance working capital, banks allow businesses to release their own internal funds to finance fixed long-term capital. Banks and firms may also enter into explicit agreements whereby short-term loans are periodically renewed, which ultimately converts these loans into long-term finance. Such financing arrangements were prevalent during the English industrial revolution.[33]

At their current level of development and given their immense needs for financing physical capital accumulation in infrastructure, African countries will benefit from fostering the development of a sound banking system. At the same time, they must forge ahead with policy reforms that encourage the development of bond and equity markets. The emphasis should be on providing the proper macroeconomic and institutional environment that facilitates financial intermediation in general. In such an environment, both banks and stock markets are likely to prosper.

D. FINANCIAL INTERMEDIATION AND THE CAPITAL FLIGHT PROBLEM

According to recent studies, Africa as a region has the highest amount of private assets held abroad compared to other developing regions.[34] Capital flight is pervasive, especially in the severely indebted low-income countries, which at the same time are overburdened by high levels of indebtedness.[34a] The illicit outflows of capital impose high costs on African economies and must be regarded by policymakers as an urgent matter of concern.

Some studies have investigated the causes or determinants of capital flight from Africa using both cross-country data and country-specific case studies. These studies find that capital flight is higher in countries (or episodes) with high corruption, bad governance, and high political instability. Olopoenia found that capital flight in Uganda was higher during the periods of political and economic instability in the 1970s and the first half of the 1980s. Excessive monetary expansion, high inflation, and high fiscal deficits also tend to be correlated with high capital flight. The cross-country study by Hermes and Lensink, the study by Nyoni on Tanzania, and the study by Olopoenia on Uganda provide some evidence that supports this prediction.

Another important factor of capital flight is market distortions, especially in the form of overvalued exchange rates and repressed interest rates. Nyoni finds that the black market premium, which is an indicator of market distortions, influences the level of capital flight. Based on data from Côte d'Ivoire, Nigeria,

Sudan, Tanzania, Uganda, and Zaïre, the study by Lensink *et al.*, shows that financial liberalization is associated with a decline in capital flight, indicating that reducing market distortions can contribute to reducing capital flight.[35] High country-specific risk leads to high capital flight, as a result of portfolio management by market participants. Using a portfolio choice approach, Collier *et al.*, concluded that high capital flight from Africa was due, among other things, to overvalued exchange rates, high country-specific risk, and high indebtedness.[36]

High capital flight is an impediment to financial market development in various ways. Past and current capital flight constitutes a drain on national resources and depresses private saving and investment. Capital flight contributes to increasing macroeconomic uncertainty, which discourages saving and lending. This is because market participants interpret high capital flight as a signal of loss of control over economic policy by the national authorities. Through herd effects, capital flight can lead to more capital flight as agents seek to minimize expected portfolio losses in the event that economic (and political) conditions deteriorate further. This discourages saving in the domestic financial system, which consequently retards financial development.

V. SUMMARY

Empirical research on the links between financial development and economic growth in Africa is still limited. However the existing evidence suggests that financial market development is positively related to the growth rate of real income. Research in this area is constrained by the lack of detailed information that can allow us to assess the extent to which financial systems fulfill their roles of facilitating exchange, identifying productive investment projects, mobilizing saving, managing risk, and monitoring management. Such information is necessary not only for research but also for formulating appropriate strategies for financial development and economic growth.

The evidence discussed in this chapter indicates that financial systems are still relatively underdeveloped in the majority of African countries. Aggregate (traditional) measures of financial intermediation show that credit supply has either stagnated or declined in most Sub-Saharan African countries in the past two decades. However, recent structural and institutional indicators of financial market development paint a relatively more optimistic picture. These indicators show that a number of countries have made significant progress in promoting an environment that is conducive to financial intermediation. This is typically the case for countries that have consistently pursued macroeconomic reforms, especially through fiscal discipline, which has promoted a stable business environment. Much progress is still needed, however, especially to strengthen the institutional framework for banking regulation, promote monetary policy autonomy, establish government and central bank credibility, and develop banking supervision capacity (through investment in technology and human capital), which will create an environment that is conducive to investment and saving. Progress in those areas not only will promote financial market development but will also foster economic growth.

ACKNOWLEDGMENT

The author is grateful for funding from the Ford Foundation and the Political Economy Research Institute (PERI) at the University of Massachusetts. He also appreciates comments from participants at the PERI international workshop on "Finance and Investment," October 27–28, 2000, at the University of Massachusetts. Jane D'Arista, Mark Brenner, and three anonymous reviewers provided helpful comments on an earlier draft of this manuscript. Research assistance from Lawrance Evans is very well appreciated.

DISCUSSION QUESTIONS

1. What is the role of the central bank in promoting the stability of the financial system?
2. Should African countries focus on developing stock markets or banks? How relevant is this issue?
3. What are the effects of fiscal deficits on financial development and financial stability?
4. How important is the legal system for financial intermediation?
5. African countries are generally regarded (by investors) as risky. How does this perception affect financial intermediation?
6. Many African banking systems have experienced high default rates. What are the economic and institutional factors that contribute to the poor performance of African banking systems?
7. Identify the effects of financial openness on financial development in African countries.
8. How does capital flight affect financial intermediation?
9. What are the expected effects of financial development on capital flight?
10. What is the relevance of central bank independence for financial intermediation?
11. Information imperfections in financial markets are probably higher in African countries than in developed countries. Why?

NOTES

[1]Beck, T. and Levine, R. (2000) *New Firm Formation and Industry Growth: Does Having a Market-Based or Bank-Based System Matter?*, Working Paper 0004, University of Minnesota, Carlson School of Management; Beck, T., Levine, R., and Loayza, N. (1999) *Finance and the Sources of Growth*, Working Paper 9907, University of Minnesota, Carlson School of Management; King, R.G. and Levine, R. (1993) "Finance, Entrepreneurship, and Growth: Theory and Evidence," *Journal of Monetary Economics*, 32, 513–542; King, R.G. and Levine, R. (1993) "Finance and Growth: Schumpeter Might Be Right," *Quarterly Journal of Economics*, 108(3), 717–737.

[2]Ndikumana, L. (2000) "Financial Determinants of Domestic Investment in Sub-Saharan Africa: Evidence from Panel Data," *World Development*, 28(2), 381–400.

[3]Pagano, M. (1993) "Financial Markets and Growth," *European Economic Review*, 37, 613–622.

[4]Myers, S. and Majluf, N. (1984) "Corporate Financing and Investment Decisions When Firms Have Information That Investors Do Not Have," *Journal of Financial Economics*, 13, 187–221.

[5]Stiglitz, J. and Weiss, A. (1981) "Credit Rationing in Markets with Imperfect Information," *American Economic Review*, 71(3), 393–410.

[6]Diamond, D. (1984) "Financial Intermediation and Delegated Monitoring," *Review of Economic Studies*, 51(3), 393–414.

[7]Robinson, J. (1952) *The Role of Interest and Other Essays*, London: Macmillan. Schumpeter, J.A. (1934) *The Theory of Economic Development*, Cambridge: Harvard University Press.

[8]Levine, R. (1997) "Financial Development and Economic Growth: Views and Agenda," *Journal of Economic Literature*, 35, 688–726.

[9]Rousseau, P., and Silla, R. (1999) "Emerging Financial Markets and Early U.S. Growth," NBER Working Paper 7448; Rousseau, P. and Wachtel, P. (1998) "Financial Intermediation and Economic Performance: Historical Evidence from Five Industrialized Countries," *Journal of Money, Credit and Banking*, 30(4), 657–678.

[10]Corosso, V. (1970) *Investment Banking in America*, Boston, MA: Harvard University Press; Haber, S. (1991) "Industrial Concentration and the Capital Markets: A Comparative Study of Brazil, Mexico, and the United States, 1830–1930," *Journal of Economic History*, 51(3), 559–580. For more references on this topic, see Levine, R. (1997) "Financial Development and Economic Growth: Views and Agenda," *Journal of Economic Literature*, 35, 688–726. Cameron, R., Crisp, O., Patrick, H., and Tilly (1967) *Banking in the Early Stages of Industrialization. A Study in Comparative Economic History*. New York: Oxford University Press.

[11]Rajan, R. and Zingales, L. (1998) "Financial Dependence and Growth," *American Economic Review*, 88(3), 559–586; Demirgüç-Kunt, A. and Maksimovic, V. (1996) "Stock Market Development and Financing Choices of Firms," *World Bank Economic Review*, 10(2), 341–369; Beck, T. and Levine, R. (2000) *New Firm Formation and Industry Growth: Does Having a Market-Based or Bank-Based System Matter?*, Working Paper 0004, University of Minnesota, Carlson School of Management; Fazzari, S., Hubbard, G., and Petersen, B. (1988) "Financing Constraints and Corporate Investment," *Brookings Papers on Economic Activity*, 1, 141–195.

[12]Demirgüç-Kunt, A. and Levine, R. (1999) "Bank-based and Market-based Financial Systems: Cross-Country Comparisons," The World Bank, Policy Research Working Paper 2143.

[13]Mehran, H., Ugolini, P., Briffaux, J.P., Iden, G., Lybek, T., Swaray, S., and Hayward, P. (1998) *Financial Sector Development in Sub-Saharan African Countries*, Occasional Paper 169, International Monetary Fund; Gelbard, E. and Leite, S.P. (1999) *Measuring Financial Development in Sub-Saharan Africa*, Working Paper 99/105, International Monetary Fund.

[14]Gelbard and Leite's survey covered only 1997. The information for 1987 was compiled retroactively by the authors from various sources. This information was then reviewed by IMF country economists, who obtained input from country authorities and IMF resident representatives. See also

Barth, J.R., Caprio, Jr., G., and Levine, R. (2000) "Banking Systems Around the Globe: Do Regulation and Ownership Affect Performance and Stability?" World Bank, Working Paper 2325 and Demirgüç-Kunt and Levine (1999). See Reference in Footnote 9.

[15]For surveys of the recent literature on economic performance in Africa, see Collier, P. and Gunning, J.W. (1999) "Explaining African Economic Performance," *Journal of Economic Literature*, 37(1), 64–111.

[16]Easterly, W. and Levine, R. (1997) "Africa's Growth Tragedy: Policies and Ethnic Divisions," *Quarterly Journal of Economics*, 112(2), 103–1250; Chari, V.V., Kehoe, P.J., and McGrattan, E.R. (1997) "The Poverty of Nations: A Quantitative Investigation," Staff Report 204, Research Department, Federal Reserve Bank of Minneapolis.

[17]Mecagni, M. and Sourial, M. (1999) *The Egyptian Stock Market: Efficiency Tests and Volatility Effects*, Working Paper 99/48, International Monetary Fund.

[18]Levine, R. and Zervos, S. (1998) "Capital Control Liberalization and Stock Market Development," *World Development*, 26(7), 1169–1183.

[19]UNCTAD (1992–2000) *World Investment Reports*, New York: United Nations; UNCTAD (1995) *Foreign Direct Investment in Africa*, New York: United Nations.

[20]Mehran, H., Ugolini, P., Briffaux, J.P., Iden, G., Lybek, T., Swaray, S., and Hayward, P. (1998) *Financial Sector Development in Sub-Saharan African Countries*, Occasional Paper 169, International Monetary Fund; Gelbard, E. and Leite, S.P. (1999) *Measuring Financial Development in Sub-Saharan Africa*, Working Paper 99/105, International Monetary Fund.

[21]Gelbard, E. and Leite, S.P. (1999) *Measuring Financial Development in Sub-Saharan Africa*, Working Paper 99/105, International Monetary Fund.

[22]Mehran, H., Ugolini, P., Briffaux, J.P., Iden, G., Lybek, T., Swaray, S., and Hayward, P. (1998) *Financial Sector Development in Sub-Saharan African Countries*, Occasional Paper 169, International Monetary Fund.

[23]Odedokun, M.O. (1996) "Alternative Econometric Approaches for Analyzing the Role of the Financial Sector in Economic Growth: Time-Series Evidence from LDCs," *Journal of Development Economics*, 50, 119–146; Spears, A. (1992) "The Role of Financial Intermediation in Economic Growth in Sub-Saharan Africa," *Canadian Journal of Development Studies*, 13(3), 361–380.

[24]Allen, D. and Ndikumana, L. (2000) "Financial Intermediation and Economic Growth in Southern Africa," *Journal of African Economics*, 9(2), 132–160.; Gelbard, E. and Leite, S.P. (1999) *Measuring Financial Development in Sub-Saharan Africa*, Working Paper 99/105, International Monetary Fund. In Gelbard and Leite's regressions, the change in the financial development index is statistically significant only when it is entered simultaneously with the index of initial level of financial development.

[25]King, R.G. and Levine, R. (1993) "Finance, Entrepreneurship, and Growth: Theory and Evidence," *Journal of Monetary Economics*, 32, 513–542.

[26]Gelbard, E. and Leite, S.P. (1999) *Measuring Financial Development in Sub-Saharan Africa*, Working Paper 99/105, International Monetary Fund.

[27]See Levine, R., Loayza, N., and Beck, T. (2000) "Financial Intermediation and Growth: Causality and Causes," *Journal of Monetary Economics*, 46(1), 31–77.; Beck, T., Levine, R., and Loayza, N. (1999) *Finance and the Sources of Growth*, Working Paper 9907, University of Minnesota, Carlson School of Management.

[28]Aryeetey, E. and Senbet, L. (2000) *Essential Financial Market Reforms in Africa* [mimeo], University of Ghana and University of Maryland.

[29]Stasavage, D. (2000) "The Franc Zone as a Restraint," in P. Collier and C. Pattillo, Eds., *Investment and Risk in Africa*, New York: St. Martin's Press, pp. 275–304.

[30]The conventional assumption is that central bankers are more conservative (have a stronger tolerance level for the costs associated with achieving low inflation) than the society as whole. See Rogoff, K. (1985) "The Optimal Degree of Commitment to an Intermediate Monetary Target,"

Quarterly Journal of Economics, 100(4), 1169–1189. This motivates the emphasis on central bank independence as a means to achieving price stability.

[31]Cameron, R., Crisp, O., Patrick, H., and Tilly, R. (1967) *Banking in the Early Stages of Industrialization: A Study in Comparative Economic History*, New York: Oxford University Press.

[32]For further evidence on the composition of outside finance for nonfinancial firms, see Fazzari, S., Hubbard, G., and Petersen, B. (1988) "Financing Constraints and Corporate Investment," *Brookings Papers on Economic Activity*, 1, 141–195; Mayer, C. (1990) "Financial Systems, Corporate Finance, and Economic Development," In Hubbard, G., Ed., *Assymetric Information Corporate Finance and Investment*, Chicago: University of Chicago Press, 307–332.

[33]Cameron, R., Crisp, O., Patrick, H., and Tilly, R. (1967) *Banking in the Early Stages of Industrialization: A Study in Comparative Economic History*, New York: Oxford University Press.

[34]Collier, P., Hoeffler, A., and Pattillo, C. (2001) "Flight Capital as a Portfolio Choice." *World Bank Econiomic Review*, 15(1), 55–80.

[34a]Boyce, J.K. and Ndikumana, L. (2001) "Is Africa a Net Creditor? New Estimates of Capital Flight from Severely Indebted Sub-Saharan African Countries 1970–1996," *Journal of Development Studies*, 38(2), 27–56.

[35]Olopoenia, R. (2000) "Capital Flight from Uganda, 1971–94," in I. Ajayi and M. Khan, Eds., *External Debt and Capital Flight in Sub-Saharan Africa*, Washington, D.C.: The IMF Institute, pp. 238–264; Hermes, N. and Lensink, R. (1992) "The Magnitude and Determinants of Capital Flight: The Case for Six Sub-Saharan African Countries," *De Economist*, 140 (4), 515–530; Nyoni, T. (2000) "Capital Flight from Tanzania," in I. Ajayi and M. Khan, Eds., *External Debt and Capital Flight in Sub-Saharan Africa*, Washington, D.C.: The IMF Institute, pp. 265–299; Lensink, R., Hermes, N., and Murinde, V. (1998) "The Effect of Financial Liberalization on Capital Flight in African Economies," *World Development*, 26(7), 1349–1368; Ndikumana, L. and Boyce, J.K. (2002) "Public Debts and Private Assets; Explaining Capital Flight from Sub-Saharan African Countries," University of Massachusetts, Department of Economics and Political Economy Research Institute, Working paper 2002-2, forthcoming in *World Development*, January 2003.

[36]Collier, P., Hoeffler, A., and Pattillo, C. (2001) "Flight Capital as a Portfolio Choice," *World Bank Econiomic Review*, 15(1), 55–80.

CHAPTER 17

Saving, Investment, and Growth in Sub-Saharan Africa

SEYMOUR PATTERSON

Department of Economics, Truman State University, Kirksville, Missouri 63501

KEY TERMS

Absolute income hypothesis	Human capital formation
Allocative efficiency	Iddir
Democracies	Institutional factors
Dependency	Investment
Deterrent effect of investment	Life-cycle hypothesis
Developing countries	Marxism
Economic growth	Neoclassical growth
Endogenous growth	Physical capital formation
Financing gap	Political instability
Foreign aid	Relative income hypothesis
Foreign capital	Resource balance
Foreign exchange earnings	Social costs
Harrod–Domar growth model	Solow–Swan growth model
Human capital	

I. INTRODUCTION

In recent years, economic performance in Sub-Saharan Africa (SSA) has been increasingly bleak. Population growth rates have been running ahead of real output growth rates, implying that output per capita has been declining. Many views have been put forward to explain Africa's poor performance relative to other regions. One old but important view holds that SSA has an abundance of labor and a shortage of capital required for growth. Indeed, the general consensus is that fixed physical capital formation is essential to economic

African Economic Development

growth and development through its effects on productivity. The problem for SSA is that domestic saving under-performs domestic investment. That is, SSA faces a financing gap, which might be filled by means of exports, foreign credit, and foreign aid. The purpose of closing the finance gap is to ensure capital formation that would stimulate growth in SSA. However, despite some evidence of a strong correlation between investment and output growth in industrialized countries, the evidence supporting such a relationship in developing countries is unsettled.

For its part, saving depends largely on income and on whether income is seen as permanent (or life-cycle income) or temporary. Saving rates and income rates are believed to be positively correlated in developed economies. However, is this generally true for SSA as well? Traditionally, saving behavior in SSA differs from saving behavior in the Western economies. People have trust in fully developed financial institutions that also characterize Western economies. These institutions are the sources of funds that find their way into investment. In the West, people save in an attempt to smooth out consumption over time. Saving behavior in Africa may be different qualitatively and still be based on a desire to smooth out consumption over time. That is, in Africa saving might be equally intended to maintain standards of living in the face of income volatility and uncertainty over time.

Across countries the conventional wisdom is that saving as a share of income tends to be higher in high-income countries than in low-income countries. Investment as a proportion of GDP range from 15% to about 27% in a selected group of SSA countries. Capital accumulation financing relies heavily on export earnings, foreign credit, and foreign aid as sources of finance. Foreign credit has increased the outstanding liability, external debt, of many SSA countries. Servicing the debt imposes a drag on output performance and siphons off funds that could flow into investment. So one has to ask, will debt relief increase investment and, hence, output? The counterintuitive answer is no. The problem is simple. Max Corden of the International Monetary Fund has argued that debt forgiveness can be an investment disincentive. His argument can be summarized as follows. If there is no debt payment of principal and interest, the country will have no need to produce more in the current period, so investment will be lower and consumption will be higher. If the country has to make a scheduled payment in the next period, it will have an incentive to invest more in the current period, so consumption will be lower.

The interaction of saving, investment, and growth is explained by a number of models. Saving models include the Keynesian absolute income hypothesis, the permanent income hypothesis, and the life-cycle hypothesis. Also the neoclassical growth model, Harrod–Domar model, and Solow–Swan model can explain the effects of investment on growth. It is important to ask how relevant these models, which were developed by Western thinkers in the context of their own experience, are to the SSA experience. The neoclassical model is frequently used to study economic performance in SSA. The Harrod–Domar model overstates growth in SSA, and the Swan–Solow model may not be applicable to SSA because of its relatively capital-intensive emphasis and its inclusion of depreciation.

Endogenous growth models are also being used to address issues of growth in SSA countries. These models have the virtue that they rely largely on domestic actions or permanent changes in certain policy variables that have long-term effects of economic growth. There is a class of endogenous growth models that are driven by technological change that come from research and development efforts of profit maximizers, which provide the justification or the rationale for subsidies to research and development (R&D) and other government policies that may influence the long-run rate of economic growth. While the shortage of R&D in Africa seems to remove the R&D models from consideration, other variants of the endogenous growth models have been used successfully to explain why growth in Africa is low.

Noneconomic factors can, of course, influence economic performance. Political instability—revolutions, wars, coups, and assassinations—can have deterrent consequences for investment. These factors can reduce growth through their negative influence on investment.

In an interesting article, Scully (1988) provides evidence that the nature of political institutions can make a significant difference in the way scarce resources are allocated within a country. He demonstrated that democracies coupled with market capitalism that observe property rights, freedom of choice, and the profit motive are more efficient economic systems than other alternatives.[1]

The remaining task for policymakers in SSA is to determine what growth rate is desired and the level of saving and investment needed to achieve it. This is possible only if output, saving, and investment are in fact correlated in some consistent and stable way.

II. ECONOMIC GROWTH, SAVING, AND INVESTMENT

Table 17.1 shows that for the period 1990 to 1998 real gross domestic product (GDP) growth rates were mostly positive for SSA countries. The rates are modest and highlight just how daunting is the problem of growth SSA faces and the need for African countries to find ways to increase their growth rates and turn their economies around. One solution is to raise the level of investment on the assumption that growth and investment are positively correlated. The ratio of investment to GDP is listed in column four of the table, which shows that investment is an important part of GDP. The saving ratio is also depicted in the table. The saving ratios in column three are less than the investment ratios in all

TABLE 17.1   Economic Growth, Saving and Investment

Countries	Real Growth, 1990–1998 (%)	Saving/GDP (%)	Investment/GDP (%)	Financing Gap (%)
Algeria	1.20	33	27	6
Angola	−0.04	13	25	−12
Benin	4.60	9	16	−8
Botswana	4.80	35	25	10
Burkina Faso	3.50	11	26	−14
Burundi	−3.20	−1	8	−9
Cameroon	0.06	20	18	2
Central African Republic	1.50	4	14	−9
Chad	4.60	1	19	−18
Congo, Democratic Republic of	−5.10	9	8	2
Congo Republic	1.00	26	35	−9
Côte d'Ivoire	3.50	24	18	6
Egypt, Arab Republic of	4.20	10	19	−9
Eritrea	5.20	−29	41	−70
Ethiopia	4.90	9	20	−11
Ghana	4.20	13	23	−10
Guinea	5.00	19	22	−3
Kenya	2.20	13	18	−5
Lesotho	7.20	−43	49	−91
Madagascar	1.30	5	13	−8
Malawi	3.90	5	18	−13
Mali	3.70	10	21	−11
Mauritania	4.20	7	22	−15
Morocco	2.10	18	22	−3
Mozambique	5.70	1	21	−20
Namibia	3.50	19	19	0
Niger	1.90	3	10	−7
Nigeria	2.60	12	20	−8
Rwanda	−3.30	−7	10	−17
Senegal	3.00	15	20	−5
Sierra Leone	−4.70	−1	8	−9
South Africa	1.60	17	16	1
Tanzania	2.90	6	16	−10
Togo	2.30	7	14	−7
Tunisia	4.40	24	25	−2
Uganda	7.40	6	15	−10
Zambia	1.00	5	14	−9
Zimbabwe	2.00	20	21	−2

Source: World Development Report 2000, pp. 250, 254, and 255.

but four countries—Algeria, Botswana, Cameroon, and Côte d'Ivoire. Investment can increase output so the solution to Africa's problem would appear to be devising a strategy that would lead to more investment. The financing gap represents the difference between domestic saving and investment as a proportion of GDP. Saving is the portion of GDP that can be used to finance investment. Absent sufficient domestic saving, the country would have to resort to foreign aid or debt. Foreign aid such as grants and concessional loans contributes to growth by relieving bottlenecks associated with low incomes. Rapid growth may require a rate of investment that is beyond what can be financed from low saving due to subsistence income. By filling the saving gap foreign aid can enable the achievement of short-run growth targets. In the long-run structural changes will be needed for long-run growth in SSA.

If SSA wishes to raise output, it must raise the level of investment. Higher investment would raise income with a multiplier effect and higher income will positively impact saving and investment. Policymakers will have to find a way to channel the resulting saving from higher output into investment.

It is also interesting to note that investment as a proportion of GDP is between 8 and 49% for the selected SSA countries shown in Table 17.1. Real GDP growth appears to be negatively correlated to the financing gap. This suggests that the indebted countries must increase the inflow of funds from abroad. In fact, in 1998, few African countries had saving ratios that exceeded the investment shown in Table 17.1. Algeria, Botswana, Cameroon, the Democratic Republic of the Congo, Côte d'Ivoire, and South Africa had a positive financing gap, except Namibia where investment just equaled saving and the financing gap was zero. However, most of the countries, the remaining 31 countries, displayed negative signs, meaning that these countries were not generating sufficient domestic saving to finance investment. This fact points to three possible scenarios for the countries. First, despite some arguments to the contrary, there is evidence that more investment will translate into higher output growth rates. The correlation coefficient between growth rates and investment/GDP ratio is 0.55 for the data in Table 17.1. Without ascribing any causality to the correlation coefficient, the only inference it is that growth and the investment/GDP ratio move together. More significantly, because a negative financing gap means that the indebted African countries will be forced to seek financial assistance from the rest of the world, these countries will have to subject themselves to restrictions of both private and official foreign lending organizations. The debt overhang might also have a negative effect on economic growth.

A simple regression analysis shows the relationship between changes in a dependent variable due to changes in one or more independent variables. The simple regression for the available data in Table 17.1 appears in the notes.[2] It illustrates the relationship between investment–GDP growth and GDP growth. It implies that a one-unit rise in the investment-GDP ratio would raise GDP growth by about 0.191%. Second, even if investment and income were positively correlated, the direction of causality would be uncertain. It is possible that increases in investment are associated with increases in output. There is obviously some feedback between output and investment that policymakers must consider.

A. Economic Growth in Sub-Saharan Africa

Some people have used the word *bleak* to describe Africa's economic prospects. Others have said that since 1960 Africa's economic history can be described as a tragedy because it is a story of unfulfilled potential. Botswana was one remarkable exception. In the 1980s, Botswana experienced a boom period with real growth rates averaging over 10% per year. At this rate of growth per capita GDP was doubling every 7.2 years. But the economy took a turn for the worse in the early 1990s and plunged into recession in 1992/1993. This was at a time when the price of diamonds on the world market was declining. Botswana's experience in this period highlights the problem of many African countries that depend on one commodity as a major source of foreign exchange earnings. A more serious problem for Africa is that real negative growth rates mean that SSA countries could never catch up to rich countries. SSA and Western economies are like two vehicles on a highway traveling in opposite directions. The notion of 'catch up' is meaningless in this context. Catch up would occur only if a negative growing country reverses direction and grows faster than countries with a positive growth rate.

Africa's poor economic performance can be traced to characteristics that African countries share with each other. Government failure is due to misplaced priorities, wasteful spending and mismanagement of investments with low or negative returns, poor planning and implementation of policies, inflation in public goods and poor quality services, and corruption and abuse of public office that cost local taxpayers millions. Trade restrictions and exchange rate controls plague many African countries and negate the benefits from trade—the gains from comparative advantage and specialization. Government subsidies to business, such as foreign aid, foster a culture of dependence, and government intervention favors the few at the expense of the many. These are some shortcomings of the SSA experience that are responsible for poor economic performance and deteriorating living standards in Sub-Saharan Africa.

Elimination of distortions in the economy does not always improve economic performance. For example, the failure of the Russian economy to respond to market signals and takeoff into high growth rates illustrates this point. But, adding distortions can restrain growth, too. For example, the government of Ethiopia has imposed many taxes on the people. There is a direct tax on income, business, agriculture, dividends, and chance winnings. There is a land use tax. There is a tithe on land. There is an education tax, a health tax, and a cattle tax. There is an indirect tax that includes a sales tax, stamp duties, and a salt tax. There are also import and export duties, excise tax on imported products, and a sales tax on imported goods. Taxes tend to distort market signals and can lead to a misallocation of resources. It is no surprise that Ethiopia is among the poorest countries on Earth.

The solution to many of SSA's problems seems clear. Government subsidies and government intervention could be reduced or eliminated. Reducing the size of government as a share of GDP would free up resources that the private sector can add to its production mix in response to market signals to produce goods and services. A small government share of income might reduce interest rates and lead to greater investment, even as the urban sector serves as a magnet pulling people to it from the countryside.

B. INVESTMENT PATTERNS IN SUB-SAHARAN AFRICA

In the short term, more inputs (capital and labor) can be expected to generate more output. But if SSA wants long-term economic growth, increasing inputs will not do it. The data in Table 17.1 suggest that investments that are in short supply may have a role to play in growth. The proceeds from exports can be used to pay for imported capital. The problem with that strategy is the country might have nothing to export or the rest of the world may not want what it wishes to export. Another strategy is to borrow from international lenders to finance imported capital. The immediate problem with that strategy is the repayment of the loan (principal and interest), which must demand significant levels of growth in the borrowing country. A third possibility is foreign aid, but this depends on the fickleness of foreign donors whose motives may be at odds with the goals of the borrowing country. A fourth ploy is to encourage foreign investment into the country by creating a climate friendly to foreign investors. This ploy depends on the credibility that the local government will live up to its commitments to foreign investors. Lock-in mechanisms can be put in place to make it unlikely that future governments will change and be unfriendly to foreign investors, so that foreign investors will feel that their investment will be safe.

After its defeat in Word War II, Japan's infrastructure was in ruins. Yet, 50 years later Japan has become one of the world's richest countries. The Dodge Plan was a Marshall Plan for Japan. But more important than foreign aid, the Japanese controlled access to their market. The government controlled the conditions under which capital, technology, and manufactured goods would leave and enter the country. This strategy allowed the Japanese to open packages of technology and capital. The Ministry of Finance exercised selective control over incoming foreign investment and controlled technology imports to force foreigners to sell raw technology in the form of patents, licenses, and expertise.[3] SSA countries may not be in a position to exercise that kind of leverage over the rest of the world, but they may still be able to do it to a limited degree. It makes no sense for SSA countries to allocate their scarce resources to develop capital that is already in existence. It is far cheaper to open the package and to study what is inside it. Ethiopia is already doing this. Enterprising Ethiopians are manufacturing crude but functional satellite dishes in Ethiopia.

Another way to overcome the investment crunch in SSA is to jump-start these countries with high productivity and capital-intensive industries that employ large numbers of people and accelerate the marginal rate of substitution capital for labor. Technology that contains investments that create new capital stock for projects with low capital/output ratios (fast-time breakeven on capital inputs such as the petrochemical, pharmaceutical, and financial and information sectors) accelerates economic growth by raising income levels. It encourages a better income distribution as higher paid workers get a larger share of GDP and enter the marketplace as consumers and savers.[4]

In Ethiopia the approach to investment and growth is quite comprehensive. Ethiopia embarked on a sector investment program (SIPs) by targeting agriculture, education, health, and roads. It envisions achieving industrialization and economic growth through investment in agriculture. In the early 1990s, the transitional government of Ethiopia pursued a strategy of broadening the agricultural production base through improvement in productivity. The agricultural sector is dominant and accounts for 50% of Ethiopia's GDP, and approximately 85% of the Ethiopian population ekes out a living in the sector. Coffee accounts for 90% of export earnings. The government's strategy includes making the sector a supplier of basic goods and a source of demand for processed agricultural and manufactured goods. In practice, spending in agriculture as a share of GDP declined during the 1990s in Ethiopia.

Education sector development program recognizes that education is an important component of investment in human capital. Education must be regarded as an input in the production function. Like other inputs, broadening access to and improving the quality of education can increase output, but it is shortsighted to depend too much on education for long-term growth. In fact, in Ethiopia the returns to primary education in the labor market have not been very promising. The social returns to primary education are 4.1% for girls and 2.4% for boys. Ironically, the opportunity cost of sending girls to school is high in poor families. Positive social externalities stem from education in general but the job-specific private benefits increase with the level of education, so the government seems willing to completely subsidize primary and secondary education and make at least part of the payments for tertiary education an individual responsibility.

Although education is investment in human capital, which can increase output and also has intrinsic value, it is not a panacea for Africa's problem of low growth. Output can rise with more input of labor or if labor has more capital at its disposal, but the key to long-term economic growth is finding efficient ways of doing things. For example, output would be unchanged whether an uneducated person or an educated person digs a ditch with her hand. A shovel in the hands of either person would increase output. The point is that output depends on more input as well as in the efficient use of these inputs. The key to long-term growth rests on changes in the way things are done, so as to increase total factor productivity. Some African countries are using this two-prong attack (more input and efficiency growth) to solve their slow growth problem. It is a strategy that Ethiopia appears to understand and is willing to put to work.

III. DETERMINANTS OF SAVINGS IN AFRICA

The need for saving to pay for investment in SSA countries cannot be overstated. For there to be domestic savings, production must exceed consumption in the current period. If income is so low that no saving is carried out, then it will not be possible for SSA countries to increase future output and consumption. Imagine for simplicity that there are only two time periods, namely the present and the future. Saving will be the outcome of the choice the countries make between current production and consumption. In the current period, saving occurs when production exceeds consumption. Saving channeled into investment will increase future production and consumption at the rate r, which is the rate of time preference (or alternatively the rate of interest). The budget constraint facing a country is

$$(Q_p - C_p)(1 + r) = (C_F - Q_F),$$

where Q denotes output and C consumption, respectively. From this relationship it is easy to see that present saving $S_p = (Q_p - C_p)$, and Q_p exceeds C_p. Present saving or excess supply can be transformed into future excess demand (or consumption) $(C_F - Q_F)$, where C_F exceeds Q_F at the rate $(1 + r)$. Thus, future consumption C_F can be found to equal $S_p(1 + r)$. Numerically, if $Q_p = 200$, and $C_p = 100$, and $r = 0.05$, then $S_p(1 + r) = 100(1.05) = 105$.

A more realistic way to think of total savings for an economy is in terms of the various components of saving: private, government, and foreign savings. Total saving is the sum of private saving (S_p), government saving (S_g), and foreign savings. Private saving has two components: household and corporate saving. Household saving is calculated as the sum of income, plus interest, plus a factor of income from abroad, plus transfers minus taxes less consumption. Corporate saving is undistributed after-tax corporate profits. Government saving consists of revenues from taxes less government spending, less interest payments, and less transfer. Finally, foreign saving consists of debt finance and equity finance. Or foreign saving can be viewed as the trade deficit plus net inflows from foreign investments. Table 17.2 shows the components and value of Ethiopia's output in

TABLE 17.2 National Accounts for Ethiopia for Fiscal Year
1995/1996 (birr million)

Private consumption	31,240.3
Government spending	4,035.1
Gross investment	7,169.6
Net exports	9,572.3
GDP	52,017.3
Net factor income from abroad	−359.5
GNP	51,657.8
Total tax revenue	6,839.8

Source: *Ethiopia Statistical Abstract* (1997), pp. 252 and 262.

birr for 1998. There are about birr 8 to a U.S. $. This information can be used to calculate total saving for this country.

$$\text{Private savings} = \text{GNP} + \text{net factor income}$$
$$- \text{total tax revenue} - \text{consumption}$$
$$= 51,657.8 + 359.5 - 6839.8 - 31,240.3$$
$$= 13,577.7 \text{ birr.}$$

$$\text{Government savings} = \text{total tax revenue} - \text{government} = 6839.8 - 4035.1$$
$$= 2804.7 \text{ birr.}$$

$$\text{Foreign savings} = -\text{net exports} - \text{net factor income from abroad}$$
$$= -9572.3 - (-359.5) = -9,212.8 \text{ birr.}$$

Total savings equal the sum of private, government, and foreign saving; that is, $S_t = S_p + S_g + S_v = 13,577 + 2804.7 + (-9212.8) = 7169.6$.

This result is none other than the amount of investment, 7169.6, in Table 17.2. So gross investment equals total saving, as must be the case because gross investment contains inventory, which must rise when saving exceeds investment and fall when investment exceeds saving. The problem for a low-income country such as Ethiopia is that efforts to expand collective saving might impoverish the country further. Forced saving in the form of a plethora of taxes and tariffs can have a similar effect. This is the paradox of thrift whereby a rise in collective saving will raise saving in the short term for a given level of income and investment. Long term, however, the implicit reduction in consumption means that income must fall. This illustrates the possibility that an increase in saving can have adverse effects on growth in SSA.

TABLE 17.3. Ratio of Saving to GDP by Income for Selected Countries in 1998

Low Income ($760 or less)	Saving/ GDP (%)	Low-Middle Income ($761–$3030)	Saving/ GDP	Upper-Middle Income ($3031–$9360)	Saving/ GDP (%)
Cameron	20	Algeria	33%	Botswana	35
Chad	1	Egypt	10%	Gabon	Not available
Côte d'Ivoire	13				
Ethiopia	9				
Ghana	13				
Kenya	13				
Nigeria	12				
Mozambique	1				
Senegal	15				
Zambia	5				
Zimbabwe	20				

Source: World Development Report 2000.

A. Domestic Saving in Sub-Saharan Africa

The World Bank furnishes data on gross domestic saving, the difference between GDP and total consumption for SSA. Table 17.3 shows that saving rates had not improved from 1980 to 1998. In 1980, three countries in the group— Algeria, Cameroon, and Nigeria—had positive resource balances. A positive resource balance means domestic saving as a percent of GDP exceeds domestic investment as a percent of GDP. The saving/investment ratio for Algeria was 110 in 1980 and 122 in 1998—an 11% rise. Similarly, for Cameroon the saving–GDP ratio went from 1% in 1980 to 2% in 1998, which represents a rise from 105 in 1980 to 111 in 1998. Nigeria had a reversal of fortunes when its ability to finance investment from domestic saving took a turn for the worse in 1998 when the saving/investment ratio was 148%, which declined by 59–60% in 1998.

Trade deficits, negative net exports, imply than the country is consuming more than it is producing in a given period of time. Trade deficits also mean an excess demand for foreign exchange. The country's currency might depreciate and make the importation of foreign capital goods more expensive and slow down their import. To consume more than it produces a country must secure foreign credit. It must borrow from foreign countries. On the other hand, foreign countries must have positive saving balances and be willing to make loans to deficit countries. Thus, the financing gap in Table 17.1 indicates inflows from foreign countries that add to the deficit country's external debt total, the change in which is the sum of the trade deficit plus the interest of the existing debt.

Another way to think of financing gap is as the difference between income and domestic absorption (i.e., consumption and investment). Both consumption and investment (domestic absorption) are assumed to be functions of income, and the marginal propensities to consume and to invest are positive. Further, absorption is inversely related to devaluation of the exchange rate. The sum of the marginal propensity to consume and to invest is believed to be greater than one. When output is below potential (full employment) devaluation would increase exports and output. However, at full employment output, expansion of net exports is possible only if domestic absorption is curtailed. Increases in income and devaluation would result in inflows.

Many Sub-Saharan African countries use overvaluation to aid in sustaining foreign credit to deal with their investment problems. Long term this is not a good strategy. The World Bank and the IMF may force countries to adopt structural adjustment programs (SAPs), including elimination of currency controls, as a condition for official credit. SAPs cause currency devaluation. Theoretically devaluation will increase exports and income via a multiplier effect. In the first instance, the increase in income due to devaluation will cause both saving and investment to rise, as they are functions of income. The effect on the saving gap is ambiguous. If the increase in saving is greater than the increase in investment the saving gap will narrow. On the other hand, if the rise in saving is less than the rise in investment the saving gap will widen. Finally, if the increase in saving equals the increase in investment the saving gap will remain the same.

Devaluation can also cause the terms of trade to worsen and real income to fall. We can think of devaluation as an increase in prices of traded goods. The resulting deterioration in the terms of trade will cause real income, saving, and investment to fall in the country. The net effect on the saving gap is uncertain. The data for Cameroon illustrate this point. The saving–income ratio in 1980 was 0.22 and in 1998 it was 0.20—a decline of 0.02. On the other hand, the investment–income ratio in 1980 was 0.21 and in 1998 it was 0.18—a decline of 0.03. These changes represent a saving gap improvement of −0.01.

B. The Saving Function in Africa

About 67% of the population in sub-Saharan Africa earns a living in the agrarian sector. A small proportion of the population resides in the urban sector and is employed in industries that pay wages. In 1998 the SSA urban population was 33%. The number of companies in the region is 1077 and represent domestic banking sector credit as a proportion of GDP of 45.5%. Specifically, in Botswana, there were 12 companies that received credit from the banking sector. Kenya has 58 companies receiving a 51.7% credit as a share of GDP from the banking sector at a cost of 11.1% above deposit rates. Nigeria listed 182 companies, which got 14.2% credit from the banking system at

13.1% above deposit rates. The cost of credit (lending less deposit rate) was 4.8%. Average interest rates tend to be high because capital is scarce. Saving has been not very sensitive to these rates of interest because the culture of banking is not well developed in SSA. In Ethiopia the alternative to banks and insurance companies as sources of savings is the Iddir. The Iddir is a grassroots insurance program administered by a community or group to meet emergency situations.[5]

Table 17.3 illustrates that most of the selected 11 countries are low-income economies, where the World Bank defines low income as $760 annually or lower. Saving as a percent of GDP for these countries runs from as little as 1% in Chad and Mozambique to as high as 20% in Zimbabwe and Cameroon. Two countries were classified as low-middle income, Algeria and Egypt, and two as upper-middle income, Botswana and Gabon. None was upper income. It is difficult to discern any pattern from the information in Table 17.3 (perhaps because no allowance is made for the equality of income distribution). However, economists have long held that at any given point in time rich people save more as a percent of income than poor people. Further, in any given economy the saving ratio tends to be constant within a country, but, as the table attests, there is no systematic variation of saving ratios across countries. We have already seen that between 1980 and 1998 saving ratios rose among our selected countries. Tables 17.1 and 17.3 show that saving rates vary across countries. What cannot be deduced from the tables is the hypothesis that rich people save more than poor people.

There are several saving hypotheses that can reconcile at least partially the notion that the propensities to save vary across income and also across countries. These may not all apply to the African experience. For example, in some African countries wage income will not be an important determinant of saving. And because the business sector in the urban landscape is small in proportion to the rest of the economy, profits are not important determinants of investment. To compound matters, the financial infrastructure is often rudimentary, as is the physical superstructure of roads, canals, and rail systems. These facts, coupled with customs and traditions that do not "trust" banks and insurance companies as repositories of funds mean that the practice of saving and investing in the Western sense might be foreign to many Africans. With these caveats aside it is well known in economics that saving and income are positively correlated. The Keynesian absolute income hypothesis informs us that saving is a linear function of disposable income. It is composed of autonomous saving and marginal propensity to consume out of income. The marginal propensity to save is the additional saving arising from additional income. Autonomous saving is independent of the level of disposable income:

$$S = -a + sY_d \qquad (17.1)$$

where S is saving, a is autonomous saving, s is the marginal propensity to save (whose value lies between 0 and 1) and Y_d denotes income minus taxes or disposable income. For low levels of income autonomous saving is negative—there is dissaving. Equation (17.1) implies that over time as income rises the average propensity to save (S/Y) rises.

Duesenberry of Harvard presents an alternative hypothesis. His hypothesis links consumption not only to current income but also to the previous highest level of consumption of the household. The formulation suggests that in the short-run households will attempt to keep consumption proportional to the previous high level of consumption. As income rises over time people will ratchet up their consumption. That is, consumption in subsequent periods will be higher due to changing the values of the highest previous consumption levels. In terms of the saving function, Eq. (17.2) can be rewritten as

$$S = -a + [1 - b(1 - \tau)Y] - eC_h \qquad (17.2)$$

Equation (17.2) shows that increases in income will cause saving (S) to expand by $[1 - b(1 + \tau)]$ and to decrease by e due to changes in C_h, the highest previous level of income. For example, suppose the autonomous consumption (a) is -100, the marginal propensity to consume (b) is 0.90, tax rate τ is 0.2, income is \$1000, the marginal propensity to consume out of the highest previous level of income (e) is 0.3, and the previous level of income is \$500, then saving is

$$S = -100 + [1 - 0.9(1 - 0.2)] * (1000) - 0.3(500) = 300 \qquad (17.3)$$

Remove the last term on the right-hand side of Eq. (17.3) and saving would be higher by \$150. This hypothesis addresses several issues alluded to before. First, it demonstrates that saving and income are positively related, so that increases in income will cause saving to increase, too. Second, the rich save more than the poor. Differences in income between the poor and the rich are manifested in differences in saving rates. Third, cross-country saving patterns are amorphous. This is illustrated in Table 17.4. Low-income countries had higher saving rates than high- and middle-income countries, and middle-income countries saving rates also exceeded high-income countries' saving rates. During the 1980s and 1990s high-income countries (mainly the United States) grew and low-income countries (particularly sub-Saharan African countries) did not grow. Yet, the saving rates in low-income countries rose from 28% to 32%, while high-income countries saw saving ratios decline from 24% to 20%.

In addition, the elite in developing countries buy luxury automobiles; all the kitchen appliances from the West; electronics equipment, such as televisions and VCRs; suits, leather jackets, and jeans; watches; etc. This kind of consumption behavior was more notable in Botswana than in Ethiopia. Cairo has a subway system, expensive modern hotels, and suburbs that look much like a suburb in Kansas City, MO, or Houston, TX. Obviously, the difference between Botswana and Ethiopia might be explained by the huge gap in per capita income between the two countries: however, in both places the middle class emulates the consumption

TABLE 17.4   Saving to GDP Ratios Across Income Levels

	1980	1998
Low income	28	32
Sub-Saharan Africa	26	15
Middle income	25	23
Lower	na	22
Upper	25	21
High income	24	19

Source: World Development Report 2000.

behaviors of Western consumers. The lower classes follow suit by emulating the consumption behavior of the elite in their country. The result of this demonstration effect is that saving across countries varies nonsystematically.

Milton Friedman gives us yet another explanation for the behavior of saving. Friedman's mode of consumption behavior is the permanent income hypothesis. Two kinds of noncorrelated incomes and consumption are identified—permanent income and transitory income, and permanent consumption and transitory consumption. Transitory income originates from unexpected increases in asset value, windfalls, lottery winnings, and capital gains. Consumption (saving) is assumed to depend on permanent income, which is the average expected income over the life of the household. Applied to African, Egypt benefits from annual transfers of income from the United States. This is permanent income. Botswana's foreign exchange earnings from mineral exports make the country more self-sufficient. Similarly, Botswana's income from diamond exports can be viewed also as permanent income. In fact, in 1994 Botswana had stashed away enough reserves to cover imports for 28 months,[6] a proportion of which could be considered permanent income if it were invested at a fixed rate of interest. The consumption function is

$$C = \beta(1 - \alpha)Y_p + \beta\alpha Y_t,$$

where $0 < \alpha < 1$ and $0 < \beta < 1$ is the long-run marginal (average) propensity to consume. From this, the saving function can be written as:

$$S = \alpha + \beta Y_p + \delta Y_t \qquad (17.4)$$

Equation 17.4 implies that all of and only transitory income will be saved if $\beta = 0$, $\alpha = 0$, and $\delta = 1$. Certainly, this would be an extreme case. It is more likely that a large fraction (not all) of transitory income would be saved. An individual who wins the lottery is unlikely to save all the winnings in low-income countries, and it is quite likely that a larger share of transitory income is saved than permanent income. As an aside, in Ethiopia part of the chance winnings is taxed (forced saving) by the Government of Ethiopia to the tune of birr 3.6 million a year.

Another interesting explanation of saving behavior is the life-cycle hypothesis. One version of it has consumption being proportional to the product of working years divided by life expectancy times annual earnings. These relationships can be expressed as

$$C = A/(n - t) + [(w - t)/(n - t)](Y_L),$$

where C is consumption, A is initial assets divided by n, w is working years, n is life expectancy, t is time, and Y_L is annual income. The formula for saving is

$$S = Y - C, S = Y_L - (A/(n - t) + Y_L - [(w - t)/(n - t)]Y_L).$$

Thus, if a worker expects to work for 40 years and live for 55 years and earn $100 a year and starts out with nothing, then saving will be,

$$S = -0 + 1 - (40/55) * 100 = \$27 \qquad (17.5)$$

Saving behavior in low-income countries is not driven by a desire to accumulate but from a desire to protect standard of living in the face of insecurity and income volatility. When income rises saving also rises and when it falls saving falls as well. Most Ethiopians make a meager living in the agricultural sector. The per capita income of Ethiopia is about $100. Most of this income is spent on consumption and saving and the Government of Ethiopia largely undertakes investment. Taxes and high prices are the means by which forced saving takes place. An overpriced currency, government spending, and foreign aid are often sources of finance for domestic investment.

IV. DETERMINANTS OF INVESTMENT IN AFRICA: INVESTMENT AS A SHARE OF GROSS DOMESTIC PRODUCT

Table 17.3 shows investment as a share of GDP for 18 selected countries in Africa. What is striking is the high ratio of investment to income. These ratios run the gamut from 14% in Zambia to as high as 27% in Algeria. The ratios seem to indicate that the countries understand the relationship between capital accumulation and economic performance.

Sub-Saharan African countries fit the profile of developing countries with scarce capital, high risk levels, low levels of information that lead to much uncertainty about the profitability of new investment, and, finally, low levels of income, which mean greater risk aversion. Confronted with these constraints, how do policymakers in SSA countries attract foreign and domestic investment? An important part of the answer to this question is an identification of the variables in the investment function. On the demand side, the marginal productivity of capital determines investment at the micro level. Investment increases the productivity of labor at a decreasing rate, so the marginal benefit of investment is the value of labor released from production. At the macro level, investment is a positive function of income and a negative function of the interest rate. The effect of income on investment is not clear cut because it depends on the income elasticities of demand for investment. In competitive markets the price of capital in industrialized countries will tend to equal its expected annual return divided by market interest rate plus depreciation. Firms in competitive markets will be able to determine their desired level of capital by equating the supply price (which is infinitely elastic) to the demand for capital. For the typical firm in a SSA country, the supply of foreign capital is perfectly elastic.

An increase in demand for the country's output will increase the demand for the input used intensively in production. If that input is capital, the investment–GNP ratio shown in Table 17.1 will rise. SSA countries are not capital rich. By and large they are producers and exporters of agricultural goods and minerals— Botswana's major source of foreign exchange earnings is diamonds and Ethiopia's might just be coffee. Attracting foreign investment might increase domestic investment provided that certain critical conditions are present. A fixed exchange rate environment is an implicit assurance to borrowers that they can ignore the exchange rate risks in the foreign short-term capital market. Such an assurance will encourage inflow of short-term capital but can also increase reliance on short-term foreign debt. The loss of credibility in the regime could have the adverse effect of causing substantial outflows. Long-term capital inflows such as foreign direct investment on growth have an export bias. That is, countries that promote exports have a higher rate of growth than countries that follow import-replacement policies. That may be the case because international companies must be competitive in the global market to garner larger international market shares. One way to be competitive is for multinational corporations to transfer technology to their host countries and train local workers. SSA countries stand a better chance to grow if they focus on exports to earn foreign exchange (to pay for capital imports) rather than concentrate on import replacement. SSA countries can increase the likelihood of becoming host countries for multi-national corporations if they pursue trade liberalization policies.

V. SAVING AND ECONOMIC GROWTH

A. NEOCLASSICAL GROWTH MODELS WITHIN THE AFRICAN CONTEXT

The question of relevance of Western theories to less developed countries is unavoidable. This is no less true of Africa, where assumptions about marginalism, open and competitive markets within the *laissez-faire* framework, do not apply. African markets are characterized by rigidities, lack of information, government ownership of productive resources, regulated exchange rates, and closed markets. In Africa there is a conflict between consumption and growth. When income is low, consumption trumps saving. Furthermore, there is a tendency for Africans to try to emulate the saving behavior of people in more advanced countries, a phenomenon known as the demonstration effect. In fact, the demonstration effect can be observed in the African's penchant for Mercedes automobiles, imported clothes and music, and to some degree Western foods. Far more important is the purchase of military hardware from the West. As a case in point, the war between Ethiopia and Eritrea has been waged with pricey Russian and Japanese fighter jets, tanks, personnel carriers, and other kinds of weapons, none of them produced in the warring countries. It makes one wonder how it is possible for poor countries to wage wars that carry such enormous price tags.

The neoclassical model is based on a production function that consists of labor, capital, and technology. It is the kind of function that assumes that you can double your output by doubling your inputs. It also assumes that when one factor, say labor is increased, while the other factor, capital, is held constant, output will still increase but at a decreasing rate. The technology in the function implies that, if you want to produce the computer on which this chapter is being typed, not only do you need capital and labor, but you also must know how to make the computer. The neoclassical model can be used to show that the growth rate of output is positively related to the growth rate of the capital–labor ratio. Suppose this positive is a constant of value 3.5. During the period 1990–1998, GDP in Ethiopia grew by 4.9%. Then it is possible to estimate the rate of growth of the capital–labor ratio needed to achieve 4.9% per capita GDP growth. The answer, of course is 1.4. If this model can be applied to SSA, the policymaker could set a target rate of growth for real per capita GDP. Estimates of the elasticity can be found from actual data for real GDP, capital, and labor for each country. The problem (which will not go away) for these countries is their lack of capital. So, even if they can determine just how much capital they need to achieve a desired rate of growth of real per capita GDP, they still have to figure out how to get it.

B. THE SOLOW–SWAN MODEL

What is the steady-state growth rate for SSA and what is the level of saving that this growth rate requires? This is not an easy question to answer because African countries are not monolithic. But the neoclassic model might help us in a search for an answer to these questions. To determine the theoretic performance of the saving rate, recall that *ex post* investment equals the sum of total saving originating in the government sector, the private sector, and the foreign sector. It follows that the change in net investment at a given point in time is equal to gross investment less depreciation. Because saving equals investment the change in capital at a point in time can be expressed in terms of the saving rate and income. That is, investment can be set to equal the saving rate times output, which is a function of capital (K), labor (L), and technology (t); i.e., $F(K, L; t)$. The assumption, of course, is that the marginal productivities of capital and labor are positive but decreasing. The production function is written in intensive form. The change in capital per unit of labor (k) at a point in time is equal to the saving rate s times output Q (i.e., capital/saving) less the sum of the growth rate of labor n and the rate of depreciation α times the capital–labor ratio k. The final result can be written as:[7]

$$d(k)/dt = sQ/L - (n + \alpha)k \qquad (17.6)$$

It follows from Eq. (17.6) that an increase in the capital–labor ratio will cause output per unit of labor to rise. If there are no saving ($s = 0$), the change in the capital–labor ratio will decline by α partly due to the rise in labor at the rate n. We do not yet have enough information to determine the optimal saving rate. But Eq. (17.6) represents forces at work, sQ/k, which are decreasing, and the constant $n + \alpha$. The steady state for the country occurs when Eq. (17.6) equals zero. So, the steady-state rate of growth of saving is $(n + \alpha)k/Q$. That is, the steady-state rate of growth of a country with a population growth rate of 2.8%, depreciation of 3%, a capital–output ratio of 5, and population of 60 (million) yields a steady-state rate of 0.45%. A more interesting question is whether poor countries grow faster than richer ones. To answer this question we differentiate Eq. (17.6) with respect to k, which yields:

$$d(dk/k)/dk = s[dQ/L - Q/k]k < 0 \qquad (17.7)$$

Equation (17.7) shows that lower values of k are associated with higher capital–labor growth rates. In other words, does this mean all else being equal that poor countries (countries with lower capital per person) grow faster in terms of per capita income? If they do, then one would expect poorer countries to catch up (i.e., converge) to richer ones. Perhaps the poorest country in the group of SSA countries in Table 17.3 is Ethiopia. Then, according to Eq. (17.7), in the long run Ethiopia's economic performance would converge to that of the higher income countries if the parameters (growth of population, depreciation, and the saving rate) are the same for all the countries.

C. Harrod–Domar Model

After World War II economists found a strong relationship between investment as a proportion of GDP and growth rates, which led De Long and Summers to conclude that the rate of investment as a proportion of income determined the rate of a country's economic growth.

In 1946, Domar believed that the target rate of growth is proportional to the product of the inverse of capital–output ratio and investment. It follows immediately from this reasoning that the level of investment is equal to the growth in output (GDP) times the capital–output ratio. As a first approximation, the change in output Q is equal to a constant (reciprocal of the capital–output ratio v) times investment I. The rate of growth in output is proportional to the ratio of investment to output.[8] Thus,

$$dQ/Q = (1/v)(I/Q) \qquad (17.8)$$

Equation (17.8) can be used to calculate the growth rate of output for a known value of v, which is assumed to be approximately 3.5. When the investment-to-GDP ratio of a country such as Ethiopia is 20%, the rate of growth of GDP would be 5.7% ($= 0.20/3.5$). But, population growth in Ethiopia during the period 1990–1998 was 2.6%, meaning that per capita GDP growth rate was 3.1%. Put differently, investment in Ethiopia of less than ($= 2.6 \times 3.5$) 9.1% would not increase per capita GDP. That level of investment may not be forthcoming.

Always lurking in the mind is the question of the relevance of Western economic models to Sub-Saharan African countries. An abundance of labor and a shortage of fixed physical capital characterize African countries. We have seen that the Harrod–Domar model works quite well in industrialized countries characterized by an abundance of capital, but there is strong evidence that it does not work in African countries. Output growth in Africa is constrained by insufficient physical capital, so increases in capital will overcome the growth problem. The problem of growth is essentially one of obtaining the physical capital resources necessary to generate a target rate of growth. The model predicts more rapid rates of growth than have been realized with high rates of investment in Africa,[9] but there is some evidence to indicate that this is not the case.[10] Some doubt exists about the investment–growth connection. Other factors such as education, political stability, and the infrastructure may play a more significant role than investment in the growth process. Yet, there is the stubborn feeling that investment is the answer to slow growth and that industrialization is the key to economic development. In recent years efforts have been made to shift the focus of investment from the public to the private sector. Because the private sector appears to work well in developed countries, it seems appropriate to apply it to developing countries and hope that the results will be the same as in developed countries. The recent thrust to privatization in African countries is a response to the perception that the private sector is more efficient in allocating scarce resources than the public sector.

Table 17.3 shows that the proportion of private investment to gross domestic investment rose from 1980 to 1997 in all the selected countries with the exception of Botswana. It is not clear yet whether the shift to private investment has paid any dividends, as economic growth in SSA countries lagged behind other regions of the world during the 1980s and 1990s. Botswana's mining industry represents about 37% of total GDP, and the government's share of GDP is about 21%. Botswana is the most successful economy in Africa and, despite the fall in investment as a proportion of GDP, the driving force behind its performance has been government investment and exports of minerals, mainly diamonds, but also copper–nickel matte and, until not so long ago, soda ash. Reliance on diamond exports makes the country a captive of the whims of economic performance in the rest of the world. Diversification of production is a possible answer to this problem. Diversification will also require physical capital formation and financing.

Many African countries have seen investment rates plummet from 1980–1998. That may explain why growth in the region has been amoebic. To compound matters income levels in Africa are low. For example, according to World Bank figures, GDP in 1998 in SSA was $316,517 million. GNP is a better measure of how the countries are doing. Individual African countries run the gamut from $100 per capita in Ethiopia to $3600 per capita in Botswana. For this reason poor African countries will be unable to generate enough saving to finance the required level of investment to meet their target growth rates.

We have noted also that the difference between domestic saving and required investment is the financing gap, which can be filled with foreign aid to attain the target growth rate. Foreign aid has unintended consequences by acting as a drag of growth. This is possible for two reasons. First, the external debt service requirements of foreign aid represent a transfer to donors that might otherwise be used by the developing country for capital formation; in 1966, Bhagwati was concerned about the consequences of excessive foreign indebtedness to donors.[11] Second, in 1972, Bauer noted that new loans would be needed to service existing ones, thus depriving the country of resources needed for investment and growth.[12] But, even if we accept the notion that investment is critical to economic growth, it is possible that African countries might divert foreign aid (in the form of debt relief) to consumption rather than investment, as noted earlier. Highly indebted countries, and for that matter their international creditors, confront a debt-relief problem. If international creditors refuse debt relief to highly indebted countries (HICs), these countries will have little incentive to invest for growth to honor their future financial obligations to creditors. If debt relief is extended to HICs, then those countries would have no need to invest for growth because they will not have any financial obligations to honor in the future.[13]

It was pointed out before that the crucial role of saving and investment in fostering output growth in developed countries is well established. However, the evidence for developing countries is not conclusive. For example, in 1987 Lipsey and Kravis[13a] found that growth in output led to growth in investment and not vice versa. Blomstrom *et al.* used pooled times series and cross-section data and the Granger–Sims causality framework to test the direction of causality and found no evidence that fixed investment is the key to economic growth.[14] In 1998, Easterly argued that the connection between foreign aid and growth is weak. Suppose all foreign aid went into investment and that the capital–output ratio is 3.5. Then, for a country such as Zambia, foreign aid would predict a per capita income of $20,000 by 1994. However, all the levels of aid, and high initial investment resulted in a per capita income of merely $600.[15] On the other hand, in 1978, Voivodas[16] used the Harrod–Domar model to examine the effects of inflows from exports and foreign capital. The financing gap can be filled from exports or foreign capital inflows, which are used to pay for capital goods imports, i.e., investment. Voivodas concluded that instabilities in foreign exchange earnings and foreign credit used to finance capital goods imports were not detrimental to economic growth. In a similar kind of analysis, in 1991, Gyimah-Brempong looked at the relationship between growth in Sub-Saharan Africa controlling for export growth, population growth, investment as a proportion of GNP, and various measures of export instability. He found that investment instability due to export instability that causes instability in export earnings has a negative effect on economic growth.[17] Because we are interested in the effect of investment on growth, we can ignore the other independent variables. In the Gyimah-Brempong study, the investment–GNP coefficient turned out to be positive (i.e., 0.095) and significantly different from zero. Thus, a 1% rise in the investment-GDP ratio would raise GDP in Sub-Saharan Africa by 0.095, assuming, of course, that nothing else changes.

VI. INVESTMENT AND ECONOMIC GROWTH

A. The Impact of Investment Instability on Economic Growth in Africa

It is not absolutely clear whether investment and economic growth are correlated, as noted from Easterly's Zambia example. Many economists believe that investment leads to growth. This is a generally held view among policymakers around the world. Industrial countries of the West that have a comparative advantage in producing goods that require more capital relative to labor have higher incomes than countries in SSA that have very little capital. So on the face of it, countries with a lot of capital are rich and countries with abundance of labor are poor. This implies that the path to wealth for poor countries is capital accumulation. That gives credence to the conventional wisdom regarding the relationship between investment and output.

However, given that SSAs are primary producers, exports of primary goods play a more significant role in increasing growth rates in SSA than investment. True, export earnings can be used to finance capital imports, which are scarce in SSA countries, but fluctuations in earnings translate into fluctuations in capital imports and reductions in growth rates.

Sub-Saharan African countries generally depend on earnings from the sale of primary goods to finance capital goods imports—that is, investment. Some believe that fluctuation in export earnings in developing countries causes similar fluctuation in their ability to import because reserves are limited and aid and foreign direct investment from developed countries are not compensating. The result is that growth will be sporadic and sustained growth difficult.

Unfortunately, earnings from exports are unstable in the region. The fact is commodity prices (and therefore foreign exchange earnings) tend to decline in the long run. The decline comes also from short-run fluctuations around the trend. The problem appears to stem from the nature of African production. Again, many African countries are single-product economies such as Ethiopia (coffee), Botswana (diamonds), and Ghana (cocoa). But, the effect of earnings instability on investment and growth is not quite so straightforward. Instability of earnings might have a positive effect on growth if developing countries reduce consumption, increasing saving and investment, but that is not conclusive. It is quite possible that there might be no correlation between earnings fluctuation and growth because the developed country anticipates earnings fluctuations and plans for such fluctuations. In this way, earnings instability has no appreciable effect on growth. However, Gyimah-Brempong, using a neoclassical growth equation with export growth and its instability as additional explanatory variables for 34 SSA countries, found that export instability had a negative and significant effect on economic growth. Low African economic performance in the 1960s through 1990s begs for some explication. To say Africa's performance is low is to be kind. In 1997, Easterly and Levine said that on average real per capita GDP in African did not grow between 1965 and 1990. East Asia and the Pacific experienced per capita GDP growth of over 5%, while in Latin America growth was almost 2% per year. The human face they put on Africa's tragedy is the average African mother who cannot expect all her children to grow up to become adults. Worse, this mother has only a 30% chance that all her children will survive to age 5 and average life expectancy is a mere 48 years. Similarly, in 1999 Collier and Gunning[17a] wrote that Africa's economic performance lagged behind that of other regions. They say that Africa's low growth can be explained by variables that are generally important for the growth process. However, these variables (lack of social capital, lack of openness to trade, etc.) are markedly low in Africa.

Easterly and Levine examined the literature for a wide variety of indicators to explain long-run economic growth in Africa. Their focus is the relationship between public policies and a country's choice of public policies. The variables in their regression are initial income, schooling, political stability, and public policies. Ethnic diversity, the result of "a tragicomic series of negotiations between European powers in the nineteenth century that split up ethnic groups and exacerbated preexisting high levels of ethnic and linguistics diversity," hinders growth. They argue that ethnic diversity can slow growth by making agreement on the provision of public goods and policies that promote growth more difficult.

B. Endogenous Growth Models

In the 1980s and 1990s economic growth in the SSA countries was a source of alarm. Some of the words used to qualify economic performance of Africa were tragedy and bleak. The neoclassical growth models rely on forces beyond the control of the countries, such as growth in income abroad to fuel demand for primary goods. The endogenous growth models include a class in which research and development drive technological change. This justifies subsidies to R&D, and other government policies, that may influence long-run growth rates. R&D is central to one version of the endogenous growth models, which have a prediction of scale effects. If the level of inputs allocated to R&D—for example, the number of scientists and engineers engaged in R&D—were to double, then growth rate of per capita output would also double. In 1995, Jones[17b] summarized the scale effects of these models by two equations. Equation (17.9) is a Cobb–Douglas-type production function with constant returns to scale:

$$Y = K^{1-\alpha}(AL_y)^{\alpha} \qquad (17.9)$$

$$\mathring{A}/A = \delta L_A \qquad (17.10)$$

where Y represents output, K refers to capital, and A denotes productivity or knowledge, as an input is neither a conventional or public good. A share of labor L_y is used to produce the output and a share is employed in R&D. In Eq. (17.10), $\mathring{A}/A$ denotes total factor productivity growth rate, which depends on the number of units of labor engaged in R&D and a constant δ. The constant δ denotes the arrival rate of new knowledge or ideas. The model predicts that by increasing the level of resources devoted to R&D the growth rate of the economy should also increase. The model also implies a scale effect whose source is the R&D in Eq. (17.10), which implies that total factor productivity growth is proportional to the number of units of labor devoted to R&D. R&D trades current costs for a stream of benefits in the future, making the rate of technology sensitive to interest rates. It implies a role for government action—a subsidy to R&D or to accumulation of total human capital. Total human capital is directly related to faster growth and free international trade can act to speed up growth.

The problem for Africa is that very little research and development effort is evident on the continent. R&D is not an area in which poor countries have a comparative advantage. The rational thing for poor countries is not to expend scarce resources on R&D. It would make more sense for these countries to import technology from advanced countries. The underlying meaning of Eqs. (17.9) and (17.10), that increases in total factor productivity would increase the growth rate of output, seems not to be appropriate for Africa. In fact, according to Jones, it may not even apply well to developed countries. That is because over the years in developed countries more scientists are engaged in R&D, but growth rates have constant means and in some instances might even have declined on average. However, this model might be inapplicable to Africa, not because it does not apply even to developed countries, but because Africa can hardly be considered to have the resources to be on the cutting edge of technology. In many African countries, spending on R&D is modest at best; in others, spending on R&D is nonexistent. It might be better for Africa to leave R&D to developed countries in which they have a comparative advantage, then Africa, as countries in Asia (Japan, for example) have done, could simply import technology from developed countries.

Romer offers another approach to endogenous growth. He maintains that technological change lies at the heart of economic growth, technological change is motivated by profit-maximizing agents, and "instructions for working with raw materials are inherently different from other economic goods." The cost of creating a new set of instructions is seen as fixed. Using the new instructions over and over again incurs no additional cost. The argument used here for economic growth is based on these three premises. There is an element of both rivalry and excludability in the R&D efforts of workers. Rival goods tend to be excludable. Technology, such as new instructions, is a non-rival input because it is not excludable. However, for profit minded agents to risk capital and improve technology their efforts may confer benefits that are at least partially excludable. From this it follows that growth depends on the accumulation of partially excludable, non-rival input. Romer gives us a very good example of excludable, non-rival input using a design for a new good. The new design comes from research and development by profit-maximizing firms. Once the new design comes on line it can be "used as often as desired, in as many productive activities as desired." This is qualitatively different from human capital such as the ability to add, which is tied to the human body in a way that design is not. The ability to add is rivalrous because a person with this ability can only be in one place at a time and can only work some one problem at a time.

Whether the unit of analysis is neoclassical or not, what seems clear is that saving is still important. If a country wishes to allocate more of its labor to R&D

it would have to subsidize that effort from high taxation or money growth inflation or both. Growth is not limited to R&D effort, as we have already seen. R&D effort is not costless, because for poor countries the debt that must often be incurred to finance it can also affect how the economy performs.

C. The Influence of Debt Relief on Economic Growth

Foreign aid can make up for low income, but as saving as a proportion of income rises the need for aid diminishes; however, there is a downside to all this: the possibility that aid can lead to unintended consequences. Foreign aid can lead to dependency by displacing processes of institutional maturation that are necessary for development.[18] In 1988, Corden addressed a question related to foreign aid, which was the view that debt relief could lead to investment. Although the conclusion is ambiguous, depending on initial assumptions, it does contain the notion that foreign creditors may benefit from debt relief. He argued that there are opposing incentive consequences of such relief. Under the right circumstances, therefore, the unintended consequence of long-term foreign aid can be poor economic performance, if dependency takes hold.[19] A country's external debt may be interpreted as mirroring the saving gap of the country. The saving gap is variously referred to as financing gap or resource balance. It occurs when investment—part of domestic spending—exceeds saving. It means that imports are greater than exports. Foreign credit is needed to adjust for excess domestic spending over domestic output. In a flexible exchange rate environment, the exchange rate would depreciate and the excess of imports over exports would vanish. Under a fixed exchange rate system, the trade deficit adds to the country's external debt. In SSA, where shortages of capital exist, the deficit can be a source of foreign capital.

What matters most is the way a country chooses to use the inflow from foreign saving or credit. SSA countries have large external debts, for which the repayment of principal and interest acts as a drag on output. That is, transfers from SSA to international creditors mean that investment requirements will not be realized. Debt relief will reduce transfers to the West from SSA, but some people believe that debt relief reduces the incentive of debtor countries to increase output. Without debt relief there is little incentive for the country to change investment and output because the benefits from increased output will go to foreign creditors. In the first instant debt relief might not increase output because no transfers will have to be made. The debt causes transfers to the West and reduces the indebted country's incentive to increase output in the country. In either case, a highly indebted SSA country will have no incentive to increase output.

Effect of debt relief can reduce investment. Imagine that a country exists in three time periods and incurs a foreign debt in time period 1. If it does not have a debt service obligation in period 3, its investment in period 2 will be I_R and output will be Q_R. If there is a debt service obligation in time period 3, investment will be I_S and output will be Q_S. Investment I_R is less than investment I_S but output Q_S is greater than Q_R. Complete debt relief means that investment in period 2 will decrease by $I_R - I_S$. In period 3 debt payment relief falls so much that consumption actually increases.

Output will be greater when the country may make a payment in period 3. To meet this obligation, investment in period 2 must be higher than it would be in the absence of debt service obligation. Consumption, however, will be lower. If there is no payment requirement, output and consumption will be higher. So debt relief will reduce investment in period 2 but raise output and consumption in period 3. Thus, a country that wants to pay its debt will increase investment and output. The difference between output and consumption is the amount paid to foreign creditors. One can infer that debt relief would reduce investment and output, but raise consumption.

VII. NONECONOMIC FACTORS INFLUENCING INVESTMENT AND ECONOMIC GROWTH

Economic growth depends on more than increases in inputs and technological progress. The political climate of the country, the level of corruption in the public and private sector, and the institutional framework prevalent in the country all have an influence on investment and on economic growth. And political instability adversely affects growth through its negative effect on investment. The verdict on corruption is mixed. Some economists believe that corruption can lead to greater allocative efficiency. Others feel that the net effect of corruption on investment is negative. The conventional wisdom has it that market economies outperform command economies.

A. THE DETERRENT EFFECTS OF POLITICAL INSTABILITY ON INVESTMENT

Political instability such as wars, strikes, coups, demonstrations, and assassinations tend to have a negative effect on economic growth through their impact on investment. Foreign investors are risk averse and would prefer to accept less return on investment for greater safety. Similarly, domestic investors are also risk averse and skittish to commit time and resources to a project in the face of political instability. We know that people with low income tend to be more risk averse and would prefer more certainty to more output. If a typical farmer in an African country has the option of two yields in a two-period cycle—option A is 75 and 25 and option B is 50 and 50, Option B has the lowest (zero) variance and hence lowest (zero) risk and is likely to be chosen over option A. Even if option A were 100 in period 1 and 0 in period 2, the farmer might still choose option B.

The presence of political instability in many African countries might go a long way to explaining poor economic performance. In 1991, Barro used 1979 datasets from banks to measure political instability. The variables were revolutions and coups per year and political assassinations per year per million population. He found that each of the variables was significantly negative for growth. The revolutions variable was also significantly negative for investment as was the assassinations variable. He interpreted the results to mean that these variables have adverse influences on property rights and thereby negatively influence investment and growth.[20] This is not the only way to think about these relationships. It is possible that growth has a positive influence on political stability. The notion is important for SSA countries beset by political instability as it implies that the solution to instability is economic growth. This is worth repeating. Fostering economic growth in SSA countries could go a long way to reducing conflict in the region.

B. ROLE OF POLITICAL INSTITUTIONS IN PROMOTING INVESTMENT

Some political systems perform better than others. Marxist systems in Ethiopia and Tanzania tended to under-perform the democratic system in Botswana. The basis for the difference in performance is that democracy and capitalist markets foster incentives of freedom of choice and enterprise and prices and profits act as signals that direct resources to profitable investment opportunities. Performance is greater in democratic/capitalist systems because they permit a great deal of individual initiative, choice, and responsibility, and information flow may simply be better in democracies. Autocratic rule and economic planning take away individual initiative and responsibility. After independence, many African countries chose socialism and economic planning as their roadmap to economic development. The President of Tanzania, Julius Nyerere, an ardent proponent of the one-party system, argued that in the absence of division over fundamental issues, a multiparty arrangement is not justified in Africa and may in fact result in counter productive factionalism, which the one-party system overcomes. Without irreconcilable groups in society, political debate is more effectively advanced under a one-party system. Mr. Nyerere, like Moi of Kenya, believed that the one-party system tended to reduce conflicts and to permit talented Africans to use their energies to solve Africa's problems. Mr. Nyerere also believed that traditional African societies were not divided along class lines and that a one-party system reflects this tradition.[21] If political instability reduces investment that is needed for economic growth, then a one-party system reduces conflicts and facilitates economic growth. All of this flies in the face of common sense. The collapse of the Soviet Union marks a shift in emphasis from the state to the individual, from a closed to an open economy, and from a command economy to a market economy.

Many African countries that experimented with Marxism and have seen the collapse of the Soviet Union and have changed to market-driven forces, recognize that the Soviet model is inconsistent and internally flawed. The state is no longer viewed as all knowing in matters related to intervention and regulation of production and distribution. One important lesson we learned from this is that market economies perform better than a command economy. This has led to efforts in Africa to remove exchange controls (in Botswana and Ethiopia), privatization, and trade liberalization designed to increase efficiency and growth.

One way to deal with institutional factors that influence investment and economic performance is to compare the efficiency change of one over some other. Growth and efficiency are correlated. So, for equal rates of capital formation, one would expect that SSA countries that transform inputs into output relatively inefficiently would grow more slowly than efficient economies. Many SSA countries seriously started transforming their economies in the 1980s. Many have become democracies after years of flirtation with Marxist governments. Let us assume that democracies outperform the neo-Marxist systems. To determine whether that is true we turn to a study done in 1988 by Scully at the University of Chicago, in which he focused on the institutional framework in which economic activity takes place. His objective was to determine the relative efficiency of the production within different institutional frameworks. The institutional framework consists of open economics, closed economics, individual rights versus state rights, and free market versus command economy. He found that politically open societies grew faster than politically closed ones. Similarly, on average, societies that emphasized individual rights grew faster than societies that extolled state rights. Finally, societies that subscribed to property rights and market allocation of resources also grew faster than societies that did not.[22] The implication for SSA countries is that their transformation to democracies and market economies will increase growth rates because they will be able to convert inputs into output more efficiently, even if there is no change in the rate of capital formation (investment).

VIII. SUMMARY

Sub-Saharan African countries are noted for an abundance of labor, a shortage of capital, and low output and growth. Many economists believe that economic growth is correlated to investment, so that for SSA the solution to low growth is physical capital formation. The problem is that SSA countries have a saving gap. The saving gap means that investment requirements of the country are greater than the country's capacity to finance them from domestic saving alone. Real growth for much of the 1990s in SSA has been quite abysmal. For the selected SSA countries, the rates were negative. If those growth rates persist, these countries can never hope to catch up with the developed countries.

Saving in SSA can be thought of as occurring when current consumption is curtailed at some interest rate to increase future consumption, but saving can also be defined in terms of private, government, and foreign saving. Total saving is the sum of private, government, and foreign saving. At the end of the fiscal year for the country, total saving must equal gross investment. To the extent that investment exceeds saving, foreign credit or aid might be needed to close the financing gap. The saving rate as a proportion of GDP in SSA is variable. It is as high as 35% in Botswana and as low as 1% in Chad and Mozambique. Government can use various devices to increase saving, including inflation, overvalued exchange rates, taxes, and lotteries. People can save on their own by creating informal saving institutions such as the Iddir in Ethiopia. Several theories explain saving behavior in developed countries that may (or may not) be applicable to developing countries generally or SSA in particular. These theories are the absolute income hypothesis, the life-cycle hypothesis, the permanent income hypothesis, and more recently endogenous growth models of various sorts.

Investment as a share of GDP in SSA is also variable—about 14% in Zambia and 27% in Algeria. Investment is important because it increases the productivity of labor. Investment is important in other ways, too, in developing countries. It can be shown that education (i.e., investment in human capital) is directly related to economic growth, but physical capital formation such as foreign direct investment and human capital formation can influence economic growth in a positive way.

Investment influences growth in slightly different ways depending on the model used. One version is the neoclassical model, which relates investment to economic growth through the capital–labor ratio elasticity. Countries that are more efficient in allocating capital to the production mix will grow faster. The Solow–Swan model is used to find the steady-state rate of growth of the capital–labor ratio used in the production of goods, and the Harrod–Domar model relates the growth in output to the investment–output ratio via the reciprocal of the incremental capital–output ratio. Various versions of Harrod–Domar have been used to examine growth in SSA. Do these models apply to Africa?

Export earnings are used to finance investment and growth. In this context, Gyimah-Brempong showed that the investment–GNP ratio turned out to be positive and significantly different from zero, but export instability was found to exert a negative and significant effect on the economic rate of growth in SSA countries.

Debt relief can be shown to have a positive or negative effect on investment. When a country faces the prospect of paying principal and interest, it may have no incentive to invest because the output would have to be transferred to foreign creditors. If foreign creditors offer debt relief, the country will have no incentive to increase investment, so current consumption will rise. The solution is to tie the country to specific investment use of any saving as a condition of debt relief. One way is to ensure that inflows will raise investment.

Political instability—wars, strikes, coups, and assassinations—can affect economic growth through its negative impact on investment. Barro has provided some empirical evidence that political instability reduces output growth.

DISCUSSION QUESTIONS

1. SSA countries have had very poor economic growth rates in the decades of the 1980s and 1990s. We have seen that the growth rates were negative. Reversing the trend is important. Within the framework of saving and investment, how can SSA reverse its poor economic performance?
2. Explain how government interference in the economy can lead to corruption.
3. Easterly argued that the Harrod–Domar model overstates the effect of investment on economic growth. Explain.
4. Why would models of investment, saving, and growth not be applicable to the SSA experience?
5. How do endogenous growth models differ from the neoclassical growth models?
6. What is the resource balance? What does it say about the saving gap of a country?
7. What is the role of education in the growth process in SSA?
8. There is evidence that the consumption is greater in poor countries than in rich ones. How can this be explained?
9. It has been argued that countries with higher levels of education and foreign direct investment grow faster. How can that be in the face of questions about the correlation between investment and growth and the fact that education as input is subject to diminishing returns?
10. H.R. 434 is an attempt by the United States to increase trade and investment in SSA. What is this expected to accomplish and why?

11. Compare and contrast the Solow–Swan model and the Harrod–Domar model and determine their relevance to SSA.
12. Political instability, which seems to plague SSA, affects growth through its impact on investment. Explain.
13. In the endogenous growth models discussed in the chapter, what drives total factor productivity growth?

NOTES

[1]Scully, G. W. (1988) "The Institutional Framework and Economic Development," *Journal of Political Economy*, 96(3), 652–662.

[2]$dGDP/GDP = -1.31 + 0.191d(INV/GDP)$ is based on 38 observations from Table 17.2.

[3]Borrus, M., Tyson, L.D., and Zysman, J. (1990) "Creating Advantage: How Government Policies Shape International Trade in the Semiconductor Industry," in P. R. Krugman, Ed., *Strategic Trade Policy and the New International Economics*, Cambridge, MA: MIT Press, p. 98.

[4]Jonnard, C.M., Griffith, J.R., and Dickinson, F. (1999) "Appropriate Technologies for Sustained Economic Growth and Development," in *Civilization, Modern Technology and Sustainable Development*, Abstracts Book, paper presented at the 8th Int. Conf. on Management of Technology, March 15–17, Cairo, Egypt, p. 41.

[5]See Dejene (1993), pp. 77–90.

[6]Jefferis, K.R. (1995) "The Economy in 1994," in *Barclay's Botswana Economic Review*, 1st ed., pp. 1–24.

[7]Simple Swan–Solow model; investment of a point in time equals gross investment less depreciation:

$$dK/dt = I - \alpha K$$

where I is investment and K is the capital stock. Because $S = I$, the above expression can be expressed in terms of the saving rate and income:

$$dK/dt = sQ - \alpha K$$

where s is the saving rate and Q is output, which is a function of capital and labor; that is, $F(K, L; t)$. The assumption, of course, is that the marginal productivities of capital and labor are positive but decreasing. If we write the production function in intensive form, we have:

$$d(K/L)/dt = L(LdK - KdL)/L^2 = dK/L - nk$$

which can be written as:

$$d(k)/dt = sQ - (n + \alpha)k$$

[8]Harrod–Domar model; as a first approximation, the formula for growth in Africa is

$$dQ = (1/v)I$$

where dQ is the change in output, v is the capital-output ratio, and I is investment. For example, if you divide Eq. (1) by output Q you will find that the growth in output is proportional to the ratio of investment to output. Thus,

$$dQ/Q = (1/v)(I/Q)$$

[9]Easterly and Levine (Easterly, W., and Levine, R. (1997) "Africa's Growth Tragedy: Policies and Ethnic Divisions," *Quarterly Journal of Economics*, November, 112(4), 1203–1250.) make the case

that SSA's ills are the result of bad policies, poor education, political instability, and inadequate infrastructure. They propose that ethnic diversity explains a substantial part of the cross-country differences in public policies, political instability, and other economic factors related to secular growth.

[10]Easterly, W. (1998) "The Quest for Growth: How We Wandered the Tropics Trying to Figure Out How To Make Poor Countries Rich," www.worldbank.org.

[11]Bhagwait, J. (1966) *The Economics of Underdeveloped Countries*, New York: McGraw-Hill.

[12]Bauer, P.T. (1972) *Dissent on Development: Studies and Debates in Development Economics*, Cambridge, MA: Harvard University Press.

[13]These results are contradictory and depend on some initial assumptions. See Corden (1988); also Note 19.

[13a]Lipsey, R., and Kravis, I. (1987) *Saving and Economic Growth: Is the United States Really Falling Behind?*, New York: The Conference Board.

[14]Blomstrom, M., Lipsey, R. E., and Zejan, M. (1996) "Is Fixed Investent the Key to Economic Growth?," *Quarterly Journal of Economics*, February, 269–276.

[15]See Easterly (1998) in Note 10.

[16]Voivodas, C.S. (1978) "The Effect of Foreign Exchange Instability on Growth," *Review of Economics and Statistics*, 60(3), 410–412.

[17]Gyimah-Brempong, K. (1991) "Export Instability and Economic Growth in Sub-Saharan Africa," *Economic Development and Cultural Change*, 815–828.

[17a]Collier, P., and Gunning, J.W. (March 1999) "Explaining African Economic Performance," *Journal of Economic Literature*, XXXVII, 64–111.

[17b]Jones, C.I. (1995) "R & D-Based Models of Economic Growth," *Journal of Political Economy*, 105(4), 759–784.

[18]Azam, J.-P., Devarajan, S., and O'Connell, S.A. (1999) *Aid Dependence Reconsidered*, Working Paper No. 99.5, Centre for the Study of African Economies.

[19]Corden, M.W. (1988) "Debt Relief and Adjustment Incentives," *International Monetary Fund Staff Papers*, 35(4), 628–643.

[20]Barro, R. J. (1991) "Economic Growth in a Cross Section of Countries," *The Quarterly Journal of Economics*, 106(2), 407–444.

[21]See Nsibambi, p. 27.

[22]See Scully (1988) in Note 1.

Africa and the International Environment

Trade and Economic Development

VICTOR IWUAGWU OGULEDO

Department of Economics, College of Arts and Sciences, Florida Agricultural and Mechanical University, Tallahassee, Florida 32307

KEY TERMS

Absolute advantage	Less developed countries (LDCs)
Appropriate technology	Multinational corporations (MNCs)
Basic human needs	Nontariff barrier to trade
Comparative advantage	Nontraditional exports
Division of labor	Optimum-size plant
Dynamic benefits from trade	Price and income elasticities of demand
Economic development	Relative factor abundance
Economic growth	Ricardian theory
Economic infrastructure	Social infrastructure
Foreign direct investment (FDI)	Specialization
Gains from international trade	Static gains from trade
Gross domestic product (GDP)	Structural adjustment program (SAP)
Hard currencies	Synthetic substitutes
Heckscher-Ohlin theory	Tariff barrier to trade
Infant industry	Terms of Trade
Institutional infrastructure	Trade pessimism
Intra-African trade	Trans-Saharan trade

I. INTRODUCTION

This chapter discusses the role of international trade in the economic development of Africa. Specifically, it focuses on the contributions that international trade makes or could make in the economic development of African countries. Economic theory and real-life experience suggest that trade could be a boost to the economic development of a country. This means that trade could serve as one of the engines of economic growth and development of African countries.

African Economic Development
441

Any development strategy that neglects the role of international trade may not be able to achieve its full potential.

Given the potentially positive role that trade could play in growth and development of a country, the crucial questions that this chapter investigates include how well trade has served as an engine of growth of African economies. What does it mean when one says that trade could serve as an engine for growth and development of African countries? Answers to these trade and development questions constitute the essence of this chapter.

Economic development includes social development of the population, which ensures uplifting the quality of human life and dignity. The provision of basic human needs creates a favorable atmosphere for social cohesion and a focus on issues that could launch a country toward a more promising path. Otherwise, growth without development, which manifests itself in rising inequalities in income and opportunities, will derail any development effort due to social and political tension that is bound to arise.

The contribution of international trade to fulfilling basic human needs in the economic development process of African countries is the main focus of this chapter. One should not minimize the fact that this type of investigation can be controversial. Some economists are of the view that international trade promotes economic growth and development in Africa, while some say that it retards it. This chapter provides information that helps to reduce this controversy.

Theories of trade are presented, followed by a discussion of the relationship between trade and economic development in Africa. The next issue discussed is opposition to unfettered free trade. Policy suggestions are proffered, and finally, a summary of the chapter is made.

II. THEORIES OF TRADE

International trade takes place when citizens of one country exchange products they produce at home with products produced by citizens of other countries. This process has been taking place since recorded human history. During the 18th and 19th centuries, Adam Smith and other classical economists made a case for freer and more open trade. Smith's *Wealth of Nations* is one of the early studies that laid the foundation for the systematic study of economics. Smith's work synthesized earlier writings on economics. In this seminal work, he extolled the virtues and benefits of free trade. Thus, one can say that international trade is the oldest branch of economics.

Interest in trade did not die with Smith. His contemporaries, especially David Ricardo,[1] refined and expounded Smith's idea about trade into the theory of *comparative advantage*. This theory states that a country should produce and export products that it can produce at a relatively lower cost at home and import

TABLE 18.1   Example of Absolute Advantage

Country	Output of One Person per Day of Labor
Nigeria	300 lb of groundnuts or 100 lb of cashew nuts
Ghana	100 lb of groundnuts or 50 lb of cashew nuts

those products that it can only produce at a relatively higher cost at home. For the former group of products, the country is said to have a comparative advantage, while for the latter it is said to have a comparative disadvantage.

One should note that there is a difference between *comparative advantage* and *absolute advantage*. Absolute advantage means that one trading country may produce all tradable goods at a lower cost per unit than its trade partners. This is because one day of labor in this particular country produces more of the tradable goods than its trade partners are able to produce. To further illustrate the difference between comparative advantage and absolute advantage, consider two countries in the world (Nigeria and Ghana), two commodities (groundnuts and cashew nuts), and a homogeneous factor of production (labor) in these two countries. With the latter assumptions, a stylized numerical illustration is given in Table 18.1.

From the illustration in Table 18.1, it can be seen that Nigeria has an absolute advantage over Ghana in production of both groundnuts and cashew nuts, but this does not mean that Nigeria should produce both products when trade opens between the two countries and that Ghana should produce none. If the latter is done, the mutual benefits from international trade will be unrealised; rather, the driving force of international trade is comparative advantage.

In this example, even if Nigeria has an absolute advantage in both products (and Ghana has an absolute disadvantage in both), its degree of productivity (or cost) advantage is relatively higher in production of groundnuts than in cashew nuts. That is, Nigeria is relatively more efficient in groundnut production; Nigeria is three times more productive than Ghana in production of groundnut. On the other hand, Nigeria is two times more productive than Ghana in production of cashew nuts. Nigeria and the world at large will benefit more from trade if it specializes in production and export of groundnuts to Ghana. On the other hand, Ghana should specialize in production and export of cashew nuts, because its comparative disadvantage is relatively lower in this product. The conclusion one can draw from this illustration is that Nigeria has a comparative advantage in groundnuts, while Ghana has a comparative advantage in cashew nuts.

If both countries reallocate their existing resources according to their comparative advantage, global output of groundnuts and cashew nuts will increase, even if global resources remain constant, hence the benefit of international trade based on comparative advantage. This stylized example can be extended to multiproduct and multicountry situations. That is, several trading countries can specialize in more than one product if they have comparative advantage in them.

According to the theory of comparative advantage, also known as the *Ricardian theory*, trading countries and the world as whole will benefit from trade if each country specializes in producing and exporting product in which it has comparative advantage. This is because, with specialization, labor (assumed to be the only resource) will be organized in such a way that it produces what it can best produce. This maximizes productivity and lowers world cost and price, and real global welfare will rise. A given quantity of world resources will produce more than in the absence of trade.

It is also important to note that a comparative advantage is caused either by the inherent (physical and social climatic) characteristics or the nature of the resource (labor) or by the technology used in production process. This means that a comparative advantage can be induced by deliberate human effort, such as investment (in human and physical capital), to improve technology.[1a] *Ceteris paribus*, investment increases the productivity of labor and capital. This in turn lowers cost per unit and may give the country a comparative advantage in some products which otherwise would not have been possible without the (increased) investment. This means that technological development influences the evolution of comparative advantage.

The Ricardian theory of trade was extended by Hechscher and Ohlin (H–O). They made Ricardian theory more realistic by explaining basically the same idea (comparative advantage) with relative factor abundance. For example, a country with a relatively large endowment of arable land should export agricultural products, and a country with a relatively large endowment of capital should export manufactured goods, etc. Contemporary trade economists in turn extended both the Ricardian and H–O trade models by introducing the element of *dynamism* to them. The dynamic trade models not only consider the static or direct benefits of trade due to comparative cost advantage, but also highlight its dynamic benefits.

The dynamic benefits of trade are the indirect, productivity-enhancing benefits to participating countries. For example, trade could serve as a source of material means indispensable for economic development such as machinery and other capital goods and raw and semifinished materials; as a means and vehicle for transmission of technological knowledge, ideas, know-how, skills, managerial talents and entrepreneurship; as an antimonopoly pressure and the best guarantee of healthy competition; and as a vehicle for international movement of capital from areas of low capital productivity to areas of high capital productivity.

Therefore, trade not only promotes effective and efficient utilization of existing resources of a country, but it also promotes the growth in the amount of resources available to a country over time. This points to the fact that trade could be an engine of growth and development of a country. These benefits are realizable if trade is free, with minimum intervention at the margin.

III. THE RELATIONSHIP BETWEEN TRADE AND ECONOMIC DEVELOPMENT OF AFRICA

A. An Overview of Trade in Africa

Africa has been an important participant in world trade since recorded history. Before the official, recorded contact with the Europeans around the 12th century, African countries played an important role in world trade and commerce, the most dramatic example being, trade across the Sahara, known as the *trans-saharan trade* or *gold trade*, which peaked between the 3rd and 13th centuries. The Sahara constitutes a natural corridor between the Sub-Saharan African countries on the one hand, and the Mediterranean and European countries on the other.

Tropical products such as kola nuts, cowries, ivory, hides and skins, wood products, and gold were exchanged for products from the Mediterranean and Europe such as salt, copper, dried fruits, cloth, horses, trinkets, and books. The trans-Saharan trade waned during the 16th and 17th centuries due to technological innovation in sea transportation and communication and development of maritime trade along the coast of Africa known as the *trans-Atlantic trade*, and the competition it brought to bear on it.[2]

The trans-Atlantic trade pattern was an extension of the trans-Saharan trade, based on international specialization in production and trade along area of comparative advantage. In either trade regime, African countries specialized in production and export of primary products: agricultural products and raw materials, tropical beverages, minerals, fuels, etc. (see Table 18.2). These export products have a common characteristic of being unprocessed or semiprocessed. This export pattern of African countries has continued largely unchanged into the 21st century.

As of now, manufactured products are not important components of Africa's total exports; primary products still predominate its exports (see Tables 18.3 and 18.4). In more than 75% of select African countries in Table 18.3, primary products constitute more than 60% of their total exports. This indicates that shocks (positive or negative) in primary export market will have significant effect on most African countries. Tables 18.3 and 18.4 also shows that African countries are important world exporters of primary products. In the majority of primary products included in Tables 18.3 and 18.4, the continent of Africa accounts for 10% or more of their world exports.

TABLE 18.2   Africa's Share of World Trade in Select Primary Products: Export*

											World Market Share									
Commodity	1970	1975	1981	1982	1983	1984	1985	1986	1987	1988	1989	1990	1991	1992	1993	1994	1995	1996	1997	1998
									Percentage Share of Value											
Aluminum	3.8	0.3	2.7	3.2	2.5	2.4	2.6	1.8	3.5	3.0	3.5	3.5	2.9	3.4	2.3	2.8	2.4	2.3	3.6	1.5
Bauxite	3.4	20.4	32.4	36.3	42.2	39.1	44.5	46.7	46.5	45.4	45.1	43.0	41.1	42.3	41.7	41.1	41.1	39.3	40.5	35.7
Cocoa beans	81.0	73.2	69.1	65.8	62.0	59.9	59.8	66.3	62.4	61.9	67.1	67.0	67.2	64.2	66.5	36.3	44.7	49.9	47.5	52.0
Coffee	28.9	29.6	23.8	23.9	22.3	21.6	22.5	21.5	19.9	19.4	19.4	17.8	14.5	13.7	18.1	11.7	13.1	13.1	11.8	12.4
Copper, ore	1.6	4.2	3.6	4.3	5.0	5.0	4.8	3.7	3.4	3.9	2.6	2.5	2.3	2.3	1.9	3.8	3.6	3.9	3.1	2.6
Cotton, raw	4.1	27.6	20.6	23.5	23.7	18.4	15.0	27.4	17.0	16.2	16.7	15.7	16.2	15.1	14.9	15.3	15.9	14.6	18.2	19.7
Cotton, yarn	11.3	6.3	5.2	4.7	6.8	7.6	7.6	6.7	13.0	13.8	13.8	10.1	9.5	8.8	11.5	2.5	2.1	1.6	1.8	1.7
Fish	3.1	3.6	3.6	3.6	3.9	4.0	4.2	4.5	4.1	4.1	3.9	4.3	4.4	4.2	5.0	3.0	3.1	2.9	3.0	3.7
Iron, ore	12.5	10.6	6.6	6.8	6.2	6.2	6.1	5.6	5.1	4.9	5.8	3.7	2.6	2.5	2.6	2.4	2.6	2.4	2.4	2.1
Live animal	3.8	2.9	2.7	3.2	2.5	2.4	2.6	1.8	1.8	1.6	1.5	1.5	1.4	1.3	1.9	1.3	1.1	0.8	0.8	0.9
Petroleum, crude	26.1	17.2	14.8	12.7	15.9	14.5	15.8	22.2	13.0	13.0	13.4	15.8	16.2	16.1	19.6					
Phosphate rock	55.3	53.0	48.2	44.1	40.6	43.7	43.0	42.3	40.2	46.3	42.8	44.3	45.9	45.5	50.0	43.5	42.4	44.5	48.4	46.7
Sugar, raw+	7.4	4.9	4.7	5.0	4.9	4.5	4.7	6.0	6.5	6.3	5.9	7.1	6.8	5.5	6.1	6.7	5.8	6.8	5.9	5.9
Tea	14.4	14.6	17.0	20.6	16.8	18.5	15.5	16.5	14.4	14.6	15.4	14.7	15.6	18.5	16.0	20.6	18.6	19.9	19.7	22.9
Tobacco	4.0	4.3	5.5	13.4	13.7	11.6	9.0	20.8	11.5	12.0	11.4	13.3	14.7	13.5	19.2	18.4	16.2	17.8	14.4	14.7
Natural rubber	3.9	6.2	4.8	4.7	4.5	4.6	5.6	5.7	5.2	5.1	7.3	6.6	4.7	5.2	5.6	3.8	4.6	6.1	6.5	5.8
Ground nuts	13.1	38.1	16.3	12.4	11.3	11.6	6.1	5.0	4.7	8.0	5.4	6.3	5.4	3.5	3.5					
Ground nut oil	15.0	50.0	16.1	37.6	36.5	40.5	20.5	26.5	42.2	41.9	47.2	46.8	31.9	32.2	22.7					
Coconut/copra	1.5	3.8	7.0	5.8	7.7	3.6	5.9	6.2	5.9	6.5	3.8	7.2	10.7	6.7	8.7					
Coconut oil	13.8	1.0	1.3	1.6	2.3	2.2	2.7	1.8	1.8	1.6	1.8	1.9	2.7	1.9	2.2					

Notes: *=Information in this table excludes Republic of South Africa; and +=1985–1986 percentages are for raw and refined sugar combined.
Source: UNCTAD, Commodity Yearbook, 1992, 1994, 1995 (for 1970 to 1993 data); UN, International Trade Statistics Yearbook 1992, 1994, 1995; and UNCTAD, Handbook of World Mineral Trade Statistics, 1993–1998.

TABLE 18.3 Total Value of Export of Primary Commodities for Select African Countries, Excluding Fuels, (Millions of U.S. Dollars)*

Country	1970	1975	1981	1982	1983	1984	1985	1986	1987	1988	1989	1990	1991	1992	1993	1994	1995	1996	1997	1998	1999
Algeria	230.6	230.2	209.1	149.4	106.4	110.7	97.2	87.8	70.9	102.5	93.1	98.6	111.4	124.2	106.4	120.8	168.4	222.0	158.8	192.4	223.3
Botswana	15.8	92.5	203.9	168.5	162.1	151.3	135.1	190.3	173.5	30.4	362.4	270.3	248.0	230.1	226.0	179.8	196.7	255.3	263.1	229.9	240.0
Cameroon	206.7	399.0	578.2	517.9	554.6	592.4	669.2	741.7	667.8	689.0	905.3	884.5	667.9	733.2	764.0	905.5	968.0	982.7	1,070.2	1,414.8	1,177.4
Chad	32.9	59.6	125.7	103.8	128.8	141.9	155.4	80.0	90.6	114.6	114.3	135.8	122.9	94.1	84.4	–	–	–	–	–	–
Comoros	3.2	6.5	14.6	17.6	18.0	12.4	14.1	18.1	9.4	18.3	13.4	10.8	19.9	16.2	18.3	11.4	11.4	11.3	9.8	8.2	7.3
Cote d'Ivoire	438.8	967.1	2,086.4	1,744.8	1,603.8	2,166.8	2,421.9	2,709.7	2,356.8	2,015.2	2,108.9	2,054.1	1,924.0	1,885.0	1,738.0	2585.2	2,704.6	2,702.8	2,559.8	2,619.2	2,858.0
Egypt	516.9	789.8	875.7	791.3	828.8	894.3	832.4	802.2	839.8	794.6	812.3	668.9	567.9	617.9	519.2	571.5	768.0	728.0	691.5	801.0	751.2
Ethiopia	113.3	201.0	345.6	369.7	362.9	362.2	277.7	460.9	326.3	401.0	382.6	237.3	190.6	150.3	190.1	317.5	362.9	632.6	400.1	523.1	582.2
Gabon	58.5	151.6	367.0	304.1	319.8	284.1	268.1	308.2	314.7	335.3	490.6	649.9	406.7	300.9	483.3	485.6	478.0	481.3	613.9	599.2	609.2
Ghana	422.2	695.0	708.5	684.7	460.4	556.1	594.3	796.4	864.9	883.2	811.1	835.8	705.9	704.9	757.7	1194.6	1,280.1	1,455.5	1,260.7	1,511.1	1,600.0
Kenya	182.9	318.8	630.2	607.4	646.2	761.5	692.8	937.2	708.8	780.7	716.2	751.9	726.0	698.3	795.0	870.6	1,210.0	1,323.3	1,400.0	1,451.0	1,390.1
Mauritius	66.1	260.9	206.8	247.2	249.6	218.5	217.3	293.7	367.9	373.7	360.1	377.0	410.4	422.8	407.9	382.0	453.7	536.9	398.4	390.9	411.2
Mozambique	130.1	162.8	165.3	168.2	105.9	84.8	81.5	87.3	99.6	104.4	98.0	102.1	119.6	122.6	121.2	124.3	145.5	185.5	155.7	138.4	149.1
Nigeria	498.4	495.0	498.4	391.9	496.5	408.5	386.1	398.4	272.0	457.4	291.9	266.4	331.7	286.7	321.9	409.0	285.7	412.8	609.1	805.6	698.4
Senegal	116.6	381.2	246.3	388.8	382.6	364.3	277.8	435.7	345.6	419.5	490.9	508.9	466.7	349.3	309.2	156.0	183.4	170.8	169.9	201.1	198.2
Uganda	256.9	269.2	245.5	353.9	365.2	388.7	433.9	404.6	316.2	272.2	271.1	174.4	171.9	144.5	189.2	411.2	560.5	633.7	505.3	482.7	490.0
Zambia	992.4	797.1	1,098.9	1,015.6	1,041.4	76.5	780.9	695.1	821.9	1,099.9	1,280.5	1,165.8	870.1	923.3	837.5	910.0	984.0	754.2	895.0	585.2	708.2
Zimbabwe	124.6	388.3	868.8	719.9	669.5	636.9	652.9	706.0	766.7	809.5	856.5	989.5	915.2	779.4	797.8	980.2	1,136.5	1,436.5	1,481.1	1,510.4	1,610.5
Total: Africa	7,637.9	12457.9	17,209.2	15,742.9	15,112.4	15,999.2	15,505.1	17,817.6	17,397.9	18,587.9	19,429.3	19,038.4	17,318.1	16,165.1	15,673.5	19,733.0	22,005.0	23,854.0	24,265.0	22,153.0	21,317.0

Note: *=These countries have been chosen to reflect Africa's geographical realities, major ecological zones, small and large countries, language differences, and availability of consistent data.

Source: Europa Publications: Europa World Yearbook, 2000; UN, International Trade Statistics Yearbook, 1998; and UNCTAD, Commodity Yearbook, 1992, 1993, 1994, 1995; UNCTAD, Handbook of Statistics, 2000–2001.

TABLE 18.4 Value of Primary Commodity Export as Percentage of Total Export of Select African Countries*

Country	1970	1975	1981	1982	1983	1984	1985	1986	1987	1988	1989	1990	1991	1992	1993	1994	1995	1996	1997	1998	1999
Algeria	22.9	4.9	1.6	1.3	1.0	1.0	1.0	1.1	1.0	1.3	1.1	1.0	1.0	1.1	1.1	1.4	1.6	1.8	1.1	1.9	1.7
Botswana	71.8	65.1	51.0	36.9	17.3	22.4	18.2	10.2	10.9	2.1	26.6	20.9	18.3	13.2	13.1	10.7	9.2	10.1	9.3	11.8	16.0
Cameroon	89.1	89.1	51.5	50.8	59.1	67.2	92.7	95.0	80.6	74.6	99.0	43.8	41.7	39.8	40.6	66.4	58.6	55.6	60.5	69.8	55.8
Chad	99.0	99.0	100.0	100.0	99.8	99.0	99.0	88.9	81.6	81.3	83.4	99.1	53.4	51.7	63.9	—	—	—	—	—	—
Comoros	64.0	65.0	91.3	88.0	94.7	99.0	88.1	90.5	78.3	87.1	74.4	60.0	82.9	73.6	83.2	95.6	94.1	80.5	89.0	91.1	81.2
Cote d'Ivoire	93.6	81.8	82.3	78.1	77.6	80.3	82.4	80.8	75.8	65.0	71.0	62.2	65.2	66.4	69.0	94.3	74.2	63.2	61.3	64.0	70.1
Egypt	67.8	56.3	27.1	25.4	25.8	28.5	45.3	36.2	41.2	37.5	31.7	25.9	15.7	20.3	23.1	16.4	22.3	20.6	17.6	25.8	21.1
Ethiopia	92.9	83.8	88.8	91.5	90.3	86.9	82.2	99.3	88.0	89.9	91.1	80.7	99.9	88.9	95.5	85.3	85.8	95.0	68.2	93.2	96.2
Gabon	48.3	16.1	16.7	14.1	16.2	14.1	13.6	24.2	24.4	27.9	42.3	26.3	17.9	14.5	21.1	20.7	18.0	14.6	19.7	24.1	20.7
Ghana	92.2	86.1	66.7	78.4	91.5	99.0	95.4	99.8	95.1	87.1	79.5	76.0	56.0	56.3	66.9	83.8	74.3	87.2	77.1	84.2	93.7
Kenya	60.0	49.5	53.0	62.2	65.7	70.3	72.3	78.1	73.6	72.9	64.5	71.5	64.5	52.2	59.5	54.9	64.4	64.0	68.2	72.3	77.2
Mauritius	95.8	87.6	63.8	67.4	69.1	58.6	50.0	43.5	40.7	38.2	36.5	31.6	34.4	32.6	31.4	28.4	29.5	29.8	25.0	23.8	26.6
Mozambique	86.7	80.6	58.8	73.4	80.2	88.3	81.5	90.0	98.6	94.1	97.0	97.3	74.8	88.2	91.8	82.9	86.6	961.1	77.9	65.9	68.7
Nigeria	40.2	6.2	2.8	2.9	4.7	3.4	2.9	6.8	3.7	6.5	3.2	2.1	2.7	2.4	3.2	4.3	2.4	2.6	4.0	8.3	5.8
Senegal	76.7	82.9	49.3	70.9	70.8	68.2	50.1	70.2	57.0	76.3	81.8	69.7	64.8	51.9	48.5	19.7	18.9	17.3	18.8	20.8	18.0
Uganda	91.1	99.2	98.1	98.3	94.9	96.7	94.3	92.8	99.1	99.3	99.3	92.9	85.5	71.2	98.5	95.8	93.6	90.4	91.0	96.3	94.8
Zambia	99.1	98.4	100.0	99.4	100.0	95.5	96.4	79.4	94.1	93.4	95.1	100.0	94.6	78.4	83.7	98.2	94.6	72.7	97.8	61.6	76.4
Zimbabwe	34.0	42.1	61.8	56.6	59.4	55.5	58.9	54.3	54.0	59.5	65.9	57.4	70.4	54.1	51.0	52.1	53.8	59.7	60.1	81.0	80.5

*These countries have been chosen to reflect Africa's geographical realities, major ecological zones, small and large countries, language differences, and availability of consistent data.

Source: UNCTAD, Commodity Yearbook, 1992, 1993, 1994, 1995; Europa Publications: Europa World Yearbook, 2000; UN International Trade Statistics Yearbook, 1998; UNCTAD, Handbook of Statistics, 2000–2001.

African exports, mainly primary products, could play a crucial role in its growth and development.[3] Trade promotes effective and efficient utilization of the existing resources of African countries. It also promotes growth in the amount of resources available to them over time. This means that trade serves as an important source of growth and development of African countries. This conclusion has to be qualified because of the poor linkage and low multiplier effect of international trade on African economies.[4] This is because its major exports are primary or semiprocessed products, which promote investment and growth in certain limited areas or enclaves of African economies where they are produced, mainly for export. Under this situation, which has not changed much since the colonial period, the African countries where these export activities take place may be experiencing economic growth without significant economic development.

This enclave of investment and growth does not create significant employment and other basic needs for the masses which economic development entails. This less-than-expected effect of trade on African countries may be due to the slow growth of export earnings from primary commodities, the accompanying risk in Africa's current degree of specialization in exports, and the difficulty of access to foreign markets for a more diversified range of exports.[5]

International trade constitutes a very important economic link between Africa and the rest of the world. The magnitude of this link is measured by the share of export and import in the total economic activities or gross domestic product (GDP) of African countries. The share of export in the GDP of the select African countries, on average, is more than 20% (see Table 18.7). This is also true of imports (see Table 18.8). Given these insights, the benefits of trade to African countries could be enormous and numerous.

Thus, African countries engage in international trade because of its benefits to them. These benefits can be static or dynamic in nature. Static gains result from specialization and using the existing resources in Africa more efficiently due to trade than otherwise. On the other hand, dynamic benefits of trade arise from the fact that trade leads to growth of Africa's resources over time. That is, trade leads to an increase in Africa's production capacity, resulting from the cumulative effect of trade on its economies. These dynamic benefits will be realized to a higher degree if the appropriate domestic policies and public investment in human and physical capital are made in Africa. Public investment will increase the absorptive and productive capacity of African countries, while appropriate domestic policies give economic agents the correct signal and incentive to adopt efficiency- and productivity-enhancing method of production in Africa.

However, analysis of the benefits from international trade should take into account the instability of international prices of agricultural products and other raw materials in which African countries specialize and export. This can cause uncertainty in planning economic development in African countries. There is also the problem of unequal exchange arising from the nature of the mainly primary products which African countries export. This problem manifests itself in long-term movement in terms of trade against African countries. Trade could only play its expected role in Africa's development process if it is mutually beneficial. Therefore, deteriorating terms of trade of African countries means that most of the benefits from specialization and trade goes to exporters of manufactures, mainly the advanced industrial countries; hence, the unequal exchange inherent in the current international trading system.

Only very few countries in the world are self-sufficient. Given this, most countries in the world must trade with each other to enjoy a rising standard of living resulting from trade, and this is also true of African countries. African countries must trade with each other and other countries in the rest of the world in order to obtain products or services they need for their growth and development.

These products are either not produced at all at home or produced at a relatively higher cost. They are products in which African countries have comparative disadvantage. These products may be needed by African countries to develop and diversify their economies, which leads to structural transformation. Structural transformation means changes in the pattern of employment and other economic activities and changes in institutions and attitudes. This structural changes must be for the better. That is, it should provide secure jobs, adequate nutrition and health, clean water, cheap transport, and education for the children. It may not be possible to have rapid structural transformation of African economies without some strategically important imported goods and services. So, no matter how it is viewed, trade is indispensable in their economic growth and development process.

B. The Potential Benefits of Trade: Static and Dynamic

Trade has many benefits. It is a source of revenue, foreign exchange, and employment. Trade also facilitates technology transfer and foreign investment. International trade serves as a source of revenue to African governments. Many African countries export significant quantities of tropical foods and beverages or other tropical products. The governments of these countries heavily intervene in the export markets of these commodities. One such intervention is through government parastatals which set the producer price for these commodities way below its international price. The difference between the world price and the price paid to the producers constitutes a source of revenue to the African government exercising such power. The lower price serves as a tax to the producers (exporters). This type of government intervention is going out of fashion, however, because it squeezes producers.

Foreign trade serves as a source of foreign exchange or foreign currency for African countries. This is derived from their export of goods and services to the rest of the world. Foreign exchange is needed to import certain goods and services from abroad. Foreign exchange could constitute a serious constraint on growth and development of African countries. They need foreign exchange to import certain foods, enough of which are not produced at home, to feed their population; intermediate inputs and raw materials to run their factories; and capital equipment to develop their industries, infrastructure, and other developmental projects.

Trade serves as a source of employment and income to African countries. The primary products and the embryonic manufacturing sectors producing for export provide an important source of employment and income to their economies. Due to involvement in trade, home producers produce on a larger scale for both home and foreign markets. This raises African economies' potential to produce for export and to provide employment and income. Large-scale production also allows African exporters to reap the benefits of economies of scale: larger output and lower cost per unit. This, in turn, makes them more competitive in the world markets.

Trade makes it possible to transfer technology, skills, and marketing expertise to African countries. With the participation of African countries in international trade, multinational corporations (MNCs) trying to avoid artificial and real barriers to trade have the incentive to locate the subsidiaries of their activities in Africa. These MNCs are mainly engaged in extractive industries which are capital and technology intensive in nature. Some of the MNCs producing in Africa, however, are engaged in manufacturing activities.

The activities of these corporations over time lead to the transfer of technology, skills, and marketing expertise to indigenous Africans. The latter inputs are sorely needed in Africa for its economies to exploit their full potentials and to acquire the dynamism they need to compete in the globalized 21st century. There are some people, however, who argue that the potential costs of the activities of the MNCs on the economies of Africa outweigh the potential benefits. A more pragmatic way to view this cost–benefit dilemma is that it depends on the government policies of the various African countries toward these footloose global firms. The more streamlined and sophisticated these policies are, the more the expected benefits from the MNCs could serve as a significant source of revenue to African governments and employment to the economy as a whole.

As a corollary to the above benefit, foreign trade could be a source of foreign direct investment (FDI). Good and friendly trade policies; credible, efficient, and effective domestic policies; and favorable profit repatriation policies attract FDI. FDI enhances the growth and development of African economies by helping them to exploit their comparative advantage. For example, Africa's mineral mines and plantation agriculture attract FDI, which in turn increases investment, technological progress, and economic growth and development. However, FDI may, if unchecked, accentuate or perpetuate enclave development and colonial patterns which are not in the best interest of African countries. Therefore, carefully designed fiscal and other policies and government regulation of FDI in the export sector could increase their linkage and multiplier effects in African economies. Such policies include a local resource content requirement; an efficient, effective, and honest tax system; a requirement to participate in economic and infrastructural development beyond the immediate area of operation; licensing and leasing agreements on technology; and employment requirement.

Foreign direct investment in African countries to exploit mineral, agricultural, and tropical products makes it incumbent upon multinational corporations to invest in development of transportation and communication facilities in Africa. Such facilities as roads, railroads, river transportation, seaports, airports, and telephones mainly provide links between the location of production activities to the seaport or airport of export. Even if in most cases these facilities are not established with the overall development of African countries as a priority, they do, however, provide a springboard from which a well-planned and coordinated economic infrastructure could be developed.

Some economists argue that the development of these types of physical infrastructure has rather undermined the development of African economies. They are of the view that it has led to development of economic enclaves and balkanization of African economies, with the accompanying social and economic tension. These physical infrastructure in most cases run direct from the agricultural plantations, mines, and manufacturing sites where FDI has been made to the ports (air or sea) of export, without linking or including other parts of the country or region.

This type of infrastructural development creates a dual economy within the same region or country: one part that has almost all the modern amenities of life and another part with little or no amenities. This situation does not promote economic development through further investment, especially by indigenous entrepreneurs. In most cases, the infrastructure is set up in such a way to frustrate potential local competitors.

Foreign trade applies competitive pressure, curbs monopoly power, and leads to improved efficiency of the economies of Africa. By engaging in trade with the rest of the world, African producers are forced to be more efficient and cost effective due to competition from foreign producers. This enables African producers to improve the quality and value of their products. Foreign competition also curbs domestic monopolistic activities, especially in the tradable sector of the economy which produces goods that are sold abroad. This in turn reduces cost of production and improves efficiency in resource use and allocation.

Foreign exchange earnings from exports increase the ability of African countries to attract additional foreign credit needed to finance import of goods and services for development purposes. This is because foreign exchange serves as potential collateral to potential foreign lenders. The ability to earn foreign exchange is an indicator of a country's capacity to service and pay back its foreign loans. Without export earnings playing such a role, the growth and development effort of African countries can be stifled.

Thus, foreign exchange earning is an important source of wherewithal needed for servicing foreign loans taken by African countries. Foreign loans could be useful for growth and development of African countries. However, because most loans taken by African countries are not used productively, they have instead constituted a drag on Africa's economic progress.[5a] This means that dynamic gains from trade depend on productive or efficient use of foreign exchange. When foreign exchange is used in ways not consistent with development, development does not follow trade. That is, in allocating foreign exchange earnings, African governments must give priority to economic activities, which are most likely to give the highest marginal benefit to their respective economies. More often than not, African countries do not follow the latter suggestion.

International trade allows African countries to share in the gains from the more rapid technological advancement of the developed countries in the form of lower prices or better quality imports. However, some economists argue that the gains from technological progress tend to be distributed to the producer in the form of higher incomes rather than to the consumer in the form of lower prices. Strong labor unions in advanced industrial countries ensure that wages are raised due to increase in productivity rather than price being lowered.

Despite the fact that international trade accounts for a significant share of economic activities (GDP) in Africa (see Tables 18.7 and 18.8), its economic growth and development performance over the past three decades has been dismal or at best anemic. This is partly due to adverse market conditions facing African exports. These market conditions include long-term deteriorating terms of trade (see Table 18.5) and tariff and non-tariff barriers to trade which the major exports of Africa confront in advanced industrial countries.[6]

The implication of deteriorating terms of trade is that the volume of Africa's exports could be growing, while export revenue declines. On the other hand, tariff and non-tariff barriers create uncertainty for exporters and artificially restrict demand for their exports. Given the relative inelasticity of supply of Africa's major exports, their prices and revenue are depressed. These two adverse market conditions make it difficult to plan economic growth and development with a credible degree of certainty, because export revenue falls and becomes unpredictable. Because of the latter, the expected level of export revenue needed in Africa's development process more often than not falls below target. This uncertainty emanating from the foreign sector is inimical to economic growth and development. It means that certain crucial intermediate and capital goods needed for economic growth and development may not be forthcoming at each

TABLE 18.5 Terms of Trade of Select African Countries (1980 = 100)

Country	1970	1975	1981	1982	1983	1984	1985	1986	1987	1988	1989	1990	1991	1992	1993	1994	1995	1996	1997	1998	1999
Algeria	18	53	116	110	100	101	101	55	58	46	53	63	58	55	48	44	43	51	52	39	49
Botswana	70	69	80	75	82	79	50.1	57.7	81.9	81.0	98.4	100.0	109.4	114.9	140.9	128	125	149	152	172	169
Cameroon	91	74	81	75	74	85	78	86	69	71	62	56	55	53	54	55	51	51	53	51	36
Chad	75	104	100	105	113	110	114	107	115	123	127	121	121	116	118	111	123	138	101	98	96
Comoros	75	104	–	–	–	110	114	107	115	123	127	121	120	116	118	65	60	55	49	47	62
Cote d'Ivoire	83	76	89	81	77	86	85	88	78	75	67	65	62	62	63	62	71	63	62	73	70
Egypt	88	103	118	113	102	103	103	67	71	63	70	80	74	71	67	63	69	71	75	70	69
Ethiopia	132	104	71	77	76	87	82	123	69	77	66	53	51	46	51	90	119	97	109	95	89
Gabon	17	60	115	113	103	104	102	60	66	55	67	80	73	69	59	54	52	63	61	44	60
Ghana	89	80	73	64	63	71	59	66	64	64	52	47	40	42	41	60	65	63	62	79	68
Kenya	79	100	93	92	88	92	91	91	73	72	68	66	64	59	59	126	117	121	143	131	110
Mauritius	103	217	103	98	101	95	95	115	123	131	128	137	146	132	148	94	96	99	101	98	96
Mozambique	95	113	103	89	88	101	94	90	83	91	102	99	96	101	102	97	97	100	98	96	94
Nigeria	19	56	114	107	95	95	93	51	57	45	53	64	57	55	48	40	40	52	53	55	52
Senegal	89	154	108	95	90	102	102	99	96	103	103	104	108	101	102	79	79	78	79	75	70
Uganda	91	69	76	75	78	97	94	108	63	69	54	42	47	31	37	133	221	158	134	154	120
Zambia	232	108	86	76	84	75	76	73	85	104	112	97	86	83	72	90	100	77	94	84	84
Zimbabwe																101	107	117	118	115	110

Source: UNCTAD, Handbook of International Trade and Development Statistics, 1986–1989, 1996–1997; IMF, Staff Country Report (various countries, 1995–2000); UNCTAD, Commodity Yearbook, 1992, 1993, 1994, 1995; and UNCTAD, Handbook of Statistics, 2000–2001.

TABLE 18.6 Total Exports of Select African Countries (Millions of U.S. Dollars)

Country	1970	1975	1981	1982	1983	1984	1985	1986	1987	1988	1989	1990	1991	1992	1993	1994	1995	1996	1997	1998	1999
Algeria	1,009	4,699	13,320	11,414	11,177	11,886	10,149	7,831	8,186	8,164	8,600	11,011	11,790	11,130	10,230	8,880	10,240	12,620	13,894	10,126	13,133
Botswana	22	142	400	457	636	674	744	865	1,587	1,418	1,360	1,292	1,358	1,742	1,722	1,848	2,142	2,537	2,842	1,948	1,500
Cameroon	232	448	1,122	1,000	939	882	722	781	829	924	900	2,019	1,600	1,840	1,883	1,364	1,651	1,769	1,860	2,027	2,110
Chad	30	48	83	58	104	131	88	99	111	141	137	230	194	182	1,332	148	252	229	237	261	277
Comoros	5	10	16	20	19	7	16	20	12	21	18	18	24	22	22	11	11	14	11	9	9
Cote d'Ivoire	469	1,182	2,535	2,235	2,067	2,698	2,939	3,354	3,110	3,100	2,970	3,300	2,950	2,840	2,519	2,742	3,645	4,278	4,179	4,092	4,077
Egypt	762	1,402	3,233	3,120	3,215	3,140	1,838	2,214	2,037	2,120	2,565	2,582	3,617	3,051	2,244	3,476	3,450	3,539	3,921	3,130	3,559
Ethiopia	122	240	389	404	402	417	338	464	371	446	420	294	189	169	199	372	423	417	587	561	480
Gabon	121	942	2,200	2,160	1,975	2,018	1,974	1,271	1,288	1,200	1,160	2,474	2,273	2,082	2,295	2,350	2,713	3,307	3,110	2,491	2,940
Ghana	458	807	1,063	873	503	540	623	862	909	1,014	1,020	1,100	1,260	1,252	1,133	1,425	1,724	1,669	1,635	1,975	1,707
Kenya	305	644	1,188	977	983	1,083	958	1,200	961	1,071	1,110	1,052	1,125	1,339	1,336	1,587	1,879	2,068	2,054	2,008	1,800
Mauritius	69	298	324	367	361	373	435	675	901	979	987	1,193	1,192	1,297	1,299	1,347	1,538	1,802	1,592	1,645	1,546
Mozambique	150	202	281	229	132	96	77	79	101	111	101	126	162	13	132	150	1,668	193	200	210	217
Nigeria	1,239	7,994	18,087	13,665	10,662	12,020	13,113	5,899	7,383	7,000	9,000	12,912	12,254	11,886	9,916	9,415	11,725	16,153	15,213	9,729	12,082
Senegal	152	460	500	548	543	534	554	620	606	550	600	730	720	673	637	791	969	986	905	968	1,100
Uganda	282	267	250	360	385	390	460	436	319	274	273	152	201	203	192.0	409	461	587	555	501	517
Zambia	1,001	810	1,074	1,022	825	801	810	875	873	1,178	1,347	1,255	920	117	1,001	927	1,040	1,037	915	950	927
Zimbabwe	367	923	1,406	1,273	1,128	1,148	1,109	1,301	1,419	1,360	1,300	1,723	1,300	1,442	1,565	1,881	2,114	2,406	2,464	1,864	2,000

Source: UNCTAD, *Handbook of International and Development Statistics,* 1986–1989; 1996–1997; UNCTAD, *Handbook of Statistics,* 2000–2001; and UNCTAD, *Commodity Yearbook,* 1992–1995.

TABLE 18.7 Exports as Share of GDP for Select African Countries (Percent)

Country	1970	1975	1981	1982	1983	1984	1985	1986	1987	1988	1989	1990	1991	1992	1993	1994	1995	1996	1997	1998	1999
Algeria	20.7	12.2	24.9	20.0	18.6	18.7	15.0	11.7	12.2	12.4	12.3	15.9	16.8	15.5	16.8	14.5	16.0	18.9	20.0	21.4	27.9
Botswana	25.6	32.2	45.0	47.9	57.6	54.9	56.4	61.0	96.6	79.4	67.4	60.5	58.4	70.3	72.0	43.8	49.2	54.5	57.8	39.8	25.0
Cameroon	20.1	9.5	12.3	10.7	9.3	7.7	6.3	6.3	6.9	8.4	8.1	19.7	16.6	20.2	25.1	11.8	13.6	14.1	14.3	22.8	24.0
Chad	9.2	6.4	14.3	9.5	14.6	17.9	10.0	11.8	13.6	14.8	13.7	22.8	18.0	16.9	18.2	11.5	19.0	16.9	17.0	16.2	17.6
Comoros	–	–	10.0	3.3	10.7	3.8	8.4	10.4	6.1	10.4	9.1	9.0	11.0	10.6	12.1	4.3	4.3	5.4	4.2	4.5	4.6
Cote d'Ivoire	12	14.5	24.5	21.6	20.0	27.7	20.8	31.8	30.0	30.5	29.5	33.3	29.3	28.9	35.1	25.1	31.3	34.6	32.4	33.4	36.4
Egypt	9.9	9.8	12.9	8.3	10.8	9.9	5.4	21.0	19.6	20.9	25.5	26.1	9.1	7.5	11.5	6.4	6.1	5.9	6.2	3.8	4.0
Ethiopia	6.8	5.9	8.0	8.2	7.8	8.2	7.2	9.2	6.7	7.9	7.4	5.2	3.4	3.3	5.5	3.5	3.9	3.4	4.6	8.6	7.4
Gabon	36.2	23.1	56.8	56.6	50.0	47.6	47.7	31.0	37.9	34.3	28.3	58.3	55.3	49.5	58.1	39.1	43.5	51.0	46.5	55.9	65.9
Ghana	20.7	18.5	23.5	20.7	12.5	12.3	13.5	17.8	17.9	18.9	18.1	19.0	30.0	29.8	26.8	19.2	22.2	20.5	19.0	23.9	22.5
Kenya	19	14.1	18.5	15.0	14.8	16.1	13.6	15.9	12.1	12.7	12.5	11.4	12.0	14.2	12.9	17.9	20.3	21.5	20.9	17.3	17.2
Mauritius	35.9	30.0	25.5	27.3	26.8	26.4	28.8	40.5	49.2	50.3	44.7	54.4	52.3	53.8	66.0	43.4	47.4	52.5	44.0	40.4	36.6
Mozambique	–	–	17.2	14.2	9.6	6.7	5.6	5.7	6.9	7.2	6.2	7.7	10.2	8.0	13.1	8.2	9.0	9.9	9.9	5.4	5.4
Nigeria	15.7	32.0	65.7	50.0	41.8	49.2	49.1	21.7	27.2	23.5	28.4	38.5	34.8	32.4	36.1	26.0	31.6	42.1	38.4	23.5	27.9
Senegal	17.6	13.4	13.8	13.2	12.8	13.1	13.1	14.0	13.2	11.4	12.5	14.5	14.1	12.8	13.4	13.6	15.8	15.3	13.3	20.6	22.9
Uganda	21.4	11.6	14.1	16.0	8.5	9.2	9.6	10.7	7.4	5.9	5.5	2.9	3.7	3.7	4.3	8.4	8.6	10.4	9.3	7.4	8.2
Zambia	55.9	41.6	51.2	50.1	44.3	40.4	40.2	43.4	42.0	53.7	62.0	57.5	43.2	44.8	51.2	22.9	26.3	24.6	21.0	27.9	28.1
Zimbabwe	24.3	22.1	28.3	25.0	21.8	22.7	20.5	24.0	26.4	23.5	21.5	27.9	20.1	24.2	30.1	20.6	23.1	24.5	24.3	29.6	35.7

Source: UNCTAD, Handbook of International Trade and Development Statistics, 1986, 1987, 1988, 1989, 1996–1997; UNCTAD, Handbook of Statistics, 2000–2001; World Bank, World Tables (various issues).

TABLE 18.8 Imports as Share of GDP for Select African Countries (Percent)

Country	1970	1975	1981	1982	1983	1984	1985	1986	1987	1988	1989	1990	1991	1992	1993	1994	1995	1996	1997	1998	1999
Algeria	25.8	15.6	21.1	18.2	17.3	16.2	14.6	13.8	10.6	11.2	12.0	14.1	11.0	11.9	15.2	15.2	16.0	13.2	12.5	19.7	21.3
Botswana	69.5	49.4	90.0	72.1	66.7	57.6	44.2	50.3	57.0	57.9	52.1	92.0	84.7	75.1	80.1	38.8	43.9	37.0	46.0	48.7	38.3
Cameroon	20.9	12.6	15.7	13.3	12.1	10.4	10.0	13.8	14.5	11.6	11.9	16.1	17.6	12.8	18.5	6.2	9.9	9.7	10.5	19.1	20.5
Chad	18.7	17.7	18.6	17.8	22.1	24.8	27.1	34.2	44.7	44.0	43.5	47.6	48.3	22.5	32.1	13.7	16.6	18.9	17.7	16.4	17.2
Comoros	–	–	21.3	19.4	19.1	23.2	18.9	19.2	26.5	29.7	30.3	30.0	34.3	33.2	28.5	20.5	24.9	61.5	60.4	91.4	91.9
Cote d'Ivoire	16.5	13.9	23.1	20.2	18.0	15.5	17.1	19.5	21.6	23.0	23.6	21.8	21.2	23.6	20.4	17.5	25.2	23.4	21.6	26.1	29.2
Egypt	10.2	27.4	35.3	32.7	34.4	34.0	16.3	25.0	21.4	23.4	19.5	23.6	19.4	20.6	22.1	18.8	20.7	21.9	20.9	19.5	18.0
Ethiopia	9.6	7.5	15.2	16.0	16.9	18.6	20.9	22.0	20.0	19.1	19.3	19.2	8.5	18.0	16.5	9.7	10.5	11.6	11.1	22.1	20.1
Gabon	23.9	11.5	21.7	18.9	21.6	20.9	23.4	21.1	21.5	26.5	23.2	18.2	20.1	16.7	19.0	12.6	14.1	14.8	16.5	25.3	29.3
Ghana	18.6	18.1	24.5	16.7	13.4	13.8	18.7	16.1	17.6	16.9	16.7	22.4	18.4	34.4	23.3	28.4	24.6	25.9	27.1	34.2	46.1
Kenya	27.6	21.5	32.3	24.7	20.5	23.0	20.4	21.4	22.0	23.6	23.7	24.1	19.2	18.2	19.5	23.6	32.4	30.7	33.4	27.6	26.7
Mauritius	39.6	33.4	43.7	34.5	32.3	33.5	35.0	41.1	55.3	66.1	60.0	73.9	69.1	67.6	72.0	62.2	60.9	66.7	60.5	50.9	53.3
Mozambique	–	–	49.0	52.0	46.3	37.4	30.9	39.2	42.9	46.4	42.0	54.0	54.3	54.1	55.2	55.6	41.9	38.2	37.6	23.4	24.6
Nigeria	13.5	24.2	74.2	54.9	35.5	24.0	23.2	14.8	14.4	12.8	11.3	12.9	17.8	22.1	17.9	20.5	21.3	18.1	26.1	24.2	32.7
Senegal	22.3	17.0	23.8	23.9	24.5	24.8	19.2	21.7	22.2	24.4	23.9	25.2	25.5	19.7	21.6	17.5	23.1	22.2	19.6	30.6	34.3
Uganda	13.1	8.7	–	–	8.3	8.1	7.2	7.5	12.9	11.8	13.2	5.6	3.6	8.0	9.5	17.9	19.7	21.0	22.1	20.8	21.3
Zambia	26.6	47.5	50.7	49.1	35.2	30.7	34.4	29.9	35.6	38.3	40.2	57.0	37.6	40.2	51.0	14.7	17.7	19.8	18.8	26.6	26.2
Zimbabwe	21.7	19.2	29.7	28.0	20.3	18.9	16.2	18.1	19.4	18.5	18.0	30.0	25.5	37.0	29.3	24.6	29.1	28.6	30.3	42.9	45.5

Source: UNCTAD, Handbook of International Trade and Development Statistics, 1986, 1987, 1988, 1989, 1996–1997; World Bank, World Tables (various issues); and UNCTAD, Handbook of Statistics, 2000–2001.

planning cycle. This does not augur well for Africa's economic development; trade turns out to be a drag on its economies.[7]

Another likely reason for the poor growth of African countries despite large share of foreign trade in their economic activities is their domestic policies on the use of foreign exchange realized from exports. In most African countries, the domestic currencies are overvalued. This policy penalizes exporters, brings in relatively small amount of revenue when export earnings are converted to local currency, discourages exporters in their effort to diversify into high-valued-added export products and sets in motion the vicious cycle of poor export performance, and creates excess demand for foreign exchange which forces the government to introduce foreign exchange control.

The introduction of foreign exchange control gives the government the upper hand in deciding who gets what share of the foreign exchange. Due to the fact that most governments in Africa are corrupt, the allocation of this scarce foreign exchange in most cases will not align with the development needs of their countries. Instead of using this valuable resource to import goods and technology needed for economic development, they are spent on frivolous and expensive imported consumer goods. A significant portion of this scarce foreign exchange is also locked away in the personal foreign bank accounts of African leaders. Thus, despite the dwindling revenue from Africa's exports, the little that are realized are misused, hence the low contribution to economic growth and development. If foreign exchange earnings are better managed in Africa, its economic development condition can improve.[8]

IV. OPPOSITION TO FREE TRADE

A. THE ALLEGED HARMFUL EFFECTS OF FREE TRADE

Despite the contributions of trade to growth and development of African economies, its potential is not fully realized. This is due to the nature of the major export commodities of Africa. As discussed above, Africa's major exports are primary commodities, and there are unique conditions, which primary products confront on the world markets. These conditions have become a lingering, long-term problem and offsetting force to the contribution of trade to growth and development of African countries.

The problematic situation which the major exports of Africa are said to confront include deteriorating terms of trade; low price and income elasticities of demand; development of synthetic substitutes; escalated tariffs in the major export markets of the United States, European Union, and Japan; and non-tariff barriers such as voluntary export restraint (VERs), minimum import expansion (MIE), border taxes, variable levies, health and sanitary requirements, etc.

These problems have led some economists to argue that trade is harmful to growth and development of African countries.

These economists advocate that instead of allowing an unfettered free trade to influence their growth and development, African countries should use targeted and temporary trade policy to regulate trade and to protect certain (infant) industries in their economies, which could in the long run compete in the world markets. They argue that Africa's link to the outside world through trade could be harmful except when appropriately guided policy is followed. Even if there may be some benefits associated with free trade, such benefits, they argue, may be outweighed by the potential cost of unfettered free trade. These trade pessimists suggest active policy to guide trade, promote export diversification, and shield infant industries that may eventually be able to export.

Trade pessimists believe that successful growth and development policies are homegrown and that African countries should not depend on foreign dictates if they are to use trade as an effective instrument to promote growth and development. African countries should use targeted and time-limited policies that protect certain economic activities in which they expect to enjoy comparative advantage over time.

Furthermore, African countries should encourage diversification of their exports away from traditional to nontraditional products. Increasing investment in economic and social infrastructure such as telecommunication, power, transport, water, health and nutrition, education, and sanitation could do this. These types of investment will boost productivity and reduce transaction cost of economic activities in their respective economies, and make Africa a better business address. This also will facilitate development of new areas of comparative advantage and improve competitiveness of African countries in the world markets. Good domestic policies should complement this investment effort.

The major reasons why trade pessimists distrust unfettered free trade are as follows. First, market imperfections in most African economies do not allow factors of production to freely move from nontradable to tradable sectors of the economy to take advantage of higher productivity and better opportunity in the export sector.[9] This means that resource usage does not respond effectively to international market price signal. Social and institutional factors are responsible for such low resource mobility. Such factors include lack of education and information, poverty, social taboos associated with working in the formal sector of the economy (such as the export sector), lack of a precise definition of private property rights and lack of respect for rule of law.

In some African countries, such as Nigeria, for example, the state or the government legally owns land. This makes it difficult, if not impossible, to buy or sell land to produce products on a commercial basis for export. Investments in land to increase productivity and to exploit comparative advantage are hindered.

Market imperfection is also due to low coverage of market and lack of frequent periodicity of market. The degree of monetization or use of money for economic transactions in the rural areas where the majority of Africa's population lives is still very low. Therefore, serious effort by African governments to introduce and strengthen financial, social, and institutional infrastructure in the rural areas of Africa will contribute immensely to its economic development and progress. The rural sector of Africa can serve as a sponge or an untapped source of ingredients of economic growth and development if appropriate, rational, and adequate investments in the infrastructure and domestic policies are made.

Second, it is argued by trade pessimists that benefits from trade are unpredictable because of the restrictions put by importing countries on products in which African exporters have comparative advantage. These restrictions take various forms both tariff and non-tariff. *Ad valorem* and specific tariffs are taxes imposed on finished imported goods. Even if trade distorting, they are not as restrictive as escalated tariffs. Escalated or graduated tariffs on the other hand, are tariffs based on stages of production of an import. They can have serious adverse effects on economic growth and development of the primary exporting countries of Africa. This is because escalated tariffs discourage processing and manufacturing of these products in African countries.[10]

Let us illustrate the discouraging effect of escalated tariff with a hypothetical example using Ghana, which is a major exporter of cocoa in the world. Ghana exports its cocoa products to advanced industrial countries of Europe, Japan, and the United States. If Ghana exports raw cocoa beans to these countries, the tariff on them is close to zero or is zero. But, if Ghana processes its cocoa beans into cocoa butter, the tariff on the cocoa butter escalates to 25%. If Ghana further processes its cocoa beans to chocolate or candy bars, the tariff on them is raised to say 110%! Now, given this hypothetical example, does it make sense for Ghana to produce candy bars for exports? The answer definitely is no, but manufacture and export of candy bars creates more added value, income, and employment in Ghana than production and export of only raw cocoa beans. What this simple hypothetical example illustrates is that tariff escalation reduces, if not wiping away completely, the multiplier effect or engine of growth effect of international trade for primary exporting countries of Africa.

On the other hand, non-tariff barriers to trade such as import quotas, voluntary export restraints, minimum import expansion, the Multifiber Agreement (MFA), etc., put quantitative restrictions, directly or indirectly, on the amount of Africa's exports to advanced industrial countries. Major African exports affected by these types of restrictions include: cotton, groundnuts, vegetable oils, and other tropical agricultural products (see Table 18.2). Almost all of the major exports of Africa are affected by these non-tariff barriers to trade. In addition to the uncertainty they cause exporters, these trade restrictions significantly reduce the export earnings of African countries.

Third, trade pessimists point to the poor prospects and low demand for the export products of interest to African countries, which are mainly raw materials and unprocessed tropical products (see Table 18.2). The reasons for poor demand prospects include low price and income elasticities of demand, availability of synthetic substitutes, and new technologies that economize on the use of raw materials.

Low price elasticity of demand is a problem because expansion of production and export of these products pushes down their world prices. However, lower world price does not necessarily lead to a proportionate increase in quantity consumed. For example, if the price of coffee falls by 50%, coffee drinkers generally are not necessarily going to increase their consumption by 50%. This leads to a loss in foreign exchange earnings to major African exporters of coffee such as Côte d'Ivoire, Kenya, Ghana, and Tanzania.

Low-income elasticity of demand hinders export of primary products by African countries because, as the standard of living of the advanced industrial countries increases, they consume proportionately less food (cocoa, coffee, tea, spices, etc.) and consume proportionately more services, especially entertainment. Thus, low income and low price elasticities of demand imply that as primary exporting countries of Africa strive to expand the production and export of the products of their comparative advantage, the demand and terms of trade of these products deteriorate (see Table 18.5).

Discovery of synthetic substitutes and new technologies that use smaller quantities of raw materials also have a dampening effect on demand and price of the major exportables of African countries. Because of the primary export boom that occurred during the few years following World War II due to the post-war recovery effort and the Korean War, the prices of export products of interest to the majority of African countries and other less developed countries (LDCs) skyrocketed. This gave an incentive to manufacturers in the advanced industrial countries to start looking for synthetic substitutes and to adopt technologies that use fewer imported raw materials. These efforts led to a fall in demand and price of raw materials in the world markets.

The above market factors, trade pessimists argue, collectively put downward pressure on demand and the price of primary exports of interest to African countries. This, they claim, has led to a long-term deterioration of terms of trade of the primary exporters. Worsening terms of trade in turn lead to falling income, employment, and foreign-exchange earnings of African exporters. Falling foreign-exchange earnings put a significant constraint on economic growth and development of African countries. The constraint manifests itself in the inability of African countries to buy industrial raw materials, food, capital equipment, and technology much needed for economic development and improvement of the quality of lives of their citizens.

Deteriorating terms of trade and the accompanying shortage of foreign exchange also limit the ability of African countries to import the technology and other inputs they need in order to exploit new areas of comparative advantage. This is especially crucial for import of materials and equipments needed to develop their economic and social infrastructure. That is, the dynamic benefits of specialization and trade may be lost due to less-than-favorable terms of trade that Africa's exports face on the world markets. The declining foreign exchange earnings as mentioned earlier, also make it difficult for African countries to service their foreign debt.

Fourth, it is argued by trade pessimists that African countries are over-dependent on exports, measured by the share of exports in their GDP. However, this argument can be viewed as seeing the cup as half empty instead of half full. This dependence, it can be argued, makes African countries vulnerable when external shocks occur because they can neither control nor easily adjust to such conditions. This situation in turn affects the predictability of investment and growth of African countries. For example, some African countries derive more than 70% of their total export earnings from export of one or two primary commodities.

However, appropriate trade policy can help to ameliorate this vulnerability. Using trade surpluses in upswing years to smooth out the deficits in the downswing years could do this. Furthermore, with appropriate domestic monetary and credit policy and financial deepening, domestic investment can be increased despite the less-than-stable foreign source of investment. Appropriate domestic monetary policy can also reduce the excessive dependence on foreign source of investment finance that precipitated the debt crisis of the 1980s, which devastated most African countries.

Despite the fact that the trade pessimists are in the minority in the debate about the role of foreign trade in development process, their argument and pessimism must be given serious attention if African countries are to cover the grounds they lost in world trade in the past century and become major global players in the 21st century. These concerns have to be given serious attention if African countries want to claim a stake in the 21st century. Africa's present comparative advantage is a product of colonial investments and policies reflecting colonial priorities, reinforced by post-colonial (or neo-colonial) governments. Given this situation, Africa's comparative advantage can be changed by making appropriate and deliberate changes in its public investment and domestic policies.

What this situation highlights is that African countries can alter their current comparative advantage through a deliberate effort to increase public investment that reflects Africa's current needs, priorities, and efforts to be competitive in the global environment of the 21st century and beyond. It also means that comparative advantage is not a given; it can change over time when a country makes a deliberate effort to influence it.

Such deliberate efforts include policy of limited protection and public sector investment in economic and social infrastructure aimed at developing new areas of comparative advantage.[11] The latter types of investment reduce transaction cost of producing goods and services. Without these types of investment, these new areas of comparative advantage will not develop. Sound domestic policies and the political will and commitment to carry them through are crucial for induced comparative advantage to materialize.

To reap the dynamic benefits of trade, these deliberate efforts must be made by African countries and their leaders. Japan and the rest of the Southeast Asia countries are living examples of this model of limited and targeted intervention by the government to influence comparative advantage. In these Asian countries, some sectors of their economies are designated for protection with the aim of helping them to grow. As they grow stronger and become able to reap the benefits of economies of scale, the protection and help are phased out as they become effective competitors in the world markets. Initially most of these economies started with export of labor-intensive products dictated by the inherent nature of their resources. But, with targeted protection of some sectors, over time they acquired comparative advantage in the export of light manufactures, such as electronics, and are now major exporters of heavy industrial and high-technology products.[12]

A similar situation can be replicated in Africa if the will and determination exist. Investment in human and physical capital should be given the highest priority if Africa is to escape from the situation it is locked into by the current world trading and economic system. These types of investment will unleash the entrepreneurial power of the economic agents in their economies, boost productivity, and increase their competitiveness in the world markets. This will help make trade actually play its expected role in the growth and development of Africa.

These deliberate efforts to influence trade will also set a virtuous cycle in motion in Africa. This is because it will boost both domestic and foreign investment in the continent and put it on a higher growth trajectory. These government efforts should be highly selective and temporary in nature, because it is essential to overcome market failure involved in the process of technological progress. Such market failure is endemic to original technological progress. Removing it through public investment is crucial to the effort to transfer products, processes, and organizational innovations from countries that have achieved economic progress, such as East Asian countries, to African countries.[13]

Furthermore, the dynamic comparative advantage that limited intervention creates will implicitly help African countries to diversify their export base. This will reduce their vulnerability and heavy dependence on primary products, whose terms of trade have been on a long-term downward trend in the past two decades (see Table 18.5).

B. The Problem of Deteriorating Terms of Trade

The theory of deteriorating commodity terms of trade of the LDCs was first launched independently (and simultaneously) in 1950 by Prebisch and Singer.[14] The barter terms of trade measure the direction of the share of a country in gains from trade. It is the ratio of a country's export price index to its import price index. A rise in the barter terms of trade for a country for a long period of time suggests that the country's share in world gains from trade is rising and vice versa.

African primary product exporters suffered deteriorating terms of trade between 1870 and 1938. But after World War II, one cannot categorically determine the terms of trade trend for the primary exporters of Africa and primary exporters as a whole. This is because during the early 1950s the terms of trade for the primary exporting countries of Africa were at their peak. On the other hand, during the late 1950s, their terms of trade sharply declined. However, if the average terms of trade are taken for the entire period of the 1950s, the deteriorating terms of trade hypothesis may not hold.[15] As Table 18.5 shows, the commodity terms of trade, on average, deteriorated for African countries during the 1970s and up to the early 1990s. Unless a major global event occurs in the near future, this trend may continue, given the nature and characteristics of primary product export.

A country's commodity terms of trade should, however, be interpreted with caution. Declining terms of trade may be due to (global) increase in productivity. In this case, export revenue can be maintained by an increase in the volume of exports. The danger with the latter is that if every exporter expands output, it may lead to an "adding up" or a "fallacy of composition" problem, which occurs when an attempt by all producers to increase export leads to a drastic fall in export price and revenue.

On the other hand, a rising terms of trade may be due to a fall in productivity and rising cost of production. This may be accompanied by a fall in the volume of exports and revenue. In either of these scenarios, a change (fall or rise) in commodity terms of trade may not necessarily be a good indicator of how benefits from trade are distributed among trading partners. Therefore, one has to be careful in interpreting the terms of trade trend for African countries and their effect on economies.

The above less-than-favorable conditions that African exports experience in the world markets have led trade pessimists to advocate that African countries should manage their involvement in world trade. They advocate deliberate policy to promote export diversification and to protect production areas of potential comparative advantage. Deliberate effort should be made to pinpoint economic activities in which African countries have potential comparative advantage. These types of activities should be protected with time-specific, targeted, and time-phased policies that allow them to grow and be able to export within a time frame.

It should be noted, however, that the advanced industrial countries do not create some of these obstacles to trade confronted by African countries. Rather, the nature of the exports of African countries is partly responsible. For example, deteriorating terms of trade and low price and income elasticities are not the creation of industrial countries. These are economic phenomena that will occur regardless of who exports primary products. On the other hand, the capitalist force that led to production of synthetic products is a major culprit, which set off the downward trend in terms of trade of African countries. Furthermore, tariff and nontariff barriers to Africa's trade are artificial barriers, which the advanced industrial countries should abolish if they are really serious and interested in faster economic growth and development of Africa.[16]

The crucial question to ask, given the deteriorating terms of trade confronting African countries, is why the product mix exported by African countries has not changed much. The explanation for this situation is economic, social, and institutional. First, the economic explanation is poor or absent economic infrastructures such as telecommunication, water, power, and transportation. The absence of these infrastructures makes it difficult, if not impossible, to produce transaction-intensive products such as manufactures and services.[17] Where the latter products are produced at all, their cost per unit is usually very high, thus making it difficult for African countries to compete both at home and in foreign markets. What this means is that nontraditional exports are never produced and exported, and diversification is very difficult despite deteriorating terms of trade facing African primary exporters.

Second, social infrastructures such as education, health, and sanitation are equally as poor, if not appalling, in Africa, but these types of infrastructure are very crucial for the nurture, growth, and improvement in skills of Africa's population and the labor force, in particular. Without a well-educated, healthy, and skilled labor force, it becomes next to impossible to venture into nontraditional production activities. An unskilled labor force creates low productivity and high cost if production of nonprimary products is ventured. Because of this situation, the incentive and opportunity are not there to diversify out of the primary product export. East Asia provides a good example of the role that investment in social infrastructures can play in a region's economic progress.

Investment in social infrastructures is investment in human capital, which in turn boosts productivity and lowers cost. Lower cost increases exporters' competitiveness in the world markets. For African countries to escape the current predicament of being locked into exporting primary products, they must be willing and committed to invest significant amounts of their public budgets in social infrastructures in the years to come.

Third, institutional infrastructures such as banking services, rule of law (especially contract enforcement), and government bureaucracy are very weak in most African countries. These institutional variables are very crucial for efficient production and export of nontraditional products such as manufactures. Long delays in banking transactions and in clearing imported inputs at the port of entry, corrupt customs services, and an inability to enforce contracts all combine to raise business uncertainty and the cost of doing business that requires speed, fulfillment of obligations, and frequent periodicity. Because this mostly depicts the situation in African countries, they have a bad reputation. Entrepreneurs, domestic and foreign, are unwilling to enter into nontraditional export business, hence the inability of African countries to diversify out of traditional primary exports.[18] To improve on their situation, African countries need a radical institutional overhaul to attract businesses that could produce and export nontraditional products.

V. POLICY SUGGESTIONS

A review of the literature on Africa's trade and economic development does not paint a hopeful and optimistic picture for the continent. Despite this situation, trade is an important economic force in Africa's attempt to grow and develop into modern economies. Africa's economic performance in the last four decades is little better than dismal. There are many reasons for this anemic economic performance. Good trade performance can help in Africa's struggle for economic development. Trade could be one of the major engines that propel Africa's growth and development.

No matter how it is looked at, trade is an important factor in Africa's growth and development. The real issue to consider is how Africa's trade can be restructured. This calls for policy recommendations to help revamp its ailing trade sector. These policy suggestions are not all-embracing but they help to highlight the problems confronting Africa's trade and how these problems can be ameliorated or solved.

There is an urgent need for African countries to diversify from their traditional exports of mainly primary products. African countries should strive to produce and export more manufactured products. This is one of the major ways through which the Southeast Asia countries significantly overcame the inherent problem of primary exporting. On the part of African countries, it will entail a restructuring and improvement of their basic economic and social infrastructures. Improvement in health and education is crucial to providing the skilled labor necessary to run the manufacturing factories. It will also entail a deliberate, massive public investment in physical infrastructure. This will in turn help in creating new areas of comparative advantage in the manufacturing sector. East Asian economies once again provide a good example of this development strategy.

A serious effort also should be made to develop appropriate technology for Africa—technology that will take Africa's resource endowment and its other unique and environmental conditions into consideration. This may involve adapting imported technology to Africa's economic and social environment. It will usher in a new method of work, improve productivity and quality of life, and ensure sustainable development.

The political and economic leaders of Africa should encourage intra-African trade. This is important given that more than 80% of Africa's trade is with the advanced industrial countries. Because these markets have built-in obstacles against primary exports and also are saturated with primary exports, it is a good idea for African countries to aggressively encourage trade among themselves. This is especially important for complementary primary exports.

However, one should realize that this strategy may be handicapped because it may not provide the badly needed "hard currencies" of the Western countries. In this sense, trade pessimists make a salient point by pointing out that the current international trade and financial system is stacked against the developing countries, and African countries in particular. The hard currencies are needed to import food, and intermediate and capital goods needed to execute economic and social development projects. Increased trade with the emerging market economies may somewhat ameliorate this problem.

Intra-African trade will also encourage development of optimum-size manufacturing plants in various regions of Africa. Instead of having many manufacturing plants operating below capacity, as they are now, one large-sized plant can produce for an entire region in Africa, with the attendant benefits of large-scale operation such as lower cost and price. This could prepare African manufacturers to compete in the global market.

There is the need for massive investment of Marshall Plan magnitude in the development of the basic infrastructures in African countries. Such infrastructures include land transportation, telecommunication, public utilities, seaports, and airports. This will help to increase production capacity, improve economic efficiency, and reduce other supply constraints that face African countries today. This is essential because Africa's trade problem is both demand side and supply side in nature.

One has to admit, however, that the conditions surrounding the Marshall Plan were relatively simple given that the countries involved were destroyed by war. The plan to rebuild was based on a clean slate, and the majority of European countries involved were similar in structure, economically and socially. This is different from the current restructuring or structural adjustment programs (SAPs) applied on African countries and other LDCs by the International Monetary Fund and the World Bank. The SAPs in most cases have stifling conditions which make matters worse for African countries. Unlike the Marshall Plan, local or national input in designing the SAPs is very small, which tends to undermine its chances of success. This is manifested by frequent policy reversals in some African countries that have embraced the SAPs.

African countries on their own should strive to reduce, if not abolish, their trade restrictive measures. It will save African countries the counter accusation which the advanced industrial countries level against them when they are requested to abolish the trade barriers in their markets which mainly target African exports. Reduced trade barriers will also promote domestic policy changes and intra-African trade.

African countries should pursue good, credible, and stable macroeconomic policies: fiscal, monetary, and exchange rate. Such policies will create a favorable and conducive atmosphere for domestic and foreign investment in the export sector of their economies. Trade will be encouraged as foreign investors are attracted to invest in export industries. This will in turn promote economic growth and development.

Africans and African leaders should encourage and promote democratization and smooth transfer of political power and a stable government which is a noneconomic factor with a great implication for economic growth and development. Political stability is a precursor to economic development; it creates growth-enhancing environment. Political stability in African countries reduces capital flight, promotes trade, and increases focus on national debates on how best to promote economic progress.

Political stability is especially important for Africa to claim the 21st century because the majority of African countries are plagued by civil and military strife and conflicts. Political instability is a major hindrance to Africa's economic development. Every effort should be made by Africans and the rest of the world to resolve these conflicts, some of which have lasted many decades. These conflicts contributed significantly to making the second half of the 20th century lost decades for Africa.

As a policy suggestion exogenous to African countries, the advanced industrial countries should seriously consider reducing, if not abolishing, trade-restrictive policies that adversely affect Africa's exports. This is needed if the advanced industrial countries are interested in and serious about increased participation of African countries in world trade and also in their economic growth and development. It is important that this issue is given serious consideration because it may take quite some time for African countries to diversify out of their current pattern of trade that is not favorable for their economic development. Favorable trade policies in the advanced industrial countries will promote industrialization effort in Africa.

African countries should strive to diversify their trade partners from the current situation of concentration of trade with their former colonial rulers. Other parts or countries of the world are also economically growing and may provide trading opportunities and new markets. The newly emerging market economy countries are typical examples of such new markets.

VI. SUMMARY

This chapter evaluated the role of international trade in the economic development process of Africa. To achieve this objective the theories of trade were reviewed, and the contribution of international trade to the economic development of African countries was discussed. The static and dynamic benefits of trade to African countries were analyzed in detail. On balance, African countries stand to benefit from trade, especially if they pursue credible liberal trade policies and increase public investment in economic and social infrastructure. Some economists, led by Prebisch and Singer, are of the view that trade could be harmful to growth and development of African countries, in particular, and LDCs, in general, if efficient, targeted policy intervention is not made. They argue that the international market conditions facing African countries and the way the international economic system is currently set up put Africa on the losing side of international trade. They are of the view that most, if not all, of the gains from trade accrue to the advanced industrial countries, manifested in the deteriorating commodity terms of trade of African countries. However, such observations should be interpreted with caution. Irrespective of this seemingly persuasive argument, trade can still play a very supportive role in Africa's economic development. Despite the bleak picture facing African countries in the international economic system, the positive role that trade could play in the development process, provides some hope, especially if appropriate domestic policies and public investments are made. On this basis, policy suggestions were proffered to both African countries and advanced industrial countries. Some of the suggestions point to problems that African countries must solve internally, such as restructuring their economies, dismantling trade barriers, and pursuing effective and credible domestic policies. Required policy changes external to African countries are mainly those instituted by the advanced industrial countries, which hurt Africa's exports.

DISCUSSION QUESTIONS

1. Explain the difference between absolute advantage and comparative advantage in international trade.
2. How does specialization and division of labor benefit trading partners?
3. What are the main obstacles confronting trade among African countries?
4. Discuss the main trade barriers which limit African countries', trade with the advanced industrial countries.

5. What are the static and dynamic benefits from free trade?
6. Why do some economists argue against free trade?
7. Why have the terms of trade of the African countries and other LDCs been deteriorating since the past three decades?
8. Why is adequate economic and social infrastructure considered a *sine qua non* for Africa's trade and economic development?
9. What are the benefits and shortcomings of the activities of the multinational corporations (MNCs) in trade and economic development of African countries?
10. From your reading of Chapter 18, would you advise African countries to promote outward-oriented (export-led) policy or inward-looking (trade restrictive) policy as a development strategy?
11. Should a policy such as the Marshal Plan be implemented for African countries? Explain the feasibility or otherwise of such a policy for African countries.

NOTES

[1]Ricardo, D. (1996) *The Principles of Political Economy and Taxation*, 3rd Ed., Amherst, N.Y.: Prometheus Books.

[1a]Krueger, A.O. (1995) *Trade Policies and Developing Nations*, Washington, D.C. The Brookings Institution.

[2]Fage, J.D. (1969) *A History of West Africa: An Introductory Survey*, 4th ed., London: Cambridge University Press; Neumark, S.D. (1964) *Foreign Trade and Economic Development in Africa: A Historical Perspective*, Stanford, CA: Stanford University.

[3]Diversification and economic growth of African economies in the foreseeable future will depend on the expansion of earning from primary exports. See, for example, Royal Institute of International Affairs (1964) *Direction for World Trade*, London: Oxford University Press, pp. 161–212; and Helleiner, G.K., Ed. (2002) *Non-Traditional Export Promotion in Africa: Experience and Issues*, New York: Palgrave.

[4]Lydall, H.F. (1975) *Trade and Employment*, Geneva, Switzerland: International Labor Office.

[5]UNCTAD (1999) *African Development in a Comparative Perspective*, Asmara, Eritrea: African World Press, pp. 89–95.

[5a]Pattillo, C., Poirson, H., and Ricci, L. (2002) "External Debt and Growth," *Finance and Development*, 39(2), 32–35; Kremer, M. and Jayachandran, S. (2002) "Odious Debt," *Finance and Development*, 39(2), 36–39.

[6]Erzan, R. and Svedberg, P. (1991) "Protection Facing Exports From Sub-Saharan Africa in the EC, Japan, and the US," in Frimpong-Ansah, J.H. *et al.*, Eds., *Trade and Development In Sub-Saharan Africa*, pp. 97–151; Svedberg, P. (1991) "The Export Performance of Sub-Saharan Africa," *Economic Development and Cultural Change*, 39(3), 549–566.

[7]Lall, S. (1993) "Trade Policies For Development: A Policy Prescription For Africa," *Development Policy Review*, 11, 44–65; Wheeler, D. (1983) "Sources of Stagnation in Sub-Saharan Africa," *World Development*, 12(1), 1–23; Ghosh, P. K. and Ghosh, D., Eds. (1984) *International Trade and Third World Development*, London: Greenwood Press, pp. 7–28; Commins, S.K., Ed. (1988) *Africa's Development Challenges and the World Bank: Hard Questions, Costly Choices*, London: Lynne Rienner Publishers.

[8]Lall, S. (1993) "Trade Policies For Development: A Policy Prescription For Africa," *Development Policy Review*, 11, 44–65; Wheeler, D. (1983) "Sources of Stagnation in Sub-Saharan Africa," *World Development*, 12(1), 1–23; Ghosh, P.K. and Ghosh, D. Eds. (1984) *International Trade and Third World Development*, London: Greenwood Press, pp. 7–28; Commins, S.K., Ed. (1988) *Africa's Development Challenges and the World Bank: Hard Questions*, London: Lynne Rienner Publishers.

[9]Morton, K. and Tulloch, P. (1977) *Trade and Developing Countries*, New York: Wiley; Wade, R. (1988). "The Role of Government in Overcoming Market Failure: Taiwan, Republic of Korea, and Japan," in H. Hughes, Ed., *Achieving Industrialization in East Asia*, New York: Cambridge University Press.

[10]Ghosh, P.K. and Ghosh, D., Eds. (1984) *International Trade and Third World Development*, London: Greenwood Press, pp. 190-218; Lankes, H.P. (2002) "Market Access for Developing Countries," *Finance and Development*, 39(3), 8–13.

[11]Balassa, B. (1988) "The Lesson of East Asian Development: An Overview," *Economic Development and Cultural Change*, 36 (suppl.), S273-290; Frank, C.R. (1975) *Foreign Trade Regimes and Economic Development: South Korea*, New York: Columbia (for NBER); Luedde-Neurath, R. (1986) *Import Control and Export-Oriented Development: A Reassessment of the Korean Case*, Boulder, CO: Westview; Petri, P. (1988) "Korea's Export Niche: Origins and Prospects," *World Development*, 16, 47–63; Rhee, Y., Ross-Larson, B., and Pursell, G. (1984) *Korea's Competitive Edge: Managing the Entry into World Markets*, Baltimore: Johns Hopkins University (for World Bank); Wade, R. (1988) "The Role of Government in Overcoming Market Failure: Taiwan, Republic of Korea, and Japan," in H. Hughes, Ed., *Achieving Industrialization In East Asia*, New York: Cambridge University Press; World Bank (1993) *The East Asian Miracle: Economic Growth and Public Policy*, New York: Oxford University Press.

[12]Balassa, B. (1988) "The Lesson of East Asian Development: An Overview," *Economic Development and Cultural Change*, 36(suppl.), S273-S290; Frank, C.R. (1975) *Foreign Trade Regimes and Economic Development: South Korea*, New York: Columbia (for NBER); Luedde-Neurath, R. (1986) *Import Control and Export-Oriented Development: A Reassessment of the Korean Case*, Boulder, CO: Westview; Y. Petri (1988), Petri, P. (1988) "Korea's Export Niche: Origins and Prospects," *World Development*, 16, 47–63; Wade, R. (1988) "The Role of Government in Overcoming Market Failure: Taiwan, Republic of Korea, and Japan," in H. Hughes, Ed., *Achieving Industrialization in East Asia*, New York: Cambridge University Press; World Bank (1993) *The East Asian Miracle: Economic Growth and Public Policy*, New York: Oxford University Press; World Band (2000) *Can Africa Claim the 21st Century?*, Washington, D.C.: World Bank.

[13]Wade, R. (1988) "The Role of Government in Overcoming Market Failure: Taiwan, Republic of Korea, and Japan," in H. Hughes, Ed., *Acieving Industrialization in East Asia*, New York: Cambridge University Press; World Bank (2000) *Can African Claim the 21st Century?*, Washington, D.C.: World Bank; Rapley, J. (1996) *Understanding Development: Theory and Practice in the Third World*, Boulder, CO: Lynn Rienner Publishers.

[14]Prebisch, R. (1962) "The Economic Development of Latin America and Its Principal Problem," *Economic Bulletin For Latin America*, 7, 1–22 (first published as an independent booklet by UNECLA in 1950); Singer, H. (1950) "The Distribution of Gains Between Investing and Borrowing Countries," *American Economic Review*, 40, 473–485; Lewis, W.A. (1969) *Aspects of Tropical Trade, 1883–1965*, Stockholm: Almgvist and Wiksell.

[15]Spraos, J. (1983) *Inequalizing Trade?*, London: Clarendon Press.

[16]For a detailed discussion of non-tariff barriers facing primary product exporters, See Baldwin, R.E. (1970) *Non-Tariff Distortions of International Trade*, Washington, D.C.: Brookings Institution; Baldwin, R.E. (1989) *Measuring Non-Tariff Trade Policies*, Cambridge, MA: National Bureau of Economic Research; IMF (2002) *Finance and Development*, September, 39(3), 4–21.

[17]World Bank (2000), *Can Africa Claim the 21st Century*, Washington, D.C.: World Bank, especially Chapter 5.

[18]World Bank (2000) *Can Africa Claim the 21st Century?*, Washington, D.C.: World Bank, chpts. 2, 5, and 7; and Helleiner reference in Note 3.

CHAPTER 19

Regionalism and Economic Development

FEMI BABARINDE

American Graduate School of International Business, Thunderbird University, Glendale, Arizona 85306

KEY TERMS

Common market
Customs union
Dynamic effect of integration
Economic and monetary union
Federalist approach
Free trade area
Functionalist approach

Neofunctionalist approach
Objectives of integration
Political union
Regionalism
Static effect of integration
Trade creation
Trade diversion

I. INTRODUCTION

This chapter discusses using regionalism to explain African economic development. A recurring theme of this volume is how daunting, overwhelming, and complex the challenges of economic development in Africa are. Various chapters have also offered some optimism, even if cautiously. This chapter continues the discussion by employing regionalism as a tool for explaining why economic development, in all of its manifestations, which are all too familiar to Americans, Europeans, Japanese, and others, has eluded the African people. In that same vein, the discussion endeavors to elucidate how regionalism can be utilized to advance the continent's economic development.

The remainder of the chapter fleshes out some of the aforementioned issues. It begins with a brief review of the African plight. It then discusses, among other things, the broad theoretical underpinnings and nuances of regionalism in general terms, the extent to which regionalism has a place in the economic development of Africa, and African countries' experimentation with regionalism at the continental and subcontinental levels.

African Economic Development
Copyright © 2003, Elsevier Science (USA). All rights reserved.

II. THE AFRICAN CONDITION

Media reports on Africa at the dawn of the 21st century are littered with unflattering caricatures and characterizations. It was only a couple of years earlier that the same media, in describing the future of the African continent, painted such a bright and optimistic picture that it even made many Africans blush. What gave rise to such optimism ostensibly were the impressive economic growth in some African countries, the transition to civilian rule in some, and the cessation of civil strife in others. Nowadays, however, one is more apt to encounter images of war, child soldiers, and the scars of civil strife—the aftermath of sectarian, ethnic, and racial confrontations in media reports. It is no wonder, therefore, that "African Renaissance," "The Last Frontier," and similar captions are quickly giving way to new headlines, such as "The Hopeless Continent."

As variously noted in other chapters, the African condition at the dawn of this century, in relative and absolute terms, is in an appalling state. Consider the following. In 2000, the total gross national product (GNP) of the African continent was $520 billion and $310 billion for Sub-Saharan Africa (SSA) in constant terms, thus representing roughly 1.7% and 1.0%, respectively, of the world's total GNP.[1] Contextually, it means that roughly 800 million Africans produced a combined GNP that was roughly 5% the national output generated by an estimated 282 million people of the United States. Other countries with much smaller populations whose individual gross national output exceeded Africa's aggregate performance in 2000 included Spain ($595 billion), Canada ($650 billion), and Brazil ($610 billion). Viewed from another perspective, many in the world league of Fortune 500 multinational companies (MNCs) boast annual turnovers that exceed the national output of most countries in Africa. For example, in 2000, 4 of the top 15 MNCs worldwide recorded at least $100 billion sales receipts each, a feat that was matched in gross national output only by the Republic of South Africa (RSA) at $130 billion.[2] If we lower the bar to $30 billion, 12 of the top 15 MNCs enjoyed that much in sales income, compared to the individual gross national output of only 5 African countries.

Furthermore, whereas some African economies grew at an impressive 4–6% per annum variously between 1990 and 2000, the average economic growth in real terms was less than 3% for much of the continent. The average per capita income was roughly $470 and $600 for SSA and Africa, respectively, in 2000, hardly enough spending money for an American or a European university student during a semester. It is thus not surprising that in its 2000 classification of countries by per capita income, the World Bank placed 38 (79%) SSA countries in the unenviable category of "low-income" countries, which represented 60% all such countries worldwide.[3] That means the average African survives on less than $2 per day, far less than the typical secondary school pupil collects in daily allowances in much of Europe and North America. In fact, it is estimated that almost one in every two Africans lives in poverty, according to the World Bank and the United Nations (UN).

The African condition is exacerbated by the continent's population explosion (2.7%), which exceeded the average annual growth rate (2% in real terms) of the economy over the 1980–2000 period. Moreover, agricultural output growth increased modestly from 2.3% (1980–1990) to 2.8% (1990–2000), the average annual growth of manufacturing output slightly declined from 1.7% (1980–1990) to 1.6% (1990–2000), and the service sector output growth marginally improved between the two periods in question.[4] In short, many African countries are unable to feed themselves; hence, they have to rely on food imports, complicating their trade balances with the rest of the world. This condition is worsened by African countries' propensity to produce what they do not consume and consume what they do not produce. Moreover, while Africa's growth in total exports was positive during most of the 1990s, it declined sharply after the peak period of 1996. What is even more, the share of intra-African trade of the continent's total trade volume has hovered at 10%, especially during the latter half of the 1990s.[5] What this means is that for a variety of reasons, explicable and otherwise, the typical African country is more likely to procure a commodity from Europe or North America than from its neighbors. This has translated into trade imbalances and concomitant mountains of debt for the continent. For instance, the debt burden for the continent (SSA) soared from $112 billion ($61 billion) in 1980 to $300 billion ($216 billion) in 2000.[6]

Compared to other parts of the world, especially in the Southern Hemisphere, the African condition is equally troubling. Indeed, in just about every category of social, economic, and even political measurements, African countries prop up global rankings. For example, foreign aid as a proportion of national income in 2000 was 5% (SSA), compared to 0.7% (South Asia) and 0.2% (Latin America and the Caribbean). Even when the rate of return on investment for MNCs is higher in Africa than in any other region, as depicted in Table 19.1, Africa still lags in capital inflow. For example, the flow of per capita direct foreign investment (DFI) into Africa was almost $11 in 1998, a stark contrast to Latin America's roughly $145, Asia's $25 (excluding Japan), the European Union's

TABLE 19.1 Rates of Return on U.S. Direct Foreign Investment by Region (%)

	1990	1991	1992	1993	1994	1995	1996	1997
Africa	24.2	30.6	28.4	25.8	24.6	35.3	34.2	25.3
Asia	27.6	23.8	22.6	20.7	18.4	20.2	19.3	16.2
Latin America	13	12.1	14.3	14.9	15.3	13.1	12.8	12.5
Less developed countries	17.2	15.9	17.2	16.9	16.5	15.8	15.3	14

Source: World Investment Report (1998). Trends and Determinants, New York: United Nations.

$615, and the United States' $706 for the same period.[7] Additionally, Africa's share of global DFI in 1998 was an abysmal 1.2% in 1998, compared to Latin America's 11.1%, Asia's 13.2%, the European Union's 36%, and the United States' 30%. Even in trade, the share of the continent's aggregate exports in global exports has remained at roughly 2%. In a global context, therefore, African economies are profoundly susceptible and peripheral.

Furthermore, measured in terms of the Human Poverty Index, Human Development Index, Physical Quality of Life Index, and per capita HIV/AIDS infection, African countries and the African people occupy the unenviable position of being (among) the poorest and most vulnerable in the world. According to several studies by the United Nations Economic Commission for Africa (UNECA) and the World Bank, it is estimated that in order for abject poverty to even be halved on the African continent by 2015, its countries would have to grow their economies by at least 7% per annum. This is quite a daunting task, given the continent's precarious history since the 1960s and given the limited efficacy of myriad economic strategies that have been attempted in the past to kindle its development. In this era of globalization and economic liberalization, it seems African countries would need to reconsider increased trade and investment, the twin engines of economic growth in the industrialized West, to reverse their misfortunes, augment their strength, and make the continent more relevant to the international political economy. But, where do they even begin? One plausible starting point in a wholistic approach is regional integration.

III. REGIONALISM: A THEORETICAL DISCOURSE

A. WHAT IS REGIONALISM?

Consistent with the relevant literature, regionalism is employed in this chapter to mean regional integration, which broadly refers to the process of peacefully creating a larger coherent entity out of previously separate units, each of which voluntarily cedes part of its sovereignty to a supranational authority and renounces the use of force for the settlement of disputes between member states.[8] In other words, regional integration refers to the establishment and/or management of a mutually interdependent relationship that involves two or more countries, presumably in the same geographical zone, to jointly produce that which they separately lack or could not optimally produce. It also broadly means the establishment of joint institutions and some shared autonomy. A few quick points are in order here. First, as is later demonstrated, regional integration is a process and not an event. Second, implicit in the aforementioned definition is the observation that regional integration can be political, particularly where sovereignty issues are involved. Third, to the extent that economics and politics are inextricably intertwined, regional integration is thus political and economic. The pooling of previously separate economies, presumably for economic purposes, is undoubtedly a political act.[9] Likewise, the process of creating larger political communities, even if it means very little or no bureaucratization and institutionalization, has economic consequences.[10] Besides, and fourth, regional integration can also be social and cultural, especially as its implementation encompasses the whole system/society.

Regional integration is in vogue nowadays around the world, as virtually every continent implements one scheme or another. The most renowned and in the vanguard of regional integration in contemporary experience is the European Union (EU), which is comprised of 15 member states. Also in the European theatre are the European Free Trade Association (EFTA), the European Economic Association (EEA), and the Central European Free Trade Agreement (CEFTA). Other notable examples are the North American Free Trade Agreement (NAFTA), the Common Market of the Southern Cone (MERCOSUR), the ANDEAN Group, and the Caribbean Common Market (CARICOM) in the Western Hemisphere. In the Asian peninsular are the Asia Pacific Economic Cooperation (APEC), the Association of Southeast Asian Nations (ASEAN), and the South Asian Association for Regional Cooperation (SAARC).

B. Why Integrate?

Against the backdrop of the aforementioned examples, why do sovereign nations integrate? Why are sovereign countries prepared to cede and share their sovereignty with others? What do nation-states hope to gain from regionalism, or what are the objectives of regional integration? Generally, sovereign nations participate in regionalism because it arguably serves as a means to an end, however defined or construed by them.

1. Regional Stability Imperative

The foremost purpose of regional integration for many participating countries is the promotion of regional stability. This is particularly critical and relevant in those regions that, historically, have been bedeviled by interstate strife. All too often, even under the best domestic circumstances and where the soundest macroeconomic policies are being implemented, interstate regional strife can compromise and undermine anticipated promising results. In other words, poor neighborhoods can emasculate even the soundest economic policies. It is therefore imperative that the neighborhood be tranquil if sound economic policies are to yield meaningful and sustained results. Not only can regional strife drain and divert scarce resources, but it can also disrupt and sever economic/trade relations. In addition, a poor neighborhood can increase the political and commercial risks of doing business in the region, thus increasing the overall cost for the business community and scaring away much-needed capital. In short, member countries must eschew military conflict for resolving disputes and make interstate war unthinkable and improbable.

2. Economic Rationale

Another primary reason for participating in regional integration is the opportunity to raise the overall welfare/standard of living of a people. According to neoclassical economic thought, countries contemplate and join regional integration because of the resultant dynamic and static benefits. The dynamic benefits argument is that the pooling of two or more economies and the coordination of business/industrial policies under the auspices of regionalism creates opportunities for economies of scale for business and industry and simultaneously increases business and economic activities. The enlarged market from regional integration, the concomitant economies of scope, and the resultant "protection" from third countries provide the business communities in the member countries the opportunity to establish new manufacturing activities/industries that otherwise might not have been created. The static benefits argument for regional integration is the positive net result of what Viner, in his seminal study, described as "trade creation" and "trade diversion" effects.[11] A trade creation effect is believed to have occurred when production or consumption is transferred from less efficient, high-cost member countries to more efficient lower cost ones, as a result of common external barriers and the removal of internal barriers. Conversely, trade diversion is said to have taken place when, consequent to the establishment of common external barriers and the removal of internal barriers, consumption and production are relocated from, say, an efficient low-cost third country to a less-efficient and higher cost member state. Trade diversion, therefore, means a redirection of consumption or production from an optimal resource allocation, because the more efficient non-member country represents a lower real supply cost. *Ceteris paribus*, regional market integration is more sensible and desirable to member countries when trade creation exceeds trade diversion.

3. Political Rationale

It is also widely argued[12] and corroborated that nation-states decide to participate in regional integration schemes, including market integration, largely for political reasons. In other words, market integration or other manifestations of regional integration are not meant to be an end in and of themselves, but as a means to an ultimate (political) end, this argument dovetails the sustained regional peace justification. Participating countries that rationalize their membership in regional integration on this basis tend to aspire to the highest level of integration (which is discussed next). What participating countries hope to gain from this level of integration includes the opportunity for collective decision-making via institutional integration, enhanced visibility on the international stage (especially for small countries) via, say, policy integration, and so on. In short, regionalism can augment the bargaining power and confidence of participating states in the global arena. After all, there is strength in numbers.

C. WHAT KIND OF INTEGRATION?

Having rationalized the reasons for indulging in regionalism, each country or the group must also determine how the scheme should be structured or the extent of the integration. After all, as noted earlier, regional integration is not an event but a process. In other words, regional integration can vary according to the depth and breadth of its agreements, interactions, policies, and so on. Economists and political scientists have identified the following stages of regional integration:[13]

1. *A free trade area* (FTA) occurs whenever two or more countries agree to lower and ultimately remove internal barriers to trade, while maintaining their respective external tariffs against other countries. In other words, if countries X, Y, and Z have entered into a free trade agreement, they will gradually reduce or remove tariffs on trade among themselves over a period of time. However, each country will maintain its own external tariffs against other (nonparticipating) countries.

2. *A customs union* (CU) refers to an arrangement whereby two or more countries agree not only to remove trade barriers among themselves, but also to maintain a common external tariff (CET) against products from other countries. Again, if we assume that countries X, Y, and Z have concluded a customs union agreement, it means that in addition to the obligations of a FTA, they will be obliged to maintain a common tariff on imports from nonparticipating countries. In other words,

$$\text{Customs union} = \text{FTA} + \text{common external tariff} \qquad (19.1)$$

3. *A common market* (CM) is an arrangement that obliges two or more participating countries to remove internal trade barriers, adopt common external barriers against trade from third countries, and promote the free movements of goods and services, labor, capital, and technology. Thus, a common market of X, Y, and Z would require compliance with the obligations of a customs union plus the promotion of the unfettered movement of the factors of production. That is,

$$\text{Common market} = \text{CU} + \text{factor mobility} \qquad (19.2)$$

4. *An economic and monetary union* (EMU) is an arrangement that requires participating countries to eliminate trade barriers among members, maintain a common external tariff against third countries, promote the free movement of goods and services and of factors of production, and coordinate their economic policies in order to achieve a common currency. This stage of regionalism is designed to facilitate economic (nominal) as well as monetary (real) convergence. The argument here is that without a single currency, the full benefits of regional integration cannot be realized, as the market will not operate at Pareto optimality. An EMU linking X, Y, and Z means that in addition to the obligations of a common market, the three countries agree to eventually adopt a common currency purposely to consolidate and augment the achievements of a common market. Thus,

$$\text{Economic and monetary union} = \text{CM} + \text{single currency} \qquad (19.3)$$

5. *A political union* (PU) is the final stage of regional integration, because it means that in addition to the cumulative obligations of an economic and monetary union, participating countries will share political decision-making over foreign policy, security policy, and so forth. It is a *de facto*, if not a *de jure*, federal arrangement. Thus, a political union of countries X, Y, and Z would mean ceding sovereignty over security policy, foreign policy, and other political decisions to a supranational authority, with its own executive, legislature, judiciary, and bureaucracy. Stated differently,

$$\text{Political union} = \text{EMU} + \text{common foreign and security policy} \qquad (19.4)$$

Some general observations can be made from the foregoing. First, regional integration is a process and not an event, which means that a group of countries is always working toward certain goals of integration and may thus find it difficult if not impossible to stop integrating, unless, of course, the scheme is discontinued. Second, with the exceptions of the first (free trade area) and the last (political union) stages, each successive stage or level of regional integration is a cumulation of the previous stages, plus more. This means that a group of countries can choose the stage or level of regionalism it deems suitable for it. Third, it is usually the dynamics of the market that pressure countries to deepen and widen the scope of integration into other policy areas, sectors, and so forth. This phenomenon is known as the "spillover effect." The extent to which regional integration may suffer setbacks or backlashes, for whatever reasons, any retreats by the group or its members may have a haltingly damaging effect on integration, otherwise known as "spillback effects."[14]

D. How Is Integration Achieved?

Once the level of integration has been decided, another vitally important issue to deal with is the approach to integration—that is, how to go about integrating. Lodge offers three broadly defined approaches.[15]

1. Functional

This approach is at one end of the spectrum and merely requires functional economic cooperation among participating countries on noncontroversial issues. It is a rather loose arrangement that requires joint action and very little bureaucratization and leaves sovereignty intact. For many critics and proponents of regionalism, this approach is really noncommittal and is unlikely to yield, let alone advance, any significant benefits of regional integration. Thus, this can be characterized as the "no bang" approach.

2. Federal

This approach is at the other end of the spectrum, not the least because it requires the immediate adoption of a constitutional/treaty division and regulation of power between supranational organs and national institutions. Thus, previously separate political entities are transformed into a coherent federated structure that amounts to immediately transferring a large chunk of their sovereignty to the supranational level. This means the establishment of governmental organs (executive, legislative, judicial, and bureaucratic) at the federal/supranational level, with which national governments will be obligated to share decision-making powers. For many countries, this is asking too much of them, and this approach can be characterized as "big bang."

3. Neofunctional

This approach is essentially a hybrid of the other two, as it strives for a compromise in order to keep the momentum for integration. This middle-of-the-road approach normally requires the creation of some supranational structures because of the shared belief that certain policies are best implemented at that level. The onus, however, is on the supranational organs to demonstrate that results in the mandated areas are indeed best attained through policies that are adopted at that level, rather than at the national level. If such a case were persuasively made, the argument goes, member states would be prepared to cede more national autonomy over other issues. In other words, successful integration in a given area would, *ceteris paribus*, spill over to other sectors or policies. In essence, this approach has the logic of integrating one sector at a time (a sector-by-sector strategy) until the relevant sectors or policies are integrated. Not surprisingly, this seems to be the most preferred of the approaches across the globe, because it portends some commitment and simultaneously allows participants some breathing room. This approach underscores the widely held dictum that regional integration is a process, thus its characterization as a "gradualist" strategy.

IV. IS REGIONAL INTEGRATION RELEVANT TO AFRICA?

Having discussed the theoretical nuances of regionalism, we now turn our attention to the relevance of regional integration to Africa. In other words, is there a place for regional integration in advancing economic development in Africa? In essence, therefore, the discussion here is about regionalism as a cure for the seemingly endless (economic) crises of Africa. In fact, there is renewed interest among development scholars and practitioners in regionalism as a means to the economic development of Africa. In light of the perilous state of the African economy and society, the ostensible failure of countless development initiatives attempted to date, and globalization, it is not surprising that African policymakers are reconsidering regionalism as a strategy for the development of the continent.[16] The renewed interest in regionalism as a strategy for the economic development of Africa is boosted by both its growing popularity and the encouraging results of regional schemes in many parts of the world. *Can regionalization turn around Africa's misfortunes?*

A. A "REGIONAL INTEGRATION IS NECESSARY" VIEW

The thrust of the contention here is not that regional integration is necessary and sufficient, but that it is indispensable for the economic development of Africa.

- One of the central reasons often cited for Africa's abysmal economic performance since the independence decade of the 1960s is its fragmentation into 53-odd countries of varied population and economic sizes. The balkanization of the continent makes it very difficult to attract much-needed DFI and technology, to expand the export market, and to enable increased domestic capital formation, all of which are catalysts for economic growth, because individual African markets are not large enough to support viable economic activity. Of the 53 sovereign countries on the continent, only Nigeria, Egypt, Ethiopia, the Democratic Republic of Congo (DRC), and the RSA have populations of at least 40 million each. Conversely, roughly 22 countries, mostly in SSA, have populations of roughly 5 million each, while 34 mostly SSA countries have population of roughly 10 million each. Other things being equal, regional integration will thus be an avenue for African countries to pool their scarce resources in order to increase their collective market size, increase capacity, coordinate/rationalize their economic and industrial policies, and improve their appeal to local and foreign investors. Regionalism, therefore, provides an avenue for African countries to surmount their size constraint and its attendant costs.

- In view of the neoclassical economic view that trade is an engine of growth, regional integration can serve as a catalyst for the economic development of Africa by boosting intra-African trade. The static gains that are likely to accrue to African countries through regional integration can catalyze their individual and collective development. Because most African, particularly neighboring, countries engage in similar if not competitive production, the resultant trade creation will not only increase trade exchange, but also spur ancillary economic activities, create new job opportunities, kindle economic growth, raise living standards, and ultimately economic development, *ceteris paribus*.

- Regionalism can also address the notorious problem of duplicated economic activity whereby, due to the legacy of colonial experience, economic nationalism, and other factors, post-independent African countries, oftentimes in the same subcontinent, end up producing essentially the same commodities and competing in the same international market. For example, in West Africa, Côte d'Ivoire, Ghana, Togo, Benin, and Nigeria are all known to be exporters of cocoa, while in East Africa Kenya, Uganda, and Tanzania grow and export tea and/or coffee. Regionalism can enable them to consolidate and rationalize such duplicated economic activities through specialization in the production of those goods in which countries enjoy comparative advantage.

- Another related problem that is typically associated with the under-development of Africa is its low industrial base, which is critical to economic development.[17] This problem is typically associated with the absence of economies of scale and protective barriers at the national frontiers. Regional integration can thus encourage higher research and development (R&D) spending and enable new economic activities, particularly those that require economies of scale from large-scale production (e.g., industrial sector) to flourish in Africa. Such large-scale industrial production of (semi) finished goods on the continent can, in turn, help African countries to reduce their individual and collective dependence on the exports of price inelastic primary commodities. These dynamic effects of regional integration in the manner of new economic activities can thus advance Africa's economic growth and development.

- As discussed earlier in the chapter and variously in the book, flashpoints abound in Africa. A consequence of these ostensibly incessant problems is that they derail and/or undermine even the best-conceived macro-economic strategies. Worse, the rest of the world is getting fatigued from the waltz of deploying troops in Africa for peacekeeping and peace enforcement purposes under the aegis of the UN. Africa is thus left with applying homegrown solutions to continental conflicts, an idea that has been mooted by Africans and non-Africans alike. Regionalism may thus be the only viable option for African countries to jointly develop and implement solutions to continental conflicts. Besides, as noted earlier, a viable and functioning regionalism makes each member its "brother's keeper," and makes all of them stakeholders in the scheme. Whereas such undertakings have not always been successful in resolving or preventing conflicts on the continent, the relative success of the Monitoring Group of the Economic Community of West African States (ECOMOG), at least in containing the spread of the intermittent civil wars in Liberia and in Sierra-Leone, is encouraging. In short, a peaceful neighborhood, which is a *sine qua non* of economic development, can be promoted and sustained in Africa through regionalism.

B. A "REGIONAL INTEGRATION IS NECESSARY BUT INSUFFICIENT" VIEW

The contention here is that while regional integration may be a logical antidote to Africa's myriad problems, it is not sufficient to advance the continent's economic development. After all, as noted in the following, regional integration is not new to Africa, and the reasons why previous or current regional initiatives or alternative strategies have failed to advance the economic development of Africa persist and must be tackled.

- In order to optimize the welfare gains of regional integration, it is imperative that information be available and accessible to economic actors in a timely manner within the integration zone. Goods, scarce resources, and production factors must flow to areas of highest potential returns in a timely manner, and an efficient communication and transportation system or network must also exist; otherwise, regionalism will be operating suboptimally. It is well established, however, that African countries suffer from a poor and inadequate infrastructure. In SSA, for example, only 12.3% of the road network is paved, there are only 14 telephone lines for every 1000 people, and the average waiting period for telephone connection is over 4 years. Undoubtedly, the cost of setting up and doing business in such an environment will likely be prohibitive.

- Additionally, the post-colonial African economy is one that is dominated by the state and its agents. Any regional scheme, however, must encompass the grassroots, civil society, and other nongovernmental actors for it to augment living standards and advance economic development. Not only must the civil society be enlightened and involved, but also (overzealous) bureaucrats must equally be properly trained and equipped to handle pertinent matters in the least disruptive or costly manner.

- Another vital factor that has undermined economic development in Africa is the absence of currency convertibility and auxiliary institutional infrastructure, such as clearinghouses. Whereas *de jure* and *de facto* currency zones exist, respectively, in Western and Central Africa (the CFA) and in Southern Africa (the Rand), currency convertibility problems still exist between currency zone and non-zone countries within the same regional bloc. African nations must endeavor to make their national currency convertible with one another in order to enable optimal economic performance in a regional bloc. Better yet, they need to consider a common/ single currency, because it is likely to boost trade and ancillary economic relations among them. In that same vein, they need clearinghouses to facilitate timely payments between economic actors.

- It is also well documented that African countries suffer from skill shortages, which will be needed to compete for scarce capital from the international market. Unless there are appropriate and adequate skills for particular (capital- or labor-intensive) economic activity—say, in the manufacturing sector—it is unlikely that foreign (local) investors will pitch their widget-making tents in the area. That, however, will only happen if the appropriate skills are available and are adequate. In a continent where the literacy rate is low and brain drain is rife, the problem of skill shortages must be tackled. A liberal global employment policy that recruits from within the region and elsewhere, while theoretically sensible, may be tantamount to political suicide, particularly in the face of high and growing unemployment in many African countries.

- More than four decades after independence, the links between many African countries and their colonial powers are still strong. Although the mindset is changing, perhaps at a snail's pace, African countries still look to European and North American countries for market, capital, aid, and security. Many African countries do so largely because of their own abject poverty. It is also sometimes easier for them to buy on credit from Europe and North America than to expend their limited cash on purchases from neighboring African countries, especially if the selling country is itself cash strapped and cannot afford to accept an IOU. Whatever the reasons for this propensity among African countries, as noted earlier, it has translated into low economic interaction among them. While this is precisely one of the problems regional integration hopes to remedy, the neocolonial North–South mentality or legacy of looking to the Northern Hemisphere, vis-à-vis trade and associated relations, must recede. Besides, African countries still have to countenance market access problems in the industrialized nations, whose economic policies may be inimical to the economic development of Africa.

- It is often argued that the net welfare gains of regional integration will be negligible when member countries engage in competitive rather than complimentary production. To the extent that the production systems of African countries are too similar and too limited, the net static welfare effects of regional integration in Africa may be few or nonexistent.

- In order for regional integration to work and advance economic development in Africa, rule of law must prevail and be sacrosanct. Even if other challenges of regional integration in Africa are surmounted, how disputes are resolved and how the welfare benefits of regionalism are apportioned among its participants are arguably the most vital. The inability to overcome this constraint but instead to allow national ideology and personal egos to eclipse the justifications for regionalism had either led to the demise of previous regional integration schemes or prevented the inauguration of others in Africa. It is thus imperative that rule of law prevails.

V. AFRICA'S PRACTICAL EXPERIENCES WITH REGIONAL INTEGRATION

Certainly, Africa is no stranger to regionalism, nor are regional integration schemes a post-colonial phenomenon in Africa.[18] To be sure, Africa's flirtation with regionalism included the short-lived 1959 Union Douanière de l'Afrique de l'Ouest and the 1981 Sene–Gambia confederation, as well as the stillborn 1965 Maghreb Permanent Consultative Committee. However, many other initiatives are still being actualized, as discussed below. In any case, regionalism was, and is, viewed by many proponents as an instrument for countervailing the fragmentation of the continent along political frontiers. Relying on the theoretical approaches to regionalism (discussed in Section III), we will now briefly discuss Africa's intellectual and practical experimentation with regionalism.

African federalists[19] are those leaders and intellectuals who subscribe, especially during the independence period, to a pan-African political integration as a prelude to eventual economic integration, because they viewed political regionalism as a precursor of economic regionalism. Earlier pan-Africanists included Modibo Keita (Mali), Sekou Touré (Guinea), and Kwame Nkrumah (Ghana), who basically argued that it was strategically prudent to "seek first the political kingdom."[20] In essence, they preferred a "big bang" approach to African integration that would entail the immediate creation of pan-African supranational strictures and structures, including an African government.

African neofunctionalists, who reject the aggressiveness of the pan-Africanists, espouse an alternative strategy. In this category of integrationists, especially during the 1960s, were Leopold Senghor (Senegal), Houphet Boigny (Côte d'Ivoire), and Jomo Kenyatta (Kenya). For these leaders, it was rather too soon after independence to relinquish national political control to a supranational entity. Besides, they further contended, the pursuit of a pan-African government was ill-advised, because it was like putting the cart before the horse. For them, economic regionalism must precede political regionalism. In general, proponents of this school of thought associate a pan-African government with the final and highest level of regional integration. To get to that stage of regionalism, they argue, relevant sectors of the economy must first be integrated. Thus, they subscribe to a "gradualist" step-by-step, sector-by-sector strategy. This is the more prevalent of the two schools of thought with regard to Africa's myriad experimentation with regionalism. This progressive strategy underpins varied intellectual discourses, symposia, and colloquia, as regards regional integration in Africa. Even the defunct Organization of African Unity (OAU) emphasized this strategy in its call for an African Economic Community, first in the 1980 Lagos Plan of Action and the Final Act of Lagos (LPA), and in the 1991 Treaty of Abuja.

Next, we turn to a brief discussion of some of the notable regional integration schemes in Africa. Indeed, virtually every African country belongs to at least one of the continent's integration schemes (Table 19.2). Given that it is estimated that as many as 200 regional schemes exist in Africa, only the notable arrangements at the (sub) continental levels will be discussed. The intent here is to describe each arrangement with respect to origin, membership, key socioeconomic indicators, challenges, and major achievements.

A. AFRICAN ECONOMIC COMMUNITY

The African Economic Community (AEC) was inaugurated when the OAU signed the Treaty of Abuja in June 1991, thus resuscitating an old idea that was enshrined in the LPA and its precursors. The initiative was not only commendable but was also a reaffirmation of the acknowledgment by African countries that regional cooperation and integration are essential to the continent's development strategies. A perusal of the articles of the treaty strongly suggests that its architects patterned the AEC after the EU. Article 4, Chapter II, of

TABLE 19.2   Membership in a Sample of African Regional Groups

Country	AEC	AMU	COMESA	EAC	ECCAS	ECOWAS	SADC
Algeria	X	X					
Angola	X		X				X
Benin	X					X	
Botswana	X						X
Burkina Faso	X					X	
Burundi	X		X		X		
Cameroon	X				X		
Cape Verde	X					X	
Central Afr Republic	X				X		
Chad	X				X		
Comoros	X		X				
Congo	X				X		
Democratic Republic of Congo	X		X		X		X
Côte d'Ivoire	X					X	
Djibouti	X		X				
Egypt	X		X				
Equatorial Guinea	X				X		
Eritrea	X		X				
Ethiopia	X		X				
Gabon	X				X		
The Gambia	X					X	
Ghana	X					X	
Guinea	X					X	
Guinea-Bissau	X					X	
Kenya	X		X	X			
Lesotho	X						X
Liberia	X					X	
Libya	X	X					
Madagascar	X		X				
Malawi	X		X				X
Mali	X					X	
Mauritania	X	X				X	
Mauritius	X		X				X
Morocco		X					
Mozambique	X		X				X
Namibia	X		X				X
Niger	X					X	
Nigeria	X					X	
Rwanda	X		X		X		
Snao Tomé and Principe	X				X		
Senegal	X					X	
Seychelles	X		X				X
Sierra Leone	X					X	
Somalia	X		X				

(Continues)

TABLE 19.2   *(Continued)*

Country	AEC	AMU	COMESA	EAC	ECCAS	ECOWAS	SADC
South Africa	X						X
Sudan	X		X				
Swaziland	X		X				X
Tanzania	X		X	X			X
Togo	X					X	
Tunisia	X	X					
Uganda	X		X	X			
Zambia	X		X				X
Zimbabwe	X		X				X

the AEC Treaty of Abuja outlines four main objectives:

1. Promote economic, social, and cultural development and the integration of African economies.
2. Establish a framework for the development, mobilization, and utilization of Africa's human and non-human resources.
3. Promote cooperation in all fields of human endeavor so as to raise the continent's living standards.
4. Coordinate and harmonize policies among existing and future economic communities.

In order to redistribute the associated costs and benefits of the AEC, the treaty provides for the eventual establishment of a Fund for Community Solidarity, Development, and Compensation. Another notable element of the treaty is contained in Article 6, Chapter II, where signatories have committed to a 34–40-year timetable for the completion of the AEC, which requires the development and/or strengthening of regionalism at the subcontinental level. The pan-African integration process is intended to be implemented in six phases, culminating in the functioning of, among others, a pan-African Economic and Monetary Union, an African Central Bank, a single African currency, and a pan-African Parliament.

B. Arab Maghreb Union

The Arab Maghreb Union (AMU) was established in 1989 to foster regional cooperation and integration among Algeria, Libya, Mauritania, Morocco, and Tunisia. Whereas the aforementioned arrangements have been located south of the Sahara and include mostly SSA countries, the AMU is the notable regional grouping north of the Sahara, exclusively for North African states. It has an estimated total population of 77 million and roughly $130 billion in GNP.[21]

TABLE 19.3   Intraregional Bloc Exports ($ million)

	1970	1980	1985	1990	1995	1996	1998	2000
AMU	60	109	274	958	1124	1142	740	1081
COMESA	412	616	466	963	1184	1582	1516	1534
EAC[a]	142	212	140	229	334	394	458	504
ECCAS	37	89	131	163	156	212	239	181
ECOWAS	86	692	1026	1533	2015	2338	2461	3331
SADC	76	96	294	930	3744	4137	4540	4419

[a]*Direction of Trade Statistics*, 2000 and 2001.
Source: 2000 and 2002 World Economic Indicators.

TABLE 19.4   Intraregional Bloc Exports (% of Total Exports)

	1970	1980	1985	1990	1995	1996	1998	2000
AMU	1.4	0.3	1	2.8	3.6	3.4	3.3	2.3
COMESA	9.1	6.1	4.7	6.6	6.6	7.9	7.7	6
EAC[a]	16.9	8.9	7.1	13.3	10.4	11.36	14.4	17.6
ECCAS	2.2	1.4	1.7	1.4	1.5	1.6	2	1
ECOWAS	2.9	10.1	5.2	7.8	9.3	8.8	10.8	10.8
SADC	1.4	0.3	1.4	2.8	10.1	10.3	10.2	12.2

[a]*Direction of Trade Statistics*, 2000 and 2001.
Source: 2000 and 2002 World Economic Indicators.

According to Tables 19.3 and 19.4, intra-AMU trade volume grew from $60 million (1970) to $109 million (1980), $958 million (1990), and $1081 million (2000), thus representing 82% growth between 1970 and 1980, 78% between 1980 and 1990, but by only 13% between 1990 and 2000. Moreover, the share of intra-AMU trade in the group's aggregate exports ranged between 1.4% (1970) and 2.3% (2000).

C. COMMON MARKET FOR EASTERN AND SOUTHERN AFRICA

The Common Market for Eastern and Southern Africa (COMESA) was established in 1993 to replace the Preferential Trade Area (PTA), which had been created in 1981 at the behest of the UN's Economic Commission for Africa (ECA) and entered into force in 1984. COMESA exemplifies the ECA's urging for an introverted free-trade area, which currently traverses 21 African states, connecting Northern and Southern Africa. The arrangement aimed to establish a free trade by 2000, implement a common external tariff by 2004, and later a common market. Among its institutional organs are the Authority of Heads of State/Government, a Council of Ministers, a Court of Justice, and a Secretariat in Lusaka, Zambia. Currently, it boasts a total population of about 380 million and roughly $170 billion in GNP. Egypt accounts for 56% of the bloc's aggregate output. Among the stated goals of the group are the improvement of commercial and economic cooperation in the region and the transformation of the production structure of participating countries. Thus far, it has managed to increase intraregional trade volume from $412 million (1970) to $616 million (1980), $963 million (1990), and $1534 million (2000) as reported in Table 19.3. Contextually, intraregional trade as a percentage of total COMESA trade increased from roughly 6% in 1980 to almost 7% in 1990, and 6% in 2000 (Table 19.4). Additionally, intra-COMESA trade volume increased by almost 50% during the 1970s, declined by 24% between 1980 and 1985 (following the inception of the PTA), but increased by 56% during the 1980s, 23% between 1990 and 1995 (following the birth of COMESA), and roughly 60% during the 1990s.

D. East African Community

The East African Community (EAC) is on again, as it was revived in late 1994, albeit some issues have yet to be resolved by its member states—Kenya, Uganda, and Tanzania.[22] The rebirth of the EAC followed a hiatus of almost two decades, because the arrangement, which was initially launched in 1967, was dissolved in 1977 following acrimonious charges and countercharges about the unequal distribution of the gains of integration. The region boasts a population of 86 million and a GNP of $26 billion. Since its revival, the moribund EAC has announced the convertibility of the currency of its member states. According to Tables 19.3 and 19.4, intra-EAC trade steadily increased from $142 million (1970) to $212 million (1980), $229 million (1990), and $504 million (2000), while the group's share of intraregional exports in total exports generally increased from 9% in 1980 to 18% in 2000. Intra-EAC trade volume grew by 49% during the 1970s and only 8% in the 1980s, 46% between 1990 and 1995 (following the rebirth of the EAC), and 120% during the 1990s.

E. Economic Community of Central African States

The Economic Community of Central African States (ECCAS) was set up in 1983 under the auspices of the OAU and the ECA. It is an arrangement that links 11 countries to promote financial and commercial cooperation by eliminating internal trade barriers and adopting a common external tariff. The group aspires to eventually create a common market that will allow free movement of the factors of production and ultimately advance the region's development. The ECCAS, like many of Africa's regional blocs, consists of a divergent group of countries that includes low income, lower-middle income, and upper-middle income countries. Its population is about 90 million and GNP is $19 billion. Whereas intra-ECCAS trade volume, reported in Table 19.3, increased from $37 million (1970) to $89 million (1980), $163 million (1990), and $181 million (2000), the actual share of intraregional trade in total trade ranged between 2% in 1970 and 1% in 2000 (Table 19.4). On the other hand, intra-ECCAS trade volume increased by 140% during the 1970s, 47% between 1980 and 1985 (after the inauguration of ECCAS), 83% in the 1980s, and only 11% during the 1990s. It seems the low volume of trade, particularly in the 1990s, can be attributed to the raging crises that involve many of the regional bloc's members.

F. ECONOMIC COMMUNITY OF WEST AFRICAN STATES

The Economic Community of West African States (ECOWAS) was officially founded in 1975 to promote cooperation and development in economic, social, and cultural activity.[23] The agreement also sets out to raise the standard of living of its citizens, increase and maintain economic stability in the region, coordinate external tariff and macroeconomic policies, improve relations among member states, and contribute to the development of the continent. Through five specialized commissions, the agreement also seeks to foster regional cooperation and development in, *inter alia*, transport, telecommunications, industry, agriculture, energy, and monetary issues. To assure an equitable distribution of the benefits that accrue from the undertaking, a Fund for Cooperation, Compensation, and Development was set up, to which Nigeria contributes the lion's share of 32%; both Côte d'Ivoire and Ghana contribute 13% each. Currently, the 16 member states have a total population of roughly 236 million and an estimated gross national income of at least $70 billion. Nigeria, the dominant partner, accounts for 54% of the bloc's population and about 47% of its GNP. Its operating organs include a Conference of Heads of State, a Council of Ministers, and a Secretariat that is located in Abuja, Nigeria. In consonance with the gradualist approach that underpins most regional integration schemes, the ECOWAS group aims to deepen its integration by establishing a common market by 1990. Whereas this goal has yet to materialize, the regional bloc has managed some success in other areas. Foremost, there is evidence of trade creation since the inception of the ECOWAS. According to Tables 19.3 and 19.4, official intra-ECOWAS trade volume (share of its total trade) has significantly increased from $86 million (1970) to $692 million (1980), $1533 million (1990), and $3331 million (2000), thus representing a marked jump from 3% of its total trade in 1970 to 12% in 2000. Additionally, intra-ECOWAS trade volume significantly increased by 705% between 1970 and 1980 (following the launch of ECOWAS), 122% between 1980 and 1990, and 117% between 1990 and 1998. Finally, in 1999, the group initiated a traveler's check program to facilitate trade and the movement of people within the region.[24]

G. SOUTHERN AFRICA DEVELOPMENT COMMUNITY

The Southern Africa Development Community (SADC) was founded in 1992 by 10 southern African states to defuse the potential economic threat from a more powerful post-apartheid South Africa.[25] It evolved from the Southern African Development Coordination Conference (SADCC) that was founded in 1980 to reduce the economic dependence of the member countries on the RSA and on the West by promoting collective self-reliance. The regional bloc aims to further evolve into a fully developed common market. In addition to a Council of Ministers, a Standing Committee of Senior Officials, and a Secretariat in Gaborone, Botswana, the SADC assigns to each of its member states the responsibility of promoting and coordinating specific regional policies and programs on behalf of the group. The 14-member SADC has an estimated population of roughly 200 million and a GNP of roughly $170 billion and is dominated by the RSA with its 77% share of the bloc's output and 22% of its population. Intra-SADC trade volume increased from a meager $76 million in 1970 to $96 million in 1980, $930 million in 1990, and $4419 million in 2000 (Table 19.3). It must, however, be noted that the inauguration of the first post-apartheid government in the RSA and the accession of the RSA to the SADC in 1994 perhaps contributed immensely to the significant jump (303% in intraregional trade between 1990 and 1995. Notwithstanding, the proportion of intraregional trade in the SADC's total trade (Table 19.4) increased from 1.4% (1970) to 12.2% (2000). Moreover, intra-SADC trade volume increased by only 26% between 1970 and 1980, but markedly increased by 206% between 1980 and 1985 (following the inauguration of the SADCC) and 75% between 1990 and 2000.

VI. SUMMARY

In this chapter, we have discussed the relevance of regionalism to economic development in Africa. The chapter begins with a cursory review of Africa's chronic problems in absolute and relative contexts. The chapter then discusses some theoretical nuances of regional integration, including the aims, stages, and approaches to regionalism. In the ensuing section, a sample of some of the notable regional integration arrangements in Africa is presented and discussed.

Against the background of the foregoing discussion, particularly when measured in terms of their trade-creation welfare effects, it is arguable that regional integration has a place in advancing economic development in Africa. In this era of the post-Cold War, globalization, liberalization, and democratization, African countries have to band together and pool their limited resources. However, in order for regional integration to work for Africans, many of the constraints that are identified above will have to be tackled. Among others, African countries have to demonstrate a better commitment to regional agreements, uphold the rule of law, resolve disputes amicably, avoid military solutions, upgrade or develop requisite infrastructures, and so on. Additionally, African governments have to better educate the populace, involve civil society and other nongovernmental factors, and train government officials at the frontiers. Imagine the amazement of a West African investor who had traveled to another ECOWAS country to explore business opportunities. Upon arrival at the immigration post of the host country, he was asked the purpose of his visit, to which he quickly and gleefully responded, "to explore investment opportunities." Sadly, the immigration officer queried why the visiting industrialist did not invest in his own (home) country. Needless to say, the shoddy reception deflated his enthusiasm.

However it comes about, an unavoidable consequence of multiple regionalism and membership therein is overstretched and divided loyalty (measured in ability to fulfil their obligations) among member countries. As many as 200 regional initiatives exist in Africa, 34 of which are in West Africa alone.[25] In some instances, the demands of membership may even be contradictory, as is the case with many African countries that belong to two or more subcontinental regional integration schemes. Such is the dilemma that has informed a recent debate in the Tanzanian polity regarding its membership in COMESA and EAC. The point is that African countries ought to consolidate their myriad regional integration arrangements. Besides, it is doubtful that the marginal gains from additional membership are significant, especially when they are not necessarily designed to complement one another in the manner that the AEC is designed to dovetail subcontinental arrangements.

As also noted and argued in Section IV above, whereas regional integration is a necessary tool in the arsenal that may be used to tackle the continent's abject poverty and ancillary crises, it must be employed as part of an all-encompassing strategy. While regional integration is by no means *the* answer, it is an essential ingredient in a cocktail of panacea that will lift the people and countries of Africa out of the doldrums of abject poverty onto the path of economic development. One of the arduous tasks of any regional integration scheme is getting every member to travel at the same speed without hampering the inexorable movement of the group towards its stated goals. This is aptly pertinent to the African situation. After all, none of the regional blocs discussed earlier has achieved its ultimate goal of a common market or an economic union in the instance of the AMU. Given that integration is a process, how synchronized and how quickly they travel may well determine if they arrive at their destination and use regionalism to advance their own development. Only time and due diligence will tell.

DISCUSSION QUESTIONS

1. What is regionalism?
2. Identify some of the notable regional integration schemes around the world.
3. Is regional integration relevant to the economic development of Africa?
4. What are the theoretical justifications for regional integration?
5. Identify and explain the stages of integration.
6. How would you characterize the levels of regional integration to which the African regional blocs that are discussed in this chapter strive?
7. How would you defend the argument that regional integration is necessary but not sufficient for advancing economic development in Africa?
8. How would you characterize the integration strategy of the African Economic Community as conceived and implemented by the OAU in the 1991 Treaty of Abuja?
9. What are the different avenues available to a group of countries that might be exploring the possibility of regional integration?
10. Of the different approaches to regionalism discussed in this chapter, which one do you believe is most appropriate for any groups of African countries, and why?

NOTES

[1]The data for these and related comparisons in this section of the chapter were obtained from World Bank (2002) *World Economic Indicators 2002*, Washington, D.C.: World Bank.

[2]This and subsequent comparisons were based on data in the "Financial Times Survey: FT 500," *Financial Times*, May 4, 2000, p. 6; World Bank (2002) *World Economic Indicators 2002*, Washington, D.C.: World Bank.

[3]This and subsequent comparisons were based on data from World Bank (2000) *World Economic Indicators 2002*, Washington, D.C.: World Bank.

[4]This and subsequent comparisons were based on data from World Bank (2002) *World Economic Indicators 2002*, Washington, D.C.: World Bank.

[5]IMF (various years) *Direction of Trade Statistics Yearbook*, Washington, D.C.: International Monetary Fund.

[6]World Bank (2002) *World Economic Indicators 2000*, Washington, D.C.: World Bank. The figure for Africa's total debt for 1980 does not include Libya, for which relevant information was unavailable.

[7]The data for these and related comparisons were obtained from World Bank (2002) *World Economic Indicators 2000*, Washington, D.C.: World Bank.

[8]See, among others, Deutsch, K. (1971) *The Analysis of International Relations*, Englewood Cliff, NJ: Prentice-Hall; Haas, E. (1970) "The Study of Regional Integration: Reflections on the Joy and Anguish of Pretheorizing," in Lindberg, L. and Scheingold, S. (1970) *Europe's Would-Be Polity*, Englewood Cliffs, NJ: Prentice-Hall; Lodge, J. (1983) *The European Community: Bibliographical Excursions*, London: Frances Pinter.

[9]Such an economic undertaking, for instance, would have to be signed and ratified by the participating countries—a political act.

[10]At the very least, any institution set up by a group of countries would, presumably, have a budget to manage its affairs—an economic consequence.

[11]Viner, J. (1950) *The Customs Union Issue*, New York: Carnegie Endowment for International Peace.

[12]This is a viewpoint that is prevalent among political economists and political scientists. For a trenchant argument, see, for example, Karl Deutsch, K. (1971) *The Analysis of International Relations*, Englewood Cliffs, NJ: Prentice-Hall.

[13]See, for example, Balassa, B. (1961) *The Theory of Economic Integration*, London: Allen & Unwin.

[14]For more on spillover and spillback effects, see, among others, Lodge, J. (1983) *The European Community: Bibliographical Excursions*, London: Frances Pinter.

[15]For more, see Lodge, J. (1983) *The European Community: Bibliographical Excursions*, London: Frances Pinter.

[16]Two recent illustrations of this are the adoption of the New Partnership for Africa's Development (NEPAD) and the establishment of an African Union (AU) by African governments in 2002.

[17]Neoclassical economic thoughts tend to emphasize the importance of industrialization to sustained economic growth and development.

[18]One of the earliest regional integration arrangements in Africa was the customs union between Kenya and Uganda in 1900. Prior to the independence period, indigenous movements in favor of African regionalism existed, some of which evolved into pan-African arrangements. See, among others, Olatunde Ojo, O. (1985) "Regional Co-operation and Integration," in O. Ojo, D.K. Orwa, and C.M.B. Utete, *African International Relations*, London: Longman.

[19]The classification of African leaders here was influenced by the discussion in Martin, G. (1992) "African Regional Cooperation and Integration: Achievements, Problems and Prospects," in A. Seidman and F. Anang, Eds., *Towards a New Vision of Self-Sustainable Development*, Trenton, NJ: Africa World Press.

[20]Kwame Nkrumah, K. (1963) *Africa Must Unite*, New York: Praeger.

[21]The reported figures for AMU and other regional associations, which are subsequently discussed in the chapter, were obtained from World Bank (2000 and 2002) *World Economic Indicators*, Washington, D.C.: World Bank; IMF (various years) *Direction of Trade Statistics Yearbook*, Washington, D.C.: International Monetary Fund.

[22]See "East Africa Born Again," *New African*, February 1995, pp. 24–25; "East Africa Stopped at the Start," *New African*, May 1995, pp. 24–25; "E. African Leaders To Co-operate," *Financial Times*, January 26, 1996, p. 6; "East African Community: Treaty Signals Rebirth of Union," *African Business*, January 2000, pp. 36–37.

[23]The *Communauté Economique de l'Afrique de l'Ouest* (CEAO) is the francophone version of regional economic cooperation in West Africa. Created in 1974 out of anxiety over a potential Nigerian dominance in the region, its current membership of seven states is comprised of 57 million people and a total gross national output of about $26 billion.

[24]Additional achievements of ECOWAS include a trans-African highway, a trans-African pipeline that supplies Nigeria's natural gas to some member countries, and the abolition of visa requirements for ECOWAS citizens.

[25]See "African Leaders Sign Treaty," *Financial Times*, August 18, 1992, p. 3. The RSA (1994), Mauritius (1995), Democratic Republic of the Congo (1997), and Seychelles (1997) have since acceded to the SADC, bringing its membership to 14.

[26]Other manifestations of regionalism include the *Communnauté Economique de l'Afrique de l'Ouest* (CEAO) and Mano River Union (MRU) in Western Africa, *Union Douaniere et Economique de l'Afrique Centrale* (UDEAC) in Central Africa, and the Southern Africa Customs Union (SACU) in Southern Africa.

CHAPTER 20

Globalization and Development

RICHARD E. MSHOMBA

Department of Economics, LaSalle University, Philadelphia, Pennsylvania 19141

KEY TERMS

Common market	Most favored nation principle
Customs union	Multinational corporations
Economies of scale	Quota
Export processing zones	Regional economic integration
Export subsidies	Tariff
Foreign direct investment	Terms of trade
Free trade area	Trade creation
Generalized system of preferences (GSP)	Trade diversion
International commodity agreements	Voluntary export restraint
International portfolio investment	

I. INTRODUCTION

This chapter considers the trend toward greater globalization and discusses the benefits and challenges of globalization for African countries. It considers ways in which African countries can work to increase the benefits and meet the challenges of globalization. It also suggests how the benefits associated with globalization can be used to foster real economic development. These issues are explored through a discussion of the operation and impact of key international organizations. The focus here is on the World Trade Organization (WTO), which has emerged as a symbol of the globalization trend. This discussion highlights some common issues developing countries face with other international institutions as well, such as the World Bank and the International Monetary Fund (IMF). Special attention is also given to regional economic integration in Africa, a strategy often suggested for trade and development in Africa.

The term *globalization* is used in this chapter to refer to the ongoing trend whereby countries increasingly interact with each other, directly or indirectly, either by choice or by circumstances. Globalization is not a new phenomenon, although it is often discussed as if it were. Of course, the actual forms and means of linkages continue to evolve and globalization is gaining momentum. This is due, in part, to (1) the gradual but significant reduction in trade barriers in the world, especially since the end of World War II; (2) the development of new and less expensive forms of transportation, communication, and global media; (3) increased awareness of the global nature of many problems; (4) various efforts to find international and standardized solutions to problems; and (5) the collapse of the former Soviet Union, which has allowed more countries to embrace the ideology of the market system, a system more conducive to foreign direct investment and international trade.

A significant institutional impetus for greater globalization came from the founding of the United Nations (UN) in 1945 to promote peace and international cooperation. Since then, many institutions and programs have been established by the UN or under the aegis of the UN to support various international initiatives.

II. AFRICA AND GLOBALIZATION

With the exception of a few African countries such as Côte d'Ivoire and Ghana with cocoa, Libya and Nigeria with oil, and Botswana with diamonds, most African economies are too small to have a noticeable impact on the world economy. Even in aggregate, Africa's 55 countries contribute only about 2% of the world's exports.[1] However, the world economy and the overall globalization trend have a significant impact on African economies. As such, African countries cannot afford a passive attitude towards globalization any more than they can afford a cavalier attitude towards development.

On the basis of membership in international institutions and organizations, Africa cannot be accused of being passive. For example, all African countries are members of the United Nations. In 2002, 41 of the 141 members of the WTO were African countries; another 5 African countries were observers. All African countries are members of the World Bank and the IMF. They also belong to international commodity agreements. In addition, all African countries belong to at least one regional economic group. African countries are also active in trying to attract multinational corporations.

III. AFRICA AND THE WORLD TRADE ORGANIZATION

The WTO was established in 1995 to succeed the General Agreement on Tariffs and Trade (GATT), which had been in operation since 1948. The main objective of GATT, and its successor, the WTO, has been to liberalize trade among member countries. This is usually achieved through rounds of negotiations to reach agreements to reduce trade barriers for specific industries. The last round of negotiation under GATT was the Uruguay Round (1986–1993) from which the WTO was born. Among the key agreements reached in this round of negotiations were the Agreement on Agriculture and the Agreement on Textiles and Clothing, which brought these two sectors under the jurisdiction of the WTO.

One of the guiding principles of the WTO and its predecessor, GATT, is non-differentiated treatment, commonly called the *most favored nation* (MFN) principle. This principle guards against arbitrary discrimination by member countries. Under this principle, a member country must treat all other members equally. Thus, for example, if Japan (a member of the WTO) decreases a tariff rate on a product coming from Brazil (also a member of the WTO), Japan must also decrease, equally, the tariff rate on that commodity coming from all other WTO members.

There are two important exceptions to the MFN principle. One is that regional economic blocs, such as free trade areas or customs unions, are allowed to reduce tariffs below the MFN rates on interregional trade.[2] Another exception to the MFN principle is that developed countries are allowed to give preferential treatment to goods they import from developing countries.

In 1999, the WTO Ministerial Conference was held in the United States, with a goal of setting agenda items for a new round of global negotiations. However, this was not achieved, due in part to (1) demonstrations against the WTO, and (2) President Clinton's effort to court the support of labor unions by insisting that labor laws be a direct mandate of the WTO.

The complaints against the WTO and its rules—and other international institutions such as the World Bank and the IMF—are many and varied. Those that are raised by developing countries, or for the perceived interests of developing countries, include the following: (1) the WTO reduces the ability of developing countries to formulate independent domestic policies; (2) developing countries are limited in their capacity for fair and effective negotiations; (3) there is an unfair distribution of the gains from trade; (4) developed countries are not open enough for goods coming from developing countries; and (5) the WTO facilitates exploitation of workers in developing countries by multinational corporations. Let us evaluate these assertions in more detail.

A. REDUCED ABILITY TO FORMULATE INDEPENDENT DOMESTIC POLICIES

African countries and other developing countries have special challenges. These challenges may require domestic policies that may not be congruent with

WTO initiatives. For example, the objective to diversify their economies and indus-trialize may require temporary subsidies and/or protection to help potentially viable, infant industries grow. Kenya may have a viable textile and clothing industry which eventually could compete successfully with imports of clothing into Kenya, if the industry was temporarily protected from such competition. This argument for protection, usually referred to as the "infant industry" argument, is not necessarily in conflict with the principle of free trade.[3]

Likewise, the dependence of many developing countries on import and export duties may limit the ability of these countries to reduce trade-related taxes. Characteristic of developing countries, African countries, especially those in Sub-Saharan Africa, have limited sources of government revenue. A relatively large proportion of output in these countries does not enter commercial channels. In addition, most transactions are not recorded. Therefore, governments have not been able to rely much on income or sales taxes. For this reason, tariffs may be used not primarily as a trade barrier, as they are in developed countries, but rather to generate revenue. The share of revenue generated by import and export duties is more than 20% for some African countries. For most developed countries the share of revenue generated by these duties is less than 1%.[4]

Certainly the WTO must be cognizant of the special challenges faced by African countries and other developing countries. Trade agreements must not hinder development initiatives; even more important, they should support those initiatives. Some WTO agreements reflect this kind of awareness and concern (although perhaps not in ways or to the extent some people would like). For example, at the conclusion of the Uruguay Round, developing countries, in general, were asked to reduce their trade barriers by relatively smaller margins than other countries. In some cases, developing countries were asked to "just give us a number" at which to bind the tariffs. In the same general spirit, developing countr-ies were given a longer period to complete the implementation of the agreements.

While it is necessary to be sensitive to the salient problems of developing countries, the WTO would not be effective in promoting trade if it allowed unlimited trade barriers. Moreover, many African countries implemented policies in the 1970s and 1980s which led to price distortions and corruption; some African officials would still like to return to those policies today. The WTO plays an important role as a deterrent to such misguided policies.

B. Developing Countries are Limited in Their Capacity for Fair and Effective Negotiations

In theory, the WTO is a democratic body, with each member country having one vote. In practice, agenda items are often set by developed countries, and negotiations are guided by the interests of and maneuvered by the overbearing capacity of those countries. When developing countries have tabled an agenda item, it is usually in reaction to some action(s) by developed countries. For example, developing countries made agriculture and textiles and clothing their main issues in the Uruguay Round of GATT in protest to export subsidies and trade barriers in developed countries which hurt developing countries. Nonetheless, their capacity to negotiate is quite limited.

Agreements are negotiated in various committees, each one requiring specific technical skills. African countries do not have the technical and diplomatic capacity to participate in these committees effectively. Whereas developed countries have specialists for each specific area of negotiation, African countries are typically represented by generalists in trade negotiations. For example, the Uruguay Round consisted of many complex agreements. In the final negotiations of that Round in 1993 in Geneva, Japan had more than 100 representatives, Tanzania had two, Ghana had one, and Angola had none.

Competent as those few African representatives may have been, they were too few in number and their resources too limited to fathom all the intricacies of economics, law, science, strategy, and politics involved. As such, many African countries signed off on the agreements without fully understanding them, let alone their likely long-term impact. They signed off on the agreements because they knew it would be difficult to join the WTO later; they subsequently requested and attended workshops by the WTO to help them understand the agreements better.

African countries need technical assistance. The United Nations Conference on Trade and Development (UNCTAD) performs the very useful function of providing valuable technical assistance to developing countries. In addition, developing countries, for their part, use a group system to share information and formulate strategies together, where they can identify common interests. African countries also try to form regional coalitions (often without much success) based on regional economic blocs. Kenya has a "National Committee on WTO," which includes participants from the government, the business sector, professional associations, and research institutions. Kenya's commercial attaché in Geneva communicates and consults with the Committee on a regular basis to determine Kenya's interests and positions on various proposals.

However, while these initiatives, especially the UNCTAD technical assistance, help to bridge the information disparity between developed and developing countries, there is still significant information and technical asymmetry in the WTO negotiations. Thus, in addition to technical assistance, African countries should be given ample time to study and understand different proposals. For their part, African countries should emulate Kenya's model and try to expand their negotiating capacity at WTO negotiations.

C. THERE IS AN UNFAIR DISTRIBUTION
OF THE GAINS FROM TRADE

Raul Prebisch, UNCTAD's first president, forcefully articulated the argument that the terms of trade were deteriorating for developing countries that were dependent on natural commodities. A country's terms of trade are the price of the country's export goods relative to the price of its import goods. For example, suppose Côte d'Ivoire must export one ton of cocoa to buy one imported tractor. If Côte d'Ivoire were only exporting cocoa and importing tractors, we would say Côte d'Ivoire's terms of trade have deteriorated if it now took more than one ton of the same type and quality of cocoa to buy an identical tractor.

Empirical evidence on the trend of the overall relative price of primary products in general has been mixed. However, the terms of trade for Africa have been deteriorating over time. Between 1980 and 1995, the average annual percentage change of the terms of trade index has been as follows: developed countries, 0.84%; developing countries as a whole, -2%; and Africa specifically, -2.25%. This means the terms of trade for Africa deteriorated by an annual average of 2.25% between 1980 and 1995.[5] As such, on average, those African exports that were able to pay for 100 tractors in 1980 would only pay for 66 tractors in 1995.

Because of this phenomenon, and the obvious poverty in most of Africa, international organizations and institutions are often challenged to support African countries and help them diversify their economies. International commodity agreements such as the International Cocoa Agreement and the International Coffee Agreement were seen in the 1960s and 1970s as a way to support prices of commodities and, thus, to support developing countries. However, because of the operational challenges of such agreements and the price distortion they create, international commodity agreements with provisions to control prices are becoming things of the past.

International commodity agreements continue to function, however, as study groups—collecting and disseminating information, sponsoring research on consumption and production, helping developing countries diversify their economies, and supporting processing in developing countries. In addition, the Common Fund for Commodities (CFC) was established in 1989, at the initiative of UNCTAD, with a membership of over 100 countries plus the European Community, the Organization of African Unity (OAU), and Common Market for Eastern and Southern Africa (COMESA). The CFC finances research and development projects that are geared toward improving productivity, competitiveness, diversification, and the optimal use of natural resources.[6] The CFC does not violate the spirit of free trade; if anything, the CFC enhances it. For this reason, the WTO should find ways to contribute to the CFC. Perhaps this could be done by channeling some WTO technical assistance through the CFC. Efforts such as these are important in addressing the issues of the distribution of the gains from trade.

D. Developed Countries are not Open Enough for Goods Produced by Developing Countries

There has been a long history of developed countries protecting sectors in which developing countries have a comparative advantage, particularly textiles and agriculture. This may indeed have exacerbated the deterioration of the terms of trade for developing countries. At the inception of GATT in 1947, developed countries protected these sectors from the jurisdiction of GATT. The agricultural sector has been protected by tariffs, quotas, voluntary export restraints, and other trade barriers. It has also been supported by production and export subsidies. Developed countries used the Multifiber Agreement (MFA) to set quotas for textiles and apparels imported from developing countries.

It should be noted, however, that with the exception of Mauritius and Kenya, the MFA did not have much negative impact on Africa. In fact, the MFA helped Africa by insulating its exports from fierce competition with Asian producers who, under free market conditions could easily have been exporting beyond their quotas. However, the MFA quotas set by the United States limited imports of textiles from Mauritius and Kenya.

It took a great deal of effort on the part of developing countries, in the Uruguay Round of GATT, to bring the agricultural sector under WTO rules and to lay the foundation for incorporating textiles and apparel into the WTO. While this is a significant accomplishment in itself, the implementation of the Agreement on Agriculture and the one on Textiles and Clothing has been deliberately slow.[7]

A fair presentation of the trade policies of developed countries must also acknowledge the preferential treatment that these countries extend to goods originating from Africa and other developing countries. This preferential treatment has taken a number of forms, such as the Generalized System of Preferences (GSP), the Lomé Convention, and the U.S. African Growth and Opportunity Act.

Under the GSP program, developed countries give preferential treatment to goods imported from developing countries. Developed countries choose which developing countries and which goods from those developing countries receive the preferential treatment.[8] Goods covered by this program enter a developed country duty free or on a GSP tariff rate, which is less than the MFN tariff rate. The difference between the MFN tariff rate and the GSP tariff rate is the margin of preference.

African countries have sometimes protested against reductions of MFN tariff rates because such a broad liberalization erodes the margin of preference.[9] However, African countries have not been able to gain much from the GSP program anyway.[10] This has been due to various domestic institutional constraints within African countries and limitations within the GSP programs themselves, such as the limited product coverage. In 1980 and 1994, only about 1 and 3%, respectively, of all imports by the United States from Africa received duty-free access under the U.S. GSP program. Table 20.1 shows the percentage of U.S. imports from a selected group of countries that received GSP duty-free access in 1980 and 1994.

Under the Lomé Convention, over 95% of all dutiable imports from the African, Caribbean, and Pacific (ACP) states enter the European Union duty free.[11] The first Lomé Convention was signed in 1975, succeeding the Yaoundé Convention, which came into effect in 1963.

TABLE 20.1 GSP Duty-Free Imports and Total Imports by the United States in 1980 and 1994 (U.S. $1000)

Country	1980			1994		
	GSP Duty-Free Imports	Total Duty-Free Imports	Imports as a Percent of Total Imports	GSP Duty-Free Imports	Total Duty-Free Imports	Imports as a Percent of Total Imports
Algeria	0	6,576,163	0.00	0	1,525,281	0.00
Botswana	43	87,186	0.05	480	13,655	3.52
Cameroon	2319	604,098	0.38	1400	55,189	2.54
Chad	0	1	0.00	0	1806	0.00
Comoros	15	3257	0.46	0	5995	0.00
Côte d'Ivoire	17,626	287,962	6.12	10,693	185,354	5.77
Egypt	2200	458,642	0.48	22,055	548,378	4.02
Ethiopia	167	86,912	0.19	147	34,100	0.43
Gabon	0	278,496	0.00	0	1,154,585	0.00
Ghana	317	206,552	0.15	2,869	198,486	1.45
Kenya	2557	53,565	4.77	9112	108,674	8.38
Mauritius	29,248	49,6575	8.90	15,682	217,131	7.22
Mozambique	17,383	104,7481	6.60	11,634	15,328	75.90
Nigeria	0	10,905,288	0.00	0	4,429,839	0.00
Senegal	253	8909	2.84	1,376	11,432	12.04
Uganda	0	125,753	0.00	275	34,858	0.79
Zambia	105,726	199,8495	2.90	168	63,477	0.26
Zimbabwe	7198	38,898	18.50	40,195	102,402	39.25
Africa	275,670	32,239,981	0.86	394,781	14,112,767	2.80
North Africa	17,419	14,253,819	0.12	62,672	2,319,440	2.70
SSA	258,251	17,986,162	1.44	332,109	11,793,327	2.82

Note: SSA = Sub-Saharan Africa.
Source: U.S. Department of Commerce.

In May 2000, the U.S. House of Representatives and the Senate approved a trade bill, the African Growth and Opportunity Act (AGOA), which promotes trade with Sub-Saharan Africa. The bill lowers trade barriers, notably for textiles and clothing, on U.S. imports from these regions. This bill is likely to provide a significant boost to Kenya and Mauritius, which were hurt by MFA quotas. The textile and clothing sector of other African countries will also benefit from this bill.

E. THE WTO FACILITATES EXPLOITATION OF WORKERS IN DEVELOPING COUNTRIES BY MULTINATIONAL CORPORATIONS

This criticism is voiced by those who are concerned with the welfare of workers in developing countries (the labor standard argument) and also by those concerned with the potential loss of jobs in some sectors in industrialized countries (the cheap labor argument). These arguments reflect legitimate concerns.

However, two points are often overlooked when considering these arguments. First, wages reflect labor productivity. Second, production does require more than just labor. For example, capital is relatively more expensive in developing countries than it is in developed countries. Thus, even if the "cheap labor" argument were a valid argument in developed countries, it could be countered with the "cheap capital" argument in developing countries. In other words, while those in developed countries can argue they are losing jobs to cheap labor in developing countries, those in developing countries can argue they are losing jobs to cheap capital in developed countries. In fact, it is the differences in relative resource costs that contribute to the mutual gains from trade.

Nonetheless, President Clinton succumbed to pressure from labor unions and insisted that labor laws be a direct mandate of the WTO. Developing countries did not agree, for good reasons. The WTO cannot encompass all facets of commercial production. Other international institutions, such as the International Labor Organization, the World Health Organization, United Nations International Children's Emergency Fund, and the United Nations Environment Program, are charged with specific areas of responsibility. Instead of requiring the WTO to set standards in these areas, the WTO should be required to adhere to the standards set by other international institutions in resolving trade disputes.

In addition, while countries must have labor laws to protect workers (and employers), countries cannot have uniform sets of standards. Labor standards are determined by, among other factors, economic development. Among ways to raise labor standards, one which is very effective, is to create jobs. Here are two examples that illustrate this and other dynamic gains from trade.

Up until the late 1960s, Mauritius depended mainly on sugar exports for foreign exchange. In the 1970s, Mauritius attracted investors with tax holidays, cheap labor, and undoubtedly lower labor standards compared to those in developed countries. By the mid-1990s, the textile industry in Mauritius had grown to generate 50% of the country's foreign exchange. Work conditions improved and wages increased to the point where in the late 1990s Mauritius started to lose its competitive advantage in textiles and began to prepare its labor force to move into the second phase of industrialization. That involved diversifying within the clothing industry and also moving into service industries and technology-intensive industries. Kenya tried to follow Mauritius' model until it was hit by protectionist policies in the United States in 1994 on its exports of pillowcases and shirts to the United States.[12]

A second example comes from Tanzania. In the early 1990s, a number of European producers established farms for cut flowers (for export) in Arusha, Tanzania, following economic reforms in Tanzania. These farms currently employ about 3000 workers, over 80% of whom are women. This is significant because, for a variety of reasons, women, in general, have fewer good job opportunities. Competition for reliable workers among flowers producers, the increase in labor productivity emanating from experience, and the quiet but growing pressure from the workers have combined to improve benefits for workers. In addition to a paid 28-day leave, the only initial benefit, workers now receive other benefits such as medical services and limited, but important, round-trip transportation to the farms. In the mid-1990s, after learning from foreign investors, local Tanzanians established their own cut-flower farms. Out of eight such farms in Arusha in the year 2000, three were owned and managed by Tanzanian entrepreneurs.

While the working conditions and benefits for workers in the cut-flower farms in Tanzania have improved, their work conditions are still not on par with those of their counterparts in Europe. However, if one were to demand that the labor standards of the cut-flower industry in Europe be applied in Tanzania, Tanzania's flowers (produced solely for export) would be barred from Europe. Thousands of poor workers in Tanzania would lose their jobs, and this opportunity for them to improve their work and economic conditions would be lost.

Good labor conditions are not simply a result of labor laws; they are also the result of an increase in employment. To the extent trade is expanded by a reduction in tariffs and non-tariff barriers to trade, causing a net increase in jobs, the WTO will contribute to an improvement in labor standards.

IV. REGIONAL ECONOMIC INTEGRATION

Regional economic integration refers to special economic arrangements between countries. Countries forming a regional economic bloc agree to reduce trade barriers on interregional trade to increase economic activities between member countries.

Regional economic integration is advocated by African leaders and most development economists as a way to increase cooperation and competition among and between African countries and as a way for Africa to forge a better position to compete in the wider world market. The overall impact of economic integration can be divided into two categories, static and dynamic.

The static impact refers to the change in market price and quantity as a result of economic integration. This impact can be analyzed in terms of *trade creation* and *trade diversion*. Trade creation occurs when economic integration leads a product source to shift from high-cost domestic producers to low-cost producers in a member country. For example, suppose Zimbabwe has a tariff on sugar imports from Mozambique to protect its own sugar growers. When Zimbabwe and Mozambique, alone or with other countries, form a regional economic bloc, Zimbabwe will reduce or eliminate tariffs on sugar imports from Mozambique. As a result, Zimbabwe will increase its imports of sugar from Mozambique, the price of sugar in Zimbabwe will decrease, and some (high cost) producers of sugar in Zimbabwe will be forced to stop producing sugar. Note that trade creation reflects movement toward free trade. It produces a net welfare gain in Zimbabwe because the gains as a result of low prices, to consumers and firms that use sugar as an input, will exceed the sum of the losses by producers and the government (lost tariff revenue).

Trade diversion occurs when integration causes a product source to shift from a low-cost nonmember country to a high-cost member country. Suppose, initially, Zimbabwe has a uniform tariff rate on all imports of butter. Because Kenya produces butter at a lower cost than Mozambique, Zimbabwe imports butter from Kenya. The price of butter produced in Kenya (P^K) is lower than the price of butter produced in Mozambique (P^M). However, when economic integration is established between Zimbabwe and Mozambique, Zimbabwe reduces or eliminates tariffs on butter imports from Mozambique, but not on imports from Kenya. If Zimbabwe shifts its source of butter imports from Kenya to Mozambique, solely due to reduced tariffs on imports from Mozambique, this would be trade diversion.

Trade diversion may cause a net welfare gain or loss to Zimbabwe. When economic integration is established, trade diversion occurs when the price of butter from Kenya plus the tariff rate ($P^K + t$) exceeds P^M. In that situation, the domestic price of butter in Zimbabwe would go down thus reducing distortion in domestic consumption and domestic production. That is a gain. However, Zimbabwe will now be paying a higher "world" price for its imports of butter (P^M instead of P^K) and that is a loss.

The dynamic impact of economic integration includes increased competition and efficiency, increased investment in the region induced by an enlarged market, increased opportunities for firms to take advantage of economies of scale,[13] and political and economic leverage in multilateral negotiations.

Every African country except Somalia belongs to at least one of these five economic blocs: the Common Market for Eastern and Southern Africa (COMESA), the Economic Community of Central African States (ECCAS), the Economic Community of West African States (ECOWAS), the Southern Africa Development Community (SADC), and the Arab Maghreb Union (UMA), as shown in Table 20.2.[14] In addition, all African countries belong to the African

TABLE 20.2 Membership of African Countries in Five Regional Economic Blocs

Country	COMESA	ECCAS	ECOWAS	SADC	UMA
Algeria					X
Angola	X	X		X	
Benin			X		
Botswana				X	
Burkina Faso			X		
Burundi	X	X			
Cameroon		X			
Cape Verde			X		
Central African Republic		X			
Chad		X			
Comoros	X				
Congo		X			
Côte d'Ivoire			X		
Democratic Republic of Congo	X	X		X	
Djibouti	X				
Egypt	X				
Equatorial Guinea		X			
Eritrea	X				
Ethiopia	X				
Gabon		X			
Gambia			X		
Ghana			X		
Guinea			X		
Guinea-Bissau			X		
Kenya	X				
Lesotho				X	
Liberia			X		
Libya					X
Madagascar	X				
Malawi	X			X	
Mali			X		
Mauritania			X		X

(Continues)

TABLE 20.2 *(Continued)*

Country	COMESA	ECCAS	ECOWAS	SADC	UMA
Mauritius	X			X	
Morocco					X
Mozambique				X	
Namibia	X			X	
Niger			X		
Nigeria			X		
Rwanda	X	X			
São Tomé and Principe		X			
Senegal			X		
Seychelles	X			X	
Sierra Leone			X		
South Africa				X	
Sudan	X				
Swaziland	X			X	
Tanzania				X	
Togo			X		
Tunisia					X
Uganda	X				
Zambia	X			X	
Zimbabwe	X			X	

Source: Mshomba (2000) and UNCTAD (1996).shomba (2000) and UNCTAD (1996).

Economic Community (AEC), which was established by the Organization of African Unity (OAU). The AEC has set an ambitious schedule to integrate the whole continent into a common market by 2022.[15]

One of the challenges facing the pursuit of economic integration in Africa is schedules that are set without any real political commitment. Agreements are reached but some countries do not honor them, even though they are parties to the agreements. A country may agree to reduce tariffs on intragroup trade, only to say a few months later that it cannot do so because such an action will have a severe negative impact on government revenue. This excuse is given even by countries whose intragroup imports are less than 5% of their total imports. Likewise, countries set group objectives without linking them to national policies.

Other challenges facing African countries in connection with economic integration are overdependence on foreign countries, foreign countries' dominance, fear of uneven distribution of benefits among members of an economic bloc, and political instability. One of the potential dynamic gains from economic integration is the political and economic leverage it can accord African countries in multilateral negotiations. This potential benefit is compromised, however, by too much dependence on foreign donors. For example, there is rivalry between

COMESA and SADC and between ECOWAS and the West African Monetary and Economic Union (*Union économique et monétaire ouest- africaine*, UEMOA), partly over foreign donors.[16] Some developed countries, on their part, devise strategies to safeguard their dominant influence on Africa. Preferential treatment extended to African countries by developed countries usually comes with strings attached.

Regarding the distribution of benefits, it is important to emphasize that African countries are quite diverse in their levels of economic development. These economic differences cause concern that the benefits of integration will gravitate toward those countries whose manufacturing sectors are relatively more developed, such as Kenya, Mauritius, and Zimbabwe in COMESA; South Africa and Zimbabwe in SADC; Côte d'Ivoire, Ghana, Nigeria, and Senegal in ECOWAS; and Cameroon in ECCAS. These concerns have given rise to two phenomena that could undermine the integration process itself: compensation schemes and selective liberalization schemes.

Some regional economic blocs have put in place schemes to compensate poorer countries for the tariff revenue that they will lose. Note that the focus on lost revenues neglects the positive impact of reduced tariffs on consumers and on the efficient allocation of resources. Even if indeed losses of tariff revenues on intragroup trade cannot be sustained, then the reduction of tariffs should be more gradual, rather than setting ambitious tariff reduction schedules which are sure to be ignored or compensatory schemes which are sure to fail.

The selective liberalization schemes have delayed tariff reductions on manufactured products and primary products that have undergone industrial processing for fear that some countries would benefit much more than others. However, it is precisely in these sectors that effective economic integration can take place in Africa. Given the homogeneous nature of unprocessed primary products, tariff reductions concentrated on these products would not lead to significant intraregional trade. Needless to say, by not liberalizing the manufacturing sector, economic blocs considerably limit the potential dynamic impact of integration: competition, efficient allocation of resources, and economies of scale.

African countries must find less distortionary schemes within which relatively advanced countries can assist poorer nations without undermining the benefits of trade. For example, regional development banks can give priority to responsible governments and/or nongovernmental organizations of relatively poor countries in issuing loans.

Finally, political instability is another challenge to economic integration. While progressive political reforms took place in many countries in Africa during the 1990s, wars and political insecurity are still pervasive in some countries, such as Angola, Burundi, Central African Republic, the Democratic Republic of Congo, Guinea, Guinea Bissau, Liberia, Rwanda, Sierra Leone, Somalia, and Sudan.

Instability in one country often deters investment, not only in that country, but also in neighboring countries.

V. GLOBALIZATION AND DEVELOPMENT

The term *development* refers to improvement in the standard of living in terms of access to basic needs and social services such as education and health services. It is quite difficult, if not impossible, to develop a comprehensive and accurate index of economic development, let alone to obtain reliable data to construct the index. However, because of the need to understand and compare countries' development levels, various indices are used, notwithstanding their shortcomings.

The World Bank groups countries into four broad income categories—low income economies, lower-middle income economies, upper-middle income economies, and high income economies—based on their GNP or GDP per capita. Most of the Sub-Saharan African countries are classified as low-income economies. The United Nations Development Program (UNDP) ranks countries based on their relative development using the Human Development Index (HDI). The HDI is calculated based on life expectancy, the average years of schooling, and real GDP per capita. Many Sub-Saharan African are among those countries ranked the lowest.[17]

Needless to say, development is a process whose momentum is determined by many factors, internal and external. Some factors, such as savings, investment, income distribution, trade, health and education systems, can be influenced by policies. Other factors, such as certain weather patterns, cannot be controlled by policies. Likewise, globalization is influenced by a wide variety of factors.

Globalization is a dynamic phenomenon that has an impact on all countries. While it is determined, in part, by countries' policies, no single country, and certainly not African countries, can effectively control its momentum. However, individual countries can implement policies that can increase the benefits and reduce the costs associated with globalization.

For example, globalization has increased the mobility of capital across countries. Some African countries use export-processing zones (EPZs) to attract direct foreign investment. EPZs are geographical areas in which manufacturers are temporarily exempted from corporate income taxes and duties on imported inputs. They are also exempted from a number of bureaucratic procedures and regulations. Experience on EPZs is mixed; but they seemed to help in the early days in Mauritius.

The advantages of direct foreign investment include increased employment and spillover of technical and managerial skills. However, the magnitude and duration of investment and their benefits depend very much on the type of industries being attracted and the underlying investment environment. Successful investment requires effective educational and training programs, public investment programs in infrastructure (roads, railways, energy, water, and telecommunications), effective labor laws that protect workers and employers, political and macroeconomic stability, and a reliable judicial system. Temporary incentives alone tend to attract highly mobile investors who are mainly concerned with short-term profits; jobs can be created quickly, but they can also be lost just as quickly.

For most African countries, where major exports are raw or only semi-processed commodities, investment programs should also aim to enhance backward and forward linkages. Development of the textile industry, for example, has a backward linkage to cotton and wool production. Production of coffee or cocoa has a forward linkage to the commodity processing and packaging industry.

Most African countries' markets are too small to allow firms to take advantage of economies of scale or to attract substantial investment. This limitation can be corrected, however, with effective economic integration. Integration also allows countries to take advantage of each other's resources and infrastructure. For example, in a common market, a shortage of skilled labor in one country may be met by a flow of labor from a country with a surplus.

As for the Tanzanian cut-flower industry discussed earlier, its success has been due in part to the easy access to Nairobi International Airport in Kenya. Some of the flowers produced in Arusha, Tanzania, are transported by road to Nairobi and flown from there to Europe. This is because the nearest international airport to the flower farms in Tanzania has only a few flights a week to Europe. The relatively easy access to Nairobi International Airport is a result of the regional economic cooperation between Kenya, Tanzania, and Uganda.[18]

Acknowledging the globalization trend does not suggest that governments should wash their hands of and surrender their duty to design and implement economic and social policies. The point has already been made that effective policies are needed to increase the benefits or decrease the costs of globalization. However, economic growth that may come from trade liberalization and more economic freedom must be geared to bringing development for the whole nation. It must be used to sustain and expand the provision of services such as water, health, and education. Neither economic growth (i.e., growth in real GDP or GNP) nor economic development (i.e., the improvement in the overall standard of living) can be sustained without the other.[19]

VI. SUMMARY

1. Globalization is an ongoing trend whereby countries increasingly interact with each other. The trend toward greater economic integration manifests itself in many forms, such as increased international trade,

regional economic integration, and direct foreign investment. It also manifests itself in various institutions such as the World Trade Organization, the International Monetary Fund, and the World Bank.

2. All African countries are members of the United Nations, the IMF, and the World Bank and more than 40 African countries are members of the WTO.

3. The WTO was established in 1995 to succeed the General Agreement on Tariffs and Trade, which had been in operation since 1948. The main objective of the WTO is to liberalize trade among member countries.

4. One of the guiding principles of the WTO is nondifferentiated treatment, commonly called the most favored nation (MFN) principle.

5. A number of complaints against the WTO and its rules have been raised by developing countries, or for the perceived interests of developing countries. They include: (1) the WTO reduces the ability of developing countries to formulate independent domestic policies; (2) developing countries are limited in their capacity for fair and effective negotiations; (3) there is an unfair distribution of the gains from trade; (4) developed countries are not open enough for goods coming from developing countries; and (5) the WTO facilitates exploitation of workers in developing countries by multinational corporations. These complaints have merit of varying degrees and some are being addressed by the WTO.

6. Regional economic integration refers to special economic arrangements whereby member countries agree to reduce trade barriers on interregional trade.

7. Some of the challenges facing the pursuit of economic integration in Africa are (1) schedules which are set without any real commitment, (2) overdependence on foreign countries, (3) foreign countries' dominance, (4) fear of uneven distribution of benefits, and (5) political instability.

8. Most Sub-Saharan countries are classified as low-income economies.

9. Development is determined by internal and external factors.

10. African countries need to implement policies that can increase the benefits and reduce the costs associated with globalization.

11. Neither economic growth (i.e., growth in real GDP or GNP) nor economic development (i.e., the improvement in the overall standard of living) can be sustained without each other.

DISCUSSION QUESTIONS

1. In what ways has the nature and the momentum of globalization changed over the last two decades?

2. What is the WTO and what is its main role?

3. What would you consider to be the rationale for the "most favored nation" principle under the WTO? In what ways might the "most favored nation" principle hinder trade liberalization?

4. Which two of the complaints against the WTO are the most valid in your view? Explain. Which two of the complaints against the WTO are the least valid in your view? Explain.

5. "Multinational corporations are bad for Africa because they exploit workers." Comment.

6. What approach to regional economic cooperation should African countries take to overcome some of the challenges to economic integration?

NOTES

[1]UNCTAD (1997) *Handbook of International Trade and Development Statistics 1995*, New York: United Nations Conference on Trade and Development.

[2]A free trade area is a regional economic bloc in which member countries reduce or remove trade barriers on intragroup trade for all goods or on an agreed subset of goods. At this level of economic integration, member states set their own national trade policies with nonmembers. A customs union represents a higher level of integration than a free trade area. In a customs union, member countries not only remove trade barriers among themselves, but also maintain common trade barriers for goods imported from nonmembers.

[3]In practice, the infant-industry argument faces several challenges. How is one to determine which industries have the potential for comparative advantage? What is the likelihood of removing protection if the industry remains infant and therefore in continual need of protection or if it matures to be a strong political constituency? There is also a question of the actual type of support to be given to the industry. While a direct subsidy may not be politically popular or fiscally sustainable, it is superior to trade barriers, in terms of the overall costs to a nation.

[4]For data on government revenues and expenditures, see recent issues of *Government Finance Statistics Yearbook*, Washington, D.C.: International Monetary Fund.

[5]UNCTAD (1997) *Handbook of International Trade and Development Statistics 1995*, New York: United Nations Conference on Trade and Development, p. 42.

[6]Common Fund for Commodities (1997) *Annual Report 1996*, Amsterdam: Common Fund for Commodities, pp. 15, 59–63.

[7]Mshomba, R. (2000) *Africa in the Global Economy*, Boulder, CO: Lynne Rienner; Tangermann, S. (1996) "Implementation of the Uruguay Round Agreement on Agriculture: Issues and Prospects," *Journal of Agricultural Economics*, 47(3), 315–337.

[8]As one can imagine, while the MFN principle prevents arbitrary discrimination when it comes to setting MFN tariff rates, preference-giving countries under the GSP program may discriminate against specific developing countries.

[9]For a comparison between the gains to preference-receiving countries, as a group, of MFN tariff cuts and the losses associated with the erosion of the margin of preference, see Baldwin, R. and Murray, T. (1977) "MFN Tariff Reductions and Developing Country Trade Benefits Under the GSP," *Economic Journal* 87, 30-46; Baldwin, R. and Murray, T. (1986) "MFN Tariff Reductions and Developing Country Trade Benefits Under the GSP," *Economic Journal*, 96, 537–539; Pomfret, R. (1986) "MFN

Tariff Reductions and Developing Country Trade Benefits Under the GSP: A Comment," *Economic Journal*, 96, 534–536.

[10]For a comprehensive discussion on the impact of the GSP initiative on sub-Saharan Africa, see Mshomba, R. (2000) *Africa in the Global Economy*, Boulder, CO: Lynne Rienner.

[11]Davenport, M. (1992) "Africa and the Unimportance of Being Preferred," *Journal of Common Market Studies*, 30(2), 233–251

[12]Due in part to the U.S. trade barriers, Kenya's producers' concentration on a single market, and poor and corrupt governance within Kenya, about two-thirds of jobs in Kenya's textiles and clothing industry were lost. See Phillips, M. (1996) "U.S. Rethinks Trade Policy with Africa," *The Wall Street Journal*, July 15, p. A2; Jacobs, B. (1997) "H.R. 1432 Could Propel Sub-Sahara Sourcing," *Bobbin*, 38(11), 88–89.

[13]A firm experiences economies of scale when its long-run average cost of production decreases as it produces more (internal economies of scale) or as more firms enter the industry (external economies of scale).

[14]There are many other smaller regional blocs in Africa, some of which are subsets of these five.

[15]A common market is a stage of integration which extends the customs union by allowing free movement of factors of production (that is, labor and capital) within the economic bloc.

[16]UEMOA is a subset of ECOWAS. UEMOA members are Benin, Burkina Faso, Côte d'Ivoire, Guinea-Bissau, Mali, Niger, Senegal, and Togo. As all of them except Guinea-Bissau are former French colonies, UEMOA receives special treatment from France which other members of ECOWAS do not receive.

[17]United Nations Development Program (UNDP) (1999) *Human Development Report*, New York: Oxford University Press, pp. 134–137.

[18]Kenya, Tanzania, and Uganda had a customs union, the East African Community (EAC), which existed from 1967 to 1977. When the EAC collapsed, the border between Kenya and Tanzania was closed. A business that depended on resources and infrastructure from or in both countries could not have survived then. The border was opened in the 1980s and Kenya, Tanzania, and Uganda started to rebuild an economic bloc in the mid 1990s. In November of 1999, the three countries agreed to reestablish a customs union by the end of 2004.

Other important publications dealing with globalization include the following: Organization of African Unity (1991) *Treaty Establishing the African Economic Community*, Bellville, South Africa: Centre for Southern African Studies, University of the Western Cape; UNCTAD (1996) *Handbook of Economic Integration and Cooperation Groupings of Developing Countries. Vol. I. Regional and Subregional Economic Integration Groupings*, New York: United Nations Conference on Trade and Development; U.S. International Trade Commission (1997) *Likely Impact of Providing Quota-Free and Duty-Free Entry to Textiles and Apparel From Sub-Saharan Africa*, USITC Publ. No. 3056, Washington, D.C.: U.S. International Trade Commission.

CHAPTER 21

Information and Communication Technologies

Francis A.S.T. Matambalya

Department of Marketing, University of Dar es Salaam, Dar es Salaam, Tanzania

KEY TERMS

Decoupling property of ICTs	Information economy (IE)
Dynamic complementarities	Information poverty
East African Community (EAC)	Intellectual property rights (IPRs)
Efficiency	Knowledge
Efficiency channel	Large-scale enterprises (LSEs)
ICT capability	Macro-level survey
ICT infrastructure	Micro-level productivity
ICT investments	New technologies (NTs)
ICT literacy	Pervasive quality of ICTs
ICT policies	Productivity
ICT returns	Productivity paradox
ICT-economic development linkages	Productivity surge
ICTs externalities	Restricted diffusion of ICTs
ICTs resources	Returns to investment
ICTs thresholds	Scale channel
Information	Small and medium-scale
Information and communications	enterprises (SMEs)
technology (ICT)	Technical efficiency
Information channels	Technological change

I. INTRODUCTION

Generally, technological change, which is manifested by the diffusion and application of new technologies (NTs), is postulated to stimulate development by enhancing the level of efficiency at which human activities in various economic and social spheres are carried out. The high expectations tied to NTs may be traced back to the catalytic effect of evolutionary technologies on economic evolution and growth. Information and communication technologies (ICTs), which present one major category of NTs within the contemporary context, are heralded to provide unique opportunities for economic development. Furthermore, their unique properties have given hope that they present a novel technology that may more effectively help developing countries to catch-up, with relatively less efforts.

The optimism tied to ICTs centers on the role of new knowledge and information in facilitating productivity and a range of benefits associated with it. The popular view derives from the recognition of information as a critical input in the economic production system, and the essence of a critical mass of knowledge as a basis for sustainable competitiveness within the framework of new competition. In this context, such excellent scholars as Romer (1983) and Stiglitz (1989) have emphasized the role of knowledge in development. Also, the subject has enjoyed the attention of the World Bank (1998). Inasmuch as ICTs support easier access to such knowledge and information, they bridge the knowledge/ information gap.

Arguing from another perspective, optimistic proponents of ICTs see them as tools with great potential for the creation of a level playing field by bridging the knowledge/ information gap between weaker and stronger economic units. Thus, inasmuch as they make it easier for developing economies to amass critical masses of knowledge necessary for development, they constitute versatile technologies capable of tackling a wide range of development deficits in the economic and social spheres. Hence, in broad terms, ICTs are postulated to *inter alia* increase economic productivity, accelerate economic growth, promote employment and income, prop up the efficiency of public administration, and result in greater public participation and democracy (Pohjola, 2000; Bedi, 1999; Kenney, 1995; Braga, 1996; Hadden, 1996). For instance, by reducing the information-related market imperfections, they promote mutually beneficial business exchanges. The power of modern ICTs lies in their contribution toward a substantial reduction of information asymmetry, thereby reducing the market imperfectness attributed to information-poor environments.

Because of the unique characteristics of ICTs, the more optimistic proponents of their role even go as far as seeing in them tools which can enable developing countries to leap-frog certain stages of development (Dedrick and Kraemer, 2000; Pohjola, 2000; Bedi, 1999; Avgerou, 1998).

The foregoing arguments bear particular significance for developing economies in general and, for our study, African economies in particular. These groups of countries are known for their "information poverty." Hence, the prospects associated with ICTs give reason for some optimism about the potential of ICTs to stimulate growth and real development and to provide greater opportunities to participate in the world economy.

In this chapter, we assess how investments in ICTs can potentially affect Africa's economic development prospects. The chapter is organized as follows. Section II discusses some evolutionary properties of ICTs, while Section III introduces the causal effects empirically observed to run from ICTs to economic development.

In Section IV, we present a general overview of the impact of ICTs, as has so far been observed for Africa's economic development. In order to highlight the picture further, in this section we use selected concrete micro-level evidence of the performance prospects stimulated by ICTs. In this context, we present some aspects of the results of a survey of 150 Small and Medium scale enterprises (SMEs) in the manufacturing sector (food processing and textile) and service sector (tourism) within the framework of the *East Africa SME Survey* conducted by the Enterprise Research Programme (ERP) team.[1] This presents us with a rare opportunity to work on the basis of sound empirical evidence, in an otherwise research-deficient region.

In Section V, we discuss the factors that limit the returns to investments in ICTs in Africa and propose the way forward in Section VI. Finally, the conclusions are presented in Section VII. The chapter also contains an appendix, which portrays the reasons for restricted diffusion of selected ICTs and a list of selected references.

II. ICTs AND SOME OF THEIR EVOLUTIONARY PROPERTIES

A. ICTs as a Special Category of Technologies

According to the *Oxford Dictionary of Economics*, information is defined as "the data available to individuals, firms or governments, at the time when economic decisions have to be made" (Black, 1997). Moreover, the U.S. Bureau of Economic Analysis (BEA), defines information technology within a narrower perspective as "office, computing and accounting machinery."

A more embracing definition of information (and implicitly communication) technologies incorporates information processing (IP) equipment. Besides computers, it includes communications equipment, scientific and engineering instruments, photocopiers and related equipment, and software and related services (Brynjolfsson and Yang, 1996, p. 182). Our discussion in this chapter is based on the second more comprehensive definition, which more adequately covers ICTs.

B. Some Evolutionary Properties of ICTs

The optimism surrounding ICTs is to a great extent attributed to a number of evolutionary properties associated with them. Accordingly, ICTs support decoupling of information; convenient, instant, and cost-effective transmission of large volumes of data; and nonrival use of information networks. Evidently, they also constitute pervasive and versatile technologies whose application finds use in virtually all spheres of the society (Bedi, 1999; Pohjola, 1998; Evans and Wurster, 1997). The most novel development associated with ICTs is presumably the creation of a whole range of new economic activities, thereby ushering in a new economy.

1. Decoupling Property of ICTs

The decoupling property of ICTs is also referred to as the separation property. Accordingly, ICTs support the separation of information from the physical repository. This property supports a new form of communication, i.e., communication free of physical movement of individuals. It also enhances selective bundling and instant transmission of needed information. Generally, such information can now be transmitted at much lower prices.

The decoupling property can also support such evolutionary organization of activities as teleworking. This creates good prospects for the development of mutually beneficial interactions between developed and developing economies. Notably, it appears that, analogous to the phenomenon of outsourcing of standardized tangible goods within the framework of technological theory of trade due to comparative costs considerations, the decoupling property of ICTs opens a vent for economic units from developed economies to "outsource" routine activities. This appears to be so, even though, unlike the case of tangible products, the basis for outsourcing routine activities might not be fully in line with the product life-cycle theory.[2]

Thus, given the availability of a functional ICTs infrastructure, it is possible to imagine data entry for the U.S. medical insurance taking place in Ghana, shoebox accounting for U.K. SMEs in Uganda, and call centers for multinationals in Mauritius and Togo. Hence, inasmuch as the decoupling property of ICTs enables such economic units as enterprises to outsource various services, it facilitates intra- and international teleworking.

2. ICTs as Information Channels

Closely related to the decoupling property, ICTs are able to serve as information channels. Combined with the possibility to decouple information from its physical repository, this property allows direct access and convenient and instant transmission of (usually) large volumes of information. Also, in the long run, it provides a more cost-effective way to access and transmit information, and such information is timely. Related to economic performance, ICTs potentially increase the efficiency and productivity of economic units (e.g., enterprise, sector, country, etc.), through the ability to acquire up-to-date knowledge from the Internet.

3. Pervasive Quality of ICTs

Another characterising feature of ICTs is their pervasive nature. A technology is said to be pervasive in nature if it (1) generates a wide range of new products (both tangible and intangible), (2) generates strong industrial interests as a means for profitability and competitive advantage, (3) reduces the costs and improves the performance of processes and products of many sectors of the economy (Bedi, 1999; Avgerou, 1998). Characteristically, the pervasive quality of ICTs provides the basis for the multiplicity of ways in which ICTs can be beneficially utilized by those with access to them (Bedi, 1999; Pohjola, 1998; Evans and Wurster, 1997). Notably, the use of ICTs is not sectoral dependent, but covers virtually all categories of human activities.

4. ICTs and Information Economy

The advent of ICTs has also ushered a new era in economic evolution worldwide, by creating a whole range of new economic activities. These activities are usually captured under the acronym of a new economy popularly known as the information economy (IE). In simple terms, IE describes the economic and social transformation related to pervasive application of ICTs. Concretely, it embodies a range of economic activities necessary for the design, production, and distribution of (1) ICTs goods, and (2) a network of infrastructures and other ICTs services. Hence, the designing, production, and distribution of such ICTs products as hard- and software packages and evolutionary forms of communication as cellular phones are aspects of IE, as are efforts to develop infrastructure for e-commerce, provision of specialized ICTs services, etc.

An information economy can be seen as a distinct sector of the economy. In those economies where ICTs are well developed, this sector is quickly gaining importance. In 1999, for instance, the turnover of the global ICTs market surpassed U.S. $2 trillion in 1999 (with an annual growth rate of 10%) and is postulated to hit the phenomenal value of U.S. $3000 trillion by 2004.

III. CAUSAL RELATIONS BETWEEN ICTS AND ECONOMIC DEVELOPMENT: AN OVERVIEW

Research on the significance of NTs with regard to development is neither new nor a prerogative of one discipline. Over time, the subject has attracted the interest of a wide range of theories, ranging from producer theory to industrial economics theories to traditional trade theory to modern trade theory and, of course, to the technology theories. Individually and jointly, these theories provide useful clues on the many facets of the linkages between technological capabilities and the productivity of economic units (Matambalya, 2003). ICTs, as they are understood in the contemporary context, present a relatively new addition to NTs. Obviously, this explains, at least in part, why even though for developed countries there is already a substantial body of research evidence on many aspects related to the diffusion and development impact of ICTs, the same cannot be claimed for developing and particularly African economies. Hence, one major problem associated with writing on ICTs is the great inter-country diversity in their development and status of research. This consideration should be kept in mind in any debate on the possible impact of ICTs on Africa's economic development.

A. DEVELOPED WORLD EVIDENCE: PRODUCTIVITY PARADOX VERSUS PRODUCTIVITY SURGE

Analogous to theoretical deliberations, empirical evidences seeking to establish the relations between ICTs and performance abound. As expected, most of these studies were conducted in developed economies; however, they offer invaluable insights that can be applicable for developing economies as well. Commonly, the pertinent studies investigate the linkages between investment in ICTs and the productivity of an economic unit. The results obtained present a mosaic of observations ranging from a deep-rooted productivity paradox to a productivity surge. In the following sections, we briefly contrast evidences on the ICT productivity paradox and productivity surge, with the assistance of selected empirical studies.

1. Productivity Paradox

Several early studies, particularly those conducted in the 1980s and the first half of the 1990s (Berndt et al., 1995; Loveman, 1994; Roach, 1991; Siegel and Grilliches, 1991; Morrison and Bendt, 1990; Solow, 1987) depicted a rather questionable productivity impact for ICTs. The studies of this group observed no positive relationships between investments in ICTs and productivity. Berndt and Morrison (1995), for instance, came to the outright observations that there exists a negative relationship between investment in ICTs and productivity. Overall, this trend of observations led to the famous *productivity paradox*, asserting the absence of linkages between information technologies (ITs) and productivity improvements.

2. Productivity Surge

Though the research world is still grappling for more conclusive evidence of the role of ICTs, increasing evidence since the second half of the 1990s supports their positive performance impact. Their importance is corroborated by studies at both the micro- and macro-levels. At the macro-level, ICTs are associated with the improvement of productivity (Braga, 1996; Kraemer and Dedrick, 1994). Kraemer and Dedrick (1994), for instance, studied the payoffs (in terms of productivity and economic growth) of investments in ITs in 12 Asia Pacific Countries for the period 1984 to 1990. They observed significant positive correlation between investments in ITs and productivity and economic growth. Accordingly, economies with higher investments in ITs recorded higher macro-economic productivity and gross domestic product (GDP) growth rates for economies.

Also, the findings of a macro-level survey by the United Nations University (UNU)/World Institute of Development Economics Research (WIDER), involving 23 member states of the Organization for Economic Cooperation and Development (OECD) for the period 1980–1995, suggest strong correlations between ICT investments and economic growth. The study estimates the productivity effect of ICTs at double the effect of other fixed investments (Pohjola, 2000, p. 2).

At the micro-level, the pivotal role of ICTs is underlined in a number of studies as well. Raymond (1985), in a study of small businesses, came to the conclusion that the use of ITs improves productivity. Also, in a study involving semistructured interviews of 30 mostly manufacturing SMEs in Merseyside, England, Naylor and Williams (1994), found out that computer revolution is a source of productivity gains. Among other things, they observed that (1) 40% of the enterprises using ITs traded internationally; (2) there were evident gains for ICTs adopters in terms of such *analytical* (as opposed to purely *transactional*) functions, as sales analysis, forecasting, and the range of services offered to customers; and (3) IT adopters reported higher orders (and, implicitly, turnover and profits). However, the authors also reason that successful use of ITs requires innovative management skills, to enable effective use of the information generated. Furthermore, the cross-enterprise differences between expectations and achievements suggest that enterprise characteristics are significant for the competitiveness impact of ICTs.

A study by Diewert and Smith (1994) corroborated the observations by Raymond (1985) and Naylor and Williams (1994) that ITs improve productivity. Other studies that provide even stronger evidence of the payoffs of ICTs are those of Bryjolfsson and Hitt (1995, 2000). In their econometric estimations, where investments in ICTs are treated as one of the factor inputs, they observed significant contributions of investment in ICTs to productivity.

Of course, in the various studies, the benefits of ICTs are predicated beyond the business sector and, in a more general sense, access to information and knowledge induced by ICTs is associated with a wide range of positive developments: accelerating economic growth, increasing the efficiency of public administration, encouraging greater public participation and democracy.

3. Summarizing Observations

Judging from the foregoing observations and the current state of ICT research, there is mounting evidence against the productivity paradox and in support of a significant impact of ICTs on economic growth (i.e., productivity surge). In our opinion, a plausible explanation of the pessimistic results obtained in the first wave of studies on the relationship between investment in ICTs and productivity is that such studies suffered from several conceptual and technical deficiencies. Most notably, the amount and quality of data were restricted. This inhibited the application of more embracing analytical methodologies.

Also, many studies did not consider the fact that the impact of ICTs is associated with a time lag. This omission substantially contributed to distortion of the results. Also, the bulk of these studies were conducted in the United States, meaning that the distortion of the results can also be attributed to locational effects. Finally, by adopting a high level of data aggregation, some of the studies missed the true dynamics, which can only be captured at the micro-level of analysis.

B. Developing Country Evidence

As already mentioned above, so far relatively little comparable efforts have been undertaken to build a body of well-researched evidence for developing economies, regarding the causal effects between ICTs and economic development. One such study is attributed to the UNU/WIDER. In a macro-level survey of a sample of developing economies, researchers observed one basic difference between developed and developing countries. In the case of the former, the share of ICTs in total investment is high, while in the case of the latter it is low. However, according to the findings, there are no unambigous linkages between investments in ICTs and economic development. Pohjola (2000) attributes this deficit of such investments, which complement ICTs, as physical infrastructure and human capital.

In our opinion, another plausible explanation of the observed relationship is that it mirrors the backward status of ICT research on the African continent and other developing regions. Analogous to the observations related to the ICT productivity paradox in industrialized countries in the late 1980s and early 1990s, the studies on developing economies apparently suffer from several deficiencies: the amount and quality of data, the ommission of considerations for time lag, inappropriate empirical formulations, etc. The methodology used in the UNU/WIDER study, for instance, contains inherent deficits and is likely to produce biased results. In particular, the overall low share of ICTs in aggregate national investments typical for developing economies obscures the internal ICT returns to individual ICT-adopting enterprises therein. Therefore, productivity gains made at the micro-level cannot be sufficiently captured at the macro-level of analysis.

At the micro-level, the role of ICTs on development is equally scantly researched for developing countries. However, commendable work in this area is attributable to Lal (1996), whose study offers interesting lessons on the impact of ICT adoption on the performance of enterprises in poor economies. The study of Indian enterprises reveals that in developing countries ICTs do make a difference. Accordingly, in a survey involving 59 electric and electronic manufacturing SMEs chiefly employing less than 50 people,[3] Lal (1996) noted higher profit margins, skill intensity, and export and import intensities for firms using ITs.

IV. REFLECTIONS ON AND EVIDENCE OF THE ROLE OF ICTS IN AFRICA'S ECONOMIC DEVELOPMENT

Just as for developing countries as a whole, the status of research on the effect of ICTs on development in African economies is dismal. Some literature devoted to the subject is based on *a priori* postulations of the linkages between ICTs and development. These reports mainly constitute excerpts, which present perceptions based on the authors' knowledge of African economies, but are barely backed with hard evidence (Odedra *et al.*, 2001; Aden, 2000; Diop, 2000).

At the micro-level, in what constitutes a rare departure from the generally disappointing state of research, at least one important study has so far been conducted. In that study, the author teamed up with researchers from four universities in East Africa and Bonn University (Germany) to conduct the *East Africa SME Survey*. The regional survey had a strong emphasis on the relationship between ICTs and micro-level productivity and profitability. In this section, we first present general reflections and then complement them with empirical observations regarding the *East Africa SME Survey*.

A. ICT DEVELOPMENT IN AFRICA AND IMPLICATIONS FOR ECONOMIC DEVELOPMENT

Unfortunately, to date, the potential role of ICTs in Africa's economic development has not attracted sufficient research interest from reputable individuals and/or institutions. Thus, in attempting to understand the issue, one needs to have deep insights into the pattern of development of ICTs on the continent and try to build a case on them. Therefore, although no rigorous macro-level empirical study has so far systematically dealt with the issue, the available evidence on the development of ICTs in Africa suggests that their impact on the continent's development has so far been minimal. As pointed out by Odedra *et al.* (2001), Aden (2000), and Diop (2000):

- In terms of individual ICTs, despite inter-country differences Africa remains overall the least computerized continent. Also, its telephone density is the worst in any continent.
- Africa is beleaguered by extensive underutilization of available ICT capabilities. This deficiency can be attributed to a lack of complementary infrastructure, equipment, and personnel. For instance, very often the erratic electricity power supply, underdeveloped telephone transmission lines and networks, etc., are substantially accountable for the suboptimal use of ICT capabilities by most of African economies.
- Generally, for a very long time, African countries lacked clear and particularly favorable ICTs policies to ensure a systematic diffusion of the pertinent technologies. In Tanzania, the government banned the importation of computers from 1974–1993 (Majuva, 2000). Also, Kenya used to levy a 100% import tax on ICT investments. Despite general changes toward friendly tax regimes for ICTs imports (such as Mauritius charging 0%), given the limited diffusion of ICTs in Africa it is imperative to take concerted action. The bottom line should be to accord ICT imports special treatment and introduce moderate rates.
- Most users of ICTs in Africa are those supported by their institutions, usually through donor-funded projects. Thus, popular use of ICTs is a dream yet to be realized.

In addition to these points, we are of the opinion that the widespread ICT illiteracy and semi-illiteracy (particularly related to computers) of most decision-makers in most African institutions (such as ministries or Universities) significantly erodes the spread of ICTs and their beneficial application. In connection with this deficit, ICTs are largely used for routine transactional activities, as opposed to analytical strategic activities.

B. Overall Macroeconomic Picture

1. Correlation Between Investments in ICT Infrastructure and GDP per Capita

At the macro-economic level, the ICTs productivity hypothesis implies that countries with higher ICTs investments should record better economic development indicators. In this context, a comparison of national ICT infrastructures and gross national product (GNP) per capita are presented in Table 21.1

TABLE 21.1   Comparison of Selected ICT Infrastructure and GDP per Capita

	ICTs Infrastructure Penetration per 1000 People in 1998		GNP per Capita in 1999 in U.S. $
	Phone Mainline Penetration	Personal Computers	
Botswana	69	7.5	3,240
Morocco	54	2.5	1,200
Tanzania	4	1.6	240
South Africa	115	47.4	3,160
Sub-Saharan Africa	14	7.5	500
Uganda	3	1.5	320
For comparison:			
East Asia and Pacific	70	14.1	1,000
World	146	70.6	4,890
High income	567	311.2	25,730

Source: WB 2001: 274–275, and 310–311.

for selected African and other economies. The results, which present simple indicators of ICT–economic development linkages, reflect the existence of a correlation between ICTs infrastructure and GNP per capita. Undeniably, higher positive correlation does not necessarily prove that increased use of ICTs causes greater GNP per capita, partly because the relationship could be a reverse one; that is, economies with higher GNP per capita are likely to invest more in an ICT infrastructure.[4] However, the results also give important hints as to the relationship between the two variables and underscore a positive linkage between ICTs infrastructure and GDP per capita.

2. Effects of ICTs in View of the Overall Pattern of Economic Activity

The extent to which the application of ICTs can impact economic development depends on the overall pattern of economic activity. As discussed, low levels of economic activity, in general, are barriers to improved economic activity and substantially render the use of ICTs less effectual. Some of the pertinent factors indicative of missing development catalysts (and which are discussed further later in this chapter) include the restricted diffusion of ICTs and under-development of the information economy.

These problems are exacerbated by the apparent limited absence of a critical mass of skills in general and ICT literacy in particular, as well as the lack of a critical mass of basic infrastructure in general and ICT infrastructure (e.g., telecommunications infrastructure) in particular. The skill-related factors pose technical barriers to the utilization of available ICTs resources. The infrastructure-related factors prohibit widespread and significant use of ICTs. Also, at the skills–infrastructure interface, a range of skills is needed to ensure good maintenance of the ICT infrastructure.

Other missing catalysts for development are related to enterprise characteristics and business environment beyond the level of the enterprise (discussed further in the next section).

C. MICROECONOMIC EVIDENCE: LESSONS FROM THE EAST AFRICA SME SURVEY

Though still at an early stage of analysis, the *East Africa SME Survey* probably provides the most extensive and research-founded evidence on the potential for ICTs to be technologies that stimulate development in Africa. According to the findings of this broad-based micro-level study, inter-enterprise performance differentials are partly explained by investments in ICTs. Hence, both inter-enterprise growth and productivity differences are partly explained by investments in ICTs. Also, the ICT-driven growth can be linked to the enhancement of productivity. This is manifested by, among other things, internal ICT returns, ICT thresholds, organizational growth, employment creation, and ICT externalities. Besides, investments in ICTs bear important scale effects, which in turn affect productivity.

1. Organizational Growth and Employment Creation

The results of the *East Africa SME Survey* suggest that ICT adopters tend to grow in terms of both number of employees and investments in physical capital. Thus, beyond enhancing scale efficiency, ICTs enable enterprises in the long run to follow their (productivity-enhancing) expansion path and grow to optimal scales of operations.[5] Invariably, enterprises investing in ICTs tend to grow in terms of both number of employees and stock of investments in non-ICT physical capital (Table 21.2). Notably, on the average non-ICTs adopters are more labor intensive, but in the long run ICT adopters appear to be more significant in terms of the creation of employment.

2. Applications of ICTs and Performance: Linkages and Requirements

a. Productivity and Internal Returns of ICTs

The depictions by Lal (1996) that even in poor economies ICTs make a difference are confirmed by preliminary results of the *East Africa SME Survey*, according to which inter-enterprise productivity and profitability differences are partly explained by investments in ICTs.[6]

TABLE 21.2   Impact of ICTs on Growth in Number of Employees and Investments in Non-ICT Physical Capital

	Growth of Number of Employees, 1997–1999			Growth of Number of Employees, 1998–1999			Growth of Investments in Non-ICT Physical Capital, 1997–1999			Growth of Investments in Non-ICT Physical Capital, 1998–1999		
	%	SD	N	%	SD	N	%	SD	N	%	SD	N
Non-ICT adopters	4.7	14	29	2.7	13	29	61	72	30	19	28	30
ICTs adopters	5.2	14	63	2.1	12	63	34	165	65	10.4	61	65
Entire sample	5.1	14	92	2.3	12	92	42	141	97	12.9	52	97

Notes: N= number of enterprises in the sample; SD=standard deviation.
Source: East Africa SME Survey.

TABLE 21.3   Impact of ICTs on Costs and Profits

Enterprise Category	Average Sales Profits per Employee in 1998 in TAS[a]	Average Cost per Unit of Output in 1998 in TAS[a]
Non-ICT adopters	2825.30	9915.00
All ICT adopters	2745.70	92895
Adopters investing more than U.S. $800 in ICTs	2857.4	7898.0
Adopters investing more than U.S. $1500 in ICTs	2905.20	9555.0

[a]TAS, Tanzanian shillings.
Source: East Africa SME Survey.

As portrayed in Table 21.3, ICTs contributed to both cost reduction and increase in profits. Though *prima facie*, these results appear to be inconclusive as regards the linkages between ICTs infrastructure and profitability, more rigorous econometric estimation proved that enterprises investing more than U.S. $1500 in ICT infrastructures recorded positive ICTs internal returns. Also, enterprises investing more than U.S. $1500 in ICTs recorded comparatively high percentages of exports.

b. ICTs Thresholds

The positive ICT productivity impact appears to be tied to a minimum threshold of investment in ICTs, as reflected by the changing relationship between average sales profits and average units costs (Table 21.3). As pointed out in the previous paragraph, in one econometric estimation with a threshold variable, investments in ICTs greater than U.S. $1500 resulted in positive ICT internal returns.[7]

The results are presented in Table 21.4, for both the full baseline model and its restricted form. In the model, three indicators of ICTs ($k2$, ml_k2, and $k2 > 1500$) were used to assess the *internal returns of* ICTs and ICT *externalities*, and concrete ICT *threshold effects*, alongside other variables. The results reveal a positive impact of investments in ICTs on returns to both labor and physical capital, underscoring the existence of *internal* or *private* (i.e., to the enterprise) benefits for enterprises investing in ICTs. In the baseline model, the coefficients for l and m are statistically highly significant, while the coefficient for *size* is statistically significant at 7.2%. Also, all three variables carry the logically expected signs.

The remaining regressors are insignificant, though their coefficients carry the correct signs. Generally, limited clues on inter-enterprise profitability differentials can be drawn from the variables for *eage*, *cur*, *internal effects of ICTs*, *non-ICT capital stock*, and *tecfr* because, in part, the aggregation of data may obscure sectoral fixed effects (i.e., data drawn from food processing, textile manufacturing, and tourist enterprises). Also, there might be limitations associated with the quality of data.

The results of the reduced form of the model (which excludes most of the insignificant variables in the full baseline model) show that alongside l and m and *size*, profitability is subject to internal threshold effects in terms of investments in ICTs. The latter is manifested by the coefficient of the variable $k2 > 1500$. Enterprises with ICT capital stock valued at more than U.S. $1500 in 1997 recorded higher rates of labor profitability in 1998. Moreover, the coefficients of the variables for ml_k2 (which proxies for locational diffusion of ICTs) and *cur* carry the expected negative and positive signs, respectively, although both are not significant at conventional levels.

The observations in Table 21.4 are complemented with *scale economies* (i.e., specific scale requirements), in order for enterprises to benefit from ICTs. Hence, returns to ICTs are contingent upon fixed factors of production (hinting that a certain critical size is necessary), so that (compared to smaller enterprises), larger enterprises are more likely to benefit from pertinent investments.

c. ICTs Externalities

Negative ICT externalities appear to be constraining the productivity impact of ICTs. In the survey, the external effect was estimated by the mean locational level of investments in ICTs in the five towns where data were collected. Thus, it is a measure of the impact of the diffusion of ICTs in a location on the

TABLE 21.4   OLS Estimation of the APF for Associations between Labor Profitability and Selected Explanatory Variables: Pooled Data[a]

Variable	Coefficient	Standard Error	t-Value	t-Prob
Baseline model				
Constant	*2.133*	*1.103*	*1.917*	*0.059****
eage (in 1998)	0.075	0.121	0.625	0.534
size (in 1998)	*0.492*	*0.269*	*1.827*	*0.072****
k1 (in 1997)	0.052	0.077	0.676	0.501
k2 (in 1997)	−0.050	0.059	−0.849	0.399
k2 > 1500 (in 1997)	0.219	0.199	1.100	0.275
ml_k2 (in 1997)	−0.096	0.110	−0.870	0.387
l (in 1998)	*−0.871*	*0.135*	*−6.442*	*0.000***
m (in 1998)	*0.489*	*0.059*	*8.224*	*0.000***
tecfr (in 1997)	0.065	0.099	0.661	0.325
Cur (in 1998)	0.466	0.471	0.990	0.325
Restricted form of the baseline model				
Constant	2.468	0.959	2.574	0.012
size (in 1998)	*0.529*	*0.237*	*2.234*	*0.028*
k2 >1500 (in 1997)	*0.253*	*0.137*	*1.846*	*0.069*
ml_k2 (in 1997)	−0.133	0.099	−1.341	0.184
l (in 1998)	*−0.858*	*0.130*	*−6.607*	*0.000***
m (in 1998)	*0.489*	*0.058*	*8.375*	*0.000***
Cur (in 1998)	0.375	0.442	0.849	0.398

Regression model (extended form)		Regression model (reduced form)	
R^2	= 0.649	R^2	= 0.641
$\bar{R}^2$	= 0.602	$\bar{R}^2$	= 0.614
F-value	= 13.875	F-value	= 23.499
F-prob	= 0.000*	F-prob	= 0.000*
SEE	= 0.4412	SEE	= 0.4349
N−K	= 74	N−K	= 78

[a]The text in italics indicates the explanatory variables which are significant within up to a 10% level of significance; *=very small value, **=significant slightly above the conventional levels, ***=significant above the conventional levels but below 10%, K= number of explanatory variables including the constant term.

Notes: Modeling partial factor profitability using $r_{\pi L} = \prod / L$ as a proxy for labor profitability. Explanatory variables: mixed lagged variables, except for *eage*, *size*, *l*, *m*, and *cur*. Dependent variable: $r_{\pi l}$ in 1998. Sample size = N= 85.

productivity of local enterprises. More widespread use of ICTs in a location (e.g., as observed in the cities of Dar es Salaam and Arusha), increases the internal benefits of ICTs.[8] Overall, this evidence suggests that the restricted diffusion of ICTs in Tanzania retards the internal returns to ICTs. It also underlines our argument that the aggregation of data obscures the productivity impact of ICTs at the micro-level.

D. CHARACTERIZING THE MACROSCOPIC CHANNELS OF ICTs IMPACT ON PERFORMANCE

Based on the *East Africa SME Survey*, ICTs seem to affect enterprises by positively impacting performance through two interrelated channels: the efficiency channel and the scale channel. In terms of efficiency, ICTs improve the allocation of the scarce enterprise resources in the various factor inputs (i.e.,allocational efficiency) and augment the competency of resource use (i.e., technical efficiency). Through the scale channel, ICTs favorably affect the scale of operations and enhance scale efficiency. These effects are briefly highlighted in the following sections.

1. Improving Efficiency in the Allocation of Resources

In allocative terms, ICTs contribute to the improvement of the allocation of resources. The impact of ICTs in this area seems to be more direct. For instance, by providing the necessary information input, ICTs help enterprises to improve their price efficiency by choosing input–output combinations to minimize cost at prevailing prices of factor inputs. Hence, they improve the ability of the enterprise to use inputs in optimal proportions. This influence of ICTs (and production NTs in particular) is what economists technically refer to as *allocative* or *price efficiency*.

Together with technical efficiency, the allocative or price efficiency forms part of *economic efficiency*. Failure to choose the most cost-efficient combination of factor inputs (e.g., due to constrained access to factor markets) would result in *allocative inefficiency*. Among the sample enterprises, 92% reported that, since adopting telephones, they have managed to geographically extend their factor markets, underscoring the role of ICTs in facilitating the access of enterprises to factor markets. Likewise, 96% of the sample enterprises achieved geographical extension of their product markets with the help of telephone technology.

2. Augmenting Technical Efficiency

ICTs also augment, albeit indirectly, the *technical efficiency*. By improving access to information, they enable enterprises to cut costs through better access to both factor and product markets. Thus, an enterprise can increase output without increasing (at least) one input or can reduce input quantities without proportionally reducing the output quantity. For instance, the geographical extension of factor markets can reduce the cost of sourcing of factor inputs and improve the output–input ratio. Likewise, the geographical extension of product markets can increase the revenues of enterprises, also improving the output–input ratio. Thus, ICTs are *de facto* sourcing/marketing technologies, contributing to efficiency in this sphere. The cost and profit figures presented in Table I suggest this kind of influence for ICTs adopters.

3. Scaling Effect

ICTs further improve the performance of an enterprise by impacting its scale. In this context, the significance of the scaling effect is first underlined by the possibility that a certain critical size is necessary for competitiveness. Hence, *scale economies* or *fixed production factors* may cause productivity deficits, a situation usually attributed to the poor performance of small enterprises. Concretely, due to resource constraints (e.g., limited amounts of own factor inputs, restricted access to credit markets), smaller enterprises may fail to take advantage to move up along the productivity-enhancing expansion path. For poor economies, the significance of scale derives from the dominant position of SMEs in the enterprise sector. Hence, the findings that indicate that ICTs have a *scaling-up* effect are of great importance for developing economies.

Presumably, the combined effect of the growth of the number of employees and physical capital stock positively affect the scale of operations, bringing ICTs adopters closer to the optimal scale. Moreover, the growth seems to vary greatly among ICTs adopters. This is logical and can be attributed to, *inter alia*, the big variations in enterprise characteristics of ICTs adopters. Also, to the extent that ICTs explain productivity differentials between two enterprises of the same size, they play a role in enhancing scale efficiency. In other words, given two enterprises of the same size, the ICT adopter is likely to outperform the non-ICT adopter.

V. FACTORS THAT LIMIT RETURNS TO INVESTMENTS IN ICTS IN AFRICA

A. RESTRICTED DIFFUSION OF ICTS

The restricted diffusion of ICTs in Africa is demonstrated by several parameters. Among other things, Africa's telephone network is the least developed in the world. Also, Africa is the least computerized continent. One glaring example of the restricted diffusion of ICTs is provided by the national ICT infrastructure, as

TABLE 21.5   Diffusion and Costs of Selected ICTs in Tanzania, South Africa, and Germany, 1994–1997

	Tanzania	Republic of South Africa (RSA)	Germany	Tanzania/RSA (%)
Telephone main lines (per 1000 persons)	3	107	550	2.8
Waiting list (thousands)	37	116	—	31.9
Average cost of a 3-minute local telephone call (U.S. $)	0.1	0.07	0.14	142.8
Mobile phones (per 1000 persons)	1	37	—	2.7
Personal computers (per 1000 persons)	1.6	41.6	255	3.8
Internet hosts (per 10,000 persons)	0.04	34.02	140.58	0.1
Televisions (per 1000 persons)	21	125	—	16.8

Sources: World Bank (2000) African Development Indicators 2000, Washington, D.C.: World Bank; World Bank (1999) The Little Data Book 1999, Washington, D.C.: World Bank.

depicted in Table 21.5 which shows the pattern of ICT physical infrastructures in Germany, Tanzania, and South Africa. The depicted nationwide diffusion of ICTs in an average African economy, as shown for Tanzania is conspicuously frivolous by international standards, as is underscored by a comparison with South Africa and Germany. For instance, the intensity of telephone main lines and mobile phones is less than 4% of the comparable intensity for the South Africa.

Another important example of restricted diffusion of ICTs is presented in the micro-level pattern of ICTs diffusion as suggested by ICT investments shown in Table 21.6, with respect to enterprise level investments in ICT equipment. Notably, 56.5% of all sample enterprises invest not more than U.S. $200 in ICTs facilities such as phones, computers, etc. This puts a high number of enterprises below the critical mass in terms of investments in ICTs. Overall, the possession and use of ICTs is relatively limited: While 99% of the sample enterprises reported using face-to-face communication, only 33% used computer-based technologies for business communication purposes. The most frequently used ICT is the telephone, reportedly used by 87% of the enterprises for business communication.

Overall, the results underscore the limited capabilities of enterprises to build competitive ICT infrastructures. Also, the minimal ICT investments imply technological isolation from the rest of the world, corroborating the observation by Biggs et al. (1995) that most enterprises in Africa operate in information-poor environments. They ascribe the deficit to (1) restricted inter-enterprise horizontal and vertical linkages, (2) preference of large-scale enterprises (LSEs)

TABLE 21.6 Cumulative Stock of Investments in ICTs for Tanzania's Enterprises in 1999

Level of Investments in ICTs (U.S. $)	Proportion of Sample (%)
Up to 100	40.8
Up to 200	56.5
Up to 300	61.2
Up to 400	63.3
Up to 500	67.3
Up to 600	68.0
Up to 700	69.4
Up to 800	70.1
Above 800	29.9
Above 1500	24.5

Source: East Africa SME Survey.

for intra-enterprise vertical linkages, (3) limited subcontracting, (4) limited foreign direct investment (FDI) which in turn reduces the prospects for learning by copying and the ability to benchmark the firm's operations against internationally competitive firms in the same line of business, (5) weak training and specialized consultancy services, and (6) poor information sources for technical and business matters (Biggs et al., 1995; Matambalya, 2000a).

The limited resources of the enterprises and the high costs of procuring and using ICTs seem to be the major factors that hinder the diffusion of ICTs. This explanation was given by 91% of the enterprises surveyed that do not use computer-dependent ICTs. A lack of computers is attributed to the high costs of hard- and software (80%) and high labor costs of computer-skilled employees (62%). Besides, close to 72% of these enterprises did not even foresee the use of computer-dependent ICTs. This could result in limited business skills or a market situation where such lower order sources of competitiveness as cheap labor or raw materials still enable enterprises to be competitive.

The low level of ICT diffusion can be attributable to several factors. To borrow from the East Africa SME Survey, the reasons cited by most Tanzanian enterprises for not having computers of their own included high prices of hard and software (cited by 80% of the respondents) and high costs for computer-skilled employees (cited by 62% of all sample enterprises). An important aspect of cost-related diffusion limitations refers to regulations on proprietary rights, in accordance with the existing intellectual property rights (IPRs) regimes. Notably, many insights, ideas, etc., that can be accessed through ICTs are proprietary and underlie national and/or international laws that govern the use of such intellectual properties as patents, copyrights, trademarks, etc.

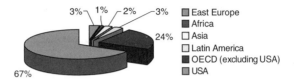

FIGURE 21.1   Internet users in 1999 as percentage of population. (From Wider, 2000, p. 8.)

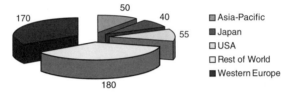

FIGURE 21.2   Estimated Internet users (million) by region in 2000. (From *Information Week*, 72, 8, 1999.)

B. UNDERDEVELOPMENT OF THE INFORMATION ECONOMY

The gross underdevelopment of the IE in Africa is depicted in Figs. 21.1 and 21.2. These figures complement the observations presented in Table 21.3. They also underscore the gap in terms of new-technology-based firms (NTBFs) in general, and local ICT providers in particular. These deficits can be attributed to many factors—most prominently, lack of requisite technological/scientific bases and local ICT providers and the relatively heavy knowledge and capital requirements. Consequently, while the turnover of the global ICT market surpassed U.S. $2 trillion in 1999 (with an annual growth rate of 10%) and is estimated to hit the phenomenal value of U.S. $3000 trillion by 2004, apparently the share of the developing economies is trivial.

Globally, the restricted diffusion of ICTs in Africa is underscored in Fig. 2. Notably, only 1% of Africa's population used the Internet in 1999, the smallest continental percentage. Implicitly, ICT-adopting enterprises, which are part of this meager 1%, have to deal with very small ICT-connected markets. Overall, the poor ICT diffusion restricts the ability of enterprises to use ICT as a tool for the extension of their factor and product markets.

VI. ESSENTIAL CONDITIONS FOR THE ENHANCEMENT OF ICTS RETURNS

While acknowledging the positive impact of ICTs, it is important to realize that ICTs are no panacea. Technically, a host of forces influence the productivity of enterprises and explain their performance differentials. Thus, whether one economic unit is more competitive than the other is, in reality, determined by a sum of enterprise-specific, sector-wide, economy-wide forces. These are complemented by influences from the international system (i.e., regional and global level forces). Therefore, in order to enhance the productivity and development impact of ICTs, it is necessary not only to improve the level of efficiency in the utilization of ICT capabilities, but also to promote other development catalysts.

A. Improve the Level of Efficiency in Utilizing Existing ICT Capabilities

In order to enhance the internal ICTs returns, it is important to improve the level of efficiency in utilizing available ICT capabilities. This is because, while the economic development impact of ICTs also depends on the level of efficiency in the utilization of ICT facilities, in practice the underutilization of ICTs is a widespread problem in African economies. This can be attributed to several reasons. Among them is the lack of human resources with the requisite expertise. Besides, although the awareness regarding the development potential associated with the use of ICTs is increasing, for many decision-makers in particular, it is still an abstract phenomenon, which they have never confronted.

The knowledge deficit by decision-makers usually translates into decisions and actions that make the application of ICTs less effectual. With corruption still rampant in many Africa countries and most ICTs users being those supported by their institutions through (usually) donor-funded projects, profitable investment in ICTs is not a pressing need. The reality is that, typically, the selection of the vendor and equipment is made by an ICT-illiterate/semi-illiterate individual without due consultation with the experts. Usually such decisions are flavored by considerations other than the stimulation of performance.

Also, at the more technical level, advance procurement of software without prior sufficient knowledge on their strengths and weaknesses is common. In addition, in Africa, ICTs are still mainly used for routine functional purposes (e.g., routine administrative activities) and rarely for analytical purposes. This problem is again closely linked to lack of expertise at various operational and strategic levels.

B. Promotion of other Development Catalysts

Research also shows the existence of dynamic complementarities between ICTs and other development catalysts. ICTs count more in combination with other factors. To sum up, some statistical analysis of the data show that there are dynamic complementarities between selected explanatory variables. For instance, the skills of the labor force and level of investments in ICTs seem to enhance each other's positive impact on productivity. The same applies for the management skills and levels of investment in ICTs. Also, scaling-up in terms of various variables (e.g., number of employees and stock of investments in ICTs) seems to bilaterally enhance each other's positive productivity impact.

The statistical analysis of the data show that in Tanzania, analogous to observations elsewhere in the world, a large part of the differences in productivity between enterprises is explained by attributes of the enterprises themselves. Hence, besides the enterprise capabilities in terms of *factor inputs* (i.e., labor, physical, and production material), such enterprise characteristics as size, capacity utilization rate, investments in NTs, and the skills of both the management staff and the labor force as a whole, are important for productivity. Productivity increases with an increasing volume of inputs and follows the general rule of scale economies (i.e., larger enterprises tend to be more productive). Also, the skills of labor and management staff (crucial for task-level efficiency) provide leverage for productivity, as in higher capacity utilization rates and more intensive use of NTs other than ICTs, the payoff of which lies in their efficiency.

Moreover, enterprises in Tanzania still face a myriad of constraints in relation to the business environment, beyond the level of the enterprise. One observation is that an inadequate public infrastructure significantly hinders productivity. According to the econometric estimations, the performance of enterprise located in areas where they face stringent infrastructural inefficiencies was substantially subdued. Also, on the average, smaller enterprises and enterprise located in smaller towns, seem to be more vulnerable to deficits in the provision of a public infrastructure.

The Appendix depicts a summary of responses to a question regarding the major obstacles to doing business. The enterprises were requested to respond to the following question: *Please indicate on a six-point scale which in your opinion pose obstacles in doing business?* The possible answers were "always," "mostly," "frequently," "sometimes," "seldom," and "never." Accordingly, of the 17 obstacles suggested, the highly ranked obstacles included unfavorable tax regulations, regulations for business start-up, business financing, corruption, reliability of the product markets, foreign trade regulations, and inflation. Tax rates of 79.3% are the biggest businessmen have to cope with. Tax regulations ("always": 79.3%) are followed by regulations for business start-up (64.4%), business financing (50.3%), inadequate supply of infrastructure (43.1%), corruption (35.2%), and the reliability of the market (32.7%). On the other hand (presumably as an expression of internal political stability), such factors as terrorism, tribalism, and crime did not seem to constitute key obstacles for doing business. Hence, 73.6 and 64.3% of the entrepreneurs reported never having faced business constraints due to tribalism and terrorism, respectively.

VII. CONCLUSIONS

The debate in this chapter underlines the importance of ICTs for economic development in the contemporary context. Potentially, ICTs facilitate the creation of a level playing field and thereby open several development opportunities for African and other developing economies. Generally, they play multiple roles as inputs into the production process and as a special kind of infrastructure that enhances the efficiency of other factor inputs. Also, they allow greater participation in the world economy.

Overall, the evidence discussed in this chapter adds to the growing body of evidence that ICTs constitute an important ingredient for economic development. ICTs increase economic productivity, accelerate growth, promote employment and income, prop up more efficient public administration, and increase public participation and democracy.

Moreover, the observations emphasize that, though the digital underdevelopment is real and does negatively impact on productivity, the challenge facing economic units in African and other poor economies goes well beyond the perceived problem of the digital divide. Thus, in order to enhance ICTs returns, besides encouraging sustained investments in ICTs in order to attain a critical level of pertinent investments and the development of ICTs infrastructure, it is also necessary to invest in complementary assets, particularly human resources and various kinds of physical infrastructures, which are equally important catalysts for sustainable development.

A. Ranking the Obstacles for Doing Business by Tranzanian SMEs

The goals for greater diffusion and application of ICTs must be pursued in conjuction with the development of the other (at least) equally important conditions for enhanced productivity. In particular, efforts must be directed at overcoming the severe resource constraints, improving the overall quality of the enterprises (in terms of such aspects as labor and management skills, capacity utilization, size relative to optimal scale of operations, or investments in NTs). Furthermore, inorder to create a stable leverage for sustainable domestic and international competitiveness, it is also important to address the many macroeconomic constraints.

VIII. SUMMARY

Several recent studies, mainly conducted in developed economies, emphasize the role that information and communication technologies (ICTs) play in economic development. Notably, ICTs enable economic units to increase productivity, thus building a base for sustainable growth. Given these facts, it is worthwhile to ask ourselves, whether, in which manner, and to what extent ICT adoption enhances the development of poor economies. In this chapter, we look critically at the links between ICTs and economic development in Africa. In our analysis, we highlight the development of ICTs in Africa and their impact on the development of the economic units thereof.

Also, we substantiate our observations by referring to empirical findings from the *East Africa SME Survey*. The survey involved collection of detailed data from the three economies of the East African Community (EAC): Kenya, Tanzania, and Uganda. We analyze 150 randomly selected enterprises in the food-processing, textile, and tourist sectors in Tanzania. We conclude that ICTs prop up productivity-propelled growth. However, ICTs present just one factor in the development equation. In order to have a better grasp of the development patterns and characteristics of the African economies, we have to bear in mind the influence of a host of other conditions as well. The *East Africa SME Survey*, for instance, provides strong evidence of the dependency of enterprise productivity and profitability on enterprise characteristics, extrinsic influences at the macro level and beyond, and dynamic interplay among the individual determinants of productivity and profitability. Thus, the underlying strategy to enhance development should be more embracing and, in a systemic way, address a broader spectrum of factors that influence production.

ACKNOWLEDGMENTS

Some of the ideas presented here are based on observations from the East Africa SME Survey. In this context, thanks are due to Alexander von Humboldt Foundation and Centre for Development (ZEF) of Bonn University for funding the East Africa SME Survey. Rebecca Neuwirth of ZEF is credited for providing useful research assistance. Among other things, she used the dataset to generate most of the tables and figures that are used in this chapter. My gratitude is also extended to Esther Ishengoma of the University of Dar es Salaam for reading the original manuscript and suggesting some constructive changes. I am also indebted to Dr. Susanna Wolf of ZEF for the scholarly support throughout the East Africa SME Survey. My sincere regards are also due to Professor Dr. Joachim von Braun of ZEF for the invaluable and intellectual guidence, and material facilitation for the East Africa SME Survey. Finally, I am grateful to the anonymous reviewer, whose critical comments were useful in revising this chapter. The views expressed here are the author's sole responsilibility.

DISCUSSION QUESTIONS

1. Which types of skills are needed to promote the effect of application of ICTs?
2. What role is played by the overall low share of ICTs in the total investment of developing economies and on the micro-level internal ICTs returns?

3. What are the appropriate empirical formulations for analysis of the development impact of ICTs in economies of various calibers?

4. What are the overriding reasons for the underutilization of ICT capacities in African and other develop economies?

5. What is the effect on the overall level of economic activity of micro-economic ICTs returns?

6. Which general ICT thresholds are needed for ICTs to be more effectual?

7. How do general ICTs diffusion differ from ICTs diffusion barriers specific to sector(s), region(s), countries, etc.?

8. Analyze the allocational, technical, and economic efficiency impact of ICTs in Africa.

9. What is the impact of ICTs on the alternative micro-economic growth dimensions: financial, organizational, strategic, and structural?

10. Do a comparative survey of the extent to which ICTs in Africa and elsewhere are used for strategic and analytical purposes versus administrative, routine purposes, and the impact of these application patterns on the ability of ICTs to stimulate performance.

11. Which types of skills are skills needed to promote the effect of application of ICTs?

NOTES

[1] The ERP is an international collaborative program partnering the Center for Development Research (ZEF) of Bonn University and four East African Universities: Kenyatta and Maseno (both Kenya), Dar es Salaam (Tanzania), and Makerere (Uganda).

[2] The theory postulates the locational link between innovation and production. Hence, new goods (i.e., those in the initial phases of product life cycle) are mainly produced and exported by adavanced (industrialized) states. Eventually, the maturity and standardization of products intrinsically leads to a shift of comparative advantage in favor of comparatively less developed economies (as the former are high-cost locations).

[3] This size category is important, as it is likely to reflect the size of enterprises in most African economies. Indeed, the *East Africa SME Survey* revealed that most of the enterprises of this category in Tanzania employ 6 to 30 persons.

[4] To get more plausible results, a temporal component could be added. Accordingly, taking countries with the same level of GDP per capita initially, the pattern of development of their GDP per capita could be analyzed in relation to changes in specified ICT infrastructure variables, such as an increase in phone line penetration, a reduction in telephone tariff, increases in the number of Internet hosts, increases in the number of personal computers, etc. This will help to determine whether there is causality running from investments in ICT infrastructure to GDP per capita.

[5] In order to investigate the scale effects of ICTs, we specified a growth function in which, enterprise *SCALE* is expressed as function of the vectors X, Z, and ϕ and Ω. The general form of a tractable scale model is specified as:

$$SCALE = \left(\beta_0 + \sum_{j=1}^{n1} \beta_j X_{jit}\right) + \sum_{\kappa=1}^{n2} \beta_k Z_{kit} + \sum_{l=1}^{n3} \beta_{lit} \Phi_{lit} + \sum_{m=1}^{n4} \beta_{mit} \Omega_{mit} + \varepsilon_{it}.$$

In this equation, the terms in the bracket represent the growth function, while those outside the bracket represent the control variables entered into the function. The subscript i indicates the observations for the ith enterprise ($i = 1, 2, 3, \ldots, N$, where N is the valid sample size), and t denotes the observation year. Also, the subscripts j, k, l and m stand for variables drawn from vectors X_{it}, Z_{it}, ϕ_{it}, and Ω_{it} for factor inputs, enterprise characteristics, influences beyond the enterprise, and complementarities among the elements of the vectors, X_{it}, Z_{it}, and ϕ_{it}, respectively. The β_s denote the coefficients of the specified explanatory variables, and ε is the error term. Also, j, k, l, and m denote the individual factors drawn from the corresponding vectors. Accordingly, $n1$, $n2$, $n3$, and $n4$ give the number of constituent variables for each vector introduced into the model.

[6]The tractable model for estimating the relationship between the specified input variables and the output variable (Y_{it}) were derived from an average production function (APF), in which, analogous to SCALE, output (productivity and profitability) is expressed as a function of the vectors X, Z, ϕ, and Ω. Hence, the general form of the APF can be expressed as:

$$Y_{it} = \left(\beta_0 + \sum_{j=1}^{n1} \beta_j X_{jit} \right) + \sum_{k=1}^{n2} \beta_k Z_{kit} + \sum_{l=1}^{n3} \beta_{lit} \Phi_{lit} + \sum_{m=1}^{n4} \beta_{mit} \Omega_{mit} + \varepsilon_{it}$$

In this equation, the terms in the bracket represent the production function, while those outside the bracket represent the control variables entered into the production function. The rest of the variables are as explained in the scale model above.

[7]Deriving from the general specifications, the model used to estimate the relationship between profit (π) as the output variable and the input variables is,

$$\pi_{it} = \begin{aligned} &(\alpha_0 + \alpha_1 k1 + \alpha_2 k2 + \alpha_3 k2 > US\$1500 + \alpha_4 l + \alpha_5 m) + \\ &(\alpha_6 eage + \alpha_7 size + \alpha_8 tcfr + \alpha_9 cur) + \alpha_{10} ml\_k2 + \varepsilon \end{aligned}$$

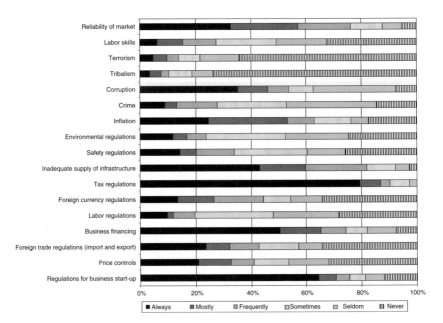

Source: East Africa SME Survey

The explanatory variables $k1$ and $k2$ denote non-ICTs and ICT capital (used to measure the internal effects of ICTs) respectively. The variable $k2>US\$1500$ is a threshold variable that indicates investments in ICT capital greater than U.S. $1500. It measures the internal threshhold effects of ICTs. The variables l and m stand for annual labor and material input costs, respectively. The variables *eage* and *size* denote enterprise age in years in 1998 and the number of employees (as a proxy for size) in 1998, respectively. The variables *tecfr* and *cur* denote investments in advanced technology as a proportion of $k1$ (as a proxy for technolgy frontier) and capacity utilization rate (in percentage), respectively. The variable *ml_k2* denotes the mean location investments in ICTs capital. The lower case letters denote that the estimations are based on logarithms. The stochastic errors are captured by the term ε.

[8]The reported estimations are based on the dataset for Tanzania. The locations are the two Lake Victoria towns of Mwanza and Musoma, the Indian Ocean coastal city of Dar es Salaam, Arusha (which is a tourist center in the north), and Zanzibar, a town on Zanzibar Island.

PART VI

Development Challenges, Policies, and Strategies

Economic Policies, Stabilization, and Reforms

SARAH BRYANT BOWER

College of Business Administration, Clarion University, Clarion, Pennsylvania 16214

KEY TERMS

Currency and money control reforms
Debt reforms
Economic growth
Economic stabilization
Financial market reforms
Fiscal reforms
GDP per capita

Government and civil services reforms
International Monetary Fund (IMF)
New Economic Recovery Program (NERP)
Parastatals
Privatization and deregulation
Structural Adjustment Programs (SAP)
Structural reforms
World Bank

I. GENERAL NATURE OF THE PROBLEM, ORIGIN, EVOLUTION, AND MANIFESTATIONS

Read almost any publication about what is going on in Africa and there are several messages that predominate. First, you see the same types of stories, again and again—those about wars, refugees and other effects of wars, droughts, floods, corruption, disease, and poverty. The second message is that there is no hope for a very long time, perhaps forever, of sustainable, positive changes taking effect. The third message is that many commentators and information sources describe Africa in the aggregate. The continent is most often discussed as if it were one country, one place, without the amazing diversity of countries. However, the issues are the same, for the most part. Governments across the continent have implemented poor domestic policies that have led to increasing debt burdens, deteriorating terms of trade, and in many ways have left their countries without the means for sustainable development. The first two messages are the ones that the people of African countries have the control to change. The third message will change as conditions improve. We, too, discuss the countries in Africa mostly in the aggregate but recognize the diversity of countries through discussion of data for individual countries.

In this chapter, we look at African economic stabilization and reform. We attempt to show that without political stability and the sustained will of governments and the people to undertake necessary steps toward improvement economic stabilization can never be achieved. We begin with some history of the political and economic circumstances of the continent in general since independence began around 1960 and recent economic performance of a sample of countries. Next, we briefly discuss relevant economic theories that are used to develop programs for stability and sustainable growth. Then, we discuss one country's experiences with structural adjustment programs. Finally, we draw conclusions and look to the future.

By way of definition, *economic stabilization* refers to policy changes that aim to achieve macroeconomic stability by reducing government spending and controlling excessive money growth that causes inflation to ultimately stabilize the domestic currency exchange rate. Closely linked are *structural reforms* that reduce government's involvement in the economy and allow for an increased role of markets. Support programs from the World Bank, the International Monetary Fund (IMF), and other donor/lending organizations (e.g., the United Nations) provide budgetary assistance, policy guidance, and other forms of assistance to bring about both microeconomic and macroeconomic reforms.

In examining economic stabilization and reform, there are several points to remember:

1. There are no easy answers. Theories can prescribe potential paths and solutions to achieve goals, but there are many caveats to consider. Theories and models are built by making assumptions, holding many factors constant, and generalizing in various ways.

2. No two countries are the same, even though discussions such as this one do generalize. There is a rich history that goes much deeper as one studies each country. However, what works for one country can provide information to guide policies for another country, but history, politics, geography, economic inputs, capabilities, and differences predominate. Some developing countries have not grown at all in the Western sense but have stayed as less developed countries, due to corruption, bad advise from outside organizations and individuals, wars and civil unrest, weather conditions, lack of know how, lack of leadership, lack of funds, or a poor geographic situation.

3. Economic stabilization does not lead to sustainable development unless there is political will on the parts of governments and people in general. As new policies are enacted, the initial reaction of the economy may be to decline before growth results. Examples of this principle are in currency devaluation or inflation control, where economic fortunes may get worse before they get better. Adverse factors, such as falling export prices, heavy debt service obligations, or low levels of education, cause discomfort, especially to the poor, that leads to strong political pressures to go back to the old, unhealthy policies that must be resisted.

4. People must trust that the government has the people's best interests at heart when making tough decisions. People must be informed and understand that changes take time. They must trust that the government is serious about sustaining efforts to improve the country's economic situation. After war, high inflationary bouts, or other destabilizing forces occur, government credibility takes years to rebuild.

II. A BRIEF HISTORY SINCE 1960: IS ECONOMIC STABILIZATION SUSTAINABLE?[1]

A country can achieve economic growth that is not sustainable. African countries' experiences in the 1960s attest to growth that was not sustainable into the 1970s or beyond. African countries gained independence at varied times from colonial masters after 1957 through about 1970, with Ghana being the first. These countries served colonial masters, with most Africans remaining in traditional farming and trading occupations. Many of the products produced went for export. After independence, in general, growth was based on export revenues from non-diversified primary products of agriculture and mining and on foreign aid. Governments took direct control of businesses, collected revenues, and directed development, with little emphasis on expansion of the private sector. Production concentrated on export products to increase government revenues and foreign exchange and on import-substitution industries that tried to replace goods from abroad. Employment increased, but primarily in the government sector.

Governments developed infrastructures, such as schools of higher education, roads, and electricity, in and around urban areas. These efforts to improve higher education were necessary to establish the next generation to run the government and infrastructure projects; however, there was little concern for rural areas. Food production was encouraged for the export sector, and there was a lack of emphasis on primary schools, health care, and local food production. Over time, these policies led to increases in overall population, heavy migration to urban areas, and dependence on imported foods. In addition, there was little comparative advantage in industry and manufacturing, little expertise within the countries, and very limited financial markets development.

Economic stability is built on political stability. Trust in a legitimate government is crucial to continuing, sustainable development. However, in the 1960s, African governments themselves proved unstable. Civil strife was common, as ethnic imbalances occurred and political power and prestige were desired. Changes in governments, often through military coups, led to reform reversals. Government spending had to be diverted from social infrastructure development to political stabilization (the famous guns-or-butter argument). "Proponents of the system, however, failed to foresee the economic stagnation that would result from the self-interest of bureaucrats; the military costs of maintaining political control; and the inefficiencies of public enterprises and price controls" (Hess and Ross 1997, p. 564).

The independence decade started out with growth that people thought could be sustained. There was much excitement at the progress made, but systems were too weak or not developed enough to lead to lasting development of the kind sought. Government spending of the 1960s could not continue without new revenue sources and positive returns on past investments to fuel continued growth and development.

Growth of the 1960s encouraged increased aid to Africa and also increased borrowing by governments from private and donor-agency sources. Debt levels increased, based on expected future revenues continuing as before. However, by the 1970s, world commodity prices fell (except oil), reducing government revenues. Increased oil prices adversely affected growth in all countries, except for the oil producers. African countries were particularly hard hit, due to vulnerabilities to changes in export conditions. Even the African oil-producing countries saw increased oil revenues being offset by deterioration in other sectors

From 1973 to 1980, growth in agriculture did not keep pace with growth in population. Devastating droughts, poor domestic government policies of heavy taxation on farmers, and negative terms of trade were some of the reasons that agricultural output declined for export and for domestic consumption. Also, other countries in the world experienced increased productivity in agriculture, leading to increasingly competitive markets. Export earnings dropped, as did growth prospects. Debt levels soared, mainly from donor agencies, as borrowing replaced revenues from exports (UNCTAD, 2000):

> The period between 1980 and 1994 witnessed a noticeable deterioration in the performance of most SSA (Sub-Saharan Africa) countries. Population grew faster than output, with per capita incomes falling, on average, by 0.6 per cent per annum. ...For every country which experienced positive per capital output growth during 1980–1994, two had negative per capita rates of growth. There were in fact only nine countries that had positive per capita growth and of these only in Botswana and

Mauritius (both already middle-income countries in 1980) was growth sufficient to tackle the challenges of economic development and poverty alleviation.

Currently, many of the same problems abound. Figures for Africa as a whole mask wide variations in growth across the continent. Table 22.1 shows data for 1995, 1998, and 1999 for 18 African countries. Income levels, as measured by GDP per capita,[2] are extremely low in most of the countries. People in Chad, Ethiopia, Kenya, Mozambique, Nigeria, Uganda, and Zambia live on about U.S. $1 per day, or less. Other countries are just above that level.

There are two bright spots, however. Botswana and Mauritius, mentioned earlier, had the highest GDP per capita at $3750 and $3500, respectively, in 1999. However, Botswana experienced high money growth in 1998 and 1999, which, if continued, could lead to destabilizing inflation. These two countries have low population growth figures, as well, compared to lower income countries.

Compare population growth rates in each country to GDP growth rates. The definition of *economic growth* is GDP rising at a faster rate than population rates. Eight of the 18 countries experienced GDP growth rates below population growth rates in at least one of the years. There is consensus of opinion among economists that African countries must grow by at least 6% to reach beyond subsistence development over the next 15 years. Only a few of these 18 countries have reached that level even in one year.

Debt accumulation over the past three decades has led to a major debt "overhang" problem, as countries struggle to pay even interest payments on monies owed to both public and private bodies. As shown in Table I, total debt service (interest payments) drains government coffers of funds needed to continue infrastructure development and maintenance and of the foreign exchange needed to pay for imports. For example, Algeria and Côte d'Ivoire spent about 10% of GDP on debt servicing in each of the years. Zambia's accumulated debt in 1998 was far greater at U.S. $5.5 billion than GDP at U.S. $3.4 billion. Problems with debt are so immense that the World Bank and IMF, as well as private lenders, have policies for debt forgiveness in place.

Correlated with high debt levels is the lack of investment in these countries. Note from the table that foreign direct investment (FDI) is low for most countries. According to the United Nations Conference on Trade and Development (UNCTAD), FDI distribution has been uneven among developing countries. In 1998, for example, developing Asian countries received 13.9%; Latin America and the Caribbean, 11.8%; and Africa, 1.3% of total world FDI, with the bulk of it going to a few countries in each region.[3] African countries have not been among the recipients of FDI, except in small amounts. Some economists lament the fact that little FDI goes to most developing countries, but it is understandable, because productive investment goes to countries that are serious about reforms. Investors invest money where returns are good and the possibility of repayment is high.

TABLE 22.1 Data for 18 African Countries[a]

		People			Economy									Trade & Finance				
Country	Year	Population, Total	Population Growth (Annual %)	Urban Population (% of Total)	GDP at Market Prices (current U.S. $)	GDP Growth (Annual %)	GDP per Capita (Thousands)	Exports of Goods and Services (% of GDP)	Imports of Goods and Services (% of GDP)	Gross Domestic Investment (% of GDP)	Current Revenue, Excluding Grants (% of GDP)	Overall Budget Deficit Including Grants (% of GDP)	Money and Quasi Money Growth (Annual %)	Foreign Direct Investment, Net Flows in Reporting Country (WDI, Current U.S. $)	Present Value of Debt (Current U.S. $)	Total Debt Service (TDS, Current U.S. $)	Short-Term Debt Outstanding (DOD, current U.S. $)	Aid per Capita (Current U.S. $)
Algeria	1995	29.1 M	2.2	56.6	41.3 B	3.8	1.42	27.5	31.2	32.2	30.6	−1.4	9.2	5.0 M	—	4.2 B	260.8 M	10.7
	1998	29.5 M	2.1	58.8	47.3 B	5.1	1.60	23.0	23.1	27.2	—	—	18.9	5.0 M	29.9 B	5.1 B	186.0 M	13.2
	1999	30.0 M	2.1	59.6	47.0 B	3.5	1.57	26.2	22.7	27.0	—	—	—	—	—	—	—	—
Botswana	1995	1.5 M	2.4	47.7	4.9 B	5.1	3.27	49.7	36.0	26.9	39.5	2.6	12.3	70.0 M	—	92.3 M	10.2 M	61.7
	1998	1.6 M	1.9	49.3	4.9 B	3.5	3.06	35.0	33.8	20.6	—	—	39.4	95.0 M	452.3 M	78.6 M	40.0 M	68.1
	1999	1.6 M	1.7	49.8	6.0 B	4.5	3.75	27.5	33.1	19.7	—	—	26.3	—	—	—	—	—
Cameroon	1995	13.2 M	2.8	44.7	8.3 B	3.3	0.63	25.7	33.1	14.5	13.0	0.2	−6.2	7.0 M	—	431.2 M	1.0 B	33.6
	1998	14.3 M	2.7	47.2	8.9 B	5.0	0.62	26.5	25.0	18.4	—	—	7.8	50.0 M	8.2 B	532.8 M	1.4 B	29.9
	1999	14.7 M	2.7	48.1	8.8 B	4.4	0.60	24.5	24.9	19.5	—	—	13.3	—	—	—	—	—
Chad	1995	6.7 M	3.7	22.2	1.4 B	1.0	0.21	22.3	34.3	10.3	—	—	48.7	13.0 M	—	15.8 M	19.9 M	35.2
	1998	7.3 M	2.7	23.2	1.7 B	8.1	0.23	19.3	31.7	15.0	—	—	−7.7	16.0 M	630.5 M	35.5 M	23.0 M	23.0
	1999	7.5 M	2.7	23.5	1.6 B	−1.0	0.21	16.5	34.7	17.8	—	—	12.2	—	—	—	—	—
Comoros	1995	492.0 T	2.6	30.4	214.6 M	−3.9	0.44	21.4	48.2	19.9	—	—	−6.1	1.0 M	—	1.0 M	10.1 M	84.8
	1998	530.8 T	2.5	32.1	197.2 M	0.0	0.37	16.7	41.9	19.8	—	—	−14.2	2.0 M	134.3 M	6.2 M	12.3 M	66.5
	1999	544.3 T	2.5	32.6	196.5 M	1.0	0.36	17.0	41.7	19.2	—	—	18.5	—	—	—	—	—
Côte d'Ivoire	1995	13.5 M	3.0	43.3	10.0 B	7.0	0.74	41.1	35.7	13.5	22.1	−3.0	18.1	211.6 M	—	1.0 B	3.9 B	89.6
	1998	14.5 M	2.0	45.2	10.9 B	4.5	0.75	44.5	38.1	18.2	21.5	−1.3	6.0	435.0 M	12.7 B	1.4 B	1.6 B	55.1
	1999	14.7 M	1.6	45.8	11.2 B	4.3	0.78	43.6	37.6	18.6	—	—	−1.7	—	—	—	—	—
Egypt, Arab Rep	1995	58.2 M	1.9	44.4	60.2 B	4.7	1.03	22.5	27.5	17.2	34.8	0.9	9.9	598.0 M	—	2.4 B	2.4 B	34.6
	1998	61.4 M	1.7	44.9	82.7 B	5.6	1.35	16.8	23.3	22.2	—	—	10.8	1.1 B	24.4 B	1.8 B	4.3 B	31.2
	1999	62.4 M	1.7	45.0	92.4 B	5.9	1.48	14.8	23.1	22.6	—	—	5.7	—	—	—	—	—
Ethiopia	1995	56.5 M	2.9	15.4	5.8 B	6.1	0.10	22.1	22.1	16.4	—	—	9.0	8.0 M	—	154.1 M	460.7 M	15.6
	1998	61.3 M	2.5	16.7	6.5 B	−1.0	0.11	15.8	27.7	18.2	—	—	−2.8	4.0 M	8.7 B	119.0 M	626.3 M	10.6
	1999	62.8 M	2.4	17.2	6.5 B	7.0	0.10	13.8	27.9	18.6	—	—	6.8	—	—	—	—	—

Country	Year																	
Gabon	1995	1.1 M	2.5	75.9	5.0 B	7.0	4.55	58.8	37.3	22.7	—	—	10.1	—	—	456.2 M	287.4 M	131.0
	1998	1.2 M	2.4	79.2	4.7 B	2.0	3.92	51.2	40.2	32.3	—	—	-1.8	-113 M	4.5 B	307.0 M	478.4 M	37.7
	1999	1.2 M	2.3	80.3	—	—	—	—	—	—	—	—	-3.0	-50 M	—	—	—	—
Ghana	1995	17.1 M	2.6	35.9	6.5 B	4.0	0.38	24.5	32.9	20.0	—	—	40.4	107.0 M	—	406.5 M	621.2 M	38.1
	1998	18.5 M	2.6	37.4	7.5 B	4.7	0.41	34.3	46.7	24.7	—	—	26.1	56.0 M	4.0 B	579.9 M	717.2 M	38.0
	1999	18.9 M	2.6	37.9	7.6 B	4.4	0.40	32.2	49.9	21.6	—	—	16.2	—	—	—	—	—
Kenya	1995	27.2 M	2.4	28.6	9.0 B	4.4	0.33	32.8	38.7	17.5	—	—	24.8	32.4 M	—	901.4 M	633.7 M	26.8
	1998	29.3 M	2.4	31.3	11.6 B	1.8	0.40	24.6	32.3	14.4	26.0	-1.3	2.6	11.0 M	5.2 B	544.6 M	858.9 M	16.2
	1999	29.4 M	2.3	32.2	10.6 B	1.6	0.36	24.7	32.8	15.3	—	—	6.0	—	—	—	—	—
Mauritius	1995	1.1 M	0.8	40.5	4.0 B	4.7	3.64	59.6	62.1	25.8	—	—	18.7	18.7 M	—	225.4 M	341.5 M	20.7
	1998	1.2 M	1.0	41.0	4.0 B	5.5	3.33	62.9	65.0	25.4	20.8	-1.2	11.2	12.0 M	2.5 B	311.8 M	573.0 M	34.2
	1999	1.2 M	0.9	41.1	4.2 B	4.7	3.50	63.9	65.9	26.0	21.2	0.9	15.2	—	—	—	—	—
Mozam-bique	1995	15.8 M	2.6	33.8	2.4 B	4.3	0.15	15.2	39.9	22.8	—	—	47.5	45.0 M	—	162.3 M	278.8 M	67.3
	1998	16.9 M	1.9	37.6	3.9 B	12.0	0.23	11.7	30.5	20.4	—	—	17.9	213.0 M	2.7 B	104.7 M	374.7 M	61.3
	1999	17.3 M	1.9	38.9	4.2 B	9.0	0.24	13.4	37.9	35.5	—	—	31.4	—	—	—	—	—
Nigeria	1995	111.3 M	3.0	39.5	28.1 B	2.5	0.25	44.3	42.2	16.1	—	—	19.4	1.1 B	—	1.8 B	5.7 B	1.9
	1998	120.8 M	2.6	42.2	41.4 B	1.8	0.34	23.5	31.7	20.0	—	—	23.2	1.1 B	29.4 B	1.3 B	6.6 B	1.7
	1999	123.9 M	2.5	43.1	43.3 B	1.0	0.35	16.9	27.5	10.6	—	—	31.4	—	—	—	—	—
Senegal	1995	8.3 M	2.7	43.8	4.5 B	4.7	0.54	34.4	40.0	16.9	—	—	7.4	32.0 M	—	281.1 M	260.2 M	79.9
	1998	9.0 M	2.7	46.0	4.7 B	5.7	0.52	33.3	38.0	19.6	—	—	8.5	40.0 M	2.7 B	322.6 M	273.0 M	55.5
	1999	9.3 M	2.7	46.7	4.8 B	5.1	0.52	33.8	41.0	21.3	—	—	13.1	—	—	—	—	—
Uganda	1995	19.2 M	3.0	12.5	5.8 B	11.5	0.30	11.8	20.8	16.2	—	—	13.9	121.0 M	—	136.7 M	92.9 M	43.3
	1998	20.9 M	2.8	13.5	6.8 B	5.6	0.33	10.3	19.7	15.1	—	—	22.9	200.0 M	2.4 B	159.5 M	135.1 M	22.5
	1999	21.5 M	2.7	13.9	6.3 B	7.8	0.29	11.4	23.1	17.2	—	—	14.1	—	—	—	—	—
Zambia	1995	9.0 M	2.7	39.2	3.5 B	-2.3	0.39	37.6	43.4	13.9	—	—	55.5	67.0 M	—	2.6 B	415.0 M	226.5
	1998	9.7 M	2.3	39.4	3.4 B	-2.0	0.35	29.4	38.4	14.3	—	—	25.6	72.0 M	5.5 B	202.1 M	329.4 M	36.1
	1999	9.9 M	2.2	39.5	3.3 B	1.3^b	0.33	28.9	39.8	16.6	—	—	14.1	—	—	—	—	—
Zimbabwe	1995	11.0 M	2.2	31.8	7.1 B	-0.5	0.65	38.2	40.9	19.6	—	—	25.5	40.0 M	—	648.6 M	685.3 M	44.6
	1998	11.7 M	1.9	33.9	6.3 B	2.5	0.54	45.9	47.8	17.2	26.7	-9.4	11.3	76.0 M	4.1 B	981.1 M	767.9 M	24.0
	1999	11.9 M	1.8	34.6	5.7 B	1.2	0.48	—	—	18.2	—	—	35.9	—	—	—	—	—

a M = million, B = billion, T = thousand.

b As reported.

Source: World Bank (2000) World Development Indicators 2000, Washington, D.C.: World Bank.

Civil unrest has continued in many areas of the continent, devastating cities and farmlands and creating millions of refugees. Ethiopia, Eritrea, Sierra Leone, and the Democratic Republic of the Congo are all examples. With its civil war, Algeria has lost access to its farmland, as thousands of land mines are buried in fields. Thousands of people have lost limbs or even their lives in accidents involving these mines. Food must be distributed through aid programs, as the farmland is considered unusable. Other costs of hostilities are widespread, beyond the countries of conflict. Neighboring countries have diverted their scarce resources into refugee management programs. These resources are being diverted from development for their own people.

Between 1987 and 1998, the percent of population across Africa living on less than U.S. $1 per day rose from 18.4 to 24.3%. Since 1998, growth has again slowed on the continent, with average GDP per capita falling by 1%, according to the World Bank.

The history of the past 40 years is one of conflict and struggle in most African countries. There have been efforts by the countries themselves and the donor community to encourage improvements in living standards of people by using economic theories to outline changes that are needed to develop economies into players on the world markets. The theories themselves have not always been correct, and, as we will see in the case of Zambia, governments have not always had the will to carry out and sustain needed reforms.

III. THEORIES OF DEVELOPMENT

Mainstream economics texts present theories of economics and of international trade and development beginning with Adam Smith in the late 1700s and going through current neo-Keynesian and neoclassical economics to spell out the necessary ingredients to achieve stable growth, ultimately through stable interest rates and exchange rates.[4] Microeconomic theories consider quantities of various goods produced and consumed, domestically and internationally. Production and consumption decisions determine jointly the relative prices of outputs and inputs of production, such as labor, capital, and land. Macroeconomic theory analyzes key impacts on the economy of changes in government spending, taxation, employment, output, money supply, and price levels on exchange rates and the balance of payments.

Based on the fundamental principles of the mainstream theories, development economics as a separate area of study began in the 1950s. The first efforts focused on "growth" models,[5] which "dominated development theory and policy in the 1950s and 1960s" (Hess and Ross, 1997, p. 143). The growth model emphasized investment and physical capital accumulation. It was thought that for economic growth to occur output and income must rise faster than the labor force or population in general (thereby raising GDP per capita, the definition of growth) (Meier, 2001):

> Believing that a developing country did not have a reliable market price system, that the supply of entrepreneurship was limited, and that large structural changes—not merely marginal adjustments—were needed, the first generation of development advisers turned to the state as the major agent of change. The government of a developmental state was to promote capital accumulation, utilize reserves of surplus labor, undertake policies of deliberate industrialization, relax the foreign exchange constraint through import substitution, and coordinate the allocation of resources through programming and planning.

Early development economists emphasized the need for physical capital and improvements in production but did not sufficiently include improvements in human capital. Theories developed from the 1960s, the second stage of development economics, responded to the earlier theories by emphasizing specific areas, such as human capital development and employment creation, using neoclassical economic principles. By providing for basic human needs through better health care, basic nutrition, and knowledge acquisition, the foundations could be laid for sustainable development.

The first stage of development economics assumed that governments in developing countries acted in the best public interest and that government intervention in the markets was required to remedy market failures. However, the result was too often government failure. The second stage assumed governments were commonly exploitative and took advantage of their powers and influence to enrich the favored few, which led to poor investments in inefficient state-owned enterprises and policies of financial repression, trade barriers, and controlled agricultural.

Since the 1980s, theories of economic development have advanced the growth model perspective and the efficiencies of markets. Focus has been on correcting government failure and promoting policy reform, with emphasis on private market development through deregulation and privatization. The World Bank and IMF use these theories to set policy agendas and goals for developing countries to benefit from donor programs. These theories are applicable to any economy. If necessary components to stability are already present, such as laws to protect individuals' rights of ownership and safety, enforcement of contracts, properly working transportation and communications systems, internal order, stable governments, and sufficiently operating financial systems to match investment and savings, then sustainable development can occur. Forming and implementing these components of growth are part of the work that donor agencies support. However, as long as the components to stability are not in place, particularly in Africa, achieving economic growth goals is difficult and far off.

Sustainable development requires stable, believable government; developed financial institutions; and government finance through taxes or domestic borrowing, not through inflationary money creation. It also takes consistent exchange-rate policies, either fixed or flexible, accompanied by free capital flows.

Note that not all elements of economic theories and policies can be expected to work in each country, as cultures, conditions, and attitudes differ. Taking theory to practice has not worked well in a number of cases. The World Bank and IMF have been criticized for putting structural adjustment programs in place in African and other countries that did not work, either because the country did not put into effect all of the necessary adjustments or because the agencies applied a standard that could not work in the given country. There are, however, at least six areas in which reforms are necessary for development to take place.

IV. STRUCTURAL REFORMS[6]

The six areas, in general, where reforms can do the most good include:

- *Fiscal reforms*: Reforms must be undertaken to ensure that governments raise needed funds through tax collection and domestic borrowing, not through inflationary money creation and continued external over-borrowing. Governments must reduce expenditures and encourage private sector development. Because developing countries have tended to have weak tax collection systems, they have funded themselves by inflationary policies, particularly by printing money. However, with high inflation, governments could not borrow long term. Therefore, short-term debt levels rose to fund longer term projects. To keep interest payments low even with high inflation, governments restricted interest rates to below market (below inflation) levels.

- *Debt reform.* Debt reform has to follow from fiscal reforms. As shown in Table 22.1, many African governments have high debt levels. Many investors consider that there is little chance of their being repaid. Instead, there are programs of debt forgiveness in use, in large part by the World Bank and the IMF, but also from governments of developed countries and the private sector (e.g., the Paris Club). Governments must find alternative sources of funding through improved tax collection and domestic borrowing, but the suggestion that governments find alternative funding sources is a tautology in that the other reforms must be in place as well, including increasing investor and public confidence in the changes in policies.

- *Financial markets.* As governments open capital markets to competition, allow private banking for domestic savings and investment, and allow the free flow of currencies, financial market integration can lead to strong economic performance (Yarbrough and Yarbrough, 2000, p. 895): "The changes associated with financial market integration also encourage domestic saving and create domestic sources of funds to finance investment projects. Even given their low incomes, developing country populations can generate impressive levels of saving-*if* convinced that the government will not expropriate those savings, erode them through inflation, or force them into instruments that pay low or even negative real rates of return."

- *Currency and money control reforms.* Whether the country uses fixed or flexible exchange rates, currencies must be freely exchangeable for other currencies and free of exchange controls. If a government is restrictive with its domestic currency, to control capital flight or to own all foreign exchange, then market forces can put pressure on the value of the currency. By allowing free currency convertibility, governments allow market forces to help correct imbalances in currency values and not lose precious foreign exchange defending the domestic currency value.

- *Privatization and deregulation.* As discussed earlier, in the first stage of economic development governments were encouraged to intervene in the markets by investing in government-owned companies, or *parastatals*, as well as to provide infrastructure spending for roads, schools, and other social programs. Government ownership of industries created problems of inefficiencies in production that increased cost structures to non-competitive levels. As a result, government subsidies and protections were needed to keep these parastatals in operation. Reforms through privatization reduce parastatals' drain on government resources and force these enterprises to be competitive or cease to exist.

- *Government and civil service reform.* The public sector has played a large role in economic activity and employment. In many cases, employment became a reward for political support of the current governments, payoffs for favors owed, or for family members. With privatization reforms, many of these employees are moved off the government roles to the private sector. This step is needed to reduce government deficits.

V. ZAMBIA: A COUNTRY'S EXPERIENCES

Since the mid-1980s, almost all African countries have undertaken structural adjustment programs under the auspices of the World Bank. Reports have been written, even by the World Bank, about the successes and failures of these programs.[7] However, the countries themselves must have the political will to make the required changes in their policies and to adhere to them. We have choosen Zambia for a case discussion to highlight its reform efforts. It is a good example of the economic performance outlined in the history section above for Africa.

Zambia is a land-locked country of about 10 million people. Over the past thirty years, it started and stopped structural adjustment programs numerous times.[8] The country performed well in the 1960s, with world prices strong for its major export product, copper; however, copper prices fell, as oil prices soared first in 1973 and then again in 1978. The economy faltered, as it had not diversified beyond copper exports during the preceding "good" times. In addition, import substitution policies to grow the manufacturing industry did not work. "The state became too entrenched in the running of most economic activities, and the types of industries that emerged were import using rather than import substitution. In the face of declining foreign exchange earnings due to the poor performance of the copper industry, capacity underutilization became the order of the day, leading to shortages of essential commodities and consequently inflation. . . .(T)he state resorted to administrative controls of prices and allocation of resources. Over time, these also bred their own problems, such as further capacity underutilization, long queues, and corruption" (Mwanza, 1997, pp. 132–133).

In 1973, Zambia entered its first agreement with the IMF for assistance and again several times over the next decade. The IMF put conditions on its help that involved limiting growth in money supply, a 20% currency devaluation, and limits on government credit. By 1978, Zambia was back to the IMF asking for more assistance. The war in neighboring Zimbabwe was limiting Zambia's progress. This time, the IMF put restrictions on credit expansion and caused Zambia to devalue its currency by 10%.

By 1981, Zambia was back to the IMF again. Copper prices had declined again, and weather conditions had caused problems in the entire region. This time, the IMF combined assistance with a World Bank loan to encourage agriculture, mining, and manufacturing. By 1982, Zambia had accumulated high debt payments and overshot credit limits. The next IMF arrangement caused the country to devalue yet again, this time for 20%, to limit money supply growth and to decrease government debt levels. The currency was allowed to float freely, but then was pegged to a basket of currencies of trading partners. With all of these measures in place, Zambia still did not improve. During the 1980s, other measures were tried. By 1987, the government abandoned its efforts with the World Bank/IMF economic and structural adjustment programs to introduce its own New Economic Recovery Program (NERP), resulting in suspension of the World Bank/IMF funds.

Under the NERP, Zambia put in place its own reforms—limiting debt service to 10% of net foreign exchange earning, fixing the exchange rate to the U.S. dollar, taking control of foreign exchange distribution, and introducing price controls. By 1988, the country was in severe difficulties. Fiscal expenditures were up, external debt service was in arrears, inflation was rising, and foreign exchange was scarce.

By 1989, Zambia was back at the World Bank and IMF for renewed assistance. Zambia renegotiated with its other external creditors. Reform programs were aimed at creating market-oriented policies. The program went off track for a time, but in 1991 a new government worked to re-engage policy requirements. Throughout the 1990s, Zambia paid off its arrears. Growth in the money supply was limited to control inflation, so that price controls were lifted; reforms occurred in the financial sector, allowing new banks to open; market exchange rates were introduced; and privatization of parastatals began, as well as other reforms.

In 1994, the Lusaka Stock Exchange opened. Privatization increased in momentum beginning in 1994, with 14 companies sold and 30 more by 1995, which helped increase the number of stocks traded on the exchange. Most of the 330 parastatals were privatized by 2000.

In 1993, GDP grew to 6.5%, but, going back to Table 22.1, by 1995, growth was negative due to droughts and the high cost of borrowing. The government again allowed excessive growth in the money supply, as seen in Table 22.1, in 1995 and 1998, although the rate of growth went down.

Currently, Zambia has a long way to go to improve, although efforts are still being made. It still has a weak court system and instances of the government interfering in the private sector. About 65% of Zambians live in severe poverty, with GDP per capita at $333 in 1999. Copper and cobalt still account for the vast majority (77%) of export revenues, so the country has not successfully diversified production.

Zambia is a good example of a country that has tried reforms on many occasions, either with the help of the World Bank and IMF or on its own, but has had disruptions to reform interrupted by natural disasters or has lacked the political will to stay the course. There have been sporadic instances of considerable growth, unsustained over the even intermediate term.

VI. SUMMARY AND CONCLUSIONS

Africa is full of a diversity of regions, individual countries, cultures, and even economic policies. These policies in African counties have been varied for many reasons, given the differences in history, educational levels, greed of those in control, and influences of "world" organizations.

In this chapter, we have looked at Africa as a whole and then discussed some sample countries. We then looked at a brief history of economic development to see where policy and reform ideas originated. We went on to present Zambia as a case study of all of the issues highlighted for the continent as a whole (Amoako, 1999):

> The central conclusion of our most recent economic assessment of the continent is that despite recent positive economic trends, most African countries do not as yet have

the conditions to sustain growth, at a level required to meet the target of reducing poverty, by half by the year 2015.

...Growth must be coupled with policies that deliberately attack poverty and promote education, health, and social safety nets. This requires an appropriate balance between short-term stabilization and adjustment measures, and longer-term consideration, including capacity building, institutional reform, human resources development and good stewardship of the environment.

The outside world needs to further recognize the importance of Africa and its component parts, to continue aid and assistance in development. It is also highly encouraging that African leaders are increasingly aware that Africans must lead economic recovery and reconstruction, with sustained peace, if any single country or, even more so, the continent is to move to its rightful place among the developed world.

DISCUSSION QUESTIONS

1. How is economic growth defined?
2. What theories have developed to guide policies for growth?
3. Discuss the four points that help us understand the limits to economic stabilization and reform.
4. How have Africa's 18 sample countries performed over the past few years?
5. What factors have led African countries to their current levels of development?
6. What policies might be put in place by governments to improve development?
7. How might world organizations respond to needed changes in Africa?
8. Trace how Zambia is an example of the history of Africa as a continent.
9. What is a parastatal? What problems arise with governments owning them?

NOTES

[1]This section is based on discussions in Hess, P. and Ross, C.G. (1997) *Economic Development: Theories, Evidence, and Policies*, New York: Dryden Press.

[2]GDP may not adequately reflect actual growth in Africa because of the non-official sectors. For a description of this issue, see Obadina, T. (2002) "Getting a Measure of African Poverty," *Africa Economic Analysis*, www.afbis.com/analysis/poverty-measure.html.

[3]www.unctad.org/templates/webFlyer.asp?intItemID=2111&lang=1

[4]It may come as a surprise to read that all economies are in development, some just more that others. We read frequently about "developed countries" and "less developed countries," as if the developed countries were through with their development process. However, developed countries can

destabilize through the same destabilizing factors that affect developing countries, such as political unrest or war, severe droughts, etc., and can quickly become less developed economies once again, even Great Britain or the United States. These countries work to remain stable by using democratic means.

[5]For a more in-depth discussion of growth models and policy implications, see Hess, P. and Ross, C.G. (1997) *Economic Development: Theories, Evidence, and Policies*, New York: Dryden Press. chpts. 3 and 4) and Meier, G.M. (2001) "The Old Generation of Development Economists and the New," in G.M. Meier and J.E. Stiglitz, Eds., *Frontiers of Development Economics: The Future in Perspective*, London: Oxford University Press.

[6]This section draws from Chapter 21 in Yarbrough, B.V. and Yarbrough, R.M. (2000) *The World Economy: Trade and Finance*, New York: Dryden Press.

[7]One such volume is Kapoor, K., Ed. (1994) *Africa's Experience with Structural Adjustment*, Proceedings of the Harare Seminar, May 23–24, Washington, D.C.: World Bank.

[8]See pages 129–146 in Mwanza, J. (1997) "World Bank-and IMF Supported Programs: A Zambian Perspective," in L. Wallace, Ed., *Deepening Structural Reform in Africa: Lessons from East Asia*, Washington, D.C.: International Monetary Fund.

CHAPTER 23

Restarting and Sustaining Growth and Development*

JAMES S. DUESENBERRY
Department of Economics, Emeritus, Harvard University, Cambridge, Massachusetts 02138

ARTHUR A. GOLDSMITH
Department of Management, University of Massachusetts, Boston, Massachusetts 02125

MALCOLM F. MCPHERSON
Belfer Center for Science and International Affairs, John F. Kennedy School of Government, Harvard University, Cambridge, Massachusetts 02138

KEY TERMS

Capital flows	Institutional deepening
Debt management	*Lagos Plan of Action*
Economic liberalization exchange rates	Macroeconomic management
Efficiency of resource use	Monetary policy
Export controls	Pan-seasonal pricing
Financial system	Politics and institutions
Fiscal policy	Price controls
Globalization	Productive resources productivity
Growth differentials	Productivity
Initial conditions	Tax policy

I. INTRODUCTION

This chapter examines how growth and development can be restarted and sustained in Sub-Saharan Africa (hereafter Africa). Though this matter has been extensively examined, we revisit it because even with major attempts at adjustment, most African countries cannot *sustain* the reforms needed to grow and develop.[1]

Reprinted with permission from and gratitude to the Journal of African Finance and Economic Development, 4(1), 102–128, 2001.

Policy reversals and economic retrogression have been the norm. Massive foreign assistance has done little to change this. Perhaps it never could, given the inconsistent conditions and shifting agendas of the donor community. But, foreign assistance can make a difference—as it has in many Asian countries— when African governments are committed to reform.[2]

Are we being too harsh? The management of the World Bank and the International Monetary Fund (IMF) have argued that Africa is "on the move."[3] In practice, however, most African governments have not made the changes that will sustain growth and development.[4]

This paper develops a framework for thinking about how to restart and sustain growth and development in Africa. Section II introduces the themes of the framework—politics and institutions, macroeconomic management, and enhancing productivity. Sections III, IV, and V discuss these themes in turn. Section VI draws the analysis together by identifying the activities needed to support growth and development. Section VII has concluding comments.

II. BACKGROUND

The Berg report and the *Lagos Plan of Action* marked a watershed in the analysis of Africa's economic problems.[5] The reports admitted officially that Africa's problems were systemic, widespread, highly complex, and not amenable to quick fixes.

Spirited debate ensued on the Berg report's "orthodox" approach *vis-à-vis* the "heterodox" action plan of the organization of African unity (OAU). Meanwhile, Africa's difficulties intensified. In response, the World Bank produced more reports and modified its assistance. It has emphasized governance and capacity building and recently argued for a "new approach" to development. The IMF and bilateral donors modified their assistance strategies as well.[6]

The *Lagos Plan of Action* had inquired, "What kind of Africa by the year 2000?" The hopeful answer was general prosperity induced by government activism and massive inflows of aid and foreign investment. The aid flowed, exceeding 20% of GDP for some countries, but growth proved elusive.

The Economic Commission for Africa and the OAU proposed an alternative approach to the IMF and World Bank's adjustment program.[7] That approach admitted the value of selective market liberalization but reaffirmed the importance of government efforts to "promote" development. As non-government organizations gained prominence, they joined the debate.[8]

So far, none of the programs has enabled any African country (besides Mauritius) to grow and develop on a sustained basis. Explanations for Africa's continued poor performance include the effects of structural characteristics (tropical location, distance from major markets), as well as weak institutions (including ineffective leadership), poor macroeconomic management, and low productivity.

These problems are not unique, although their concentration in Africa has been unusual. Cross-country research identifies the relative importance of factors generating *differences* in growth rates across groups of countries.[9] Table 23.1 reports a growth-accounting exercise for the period 1965 to 1990 for 10 countries in East/South Asia and 17 countries in Africa. Differences between the average annual growth rates are largely explained by "demography" and "policy variables." The former covers population and labor force growth and life expectancy; the latter covers "institutions," "government savings rate," and "openness."

The statistical significance of "institutions" points to government actions that increase the effectiveness of public bureaucracies, improve the competence of

TABLE 23.1 Contributions to Growth Differentials Between East/Southeast Asia and Various Regions, 1965–1990 (Percent, Annual Average)

	Contribution of Each Variable to the Difference in Per Capita Growth Relative to East/Southeast Asia		
	South Asia	Sub-Saharan Africa	Latin America
Initial conditions	0.3	0.7	−1.2
Initial GDP per capita	0.5	1.0	−1.2
Schooling	−0.2	−0.4	−0.1
Resources and geography	0.2	−1.0	−0.6
Natural Resources	0.1	−0.2	−0.2
Landlocked	0.0	−0.3	−0.1
Tropics	0.5	−0.2	0.0
Coastline/land area	−0.3	−0.3	−0.3
Policy variables	−2.1	−1.7	−1.8
Government Savings Rate	−0.4	−0.1	−0.3
Openness	−1.2	−1.2	−1.0
Institutions	−0.5	−0.4	−0.5
Demography	−0.9	−1.9	−0.2
Life Expectancy	−0.5·	−1.3	0.1
Growth in working age population	−0.3	0.1	−0.2
Growth in total population	−0.2	−0.7	−0.1
Difference in:			
Predicted growth	−2.5	−3.9	−3.8
Actual growth	−2.9	−4.0	−3.9

Note: The ten economies in the sample from East/Southeast Asia are Hong Kong, China, Singapore, Korea, Taiwan, Thailand, Malaysia, Indonesia, the Philippines, and Papua New Guinea.
Source: Radelet, Sachs and Lee (1997).

public sector administrators, promote effective implementation of public sector programs, maintain accountability, and enhance governance. The significance of the "government savings rate" is evidence of the importance of policies that maintain macroeconomic balance. The variable "openness" reflects the policies that contribute to international competitiveness, raise total factor productivity, and encourage the investment needed for growth.

In aggregate terms, the decomposition exercise focuses attention on the major elements (structure and policy) that impede growth and development in Africa. Little can be done about some of them (e.g., tropics and distance), apart from making compensating changes that improve efficiency elsewhere in the economy. Much, however, can be done to remove policy-induced impediments. Accordingly, we have been working with teams of African researchers in Ghana, Kenya, Senegal, Tanzania, and Uganda. In each country, the teams have been addressing the question: What has to be done to restart and sustain growth and development? These teams have been working with senior policymakers to identify the main issues involved, analyze them, and draw conclusions on how to move their countries forward. Non-local assistance has been confined to financial and logistical support, the sharing of cross-country experiences, and the organization of regular workshops to exchange ideas and report on progress. The framework for our research has three themes: *politics and institutions, macroeconomic management, and enhancing productivity.*

III. POLITICS AND INSTITUTIONS

Evidence in Table 23.1 suggests that institutional shortcomings have affected Africa's economic performance. These government or "non-market" failures are the corollary of "market failures." Governments fail by doing things they should not do and omitting to do things they should. Remedies for these failures are distinct. The first requires restricting the state; the second requires strengthening it. Both are politically difficult.

Most African governments became dramatically over-extended as they attempted to "promote" development. One justification for government involvement was the belief that the state could raise large amounts of resources. That happened, initially at least, but the resources were not invested efficiently. With the oil and food shocks of the 1970s, the supply of real resources fell sharply. (For oil producers, the collapse came later.) Unwilling to adjust, most governments maintained their expenditures. The resulting budget deficits absorbed domestic savings that might otherwise have been productively invested. Many state-owned enterprises (SOEs) became chronic loss-makers.[10]

Errors of omission by government have received less attention, though this is changing.[11] The most obvious has been the failure to preserve, through leadership and policy reform, the institutional setting that would support high rates of investment. The result has been to "run Thomas Hobbes in reverse." In *Leviathan*, Hobbes discussed the condition of profound uncertainty people experience when there is no central authority. In this "state of nature," human life is "nasty, poor, brutish, and short." In Hobbes' view, people forged a social contract to escape this predicament. They agreed to submit themselves to an independent political authority in exchange for social peace and "commodious living."

What happens if the social contract is broken, as has been happening across Africa? Arbitrary borders and heterogeneous populations impart less legitimacy to African states than is true elsewhere.[12] The most extreme examples are the collapsed states, such as Somalia or Liberia, where the social contract has unraveled. Some countries, Uganda for instance, have strong central governments whose authority diminishes in peripheral areas. In other places, such as Nigeria and South Africa, personal security is threatened even in central locations. For protection, Africans have fallen back on traditional and informal mechanisms. This second-best solution, as Hobbes understood, does not provide the conditions for flourishing markets and vibrant social interaction.

More is needed than restricting the government's role in the economy. Parallel efforts are required to provide basic public goods: a stable constitutional and legal order, as stressed by Hobbes, together with macroeconomic stability and conditions for raising productivity (including education, public health, and physical infrastructure). There have to be major improvements in governance.

The United Nations Development Program (UNDP) defines governance as the exercise of authority to manage a country's affairs. According to the UNDP, good governance is participatory, transparent, and accountable.[13] The World Bank has a similar definition. The Bank notes that governance is most effective when procedures are clear and leaders' decisions are responsive to public demands.[14] These definitions are consistent with classic liberal theories of what governments should do. Once considered culturally biased or politically insensitive, these theories have been embraced by international agencies as a guide for proper governance.[15] They have gained support within Africa, too.

The assumption, familiar since the Enlightenment, is that popular involvement in an organized civil society is necessary to counter arbitrary and non-representative decisions of leaders and political authorities. Without open access to decision-makers, the majority cannot press its demands. And, lacking pressure from below, leaders and governments are more likely to abuse their positions. Africa's unfortunate experiences with corrupt leaders and brutal governments largely explain why development agencies now stress the rule of law, freedom of association, respect for human rights, and democracy. Such institutions are intended to hold leaders accountable for bad economic performance. The empirical record suggests political corruption is lower under democratic conditions.[16] This is not an argument for any particular system of government.

Participatory politics covers many modes of representation. The basic principle is that people have to be able to take part in open debates over public policies that affect them.

During the Cold War, it was argued that participatory politics clashed with market-oriented growth and that authoritarianism makes economic reforms easier. These views have lost ground.[17] Autocratic regimes in Africa have a poor record of sustained reform. African democracies do no worse than the regimes they replace.[18] Furthermore, historical evidence shows that poor countries can develop under democracy, and that democracy can survive in poor countries if they develop.[19]

The rub is that improving governance can be slow. Africa has been edging toward more competitive systems since the fall of the Berlin Wall, but political reform has been fragile.[20] It is difficult to restructure political systems that have hardened around personalized power, arbitrary and unaccountable decision-making, widespread dishonesty, and repression of dissent. Like Gresham's law, bad institutions crowd out good ones.

In Africa, interest groups have not played the positive role ascribed to them by pluralist political theory. The most important groups have been based on ethnic and family loyalties. Modern interest groups that cut across ethnic and regional divisions, such as trade associations or labor unions, have yet to take a major part in sustained economic and political reform.

All public policies, including economic reform, create winners and losers. Important constituencies in Africa often lose from economic reform, especially in the short term. These groups are apt to mobilize to protect themselves from adverse outcomes. State intervention has created economic rents that officials use to maintain patronage and retain power. Typically, the dominant coalition extracts rents from the rural sector, which lacks access and influence and uses the resources to buy off urban opposition and finance government insiders. Disfavored groups are either left out of the political equation or violently repressed.[21]

Economic liberalization frequently implies political realignment in Africa. The donor community is correct to emphasize governance, thereby reinforcing incipient domestic political demands for a fairer sharing of resources. Still, the ruling elite seldom embraces economic reforms. They make the concessions they must to gain access to donor funds while simultaneously preserving as much of the *status quo* as possible to stay in power. Yet, without economic reform, the economy collapses.

It would be reassuring to believe that international agencies will continue emphasizing governance. Past practice raises doubts. Critics of the World Bank assert that it has too many ideas and too few priorities.[22] Other donors have been capricious as well, responding to demands from their own constituencies to tackle the latest fad. Lessons are forgotten, mistakes are repeated, and follow-through is lacking. Members of the international development community rarely pause to consider whether their shifting and (often) contradictory agenda is manageable in Africa. None of the stylish approaches to development is necessarily wrong. There are simply far too many initiatives, most of which are not given the time or attention before being replaced or deflected. The approach we suggest here seeks to simplify the development agenda and improve the effectiveness of each of its components.

IV. MACROECONOMIC MANAGEMENT

Accountable public institutions are essential for sound macroeconomic management.[23] At a minimum, macroeconomic management should be guided by the medical maxim "do no harm."

For almost three decades, African countries have had severe macroeconomic imbalances. These are reflected in high inflation rates, overvalued real exchange rates, capital flight, currency substitution, foreign debts that can only be serviced with foreign aid, large public sector deficits, and insolvent financial organizations. Many factors contributed to these problems. Over-ambitious development programs financed through domestic credit and foreign loans have played a major role. Governments have been unwilling to adjust fiscal and monetary policies to match changes in terms of trade and other shocks. Attempts to maintain unrealistic exchange rates reduced exports and led to capital flight.[24] Low, often negative, real interest rates raised the incentive to move capital abroad. Interest rate ceilings and credit allocation programs wasted scarce capital and led to bank insolvency.

Dealing with these problems requires the reorientation of macroeconomic management. That effort involves four interrelated tasks. The first is to achieve balance between domestic demand and potential output in ways that lead to the highest utilization of resources consistent with price stability. The second is to maintain an exchange rate that promotes rapid export growth and a sustainable current account. The third task is to develop and maintain a well-ordered financial system that balances aggregate savings and investment and provides an efficient, market-based allocation of available capital. The fourth is to ensure that public and private sector borrowing remains within prudent limits.

A. EXCHANGE RATES

With appropriate macroeconomic policies and strong political support, a fixed exchange rate may contribute to economic stability and improve the climate for investment. But, fixed exchange rates can become overvalued and the effort to maintain them creates instability. Moreover, Asian experience has shown that success in maintaining a fixed exchange rate may attract destabilizing capital flows.

However, it does not follow that floating exchange rates provide a painless solution to balance of payments problems. In principle, floating rates require minimal intervention because markets move the exchange rates to keep the external accounts in balance. That does not, of course, allow governments to conduct their monetary and fiscal policies without concern for trade and payments considerations. Exchange markets respond quickly to actual or threatened inflation.[25]

The long lags between exchange rate movements and the resulting changes in imports and exports exacerbate exchange rate volatility. Moreover, exchange rates are also driven by variations in foreign aid and remittances, as well as by interest rates and expectations about changes in capital markets. They also respond to expectations of policy change and fears of political instability.

These considerations make movements of nominal and real exchange rates difficult to explain and to forecast.[26] In time, exchange rates *do* respond to changes in relative prices and they *do* respond to changes in the factors underlying the supply of and demand for commodities.[27] However, there may be considerable unexplained and unwanted variation in exchange rates and trade flows over the short term. These will be minimized if other aspects of macroeconomic management contribute to stability.

B. Fiscal Policy

Fiscal policy is cumbersome for short-run demand management. Most of the time governments must rely on monetary policy for demand management while ensuring that fiscal policy does not add to the difficulties, but fiscal policy has a more positive role to play in response to shocks. When the terms of trade deteriorate or crops fail, as often happens in Africa, the decline in real national income must be matched by some combination of reduced domestic absorption, borrowing, or aid. Reductions in budget expenditures must play a role in the adjustment. Failure to make that adjustment in the 1970s created debt and balance of payments problems that still burden African countries.

Over the long term, fiscal policy contributes to economic growth through the efficient use of resources available through taxation, foreign aid, and foreign investment.[28] Capital is scarce in Africa and should not be wasted. In their budget management, governments should run a current surplus.[29] Capital expenditures should only exceed that surplus when it can be shown that the expenditures have a higher social return than private alternatives.[30] With levels of debt they cannot service, African governments have no justification in borrowing to finance deficit spending.

Tax policy should be designed to raise revenue with as few distortions as practicable. The heavy reliance on trade taxes in Africa creates serious distortions. Government expenditures are typically overburdened by wage and debt service payments. One goal of reducing debt should be to release resources to ensure adequate funds for operations and maintenance thereby raising the efficiency of capital.

C. MONETARY POLICY

Monetary management becomes very difficult if the central bank is expected to provide credit to finance government deficits. The availability of that money "tap" undermines budget discipline and often requires the central bank either to give up controlling inflation, or to crowd out private borrowers using high interest rates. Similarly, borrowing by SOEs has seriously weakened banking systems across Africa by creating moral hazard, encouraged imprudent lending, and generated large losses for banks and governments.

In Africa, as elsewhere, the central objective of monetary policy is to achieve the fullest utilization of resources consistent with an acceptable inflation target.[31] Even the central banks that have publicized their inflation targets also recognize the importance of output and employment considerations.[32] They accept gradual inflation and appreciate the need for monetary ease when demand weakens. However, the use of inflation targets is meant to give notice that central banks will not allow supply shocks to set off wage–price spirals. It also affirms that they will not accommodate budget deficits.

Unlike fiscal policy, monetary policy can be continually adjusted without lengthy decision or implementation lags. Unfortunately, the lags between monetary actions and their effects on economic activity are long and variable. This complicates monetary management due to the need to forecast economic conditions many months ahead.

Central banks have only one main policy instrument. They can control the supply of reserve money, usually by means of treasury bill auctions or open market operations. That allows them to control either market interest rates on short-term securities or the money supply. Currently, most central banks use their indirect control of short-term interest rates as the primary policy tool. They raise rates when they believe that too rapid demand growth will generate inflation and reduce them when they fear slow output growth.

Because of the difficulty of predicting demand movements and the response of prices to these movements, together with our imprecise knowledge of the effects of interest rates, central banks cannot prevent fluctuations in output, employment, or prices. But, in the absence of major shocks, a gradualist monetary policy together with a sound fiscal policy can be expected to keep the economy on a stable path.

While institutional weaknesses often make routine monetary operations difficult in Africa, the core central banking problems arise from supply shocks, balance of payments problems, and fiscal imbalances. An early response to shocks is required because inflation caused by excess demand will continue as long as price increases are matched by increases in nominal demand. Moreover, if the inflation is allowed to persist, expectations of continued inflation become established. Subsequent price rises make stabilization more difficult to achieve.

D. Financial System

An important concern for all African central banks is the financial system. After years of mismanagement, the banking systems of many African countries are being restored to solvency, supervision is improving, and central banks have moved toward indirect control of the supply of money and credit.[33] Even with these changes, African banking systems will still directly serve only a small segment of the economy. When working well, they provide a safe haven for those who wish to save in financial form rather than in real capital.

Financial stability is essential for efficient intermediation and financial deepening. African financial markets remain thin with few opportunities for the expansion of specialized organizations, such as merchant banks and finance houses. African governments have complicated the situation by attempting to promote financial development through various "supply-leading" financial initiatives. These have not worked as financial development largely depends on the expansion of markets and the reduction of intermediation costs.[34] These, in turn, require economic liberalization and mechanisms that more closely integrate African economies with the global financial system.

E. Capital Flows

A major objective of restoring financial stability is to reverse the trends in capital flight and currency substitution.[35] African countries now have long experience with capital outflows. We know from IMF and other data that African residents hold large deposits in foreign banks.[36] Those offshore investments represent African savings that might have been usefully invested at home. Any African country that can make investment conditions attractive enough to induce its citizens to bring their wealth home will raise investment and accelerate growth. Indeed, this is the first step in attracting foreign direct investment. To end capital outflows and encourage the return of flight capital, African governments must rebuild confidence in the future of their economies. This requires, among other things, price stability, a consistent approach to exchange rate management, and monetary and fiscal policies that help countries bring their external debt under control.

F. DEBT MANAGEMENT

There have now been many attempts, mostly by the donor community, to resolve Africa's debt problem. Initiatives include selective debt write-downs, write-offs, and concessionary refinancing. The most recent program for highly indebted poor countries (HIPC) has been seen as a "debt exit" strategy for some countries. The economic decline following the Asian crisis has reduced the prospect that African countries will grow at rates needed for such an "exit" to occur.

In principle, net aid flows are large enough to cover the debt service payments for most countries. There are frequent delays in those flows due to donor disbursement procedures or the problems of meeting conditions attached to aid. External debt is only part of the problem. Many African countries have large stocks of domestic debt due to past deficit financing, SOE losses, and loan guarantees that were called.

These debts are so large they narrow the options for macroeconomic managers. Debt is no longer a "cushion" for current operations. The shortage of foreign exchange reserves places greater stress on the need to adjust. African governments have to be far more proactive in addressing their debt problems. The "aid exit" strategy suggested later is also a "debt exit" strategy.

None of these activities is independent. Monetary and fiscal policies, exchange rate, and debt management require coordination, but interpretations of what is involved vary. In the franc zone, the regional central banks dominate monetary policy and have a role in determining fiscal limits for member countries. The exchange rate is fixed and non-negotiable. In other African countries, governments determine fiscal policy, strongly influence monetary policy, and, with few exceptions, manipulate their exchange rates.

Some countries have sought a more rational approach to macroeconomic policy by granting their central banks independence. In practice, the impact of central banks on policy rarely depends on their statutory position. Central banks do not usually act in ways that are strongly opposed by their governments.[37] More important are the governor's political influence and the central bank's reputation for economic expertise.

V. ENHANCED PRODUCTIVITY

Institutional reform and prudent macroeconomic management can provide a stable setting for growth and development, but they do not, in themselves, increase output. The sustained growth of output requires the accumulation of human and physical capital (so as to embody new technology and new information) and continued increases in the efficiency of resource use.

Important determinants of Africa's poor growth performance have been low rates of accumulation (reflecting the low savings rate) and inefficient resource use. This is evident from the aggregate data. Over the period 1975 to 1996, real output, the labor force, and the supply of capital (derived from gross investment data) increased at annual rates of 2.2, 2.6, and 2.1%, respectively.[38] Based on these data, total factor productivity rose marginally and labor productivity (i.e., output per worker) declined. By contrast, there were solid gains in total factor and labor productivity outside Africa during the same period. These have been essential features of Africa's "marginalization" within the world economy.[39]

A. INCREASING THE SUPPLY OF PRODUCTIVE RESOURCES

To increase the supply of productive resources across Africa, the rate of investment has to rise sharply. Governments cannot borrow their way to prosperity. They are already overburdened with debt and by running deficits augment that debt, nor can they expect international assistance much beyond the increases of the last two decades. Net aid to Africa (excluding Nigeria and South Africa) increased from 5.0% of GDP in 1975 to 10.1% of GDP in 1996.[40] Finally, instability and shrinking markets have led most private investors to view Africa as a last resort rather than the last frontier. The additional resources needed to sharply accelerate the rate of investment will be difficult to find. Nonetheless, an immediate response could be made through public sector savings. For the government, this would require changes in fiscal policy that eliminate the budget deficit.

Many opportunities exist. African governments have too many overseas missions. Their officials travel abroad too often with too little effect. Military budgets are excessive. Public sector capital depreciates rapidly because of poor maintenance. Losses due to corruption by public officials are large.[41] Furthermore, public revenue is reduced through tax fraud, kickbacks, the nonrecovery of debt to the public sector, and tax concessions based on cronyism. SOEs can respond similarly as well. They can eliminate losses by selling or closing loss-making activities.

Over time, the government's domestic efforts to mobilize resources will be enhanced by the effects of financial deepening (as the macroeconomy stabilizes) and residents begin to repatriate flight capital. These, in turn, will stimulate flows of foreign direct investment.

A further boost to the supply of productive resources will occur through measures that reduce the incentives for skilled workers to emigrate. Throughout Africa, many skilled workers have left rather than tolerate the excesses of one-party states and autocratic leaders.[42] Many found local salaries and conditions unacceptable. These economic refugees—doctors, teachers, university lecturers, and accountants—have been among the most productive, motivated, and innovative workers.

How long it will take to make a substantive difference in the supply of productive resources is difficult to predict. The main determinant will be the pace at which local and foreign investors become convinced that African governments are committed to sustained economic reform. Donors can support this process, but only to the extent that African governments continue to take the lead.

B. Raising the Efficiency of Resource Use

Africa's declining labor productivity is directly related to the institutional weaknesses and macroeconomic problems noted earlier. The effect can be described as "running Adam Smith in reverse" (parallel to the earlier reference to Hobbes). Smith emphasized the efficiency gains associated with specialization. He also noted that the degree of specialization and division of labor depended on the "extent of the market."[43,44]

Those advantages have been lost across Africa through collapsing real effective demand, imploding markets, and declining business opportunities. Individuals and firms have found that diversification is essential to spread their risks and minimize the decline in their incomes. Such "safety-first" or "coping" strategies make sense for individuals, even though they raise unit costs and reduce total production.

Many farmers, for example, have selectively withdrawn from the cash economy and expanded their subsistence-based activities (crops and livestock). That approach increases their chances of survival at the cost of declining production and productivity.[45] Agricultural productivity has been seriously undermined by over-taxation in various forms: price controls, rigged exchange rates, pan-seasonal and pan-territorial pricing of outputs and inputs, marketing restrictions, export controls, and high protection for manufacturing.[46] Subsidies on fertilizer, fuel, irrigation water, and credit have provided inefficient and incomplete offsets. With precarious food supplies and rising populations, it is essential that farm output throughout Africa be increased.[47] Removing the policies that adversely affect agriculture will help raise productivity and output, but the full benefit of a constructive agricultural policy cannot be obtained without substantial investment in agricultural infrastructure and rural health and education. Such changes begin to redress poverty in Africa while providing a foundation for countries to move into labor-intensive manufactured exports.[48]

Deteriorating education standards and losses due to HIV/AIDS have lowered productivity.[49] Workers entering the labor force in many sectors have fewer skills than their predecessors. Employers have adjusted by fragmenting tasks and providing additional training. Both adjustments have raised costs. Shrinking markets and declining economic activity provide new workers with fewer opportunities for "learning-by-doing," reducing the scope for innovation and initiative.[50] A related problem has been the decline in the quality of management. The reduction in business activity has diminished the scope for grooming future managers. For their part, managers have been preoccupied responding to crises, diverting their attention from the challenges of promoting growth.

Productivity has also been adversely affected by financial instability. The lack of financial development, noted above, has kept intermediation costs high. Capital that might have been invested locally has been transferred abroad. Furthermore, the financial disruption associated with deficit financing and unsustainable levels of debt has eroded the confidence needed to stimulate investment, innovation, and growth.

Opportunities for raising productivity have been limited by the lack of regional cooperation in Africa. The Global Coalition for Africa reported that more than 200 organizations dealt with regional cooperation in Africa. None functions in ways that expand regional markets. Most countries belong to several regional groups, creating duplication and confusion.[51]

Finally, bilateral trade relations in Africa have done little to enhance the confidence and stability needed for raising investment and productivity. Disputes are common among neighbors. These have restricted cross-border trade and commerce, denying producers and consumers the benefits of local comparative advantage.

VI. A FRAMEWORK FOR RESTARTING GROWTH

To restart and sustain growth and development, five issues are crucial:

1. *Public sector restraint*—To redress the excesses of the past, African governments have to permanently reduce what they attempt to accomplish. Few governments have the capacity to venture beyond education, health, infrastructure, an effective judicial system, and sound macroeconomic management. This is doubly true for countries where HIV/AIDS

prevalence rates are high. Priorities must be established and mechanisms (sale, leasing, greater private sector competition) found for disengaging from non-priority areas.[52] Government activity should not continue to subtract value.[53]

2. *Government as saver*—A practical indication of public sector restraint will be a sharp rise in government savings. Development specialists used to stress this point.[54] Few governments took heed. But, without large sustained increases in savings, African governments have no *permanent* way out of getting out of debt or moving beyond aid.

3. *Institutional deepening*—Successful economies are characterized by popular input to public decisions, competent civil services, rule of law, effective financial supervision, and prudent macroeconomic management. None of these institutions evolved overnight. All such institutional development (indeed, *all* development) is work in progress. This is especially the case with leadership. Vital at all times, effective leadership has a special role of maintaining a growth-oriented focus when key institutions are weak. An enlightened leader would encourage those institutions and foster a setting in which economic management is both efficient and accountable.[55]

4. *Responses to globalization*—The strategy of relying on "aid not trade" for three decades has bankrupted most African countries and "marginalized" the continent. Opening up involves risks, particularly when international markets become unstable.[56] Nonetheless, the benefits of expanding markets and increased specialization created by trade greatly outweigh the advantage that might accrue to any African country on the basis of its own real effective demand.[57] A constructive response to globalization will require African governments to shape their policies, starting from the constraints and opportunities within the global economy. Such an approach does not limit the sovereignty of African governments. In reality, debt, deficits, and declining real incomes impose far harsher limits.

5. *Ending aid dependency*—There is now little doubt that foreign aid only works when governments are dedicated to reform.[58] But, breaking out of the tangled web that exists between African governments and donors is difficult. One approach would be for all African governments to devise their *own* medium-term strategies for working themselves off aid. Even with such strategies, aid to Africa would not immediately diminish. It will take time and resources to deal with debt and reconstruction. Moreover, emergencies will always require a special response. Nonetheless, the process of designing an aid exit strategy will be invaluable for African governments. It will focus attention on the changes in local policies, institutions, and links with donors needed to move African countries

beyond aid. Properly conceived, such an aid exit strategy would be a debt exit strategy as well.

VII. SUMMARY

To restart and sustain growth and development, African governments should take the initiative. Several issues are important. First, economic reform has to be sustained; start–stop reform is a dead end. Second, all African governments should design and begin implementing an aid exit strategy. Third, African governments should focus on measures that stimulate accumulation and raise productivity; their own operations provide an ideal starting point. Fourth, the organizations central to economic management have to be strengthened. Fifth, African governments should recast their policies so as to take advantage of globalization; there is no future in isolation and disengagement. Bringing these strands together requires leadership. Restraint is essential, and leaders must be held accountable for their performance.

A report by the European Commission on relations between the European Union and the Africa, Caribbean, and Pacific (ACP) countries stated: "The colonial and post-colonial periods are behind us and a more politically open international environment enables us to lay down the responsibilities of each partner less ambiguously."[59] For African governments, one responsibility is a full-scale effort to restart and sustain growth and development. This paper provides a framework for beginning that process. Meeting the challenge will not be easy; however, it will be much easier than if stagnation and decline are allowed to continue.

DISCUSSION QUESTIONS

1. List and discuss the five crucial issues that the authors consider necessary for starting and sustaining growth and development in Africa. Do you agree with these issues? If so, why? If not, why not? Can you think of other issues missing from the list?
2. What is the role of macroeconomic management in growth and development in Africa and why is this role important?
3. It is often argued that politics and institutions are important issues in African growth and development and institutional shortcomings have affected Africa's economic performance. In what ways do politics and institutions affect economic development in Africa? Why is the issue of governance more than restricting the government's role in the economy?
4. Discuss the exchange rate, fiscal, and monetary policy solutions proposed in this chapter. How effective do you think that these solutions and recommendations would be?

5. A meaningful and effective macroeconomic management requires reforms in the financial system, capital flows, and debt management. Examine this statement with respect to African economic development.
6. Based on the information contained in this chapter, how can we enhance productivity in Africa?
7. Compare the contributions to growth differentials between East Asia and Africa. What factors account for these growth differentials?
8. According to the authors, what factors affect agricultural productivity in Africa? How can agricultural productivity be improved?
9. How would you bring about sustainable growth and development in Africa?

NOTES

[1]Without rapid growth and development, African countries will remain "wards of the international community" (Krugman, P.R. (1989) "Developing countries in the World Economy," *Daedalus*, 118, 183–203).

[2]Burnside, C., and Dollar, D. (2000) "Aid, Policies, and Growth," *American Economic Review*, 90, 847–868; Tsikata, T. M. (1998) *Aid Effectiveness: A Survey of the Recent Empirical Literature*, Working Paper PPAA/98/1, Washington, D.C.: International Monetary Fund.

[3]Camdessus, M. (1996) Address to the Board of Governors of the IMF, October 1, 1996, Washington, D.C.; Madavo, C., and Sarbib, J.-L. (1997) "Africa on the Move: Attracting Private Capital to a Changing Continent," *SAIS Review*, 7, 111–126.; Wolfensohn, J.D. (1997) *The Challenge of Inclusion*, Address to the Board of Governors, September 23, 1997, Hong Kong, China.

[4]McPherson, M.F., and Goldsmith, A.A. (1998) "Africa: On the Move?," *SAIS Review*, 28, 153–167.

[5]World Bank (1981) *Accelerated Development in Sub-Saharan Africa: An Agenda for Action*, Washington, D.C.: World Bank; OAU (1980) *The Lagos Plan of Action for the Implementation of the Monrovia Strategy for the Economic Development of Africa*, Lagos: Organization of African Unity.

[6]Wolfensohn, J.D. (1998) *The Other Crisis*, Address to the Board of Governors, October 6, 1998, Washington, D.C.; World Bank (1991); *The African Capacity Building Initiative*, Washington, D.C.: The World Bank. World Bank (1989) *Sub-Saharan Africa from Crisis to Sustainable Growth: A Long-Term Perspective Study*, Washington D.C.: World Bank; World Bank (1984) *Towards Sustained Development in Sub-Saharan Africa*, Washington, D.C.: World Bank; World Bank (1986) *Financing Adjustment with Growth in Sub-Saharan Africa, 1986–90*, Washington D.C.: World Bank; World Bank (1994) *Adjustment in Africa: Reforms, Results and the Road Ahead*, New York: Oxford University Press.

[7]ECA/OAU (1989) *African Alternative Framework to Structural Adjustment Programmes for Socio-Economic Recovery and Transformation*, AAF-SAP, New York: Economic Commission for Africa, United Nations.

[8]OXFAM (1995) *The Impact of Structural Adjustment on Community Life: Undoing Development*, Boston: Oxfam America.

[9]Radelet, S.C., Sachs, J.D., and Lee, J.-W. (1997) "Economic Growth in Asia," draft, Cambridge, MA: Harvard Institute for International Development; Bloom, D.E., and Sachs, J.D. (1998) "Geography, Demography, and Economic Growth in Africa," *Brookings Papers on Economic Activity*, 2, 207–274.

[10]An example is Zambia Airways. In the 3 years before being shut down in early 1995, it had lost more than $100 million. Closing the airline raised national saving and GDP and increased the supply of foreign exchange.

[11]Brautigam, D. (1996) "State Capacity and Effective Governance," in B. Ndulo and N. van der Walle, Eds., *Agenda for Africa's Economic Renewal*, Washington, D.C.: Overseas Development Council; World Bank (1997) *World Development Report 1997: The State in a Changing World*, New York: Oxford University Press.

[12]Englebert, P. (2000) *State Legitimacy and Development in Africa*, Boulder, CO: Lynne Rienner Publishers.

[13]UNDP (1997) *Governance for Sustainable Human Development*, New York: United Nations Development Program.

[14]World Bank (1994b) *Governance*, Washington, D.C.: World Bank/UNDP.

[15]USAID (1994) *Strategies for Sustainable Development*, Washington, D.C.: United States Agency for International Development; CIDA (1995) *Human Rights: Government of Canada Policy for CIDA on Human Rights, Democratization, and Good Governance*, Hull: Canadian International Development Agency; JICA (1995) *Participatory Development and Good Governance*, report of the Aid Study Committee, Japan International Cooperation Agency.

[16]Goldsmith, A.A. (1999) "Slapping the Grasping Hand: Correlates of Political Corruption in Emerging Markets," *American Journal of Economics and Sociology*, 58(4), 865–883.

[17]Bhagwati, J. (1995) "The New Thinking on Development," *Journal of Democracy*, 6, 50–62.

[18]Sandbrook, R. (1996) "Democratization and the Explanation of Economic Reform in Africa," *Journal of International Development*, 8, 1–20.

[19]Przeworski, A., and Limongi, F. (1997) "Democracy and Development," in A. Hadenius, Ed., *Democracy's Victory and Crisis*, Cambridge, U.K.: Cambridge University Press; Chaudhurie-Aziz, M. (1998) "Political Participation and Long-Run Economic Performance," paper presented to Annual Meeting of the American Political Science Association, September 3–6, Boston, MA.

[20]Thomas, T. (1996) "Africa for the Africans," *The Economist*, September 7; Joseph, R. (1997) "Democratization in Africa after 1989: Comparative and Theoretical Perspectives," *Comparative Politics*, 29, 363–383.

[21]Sandbrook, R. (1986) "The State and Economic Stagnation in Tropical Africa," *World Development*, 14, 319–332; Ayittey, G.B.N. (1992) *Africa Betrayed*, New York: St. Martin's Press.

[22]Sachs, J. (1996) "Growth in Africa: It Can Be Done," *The Economist*, June 29, pp. 19–21.

[23]Collier, P. (1991) "Africa's External Economic Relations: 1960–90," in D. Rimmer, Ed., *Africa 30 Years On*, London: The Royal Africa Society in association with James Currey; Collier, P., and Pattillo, C., Eds. (2000) *Investment and Risk in Africa*, Basingstoke: Macmillan.

[24]Ghura, D., and Grennes, T.J. (1993) "The Real Exchange Rate and Macroeconomic Performance in Sub-Saharan Africa," *Journal of Development Economics*, 42: 155–174.

[25]Quirk, P.J. (1996) "Exchange Rate Regimes as Inflation Anchors," *Finance and Development*, March, 42–45.

[26]Duesenberry, J.S. et al. (1994) "Improving Exchange Rate Management in Sub-Saharan Africa," CAER Discussion Paper No. 31, Cambridge, MA: Harvard Institute for International Development.

[27]Dollar, D. (1992) "Outward-Oriented Developing Economies Really Do Grow More Rapidly: Evidence from 95 LDCs 1976–1985," *Economic Development and Cultural Change*, 40, 523–544; Rodrik, D. (1997) "Trade Policy and Economic Performance in Sub-Saharan Africa," paper prepared for the Swedish Ministry for Foreign Affairs.

[28]Easterly, W., Rodriguez, C.A., and Schmidt-Hebbel, K. (1994) *Public Sector Deficits and Macroeconomic Performance*, New York: Oxford University Press; McKenzie, G.A., Orsmond, D.W.H., and Gerson, P.R. (1997) "The Composition of Fiscal Adjustment and Growth Lessons from Fiscal Reforms in Eight Economies," Occasional Paper No. 149, Washington, D.C.: International Monetary Fund.

[29]HIID (1997) "A New Partnership for Growth in Africa," Cambridge, MA: Harvard Institute for International Development.

[30]Squire, L. (1989) "Project Evaluation in Theory and Practice," in H.B. Chenery and T.N. Srinivasan, Eds., *Handbook of Development Economics*, Vol. 2, Amsterdam: North Holland.

[31]Fuhrer, J.C. (1997) "Central Bank Independence and Inflation Targeting: Monetary Policy Paradigms for the Next Millennium," *New England Economic Review*, Jan./Feb., 20–36.

[32]Bernanke, B.S. and Mishkin, F.S. (1999) *Inflation Targeting: Lessons from the International Experience*, Princeton, NJ: Princeton University Press; Masson, P.R., Savastano, M.A., and Sharma, S. (1998) "Can Inflation Targeting Be a Framework for Monetary Policy in Developing Countries?," *Finance and Development*, March, 34–37; FRBKC (1996) *Achieving Price Stability*, proceedings of a symposium sponsored by the Federal Reserve Bank of Kansas City, August 29–31, 1996, Jackson Hole, WY.

[33]Duesenberry, J.S. and McPherson, M.F. (1992) "Monetary Management in Sub-Saharan Africa: Key Issues," *Journal of African Finance and Economic Development*, 1, 25–36; Alexander, W.E., Balino, T.J.T., and Enoch, C. (1996) "Adopting Indirect Instruments of Monetary Policy," *Finance and Development*, March, 14–17.

[34]McKinnon, R.W. (1973) *Money and Capital in Economic Development*, Washington, D.C.: The Brookings Institution; North, D.C. (1997) "Transaction Costs Through Time," in C. Menard, Ed., *Transaction Cost Economics: Recent Developments*, Brookfield: Edward Elgar.

[35]Bhattacharya, A., Montiel, P.J., and Sharma, S. (1997) "How Can Sub-Saharan Africa Attract More Private Capital Inflows?," *Finance & Development*, June, 3–6; Gastanaga, V.M., Nugent, J.B., and Pashamova, B. (1998) "Host Country Reforms and FDI Flows: How Much Difference Do They Make?," *World Development*, 26, 1299–1314.

[36]A study by Ajayi (1997) suggests that capital flight from Africa has been modest. This contradicts numerous other studies showing the opposite (Collier, P. and Gunning, J.W. (1999) "Explaining African Economic Performance," *Journal of Economic Literature*, 37(1), 64–111.)

[37]There is now a large literature on central bank independence (Goodhart, C.A.E. (1994) "Game Theory for Central Bankers: A Report to the Governor of the Bank of England," *Journal of Economic Literature*, 32, 101–114; Blinder, A.S. (1998) *Central Banking in Theory and Practice*, Cambridge, MA: The MIT Press.) All of it favors the trend to "freeing" the central bank of government influence. Here, the best is the enemy of the good. In practice, governments and central banks are mutually dependent. Effective macroeconomic management is impossible without their joint cooperation.

[38]Sources are *World Development Indicators 1998* CD-ROM and *African Development Indicators 1998/99*.

[39]Collier, P. (1995) "The Marginalization of Africa," *International Labour Review*, 134, 541–557; Yeats, A. *et al.* (1997) *Did Domestic Policies Marginalize Africa in World Trade?*, Directions in Development Series, Washington, D.C.: World Bank; Rodrik, D. (1997) "Trade Policy and Economic Performance in Sub-Saharan Africa," paper prepared for the Swedish Ministry for Foreign Affairs.

[40]See *African Development Indicators 1998/99*, Table 12.9; South Africa and Nigeria are excluded because both received minimal amounts of aid.

[41]See IRIS (1996) *Governance and the Economy in Africa: Tools for Analysis and Reform of Corruption* College Park: Center for Institutional Reform and the Informal Sector; Bardhan, P. (1977) "Corruption and Development: A Review of Issues," *Journal of Economic Literature*, 35, 1320–1346.

[42]Ayittey, G.B.N. (1998) *Africa in Chaos*, New York: St. Martin's Press; Ayittey, G.B.N. (1992) *Africa Betrayed*, New York: St. Martin's Press; Sandbrook, R. (1986) "The State and Economic Stagnation in Tropical Africa," *World Development*, 14, 319–332.

[43]Smith (1776; Skinner edition, 1979, p. 121) wrote: "When the market is very small, no person can have the encouragement to dedicate himself entirely to one employment, for want of the power to exchange all that surplus part of the produce of his own labour...."

[44]Goldsmith, A.A. (1995) "The State and the Market in Economic Development: A Second Look at Adam Smith in Theory and Practice," *Development and Change*, 26, 633–650.

[45]Block (Block, S.A. (1994) "A New View of Agricultural Productivity in Sub-Saharan Africa," *American Journal of Agricultural Economics*, 76, 619–624) argued that productivity measured in "wheat units" had not declined in Africa. This is *not* reflected in the food security or health data (*African Development Indicators 1998/99*, Table 8.5, Part 13); agricultural productivity has improved in some areas, but it has been localized (Schioler, E. (1998) *Good News from Africa: Farmers, Agricultural Research and Food in the Pantry*, Washington, D.C.: International Food Policy Research Institute.).

[46]World Bank (1981) *Accelerated Development in Sub-Saharan Africa: An Agenda for Action*, Washington, D.C.: World Bank; ECA/OAU (1989) *African Alternative Framework to Structural Adjustment Programmes for Socio-Economic Recovery and Transformation*, AAF-SAP, New York: Economic Commission for Africa, United Nations, pp. 2–3; Eicher, C.K. and Baker, D.C. (1992) "Agricultural Development in Sub-Saharan Africa: A Critical Survey," in L.R. Martin, Ed., *A Survey of Agricultural Economics Literature*, Vol. 4, Minneapolis, MN: University of Minnesota Press for the American Agricultural Economics Association.

[47]*African Development Indicators 1998/99*, Table 2.17, pp. 5–35

[48]One clear lesson from Asia's emergence is that rapid increases in agricultural productivity preceded the shift to manufactured exports (As DB (1997) *Emerging Asia: Changes and Challenges*, Manilla: Asian Development Bank).

[49]Freeman, R. and Lindauer, D. (1998) "Why Not Africa?," draft, Cambridge, MA: Harvard University.

[50]Ironically, none of the mainstream growth theorists has seen the possibility of economic regression through "incapacity-through-inactivity" (see, for example, Solow, R.M. (1997) *Learning from "Learning by Doing": Lessons for Economic Growth*, Stranford, CA: Stranford University Press). This outcome would emerge from running an endogenous growth model backwards.

[51]GCA (1996) *African Social and Economic Trends 1995*, annual report, Washington, D.C.: Global Coalition for Africa; Gibb, R. (1998) "Southern African in Transition: Prospects and Problems Facing Regional Integration," *The Journal of Modern African Studies*, 36, 287–306.

[52]Bennell, P. (1997) "Privatization in Sub-Saharan Africa: Progress and Prospects During the 1990s," *World Development*, 25, 1785–1804; World Bank (1997) *World Development Report 1997: The State in a Changing World*, New York: Oxford University Press.

[53]Dealing with redundant public servants has delayed labor market reform across Africa. One scheme would be to identify redundant workers and keep them on the payroll at a base level of pay. These workers would contribute to improved efficiency by simply staying out of the way. This arrangement would be significantly cheaper and more effective than most redundancy schemes now in place.

[54]Heller, W.W. (1954) "Fiscal Policies for Underdeveloped Economies," in H.P. Wald, Ed., *Conference on Agricultural Taxation and Economic Development*, Cambridge, MA: Harvard Law School; IRIS (1996) *Governance and the Economy in Africa: Tools for Analysis and Reform of Corruption*; College Park: Center for Institutional Reform and the Informal Sector; Meier, G.M., Ed. (1970) *Leading Issues in Economic Development*, 2nd ed., New York: Oxford University Press.

[55]One area that has so far been poorly addressed has been the organizational consequences of the HIV/AIDS pandemic. Organizations are under severe stress through the loss of staff, the waste of staff time, the high cost of training, and increasing opportunism through the breakdown in accountability. Additional stress is being added by the requirements of reform, most of which add to rather than remove administrative and analytical burdens.

[56]FRBKC (1997) *Maintaining Financial Stability in a Global Economy,* proceedings of a symposium sponsored by the Federal Reserve Bank of Kansas City, August, Jackson Hole, WY; Pill, H. and Pradhan, M. (1997) "Financial Liberalization in Africa and Asia," *Finance and Development*, June, 7–10; Knight, M. (1998) "Developing Countries and the Globalization of Financial Markets," *World Development,* 26, 1185–1200.

[57]OECD (1998) *Open Markets Matter: The Benefits of Trade and Investment Liberalisation*, Paris: Organisation for Economic Cooperation and Development; Kreuger, A.O. (1997) "Trade Policy and Economic Development: How We Learn," *American Economic Review*, 87, 1–22; Reisen, H. (1989) "Public Debt, External Competitiveness, and Fiscal Discipline in Developing Countries," *Princeton Studies in International Finance*, November (No. 66); Goldsbrough, D. *et al.* (1996) *Reinvigorating Growth in Developing Countries: Lessons from Adjustment Policies in Eight Economies*, Occasional Paper No. 139, Washington, D.C.: International Monetary Fund.

[58]Orme, J. (1995) "The Original Megapolicy: America's Marshall Plan," in J.D. Montgomery and D.A. Rondinelli, Eds., *Great Policies: Strategic Innovations in Asia and the Pacific Basin*, Wesport, CT: Praeger; Work Bank (1998) *Assessing Aid*, Research Report, Washington, D.C.: World Bank.

[59]European Union (1996) "Green Paper on Relations Between the European Union and the ACP Countries on the Eve of the 21st Century: Challenges and Options for a New Partnership," European Commission Study Group Partnership 2000 DG VIII/1, Brussels.

GLOSSARY

Absolute advantage The ability of a person, firm, or nation to produce everything more efficiently than another person, firm, or nation.

Absolute income hypothesis Theory which states that saving is a linear function of disposable income. It is composed of autonomous saving and the marginal propensity to consume out of income.

Acquired immune deficiency syndrome (AIDS) The disease caused by the human immunodeficiency virus (HIV), which attacks and destroys the immune system. HIV causes AIDS when it enters the body through the exchange of fluids, invasive mucosal procedures using contaminated instruments, or, in the case of drug users, through the exchange of needles.

Adult literacy The Percentage of people ages 15 and above who can, with understanding, read and write a short, simple statement on their everyday life.

African Development Bank (AfDB) A multinational development bank established in 1966 to assist the development of African nations through the provision of loans and technical assistance.

AFDB is supported by 77 nations including 53 countries from Africa, North and South America, Europe, and Asia. AfDB is headquartered in Abidjan, Côte d'Ivoire. The Bank Group consists of three institutions.

African dummy Another name for the so-called *Africa effect*—an indication that simply being in Africa results in low growth—which is often used to explain Africa's dismal growth.

African economic development A multidimensional process involving an increase in income, improvement in the quality of life of Africans, and transformation in the structure of African economies, social structures, and popular attitudes.

Agglomeration externalities Spillover costs or benefits experienced by a firm or country due to proximity to spatial clustering. Positive feedbacks between firms may take the form of information contagion. They may also result from pecuniary externalities: the local provision of specialized industrial services and the local availability of a pool of qualified workers.

Agricultural development The process of improving the nature of agriculture in all its aspects—increasing basic agricultural production, improving input and credit availability, establishing research stations and effective extension services, and improving irrigation, marketing, and transportation networks.

Agricultural growth Sustained increase in the output of the agricultural sector which ultimately results in rising national output.

Agricultural productivity Output per unit of input of the agricultural sector; this may be high or low. (See also *Agricultural growth*.)

Agriculture share in GDP The value added in a country's agricultural sector as a percentage of gross domestic product.

AIDS See *acquired immune deficiency syndrome.*

Alienation The condition of physical or emotional estrangement or isolation.

Allocative efficiency The allocation or apportionment of resources toward the production of the proper mix of products most wanted by society

Anglophone English-speaking, or pertaining to a country or territory that has been colonized by Great Britain; former colonies of Great Britain in Africa.

Annual deforestation The average annual percentage change in forest area; negative numbers indicate an increase in forest area.

Annual water use per capita A country's annual water use, in a single year, divided by its population of the same year and expressed in cubic meters.

Appropriate technology Technology that takes into consideration a nation's resource endowment and its other unique and environmental conditions it involves adapting imported technology.

Assimilation The process whereby the citizens of a country or region or minority group are forced to adopt the customs and attitudes of another culture; assimilation was a conscious policy used by the French colonial administration in Africa.

Banking regulation The stated rules and guidelines that direct the commercial operation of banks and depository institutions, usually established and enforced by the central bank.

Basic human needs The essential and fundamental goods and services necessary for a minimum standard of living. They include food, shelter, clothing, sanitation, education, etc.

Beggar your neighbor Improving one's lot by impoverishing someone else through direct expropriation or appropriation of someone else's wealth by looting and raiding.

Benefit-enhancing corruption A very popular form of corruption in post-independence Africa. It occurs when civil servants allow more public benefits to accrue toward specific individuals or groups against the legally due parties. In exchange, recipients share these additional benefits with the bureaucrat based on prior arrangements.

Benefit-reducing corruption A form of corruption that occurs when civil servants illegally appropriate public benefits intended for private citizens or groups for their own use.

Bidirectional causal relationships A relationship with a feedback effect or moving in two usually opposite directions. It is a relationship where the causal variable is also an effect.

Bourgeoisie In capitalism, the wealthy middle-class business people who own property and have control over material goods and means of production.

Brain drain Also known as reverse technology transfer. It is the significant international migration of highly skilled manpower, especially scientists and technical workers, from developing countries to the more advanced countries offering better opportunities. Many educated and skilled Africans have migrated to the West in response to the poor economic situation in their home countries; the West gains, Africa loses.

Bribe A monetary payment or other inducement used to elicit illegal or dishonest activity or service.

Bureaucratic bottlenecks Also known as *red tape* or *bureaucracy*, bureaucratic bottlenecks are restrictions in the administrative system or process in which the need to follow complex procedures impedes effective action.

Bureaucratic corruption A form of corruption that occurs when public servants raise their compensation levels above and beyond the legal limit

Capabilities "doings and beings" Being adequately nourished, leading a long and healthy life, being literate, and avoiding homelessness.

Capital flight Large-scale movement or removal of financial assets, individual and corporate investment capital, and income from a country.

Capital flows Spatial or temporal movement of direct and portfolio investment or capital goods expenditures. These flows can be from individuals, corporations, commercial banks, and financial investment companies.

Carbon dioxide emissions per capita Emissions of CO_2 from the burning of fossil fuels in industrial processes and the manufacture of cement. It is calculated by dividing emissions by total population and expressd in metric tons.

Central Africa Region in central part of Africa comprising Angola, Cameroon, Central African Republic, Chad, Congo Republic, Equatorial Guinea, Gabon, São Tomé and Principe, and the Democratic Republic of Congo.

Central bank independence The ability of a central bank to conduct monetary policy and efficiently perform its supervisory and regulatory roles without interference by government and the political elite. It is also the degree to which the central bank can avoid the politicization of monetary policy and avoid fulfilling the interests of the government and the political elite, that could constrain its supervisory and regulatory efficiency.

Child malnutrition The percentage of children less than 5 years old who are underweight.

Civil war War within a nation; the act of war between opposing groups of one country.

Colonialism Policy of extending control or maintaining dominance by a nation over another country or territory.

Commodity terms of trade The price index of exports divided by the price index of imports. For example, if export prices increase 10% and import prices 22%, the commodity terms of trade would drop 10%; that is, 1.10/1.22 = 0.90.

Common market A level of economic integration that allows movement of factors of production within the economic bloc. It involves unified duty on imports for members and free movement of goods labor, and capital among member countries.

Communal land tenure A land tenure system mainly dictated by group ownership and rights over land. This group could be a family, clan, tribe, or community.

Comparative advantage The ability to produce a good or service at lower opportunity cost than a competitor or a higher relative efficiency in the production of a particular good in one country or company as opposed to another. A nation or firm has comparative advantage in some product when it can produce that product at lower domestic opportunity cost than can a potential trading partner.

Complex humanitarian emergencies A human-made crisis, in which large numbers of people die and suffer from war, physical violence (often by the state), and refugee displacement.

Conflict tradition An indicator of the justifications for political violence, based on the cultural experience of violence in the past.

Contraception A population control tool involving the deliberate prevention of conception or impregnation through the use of various devices—sexual techniques, abortion, or drugs.

Corruption Perverse or dishonest exploitation or subversion of power for personal gain, usually involving theft of public resources by civil servants; embezzlement; illegal extraction of income from state enterprises; nepotism; favoring relatives, friends, and those who are able to pay bribes in the distribution of public goods and services, employment in the civil service, etc. It is the abuse of one's public office in an effort to extract benefits for the officeholder or his relatives, friends, and supporters; capricious and selective enforcement of state regulations in an effort to benefit the enforcer or regulator; differential treatment of business owners in the expectation of a bribe from the owner of the enterprise that is enjoying the preferential treatment; and illegal taxation of private economic effort with benefits accruing to the bureaucrat.

Corruption perception index Composite index produced by various organizations including Transparency International, relating to perceptions of the degree of corruption in a country as seen by business people, risk analysts, and the general public; it ranges between 10 (highly clean) and 0 (highly corrupt).

Cost-enhancing corruption A form of corruption whereby civil servants who control stocks of public goods may attempt to extract rents from potential consumers either by demanding payment (in the case of goods that are supposed to be free to consumers) or by charging a price that is greater than the ceiling or government imposed price.

Cost-reducing corruption A type of corruption in which civil servants attempt to lower the costs imposed on a business enterprise by state regulations below their normal levels.

Crude birth rates The yearly number of live births per 1000 population.

Culture A society's shared ways of being, encompassing the beliefs, values, norms, customs, practices, institutions, and social behaviors produced by a particular nation, population, or group of people.

Customs union A level of economic integration where member countries remove trade barriers among themselves and also set common trade barriers for goods imported from nonmembers; it places unified duty on imports from the rest of the world for members.

DALYs (disability-adjusted life years) A World Bank measure that combines healthy life years lost because of premature mortality with those lost as a result of disability.

Death rates Also known as the crude death rate; the yearly number of deaths per 1000 population.

Debt service The interest and principal payments due in a given year on external debt.

Debt servicing Paying back a debt or paying only the interest on a debt, as a condition set by the lender, to allow postponing payments on the principal.

Democracy Countries that are ruled by individuals in government that have been chosen freely and equally by the people of the nation. It is the right of all citizens to participate in the selection and election of government representatives is given.

Demographic transitions theory A theory that states that all human populations move from a pretransitional stage of high fertility, high mortality, and low population growth rate through a period of high population growth rates resulting from a decline in mortality rates to another period of low population growth rates.

Dependency ratio Ratio of nonworking population (conventionally defined as 0 to 14 years and 65 years and over) to working-age population.

Diarrhea Disease or infection of the gastrointestinal system characterized by gastrointestinal upset and frequent and excessive discharging of the bowels, producing abnormally thin watery feces and spreading infection.

Diaspora The dispersion of a unified people, language, culture, or entity from its origin.

Dictatorship A nation under the despotic rule of an absolute power or authority figure.

Disguised unemployment A state of being seemingly employed but in reality being underemployed or doing jobs that may require less than full-time commitment.

Division of labor A form of specialization in production involving the separation and organization of tasks among workers within a group.

Dynamic benefits from trade The indirect, productivity-enhancing, development-generating benefits to trading countries. For example, trade could help a country obtain machinery and other capital goods, raw and semi-finished materials, technological knowledge, ideas, know-how, skills, managerial talents, and entrepreneurship. Trade could serve as a vehicle for international movement of capital from areas of low capital productivity to areas of high capital productivity.

East Africa Region in east central Africa, usually taken to consist of Burundi, Kenya, Rwanda, Somalia, Tanzania, and Uganda.

Economic and monetary union (EMU) An arrangement or economic linkage involving free-trade zones or trade blocs, a single currency, and unified monetary policy across nations. The European Union is an example of an EMU.

Economic determinism The determination of a country's political system and its relevant class structures by the nation's economies or predominant "mode of production."

Economic development The rise in per capita income, the improvement of quality of life, the reduction of poverty, and the positive fundamental change in the structure of an economy.

Economic growth Increase in output (GDP or GNP) or incomes over a period of time—a quarter or a year.

Economic infrastructure Infrastructures such as telecommunication, water, power, and transportation which make it possible to produce transaction-intensive products such as manufactures and services.

Economic integration Common and unified economic policy usually associated with a monetary union.

Economic reform Policy measure geared toward the reduction of government's involvement in the economy while allowing for an increased role of markets.

Economic regression A decline in per capita gross product.

Economic stabilization Policy changes that aim to achieve macroeconomic stability by reducing government spending and controlling excessive money growth, which cause inflation, to ultimately stabilize the domestic currency exchange rate.

Economic union Common market with harmonized economic policies; for instance, the European Community.

Economies of scale Achieved when the long run average cost decreases as output increases.

Ecosystem A localized community and the environment it lives and depends on, as a whole.

Educational attainment A measure of achievement in adult literacy (two-thirds weight) and the combined gross primary, secondary, and tertiary enrollment ratio (one-third weight).

Electorialism Leaders chosen for office without all the attendant rights to which people in advanced democracies are accustomed.

ELF index See *Ethno-linguistic fractionalization index.*

Energy efficiency Gross domestic product divided by total energy consumption of oil equivalent, expressed in constant U.S. dollars.

Energy use per capita Annual consumption of commercial energy divided by population, expressed in kilograms of oil equivalent.

Entitlement The legitimate right and claim of ownership over an item. It is central to one's livelihood and well-being and generates capabilities.

Epidemiology The scientific study of the origin, causes, distribution (transmission), and control of disease in populations.

Ethnic diversity The occurrence of disparate or dissimilar cultural traits, language, and heritage within a social group or nation.

Ethno-linguistic fractionalization (ELF) The degree to which societies differ with respect to the extent of ethnic differentiation

Ethno-linguistic fractionalization index (ELF index) A quantitative measure of how societies differ with respect to the extent of ethnic differentiation. Homogenous societies are scored zero, and the theoretical maximum of 100 would be reached if each person belonged to a distinct group. The observed range is from 0 to 93.

Exchange rate The rate at which one currency exchanges for another or a system that measures the price of one currency in terms of another.

Expansive corruption One of two types of corruption identified by Osterfeld; it involves activities (e.g., the theft of public resources by civil servants) that significantly improve and enhance the competitiveness of markets.

Export processing zones Geographical areas designed to give incentives for export-oriented production.

Export subsidies Tax breaks or subsidies given to domestic producers or foreign buyers to promote exports.

Externalities or spillovers Positive and negative outcomes resulting from production or consumption that affects or spills over to third parties or nonparticipants in the market.

Female labor force The percentage of women in the labor force.

Fertility rate Total fertility rate representing the number of children that would be born to a woman if she were to live to the end of her childbearing years and bear children in accordance with prevailing age-specific fertility rates.

Financial intermediation Service of mobilizing financial resources and savings from depositors and making them available to investors as loans.

First World Industrialized Western Europe, North America, and Pacific.

Fiscal policy Discretionary fiscal policy referring to the deliberate manipulation of taxes and government spending by government to alter real domestic output and employment, control inflation, and stimulate economic growth. "Discretionary" means the changes are at the option of the state government. Expansionary fiscal policy (creating a budget deficit) is used to combat a recession and embodies three options. Contractionary fiscal policy is used against demand–pull inflation.

Foreign direct investment (FDI) Otherwise known as direct foreign investment (DFI). International capital flows and foreign real investment in production of goods and services in which a firm in one country creates a new business or expands or merges with a firm in another.

Foreign exchange earnings Profit made from the conversion of one currency into another or the buying and selling of different currencies.

Forest coverage The percentage of total land area covered by forest and woodland.

Francophone A person or nation that uses French as a native or official language; also refers to former French colony.

Free trade area A regional economic bloc in which member countries reduce or remove trade barriers on intragroup trade for all goods or on an agreed subset of goods; a level of economic integration where members remove barriers on trade between member countries, but each country sets its own trade policies with nonmembers. At this level of economic integration, member states set their own national trade policies with nonmembers. A customs union represents a higher level of integration than a free trade area; in a customs union, member countries not only remove trade barriers among themselves, but also maintain common trade barriers for goods imported from nonmembers.

Free trade associations Elimination of duties on imports among countries involved, while charging different duties on imports from other countries. An example is the North American Free Trade Agreement (NAFTA) between the United States, Mexico, and Canada.

Freedom Index Perhaps the most widely used index for democracy; measures various subcomponents of political and civil freedoms and then ranks them from one to seven, where seven is completely authoritarian and one completely free.

Gains from international trade The benefits that result when countries sell goods and services to one another.

GDP per capita The ratio of GDP to the population; also, a measure of per capita income.

Gemeinschaft Societies characterized by community, family, geographic solidarity, blood, religious association, and rank through ascriptive characteristics.

Gender gap Difference in male/female performance or outcome.

Generalized system of preferences (GSP) A program under which developed countries provide preferential reduction or removal of tariffs on products from developing countries.

Gesellshaft Societies that are more purposeful and are based more on common interests, unbundled communities, and secular association and are ranked on merit.

Gini coefficient A measure of income concentration or inequality that sums the absolute difference between all pairs of incomes; the coefficient ranges from 0 (absolute equality) to 1 (maximum inequality, where one person receives all income).

Gini index A measure of the extent to which the distribution of income among individuals or households within a country deviates from a perfectly equal distribution. A value of 0 represents perfect equality; a value of 1, perfect inequality.

Globalization The process by which a business or company becomes global or international in its operations; increasing economic interdependence among the countries of the world in which global politics plays a key role. It involves a significant increase in trade, capital, cultural, and information flows. This multiplicity of linkages, interconnections, interdependence, and dependence has been facilitated by improvements in transportation and communications and removal of trade barriers.

GNI (GNP) The sum of value added by all resident producers plus any product taxes (less subsidies) not included in the valuation of output plus net receipts of primary income (compensation of employees and property income) from abroad.

GNP per capita growth rate The average annual percentage change in a country's real GNP per capita ($\Delta Y_t = (Y_t - Y_{t-1})/Y_{t-1}$, where Y_t is real per capita GNP in a given year t, and Y_{t-1} is the previous year's per capita GNP).

GNP per capita in international dollars (I$) Calculated by converting GNP per capita to its purchasing power parity (PPP) rate, where PPP is defined as the number of units of a country's currency required to buy the same amounts of goods and services in the domestic market as $1 would buy in the United States. If GNP per capita in mainland Tanzania in 1998 was $220, and its purchasing-power adjustment (PPP exchange rate/actual exchange rate) was 2.195, then GNP in international dollars (I$) was $2.195 \times 220 = 483$.

Gross domestic product (GDP) The market value of all final goods and services produced within a country in one year; usually comprised of output generated within the domestic economy regardless of the source of the output.

Gross national product (GNP) The sum value added by all resident producers plus any product taxes (less subsidies) not included in the valuation of output plus net receipts of primary income (compensation of employees and property income) from abroad.

Growth rates The rate at which output (GDP or GNP) changes annually; $((GDP_t - GDP_{t-1})/GDP_{t-1}) \times 100$.

Health The World Health Organization (WHO) defines health as a state of complete physical, mental, and social well-being and not merely the absence of disease or infirmity.

Heckscher–Ohlin theory Also, Heckscher–Ohlin–Samuelson (HOS) model. A theory suggesting that differences between countries in their relative factor endowments and differences between commodities in the intensities with which they use these factors determine who sells what in international trade.

Hidden unemployment A state of employment involving labor that is unproductive due to physical incapacitation, disease, lack of skill, or low productivity.

Hispanophone Former Spanish colony or a person or nation that uses Spanish as a native or official language.

Household infrastructure index An index that examines a household's access to different categories of infrastructure.

Human Development Index (HDI) A composite index based on the three indicators of life expectancy, educational attainment, and GNP per capita; measures average achievement in three basic dimensions of human development—a long and healthy life, knowledge, and a decent standard of living. The HDI rages from 0 to 1, with a value of 1 being the highest.

Human immunodeficiency virus (HIV) A virus that causes the disease acquired immune deficiency syndrome (AIDS). There are two types of HIV; the more easily transmissible HIV-1 is found in all parts of the world, and HIV-2 is found mostly in West Africa.

Human poverty A living condition that involves a lack or limitation of basic human needs and the absence or denial of choices and opportunities that allow one to live a tolerable life.

Human Poverty Index (HPI) A composite index measuring deprivations in the three basic dimensions of the Human Development Index: longevity, knowledge, and standard of living.

Illiteracy rates (adult) Percentage of people who have inadequate education measured as the percentage of people aged 15 and above who cannot, with understanding, read and write a short, simple statement on their everyday life.

IMF (International Monetary Fund) International financial institution which, like the World Bank, originated as a Bretton Woods organization in 1944; involved in the regulation of the international monetary exchanges to minimize international financial instability.

Import substitution (IS) The belief that developing countries should substitute previously imported simple consumer goods and ultimately manufactured items with domestically produced manufactures using protective import tariffs and quotas.

Income poverty The lack of a minimum level of financial resources to satisfy basic human needs.

Income terms of trade (export purchasing power) The commodity terms of trade multiplied by export volume. For example, if the commodity terms of trade should drop 10% while export volume increased by 22%, the income terms of trade would increase by 10%; that is, $0.90 \times 1.22 = 1.10$.

Indicators of development Items that determine the development performance of countries within the context of other countries.

Indirect rule A British method of governing its former colonies that attempted to govern the Africans through a semblance of African institutions on the local level.

Infant mortality rates The number of children who die before their first birthday out of every 1000 live births.

International commodity agreements Arrangements in which exporting and importing countries of a particular commodity agree to control the supply of that commodity in the world market.

International portfolio investment Foreign investment, which is purely financial in nature.

Intra-African trade Trade done by Africans within the African continent.

Investment share in GDP Gross domestic investment as a percentage of gross domestic product.

Investment The purchase of capital goods by a business (capital investment) to make a profit, or the purchase of financial assets (financial investment); it is the total market value of goods and services produced in a country or region annually, including output by foreign owned resources in the country.

Italophones Former Italian colonies; a person or nation that uses Italian as a native or official language.

Kleptocracy A government run by individuals with the specific purpose of procuring wealth and money for themselves.

Lagos Plan of Action An act signed in 1980 in Lagos, Nigeria, by African Heads of States who envisaged the creation of an African Economic Community that would be built on regional economic groupings such as SADC and ECOWAS.

Land tenure A set of rights determining who owns land; rights involving the use of land and in what manner.

Land tenure reform A process whereby existing land tenure system is overhauled, totally or partially using a variety of measures, either jointly or separately (e.g., nationalizing land and creating state-owned farms, making tenant farmers own land they farm on, and dividing large plots of land among the poor).

Learning by doing Looking inward and using a policy of encouraging indigenous technology in manufacturing based on a country's resource endowment. Inward-looking development policy.

Legitimacy The normative basis for the exercise of governmental authority.

Less developed countries (LDCs) Also known as developing countries; includes countries with low per capita income found mostly in Africa, Asia, Latin America.

Life expectancy A measure of longevity—the average number of years a newborn baby would live if patterns of mortality prevailing for all people at the time of its birth were to stay the same throughout life.

Life expectancy at birth The average number of years a newborn baby would live if patterns of mortality prevailing for all people at the time of its birth were to stay the same throughout the child's life.

Life-cycle hypothesis Views consumption as being proportional to the product of working years divided by life expectancy times annual earnings.

Literacy rates The number of people within a population who are able to read and write.

Lorenz curve A curve that shows the percentage of total income accounted for by any cumulative percentage of recipients. The further the Lorenz curve (the convex line) bends away from the 45° line, the greater is the inequality of income distribution.

Low-income (LIC) economies Those economies in which 1999 GNI per capita was $755 or less.

Low-level equilibrium population trap/ Malthusian population trap A vicious cycle of economic growth leading to high population growth, which mops up economic gains and leads to poverty and positive checks, followed by another cycle of economic progress, population growth, and so on.

Lower-middle-income (LMC) economies Those economies for which the 1999 GNI per capita was between $755 and $2995.

Lusophone A person or nation that uses Portuguese as a native or official language; also refers to a former Portuguese colony.

Macroeconomic policy A major function of government designed to stabilize and grow the economy; achieved in part by manipulating the public budget—government spending and tax collections—to increase output and employment or to reduce inflation. It also entails changes in money supply by the monetary authorities (an independent central bank). Hence, the fundamental objective of macroeconomic policy is to assist the economy in achieving a full-employment, noninflationary level of output.

Malaria An infection caused by four kinds of *Plasmodium* parasite that can be transmitted to people by the bite of infected female anopheline mosquitoes. It is a severe illness usually characterized by recurring chills and fever is caused by *P. falciparum*, which is widespread in Africa and less so in Asia and Latin America.

Malnutrition A state of inadequate or faulty nutrition usually measured by the prevalence of malnutrition—the percentage of children under age 5 who are underweight.

Malthusian population trap A vicious cycle of economic growth leading to high population growth, which mops up economic gains and leads to poverty and positive checks, followed by another cycle of economic progress, population growth, and so on.

Maternal mortality ratio A measure of survivorship of women expressed as the number of women who die during pregnancy or childbirth per 100,000 live births.

Middle-income (MIC) economies Those economies for which the 1999 GNI per capita was between $755 and $9265.

Migration A focus on how human population is distributed in geographic space; how people move from one country or region to another.

Military centrality The size of military expenditures relative to GNP.

Modernization theory Theory that held that countries with higher per capita GDP, higher levels of education, more urban dwellers, more unions, higher levels of education, and other indices of more modern society also had more demands from society for political inclusion.

Monetary policy Altering of the economy's money supply for the purpose of stabilizing aggregate output, employment, and price level. This is done to assist the economy achieve a full-employment, noninflationary level of output. More specifically, it involves increasing the money supply during a recession to stimulate spending (easy monetary policy) and restricting the money supply during inflation to constrain spending (tight monetary policy).

Moral hazard The possibility of loss or risk posed to an insurer due to uncertainty about the honesty of the insured.

Mortality A measure of the probability of dying—that is, the probability of a person dying before reaching a certain age.

Most favored nation principle The term is used in the context of the World Trade Organization to imply that a member country must treat all other members equally in respect to trade policy.

Multiethnic societies Societies that have more than one ethnic group.

Multinational corporations Firms that operate in several countries.

Nationalism Loyalty or a sense of devotion to a nation or cause by a country under foreign control or by a people desirous of a separate identity to achieve political independence.

Negative real interest rate A nominal rate of interest less than the inflation rate.

Neoclassical tradition Revival of the classical school of thought which believes that the state's role is strictly limited to the provision of essential services and to the definition of property rights within the economic system, with the goal of reducing externalities and promoting and diffusing information about existing economic opportunities.

Neo-Marxist paradigm Expectation that the state should become more activist in the development process, owning resources, producing goods and services, and planning development.

Neolithic Pertaining to the Stone Age, between about 8000 B.C. and 5000 B.C.; characterized by the development of settled agriculture and the use of polished stone tools and weapons.

Nepotism The favoring of relatives and friends in the distribution of public goods and services, employment in the civil service, etc. It is the abuse of one's power in public office in an effort to extract benefits for the officeholder or his relatives, friends, and supporters.

Net aid flows per capita Net concessional loans and grants received by a country divided by its mid-year population.

Non-bank financial institutions Financial institutions such as thrift institutions, savings and loan associations, credit unions, and mutual savings banks that provide financial services, including checking and saving facilities, financial investment, and credit facilities.

ODA (Official Development Assistance) Actual international transfer by the donor of financial resources or of goods or services valued at the cost to the donor, less any repayments of loan principal during the same period. It also includes some loans, technical cooperation assistance, and grants by official agencies of the members of the Development Assistance Committee.

OECD (Organization for Economic Cooperation and Development) An international organization based in Paris and consisting of 20 (wealthy) countries from Europe and North America whose main objective is to promote economic growth through cooperation and technical analysis of economic trends.

Onchocerciasis Also called river blindness. A worm-borne tropical disease transmitted by black flies. The symptoms include skin nodules, lesions, and blindness.

Openly unemployed Urban educated members of the labor force, usually 15 to 24 years of age without employment.

Operationalization Moving from the level of abstract concepts to concrete indicators, especially in research; requires the use of specific indicators and measures to think about logical possibilities and establish relationships.

Orthodox development paradigm Within the context of this paradigm, an economy that afforded its citizens a high level of personal income was considered developed, while an economy whose per capita GDP was relatively low was considered undeveloped and poor.

Orthodoxy (conformity) The practice of observing established social customs and definitions of appropriateness.

Panel data Pooled data in which the same cross-sectional unit is surveyed over time, such as households, a firm.

Parastatals (parastatal enterprises, state-owned enterprises [SOEs]) Public corporations and statutory boards owned by the state but responsible for day-to-day management to boards of directors, some of whom are appointed by the state; state-owned or government-controlled organization, business, or industry.

Patrimonialism A political system in which incumbents use governmental structures as instruments for their personal enrichment.

Patronage A system of political control exercised from above, which is based on the distribution of political and economic favors.

Per capita income Income per person, determined as the ratio of GDP to population.

Personal rule Situation in which incumbent politicians use public resources to purchase loyalty and thus continue to maintain a monopoly on political power and the supply of legislation.

Physical Quality of Life Index Composite index that measures the quality of life using three social indicators—live expectancy at birth, literacy rate, and infant mortality rate. PQLI values range from 1 to 100, where 1 represents the worst performance for any country and 100 the best performance. In general, countries with low PQLIs tend to have low per capita GDP.

Political instability (PI) Situation, activities, or patterns of political behavior (including wars, strikes, coups, and assassinations) that threaten to change or change the political system in a non-constitutional way. These politically unstable events often bring about sudden radical changes in property right laws and the rules governing business conduct as well as social relationships. The key attribute of PI is that it generates uncertainties about the stability of an existing political system and/or government, and this uncertainty negatively affects the authority and effectiveness of governing institutions, the judiciary included.

Political union The final stage of regional integration; in addition to cumulative obligations of an economic and monetary union, participating countries share political decision-making over foreign policy, security policy, and so forth. It is a *de facto*, if not a *de jure*, federal arrangement.

Population below income poverty line The percentage of the population living below $1 a day (the poverty line) adjusted for purchasing power parity (PPP).

Population control The limiting of numbers of people living in an area.

Population growth rate The average annual percentage change in a country's population (population$_t$ – population$_{t-1}$/ × 100), expressed as percent.

Poverty A degrading condition of having too little money and living life devoid of economic, social, and political choices.

Poverty rate Percentage of the population living on less than one U.S. dollar a day measured in purchasing power parity (PPP) dollars.

PPP GNI (PPP GNP) Gross national income converted to international dollars using purchasing power parity (PPP) rates. An international dollar has the same gross national income (GNI) purchasing power as a U.S. dollar has in the United States. GNI is the sum of value added by all resident producers plus any product taxes (less subsidies) not included in the valuation of output plus net receipts of primary income (compensation of employees and property income) from abroad.

Predatory rule Rule through coercion, material inducement, and personality politics, which tends to degrade the institutional foundations of the economy and state.

Preferential tariffs Lowering of duties on imports from member states.

Primary health care (PHC) The health care that focuses primarily on preventive rather than curative medicine involving universal children's immunization, sanitation, safe water, health education, and community involvement in healthcare decisions as well as implementation.

Primary school enrollment rates Percentage of students of official school age who are enrolled in primary schools.

Process democrats Those who look to see if the leaders were elected in free and fair elections.

Production function A technical relationship between inputs and outputs such as units of labor and units of output.

Productive resources Also known as factors of production—land, labor capital, and entrepreneurship; resources used in the production of goods and services.

Productivity Output per unit of input; that is, the ratio of output to input.

Proletariat Marxian designation of the working class or the masses.

Property rights regimes Society's institutional arrangements; an effective set of rules.

Property rights Set of rules governing ownership of property.

Purchasing power parity (PPP) A method of converting GNP per capita into international dollars by determining the number of currency units required to buy the same amount of goods and services in another country as one currency unit would buy at home. The international dollar is obtained when the exchange rates are converted by purchasing power parities to account for differences in prices across countries. Consequently, an international dollar buys the same amount of goods and services in a country's domestic market as one dollar would buy in the United States.

Purchasing power The total amount of goods and services that an amount of money, a monetary unit, or an income can command. It measures the real value of a currency in terms of the goods and services it can buy.

Quality of life Degree of fulfillment of basic needs and human welfare; the extent of satisfaction with and access to food, clothing, housing, health, educational services, good environment, and richer cultural life.

Quota A quantitative limit on imports.

Real per capita GNP Total output adjusted for price changes. The ratio of nominal GNP to the deflector.

Regional economic integration Refers to special economic arrangements between countries in a given geographical area. This implies differential treatment in trade for member countries in comparison with treatment for nonmember countries.

Regionalism The process of peacefully creating a larger coherent entity out of previously separate units, each of which voluntarily cedes part of its sovereignty to a supranational authority and renounces the use of force for the settlement of disputes between member states; the establishment and/

or management of a mutually interdependent relationship that involves two or more countries, presumably in the same geographical zone, to produce jointly that which they separately lack or could not optimally produce; the establishment of joint institutions and some shared autonomy.

Relative deprivation People's perception of social injustice resulting from a discrepancy between goods and conditions they expect and those they can get or keep.

Rent seeking Unproductive activity to obtain private benefit from public action and resources.

Restrictive corruption One of two types of corruption identified by Osterfeld; limits avenues for socially beneficial exchange. According to Osterfeld, restrictive corruption promotes the redistribution of income in favor of certain individuals and groups, thus exacerbating inequalities in income and wealth distribution.

Saving The difference between disposable income and personal consumption expressed as the amount of disposable income not spent for consumption.

Second World Industrialized centrally planned economies of Eastern Europe.

Secondary school enrollment rates Ratio of total enrollment or percentage of students enrolled in a secondary school.

Secularization The movement from less modern to a more modern society.

Southern Africa Region in southern part of Africa, usually taken to include Botswana, Lesotho, Namibia, South Africa, Swaziland, and Zimbabwe.

Specialization The use of the resources of an individual, firm, or nation to produce one or a few goods and services.

State failure A situation where the governing elites lose their capability to maintain authority, law, and political order, which indicates losing their ability to control public resources, set and maintain rules of social behavior, allocate resources effectively, control territory, and conduct an organized foreign policy.

Stock market liquidity A value measured by the value of shares traded (volume or ratio of GDP) and the turnover ratio.

Structural Adjustment Program (SAP) Economic reform programs usually recommended by the International Monetary Fund to promote growth and attain inflation-free balance of payment equilibrium. SAPs involve private and public sector reforms, including trade reforms, agricultural reforms, deregulation of markets, reform of the public enterprise, and financial reforms.

Structural reforms Policies that reduce government's involvement in the economy and allow for an increased role of markets.

Structural transformation The transformation of the productive structure of the economy from mostly agrarian to industrial or service-based. Structural transformation involves industrialization, agricultural transformation, migration, and urbanization.

Sub-Saharan Africa The 48 countries of Africa found south of the Sahara, none of which are classified as high-income economies. They include Angola, Benin, Botswana, Burkina Faso, Burundi, Cameroon, Cape Verde, Central African

Republic, Chad, Comoros, Congo Republic, Democratic Republic of Congo, Côte d'Ivoire, Equatorial Guinea, Eritrea, Ethiopia, Gabon, The Gambia, Ghana, Guinea, Guinea-Bissau, Kenya, Lesotho, Liberia, Madagascar, Malawi, Mali, Mauritania, Mauritius, Mayotte, Mozambique, Namibia, Niger, Nigeria, Rwanda, São Tomé and Principe, Senegal, Seychelles, Sierra Leone, Somalia, South Africa, Sudan, Swaziland, Tanzania, Togo, Uganda, Zambia, and Zimbabwe.

Tariff A tax or excise duty imposed on imports.

Tariff barrier to trade Usually comes in form of protective tariffs or import quotas; An excise tax or duty or duties levied by a government on imported or sometimes exported goods. It is usually used to shield domestic producers from foreign competition.

Technological change Improvement or degradation in the body of knowledge and techniques which can be used to produce goods and services.

Terms of trade (TOT) The price of exports in terms of the price of imports; that is, the number of units of the exportable obtainable for each unit of importable.

Tertiary education Higher education generally begun after high school and carried out at a university or college, and usually involving study for a degree or diploma. Normally requires, as a minimum condition of admission, the successful completion of education at the secondary level.

Third World The less developed countries found mainly in Africa, Asia, and Latin America.

Total fertility rate (TFR) The average number of children that a woman would have if she goes through her reproductive years (15–49) experiencing the current age-specific fertility rates; measures the propensity to have children.

Trade balance Exports minus imports of goods and services; a deficit if negative, and a surplus if positive.

Trade creation Takes place when economic integration leads a product source to shift from high-cost domestic producers to low-cost producers in a member country.

Trade diversion Takes place when economic integration leads a product source to shift from a low-cost nonmember country to a high-cost member country.

Trade share in GDP Exports and imports of goods and services as a percent of gross domestic product.

Trans-Saharan trade Trade across the Sahara which historically (before the era of European Colonization) involved the Western Saharan empires of Ghana, Mali, and Songhay. Also known as the "long distance trade," it involved a variety of commodities, (such as salt, gold, Kola, and slaves), merchants, trading routes, and trading centers from Fezzan to Libya. In addition, numerous primary and secondary products were transported through the trans-Saharan caravans.

Unemployment rate The percentage of the labor force that is unemployed; (number of unemployed/labor force) × 100.

Upper-middle-income (UMC) economies Upper-middle-income economies are those in which 1999 GNI per capita was between $2996 and $9265.

Vent for surplus Outlet for the surplus productive capacity resulting from international trade. The vent for surplus theory suggests that international trade provides a wider market outlet for the productive capacity that would have remained underutilized in the absence of trade, resulting in direct gains from trade.

Victimization Subjecting individuals or groups to harm or suffering through persecution, aggression, or violence as with the Jews in Europe and the Tutsi in Rwanda.

Visibly active but underutilized Members of the labor force who are neither unemployed nor underemployed but have found visible means of marking time.

Voluntary export restraint A quantitative limit on exports usually instituted as a result of pressure from the importing country.

Warlord A ruler who rejects the creation of a state, with its collective authority and bureaucratic institutions, in favor of private or personal exercise of power.

West Africa Region in western Africa that stretches from the southern part of the Sahara desert to the Atlantic Ocean and eastward up to Cameroon.

WHO (World Health Organization) A specialized agency of the United Nations with headquarters in Geneva, Switzerland, composed of 193 member countries as of 2002. WHO directs and coordinates international health work and strives to bring the highest level of health to all peoples.

World Bank Also known as the International Bank for Reconstruction and Development (IBRD). Multilateral agency or international financial institution that serves as the main source of development assistance for developing nations; borrows private funds in the capital markets of rich countries and lends them to the governments of developing countries. Includes the International Bank for Reconstruction and Development, the International Development Association, the International Finance Corp., the Multilateral Investment Guarantee Agency, and the International Centre for the Settlement of Investment Disputes.

Youth literacy Percentage of school-age people (below age 15) who can, with understanding, read and write a short, simple statement.

BIBLIOGRAPHY

CHAPTER 1: WHY STUDY AFRICAN ECONOMIC DEVELOPMENT?

Barro, R. J. (1991) "Economic Growth in a Cross Section of Countries," *Quarterly Journal of Economics*, 106: 407–443.

Basu, K. (1997) *Analytical Development Economics: The Less Developed Economies Revisited*, Cambridge, MA: MIT Press.

Bloom, D. E. and Sachs, J. D. (1998) "Geography, Demography, and Economic Growth in Africa," *Brookings Papers on Economic Activity*, 2: 207–295.

Chenery, H. (1988) "Introduction to Part 2," in H. Chenery and T. N. Srinivasan, Eds., *Handbook of Development Economics*, Vol. 1, Amsterdam: Elsevier.

Collier, P. and Gunning, J. W. (1999) "Explaining African Economic Performance," *Journal of Economic Literature*, 37: 64–111.

Easterly, W. and Levine, R. (1997) "Africa's Growth Tragedy: Policies and Ethnic Divisions," *Quarterly Journal of Economics*, 112: 1203–1250.

Freedom House (2002) *Freedom in the World 2001–2002: Select Data from Freedom House's Annual Global Survey of Political Rights and Civil Liberties*, www.freedomhouse.org/research/survey2002.htm.

Morris, D. (1979) *Measuring the Condition of the World's Poor: The Physical Quality of Life Index*, London: Cass.

Price, G. N. (2001) "Economic Growth in a Cross Section of Non-Industrial Countries: Does Colonial Heritage Matter for Africa?," paper presented at the Allied Social Science Association Meeting, New Orleans, LA, Jan. 5–7.

Stern, N. (1989) "The Economics of Development: A Survey," *The Economic Journal*, 99: 597–685.

Temple, J. (1999) "The New Growth Evidence," *Journal of Economic Literature*, 37: 112–156.

United Nations Development Program (UNDP) (2000) *Human Development Report 2000*, New York: Oxford University Press.

United Nations Development Program (UNDP) (2001) *Human Development Report 2001*, New York: Oxford University Press.

World Bank (1990) *World Development Report 1990: Poverty*, New York: Oxford University Press.

World Bank (1991) *World Development Report 1991: The Challenge of Development*, New York: Oxford University Press.

World Bank (2001) *World Development Indicators 2001 CD-ROM*, Washington, D.C.: The World Bank.

World Bank (2001) *World Development Report 2001*, New York: Oxford University Press.

CHAPTER 2: OVERVIEW OF AFRICAN DEVELOPMENT

Easterly, W. and Levine, R. (1997) "Africa's Growth Tragedy: Policies and Ethnic Divisions," *Quarterly Journal of Economics*, 112(4): 1203–1250.

Fields, G. S. (1960) *Poverty, Inequality and Development*. London: Cambridge University Press.

Frank, Jr., C. R. and Webb, R. C., Eds. (1977) *Income Distribution and Growth in the Less-Developed Countries*, Washington, D.C.: Brookings Institution.

Gillis, M., Perkins, D. H., Roemer, M., and Snodgrass, D. R. (1996) *Economics of Development*, New York: W.W. Norton.

Nafziger, E. W. (1997) *The Economics of Developing Countries*, Upper Saddle River, NJ: Prentice-Hall.

Nnadozie, E. (1998) *African Culture and American Business in Africa*, Kirksville, MO: Afrimax.

Sachs, J. D. and Warner, A. M. (1997) "Sources of Slow Growth in African Economies," *Journal of African Economies*, 6: 335–376.

Sears, D. (1973) "The Meaning of Development," in C. K. Wilber, Ed., *The Political Economy of Development and Underdevelopment*, New York: Random House.

Sen, A. K. (1973) *On Economic Inequality*, New York: Norton.

Todaro, Michael P. (2000) *Economic Development*, Reading, MA: Addison-Wesley.

UNCTAD (2001) *Economic Development in Africa: Performance, Prospects and Policy Issues*, New York: United Nations Conference on Trade and Development.

United Nations Development Program (UNDP) (1990–1994) *Human Development Report*, New York: Oxford University Press.

World Bank (2001) *World Development Indicators 2001 CD-ROM*, Washington, D.C.: The World Bank.

World Bank (2001) *World Development Report 2001*, New York: Oxford University Press.

CHAPTER 3: DEFINITION AND MEASUREMENT OF GROWTH AND DEVELOPMENT

Adler, M. J., Ed. (1994) *Great Books of the Western World*, Chicago, IL: Encyclopaedia Britannica.

Aghion, P., Caroli, E., and García-Peñalosa, C. (1999) "Inequality and Economic Growth: The Perspective of the New Growth Theories," *Journal of Economic Literature*, 37: 1615–1660.

Alesina, A. and Rodrik, D. (1994) "Distributive Politics and Economic Growth," *Quarterly Journal of Economics*, 109(2): 465–490.

Chenery, H. (1988) "Introduction to Part 2," in H. Chenery and T. N. Srinivasan, *Handbook of Development Economics*, Vol. 1, Amsterdam: Elsevier.

Morris, D. (1979) *Measuring the Condition of the World's Poor: The Physical Quality of Life Index*, London: Cass.

Perroti, R. (1993) "Political Equilibrium, Income Distribution, and Growth," *Review of Economic Studies*, 60(4): 755–776.

Persson, T. and Tabellini, G. (1994) "Is Inequality Harmful for Growth?," *American Economic Review*, 84(3): 600–621.

Sachs, J. D. and Warner, A. M. (1997) "Sources of Slow Growth in African Economies," *Journal of African Economies*, 6: 335–376.

Sen, A. (1988) "The Concept of Development," in H. Chenery and T. N. Srinivasan, *Handbook of Development Economics*, Vol. 1, Amsterdam: Elsevier.

Stern, N. (1989) "The Economics of Development: A Survey," *The Economic Journal*, 99: 597–685.

Todaro, M. P. (2000) *Economic Development*, 7th ed., Reading, MA: Addison-Wesley.

United Nations Development Program (UNDP) (1997) *Human Development Report 1997*, New York: Oxford University Press.

United Nations Development Program (UNDP) (2000) *Human Development Report 2000*, New York: Oxford University Press.

United Nations Development Program (UNDP) (2001) *Human Development Report 2001*, New York: Oxford University Press.

World Bank (1990) *World Development Report 1990: Poverty*, New York: Oxford University Press.

World Bank (1991) *World Development Report 1991: The Challenge of Development*, New York: Oxford University Press.

World Bank (2000) *World Development Report 2000: Entering the 21st Century*, New York: Oxford University Press.

World Bank (2001) *World Development Indicators 2001 CD-ROM*, Washington, D.C.: The World Bank.

World Bank (2001) *World Development Report 2001*, New York: Oxford University Press.

CHAPTER 4: GEO-ECONOMY AND HISTORY

Azevedo, M. J. (1998) *Africana Studies: A Survey of Africa and the African Diaspora*, Raleigh-Durham, NC: Carolina Academic Press.

Brooks, L. (1966) *Great Civilizations of Ancient Africa*, New York: Four Winds Press.

Cohen, D. L. and Daniel, J., Eds. (1981) *Political Economy of Africa: Selected Readings*, Harlow, England: Longman.

Curtin, P., Feierman, S., Thompson, L., and Vansina, J. (1989) *African History*, New York: Longman.

Davidson, B. (1994) *Modern Africa: A Social and Political History*, New York: Longman.

Fage, J. D. (1980) *An Atlas of African History*, New York: Africana.

Fairservis, W. A. (1962) *The Ancient Kingdoms of the Nile*, New York: A Mentor Book.

Griffiths, I. (1984) *An Atlas of African Affairs*, London: Cambridge University Press.

Grove, A. T. (1989) *The Changing Geography of Africa*, New York: Oxford University Press.

Hance, W. (1969) *The Geography of Africa*, New York: Columbia University Press.

Ki-zerbo, J., Ed. (1989) *General History of Africa*, Vol. I, Paris: UNESCO.

Raikes, P. (1988) *Modernizing Hunger: Famine, Food Surplus, and Farm Policy in the EEC and Africa*, London: Macmillan.

Rodney, W. (1972) *How Europe Underdeveloped Africa*, Dar-es-Salaam: Tanzania Publishing House.

Rotberg, R. I., Ed. (1973) *Africa and Its Explorers: Motives, Methods, and Impact*, Cambridge, MA: Harvard University Press.

Shillington, K. (1989) *History of Africa*, London: Macmillan.

Stock, R. (1995) *Africa South of the Sahara: A Geographical Interpretation*, New York: Guilford Press.

Sulaiman, M., Ed. (1990) *The Greenhouse Effect and Its Implications for Africa*, London: Institute of African Alternatives.

Temu, A. and Swai, B. (1981) *Historians and Africanist History*, London: Zed Press.

Thompson, B. W. (1965) *The Climate of Africa*, New York: Oxford University Press.

CHAPTER 5: ENGINES OF GROWTH AND AFRICA'S ECONOMIC PERFORMANCE

Aghion, P. and Howitt, P. (1992) "A Model of Growth Through Creative Destruction," *Econometrica*, 60(2): 323–351.

Aghion, P. and Howitt, P. (1998) *Endogenous Growth Theory*, Cambridge, MA: MIT Press.

Arrow, K. J. (1962) "The Economic Implications of Learning by Doing," *Review of Economic Studies*, 29: 155–173.

Arthur, W. B. (1990) "'Silicon Valley' Locational Clusters: When Do Increasing Returns Imply Monopoly?," *Mathematical Social Sciences*, 19: 235–251.

Bailey, R. (1995) *The True State of the Planet*, New York: The Free Press.

Barro, R. J. (1991) "Economic Growth in a Cross-Section of Countries," *Quarterly Journal of Economics*, May: 106, 407–443.

Biggs, T., Moody, G., Leewen, J. V., and White, E. (1994) *Africa Can Compete! Export Opportunities and Challenges in Garments and Home Products in the U.S. Market*, Washington, D.C.: The World Bank.

Boserup, E. (1965) *The Conditions of Agricultural Growth*, Chicago, IL: Aldine Publishing.

Braudel, F. (1986) *Civilization and Capitalism*, New York: Harper & Row.

Ciccone, A. and Matsuyama, K. (1996) "Start-Up Costs and Pecuniary Externalities as Barriers to Economic Development," *Journal of Development Econonmics*, 49(1): 33–59.

Ciccone, A. (1996) *Externalities and Interdependent Growth: Theory and Evidence* [mimeo], Department of Economics, University of California, Berkeley.

Collier, P. and Gunning, J. W. (1999) "Explaining African Economic Performance," *Journal of Economic Literature*, 37(1): 64–111.

Deaton, A. and Miller, R. (1996) "International Commodity Prices, Macroeconomic Performance, and Politics in Sub-Saharan Africa," *Journal of African Economies*, 5(3): 99–191. Supplement Part I.

Dervis, K., de Melo, J., and Robinson, S. (1982) *General Equilibrium Models for Development Policy*, Washington, D.C.: World Bank.

Dollar, D. and Kraay, A. (2000) *Growth Is Good for the Poor* [mimeo], Development Research Group, Washington, D.C.: World Bank.

Ehrlich, P. R. (1968) *The Population Bomb*, Ballantine Books, New York.

Elbadawi, I. and Schmidt-Hebbel, K. (1998) "Instability and Growth in the World," *Journal of African Economies*, 7(suppl. 2): 116–168.

Fafchamps, M. (2000) "Ethnicity and Credit in African Manufacturing," *Journal of Development Economics*, 61: 205–235.

Fafchamps, M. (1997) "Mobile Capital, Location Externalities, and Industrialization," *Journal of Comparative Economics*, 25(3), 345–365.

Gerschenkron, A. (1962) *Economic Backwardness in Historical Perspective*, Cambridge, MA: Belknap Press.

Grossman, G. M. and Helpman, E. (1991) "Quality Ladders and Product Cycles," *Quarterly Journal of Economics*, 106: 557–586.

Hirschman, A. O. (1958) *The Strategy of Economic Development*, New Haven, CT: Yale University Press.

Hopkins, A. G. (1973) *An Economic History of West Africa*, London: Longman.

Hummels, D. (1995) *Global Income Clustering and Trade in Intermediate Goods*, Ann Arbor, MI: University of Michigan.

Humphreys, C. and Jaeger, W. (1989) *Africa's Adjustment and Growth in the 1980s*, Washington, D.C.: World Bank/UNDP.

Jacobs, J. (1984) *Cities and the Wealth of Nations*, New York: Random House.

Jacobs, J. (1969) *The Economy of Cities*, New York: Random House.

Jones, C. I. (1997) "On the Evolution of the World Income Distribution," *Journal of Economic Perspectives*, 11(3): 19–36.

Jones, L. E. and Manuelli, R. (1990) "A Convex Model of Equilibrium Growth: Theory and Policy Implications," *Journal of Political Economy*, 98(5): 1008–1038.

Kanbur, R. (1997) *Income Distribution and Development* [mimeo], Washington, D.C.: World Bank.

King, R. G. and Rebelo, S. T. (1993) "Transitional Dynamics and Economic Growth in the Neoclassical Model," *American Economic Review*, 83(4): 908–931.

Krugman, P. R. (1991) "Increasing Returns and Economic Geography," *Journal of Political Economy*, 99(3): 483–499.

Krugman, P. R. (1991) *Geography and Trade*, Cambridge, MA: MIT Press.

Kuznets, S. (1955) "Economic Growth and Income Inequality," *American Economic Review*, 65(1): 1–28.

Lucas, R. E. (1988) "On the Mechanics of Economic Development," *Journal of Monetary Economics*, 22: 3–42.

Maddison, A. (1987) "Growth and Slowdown in Advanced Capitalist Economies: Techniques of Quantitative Assessment," *Journal of Economics Literature*, 25(2): 649–698.

Maddison, A. (1982) *Phases of Capitalist Development*, London: Oxford University Press.

Mankiw, N. G., Romer, D., and Weil, D. N. (1992) "A Contribution to the Empirics of Economic Growth," *Quarterly Journal of Economics*, 107: 407–437.

Mkandawire, T. and Soludo, C. (1998) *African Perspectives on Structural Adjustment: Our Continent, Our Future*, Nairobi, Kenya: African World Press.

Morris, C. T. and Adelman, I. (1988) *Comparative Patterns of Economic Development, 1850–1914*, Baltimore, MD: Johns Hopkins University Press.

Murphy, K. M., Shleifer, A., and Vishny, R. W. (1989) "Industrialization and the Big Push," *Journal of Political Economy*, 97(5): 1003–1026.

Myint, H. (1958) "The 'Classical Theory' of International Trade and the Underdeveloped Countries," *Economic Journal*, 68: 317–337.

Myrdal, G. (1957) *Economic Theory and Under-Developed Regions*, London: Gerald Duckworth.

Nelson, R. and Winter, S. (1982) *An Evolutionary Theory of Economic Change*, Cambridge MA: Harvard University Press.

Nurkse, R. (1953) *Problems of Capital Formation in Underdeveloped Countries*, New York: Oxford University Press.

Oyejide, A. (1998) "Trade Policy and Regional Integration in the Development Context: Emerging Patterns, Issues, and Lessons for Sub-Saharan Africa," *Journal of African Economies*, 7(suppl. 1): 108–145.

Perroux, F. (1962) *L'Economie des Jeunes Nations*, Paris: Presses Universitaires de France.

Prebisch, R. (1963) *Towards a Dynamic Development Policy for Latin America*, New York: United Nations.

Pritchett, L. (1997) "Divergence, Big Time," *Journal of Economic Perspectives*, 11(3): 3–17.

Rodriguez-Clare, A. (1996) "The Division of Labor and Economic Development," *Journal of Development Economics*, 49: 3–32.

Romer, P. M. (1990) "Endogenous Technological Change," *Journal of Political Economy*, 98(5, pt. 2): 71–102.

Romer, P. M. (1986) "Increasing Returns and Long-Run Growth," *Journal of Political Economy*, 94(5): 1002–1037.

Rosenstein-Rodan, P. (1943) "Problems of Industrialization in Eastern and South-Eastern Europe," *Economic Journal*, June 53(210/211): 202–211.

Rostow, W. W. (1956) "The Take-Off into Self-Sustained Growth," *Economics Journal*, 261(66): 25–48.

Schultz, T. W. (1961) "Investment in Human Capital," *American Economic Review*, 51(1): 1–17.

Schumpeter, J. A. (1961) *The Theory of Economic Development*, Cambridge, MA: Harvard University Press.

Solow, R. M. (1956) "A Contribution to the Theory of Economic Growth," *Quarterly Journal of Economics*, 70: 65–94.

Solow, R. M. (1956) "Technical Change and the Aggregate Production Function," *Review of Economics and Statistics*, 39: 312–320.

Steel, W. F. and Evans, J. W. (1981) *Industrialization in Sub-Saharan Africa*, Washington, D.C.: World Bank.

Steel, W. F. and Webster, L. M. (1991) *Small Enterprises Under Adjustment in Ghana*, Tech. Paper No. 138, Industry and Finance Series, Washington, D.C.: World Bank.

Stokey, N. L. (1988) "Learning by Doing and the Introduction of New Goods," *Journal of Political Economy*, 96(4): 701–717.

Winter-Nelson, A. E. (1992) "Marketing Boards and Market Power: The Case of Kenyan Pyrethrum," Ph.D. thesis, Stanford, CA: Food Research Institute, Stanford University.

World Bank (1981) *Accelerated Development in Sub-Saharan Africa: An Agenda for Action*, Washington, D.C.: World Bank (also known as the Berg report).

World Bank (1993) *The East Asian Miracle: Economic Growth and Public Policy*, New York: Oxford University Press.

Young, A. (1991) "Learning by Doing and the Dynamic Effects of International Trade," *Quarterly Journal of Economics*, May: 106, 369–405.

CHAPTER 6: POPULATION

Abou-Stait, F. (1994) "The Population Debate in Relation to Development: The Case of Sub-Saharan Africa, *Egypt Population and Family Planning Review*, 28(2): 139–161.

Abuja Declaration on HIV/AIDS, Tuberculosis and Other Related Infectious Diseases (2001), resulting from African Summit on HIV/AIDS, April 24–27, 2001 (http://www.oau-uoa.org/afrsummit).

Adegbola, O. (1990) "Demographic Effects of Economic Crisis in Nigeria: The Brain Drain Component," paper presented at the Conference on the Role of Migration in African Development: Issues and Policies for the '90s, Nairobi: Union for African Population Studies.

Adepoju, A. (1990) "State of the Art Review of Migration in Africa," in *Proc. Conference on the Role of Migration in African Development: Issues and Policies for the '90s*, Vol. 1, Dakar: Union for African Population Studies, pp. 3–41.

Adeyi, O., Hecht, R., Njobvu, E., and Soucat, A. (2001) *AIDS, Poverty Reduction and Debt Relief*, Geneva: Joint United Nations Programme on HIV/AIDS (UNAIDS).

Bloom, D. and Canning, D. (2001) "Cumulative Casuality, Economic Growth and Demographic Transition," in N. Birdsall, A.C. Kelley, and S.W. Sinding, Eds., *Population Matters: Demographic Change, Economic Growth, and Poverty in the Developing World*, Oxford: Oxford University Press, pp. 165–197.

Bongaarts, J. (1978) "A Framework for Analyzing the Proximate Determinants of Fertility," *Population and Development Review*, 4(1): 105–132.

Bongaarts, J. (1982) "The Fertility-Inhibiting Effects of the Intermediate Variables," *Studies in Family Planning*, 13(6–7): 179–189.

Bongaarts, J. and Potter, R. G. (1983) *Fertility, Biology, and Behavior: An Analysis of the Proximate Determinants*, New York: Academic Press.

Boserup, E. (1965) *The Conditions of Agricultural Growth*, London: Allen & Unwin.

Caldwell, J. C. (1982) "The Wealth Flows Theory of Fertility Decline," in C. Hohn and R. Mackensen, Eds., *Determinants of Fertility Trends: Theories Re-Examined*, Liege, Belgium: Ordina Editions, pp. 169–188.

Coale, A. (1990) *Lectures on Population and Development*, Lectures in Development Economics, No. 8, Islamabad: Pakistan Institute of Development Economics.

Cohen, B. (1993) "Fertility Levels, Differentials and Trends," in K. A. Foote, K. H. Hill, and L. G. Martin, Eds., *Demographic Change in Sub-Saharan Africa*, Washington, D.C.: National Academy Press, pp. 8–67.

ECA (1999) *Africa's Population and Development Bulletin, June–July*, Addis Ababa: Economic Commission for Africa.

Ehrlich, P. (1968/1971) *The Population Bomb*, London: Pan Books.

Furedi, F. (1997) *Population and Development: A Critical Introduction*, New York: St. Martin's Press.

Goliber, T. (1989) "Africa's Expanding Population: Old Problems, New Policies," *Population Bulletin*, 44(3).

Hardin, G. (1968) "The Tragedy of the Commons," *Science*, 162(3859): 1243–1248.

Jolly, C. and Gribble, J. (1993) "The Proximate Determinants of Fertility," in K. A. Foote, K. H. Hill, and L. G. Martin, Eds., *Demographic Change in Sub-Saharan Africa*, Washington, D.C.: National Academy Press, pp. 68–116.

Kelley, A. (1996) "The Consequences of Rapid Population Growth on Human Resource Development: The Case of Education," in D. Ahlburg, A. Kelley, and C. Mason, Eds., *The Impact of Population Growth on Well-Being in Developing Countries*, Berlin: Springer-Verlag, pp. 67–138.

Kelley, A.C. (2001) "The Population Debate in Historical Perspective: Revisionism Revised," in N. Birdsall, A.C. Kelley, and S.W. Sinding, Eds., *Population Matters: Demographic Change, Economic Growth, and Poverty in the Developing World*, Oxford University Press, pp. 24–54.

Kelley, A. and Schmidt, R. (1994) *Population and Income Change: Recent Evidence*, Discussion Paper No. 249, Washington, D.C.: World Bank.

Kuznets, S. (1975) "Population Trends and Modern Economic Growth," in *The Population Debate: Dimensions and Perspectives*, Vol. 1, New York: United Nations, pp. 425–433; reproduced as Chapter 1 in *Population and Development*, P. Demeny and G. McNicoll, Eds., New York: St. Martins Press, 1998, pp. 5–18.

Menken, J. (1994) "Demographic–economic Relationships and Development," in F. Graham-Smith, Ed., *Population: The Complex Reality*, London: The Royal Society.

National Research Council (1986) *Population Growth and Economic Development: Policy Questions*, Committee on Population, Washington, D.C.: National Academy Press.

National Research Council (1993) *Demographic Effects of Economic Reversals in Sub-Saharan Africa*, Washington, D.C.: National Academy Press.

National Research Council (1993) *Factors Affecting Contraceptive Use in Sub-Saharan Africa*, Washington, D.C.: National Academy Press.

Oucho, J. and Gould, W. T. S. (1993) "Internal Migration, Urbanization and Population Distribution," in K. A. Foote, K. H. Hill, and L. G. Martin, Eds., *Demographic Change in Sub-Saharan Africa*, Washington, D.C.: National Academy Press, pp. 257–296.

Population Reference Bureau (1976) *World Population Growth and Response*, Washington, D.C.: Population Reference Bureau.

PRB (2000) *2000 World Population Data Sheet*, Washington, D.C.: Population Reference Bureau.

PRB (2001) *2001 World Population Data Sheet*, Washington, D.C.: Population Reference Bureau.

Ross, J., Stover, J., and Willard, A. (1999) *Profiles for Family Planning and Reproductive Health Programs*, Glastonbury, CT: The Futures Group International.

Russell, S. S. (1993) "International Migration," in K. A. Foote, K. H. Hill, and L. G. Martin, Eds., *Demographic Change in Sub-Saharan Africa*, Washington, D.C.: National Academy Press, pp. 297–349.

Simon, J. (1981) *The Ultimate Resource*, Princeton, NJ: Princeton University Press.

Simon, J. (1989) "On Aggregate Empirical Studies Relating Population Variables to Economic Development," *Population and Development Review*, 15(2): 323–332.

Simon, J. (1998) "Is Population Growth a Drag on Economic Development?," in J. A. Dorn, S. H. Hanke, and A. A. Walters, Eds., *The Revolution in Development Economics*, Washington, D.C.: CATO Institute, pp. 75–91.

Sparks, D. (2001) "Economic Trends in Africa South of the Sahara, 2000," in Murison, K., Ed., *Africa South of the Sahara 2001*, London: Europa Publications, pp. 11–19.

UNAIDS (2000) *AIDS Epidemic Update: December 2000*, Geneva: United Nations Joint Program on AIDS/World Health Organization.

UNFPA (1998) *Financial Resource Flows for Population Activities in 1998*, New York: United Nations Population Fund.

UN (2000) *Levels and Trends of Contraceptive Use as Assessed in 1998*, New York: United Nations.

UN (2000) *World Population Monitoring 1999: Population Growth, Structure and Distribution*, New York: United Nations.

United Nations (1998) *National Population Policies*, New York: United Nations.

USAID (1999) *An Overview of USAID Population Assistance FY 1999*, Arlington VA: Family Planning and Logistics Management, United States Agency for International Development.

USAID (2000) *An Overview of USAID Population Assistance FY 1999*, Arlington, VA: Family Planning and Logistics Management.

USAID (2001) *Overview of USAID Population Assistance FY 2000*, Washington, D.C.: Family Planning and Logistics Management, United States Agency for International Development.

Weeks, J. R. (1999) *Population: An Introduction to Concepts and Issues*, 7th ed., Belmont, CA: Wadsworth.

Williamson, J.G. (2001) "Demographic Change, Economic Growth, and Inequality," in N. Birdsall, A.C. Kelley, and S.W. Sinding, Eds., *Population Matters: Demographic Change, Economic Growth, and Poverty in the Developing World*, Oxford: Oxford University Press, pp. 106–136.

World Bank (1994) *Population and Development: Implications for the World Bank*, Washington, D.C.: World Bank.

CHAPTER 7: POVERTY AND DEVELOPMENT

Beukes, E. P. (1989) "Theories of Economic Development: An Overview and Some Implications," In J. K. Coetzee, Ed., *Development Is for People*, Johannesburg: Southern Book Publishers.

614

Boltvinik, J. (1999) *Poverty Measurement Methods: An Overview*, SEPED Series on Poverty Reduction, New York: United Nations Development Program.

Bruntland Commission (1987) *Our Common Future*. World Commission on Environment and Development, Oxford: Oxford University Press.

Crocker, D. (1992) "Functioning and Capability: The Foundations of Sen's and Nussbaum's Developmant Ethic," *Political Theory*, 20(4): 591.

Ewert, J., Hamman, J., Tregurtha, N., Vink, N., Visser, C., and Williams, G. (1998) *State and Market, Labour and Land: The South African Wine Industry in Transition*, University of Stellenbosch, unpublished research report.

Glover, J. (1995) "The Research Programme of Development Ethics," in M. Nussbaum and J. Glover, Eds., *Women, Culture and Development: A Study of Human Capabilities*, Oxford, Clarendon Press.

Goulet, D. (1995) "Participation in Development: New Avenues," in V. K. Pillai and L. W. Shannon, Eds., *Developing Areas: A Book of Readings and Research*, Oxford: Berg Publishers.

Hettne, B. (1995) *Development Theory and the Three Worlds*, Essex, U.K.: Longman Scientific.

Jaquette, J. (1990) "Gender and Justice in Economic Development," in I. Tinker, Ed., *Persistent Inequalities: Women and World Development*, New York: Oxford University Press.

Korten, D. C. (1984) "People-Centred Development: Towards a Framework." in D. C. Korten and R. Klauss, Eds., *People-Centred Development: Contributions Towards Theory and Planning Frameworks*, West Hartford, CT: Kumarian Press.

Laderchi, C. (1999) *The Many Dimensions of Deprivation in Peru: Theoretical Debates and Empirical Evidence*, Working Paper 29 QEHWP29, Queen Elizabeth House Working Paper Series, Oxford: Queen Elizabeth House.

Leibbrandt, M. and Woolard, I. (1999) "A Comparison of Poverty in South Africa's Nine Provinces," *Development Southern Africa*, 16(1): 28–54.

Marglin, S. (1990) "Towards the Decolonisation of the Mind," in F. Apffel-Marglin and S. Marglin, Eds., *Dominating Knowledge: Development, Culture and Resistance*, Oxford: Clarendon Press.

May, J., Carter, M., and Posel, D. (1995) *The Composition and Persistence of Poverty in Rural South Africa: An Entitlements Approach*, Policy Paper No. 15, Johannesburg: Land and Agriculture Policy Centre.

Miles, I. (1992) "Social Indicators for Real-Life Economics," in P. Ekins and M. Max-Neef, Eds., *Real Life Economics: Understanding Wealth Creation*, London: Routledge.

Saraceno, E. (1994) "Recent Trends in Rural Development and Their Conceptualisation," *Journal of Rural Studies*, 10(4): 321–330.

Sen, A. (1983) "Poor, Relatively Speaking," *Oxford Economic Papers*, 35(2): 153–169.

Sen, A. (1984) "Goods and People," in A. Sen, Ed., *Resource, Values and Development*, Oxford: Basil Blackwell.

Sen, A. (1985) "Well-Being, Agency and Freedom: The Dewey Lectures 1984," *Journal of Philosophy*, 72(4): 169–221.

Sen, A. (1987) "The Standard of Living: Lecture 1, Concepts and Critiques," in G. Hawthorn, Ed., *The Standard of Living: The Tanner Lectures, Clare Hall, Cambridge 1985*, Cambridge, U.K.: Cambridge University Press.

Sen, A. (1988) "The Concept of Development," in H. Chenery and T. N. Srinivasan, Eds., *Handbook of Development Economics*, Vol. 1, Amsterdam: North-Holland.

Sen, A. (1989) "Development as Capability Expansion," *Journal of Development Planning*, 17: 41–58.

Sen, A. (1992) *Inequality Reexamined*, Oxford: Clarendon Press.

Sen, A. (1995) "Food, Economics and Entitlements," in J. Dreze and A. Sen, Eds., *The Political Economy of Hunger*, Vol. III, Oxford: Clarendon Press.

Staatz, J. M. and Eicher, C. K. (1998) "Agricultural Development Ideas in Historical Perspective," in C. K. Eicher and J. M. Staatz, Eds., *International Agricultural Development*, 3rd ed., Baltimore, MD: Johns Hopkins University Press.

Streeten, P. (1994) "Human Development: Means and Ends," *American Economic Review: Papers and Proceedings*, 84(2): 232–237.

United Nations Development Program (UNDP) (1993) *Human Development Report 1993*, New York, Oxford University Press.

Van Zyl, J. C. (1995) *Needs-Based Development Strategy and the RDP: Some Broad Issues*, Johannesburg: DBSA.

Verholst, T. (1987) *No Life Without Roots: Culture and Development*, London: Zed Books.

Vink, N., Kirsten, J., and Tregurtha, N. (1999) *Job Shedding in South African Agriculture*, background paper prepared for the Agricultural Job Summit, National Department of Agriculture, Republic of South Africa.

Vink, N. and Tregurtha, N. (1999) *Spatial Guidelines for Infrastructure, Investment and Development: Rural Issues Theme Paper*, Report to the CIU, Office of the President.

Weaver, J. and Jameson, K. (1981) *Economic Development: Competing Paradigms*, New York: University Press of America.

World Bank *South African Agriculture: Structure, Performance and Options for the Future*, Informal Discussion Papers on Aspects of the Economy of South Africa, Washington, D.C.: World Bank, Feb. 28, 1994, No. 6, Vol. 1.

World Bank (2000) *World Development Report 2000*, New York, Oxford University Press.

World Conservation Strategy, The (1981) Botanic Gardens and the World Conservation Strategy: Proceedings of an International Conferemce, Bramwell, D., ed., Published for IUCN by Academic Press, 1987.

CHAPTER 8: IMPLICATIONS OF ETHNIC DIVERSITY

Alesina, A., Baqir, R., and Easterly, W. (1999) "Public Goods and Ethnic Divisions," *Quarterly Journal of Economics*, 114(4), 1243–1284.

Anderson, B. (1983) *Imagined Communities*, London: Verso.

Angoustures, A. and Pascal, V. (1996) "Diasporas et Financement des Conflicts," in F. Jean and J.-C. Rufin, Eds., *Economie des Guerres Civiles*, Paris: Hachette.

Arcand, J.-L., Guillaumont, P., and Guillaumont, S. (2000) "How To Make a Tragedy: On the Alleged Effect of Ethnicity on Growth," *Journal of International Development*, 12(7): 925–938.

Bates, R. (1999) *Ethnicity, Capital Formation and Conflict*, Social Capital Initiative Working Paper 12, Washington D.C.: World Bank.

Benabou, R. (1996) "Inequality and Growth," in B. Bernanke and J. Rotemberg, Eds., *NBER Macroeconomics Annual*, Cambridge, MA: MIT Press.

Biggs, T., Raturi, M., and Srivastava, P. (1996) *Enforcement of Contracts in an African Credit Market*, RPED Discussion Paper, Washington D.C.: World Bank.

Bisin, A. and Verdier, T. (2000) "Beyond the Melting Pot: Cultural Transmission, Marriage and the Evolution of Ethnic and Religious Traits," *Quarterly Journal of Economics*, 115(3).

Brito, D. L. and Intriligator, M. D. (1992) "Narco-Traffic and Guerrilla Warfare: A New Symbiosis," *Defence Economics*, 3(4), 263–274.

Buchanan, J. M. and Faith, R. L. (1987) "Secession and the Limits of Taxation: Towards a Theory of Internal Exit," *American Economic Review*, 77(5): 1023–1031.

Coate, S. and Morris, S. (1995) "On the Form of Transfers to Special Interests," *Journal of Political Economy*, 103(6): 1210–1235.

Colley, L. (1992) *Britons: Forging the Nation*, New Haven, CT: Yale University Press.

Collier, P. (1999) "The Political Economy of Ethnicity," in B. Pleskovic and J. E. Stiglitz, Eds., *Annual Bank Conference on Development Economics 1998*, Washington D.C.: World Bank.

Collier, P. (2000) "Ethnicity, Politics and Economic Performance," *Economics and Politics*, 12(3): 225–245.

Collier, P. (2000) "Rebellion as a Quasi-Criminal Activity," *Journal of Conflict Resolution*, 44(6), 839–853.

Collier, P. and Garg, A. (1999) "On Kin Groups and Wages in the Ghanaian Labour Market," *Oxford Bulletin of Economics and Statistics*, 61(2): 133–152.

Collier, P. and Hoeffler, A. (1998) "On the Economic Causes of Civil War," *Oxford Economic Papers*, 50(4), 563–573.

Collier, P. and Hoeffler, A. (2000) *Greed and Grievance in Civil War*, Policy Research Working Paper 2355, Washington, D.C.: World Bank.

Collier, P., Hoeffler, A., and Pattillo, C. (2001) "Flight Capital as a Portfolio Choice," *World Bank Economic Review*, 15(1): 55–80.

Downs, A. (1957) *An Economic Theory of Democracy*, New York: Harper & Row.

Drazen, A. (2000) *Political Economy in Macroeconomics*, Princeton, NJ: Princeton University Press.

Easterly, W. and Levine, R. (1997) "Africa's Growth Tragedy: Policies and Ethnic Divisions," *Quarterly Journal of Economics*, 112: 1203–1250.

Emminghaus, W., Kimmel, P., and Stewart, E. (1998) "Primal Violence Illuminating Culture's Dark Side," in E. Weiner, Ed., *The Handbook of Inter-Ethnic Coexistence*, New York: The Continuum Publishing Company.

Esteban, J. and Ray, D. (1994) "On the Measurement of Polarization," *Econometrica*, 64(4): 819.

Fearon, J. D. and Laitin, D. D. (1999) *Weak States, Rough Terrain, and Large-Scale Ethnic Violence Since 1945* [mimeo], Stanford, CA: Department of Political Science, Stanford University.

Frank, R. (2000) "Fiji Mahogany Fuels Latest Resource Battle in Troubled Region," *The Wall Street Journal*, Sept. 13, p. A1.

Greif, A. (1992) "Institutions and International Trade: Lessons from the Commercial Revolution," *American Economic Review*, 82(2): 128–133.

Grossman, H. I. (1991) "General Equilibrium Model of Insurrections," *American Economic Review*, 81(4): 912–921.

Gurr, T. R. (1993) *Minorities at Risk: A Global View of Ethnopolitical Conflicts*, Washington D.C.: U.S. Institute of Peace.

Hardin, R. (1997) "Economic Theories of the State," in D. Mueller, Ed., *Perspectives on Public Choice*, Cambridge, U.K.: Cambridge University Press.

Hoeffler, A. (1998) "Econometric Studies of Growth, Convergence and Conflicts," D.Phil. thesis, London: University of Oxford.

Horowitz, D. (1985) *Ethnic Groups in Conflict*, Berkeley, CA: University of California Press.

Inman, R. P. and Rubinfeld, D. R. (1997) "The Political Economy of Federalism," in D. Mueller, Ed., *Perspectives on Public Choice*, Cambridge, U.K.: Cambridge University Press.

Lipset, S. M. (1960) *Political Man*, New York: Anchors Books.

MacCulloch, R. (1999) *What Makes a Revolution*, Working Paper B24, Bonn: Center for European Integration Studies.

Mehlum, H. and Moene, K. (2000) *Contested Power and Political Instability*, Discussion Paper, Oslo: Department of Economics, University of Oslo.

Meltzer, A. and Richards, S. (1981) "A Rational Theory of the Size of Government," *Journal of Political Economy*, 89: 914–927.

Miguel, T. (1999) *Ethnic Diversity and School Funding in Kenya* [mimeo], Cambridge, MA: Department of Economics, Harvard University.

Mueller, D., Ed., (1997) *Perspectives on Public Choice*, Cambridge, U.K.: Cambridge University Press.

Ognedal, T. (1998) "Comments on T. Eggertsson's 'limits to institutional reforms'," *Scandinavian Journal of Economics*, 100(1): 364–366.

Olson, M. (1991) "Autocracy, Democracy and Prosperity," in R. Zeckhauser, Ed., *Strategy and Choice*, Cambridge MA: MIT Press.

Posner, D. N. (1999) *Ethnic Fractionalization in Africa* [mimeo], Los Angeles: Department of Political Science, University of California.

Posner, R. A. (1980) "A Theory of Primitive Society with Special Reference to Law," *Journal of Law and Economics*, 23(1): 1–53.

Schofield, N. (1997) "Multiparty Electoral Politics," in D. Mueller, Ed., *Perspectives on Public Choice*, Cambridge, U.K.: Cambridge University Press.

Shubik, M. (1982) *Game Theory in the Social Sciences: Concepts and Solutions*, Cambridge, MA: MIT Press.

Singer, J. D. and Small, M. (1994) *Correlates of War Project: International and Civil War Data, 1816–1992*, Ann Arbor, MI: Inter-University Consortium for Political and Social Research.

Stigler, G. J. (1964) "A Theory of Oligopoly," *Journal of Political Economy*, 72: 44–61.

Tocqueville, A. de (1959) *Democracy in America*, New York: Vintage Books.

Weber, E. (1975) *Peasants into Frenchmen*, Stanford, CA: Stanford University Press.

Weingast, B. (1979) "A Rational Choice Perspective on Congressional Norms," *American Journal of Political Science*, 23: 245–262.

CHAPTER 9: HEALTH AND ECONOMIC DEVELOPMENT

Airhihenbuwa, C.O. (1995) *Health and Culture: Beyond the Western Paradigm*, London: Sage.

Alemayehu, M. (2000) *Industrializing Africa: Development Options and Challenges for the 21st Century*, Trenton, NJ: Africa World Press.

Azevedo, M. J. (1991) *Historical Dictionary of Mozambique*, Metuchen, NJ: Scarecrow Press.

Banque Mondiale (1994) *Pour une meilleure Afrique: les leçons de l'experience*, Washington, D.C.: World Bank.

Braun, J. von, Teklu, T., and Webb, P. (1998) *Famine in Africa: Causes, Responses and Prevention*, Baltimore, MD: Johns Hopkins University Press.

Cahill, K. (1976) *Health and Development*, New York: Orbis Books.

CDC (1991) *Africa Child Survival Initiative: Combating Childhood Communicable Diseases, 1990–1991*, Atlanta, GA: Centers for Disease Control.

Charbot, J., Harmeijer, J. W., and Streetfland, P. H., Eds. (1995) *African Primary Health Care in Times of Economic Turbulence*, Amsterdam: Royal Tropical Institute.

Curtin, P. (1998) *Disease and Empire: The Health of European Troops in the Conquest of Africa*, New York: Cambridge University Press.

Falola, T. and Ityavyar, D., Eds. (1992) *The Political Economy of Health in Africa*, Africa Series No. 60, Athens, OH: University Monographs.

Feachem, R., Kjellstrom, T., Murray, C., Over, M., and Phillips, M., Eds. (1992) *The Health of Adults in the Developing World*, London: Oxford University Press.

Gray, C., Baudouy, J., Martin, K., Bang, M., and Cash, R. (1990) *Primary Health Care in Africa: A Study of the Mali Rural Health Project*, Boulder, CO: Westview Press.

Health Systems Research (1994) *Factors Associated with Maternal Mortality*, Vol. 2, Amsterdam: Royal Tropical Institute.

Health Systems Research (1994) *Availability, Provision and Use of Drugs*, Vol. 1, Amsterdam: Royal Tropical Institute.

Hollingsworth, J., Rogers, J. H., and Hanneman, R. (1990) *State Intervention in Medical Care: Consequences for Britain, France, Sweden, and the United States, 1890–1970*, Ithaca, NY: Cornell University Press.

Ishikawa, K. (1999) *Nation Building and Development Assistance in Africa*, Tokyo: Macmillan Press.

Kwast, B. E. (1995) "Maternity Care in Developing Countries," in K. van de Velden, J. K. S. van Ginneken, J. P. Velema, F. B. de Walle, and J. H. van Wijnen, Eds., *Health Matters: Public Health in North–South Perspective*, Amsterdam: Royal Tropical Institute, pp. 175–183.

Lindenbaum, S. and Lock, M. (1993) *Knowledge, Power and Practice: The Anthropology of Medical and Everyday Life*, Berkeley, CA: University of California Press.

Mann, J. M., Tarantola, D. J., and Netter, T. W., Eds. (1992) *AIDS in the World*, New York: Cambridge University Press.

Moeller, D. (1997) *Environmental Health*, Cambridge, MA: Harvard University Press.

Nasah, B. T., Mati, J. K. G., and Kasonde, J. M. (1994) *Contemporary Issues in Maternal Health Care in Africa*, Toronto: Toronto University Press.

Over, M., Ellis, R., Huber, J., and Solon, O. (1992) "The Consequences of Adult Ill Health," in R. Feachem, T. Kjellstrom, C. Murray, M. Over, and M. Phillips, Eds., *The Health of Adults in the Developing World*, London: Oxford University Press, pp. 161–207.

Pannenborg, O. (1995) "An Economic and Financial Look at Health in Low and Middle-Income Countries," in K. van de Velden, J. K. S. van Ginneken, J. P. Velema, F. B. de Walle, and J. H. van Wijnen, Eds., *Health Matters: Public Health in North–South Perspective*, Amsterdam: Royal Tropical Institute, pp. 43–62.

Pearce, T. O. (1992) "Health Inequalities in Africa," in T. Falola and D. Ityavyar, Eds., *The Political Economy of Health in Africa*, Africa Series No. 60, Athens, OH: University Monographs, pp. 184–216.

Peters, D., Kandola, K., Elmendorf, A. E., and Chellaraj, G. (1999) *Health Expenditures, Services, and Outcomes in Africa: Basic Data and Cross-National Comparisons: 1990–1996*, Washington, D.C.: World Bank.

Rasmussen, R. and Rubert, S. C. (1990) *Historical Dictionary of Zimbabwe*, Metuchen, NJ: Scarecrow Press.

Ruttan, W. V. (1994) *Health and Sustainable Agricultural Development*, Boulder, CO: Westview Press.

Shepherd, G. and Sonko, K. N. M., Eds. (1994) *Economic Justice in Africa: Adjustments and Sustainable Development*, Westport, CO: Greenwood Press.

Stephenson, M. (1997) "Health Care," in *Encyclopedia of Africa South of the Sahara*, Vol. 2, New York: Scribners' Sons, pp. 288–293.

Stock, R. and Anyinam, C. (1992) "National Governments and Health Services in Africa," in T. Falola and D. Ityavyar, Eds., *The Political Economy of Health in Africa*, Africa Series No. 60, Athens, OH: University Monographs, pp. 217–246.

Turshen, M. (1999) *Privatizing Health*, New Brunswick, NJ: Rutgers University Press.

United Nations (2000) *Africa Recovery*, 14(1): 1–28, produced by United Nations. Published in English and French by the Library and Publications Division of the United Nations Department of Public Information, with support from UNDP and UNICEF.

Van de Velden, K., van Ginneken, J. K. S., Velema, J. P., de Walle, F. B., and van Wijnen, J. H., Eds. (1995) *Health Matters: Public Health in North–South Perspective*, Amsterdam: Royal Tropical Institute.

Vogel, R. J. (1992) *Financing Health Care in Sub-Saharan Africa*, Phoenix, AZ: Arizona State University Press.

WHO (1994) *Availability, Provision and Use of Drugs*, Vol. 1, Project on Health Systems Research for the Southern African Region, Harare, Zimbabwe: World Health Organization, pp. 69–88.

Wijk-Sijbesma, C. van and de Walle, F. B. (1995) "Environmental Hygiene and Human Health," in K. van de Velden, J. K. S. van Ginneken, J. P. Velema, F. B. de Walle, and J. H. van Wijnen, Eds., *Health Matters: Public Health in North–South Perspective*, Amsterdam: Royal Tropical Institute, pp. 103–115.

CHAPTER 10: EDUCATION

Alemaxehu, M. (2000) *Industrializing Africa: Development Options and Challenges for the 21st Century*, Trenton, NJ: Africa World Press.

Becker, G. S. (1962) "Investment in Human Capital: A Theoretical Analysis," *Journal of Political Economy*, 70(5, pt. 2): 9–49.

Bond-Stewart, K. (1970) *Education in Southern Africa*, Gweru: Mambo Press.

Bray, M., Clarke, P. B., and Stephens, D. (1988) *Education and Society in Africa*, London: Edward Arnold.

Datta, A. (1984) *Education and Society: A Sociology of African Education*, New York: St. Martin's Press.

Davidson, B. (1994) *Modern Africa*, London: Oxford University Press.

Denison, E. F. (1962) "Education, Economic Growth, and Gaps in Information," *Journal of Political Economy*, 70(5, pt. 2): 124–128.

Eicher, J. (1985) *Educational Costing and Financing of Education in Developing*, World Bank Staff Working Papers, No. 65.

Fafunwa, A. B. and Aisiku, J. U. (1982) *Education in Africa: A Comparative Survey*, London: Allen & Unwin.

Gapinski (1996) "Economics Growth and its Components in African Nations," *Journal of Developing Areas*, 30, 525–548.

Haber, C. (1989) *Politics in African Education*, London: Macmillan.

Ishikawa, K. (1999) *Nation Building and Development Assistance in Africa*, New York: St. Martin's Press.

Jolly, R. (1969) *Planning Education for Economic Development*, Nairobi: East Africa Publishing House.

Jones, T. J. (1922) *Education in Africa*, New York: Phelps-Stokes.

Leonor, M. D., Ed. (1998) *Unemployment, Schooling, and Training in Developing Countries*, London: Groom Helm.

Meier, G. M. and Rauch, J. E. (2000) *Leading Issues in Economic Development*, 7th ed., New York: Oxford University Press.

Mitchell, B. R. (1998) *International Historical Statistics. Historical Statistics: Africa, Asia, Oceania (1975–1993)*, 4th ed., New York: Macmillan.

Mungazi, D. (1991) *Colonial Education for Africans: George Stark's Policy in Zimbabwe*, New York: Praeger.

Mungazi, D. and Walker, L. K. (1997) *Educational Reform and the Transformation of Southern Africa*, New York: Praeger.

Ness, I. and Ciment, J. (1999) *The Encyclopedia of Global Population and Demographics*, Vols. 1 and 2, Armonk, NY: M. E. Sharpe.

Nwomonoh, J., Ed. (1998) *Education and Development in Africa: A Contemporary Survey*, London: International Scholars Publications.

Psacharopoulos, G. (1984) "The Contribution of Education to Economic Growth: International Comparisons," in J. W. Kendrick, Ed., *International Comparisons of Productivity and Causes of the Slowdown*, New York: Ballinger, pp. 335–360.

Rwomire, A. (1998) "Education and Development: African Perspectives," in J. Nwomonoh, Ed., *Education and Development in Africa: A Contemporary Survey*, London: International Scholars Publications, pp. 2–23.

Schultz, T. W. (1962) "Reflections on Investment in Man," *Journal of Political Economy*, 70(5, pt. 2): 1–8.

Third World Institute (1996) *A Third World Guide 1995/96*, London: OXFAM.

Thompson, A. R. (1980) *Education and Development in Africa*, London: Macmillan.

Tiesen, J. K. (1994) "A Study of the Effects of Structural Adjustment on Education and Health in Africa," in G. W. Stepherd and K. N. M. Sonko, Eds., *Economic Justice in Africa: Adjustment and Sustainable Development*, London: Greenwood Press, pp. 79–116.

Turshen, M. (1999) *Privatizing Health Services in Africa*, New Brunswick, NJ: Rutgers University Press.

UNESCO (1996) *Analysis, Agendas, and Priorities for Education in Africa: A Review of Externally Initiated, Commissioned, and Supported Studies of Education in Africa, 1990–1994*, summary prepared for UNESCO, Working Group Lead Agency, http://www.unesco.org/education/educnews/97_02_18/wgesa_eng.htm.

UNESCO (2001) "Education of Girls and Women Beyond Access," in *Education*, http://www.unesco.org/education/primary/access.shtml.

UN (1999) *United Nations Statistical Yearbook*, New York: United Nations.

Urch, G. (1992) *Education in Sub-Saharan Africa*, New York: Garland Publishing.

Weisbrod, B. A. (1962) "Education and Investment in Human Capital," *Journal of Political Economy*, 70(5, pt. 2): 106–123.

World Bank (2000) *World Development Indicators*, Washington, D.C.: World Bank.

World Bank (2000) *Entering the 21st Century: World Development Report 1999/2000*, Washington, D.C.: World Bank.

CHAPTER 11: DEMOCRACY AND DEVELOPMENT

Anderson, P. (1974) *Lineages of the Absolutist State*, New York: Verso.

Bollen, K. A. and Jackman, R. W. (1985) "Political Democracy and the Size Distribution of Income," *American Sociological Review*, 50: 438–457.

Bratton, M. and van de Walle, N. (1997) *Democratic Experiments in Africa: Regime Transitions in Comparative Perspective*, Cambridge, U.K.: Cambridge University Press.

Callaghy, T. M. and Ravenhill, J., Eds. (1993) *Hemmed In: Responses to Africa's Economic Decline*, New York: Columbia University Press.

Collier, P. and Gunning, J. W. (1999) "Explaining African Economic Performance," *Journal of Economic Literature*, 37: 64–111.

Dahl, R. A. (1971) *Polyarchy: Participation and Opposition*, New Haven: Yale University Press.

Diamond, L. (1994) "Rethinking Civil Society: Toward Democratic Consolidation," *Journal of Democracy*, 5(3): 4–17.

Diamond, L., Linz, J. J., and Lipset, S. M., Eds. (1988) *Democracy in Developing Countries: Africa*, Vol. 2, Boulder, CO: Lynne Rienner Publishers.

Foley, M. W. and Edwards, B. (1996) "The Paradox of Civil Society," *The Journal of Democracy*, 7(3): 38–52.

Geddes, B. (1999) "What Do We Know About Democratization after Twenty Years?," *Annual Reviews Political Science*, (2): 115–144.

Haggard, S. and Kaufman, R. R., Eds. (1992) *The Politics of Economic Adjustment*, Princeton, NJ: Princeton University Press.

Hodder-Williams, R. (1984) *An Introduction to the Politics of Tropical Africa*, London: Allen & Unwin, 1984.

Huntington, S. P. (1991) *The Third Wave: Democratization in the Late Twentieth Century*, Norman, OK: University of Oklahoma Press.

Kholi, A. (1986) "Democracy and Development," in J. P. Lewis and V. Kallab, Eds., *Development Strategies Reconsidered*, New Brunswick, NJ: Transaction Books.

Lindblom, C. E. (1977) *Politics and Markets: The World's Political–Economic Systems*, New York: Basic Books.

Lipset, S. M. (1959) "Some Social Requisites of Democracy: Economic Development and Political Legitimacy," *American Political Science Review*, 53(1): 69–105.

Moore, Jr., B. (1966) *Social Origins of Dictatorship and Democracy: Lord and Peasant in the Making of the Modern World*, Boston: Beacon Press.

Przeworski, A. (1991) *Democracy and the Market: Political and Economic Reforms in Eastern Europe and Latin America*, Cambridge, U.K.: Cambridge University Press.

Przeworski, A. and Limongi, F. (1997) "Modernization: Theories and Facts," *World Politics* 49: 155–183.

Quinn, J. J. (1999) The Managerial Bourgeoisie: Capital Accumulation, Development and Democracy," in R. L. Sklar and D. Becker, Eds., *Postimperialism and World Politics*, New York: Praeger, pp. 219–252.

Quinn, J. J. (2002) *The Road Oft Traveled: Developmental Policies and State Ownership of Industry in Africa*, Westport, CT: Praeger.

Schumpeter, J. A. (1942) *Capitalism, Socialism and Democracy*, New York: Harper.

Sklar, R. L. (1983) "Democracy In Africa," *African Studies Review*, 26(3/4): 11–12.

Sklar, R. L. (1987) "Developmental Democracy," *Comparative Studies in Society and History*, 29(4): 686–714.

van de Walle, N. (1994) "Review Essay: Adjustment Alternatives and Alternatives to Adjustment," *African Studies Review*, 33: 103–117.

van de Walle, N. (1999) "Economic Reform in Democratizing Africa," *Comparative Politics*, October: 21–41.

World Bank (1989) *Sub-Saharan Africa: From Crisis to Sustainable Growth*, Washington, D.C.: World Bank.

World Bank (1994) *Adjustment in Africa: Reforms, Results, and the Road Ahead*, Washington, D.C.: World Bank.

World Bank (2000) *African Development Indicators 2000*, Washington, D.C.: World Bank.

CHAPTER 12: POLITICAL INSTABILITY

Alesina, A. and Perotti, R. (1994) "The Political Economy of Growth: A Survey of the Literature," *The World Bank Economic Review*, 8(30): 351–371.

Alesina, A. S., Ozler, N., and Swagel, P. (1995) "Political Instability and Economic Growth," Working Paper No. 4173, Cambridge, MA: National Bureau of Economic Research.

Alexander, W. R. J. and Hansen, P. (1998) "Government, Exports, Instability, and Economic Growth in Sub-Saharan Africa," *The South African Journal of Economics*, 66(4): 492–511.

Apraku, K. K. (1991) *African Emigres in the United States: A Missing Link in Africa's Social and Economic Development*, New York: Praeger.

Collier, P. (2000) *Greed and Grievance in Civil War*, Policy Research Paper No. 2355, Washington, D.C.: World Bank.

Collier, P. and Hoeffler, A. (1995) "War, Peace, and Private Portfolios," *World Development*, 23: 233–241.

Collier, P. and Gunning, J. W. (1999) "Explaining African Economic Performance," *Journal of Economic Literature*, 37(1): 64–111.

Deaton, A. and Miller, R. (1995) *International Commodity Prices, Macroeconomic Performance, and Politics in Sub-Saharan Africa*, Princeton Studies in International Finance, No. 79, Princeton, NJ: Princeton University.

Devereux, M. (1996) *Political Uncertainty, Capital Taxation and Growth* [mimeo], University of British Columbia.

Dixit, A. and Pindyck, R. (1994) *Investment Under Uncertainty*, Princeton, NJ: Princeton University Press.

Easterly, W. and Levine, R. (1997) "Africa's Growth Tragedy: Policies and Ethnic Divisions," *Quarterly Journal of Economics*, 112(4): 1203–1250.

Edwards, S. and Tabellini, G. (1991) *Political Instability, Political Weakness, and Inflation: An Empirical Analysis*, Working Paper No. 3721, Cambridge, MA: National Bureau of Economic Research.

Elbadawi, I. and Sambanis, N. (2000) "Why Are There So Many Civil Wars in Africa? Understanding and Preventing Violent Conflict," *Journal of African Economies*, 9(3): 22–269.

Fedderke, J., R. H. de Kadt, and J. M. Luiz (2001) "Indicators of Political Liberty, Property Rights and Political Instability in South Africa: 1935–97," *International Review of Law and Economics*, 1(1): 103–134.

Fedderke, J. and Klitgaard, R. (1998) "Economic Growth and Social Indicators: An Exploratory Analysis," *Economic Development and Cultural Change*, 46(3): 455–489.

Feder, G. (1983) "On Exports and Economic Growth," *Journal of Development Economics*, 12: 59–73.

Fosu, A. K. (1992) "Political Instability and Economic Growth: Evidence from Sub-Saharan Africa," *Economic Development and Cultural Change*, 40(2): 823–841.

Gupta, D. (1990) *Economics of Political Violence*, New York: Praeger.

Gyimah-Brempong, K. and Munoz de Camacho, S. (1998) "Political Instability, Investment, Human Capital, and Economic Growth in Latin America," *Journal of Developing Areas*, 32(4): 449–466.

Gyimah-Brempong, K. and Traynor, T. L. (1996) "Political Instability and Savings in Less Developed Countries: Evidence from Sub-Saharan Africa," *Journal of Development Studies*, 32(5): 695–714.

Gyimah-Brempong, K. and Traynor, T. L. (1999) "Political Instability, Investment, and Economic Growth in Sub-Saharan Africa," *Journal of African Economies*, 8(1): 52–86.

Hirschman, A. O. (1956) *A Strategy of Economic Development*, New Haven, CT: Yale University Press.

Islam, N. (1995) "Growth Empirics: A Panel Data Approach," *Quarterly Journal of Economics*, 110: 1127–1140.

Jackman, R. (1978) "The Predictability of Coups d'Etat: A Model with African Data," *American Political Review*, 72: 1263–1275.

Jenkins, C. J. and Kpososwa, A. J. (1990) "Explaining Military Coups d'Etat: Black Africa 1957–1984," *American Sociological Review*, 55(6): 861–875.

Johnson, T., Skater, R. O., and McGowan, P. (1984) "Explaining African Coups d'Etat, 1960–1982," *American Political Science Review*, 78: 622–640.

Knack, S. and Keefer, P. (1995) "Institutions and Economic Performance: Cross-Country Tests Using Alternative Institutional Measures," *Economics and Politics*, 7: 207–227.

Knight, M., Loayza, N., and Villanueva, D. (1993) "Testing the Neoclassical Theory of Economic Growth: A Panel Data Approach," *IMF Staff Papers*, 40(3): 512–541.

Krueger, A. O. (1980) "Trade Policy as an Input to Development," *American Economic Review Papers and Proceedings*, 70: 288–292.

Kuznets, S. (1966) *Modern Economic Growth: Rate, Structure, and Spread*, New Haven, CT: Yale University Press.

Londregan, J. B. and Poole, K. T. (1990) "Poverty, the Coup Trap, and Seizure of Executive Power," *World Politics*, 42(2): 151–193.

Mancur, O. (1963) "Rapid Growth as a Destabilizing Force," *Journal of Economic History*, 23(4): 529–552.

Mbaku, J. M. (1992) "Political Instability and Economic Development in Sub-Saharan Africa: Further Evidence," *The Review of Black Political Economy*, Spring: 39–53.

McGowan, P. and Johnson, T. H., (1984) "African Military Coups d'Etat and Under-development: A Quantitative Historical Analysis," *Journal of Modern African Studies*, 22(4): 633–666.

North, D. C. (1990) *Institutions, Institutional Change, and Economic Performance*, New York: Cambridge University Press.

O'Kane, R. (1981) "A Probabilistic Approach to the Causes of Coups d'Etat," *British Journal of Political Science*, 11: 287–308.

O'Kane, R. (1983) "Towards an Examination of the General Causes of Coups d'Etat," *European Journal of Political Research*, 11: 27–44.

Ozler, S. and Roderik, D. (1992) "External Shocks, Politics, and Private Investment: Some Theory and Empirical Evidence," *Journal of Development Economics*, 39: 141–162.

Persson, T. and Tebellini, G. (1997) *Political Economics and Macroeconomic Policy*, NBER Working Paper No. 6329, Cambridge, MA: National Bureau of Economic Research.

Powelson, J. P. (1972) *Institutions of Economic Growth*, Princeton, NJ: Princeton University Press.

Rae, D. (1968) "A Note on the Fractionalization of Some European Party Systems," *Comparative Political Studies*, 1: 413–418.

Sachs, J. D. and Warner, A. M. (1997) "Fundamental Sources of Long-Run Growth," *American Economic Review Papers and Proceedings*, 87: 184–188.

Sachs, J. D. and Warner, A. M. (1997) "Sources of Slow Growth in African Economies," *Journal of African Economies*, 6: 335–376.

Sahn, D., Ed. (1994) *Economic Crisis and Policy Reform in Africa: An Introduction*, Ithaca, NY: Cornell University Press.

Sanders, D. (1981) *Patterns of Political Instability*, New York; St. Martin's Press.

Scully, G. W. (1988) "The Institutional Framework and Economic Development," *Journal of Political Economy*, 96(3): 652–662.

Svenson, J. (1998) "Investment, Property Rights and Political Instability: Theory and Empirical Evidence," *European Economic Review*, 42(7): 1317–1341.

Umez, B. N. (1993) "Has Social Mobilization Caused Political Instability in Africa? A Granger–Causality Test," *The Review of Black Political Economy*, Summer: 33–54.

Wells, K. (1992) "South Africa Violence Wounds Economy," *The Wall Street Journal*, September 30.

Williamson, O. (1985) *The Economic Institutions of Capitalism*, New York: Free Press.

World Bank (1997) *World Development Report 1997*, New York: Oxford University Press.

World Bank (2000) *World Development Report 1999/2000*, New York: Oxford University Press.

CHAPTER 13: INEQUALITY AND CONFLICT

International Federation of Red Cross and Red Crescent Societies, *World Disasters Report*, Dordrecht, Netherlands: Martinus Nijhoff, 1993.

Keen, D. (1998) *The Economic Functions of Violence in Civil Wars*, Oxford: Oxford University Press.

Collier, P. and Hoeffler, A. (1998) "On Economic Causes of War," *Oxford Economic Papers*, 50(4): 563–574.

Rothchild, D. (1997) *Managing Ethnic Conflict in Africa: Pressures and Incentives for Cooperation*, Washington, D.C.: The Brookings Institution.

Rummel, R. R. (1994) *Death by Government*, New Brunswick, NJ: Transaction Publishers.

Reno, W. (1998) *Warlord Politics and African States*, Boulder, CO: Lynne Rienner Publishers.

Singer, D. and Small, M. (1994) *Correlates of War Project: International and Civil War Data*, Part 2, *The Civil War File*, New Haven, CT: Yale University.

Stewart, F., Humphreys, F. P., and Lea, N. (1997) "Civil Conflict in Developing Countries Over the Last Quarter of a Century: An Empirical Overview of Economic and Social Consequences," *Oxford Development Studies*, 25(1): 11–41.

Stewart, F., Fitzgerald, V. *et al.*, Eds. (2000) *War and Underdevelopment*, London: Oxford University Press.

Stockholm International Peace Research Institute, *SIPRI Yearbook*, London: Oxford University Press, 1987–2001.

Zartman, W., Ed. (1995) *Collapsed States: The Disintegration and Restoration of Legitimate Authority*, Boulder, CO: Lynne Rienner Publishers.

CHAPTER 14: CORRUPTION AND ECONOMIC DEVELOPMENT

Adebayo, A. (1972) "Formulating Administrative Reform Strategies in Africa," *Quarterly Journal of Administration (Nigeria)*, 6: 223–244.

Adekson, J. (1981) *Nigeria in Search of a Stable Civil-Military System*, Boulder, CO: Westview, pp. 71–72.

Alam, M. S. (1989) "Anatomy of Corruption: An Approach to the Political Economy of Underdevelopment," *The American Journal of Economics and Sociology*, 48(4): 442.

Anderson, T. L. and Hill, P. J. (1986) "Constraining the Transfer Society: Constitutional and Moral Dimensions," *Cato Journal*, 6(1): 317–339.

Bardhan, P. (1997) "Corruption and Development: A Review of the Issues," *Journal of Economic Literature*, Vol. 35(3): 1320–1346.

Bates, R. H. (1981) *Markets and States in Tropical Africa*, Berkeley, CA: University of California.

Bates, R. H. (1989) *Beyond the Miracle of the Market*, Cambridge, U.K.: Cambridge University Press.

Bates, R. H. (1989) *Essays on the Political Economy of Rural Africa*, Berkeley, CA: University of California Press.

Bates, R. H. (1994) "The Impulse To Reform in Africa," in J. A. Wildner, Ed., *Economic Change and Political Liberalization in Sub-Saharan Africa*, Baltimore, MD: Johns Hopkins University Press.

Bayley, D. H. (1966) "The Effects of Corruption in a Developing Nation," *The Western Political Quarterly*, 19(4): 719–732.

Brennan, G. and Buchanan, J. M. (1985) *The Reason of Rules: Constitutional Political Economy*, Cambridge, U.K.: Cambridge University Press.

Brett, E. A. (1995) "Institutional Theory and Social Change in Uganda," in J. Harriss, J. Hunter, and C. M. Lewis, Eds., *The New Institutional Economics and Third World Development*, London: Routledge, p. 203.

Buchanan, J. M. (1991) *Constitutional Economics*, Oxford: Basil Blackwell.

Congleton, R. D. (1994) "Constitutional Federalism and Decentralization: A Second Best Solution," *Economia Delle Scelte Pubbliche (Italy)*, 11(1): 15–29.

Elliott, K. A., Ed. (1997) *Corruption and the Global Economy*, Washington, D.C.: Institute for International Economics.

Gillespie, K. and Okruhlik, G. (1991) "The Political Dimensions of Corruption Cleanups: A Framework for Analysis," *Comparative Politics*, 24(1): p. 80.

Gould, D. J. (1980) *Bureaucratic Corruption and Underdevelopment in the Third World: The Case of Zaire*, New York: Pergamon Press.

Gould, D. J. and Mukendi, T. B. (1989) "Bureaucratic Corruption in Africa: Causes, Consequences and Remedies," *International Journal of Public Administration*, 13(3): 431.

Gwartney, J. D. and Wagner, R. E. (1988) "Public Choice and the Conduct of Representative Government," J. D. Gwartney and R. E. Wagner, Eds., *Public Choice and Constitutional Economics*, Greenwich, CT: JAI Press.

Gwartney, J. D., Lawson, R., and Block, W., Eds. (1996) *Economic Freedom of the World: 1975–1995*, Vancouver: The Fraser Institute.

Hanna, S., Folke, C., and Mäler, K.-G. (1995) "Property Rights and Environmental Resources," in Hanna, S. and Munasinghe, M., Eds., *Property Rights and the Environment: Social and Ecological Issues*, Washington, D.C.: World Bank, p. 15–29.

Hope, K. R., Sr. and Chikulo, B. C., Eds. (2000) *Corruption and Development in Africa: Lessons from Country Case Studies*, London: Macmillan.

Ihonvbere, J. O. and Ekekwe, E. (1988) "Dependent Capitalism, Structural Adjustment and Democratic Possibilities in Nigeria's Third Republic," *Afrika Spectrum*, 23(3): 273–291.

Jabbra, J. G. (1976) "Bureaucratic Corruption in the Third World: Causes and Remedies," *Indian Journal of Public Administration*, 22: 673–691.

Jua, N. (1998) "Cameroon: Jump-Starting an Economic Crisis," in J. M. Mbaku, Ed., *Corruption and the Crisis of Institutional Reforms in Africa*, Lewiston, NY: Edwin Mellen Press.

Kaufmann, D. and Wei, S.-J. (1999) *Does "Grease Money" Speed Up the Wheels of Commerce?*, Policy Research Paper No. 2254, Washington, D.C.: World Bank.

Kimenyi, M. S. (1991) "Barriers to the Efficient Functioning of Markets in Developing Countries," *Konjunturpolitik (Berlin)*, 37(4): 199–227.

Kligaard, R. (1991) *Controlling Corruption*, Berkeley, CA: University of California Press.

Leff, N. H. (1964) "Economic Development Through Bureaucratic Corruption," *American Behavioral Scientist*, 8(3): 8.

LeVine, V. T. (1975) *Political Corruption: The Ghanaian Case*, Stanford, CA: Hoover Institution.

Madunagu, E. (1983) *Nigeria: The Economy and the People*, London: New Beacon Books.

Mbaku, J. M. (1990) "Military Coups as Rent-Seeking Behavior," *Journal of Political and Military Sociology*, 22: 241–284.

Mbaku, J. M. (1992) "Bureaucratic Corruption as Rent-Seeking Behavior," *Konjunturpolitik (Berlin)*, 38(4): 247–265.

Mbaku, J. M. (1993) "Markets and the Economic Origins of Apartheid in South Africa," *The Indian Journal of Social Science*, 6(2): 139–158.

Mbaku, J. M. (1996) "Bureaucratic Corruption and the Crisis of Institutional Reforms in Africa," *Business and the Contemporary World*, 8(3/4): 145–170.

Mbaku, J. M. (1996) "Bureaucratic Corruption in Africa: The Futility of Cleanups," *Cato Journal*, 16(1): 99–118.

Mbaku, J. M. (1997) *Institutions and Reform in Africa: The Public Choice Perspective*, Westport, CT: Praeger.

Mbaku, J. M. (1998) "Constitutional Engineering and the Transition to Democracy in Post-Cold War Africa," *The Independent Review*, 2(4): 501–517.

Mbaku, J. M. (1998) "Improving African Participation in the Global Economy: The Role of Economic Freedom," *Business and the Contemporary World*, 10(2): 297–338.

Mbaku, J. M. (1999) "Making the State Relevant to African Societies," in J. M. Mbaku, Ed., *Preparing Africa for the Twenty-First Century: Strategies for Peaceful Coexistence and Sustainable Development*, Aldershot, U.K.: Ashgate.

Mbaku, J. M. (2000) *Bureaucratic and Political Corruption in Africa: The Public Choice Perspective*, Malabar, FL: Krieger.

McMullan, M. (1961) "A Theory of Corruption," *Sociological Review*, 9(6): 21–47.

North, D. C. (1990) *Institutions, Institutional Change and Economic Performance*, Cambridge, U.K.: Cambridge University Press.

Nye, J. S. (1967) "Corruption and Political Development: A Cost-Benefit Analysis," *The American Political Science Review*, 61(2): 417–427.

Organization of African Unity (OAU) (1981) *The Lagos Plan of Action for the Economic Development of Africa 1980–2000*, Geneva: International Institute for Labor Studies.

Osterfeld, D. (1992) *Prosperity Versus Planning: How Government Stifles Economic Growth*, New York: Oxford University Press.

Ostrom, E., Schroeder, L., and Wynne, S. (1993) *Institutional Incentives and Sustainable Development: Infrastructure Policies in Perspective*, Boulder, CO: Westview.

Rose-Ackerman, S. (1997) *Corruption and Government: Causes, Consequences, and Reform*, Cambridge, U.K.: Cambridge University Press.

Szeftel, M. (1983) "Corruption and the Spoils System in Zambia," in M. Clarke, Ed., *Corruption: Causes, Consequences and Control*, New York: St. Martin's Press.

Tullock, G. (1967) "The Welfare Costs of Tariffs, Monopolies and Theft," *Western Economic Journal*, 5(3): 224–232.

United Nations Development Project (UNDP) (1990) *Human Development Report 1990*, New York: Oxford University Press.

Wicksell, K. (1967) "A New Principle of Just Taxation," in R. A. Musgrave and A. T. Peacock, Eds., *Classics in the Theory of Public Finance*, New York: St. Martin's Press (originally published in 1896).

Wildavsky, A. (1990) "A Double Security: Federalism as Competition," *Cato Journal*, 10: 39–58.

World Bank (1979) *Zaire: Current Economic Situation and Constraints*, Washington, D.C.: World Bank.

World Bank (1981) *Accelerated Development in Sub-Saharan Africa: An Agenda for Action*, Washington, D.C.: World Bank.

CHAPTER 15: LAND TENURE, AGRICULTURE, AND ECONOMIC DEVELOPMENT

Addison, T. and Demery, L. (1989) "The Economics of Rural Poverty Alleviation," in S. Commander, Ed., *Structural Adjustment and Agriculture: Theory and Practice in Africa and Latin America*, London: James Curry, p. 77–89.

Barrows, R. and Roth, M. (1990) "Land Tenure and Investment in African Agriculture: Theory and Evidence," *The Journal of Modern African Studies*, 28: 265–297.

Bassett, T. J. (1993) "Introduction: The Land Question and Agricultural Transformation in Sub-Saharan Africa," in T. J. Basset and D. E. Crummey, Eds., *Land in African Agrarian Systems*, Madison, WI: University of Wisconsin Press, pp. 3–31.

Bates, R. H. and Lofchie, M. F., Eds. (1980) *Agricultural Development in Africa*, New York: Praeger.

Berry, S. (1993) *No Condition Is Permanent: The Social Dynamics of Agrarian Change in Sub-Saharan Africa*, Madison, WI: University of Wisconsin Press, pp. 101–134.

Bhuduri, A. and Skarstein, R. (1997) "Introduction," in A. Bhuduri and R. Skarstein, Eds., *Economic Development and Agricultural Productivity*, Cheltenham, U.K.: Edward Elgar Publishing, pp. 1–22.

Bruce, J. W. (1993) "Do Indigenous Tenure Systems Constrain Agricultural Development?," in T. J. Basset and D. E. Crummey, Eds., *Land in African Agrarian Systems*, Madison, WI: University of Wisconsin Press, pp. 35–56.

Bruce, J. and Migot-Adholla, S., Eds. (1994) *Searching for Land Tenure Security in Africa*, Dubuque, IA: Kendall/Hunt Publishers.

Cohen, J. M. (1980) "Land Tenure and Rural Development in Africa," in R. H. Bates and M. F. Lofchie, Eds., *Agricultural Development in Africa*, New York: Praeger, p. 349–400.

du Guerny, J. and Topouzis, D. (1996) "Gender, Land and Fertility: Women's Access to Land and Security of Tenure," *Modules on Gender, Population and Rural Development with a Focus on Land Tenure and Farming Systems*, Food and Agriculture Organization, Rome, Italy.

Eicher, C. K. and Staatz, J. M., Eds. (1998) *Agricultural Development in the Third World*, Baltimore, MD: John Hopkins University Press.

Foster, P. and Leathers, H. D. (1990) *The World Food Problem: Tackling the Causes of Undernutrition in the Third World*, 2nd ed., Boulder, CO: Lynne Rienner Publishers.

Global Coalition for Africa, Economic Committee (1999) "Promoting Agricultural Productivity and Competitiveness in Sub-Saharan Africa," paper presented at Economic Committee Meeting, Nairobi, Kenya, April 1999.

Gyasi, E. A. (1994) "Adaptability of African Communal Land Tenure to Economic Opportunity: The Example of Land Acquisition for Oil Palm Farming in Ghana," *Africa*, 64: 391–403.

Jaffee, S. and Morton, J., Eds. (1995) *Marketing Africa's High-Value Foods: Comparative Experiences of an Emergent Private Sector*, Washington, D.C.: World Bank.

Lambert, V. A. and Seligson, M. A. (1997) "Asset Distribution and Access: Land Tenure Programs," in L. G. Tweeten and D. G. McClelland, Eds., *Promoting Third World Development and Food Security*, Westport, CT: Praeger, pp. 160–164.

Lastarria-Cornhiel, S. (1997) "Impact of Privatization, Gender, and Property Rights in Africa," *World Development*, 25: 1317–1333.

Lofchie, M. F., Eds. (1980) *Agricultural Development in Africa*, New York: Praeger.

Maxwell, D. and Weibe, K. (1998) *Land Tenure and Food Security: A Review of Concepts, Evidence, and Methods*, Research Paper No. 129, Madison, WI: Land Tenure Center, University of Wisconsin-Madison, p. 1.

Mellor, J. W. (1995) "Introduction," in J. W. Mellor, Ed., *Agriculture on the Road to Industrialization*, Baltimore, MD: Johns Hopkins University Press, pp. 1–22.

Mosher, A. T. (1969) *Creating a Progressive Rural Structure to Serve Modern Agriculture*, New York: Agricultural Development Council.

Place, F. and Migot-Adholla, S. (1998) "The Economic Effects of Land Registration on Smaller Farms in Kenya: Evidence From Nyeri and Kakamega Districts," *Land Economics*, 74: 360–373.

Raj, M., Kumbe, V., and Sudhir, P., Eds. (1985) *Agricultural Markets in the Semi-Arid Tropics*, Patancheru: ICRISAT.

Rhodes, J. V. and Dauve, J. L. (1998) *The Agricultural Marketing System*, 5th ed., Scottsdale, AZ: Holcomb Hathaway.

Rossmiller, G. E., Ed. (1978) *Agricultural Sector Planning*, Lansing, MI: Michigan State University Press.

Sanders, J. H., Shapiro, B. I., and Ramaswamy, S. (1996) *The Economics of Agricultural Technology in Semiarid Sub-Saharan Africa*, Baltimore, MD: Johns Hopkins University Press.

Stevens, R. D. and Jabara, C. L. (1988) *Agricultural Development Principles: Economic Theory and Empirical Evidence*, Baltimore, MD: Johns Hopkins University Press.

Timmer, P. (1998) "The Macroeconomics of Food and Agriculture," in C. K. Eicher and J. M. Staaz, Eds., *International Agricultural Development*, Baltimore, MD: John Hopkins University Press, pp. 187–211.

Van der Laan, L. H. (1984) *The Trans-Oceanic Marketing Channel: A New Tool for Understanding Tropical Africa's Export Agriculture*, New York: International Business Press.

Waiguchu, M. J., Tiagha, E., and Mwaura, M., Eds. (1999) *Management of Organizations in Africa: A Handbook and Reference*, Westport, CT: Quorum Books.

CHAPTER 16: FINANCIAL MARKETS AND ECONOMIC DEVELOPMENT

Alesina, A. and Summers, L. (1993) "Central Bank Independence and Macroeconomic Performance: Some Comparative Evidence," *Journal of Money, Credit, and Banking*, 25(2): 151–162.

Allen, D. and Ndikumana, L. (2000) "Financial Intermediation and Economic Growth in Southern Africa," *Journal of African Economies*, 9(2): 132–160.

Aryeetey, E. and Senbet, L. (2000) *Essential Financial Market Reforms in Africa* [mimeo], University of Ghana/University of Maryland.

Aryeetey, E., Hettige, H., Nissanke, M., and Steel, W. (1997) "Financial Market Fragmentation and Reforms in Ghana, Malawi, Nigeria, and Tanzania," *World Bank Economic Review*, 11(2): 195–218.

Athey, M. and Laumas, P. (1994) "Internal Funds and Corporate Investment in India," *Journal of Development Economics*, 45: 287–303.

Ball, R. (1999) "The Institutional Foundation of Monetary Commitment: A Comparative Analysis," *World Development*, 27(10): 1821–1842.

Beck, T. and Levine, R. (2000) *New Firm Formation and Industry Growth: Does Having a Market-Based or Bank-Based System Matter?*, Working Paper 0004, Carlson School of Management, University of Minnesota.

Beck, T., Levine, R., and Loayza, N. (1999) *Finance and the Sources of Growth*, Working Paper 9907, Carlson School of Management, University of Minnesota.

Bhinda, N., Griffith-Jones, S., Leape, J., and Martin, M. (1999) *Private Capital Flows to Africa: Perceptions and Reality*, The Hague: FONDAD.

Bigsten, A., Paul Collier, P. *et al.* (1999) "Investment in Africa's Manufacturing Sector: A Four Country Panel Data Analysis," *Oxford Bulletin of Economics and Statistics*, 61(4): 489–512.

Boyce, J. K. and Ndikumana, L. (2000) *Is Africa a Net Creditor? New Estimates of Capital Flight from Severely Indebted Sub-Saharan African Countries, 1970–1996*, Working Paper 2000-1, Department of Economics and Political Economy Research Institute, University of Massachusetts.

Cameron, R., Crisp, O., Patrick, H., and Tilly, R. (1967) *Banking in the Early Stages of Industrialization: A Study in Comparative Economic History*, New York: Oxford University Press.

Chari, V. V., Kehoe, P. J., and McGrattan, E. R. (1997) *The Poverty of Nations: A Quantitative Investigation*, Staff Report 204, Research Department, Federal Reserve Bank of Minneapolis.

Clark, R. (1998) *Africa's Emerging Securities Markets: Developments in Financial Infrastructure*, Westport, CT: Quorum Books.

Collier, P. and Gunning, J. W. (1999) "Explaining African Economic Performance," *Journal of Economic Literature*, 37(1): 64–111.

Collier, P. and Gunning, J. W. (1999) "Why Has Africa Grown Slowly?," *Journal of Economic Perspectives*, 13(3): 3–22.

Collier, P., Hoeffler, A., and Pattillo, C. (1999) *Flight Capital as a Portfolio Choice*, unpublished manuscript, Washington, D.C.: World Bank.

Corosso, V. (1970) *Investment Banking in America*, Cambridge, MA: Harvard University Press.

Cukierman, A. (1992) *Central Bank Strategy, Credibility, and Independence: Theory and Evidence*, Cambridge, MA: The MIT Press.

Demirgüç-Kunt, A. and Levine, R. (1999) "Bank-Based and Market-Based Financial Systems: Cross-Country Comparisons," Policy Research Working Paper 2143, Washington, D.C.: World Bank.

Demirgüç-Kunt, A. and Maksimovic, V. (1996) "Stock Market Development and Financing Choices of Firms," *World Bank Economic Review*, 10(2): 341–369.

Diamond, D. (1984) "Financial Intermediation and Delegated Monitoring," *Review of Economic Studies*, 51(3): 393–414.

Easterly, W. and Levine, R. (1997) "Africa's Growth Tragedy: Policies and Ethnic Divisions," *Quarterly Journal of Economics*, 112(2): 103–1250.

Fazzari, S., Hubbard, G., and Petersen, B. (1988) "Financing Constraints and Corporate Investment," *Brookings Papers on Economic Activity*, 1: 141–195.

Gelbard, E. and Leite, S. P. (1999) *Measuring Financial Development in Sub-Saharan Africa*, Working Paper 99/105, Washington, D.C.: International Monetary Fund.

Global Financial Data (2000) *Capitalization, Trading Volumes, and Number of Listed Companies in 1998*, Los Angeles, CA: Global Financial Data.

Grilli, V., Masciandaro, D., and Tabellini, G. (1991) "Political and Monetary Institutions and Public Financial Policies in the Industrial Countries," *Economic Policy*, 13: 341–392.

Grossman, S. and Stiglitz, J. (1980) "On the Impossibility of Informationally Efficient Markets," *American Economic Review*, 70(3): 393–408.

Haber, S. (1991) "Industrial Concentration and the Capital Markets: A Comparative Study of Brazil, Mexico, and the United States, 1830–1930," *Journal of Economic History*, 51(3): 559–580.

Hermes, N. and Lensink, R. (1992) "The Magnitude and Determinants of Capital Flight: The Case for Six Sub-Saharan African Countries," *De Economist*, 140(4): 515–530.

Hubbard, G. (2000) *Money, the Financial System, and the Economy*, Reading, MA: Addison-Wesley.

Jaramillo, F., Schiantarelli, F., and Weiss, A. (1996) "Capital Market Imperfections Before and After Financial Liberalization: An Euler Equation Approach to Panel Data for Ecuadorian Firms," *Journal of Development Economics*, 51: 367–386.

Jensen, M. and Meckling, W. H. (1976) "Theory of the Firm: Managerial Behavior, Agency Costs, and Ownership Structure," *Journal of Financial Economics*, 3: 305–360.

Kasekende, L. and Hussain, I. (2000) "The Central Bank as a Restraint: The Experience of Uganda," in P. Collier and C. Pattillo, Eds., *Investment and Risk in Africa*, New York: St. Martin's Press, pp. 169–181.

King, R. G. and Levine, R. (1993) "Finance and Growth: Schumpeter Might Be Right," *Quarterly Journal of Economics*, 108(3): 717–737.

King, R. G. and Levine, R. (1993) "Finance, Entrepreneurship, and Growth: Theory and Evidence," *Journal of Monetary Economics*, 32: 513–542.

La Porta, R., Lopez-De-Silanes, F., Shleifer, A., and Vishny, R. (1997) "Legal Determinants of External Finance," *Journal of Finance*, 52(3): 1131–1150.

La Porta, R., Lopez-De-Silanes, F., Shleifer, A., and Vishny, R. (1998) "Law and Finance," *Journal of Political Economy*, 106(6): 1113–1155.

Lensink, R., Hermes, N., and Murinde, V. (1998) "The Effect of Financial Liberalization on Capital Flight in African Economies," *World Development*, 26(7): 1349–1368.

Levine, R. (1997) "Financial Development and Economic Growth: Views and Agenda," *Journal of Economic Literature*, 35: 688–726.

Levine, R. (1998) "The Legal Environment, Banks, and Long-Run Economic Growth," *Journal of Money, Credit, and Banking*, 30(3): 596–613.

Levine, R. (2000) *Bank-Based or Market-Based Financial Systems: Which Is Better?*, Working Paper 0005, Carlson School of Management, University of Minnesota.

Levine, R. and Zervos, S. (1998) "Capital Control Liberalization and Stock Market Development," *World Development*, 26(7): 1169–1183.

Levine, R., Loayza, N., and Beck, T. (2000) "Financial Intermediation and Growth: Causality and Causes," *Journal of Monetary Economics*, 46(1): 31–77.

Lynch, D. (1996) "Measuring Financial Sector Development: A Study of Selected Asia-Pacific Countries," *Developing Economies*, 32(1): 3–33.

Mayer, C. (1990) "Financial Systems, Corporate Finance, and Economic Development," in G. Hubbard, Ed., *Asymmetric Information, Corporate Finance and Investment*, Chicago, IL: University of Chicago Press, pp. 307–332.

Mbendi Information for Africa (2000) *African Stock Exchange 1998*, Claremont, South Africa: Mbendi Information Services, www.mbendi.co.za.

Mecagni, M. and Sourial, M. (1999) *The Egyptian Stock Market: Efficiency Tests and Volatility Effects*, Working Paper 99/48, Washington, D.C.: International Monetary Fund.

Mehran, H., Ugolini, P., Briffaux, J.-P., Iden, G., Lybek, T., Swaray, S., and Hayward, P. (1998) *Financial Sector Development in Sub-Saharan African Countries*, Occasional Paper 169, Washington, D.C.: International Monetary Fund.

Merton, R. (1995) "A Functional Perspective of Financial Intermediation," *Financial Management*, 24: 23–41.

Montiel, P. (1996) "Financial Policies and Economic Growth: Theory, Evidence and Country-Specific Experience from Sub-Saharan Africa," *Journal of African Economies*, 5(3, A. R. suppl.): 65–98.

Myers, S. and Majluf, N. (1984) "Corporate Financing and Investment Decisions When Firms Have Information That Investors Do Not Have," *Journal of Financial Economics*, 13: 187–221.

Ncube, M. and Senbet, L. (1997) "Perspectives on Financial Regulation and Liberalization in Africa Under Incentive Problems and Asymmetric Information," *Journal of African Economies*, 6(1): 29–88.

Ndikumana, L. (2000) "Financial Determinants of Domestic Investment in Sub-Saharan Africa: Evidence from Panel Data," *World Development*, 28(2): 381–400.

Ndikumana, L. (2001) "A Study of Capital Account Regimes in Africa," paper prepared for the UNCTAD Workshop on Management of Capital Flows: Comparative Experiences and Implications for Africa, March 20–21, Cairo.

Ndikumana, L. and Boyce, J. K. (1998) "Congo's Odious Debt: External Borrowing and Capital Flight in Zaire," *Development and Change*, 29(2): 195–217.

Nissanke, M. and Aryeetey, E. (1998) *Financial Integration and Development in Sub-Saharan Africa*, London: Routledge.

Nyoni, T. (2000) "Capital Flight from Tanzania," in I. Ajayi and M. Khan, Eds., *External Debt and Capital Flight in Sub-Saharan Africa*, Washington, D.C.: The I. F. Institute, pp. 265–299.

Odedokun, M. O. (1996) "Alternative Econometric Approaches for Analyzing the Role of the Financial Sector in Economic Growth: Time-Series Evidence from LDCs," *Journal of Development Economics*, 50: 119–146.

Olopoenia, R. (2000) "Capital Flight from Uganda, 1971–94," in I. Ajayi and M. Khan, Eds., *External Debt and Capital Flight in Sub-Saharan Africa*, Washington, D.C.: The IMF Institute, pp. 238–264.

Pagano, M. (1993) "Financial Markets and Growth," *European Economic Review*, 37: 613–622.

Rajan, R. and Zingales, L. (1998) "Financial Dependence and Growth," *American Economic Review*, 88(3): 559–586.

Robinson, J. (1952) *The Role of Interest and Other Essays*, London: Macmillan.

Rogoff, K. (1985) "The Optimal Degree of Commitment to an Intermediate Monetary Target," *Quarterly Journal of Economics*, 100(4): 1169–1189.

Rousseau, P. and Wachtel, P. (1998) "Financial Intermediation and Economic Performance: Historical Evidence From Five Industrialized Countries," *Journal of Money, Credit and Banking*, 30(4): 657–678.

Schumpeter, J. A. (1934) *The Theory of Economic Development*, Cambridge, MA: Harvard University Press.

Shleifer, A. and Summers, L. (1988) "Breach of Trust in Hostile Takeovers," in A. Auerbach, Ed., *Corporate Takeovers: Causes and Consequences*, Chicago, IL: University of Chicago Press, pp. 33–56.

Singh, A. (1995) "The Stock Market, Economic Efficiency and Industrial Development," in P. Arestis and V. Chick, Eds., *Finance, Development and Structural Change: Post-Keynesian Perspectives*, Brookfield, VT: Elgar, pp. 71–112.

Singh, A. (1999) "Should Africa Promote Stock Market Capitalism?," *Journal of International Development*, 11: 343–365.

Spears, A. (1992) "The Role of Financial Intermediation in Economic Growth in Sub-Saharan Africa," *Canadian Journal of Development Studies*, 13(3): 361–380.

Stasavage, D. (2000) "The Franc Zone as a Restraint," in P. Collier and C. Pattillo, Eds., *Investment and Risk in Africa*, New York: St. Martin's Press, pp. 275–304.

Stiglitz, J. (1985) "Credit Markets and the Control of Capital," *Journal of Money, Credit and Banking*, 17(2): 133–152.

Stiglitz, J. and Weiss, A. (1981) "Credit Rationing in Markets with Imperfect Information," *American Economic Review*, 71(3): 393–410.

Tybout, J. (1983) "Credit Rationing and Investment Behavior in a Developing Country," *Review of Economics and Statistics*, 65(4): 598–607.

UNCTAD (1992–2000) *World Investment Report*, New York: United Nations Publications.

UNCTAD (1995) *Foreign Direct Investment in Africa*, New York: United Nations Publications.

Widner, J. (2000) "The Courts as a Restraint: The Experience of Tanzania, Uganda, and Botswana," in P. Collier and C. Pattillo, Eds., *Investment and Risk in Africa*, New York: St. Martin's Press, pp. 219–242.

World Bank (1997) *Private Capital Flows to Developing Countries: The Road to Financial Integration*, New York: Oxford University Press.

World Bank (2000) *Can Africa Claim the 21st Century?*, Washington, D.C.: The World Bank.

World Bank (2000) *World Development Indicators 2000 CD-ROM*, Washington, D.C.: World Bank.

CHAPTER 17: SAVING, INVESTMENT, AND GROWTH IN SUB-SAHARAN AFRICA

Aredo, D. (1993) "The Iddir: A Study of an Indigenous Informal Financial Institution in Ethiopia," *Saving and Development*, Milano, Italy: Finafrica Foundation.

Azam, J.-P., Devarajan, S., and O'Connell, S. A. (1999) *Aid Dependence Reconsidered*, Working Paper Series No. 99.5, Centre for the Study of African Economies.

Barro, R. J. (1991) "Economic Growth in a Cross Section of Countries," *The Quarterly Journal of Economics*, 56(2): 407–444.

Bauer, P. T. (1972) *Dissent on Development: Studies and Debates in Development Economics*, Cambridge, MA: Harvard University Press.

Benabou, R. (1996) "Equity and Efficiency," *The Review of Economic Studies*, 63: 237–264.

Bhagwait, J. (1966) *The Economics of Underdeveloped Countries*, New York: McGraw-Hill.

Blomstrom, M., Lipsey, R. E., and Zejan, M. (1996) "Is Fixed Investment the Key to Economic Growth?," *Quarterly Journal of Economics*, 3: 269–276.

Centre for the Study of African Economies (1998) *Research Summary*, London: Oxford University Press.

De Long, J. B. and Summers, L. (1991) "Equipment Investment and Economic Growth," *Quarterly Journal of Economics*, 56: 445–502.

De Long, J. B. and Summers, L. (1992) "Equipment Investment and Economic Growth: How Strong Is the Nexus?," *Brookings Papers on Economic Activity*, 1992(2): 157–211.

Deaton, A. (1989) "Saving in Developing Countries: Theory and Review," in *Proc. of the World Bank Annual Conf. on Development Economics*, Washington, D.C.: World Bank.

Domar, E. (1946) "Capital Expansion, Rate of Growth, and Employment," *Econometrica*, 14: 137–147.

Easterly, W. (1997) "The Ghost of Financing Gap: How the Harrod–Domar Growth Model Still Haunts Development Economics," July: 1–30, Washington, D.C.: World Bank, Development Research Group Series: Policy Research Working Papers, 1807.

Easterly, W. (1998) *The Quest for Growth: How We Wandered the Tropics Trying To Figure Out How To Make Poor Countries Rich*, www.worldbank.org.

Easterly, W. and Levine, R. (1997) "Africa's Growth Tragedy: Policies and Ethnic Divisions," *Quarterly Journal of Economics*, 112(4): 1203–1250.

Gillis, M., Perkins, D. H., Roemer, M., and Snodgrass, D. R. (1992) *Economics of Development*, 3rd ed., New York: W.W. Norton.

Gyimah-Brempong, K. (1991) "Export Instability and Economic Growth in Sub-Saharan Africa," *Economic Development and Cultural Change*, 39(4): 815–828.

Jefferis, K. R. (1995) "The Economy in 1994," in *Barclay's Botswana Economic Review*, 6(1); 1–24.

Johnston, M. (1997) "Public Officials, Private Interests, and Sustainable Democracy: When Politics and Corruption Meet," in K. A. Elliott, Ed., *Corruption and the Global Economy*, Washington, D.C.: Institute of International Economics, pp. 61–82.

Krugman, P. (1996) *Pop Internationalism*, Cambridge, MA: The MIT Press.

Mauro, P. (1995) "Corruption and Growth," *Quarterly Journal of Economics*, 110: 681–712.

Rose-Ackerman, S. (1997) "Corruption and Development," paper prepared for the Annual Bank Conference on Development Economies, May, Washington, D.C.

Salkin, J. S. (1994) "The Economy in 1993," in *Barclay's Botswana Economic Review*, 5(1).

Sandbrook, R. (1991) "Economic Crisis, Structural Adjustment and the State in Sub-Saharan Africa," in D. Ghai, Ed., *The I. F. and the South: The Social Impact of Crisis an Adjustment*, London: Zed Books, pp. 95–114.

Shleifer, A. (1996) *Government in Transition*, Discussion Paper No. 1783, Boston, MA: Harvard Institute for Economic Research.

Shleifer, A. and Vishny, R. W. (1993) "Corruption," *Quarterly Journal of Economics*, 108: 599–617.

Voivodas, C. S. (1978) "The Effect of Foreign Exchange Instability on Growth," *Review of Economics and Statistics*, 60(3): 410–412.

World Bank (2000) World Development Report 2000, Washington, D.C.: World Bank.

CHAPTER 18: TRADE AND ECONOMIC DEVELOPMENT

Balassa, B. (1988) "The Lessons of East Asian Development: An Overview," *Economic Development and Cultural Change*, 36(suppl.): S273–S290.

Baldwin, R. E. (1970) *Non-Tariff Distortions of International Trade*, Washington, D.C.: Brookings Institution.

Baldwin, R. E. (1989) *Measuring Non-Tariff Trade Policies*, Cambridge, MA: National Bureau of Economic Research.

Carbaugh, R. J. (2002) *International Economics*, 8th ed., Cincinnati: South-Western, College Pub.

Cashin, P. and Pattillo, C. (2001) "The Duration of Terms of Trade Shocks in Sub-Saharan Africa," *Finance and Development*, 37(2): 26–29.

Commins, S. K., Ed. (1988) *Africa's Development Challenges and the World Bank: Hard Questions, Costly Choices*, London: Lynne Rienner Publishers.

Erzan, R. and Svedberg, P. (1991) "Protection Facing Exports from Sub-Saharan Africa in the EC, Japan and the U.S.," in J. Frimpong-Ansah, S. Ravi Kanbur, and P. Svedberg, Eds., *Trade and Development in Sub-Saharan Africa*, Manchester, NY: Manchester University Press, pp. 97–151.

Fage, J. D. (1969) *A History of West Africa: An Introductory Survey*, 4th ed., Cambridge, U.K.: Cambridge University Press.

Frank, C. R. (1975) *Foreign Trade Regimes and Economic Development: South Korea*, New York: Columbia (for National Bureau of Economic Research).

Ghosh, P. K. and Ghosh, D., Eds. (1984) *International Trade and Third World Development*, London: Greenwood Press.

Gupta, S., Hammond, B., Leete, R., and Swanson, E. (2000) "Progress Towards the International Development Goals," *Finance and Development*, 37(4): 14–17.

Helleiner, G. K. (2002) *Non-Traditional Exports in Sub-Saharan Africa: Issues and Experiences*, Basingstoke, U.K.: Palgrave Publishers.

Hernandez-Cata, E. (2000) "Raising Growth and Investment in Sub-Saharan Africa: What Can Be Done?," *Finance and Development*, 37(4): 30–33.

Krueger, A. O. (1995) *Trade Policies and Developing Nations*, Washington, D.C.: The Brookings Institution.

Lall, S. (1993) "Trade Policies for Development: A Policy Prescription for Africa," *Development Policy Review*, 11: 44–65.

Lewis, W.A. (1969) "Aspects of Tropical Trade, 1883–1965," *Wicksell Lectures*, pp. 1–53.

Loungani, P. and Razin, A. (2001) "How Beneficial Is Foreign Direct Investment for Developing Countries?," *Finance and Development*, 38(2): 6–9.

Luedde-Neurath, R. (1986) *Import Control and Export-Oriented Development: A Reassessment of the Korean Case*, Boulder, CO: Westview.

Lydall, H. F. (1975) *Trade and Employment*, Geneva: International Labor Office.

Mishra, D., Mody, A., and Murshid, A. (2001) "Private Capital Flows and Growth," *Finance and Development*, 38(2): 2–5.

Morton, K. and Tulloch. P. (1977) *Trade and Developing Countries*, New York: John Wiley & Sons.

Neumark, S. D. (1964) *Foreign Trade and Economic Development in Africa: A Historical Perspective*, Stanford, CA: Stanford University Press.

Nsouli, S. M. (2000) "Capacity Building in Africa: The Role of International Financial Institutions," *Finance and Development*, 37(4): 34–37.

Petri, P. (1988) "Korea's Export Niche: Origins and Prospects," *World Development*, 16: 47–63.

Prebisch, R. (1962) "The Economic Development of Latin American and Its Principal Problem," *Economic Bulletin For Latin America*, 7: 1–22 (article originally published in 1950).

Pursell, G. (1984) *Korea's Competitive Edge: Managing the Entry into World Markets*, Baltimore, MD: Johns Hopkins Univeristy Press.

Rapley, J. (1996) *Understanding Development: Theory and Practice in the Third World*, Boulder, CO: Lynn Rienner Publishers.

Royal Institute of International Affairs (1964) *Direction for World Trade*, London: Oxford University Press, pp. 161–212.

Salvatore, D. (2001) *International Economics*, 7th ed., New York: John Wiley & Sons.

Singer, H. (1950) "The Distribution of Gains Between Investing and Borrowing Countries," *American Economic Review*, 40: 473–485.

Smith, S. C. (1997) *Case Studies in Economic Development*, 2nd ed., New York: Addison-Wesley.

Spraos, J. (1983) *Inequalizing Trade?*, London: Clarendon Press.

Svedberg, P. (1991) "The Export Performance of Sub-Saharan Africa," *Economic Development and Cultural Change*, 39(3): 549–566.

Todaro, M. P. (2000) *Economic Development*, 7th ed., New York: Addison-Wesley.

UNCTAD (1999) *African Development in a Comparative Perspective*, Asmara, Eritrea: African World Press.

Wade, R. (1988) "The Role of Government in Overcoming Market Failure: Taiwan, Republic of Korea, and Japan," in H. Hughes, Ed., *Achieving Industrialization in East Asia*, New York: Cambridge University Press.

Wheeler, D. (1983) "Sources of Stagnation in Sub-Saharan Africa," *World Development*, 12(1): 1–23.

World Bank (1993) *The East Asian Miracle: Economic Growth and Public Policy*, New York: Oxford University Press.

World Bank (2000) *Can Africa Claim the 21st Century?*, Washington, D.C.: World Bank.

CHAPTER 19: REGIONALISM AND ECONOMIC DEVELOPMENT

Anon. (1992) "African Leaders Sign Treaty," *Financial Times*, August 18, p. 3.

Anon. (1995) "East Africa Born Again," *New African*, February, pp. 24–25.

Anon. (1995) "East Africa Stopped at the Start," *New African*, May, pp. 24–25.

Anon. (1995) "Southern Africa Urged To Integrate," *Financial Times*, August 29, p. 4.

Anon. (1996) "East African Leaders to Cooperate," *Financial Times*, January 26, p. 6.

Anon. (2000) "East African Community: Treaty Signals Rebirth of Union," *African Business*, January, pp. 36–37.

Anon. (2000) "Financial Times Survey: FT 500," *Financial Times*, May 4, p. 6.

Aryeetey, E. (1998) "Sub-Saharan African Experiences with Regional Integration," in *Trade Reform and Regional Integration in Africa*, Z. Iqbal, and M. Khan, eds., Washington, D.C.: IMF Institute.

Balassa, B. (1961) *The Theory of Economic Integration*, London: Allen & Unwin.

Deutsch, K. (1971) *The Analysis of International Relations*, Englewood Cliffs, NJ: Prentice-Hall.

Dossier (1993) "Regional Integration," *The Courier*, No. 142, November–December, pp. 48–90.

Ernest Aryeetey, E. (1998) "Sub-Saharan African Experiences with Regional Integration," in Z. Iqbal and M. Khan, Eds., *Trade Reform and Regional Integration in Africa*, Washington, D.C.: IMF Institute.

Haas, E. (1970) "The Study of Regional Integration: Reflections on the Joy and Anguish of Pretheorizing," in Lindberg and Scheingold, *Europe's Would-Be Polity*, Englewood Cliffs, NJ: Prentice-Hall.

IMF (1998) *Direction of Trade Statistics Yearbook*, Washington, D.C.: International Monetary Fund.

Lodge, J. (1983) *The European Community: Bibliographical Excursions*, London: Frances Pinter.

Martin, G. (1992) "African Regional Cooperation and Integration: Achievements, Problems and Prospects," in A. Seidman and F. Anang, Eds., *Towards a New Vision of Self-Sustainable Development*, Trenton, NJ: Africa World Press.

Nkrumah, K. (1963) *Africa Must Unite*, New York: Praeger.

Ojo, O. (1985) "Regional Cooperation and Integration," in O. Ojo, D. K. Orwa, and C. M. B. Utete, Eds., *African International Relations*, London: Longman.

Omotunde, J. (1991) "Economic Integration in Africa: Enhancing Prospects for Success," *The Journal of Modern African Studies*, 29(1).

Oyejide, A. (1998) "Trade Policy and Regional Integration in Sub-Saharan Africa," in Z. Iqbal and M. Khan, Eds., *Trade Reform and Regional Integration in Africa*, Washington, D.C.: IMF Institute.

Viner, J. (1950) *The Customs Union Issue*, New York: Carnegie Endowment for International Peace.

World Bank (2000) *2000 World Economic Indicators*, Washington, D.C.: World Bank.

CHAPTER 20: GLOBALIZATION AND DEVELOPMENT

Baldwin, R. and Murray, T. (1977) "MFN Tariff Reductions and Developing Country Trade Benefits Under the GSP: A Reply," *Economic Journal*, 87: 30–46.

Baldwin, R. and Murray, T. (1986) "MFN Tariff Reductions and Developing Country Trade Benefits Under the GSP," *Economic Journal*, 96: 537–539.

CFC (1997) *Annual Report 1996*, Amsterdam: Common Fund for Commodities.

Davenport, M. (1992) "Africa and the Unimportance of Being Preferred," *Journal of Common Market Studies*, 30(2): 233–251.

Deutsch, K. (1971) *The Analysis of International Relations*, Englewood Cliffs, NJ: Prentice-Hall.

Hass, E. (1970) The Study of Regional Intergration: Reflections on the Joy and Anguish of Pretheorizing, in Lindberg and Scheingold, *Europe's Would-Be Polity*, Englewood Cliffs, NJ: Prentice-Hall.

IMF *Government Finance Statistics Yearbook*, Washington, D.C.: International Monetary Fund.

Isaak, R. (2000) *Managing World Economic Change*, Englewood Cliffs, NJ: Prentice-Hall.

Jacobs, B. (1997) "H.R. 1432 Could Propel Sub-Sahara Sourcing," *Bobbin*, 38(11): 88–89.

Lodge, J. (1983) *The European Community: Bibliographyical Excursions*, London: Frances Pinter.

Mshomba, R. (2000) *Africa in the Global Economy*, Boulder, CO: Lynne Rienner Publishers.

Organization of African Unity (1991) *Treaty Establishing the African Economic Community*, Bellville, South Africa: Centre for Southern African Studies, University of the Western Cape.

Phillips, M. (1996) "U.S. Rethinks Trade Policy with Africa," *The Wall Street Journal*, July 15, p. A2.

Pomfret, R. (1986) "MFN Tariff Reductions and Developing Country Trade Benefits Under the GSP: A Comment," *Economic Journal*, 96: 534–536.

Tangermann, S. (1996) "Implementation of the Uruguay Round Agreement on Agriculture: Issues and Prospects," *Journal of Agricultural Economics*, 47(3): 315–337.

UNCTAD (1996) *Handbook of Economic Integration and Cooperation Groupings of Developing Countries*, Vol. I, *Regional and Subregional Economic Integration Groupings*, New York: United Nations Conference on Trade and Development.

UNCTAD (1997) *Handbook of International Trade and Development Statistics 1995*, New York: United Nations Conference on Trade and Development.

United Nations Development Program (UNDP) (1999) *Human Development Report*, New York: Oxford University Press.

USITC (1997) *Likely Impact of Providing Quota-Free and Duty-Free Entry to Textiles and Apparel From Sub-Saharan Africa*, Publ. No. 3056, Washington, D.C.: U.S. International Trade Commission.

World Bank (2000) *Can Africa Claim the 21st Century?*, New York: World Bank.

CHAPTER 21: INFORMATION AND COMMUNICATION TECHNOLOGIES (ICTs)

Aden, A. (2000) "No Connection Under This Number: Africa and the Internet," in *Development and Cooperation*, 5: 24–26.

Avgerou, C. (1998) "How Can IT Enable Growth in Developing Countries?," in *Information Technology for Development*, 8: 15–28.

Berndt, E. and Morrison, C. "High Tech-Capital Formation and Economic Performance in U.S. Manufacturing Enterprises: An Exploratory Analysis," in *Journal of Econometrics*, 65(1): 9–43.

Biggs, T., Shah, M., and Srivastava, P. (1995) *Technological Capabilities and Learning in African Enterprises*, Paper No. 288, Africa Technical Department Series, Washington, D.C.: World Bank.

Braga, C. (1996) "The Impact of Internationalisation of Services in Developing Countries," *Finance and Development*, 33(1): 14–17.

Brynjolfsson, E. and Hitt, L. (1995) "Information Technology as a Factor of Production: The Role of Differences Among Firms," *Economics of Innovation Technology*, 3: 183–200.

Brynjolfsson, E. and Hitt, L. (2000) *Computing Productivity: Firm Level Efficiency*, MIT Sloan Management School/University of Pennsylvania, MIT Working Paper, No. 4210–01.

Dedrick, J. and Kraemer, K. (2000) "National IT Policies for Developing Countries," in *WIDER ANGLE*, Paper No. 1/2000, World Institute of Development Economics Research, pp. 5–6.

Diewert, W. and Smith, A. (1994) *Productivity Measurement for a Distribution Firm*, Paper No. 4812, Cambridge, MA: National Bureau of Economic Research.

Diop, O. (2000) "Impact of Electronic Communication on African Development," website notes. http://www.uneca.org/aisi/odiop.htm

ERO (1998) *The A. C. of the Lomé Convention*, Brussels: European Research Office.

Evans, P. and Wurster, T. (1997) "Strategy and the New Economics of Information," in C. Stern and G. Stalk, Jr., Eds., *Perspectives for Strategy from Boston Consulting Group*, New York: John Wiley & Sons.

Hadden, S. (1996) "Democracy on the Electronic Frontier," in G. Chapman, Ed., *Beyond the Endless Frontier*, Cambridge, MA: MIT Press.

Kenney, G. (1995) "The Missing Link: Information," *Information Technology for Development*, 6: 33–38.

Kraemer, K. and Dedrick, J. (1994) *IT and Economic Development: Lessons from the Asia-Pacific Region*, PICT Policy Research Paper No. 26, Brunel University. PICT: Program on Information and Communication Technologies, May 1994 (PRP No. 26), pp. 1–23.

Lal, K. (1996) "Information Technology, International Orientation and Performance: A Case Study of Electrical and Electronic Manufacturing Firms in India," *Information Economics and Policy*, 8: 269–280.

Loveman, G. (1994) "An Assessment of the Productivity Impact of Information Technologies," in T. Allen and M. Scott, *Information Technology and the Corporation of the 1990s: Research Studies*, Cambridge, MA: MIT Press.

Majuva, C. (2000) "Development Dynamics and Future Prospects of Electronic Commerce for Developing Economies: A Case Study of Tanzania," MBA dissertation, University of Dares Salaam.

Matambalya, F. (2000) "Information and Communication Technologies (ICTs) and the Economic Empowerment of Small and Medium Scale Enterprises (SMEs)," paper presented at the Internal Policy Dialogue: Building Coalitions Against Poverty, co-organized by World Bank, German Foundation for International Development, and German Federal Ministry for Economic Cooperation and Development, November 6–7, Bonn.

Matambalya, F. (2000) "The Significance of Information and Communication Technologies (ICTs) for Economic Productivity in Africa: Micro-Level Evidences from a Survey of Small and Medium Scale Enterprises (SMEs) in Tanzania," *Internationales Afrika Forum*, 3: 271–278.

Matambalya, F. (2002) *The Effect of Information and Communication Technologies (ICTs) on Enterprise Scale in Developing Economies: Issues and Micro-Level Evidence from East Africa*, ZEF Discussion Paper.

Matambalya, F. (2002) *Linking Participation in Technological Development and the Competitiveness of East Africa's SMEs in a Liberal Global Economy: A Case Study of Tanzania*, ZEF Discussion Paper.

Morrison, C. and Berndt, E. (1990) *Assessing the Productivity of Information Technology Equipment in the US Manufacturing Industries*, Working Paper No. 3582, Cambridge, MA: National Bureau of Economic Research.

Naylor, J. and Williams, J. (1994) "The Successful Use of IT in MSEs in Merseyside," *European Journal of Information System*, 3(1): 48–56.

Odedra, M., Lawrie, M., Bennet, M., and Goodman, S. (2001) "Information Technology in Sub-Saharan Africa," website notes. http://www.sas.upenn.edu/African_Studies/Comp_Articles/Information_Technology_117.html.

Pohjola, M. (1998) "Information Technology and Economic Development: An Introduction to the Research Issues," Working Paper, New York: United Nations University/World Institute of Development Economics Research.

Pohjola, M. (2000) "IT and Economic Growth," in *WIDER ANGLE*, No. 1/2000, Helsinki: World Institute of Development Economics Research, pp. 1–2.

Raymond, L. (1985) "Organisation Characteristics and MIS Success in the Context of Small Business," *MIS Quarterly*, 12(2): 37–52.

Roach, S. (1991) "Under Siege: The Restructuring Imperative," *Harvard Business Review*, 68: 82–92.

Romer, P. (1993) "Ideas Gap and Object Gap in Economic Development," in *Journal of Monetary Economics*, 32: 543–573.

Siegel, D. and Grilliches, Z. (1991) "Purchased Services, Outsourcing, Computers, and Productivity in Manufacturing," Working Paper No. 3678, Cambridge, MA: National Bureau of Economic Research.

Stiglitz, J. (1989) "Economic Organisation, Information and Development," in J. Behrman and T. Srinivsan, *Handbook of Development Economics*, Vol. 1, Amsterdam: North-Holland.

World Bank (1998) *World Development Report*, New York: Oxford University Press.

CHAPTER 22: ECONOMIC POLICIES, STABILIZATION, AND REFORMS

Amoako, K. Y. (1999) "The Economic Causes and Consequences of Civil Wars and Unrest in Africa," address to the 70th Ordinary Session of the Council of Ministers of the Organization of African Unity, Algeria, www.afbis.com/analysis/Africa%20war.htm.

Bryant, S. K. (2000) *Optimal Regional Trading Agreements for Developing Countries*, presented at the International Atlantic Economic Society Charleston, South Carolina.

Hess, P. and Ross, C. G. (1997) *Economic Development: Theories, Evidence, and Policies*, New York: Dryden Press.

Kapoor, K., Ed. (1994) "Africa's Experience with Structural Adjustment," in *Proceedings of the Harare Seminar*, May 23–24, Washington, D.C.: World Bank.

Meier, G. M. (2001) "The Old Generation of Development Economists and the New," in G. M. Meier and J. E. Stiglitz, Eds., *Frontiers of Development Economics: the Future in Perspective*, London: Oxford University Press/World Bank.

Mwanza, J. (1997) "World Bank and IMF-Supported Programs: A Zambian Perspective," in L. Wallace, Ed., *Deepening Structural Reform in Africa: Lessons from East Asia*, Washington, D.C.: International Monetary Fund.

Obadina, T. (undated) "Getting a Measure of African Poverty," *Africa Economic Analysis*, www.afbis.com/analysis/poverty-measure.html.

UNCTAD (2000) *African Development in a Comparative Perspective*, Asmara, Eritrea: Africa World Press.

Yarbrough, B. V. and Yarbrough, R. M. (2000) *The World Economy: Trade and Finance*, New York: Dryden Press.

CHAPTER 23: RESTARTING AND SUSTAINING GROWTH AND DEVELOPMENT

Alexander, W. E., Balino, T. J. T., and Enoch, C. (1996) "Adopting Indirect Instruments of Monetary Policy," *Finance and Development*, 33(1): 14–17.

AsDB (1997) *Emerging Asia: Changes and Challenges*, Manila: Asian Development Bank.

Ayittey, G. B. N. (1992) *Africa Betrayed*, New York: St. Martin's Press.

Ayittey, G. B. N. (1998) *Africa in Chaos*, New York: St. Martin's Press.

Bardhan, P. (1997) "Corruption and Development: A Review of Issues," *Journal of Economic Literature*, 35: 1320–1346.

Barrett C. and Carter, M. (1999) "Microeconomically Coherent Agricultural Policy in Africa," in J. Paulson, Ed., *The Role of the State in Key Markets*, New York: Macmillan Press.

Bennell, P. (1997) "Privatization in Sub-Saharan Africa: Progress and Prospects During the 1990s," *World Development*, 25: 1785–1804.

Bernanke, B. S. and Mishkin, F. S. (1999) *Inflation Targeting: Lessons from the International Experience*, Princeton, NJ: Princeton University Press.

Bhagwati, J. (1995) "The New Thinking on Development," *Journal of Democracy*, 6: 50–62.

Bhattacharya, A. P., Montiel, J., and Sharma, S. (1997) "How Can Sub-Saharan Africa Attract More Private Capital Inflows?," *Finance and Development*, 34(2): 3–6.

Blinder, A. S. (1998) *Central Banking in Theory and Practice*, Cambridge, MA: The MIT Press.

Block, S. A. (1994) "A New View of Agricultural Productivity in Sub-Saharan Africa," *American Journal of Agricultural Economics*, 76: 619–624.

Bloom, D. E. and Sachs, J. D. (1998) "Geography, Demography, and Economic Growth in Africa," *Brookings Papers on Economic Activity*, 1998(2): 207–273.

Brautigam, D. (1996) "State Capacity and Effective Governance," in B. Ndulo and N. van der Walle, Eds., *Agenda for Africa's Economic Renewal*, Washington, D.C.: Overseas Development Council.

Burnside C. and Dollar, D. (2000) "Aid, Policies, and Growth," *American Economic Review*, 90: 847–868.

Camdessus, M. (1996) Address to the Board of Governors of the IMF, October 1, Washington, D.C.

Chaudhurie-Aziz, M. (1998) "Political Participation and Long-Run Economic Performance," paper presented to Annual Meeting of the American Political Science Association, September 3–6, Boston, MA.

CIDA (1995) *Human Rights: Government of Canada Policy for CIDA on Human Rights, Democratization, and Good Governance*, Hull: Canadian International Development Agency.

Collier, P. (1991) "Africa's External Economic Relations: 1960–90," in D. Rimmer, Ed., *Africa 30 Years On*, London: The Royal Africa Society, in association with James Currey.

Collier, P. (1995) "The Marginalization of Africa," *International Labour Review*, 134: 541–557.

Collier, P. and Gunning, J. W. (1999) "Explaining African Economic Performance," *Journal of Economic Literature*, 37(1): 64–111.

Collier, P. and Pattillo, C., Eds. (2000) *Investment and Risk in Africa*, Basingstoke: Macmillan.

Dollar, D. (1992) "Outward-Oriented Developing Economies Really Do Grow More Rapidly: Evidence from 95 LDCs 1976–1985," *Economic Development and Cultural Change*, 40: 523–544.

Duesenberry, J. S. and McPherson, M. F. (1992) "Monetary Management in Sub-Saharan Africa: Key Issues," *Journal of African Finance and Economic Development*, 1: 25–36.

Duesenberry, J. S. *et al.* (1994) "Improving Exchange Rate Management in Sub-Saharan Africa," CAER Discussion Paper No. 31, Boston, MA: Harvard Institute for International Development.

Easterly, W., Rodriguez, C. A., and Schmidt-Hebbel, K. (1994) *Public Sector Deficits and Macroeconomic Performance*, New York: Oxford University Press/World Bank.

ECA/OAU (1989) *African Alternative Framework to Structural Adjustment Programmes for Socio-Economic Recovery and Transformation (AAF-SAP)*, E/ECA/CM.15/6/Rev.3, Addis Ababa: United Nations Economic Commission for Africa.

Eicher, C. K. and Baker, D. C. (1992) "Agricultural Development in Sub-Saharan Africa: A Critical Survey," in L. R. Martin, Ed., *A Survey of Agricultural Economics Literature*, Vol. 4, Minneapolis: University of Minnesota Press for the American Agricultural Economics Association.

Englebert, P. (2000) *State Legitimacy and Development in Africa*, Boulder, CO: Lynne Rienner Publishers.

European Union (1996) "Green Paper on Relations Between the European Union and the ACP Countries on the Eve of the 21st Century: Challenges and Options for a New Partnership," paper presented at the European Commission Study Group Partnership 2000, DGVIII/1, November 14, Brussels.

FRBKC (1996) *Achieving Price Stability*, proceedings of a symposium sponsored by the Federal Reserve Bank of Kansas City, August 29–31, Jackson Hole, WY.

FRBKC (1997) *Maintaining Financial Stability in a Global Economy*, proceedings of a symposium sponsored by the Federal Reserve Bank of Kansas City, August, Jackson Hole, WY.

Freeman, R. and Lindauer, D. (1998) *Why Not Africa?*, draft paper, Cambridge, MA: Harvard University.

Fuhrer, J. C. (1997) "Central Bank Independence and Inflation Targeting: Monetary Policy Paradigms for the Next Millenium," *New England Economic Review*, January/February: 20–36.

Gastanaga, V. M., Nugent, J. B., and Pashamova, B. (1998) "Host Country Reforms and FDI Flows: How Much Difference Do They Make?," *World Development*, 26: 1299–1314.

GCA (1996) *African Social and Economic Trends 1995*, annual report, Washington, D.C.: Global Coalition for Africa.

Ghura, D. and Grennes, T. J. (1993) "The Real Exchange Rate and Macroeconomic Performance in Sub-Saharan Africa," *Journal of Development Economics*, 42: 155–174.

Gibb, R. (1998) "Southern African in Transition: Prospects and Problems Facing Regional Integration," *Journal of Modern African Studies*, 36: 287–306.

Goldsbrough, D. *et al.* (1996) *Reinvigorating Growth in Developing Countries: Lessons from Adjustment Policies in Eight Economies*, Occasional Paper No. 139, Washington, D.C.: International Monetary Fund.

Goldsmith, A. A. (1995) "The State and the Market in Economic Development: A Second Look at Adam Smith in Theory and Practice," *Development and Change*, 26: 633–650.

Goldsmith, A. A. (1999) "Slapping the Grasping Hand: Correlates of Political Corruption in Emerging Markets," *American Journal of Economics and Sociology*, 58(4): 865–883.

Goodhart, C. A. E. (1994) "Game Theory for Central Bankers: A Report to the Governor of the Bank of England," *Journal of Economic Literature*, 32: 101–114.

Heller, W. W. (1954) "Fiscal Policies for Underdeveloped Economies," in H. P. Wald, Ed., *Conference on Agricultural Taxation and Economic Development*, Cambridge, MA: Harvard Law School.

HIID (1997) *A New Partnership for Growth in Africa*, Cambridge, MA: Harvard Institute for International Development.

Ibi-Ajayi, S. (1997) *An Analysis of External Debt and Capital Flight in the Severely Indebted Low Income Countries in Sub-Saharan Africa*, Working Paper WP/97/68, Washington, D.C.: International Monetary Fund.

IRIS (1996) *Governance and the Economy in Africa: Tools for Analysis and Reform of Corruption*, College Park, MD: Center for Institutional Reform and the Informal Sector.

Jenkins, M. A. (1996) "Central Bank Independence and Inflation Performance: Panacea or Placebo?," *BNL Quarterly Review*, 197: 241–269.

JICA (1995) *Participatory Development and Good Governance*, report of the Aid Study Committee, Japan International Cooperation Agency, Japan.

Joseph, R. (1997) "Democratization in Africa After 1989: Comparative and Theoretical Perspectives," *Comparative Politics*, 29: 363–383.

Knight, M. (1998) "Developing Countries and the Globalization of Financial Markets," *World Development*, 26: 1185–1200.

Kreuger, A. O. (1997) "Trade Policy and Economic Development: How We Learn," *American Economic Review*, 87: 1–22.

Krugman, P. R. (1989) "Developing Countries in the World Economy," *Daedalus*, 118: 183–203.

Madavo, C. and Sarbib, J.-L. (1997) "Africa on the Move: Attracting Private Capital to a Changing Continent," *SAIS Review*, 7: 111–126.

Masson, P. R., Savastano, M. A., and Sharma, S. (1998) "Can Inflation Targeting Be a Framework for Monetary Policy in Developing Countries?," *Finance and Development*, March, 34–37.

McCulloch, R. and McPherson, M. F. (1998) "Promoting and Sustaining Trade and Exchange Reform in Africa: An Analytic Framework," in M. McPherson, Ed., *Promoting and Sustaining Trade and Exchange Rate Reform in Africa*, Cambridge, MA: Belfer Center for Science and International Affairs, Harvard University.

McKenzie, G. A., Orsmond, D. W. H., and Gerson, P. R. (1997) *The Composition of Fiscal Adjustment and Growth Lessons from Fiscal Reforms in Eight Economies*, Occasional Paper No. 149, Washington, D.C.: International Monetary Fund.

McKinnon, R. W. (1973) *Money and Capital in Economic Development*, Washington, D.C.: The Brookings Institution.

McPherson, M. F. and Goldsmith, A. A. (1998) "Africa: On the Move?," *SAIS Review*, 28: 153–167.

Meier, G. M., Ed. (1970) *Leading Issues in Economic Development*, 2nd ed., New York: Oxford University Press.

North, D. C. (1997) "Transactions Costs Through Time," in C. Menard, Ed., *Transaction Cost Economics Recent Developments*, Brookfield, VT: Edward Elgar.

OECD (1998) *Open Markets Matter: The Benefits of Trade and Investment Liberalisation*, Paris: Organisation for Economic Cooperation and Development.

Organization of African Unity (OAU) (1980) *The Lagos Plan of Action for the Implementation of the Monrovia Strategy for the Economic Development of Africa*, Geneva: International Institute for Labor Studies.

Orme, J. (1995) "The Original Megapolicy: America's Marshall Plan," in J. D. Montgomery and D. A. Rondinelli, Eds., *Great Policies: Strategic Innovations in Asia and the Pacific Basin*, Wesport, CT: Praeger.

OXFAM (1995) *The Impact of Structural Adjustment on Community Life: Undoing Development*, Boston, MA: OXFAM America.

Pill, H. and Pradhan, M. (1997) "Financial Liberalization in Africa and Asia," *Finance and Development*, June: 7–10.

Przeworski, A. and Limongi, F. (1997) "Democracy and Development," in A. Hadenius, Ed., *Democracy's Victory and Crisis*, Cambridge, MA: Cambridge University Press.

Quirk, P. J. (1996) "Exchange Rate Regimes as Inflation Anchors," *Finance and Development*, 33(1): 42–45.

Radelet, S. C., Sachs, J. D. and Lee, J.-W. (1997) *Economic Growth in Asia*, draft paper, Cambridge, MA: Harvard Institute for International Development.

Reisen, H. (1989) "Public Debt, External Competitiveness, and Fiscal Discipline in Developing Countries," *Princeton Studies in International Finance*, November, No. 66.

Rodrik, D. (1997) *Trade Policy and Economic Performance in Sub-Saharan Africa*, paper prepared for the Swedish Ministry for Foreign Affairs.

Sachs, J. (1996) "Growth in Africa: It Can Be Done," *The Economist*, June 29: 19–21.

Sandbrook, R. (1986) "The State and Economic Stagnation in Tropical Africa," *World Development*, 14: 319–332.

Sandbrook, R. (1996) "Democratization and the Explanation of Economic Reform in Africa," *Journal of International Development*, 8: 1–20.

Schioler, E. (1998) *Good News from Africa: Farmers, Agricultural Research and Food in the Pantry*, Washington, D.C.: International Food Policy Research Institute.

Senbet, L. W. (1996) "Perspectives on African Finance and Economic Development," *Journal of African Finance and Economic Development*, 2: 1–22.

Smith, A. (1979) *The Wealth of Nations*, Books I–III, New York: Penguin Books.

Solow, R. M. (1997) *Learning from "Learning by Doing": Lessons for Economic Growth*, Stanford, CA: Stanford University Press.

Squire, L. (1989) "Project Evaluation in Theory and Practice," in H. B. Chenery and T. N. Srinivasan, Eds., *Handbook of Development Economics*, Vol. 2, Amsterdam: North-Holland.

Thomas, T. (1996) "A Survey of Sub-Sahran Africa: Africa for the Africans," *The Economist*, September 7, pp. 3–4.

Tsikata, T. M. (1998) *Aid Effectiveness: A Survey of the Recent Empirical Literature*, Working Paper PPAA/98/1, Washington, D.C.: International Monetary Fund.

UNDP (1997) *Governance for Sustainable Human Development*, New York: United Nations Development Program.

USAID (1994) *Strategies for Sustainable Development*, Washington, D.C.: United States Agency for International Development.

Wolfensohn, J. D. (1997) *The Challenge of Inclusion*, address to the Board of Governors, September 23, Hong Kong, China.

Wolfensohn, J. D. (1998) *The Other Crisis*, address to the Board of Governors, October 6, Washington, D.C.

World Bank (1981) *Accelerated Development in Sub-Saharan Africa: An Agenda for Action*, Washington, D.C.: World Bank.

World Bank (1984) *Towards Sustained Development in Sub-Saharan Africa*, Washington, D.C.: The World Bank.

World Bank (1986) *Financing Adjustment with Growth in Sub-Saharan Africa, 1986–90*, Washington, D.C.: The World Bank.

World Bank (1989) *Sub-Saharan Africa from Crisis to Sustainable Growth a Long-Term Perspective Study*, Washington, D.C.: The World Bank.

World Bank (1991) *The African Capacity Building Initiative*, Washington, D.C.: The World Bank.

World Bank (1994) *Adjustment in Africa: Lessons from Country Case Studies*, New York: Oxford University Press/World Bank.

World Bank (1994) *Adjustment in Africa: Reforms, Results and the Road Ahead*, New York: Oxford University Press.

World Bank (1994) *Governance*, Washington, D.C.: World Bank/United Nations Development Project.

World Bank (1997) *World Development Report 1997: The State in a Changing World*, New York: Oxford University Press.

World Bank (1998) *Assessing Aid*, World Bank Research Report, Washington, D.C.: The World Bank.

Yeats, A. et al. (1997) *Did Domestic Policies Marginalize Africa in World Trade?*, Washington, D.C.: World Bank Directions in Development Series.

INDEX